VISUAL QUICKSTART GUIDE

Microsoft Office

FOR WINDOWS

- **Word for Windows 6.0**
- **Excel 5.0**
- **PowerPoint 4.0**
- **Access 2.0**
- **Mail 3.2**

Steve Sagman

Microsoft Office for Windows
Visual QuickStart Guide

Steve Sagman

Peachpit Press
2414 Sixth Street
Berkeley, CA 94710
510/548-4393
510/548-5991 (fax)

Find us on the World Wide Web at: http://www.peachpit.com

Peachpit Press is a division of Addison Wesley Longman

ISBN 1-56609-166-7

0 9 8 7 6 5 4 3

Printed and bound in the United States of America

Printed on recycled paper

Thank You

To **Roslyn Bullas** at Peachpit Press for guidance, flexibility, and patience.

To **Ted Nace** and the folks at Peachpit Press for producing such outstanding books and for giving me this opportunity.

To **Elaine Weinmann** for allowing me to emulate her superb book design.

To **Canterbury Press** for their consummate imagesetting.

To **Eric** and **Lola** for their patience and love.

Book Design

Elaine Weinmann

Additional Design

Milton Zelman

About the Author

Half a million readers know Steve Sagman's books on PC software, including his international best-sellers on Harvard Graphics.

He gives classes and seminars nationwide on application software, especially presentation graphics and desktop publishing programs. His company provides training, courseware, user documentation, and user interface consulting.

He welcomes comments, questions, and suggestions and can be reached at:

Net: ssagman@pipeline.com
CompuServe: 72456,3325
MCI Mail: SSAGMAN

or at: Steve Sagman
570 Mecox Rd.
Water Mill, NY 11976.

Other Books by Steve Sagman

Using Harvard Graphics

1-2-3 Graphics Techniques

*Getting Your Start in Hollywood***

Using Windows Draw

*Mastering CorelDraw 3** **

Using Freelance Graphics 2

*Using 1-2-3 for Windows Release 4**

*Mastering CorelDraw 4** **

*The PC Bible** **

Running PowerPoint 4

*Harvard Graphics for Windows 2: Visual QuickStart Guide***

* Contributor.

** Also published by Peachpit Press.

Table of Contents

Common Office Techniques

1. Basic Windows Procedures

2. Essential Office Techniques

Word 6.0 Word Processing

Excel 5.0 Number Crunching

PowerPoint 4.0 Presenting

Access 2.0 Database Management

Combining the Office Applications

Common Office Techniques

Common Office Techniques

Basic Windows Procedures

Essential Office Techniques

Basic Windows Procedures

1

What is Windows?

Microsoft Windows runs on an IBM-compatible PC and puts a graphical working environment on the screen. Windows provides visual controls you use to run *applications* (programs that run within Windows and perform specific tasks, such as word processing). These controls include menus, buttons, scroll bars, and other onscreen items that you operate with the mouse or keyboard.

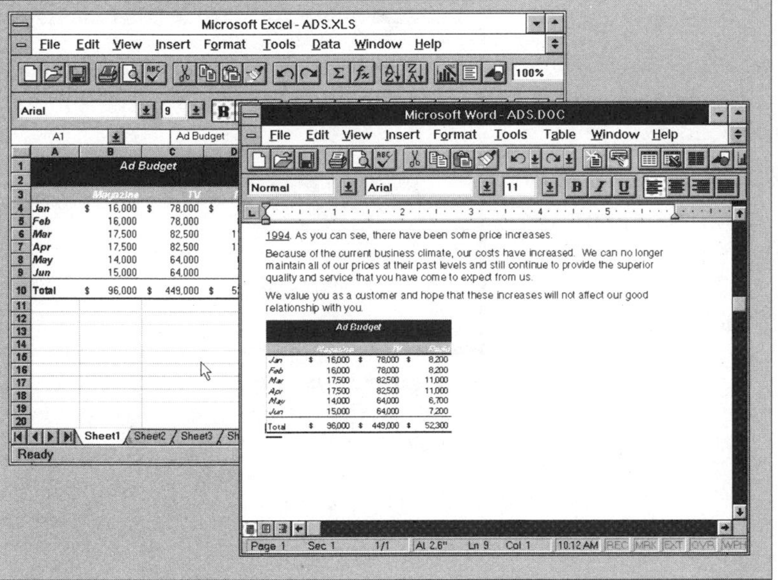

Because all Windows applications run in identical panes on the screen and sport similar menus, buttons, scroll bars, dialog boxes, and other controls, they all work alike. This makes it easy to learn and use Windows programs because you transfer your knowledge of one application to many others.

Windows provides other benefits, too. You can open more than one window and run applications on the screen side by side. You can easily transfer information from one application to another, even setting up links that update the copies in other applications when the original changes. In addition, you see your work on the screen as it will look when printed.

Starting Windows

On your system, Windows may start automatically when you turn on the computer, or it may already be running if your computer always stays on. But if you need to start Windows each morning, follow these steps:

1. At the DOS prompt, type WIN. **(Figure 1)**
2. Press Enter. Windows starts. **(Figure 2)**

✓ Tips

- Windows can have many different looks depending on how your system has been set up, so your screen might not match the opening Windows screen shown here.
- If Microsoft Office has been set to start automatically after you start Windows, you may see a Microsoft Office opening screen followed by the Microsoft Office Manager. **(Figure 3)**
- To customize the Microsoft Office Manager, click it with the right mouse button.

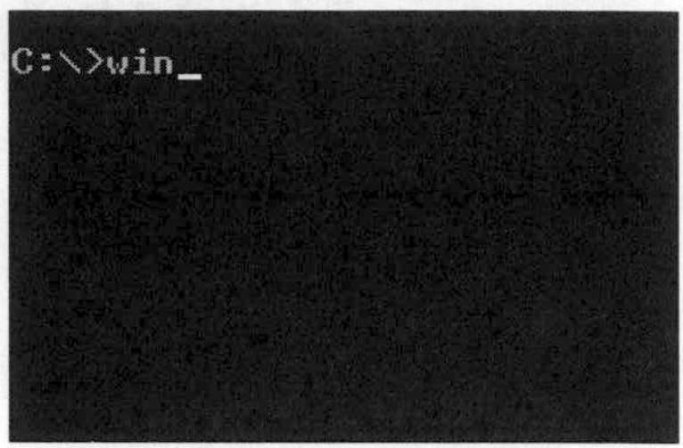

Figure 1. *Type WIN at the DOS prompt.*

Figure 2. *The Windows opening screen appears. (Your screen may show different windows and icons.)*

Figure 3. *The Microsoft Office Manager.*

Using the Mouse

Moving the mouse on the desktop moves the pointer on the screen. Use the left mouse button to click unless you have swapped the mouse buttons with the Windows Control Panel. Here are the three basic mouse techniques:

Click

Place the pointer on something and then click the left mouse button once. Click on a menu item or object to select it, or click on an onscreen button to press it.

Double-click

Place the pointer on something and then click the left mouse button twice in quick succession. Double-click to launch Harvard, select an item on a list, or select a word.

Drag

Place the pointer on something, press and hold down the mouse button, move the mouse, and then release the mouse button. Drag to highlight text, or move an object, dialog box, or window.

Terminology

Select

Click on an object on the screen. Your next action will affect the selected object. To select a menu, click its name or press Alt+underlined letter in name. To select text, place the pointer at the beginning of the text and then drag across the text. Selected text is highlighted.

Press

Press a key on the keyboard.

Drop-down list

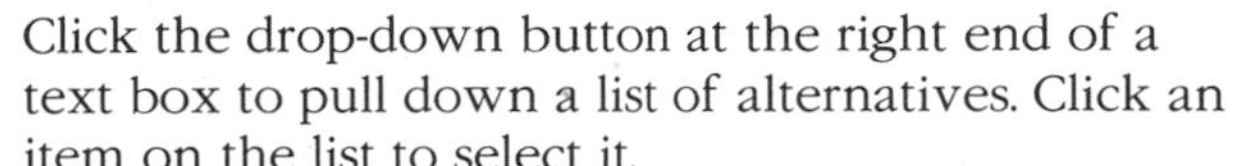

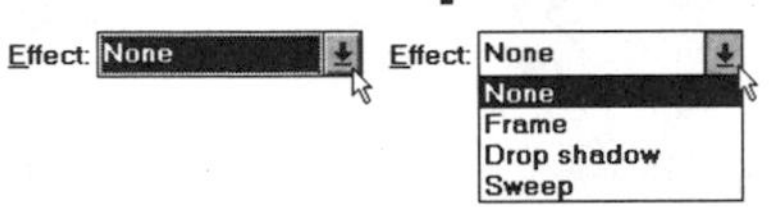

Click the drop-down button at the right end of a text box to pull down a list of alternatives. Click an item on the list to select it.

Check/ Uncheck

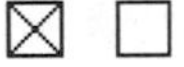

Click the checkbox next to an option to turn it on or off. A checked box indicates that the option is turned on.

Scroll

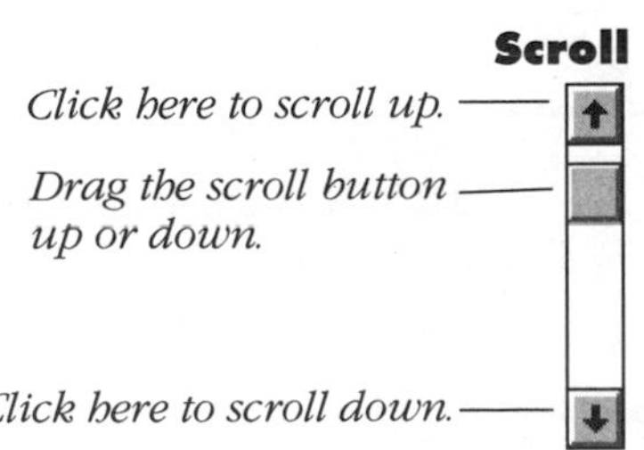

Use the scroll bar to the right of the list to move forward or backward through the list. Drag the button up or down along the scroll bar or click the up or down arrow buttons at the ends of the scroll bar.

An Application Window

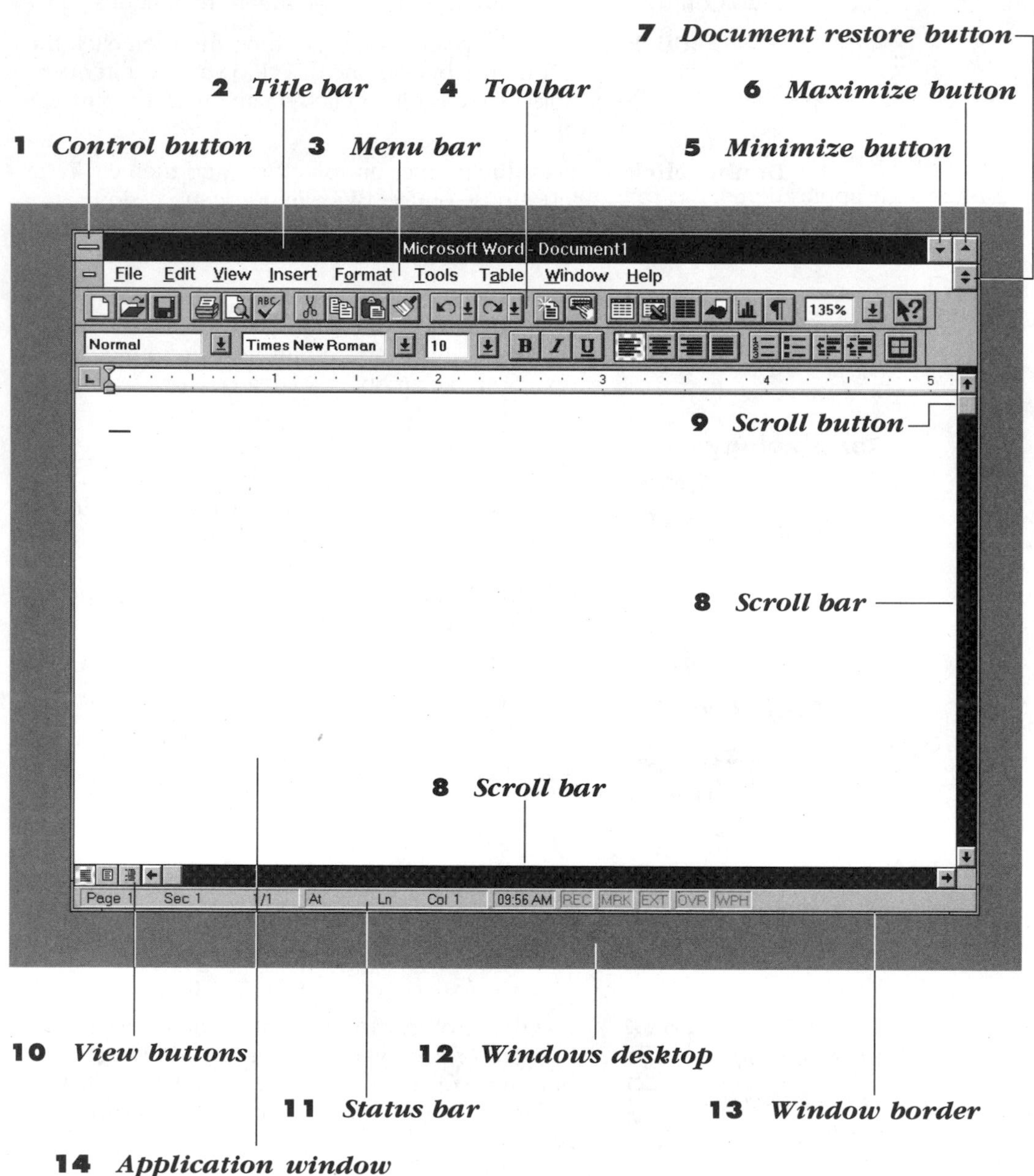
7 Document restore button
2 Title bar
4 Toolbar
6 Maximize button
1 Control button
3 Menu bar
5 Minimize button
Microsoft Word - Document1
File Edit View Insert Format Tools Table Window Help
135%
Normal
Times New Roman
10
9 Scroll button
8 Scroll bar
8 Scroll bar
Page 1 Sec 1 1/1 At Ln Col 1 09:56 AM REC MRK EXT OVR WPH
10 View buttons
12 Windows desktop
11 Status bar
13 Window border
14 Application window

Key to the Application Window

1 ***Control button***

Click here to pull down a menu of options for controlling the application window.

2 ***Title bar***

Displays the application name. Drag the title bar to move the application window. Double-click the title bar to switch between maximized and restored window.

3 ***Menu bar***

Click a menu name or press Alt+underlined letter in a menu name to pull down a menu.

4 ***Toolbar***

Click a tool to perform a frequently needed task. Place the pointer on a tool without clicking and pause to see a description of the tool in a tooltip.

5 ***Minimize button***

Click here to shrink the application window to an icon.

6 ***Maximize button***

Click here to expand the application window to fill the screen.

7 ***Document restore button***

Click here to restore the document window that is maximized within an application window.

8 ***Scroll bar***

Click the arrows at either ends of the scroll bars to move the view of a zoomed document or drag the scroll button along the scroll bar.

9 ***Scroll button***

Drag the scroll button to move the view of a zoomed document. The position of the scroll button relative to the scroll bar corresponds to the position of the view relative to the entire document.

10 ***View buttons***

Click these buttons to switch among alternate views of the document.

11 ***Status bar***

Displays the current status of the document.

12 ***Windows desktop***

The background upon which all windows are opened.

13 ***Window border***

Drag the window border to resize or reshape the applicationwindow.

14 ***Application window***

All the action in each application occurs in an application window.

Choosing From Menus in Windows

Every application has a horizontal menu bar that crosses the top of the window. Each menu name on the menu bar represents a group of commands or options on a vertical menu.

1. Click a menu name to open a vertical menu. **(Figure 4)**

   or

   Press Alt and then press the underlined letter in the word.
2. Click a command or option on a vertical menu. **(Figure 5)**

   or

   Press the underlined letter in the command or option you want.

✔ Tips

- You don't have to hold down Alt when you select a menu. You can press Alt once and then press the underlined letter in the menu name.
- To close a menu, click the menu name again without choosing a command or option.

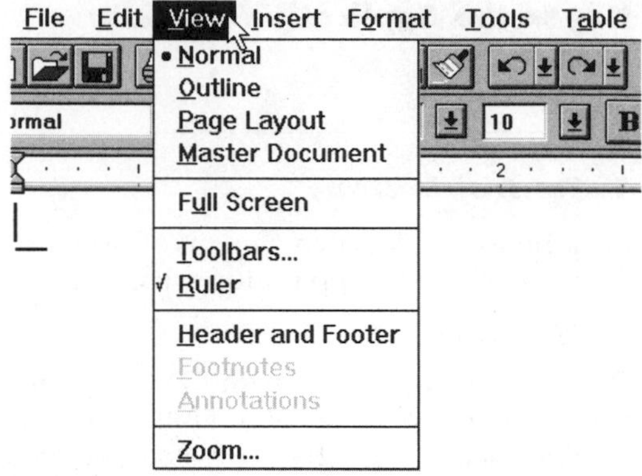

Figure 4. *Click a menu name.*

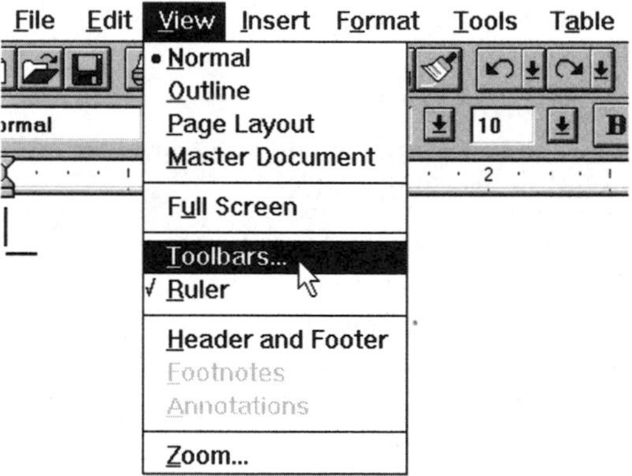

Figure 5. *A menu.*

Selecting Options in Dialog Boxes

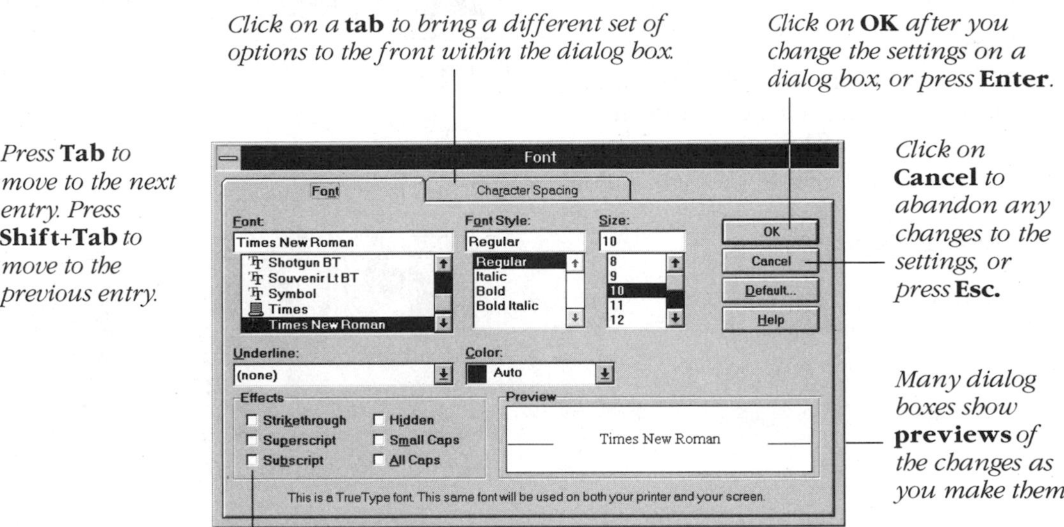

Click on a **tab** *to bring a different set of options to the front within the dialog box.*
Click on **OK** *after you change the settings on a dialog box, or press* **Enter**.
Press **Tab** *to move to the next entry. Press* **Shift+Tab** *to move to the previous entry.*
Click on **Cancel** *to abandon any changes to the settings, or press* **Esc.**
Many dialog boxes show **previews** *of the changes as you make them.*
Click on a **checkbox** *to turn the option on or off. When a checkbox is checked with an "x", the option is on. You can also press Alt+underlined letter.*
Font
Font
Character Spacing
Font:
Times New Roman
Shotgun BT
Souvenir Lt BT
Symbol
Times
Times New Roman
Font Style:
Regular
Regular
Italic
Bold
Bold Italic
Size:
10
8
9
10
11
12
OK
Cancel
Default...
Help
Underline:
(none)
Color:
Auto
Effects
Strikethrough
Superscript
Subscript
Hidden
Small Caps
All Caps
Preview
Times New Roman
This is a TrueType font. This same font will be used on both your printer and your screen.

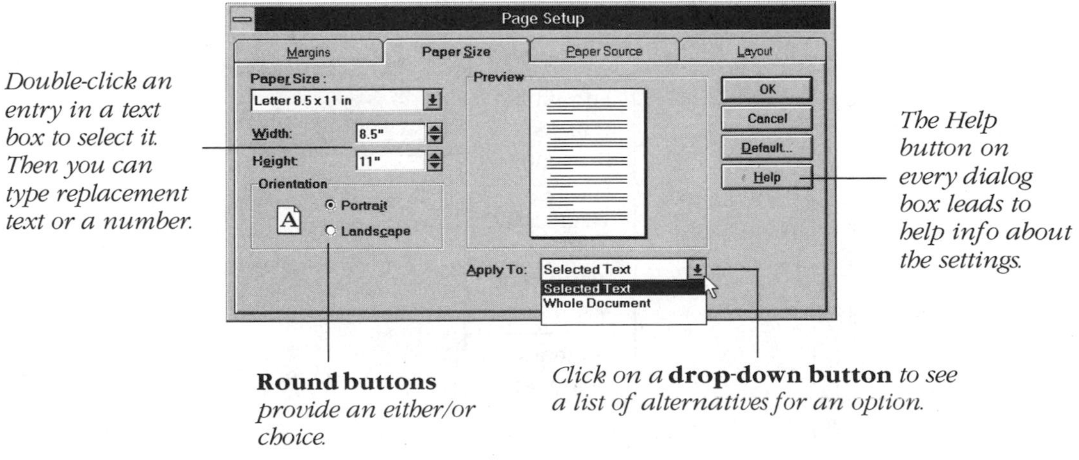

Double-click an entry in a text box to select it. Then you can type replacement text or a number.
The Help button on every dialog box leads to help info about the settings.
Round buttons *provide an either/or choice.*
Click on a **drop-down button** *to see a list of alternatives for an option.*
Page Setup
Margins
Paper Size
Paper Source
Layout
Paper Size:
Letter 8.5 x 11 in
Width:
8.5"
Height:
11"
Orientation
Portrait
Landscape
Preview
OK
Cancel
Default...
Help
Apply To:
Selected Text
Selected Text
Whole Document

Figure 6. *Two typical dialog boxes.*

Using the Toolbars

Click any toolbar button to perform an action. **(Figure 7)**

✔ Tips

- To see a Tooltip description of a button, place the pointer on the button and pause. **(Figure 8)**
- Click any toolbar with the right mouse button to get a list of other toolbars you can use. **(Figure 9)**

Figure 7. *The Chart toolbar for Excel.*

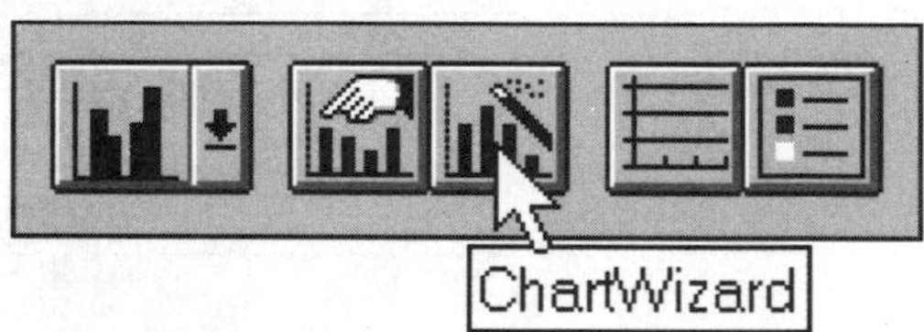

Figure 8. *Pause on a button to get a descriptive Tooltip.*

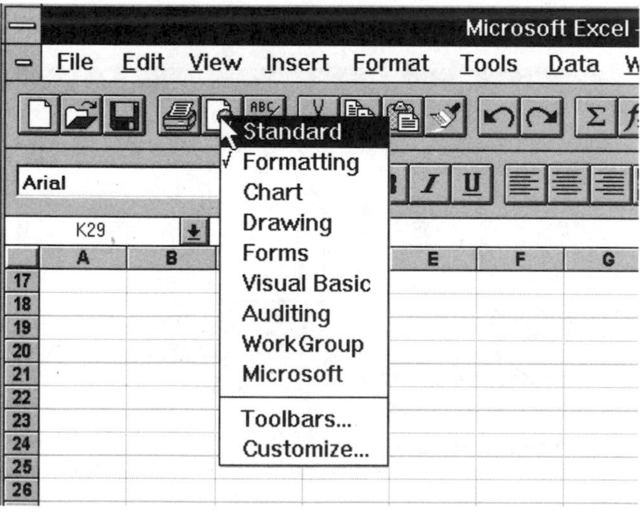

Figure 9. *The menu of toolbars in Excel.*

Figure 10. *Click the icon of the application to open.*

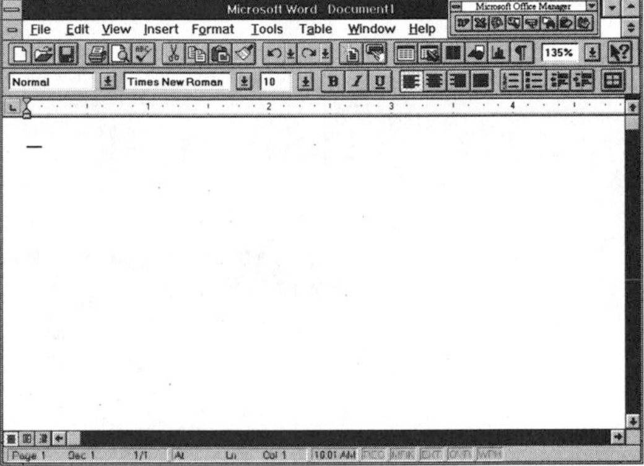

Figure 11. *Move the Microsoft Office Manager to a non-critical part of the screen.*

The Control button.

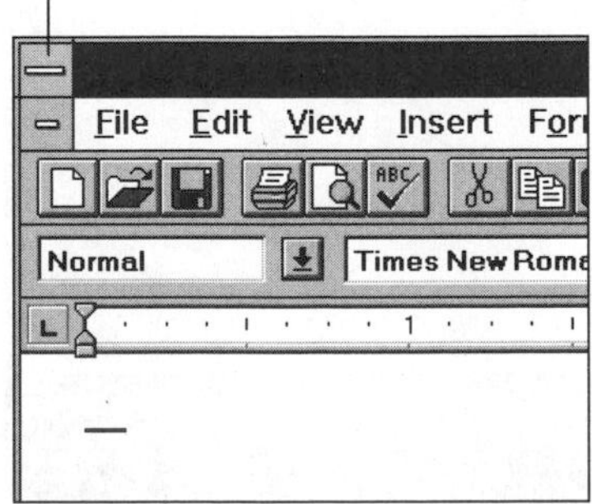

Figure 12. *The Control button.*

Starting Applications

1. On the Microsoft Office Manager, click the icon for the application to open. **(Figure 10)**

✔ **Tip**

■ The Microsoft Office Manager stays on top of all other windows. You can close the Microsoft Office Manager *(See Closing Windows, page 18.)* or you can move the Microsoft Office Manager out of the way. **(Figure 11)** *See Moving a Window, page 15.*

Exiting Applications

1. Double-click the Control button at the upper left corner of the application window. **(Figure 12)**

or

Click the Control button and choose Close from the drop-down menu that appears.

or

From the File menu, choose Exit.

or

Press Alt+F4.

✔ **Tip**

■ Windows will not let you exit an application without first asking whether to save any files that are open, so you never have to worry about losing your work by exiting prematurely.

About Manipulating Windows

As you work in an application, you might want to maximize its window to fill the screen or minimize the window to reduce it temporarily to an icon.

At other times, you may want to move windows to different areas of the screen to transfer information among windows.

Maximizing, minimizing, arranging, and switching among windows are all indispensable tasks while working in Windows.

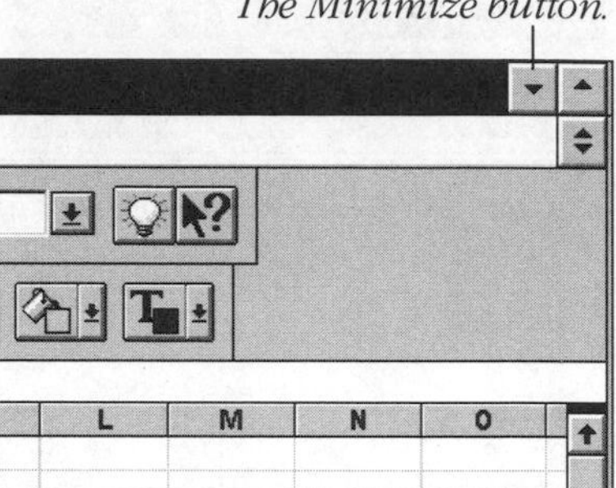

Figure 13. *The Minimize button.*

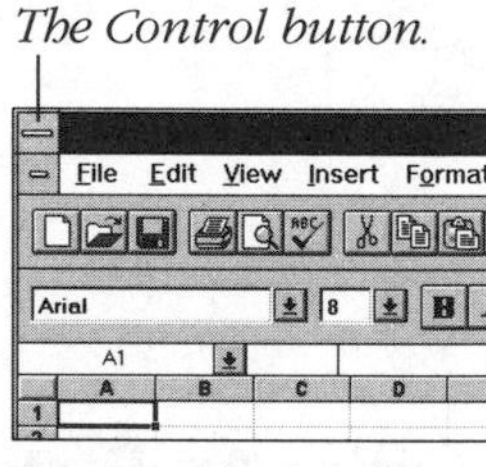

Figure 14. *The Control button.*

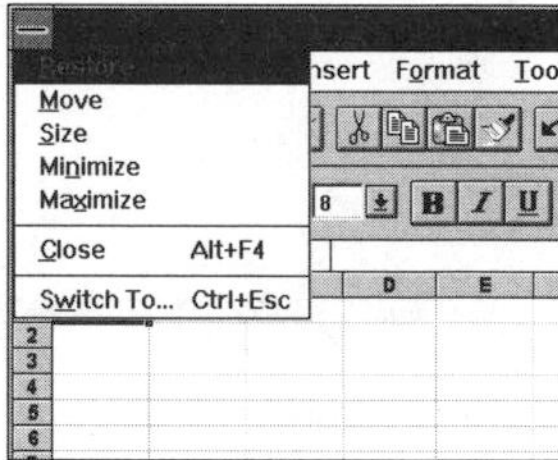

Figure 15. *The Control menu.*

Minimizing Windows

By minimizing a window (reducing it to an icon on the Windows desktop), you set aside an application but leave it running. To re-open the application's window, double-click the icon.

1. Click the Minimize button. **(Figure 13)**

   or

1. Click the Control button. **(Figure 14)**
2. Choose Minimize from the Control menu. **(Figure 15)**

✔ Tips

- Double-click a minimized icon to reopen an application.
- When you minimize an application, its icon may be hidden on the desktop behind other windows on the screen. *See Switching Among Windows, page 17, for information about reopening a hidden application.*

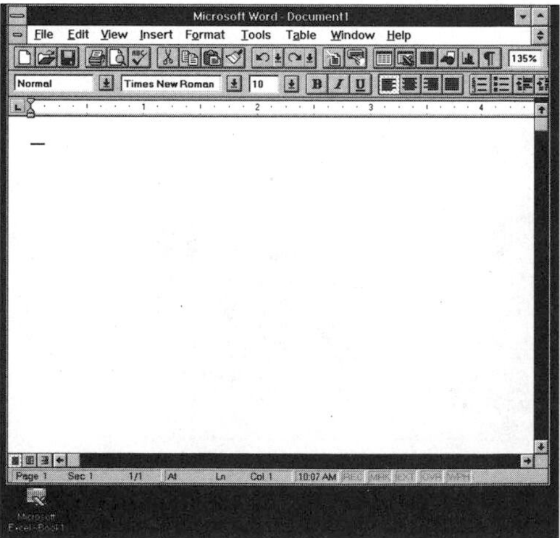

Figure 16. *A minimized application.*

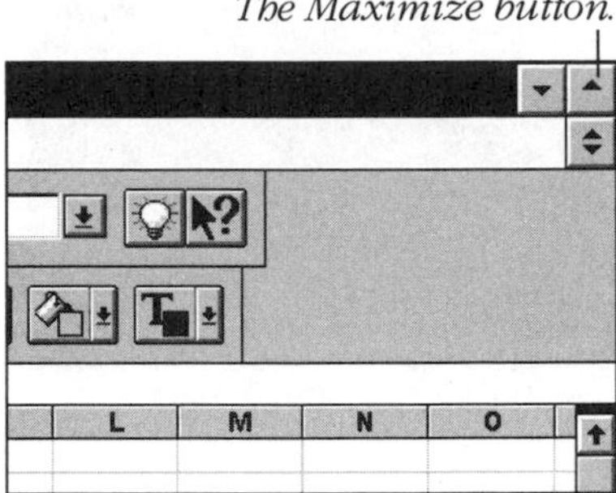

Figure 17. *The Maximize button.*

The Control button.

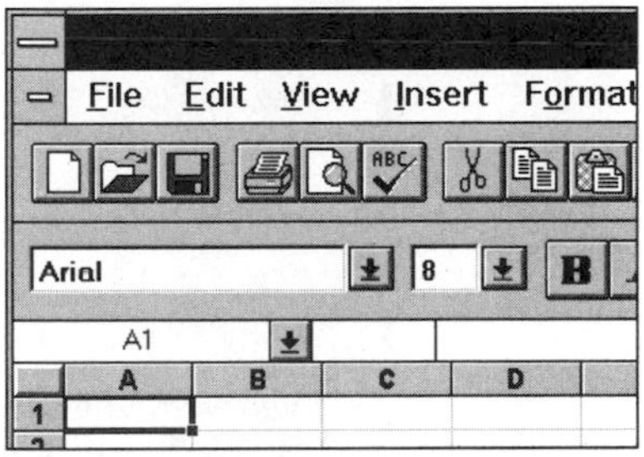

Figure 18. *The Control button.*

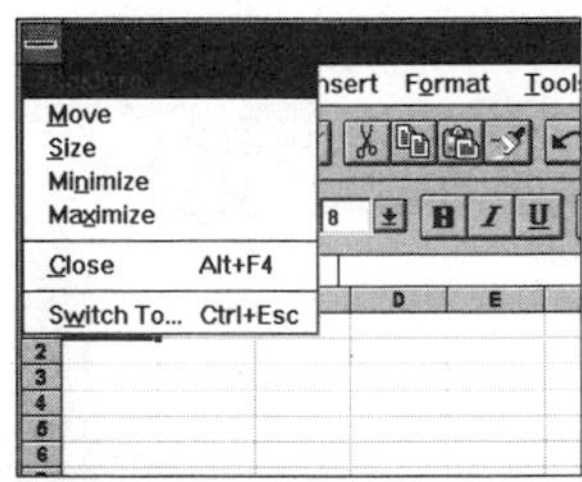

Figure 19. *The Control menu.*

Maximizing Windows

Maximizing a window enlarges it to fill the screen so you can see more of your work.

1. Click the Maximize button **(Figure 17)**

   or

1. Click the Control button **(Figure 18)**
2. Choose Maximize from the Control menu **(Figure 19)**

✔ Tips

- Because you cannot resize a maximized window, the window border disappears.
- How do you tell a maximized window in a crowded room? It's the one that has no Maximize button.

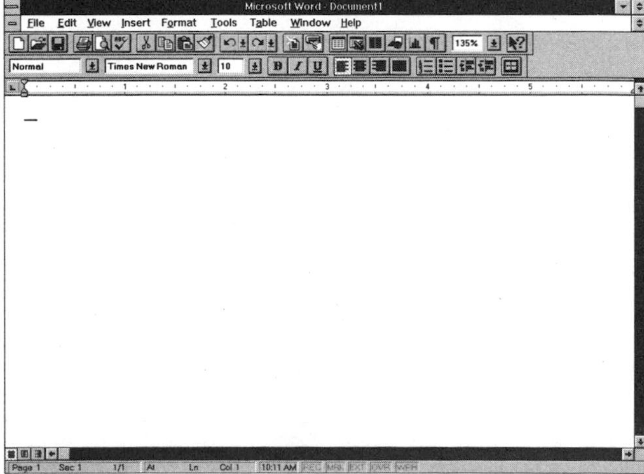

Figure 20. *A maximized application.*

Restoring Windows

A maximized window that you *restore* becomes free-floating. A minimized window returns to its last state: Either free floating or maximized.

1. Click the Restore button of a maximized window or double-click a minimized icon. **(Figures 21-22)**
or

1. Click the Control button of a maximized window or click a minimized icon once.

2. Choose Restore from the Control menu. **(Figures 23)**

✔ Tip

■ Double click a maximized window's title bar to restore the window. Double click again to maximize the window.

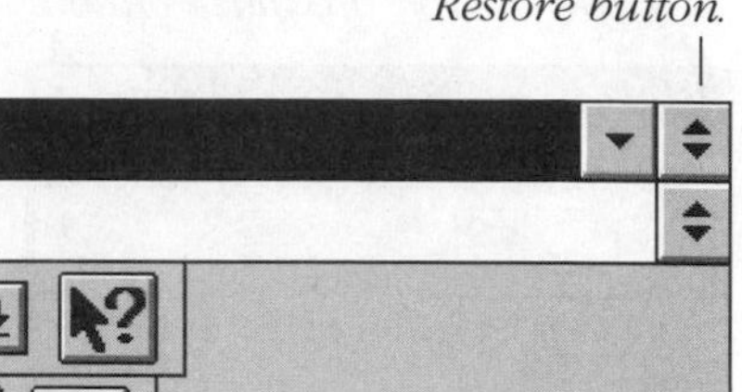

Figure 21. *The Restore button.*

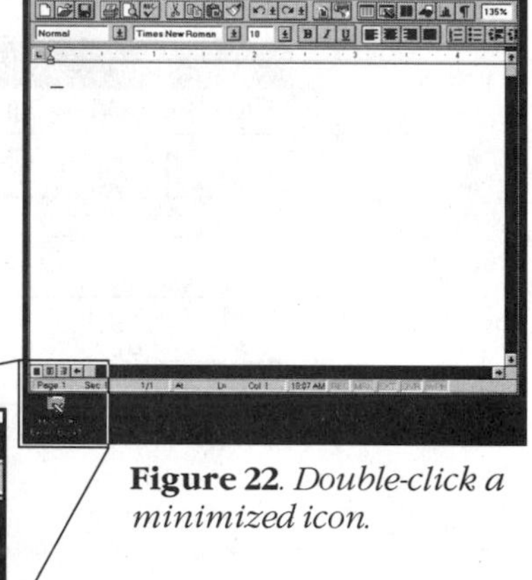

Figure 22. *Double-click a minimized icon.*

Figure 23. *The Control menu of a minimized icon.*

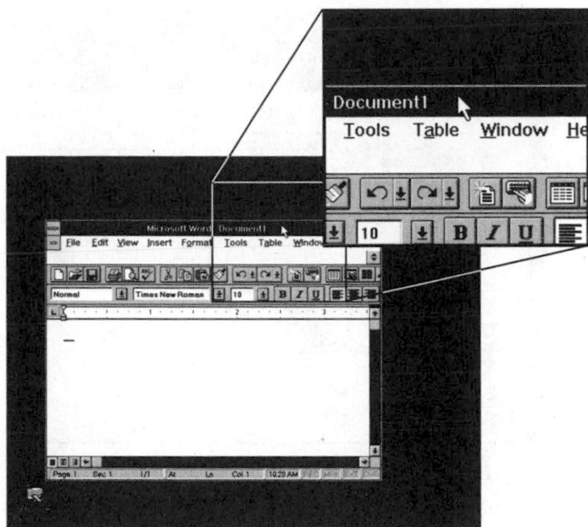

Figure 24. *The title bar.*

Moving a Window

1. Place the mouse pointer on the window's title bar **(Figure 24)**
2. Press and hold the mouse button.
3. Move the mouse to drag the window. **(Figure 25)**
4. Release the mouse button. **(Figure 26)**

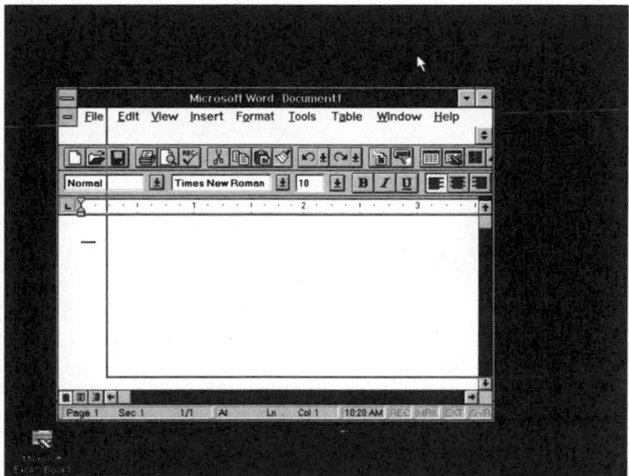

Figure 25. *Move the mouse while holding down the mouse button.*

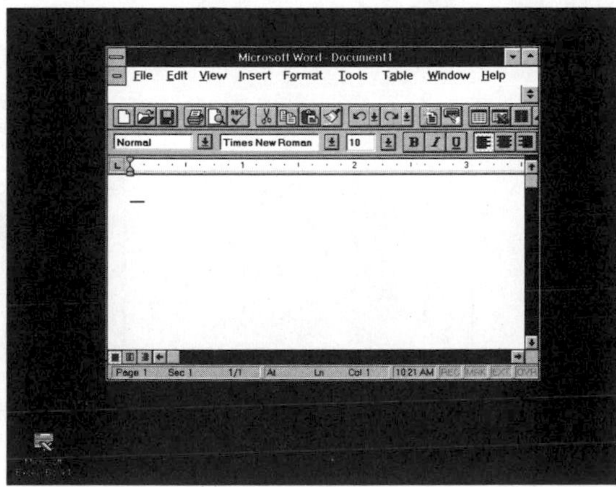

Figure 26. *The moved window.*

Resizing a Window

1. Place the mouse pointer on a window border. The pointer becomes a double arrow. **(Figure 27)**
2. Press and hold the mouse button.
3. Move the mouse to drag the border. **(Figure 28)**
4. Release the mouse button. **(Figure 29)**

✔ Tips

- You can drag a top, bottom, or side border.
- Drag the corner of the border to resize a window diagonally. **(Figure 30)**

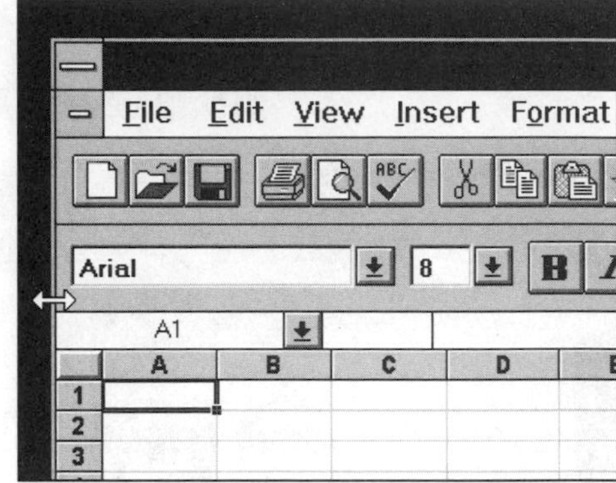

Figure 27. *The pointer becomes a double arrow when placed on any window border*

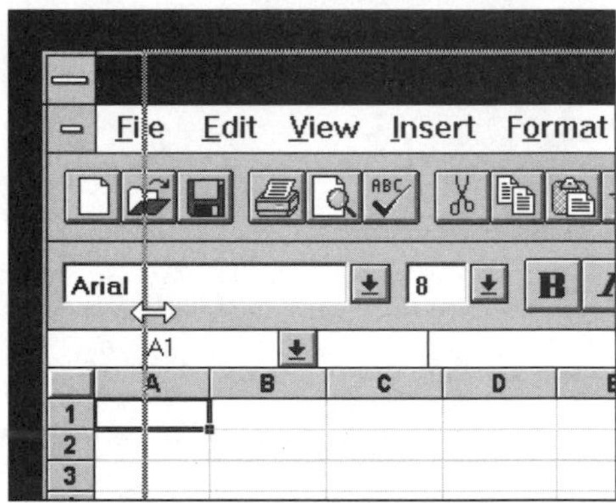

Figure 28. *Move the mouse while holding down the mouse button.*

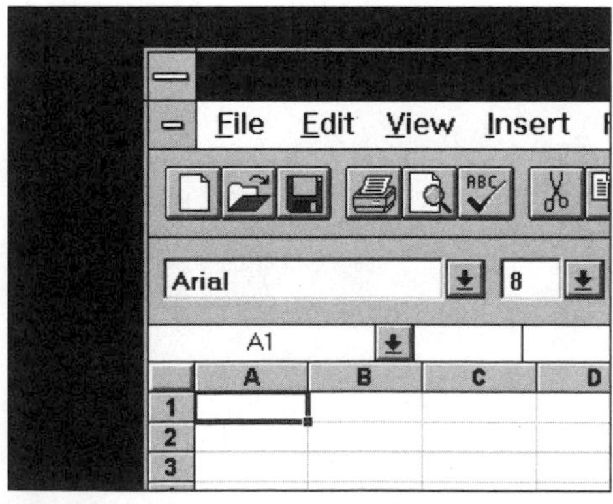

Figure 29. *The resized window.*

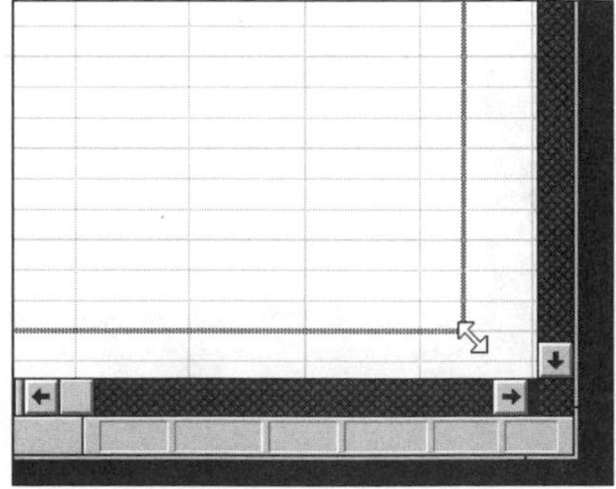

Figure 30. *Resizing a window in two directions simultaneously.*

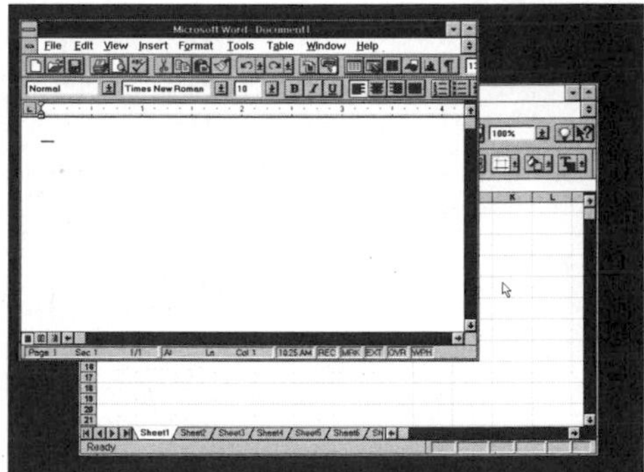

Figure 31. *To bring Excel to the front, click any visible part of the Excel window.*

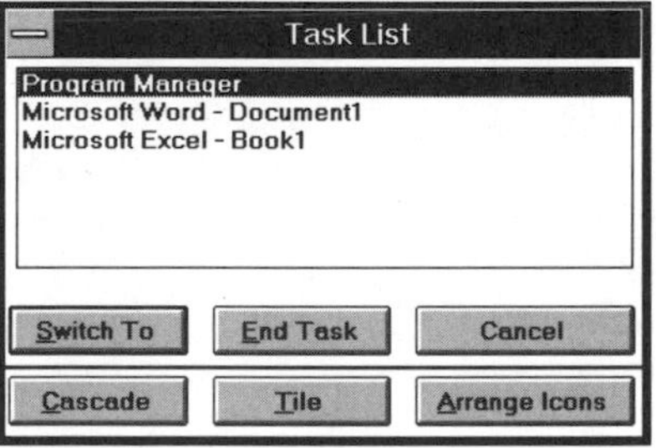

Figure 32. *The Task List.*

Switching Among Windows

1. Click any visible part of an open window. **(Figure 31)**

   or, if one window fills the screen or the window you want is covered by other windows
2. Press Ctrl+Esc to get to the Task List. **(Figure 32)**
3. Double-click an application name on the list.

✔ Tip

- To get to the Task List, you can also either: **1)** Double-click on the Windows desktop to summon the Task List, or **2)** click the Control button and choose Switch To from the Control menu.

Automatically Arranging Windows

1. Press Ctrl+Esc to bring up the Task List. **(Figure 32)**
2. Click **Tile** or **Cascade** to arrange all open windows. **(Figures 33-34)**

✔ Tips

- Only open windows are tiled. Minimized windows (icons) are not tiled.
- To arrange a window so it nearly fills the screen but leaves the desktop and icons showing at the bottom, minimize all other windows and then use Tile.

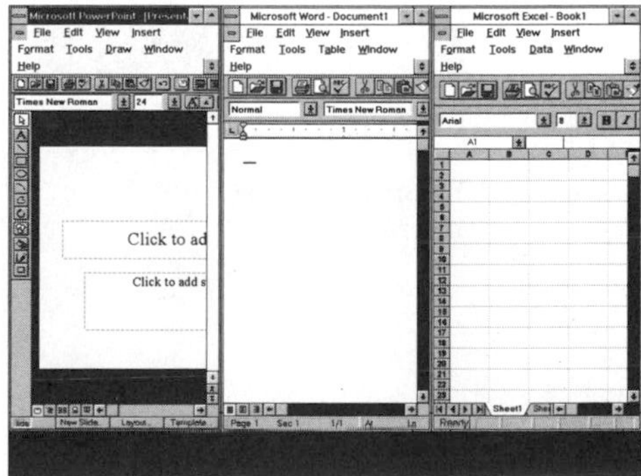

Figure 33. *Three tiled windows.*

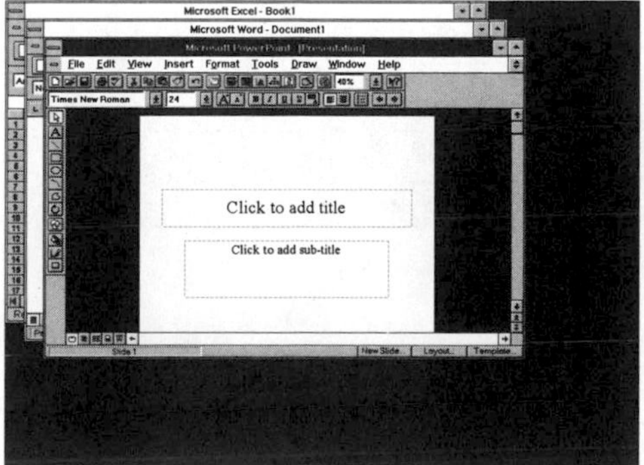

Figure 34. *Three cascaded windows.*

Closing Windows

1. From the File menu, choose Exit. **(Figure 35)**

or

Double-click the Control button.

or

Click the Control button and choose Close from the Control menu. **(Figure 36)**

or

Press Alt+F4.

✔ Tip

■ An application window will not close without offering you the opportunity to save any unsaved documents, so you should always close all applications before turning off your computer.

File
New... Ctrl+N
Open... Ctrl+O
Close
Save Ctrl+S
Save As...
Save All
Find File...
Summary Info...
Templates...
Page Setup...
Print Preview
Print... Ctrl+P
1 D-PHONES.DOC
2 BENEFIT.DOC
3 ITINRARY.DOC
4 ATSCRIPT.DOC
Exit

Figure 35. *The Word File menu.*

Figure 36. *The Control menu.*

Essential Office Techniques

Figure 1. *The Undo button.*

Edit	
Undo Clear	Ctrl+Z
Repeat Clear	Ctrl+Y
Cut	Ctrl+X
Copy	Ctrl+C
Paste	Ctrl+V
Paste Special...	
Clear	Delete
Select All	Ctrl+A
Find...	Ctrl+F
Replace...	Ctrl+H
Go To...	Ctrl+G
AutoText...	
Bookmark...	
Links...	
Object	

Figure 2. *The Edit menu.*

Click here to pull down the undo list...

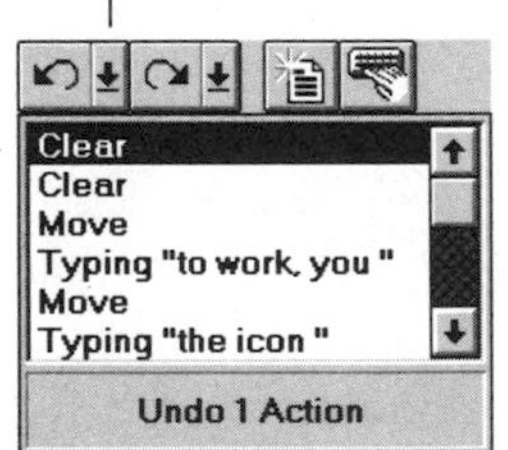

...then click an item on the list.

Figure 3. *The undo list.*

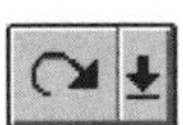

Figure 4. *The Redo button.*

About Office Techniques

One advantage of working in Microsoft Office is the body of procedures that the applications share in common. If something works a certain way in one application, it almost always works identically in all the other applications.

Become acquainted with these common techniques early and try them in any application. You'll be using them constantly.

Undoing Any Change

Remember Undo! You can undo just about any error as long as you undo it right away. If you do something else before you undo, you won't be able to undo anything you did before (except in **Word** where you can choose from a list of recent actions to undo).

1. Click the Undo button on the Standard toolbar. **(Figure 1)**

   or

   Press Ctrl+Z.

   or

   From the Edit menu, choose Undo *action.* **(Figure 2)**

✔ Tips

- In **Word**, click the pull-down button next to the Undo button to choose from a list of recent actions that you can undo. **(Figure 3)**
- To redo something you've undone, click the Redo button. Redo undoes an undo. **(Figure 4)**

Entering Text

Whenever an application is ready for you to type text, a blinking insertion point appears. Whatever you type inserts at the insertion point. **(Figures 5-6)**

1. Simply begin typing to insert text at the insertion point.

✔ **Tip**

■ To type over existing text that is to the right of the insertion point, press the Insert key to switch from Insert to Overwrite mode. **(Figure 7)**

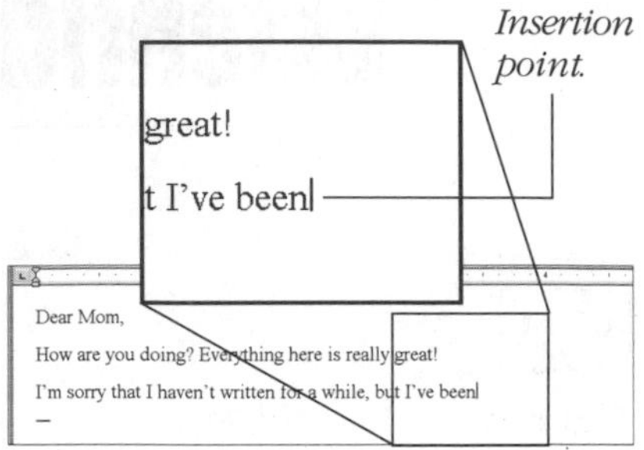

Figure 5. *The insertion point*

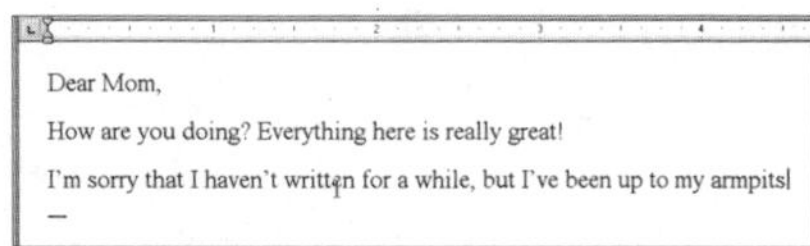

Figure 6. *Anything you type is inserted at the insertion point*

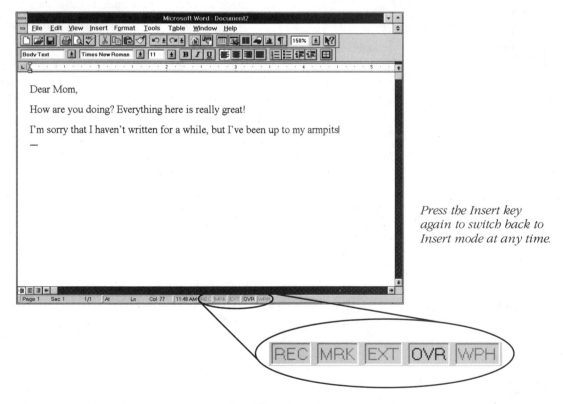

Press the Insert key again to switch back to Insert mode at any time.

Figure 7. *An OVR indicator appears when Word is in Overwrite mode.*

Click here

Dear Mom,

How are you doing? Everything here is really great!

I'm sorry that I haven't written for a while, but I've be
since the beginning of my new job. I've been given tw
don't get any training until next month. Everybody is
on them for hand holding. Needless to say, work is a l
moment, but I'm sure it will settle down quickly.

My new apartment is fantastic! I've actually enjoyed t

Figure 8. *Click at the spot to insert new text.*

Insertion point

Dear Mom,

How are you doing? Everything here is really great!

I'm sorry that I haven't written for a while, but I've be
since the beginning of my new job. I've been given tw
don't get any training until next month. Everybody is
on them for hand holding. Needless to say, work is a l
moment, but I'm sure it will settle down quickly.

My new apartment is fantastic! I've actually enjoyed t

Figure 9. *An insertion point appears.*

Moving the Insertion Point

To revise or add to existing text, you must move the insertion point to the spot for editing.

1. Click once in the existing text where you'd like to add or edit text. **(Figures 8-9)**
   or
   Press the arrow keys on the keyboard to move the insertion point.

✔ Tips

- Hold down Ctrl while pressing the right- or left-arrow key to move the insertion point a whole word to the right or left. **(Figure 10)**
- Hold down Ctrl while pressing the up- or down-arrow keys to move paragraph by paragraph.
- In **Excel**, the insertion point appears on the Edit Line.

Table 2-1. ***Other Keyboard Shortcuts***

Home	Beginning of a line
End	End of a line.
Ctrl-Home	Top of file
Ctrl-End	Bottom of file

My new apartment is fantastic! I've actually enjoyed the renovations.

Figure 10. *Hold down Ctrl and press the right-arrow key to move the insertion point a whole word.*

Using the Scroll Bars

The scroll bars show the current vertical or horizontal location in a file. They also provide a quick method for jumping to a position along the length or width of a file.

The span of each scroll bar represents the entire length or width of the document. The position of the *scroll button* along the *scroll bar* shows your extent through the document. To use the scroll bars:

1. Click an arrow button at the end of a scroll bar to move a single increment in one direction. **(Figure 11)**

   or

2. Drag the scroll button along the scroll bar to move to a particular location. **(Figure 12)**

   or

3. Press and hold the mouse button at the spot along the scroll bar that represents the extent in the document to jump to. For example, press and hold halfway down the vertical scroll bar to jump to a point halfway through a file. **(Figure 13)**

✔ Tip

- Scroll bars appear only when you can move to a point that does not show on the screen.

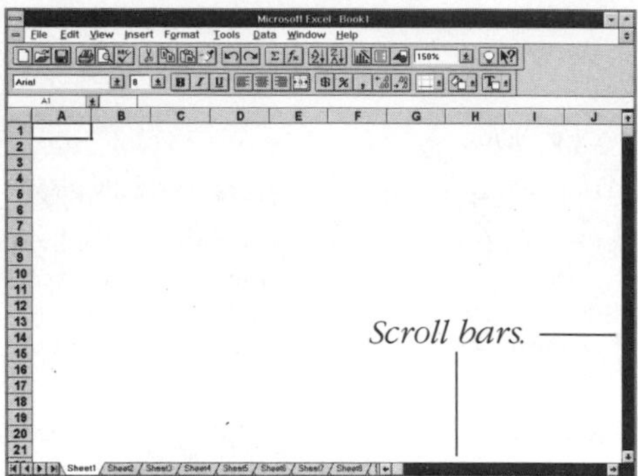

Figure 11. *The scroll bars.*

Figure 12. *Drag the scroll button to move to a new spot on the screen or in a file.*

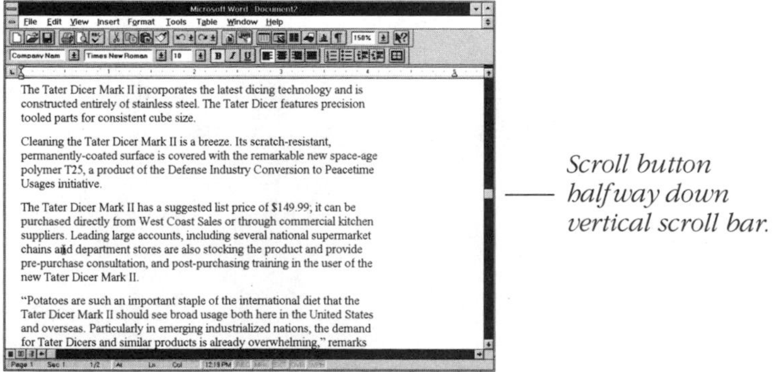

Figure 13. *Halfway down the vertical scroll bar represents halfway through the length of the entire document.*

The I-beam pointer.

I've been up to my armpits in work
iven twelve accounts to handle and I

Figure 14. *Place the pointer on the first word...*

I've been up to my armpits in work
iven twelve accounts to handle and I

Figure 15. *...then drag across the text to select.*

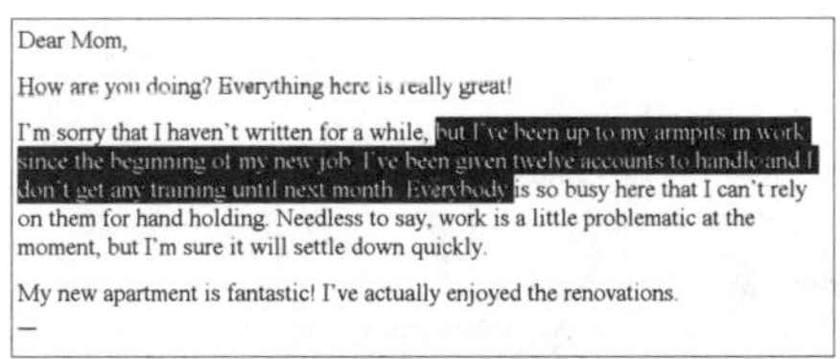

Dear Mom,

How are you doing? Everything here is really great!

I'm sorry that I haven't written for a while, but I've been up to my armpits in work since the beginning of my new job. I've been given twelve accounts to handle and I don't get any training until next month. Everybody is so busy here that I can't rely on them for hand holding. Needless to say, work is a little problematic at the moment, but I'm sure it will settle down quickly.

My new apartment is fantastic! I've actually enjoyed the renovations.

Figure 16. *Drag down to select several lines.*

Selecting Text with the Mouse: Part I

Knowing how to select text is critically important as you must **always** select text **before** you can format, copy, move, or delete it.

1. Place the I-beam pointer anywhere in the first word to select. **(Figure 14)**
2. **Hold down** the mouse button and drag to anywhere in the last word to select. **(Figure 15)**

or, to select text on multiple lines

1. Drag down through the document to highlight multiple lines. **(Figure 16)**
2. Release the mouse button

✔ Tips

- The Automatic Word Selection option guarantees that the entire first and last word of the selection are highlighted.
- In **Excel**, you must select text on the Edit Line. **(Figure 17)**
- **Mouse shortcut**: Click at the beginning of the text, press and hold Shift key, and click at the end of the text.

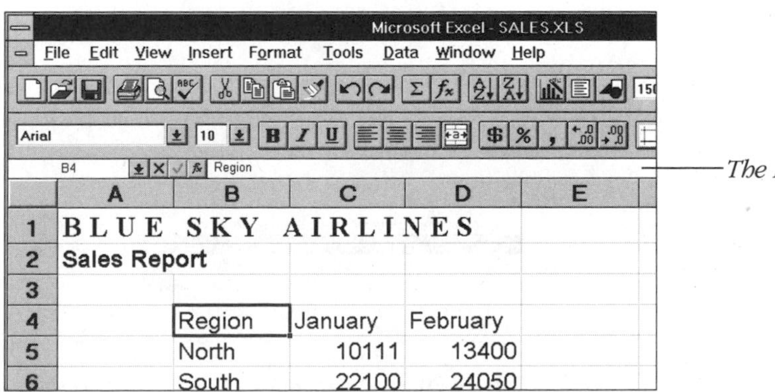

Figure 17. *The Edit Line in Excel.*

Selecting Text with the Mouse: Part II

To select a word Double-click the word. **(Figure 18)**

To select a paragraph Triple-click the paragraph. **(Figure 19)**

✔ Tips

- **Word tip**: To select an entire line of text, click in the left margin next to the line. **(Figure 20)**
- **Word tip**: To select multiple entire lines, click to the left of the first line and then drag down through the left margin.

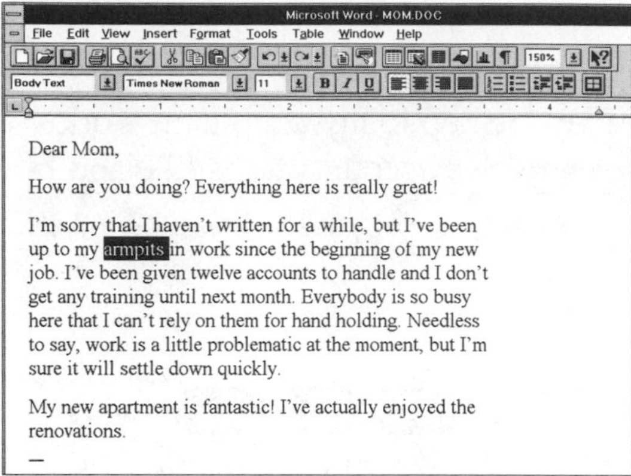

Figure 18. *Double-click any word to select it.*

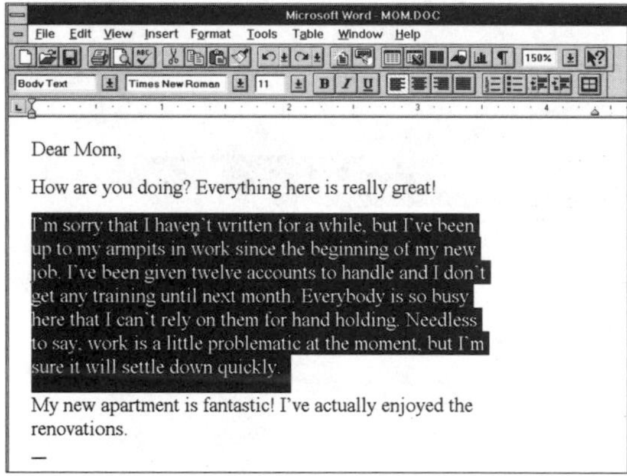

Figure 19. *Triple-click to select a paragraph.*

Click in left margin.

I'm sorry that I haven't written for a while, but I've been up to my armpits in work since the beginning of my new job. I've been given twelve accounts to handle and I don't get any training until next month. Everybody is so busy here that I can't rely on them for hand holding. Needless to say, work is a little problematic at the moment, but I'm sure it will settle down quickly.

Figure 20. *In Word, click in the left margin to select a line.*

The insertion point.

I'm sorry that I haven't written for a while, but I've been

Figure 21. *The insertion point.*

I'm sorry that I haven't written for a while, but I've been

Figure 22. *Hold Shift and move to the last character to select.*

Figure 23. *Press Ctrl+Shift+arrow key to select text word by word.*

Selecting Text with the Keyboard

1. Position the insertion point in front of the first character. **(Figure 21)**
2. Press and hold the Shift key and move the insertion point to the end of the last word to select. **(Figure 22)**

✔ Tips

- Press and hold Shift and press the down arrow key to select multiple lines of text.
- Press the Shift and Ctrl keys along with the left or right arrow keys to select a word at a time. **(Figure 23)**

Selecting and Replacing Text

To replace text in a document or in a text box on a dialog box, you can always select the text and simply type over it. The characters that are selected will be replaced when you begin typing.

1. Select the text to replace. **(Figures 24-25)**
2. Type replacement text. **(Figures 26-27)**

✔ Tip

- To quickly select an entry in a text box, double-click the entry.

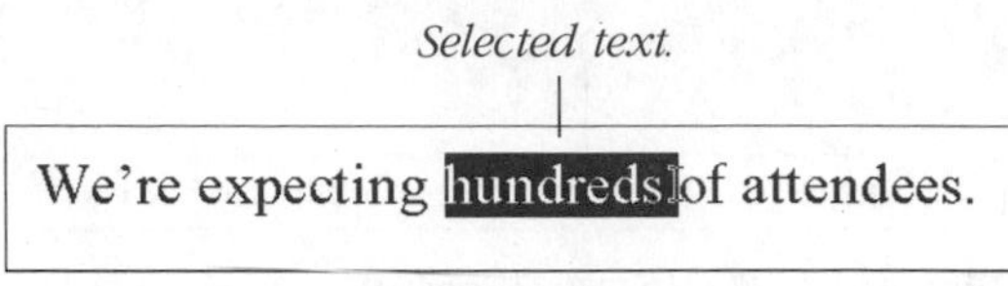

Figure 24. *Selecting text in a document.*

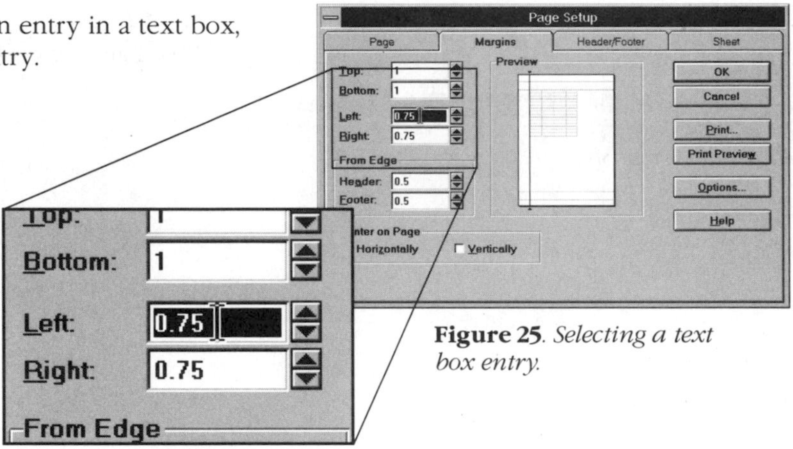

Figure 25. *Selecting a text box entry.*

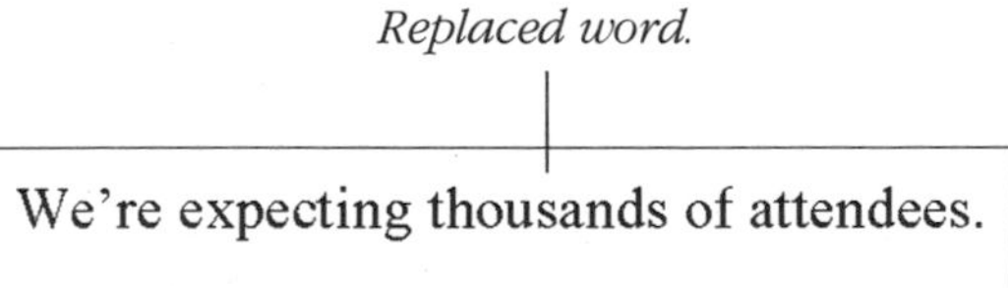

Figure 26. *Typed text replaces selected text.*

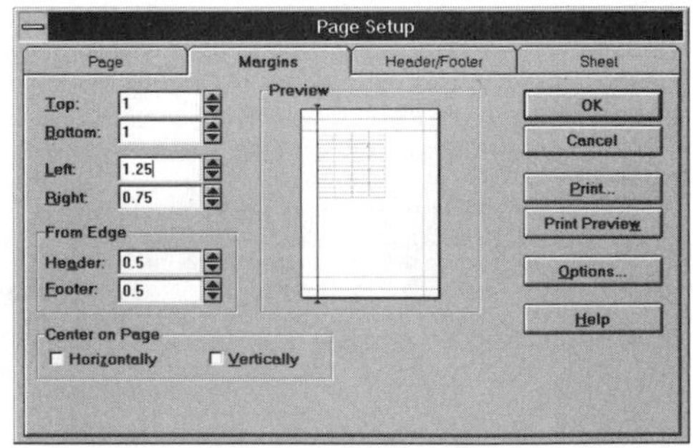

Figure 27. *A new typed entry replaces a selected entry.*

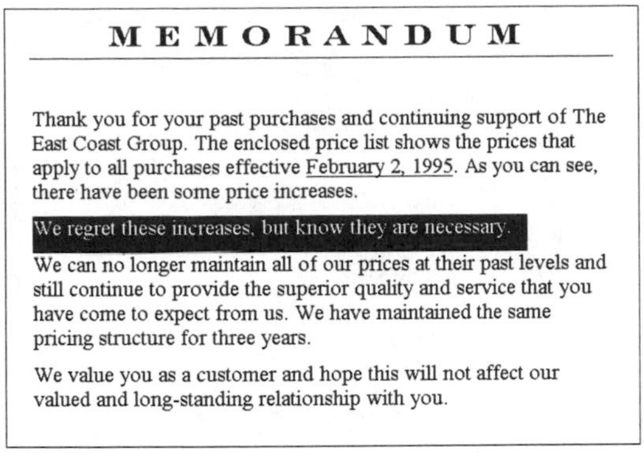

MEMORANDUM

Thank you for your past purchases and continuing support of The East Coast Group. The enclosed price list shows the prices that apply to all purchases effective February 2, 1995. As you can see, there have been some price increases.

We regret these increases, but know they are necessary.

We can no longer maintain all of our prices at their past levels and still continue to provide the superior quality and service that you have come to expect from us. We have maintained the same pricing structure for three years.

We value you as a customer and hope this will not affect our valued and long-standing relationship with you.

Figure 28. *Select the text to move.*

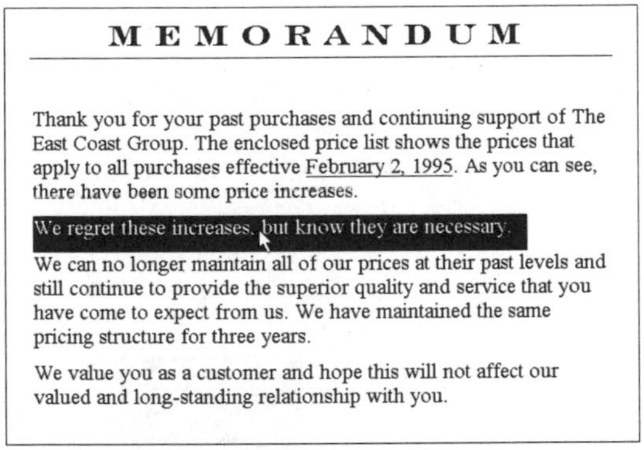

MEMORANDUM

Thank you for your past purchases and continuing support of The East Coast Group. The enclosed price list shows the prices that apply to all purchases effective February 2, 1995. As you can see, there have been some price increases.

We regret these increases, but know they are necessary.

We can no longer maintain all of our prices at their past levels and still continue to provide the superior quality and service that you have come to expect from us. We have maintained the same pricing structure for three years.

We value you as a customer and hope this will not affect our valued and long-standing relationship with you.

Figure 29. *Place the mouse pointer on the text.*

Dragging and Dropping Text

To move text in document, you can always select the text and then drag it to a new location. You can even drag text from one document to another or from one application window to another.

1. Select the text to move. **(Figure 28)**
2. Place the mouse pointer on the selected text. The mouse pointer becomes an arrow. **(Figure 29)**
3. Press and hold the mouse button and drag the pointer to the destination for the text. A gray insertion point indicates the exact spot the text will reappear. **(Figure 30)**
4. Release the mouse button to drop the text at the new location. **(Figure 31)**

✔ Tips

- To **copy** rather than **move** the text, (leaving the original intact) press and hold the Ctrl key while you drag.
- **Excel**, **PowerPoint**, **Access**, and **Mail** have other types of objects you can drag and drop using similar techniques.

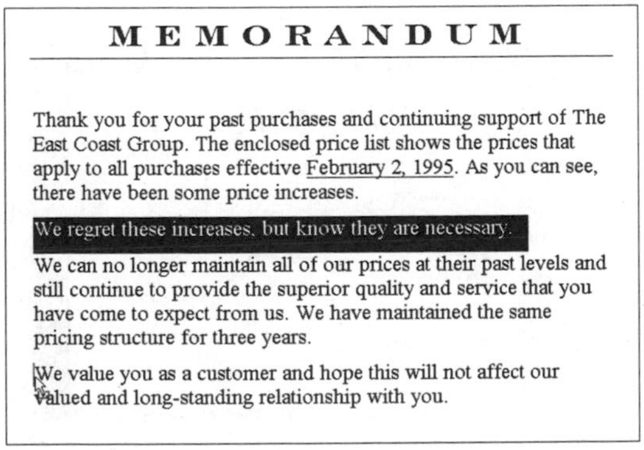

MEMORANDUM

Thank you for your past purchases and continuing support of The East Coast Group. The enclosed price list shows the prices that apply to all purchases effective February 2, 1995. As you can see, there have been some price increases.

We regret these increases, but know they are necessary.

We can no longer maintain all of our prices at their past levels and still continue to provide the superior quality and service that you have come to expect from us. We have maintained the same pricing structure for three years.

We value you as a customer and hope this will not affect our valued and long-standing relationship with you.

Figure 30. *Drag the gray insertion point to the destination.*

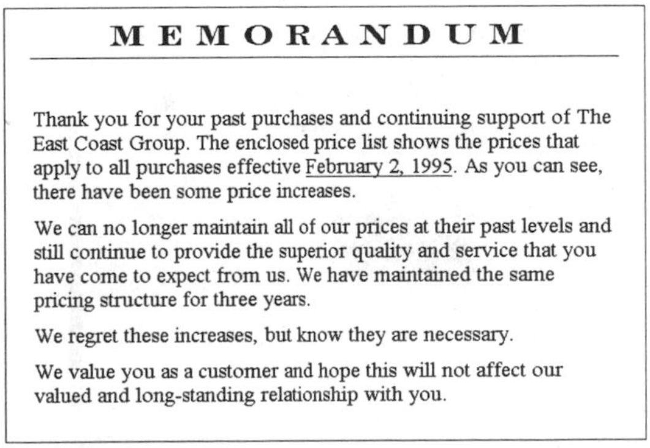

MEMORANDUM

Thank you for your past purchases and continuing support of The East Coast Group. The enclosed price list shows the prices that apply to all purchases effective February 2, 1995. As you can see, there have been some price increases.

We can no longer maintain all of our prices at their past levels and still continue to provide the superior quality and service that you have come to expect from us. We have maintained the same pricing structure for three years.

We regret these increases, but know they are necessary.

We value you as a customer and hope this will not affect our valued and long-standing relationship with you.

Figure 31. *Release the mouse button to drop the text.*

Selecting Objects

Passages of text, drawings, charts, scanned images, and other items you can select are called "objects." You can drag objects to reposition them on the page within an application, and you can usually drag them to other applications, too.

- In **Word**, select text to create an object that you can drag. **(Figure 32)**
  See Selecting Text, page xx.
- In **Excel**, drag from one corner of a range of cells to the opposite corner to create a selected range. **(Figure 33)** The selected range, now enclosed in a box, is an object that you can drag. **(Figure 34)**
- In **PowerPoint** and **Access**, each item on a page is an object. For example, a set of bulleted text items in **PowerPoint** is an object that you can drag. **(Figure 35)**

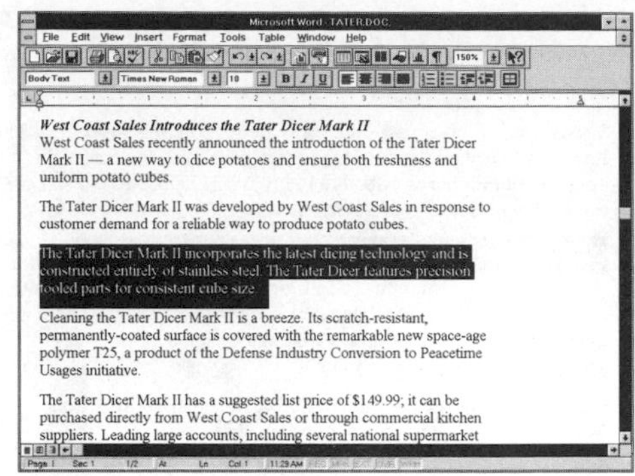

Figure 32. *Selected text is an object.*

You can insert data into the active, unhighlighted cell of a range by simply typing.

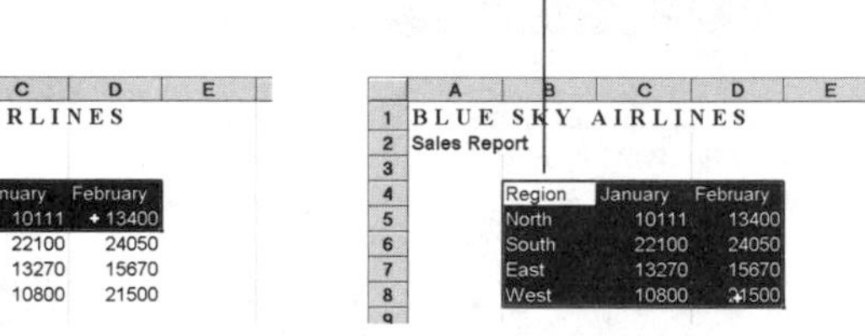

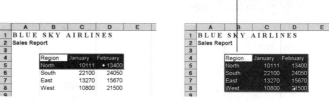

Figure 33. *Drag from the upper left corner cell to the lower right corner cell to select a range.*

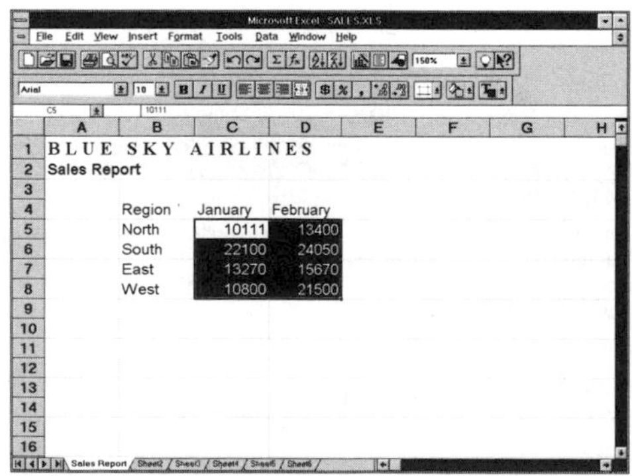

Figure 34. *A selected range of cells is highlighted and enclosed in a box.*

Figure 35. *Handles appear around selected objects in PowerPoint.*

A selected object is enclosed by handles.

Figure 36. *Selected object.*

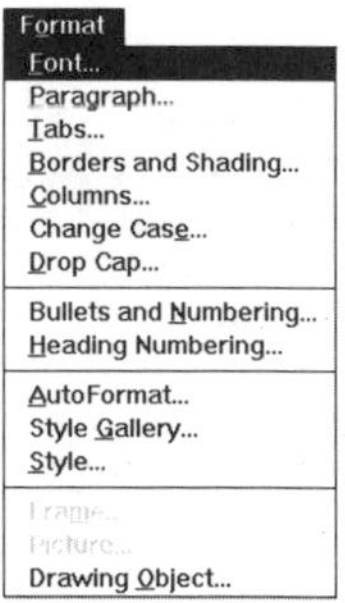

Figure 37. *The Word Format menu.*

Formatting Objects

You must always **first** select an object and **then** choose a formatting command, not the other way around.

1. Select the object to format. **(Figure 36)**
2. Choose a formatting option from the Format menu. **(Figure 37)**

   or

   Click the toolbar button for the formatting command

   or

   Use the keyboard shortcut for the formatting command...

✔ Tips

- In **Excel**, **PowerPoint**, and **Access**, the first command on the Format menu always leads to a customized dialog box with special formatting options for the object you've selected. **(Figure 38)**
- The most popular formatting commands appear as buttons on the Formatting toolbar.

Table 2-2. ***Common Keyboard Shortcuts***

Ctrl+b	Bold
Ctrl+i	Italic
Ctrl+u	Underline

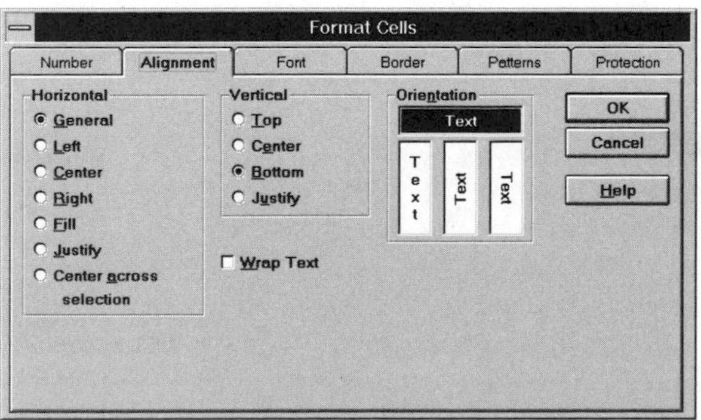

Figure 38. *The Excel Format Cells dialog box.*

Copying Formatting with the Format Painter

The Format Painter transfers formatting from one object to another.

1. Select an object that has the desired formatting. **(Figure 39)**
2. Click the Format Painter button in the Standard toolbar to pick up the object's formatting. **(Figure 40)**
3. Select the object to receive the formatting. If the object is a passage of text, drag across the text to format. **(Figures 41-42)**

✔ Tip

■ To apply formatting to an entire sentence, press and hold the Ctrl key and then click any word in the sentence.

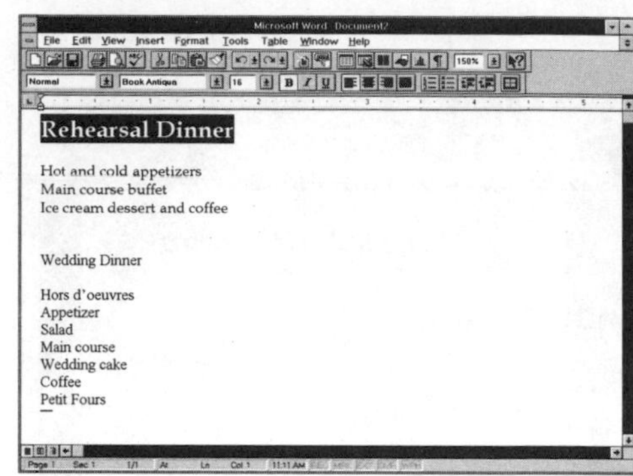

Figure 39. *Select the formatted object.*

The Format Painter button.

Figure 40. *The Format Painter button.*

Rehearsal Dinner

Hot and cold appetizers
Main course buffet
Ice cream dessert and coffee

Wedding Dinner

Hors d'oeuvres
Appetizer
Salad
Main course
Wedding cake
Coffee
Petit Fours

Figure 41. *Drag across text with the Format Painter pointer.*

Rehearsal Dinner

Hot and cold appetizers
Main course buffet
Ice cream dessert and coffee

Wedding Dinner

Hors d'oeuvres
Appetizer
Salad
Main course
Wedding cake
Coffee
Petit Fours

Figure 42. *The newly formatted object.*

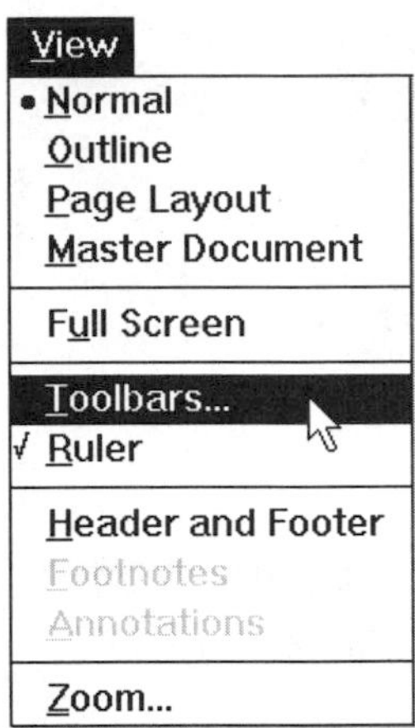

Figure 43. *The View menu.*

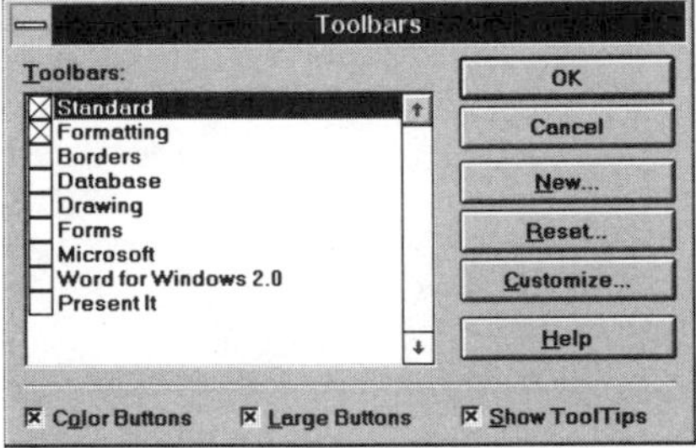

Figure 44. *Click the checkboxes for the toolbars you want and then click OK.*

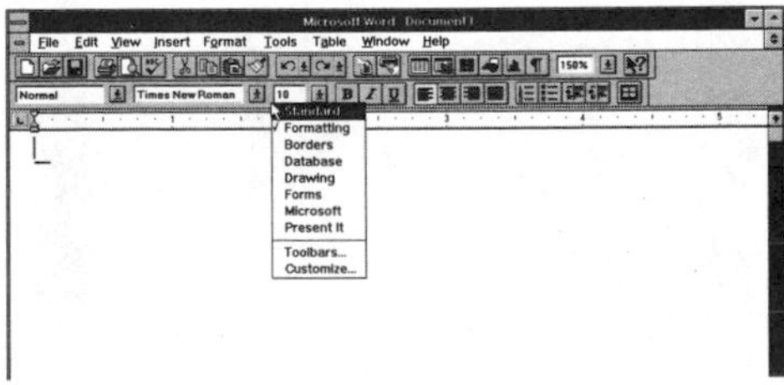

Figure 45. *Click a toolbar with the right mouse button to get to the toolbar list.*

Selecting Toolbars

A default group of toolbars appears in each application, but you can select others to add to the screen to gain access to buttons for special tasks.

1. From the View menu, select Toolbars **(Figure 43)**, click the checkboxes for the toolbars you want **(Figure 44)**, and click OK.

   or

   Click any toolbar with the right mouse button and then click the toolbar to add. **(Figure 45)**

✔ Tips

- To add new toolbar buttons to a toolbar, choose Toolbars from the View menu and then click Customize. On the Customize dialog box, choose a Category from the list and then drag the button you want from the dialog box to the toolbar. **(Figure 46)**
- To move a button within a toolbar or to a different toolbar, hold down the Alt key and drag the button.

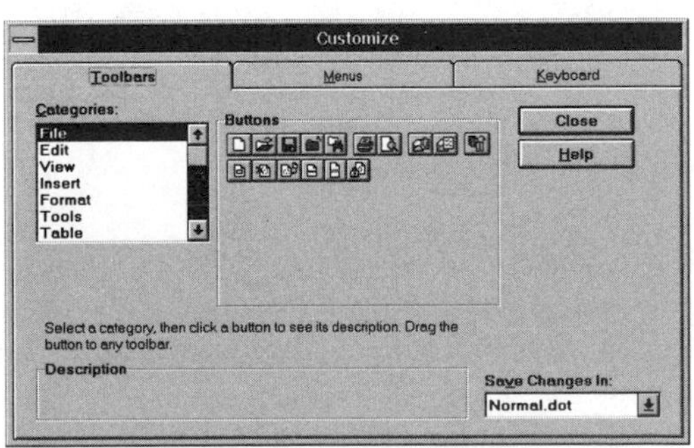

Figure 46. *The Customize dialog box.*

Getting a Shortcut Menu

A shortcut menu offers the commands you are most likely to need after you select an object. A shortcut menu shows only commands that are applicable to the object.

In **Word**, select text and click the right mouse button. **(Figure 47)**

In **Excel**, select a range of cells and click the right mouse button. **(Figure 48)**

In **PowerPoint**, select any object and click the right mouse button. **(Figure 49)**

✔ Tip

■ Click the right mouse button again to remove a shortcut menu you don't want to use.

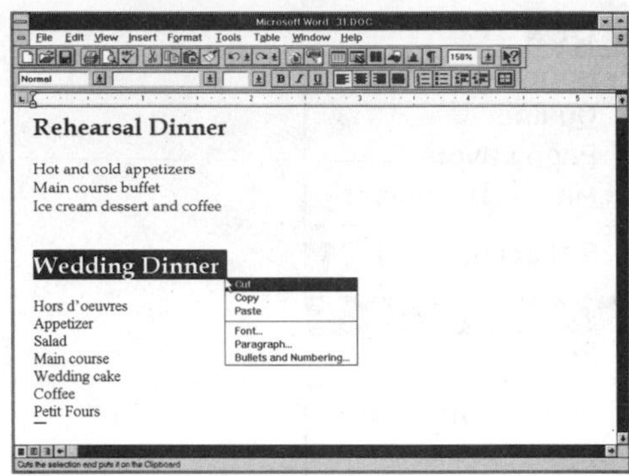

Figure 47. *Shortcut menu for selected text in Word.*

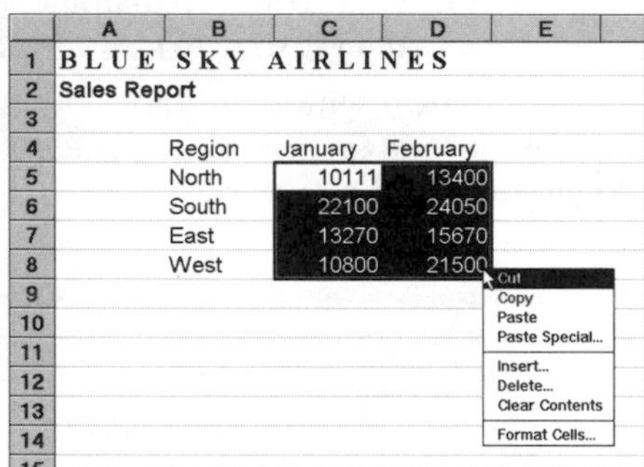

Figure 48. *Shortcut menu for a range of cells in Excel.*

Figure 49. *Shortcut menu for a PowerPoint object.*

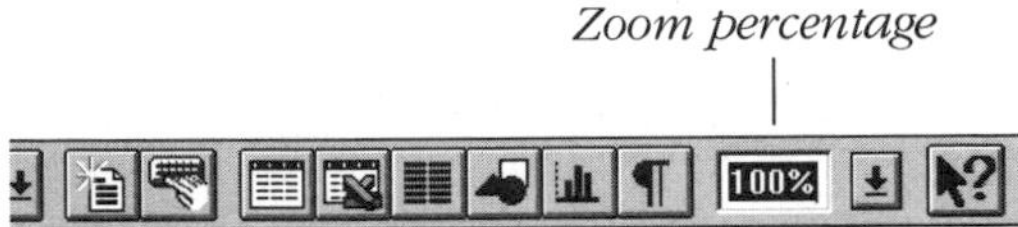

Figure 50. *Double-click the existing zoom percentage to select it and then enter a new percentage.*

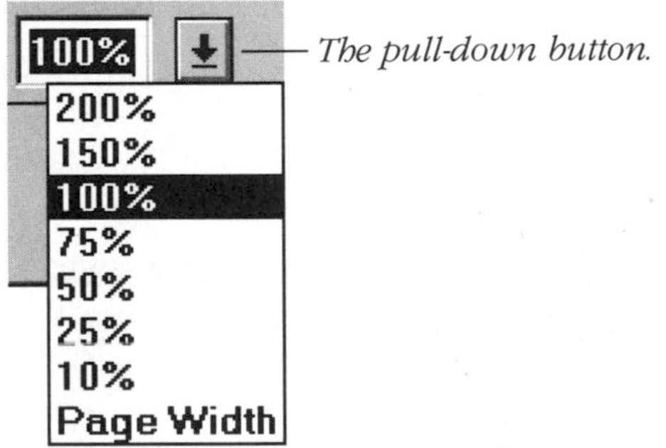

Figure 51. *The Zoom Control.*

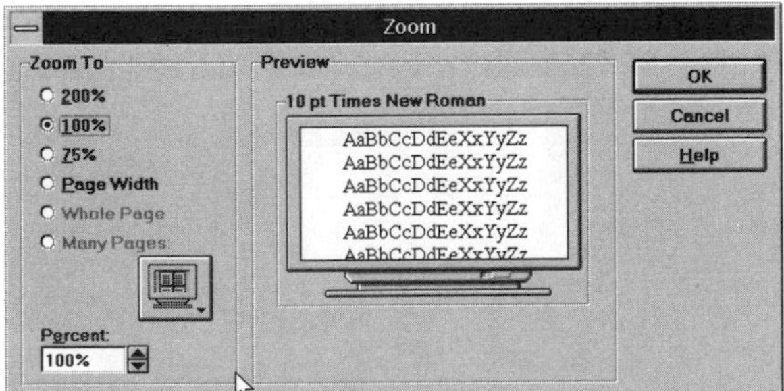

Figure 52. *The Zoom dialog box in Word.*

Zooming In and Out

To magnify your work on the screen, choose one of the preset zoom percentages or enter your own. For example: 200% would magnify everything by a power of two.

1. Double-click the current zoom percentage number, type a new zoom percentage, and press Enter. **(Figure 50)**

   or

   Click the pull-down button next to the Zoom Control and then choose a preset percentage from the list. **(Figure 51)**

   or

   From the View menu, choose Zoom and then choose a preset percentage or enter your own in the Zoom dialog box. **(Figure 52)**

✔ Tips

- In **Word**, Page Width zooms to a percentage that neatly fits the text across the screen.
- In **Excel**, Selection zooms to the percentage that neatly fits the selected range of cells to the screen.

Setting up the Page Margins

The page margins give you white space at the top, bottom, left, and right sides of the page.

1. From the File menu, choose Page Setup. **(Figure 53)**
2. On the Page Setup dialog box, click the Margins tab. **(Figure 54)**
3. Double-click and then type over the margin settings. **(Figure 55)**

   or

   Click the arrow buttons to incrementally increase or decrease each setting.

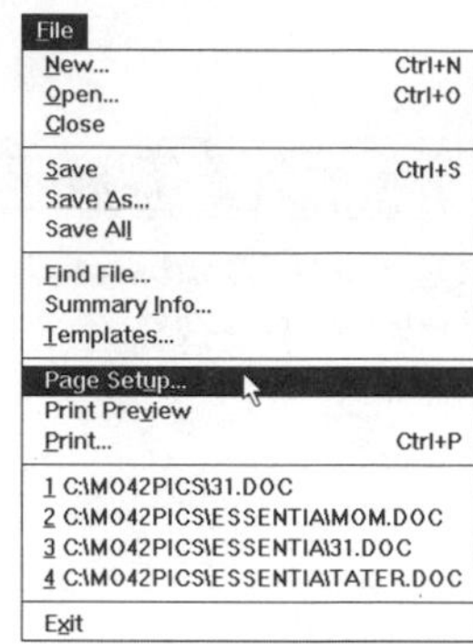

Figure 53. *The File menu.*

✔ Tips

- Click the Paper Size or Page tab to print landscape (sideways) rather than portrait, or to specify a paper size other than letter (8 1/2 x 11). **(Figure 56)**
- The Page Setup choices are stored as part of the current document. The next new document you create will revert to the original, default page setup.
- In **Word**, you can click Default after changing the Page Setup to change the default for the following new documents.

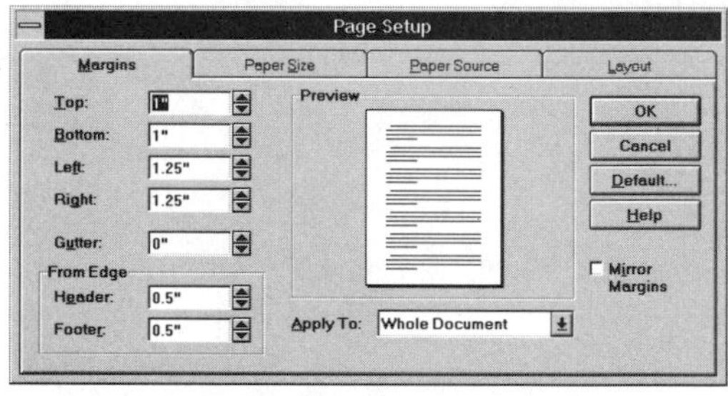

Figure 54. *The Page Setup dialog box.*

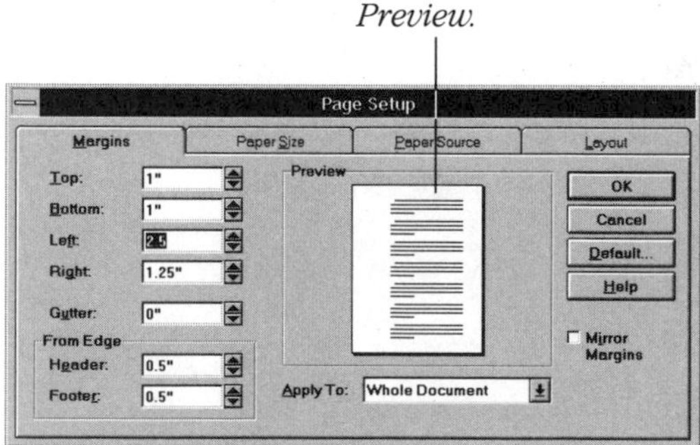

Figure 55. *The preview shows the current margin settings.*

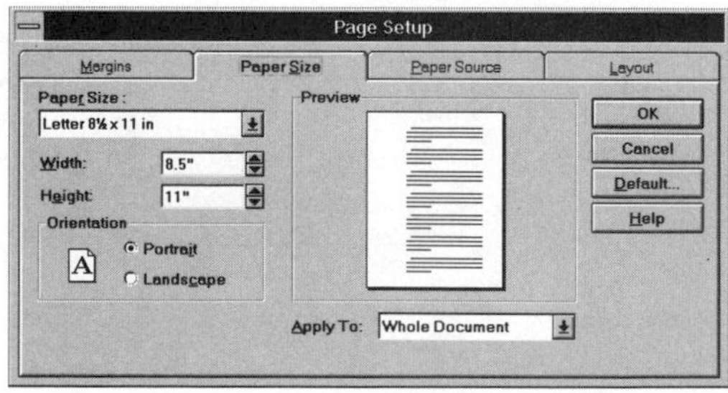

Figure 56. *The Paper Size tab in Word.*

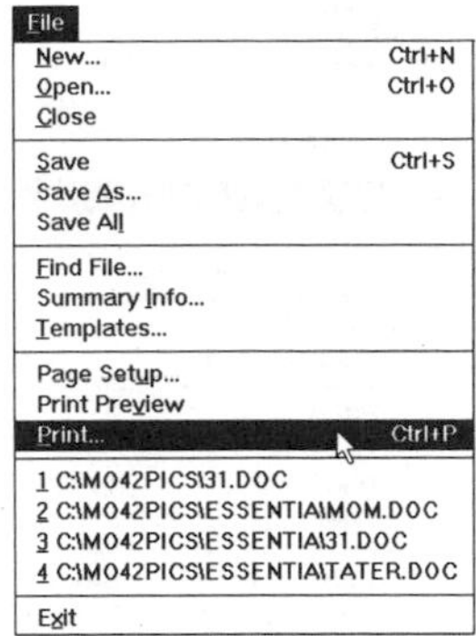

Figure 57. *The File menu.*

Choosing a Printer

If you have more than one printer available, usually when you're on a network, you can choose a printer other than the default printer.

1. From the File menu, choose Print. **(Figure 57)**
2. On the Print dialog box, click Printer or Printer Setup. **(Figure 58)**
3. On the Printer Setup dialog box, choose a printer from the list and then click OK. **(Figure 59)**

✔ Tip

- The good part about having only one printer is that you'll never need to choose a different printer with Printer Setup.

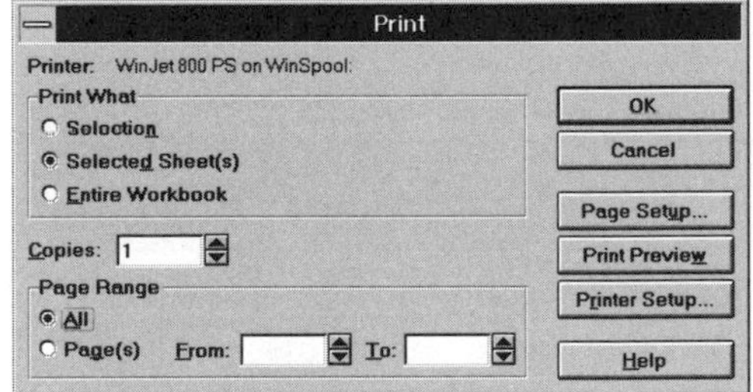

Figure 58. *The Print dialog box.*

Printing

1. From the File menu, choose Print.

   or

   Press Ctrl+P.
2. If necessary, choose a different Print What option on the Print dialog box. **(Figure 58)**
3. Modify the number of copies, if you want.
4. Click All to print the entire document or enter starting and ending page numbers.

✔ Tip

- In **Word**, you can enter a range of pages and individual pages at the same time. Entering 1-3,5 would print pages 1 through 3 and also page 5. Entering 6,12 would print pages 6 and 12.

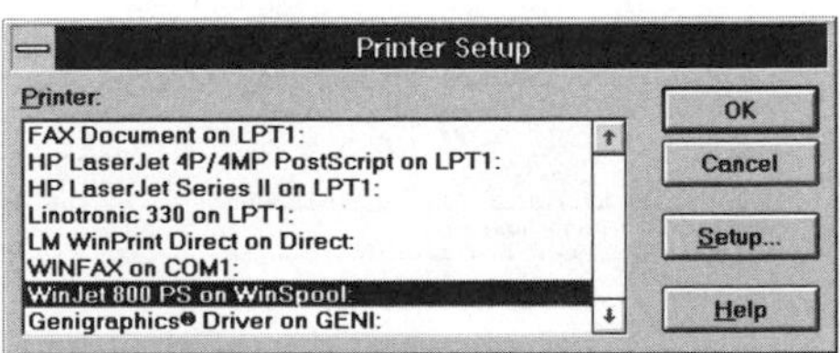

Figure 59. *The Printer Setup dialog box in Excel.*

Saving Your Work

1. From the File menu, choose Save. **(Figure 60)**
   or
   Click the Save button. **(Figure 61)**
   or
   Press Ctrl+S.
2. On the Save dialog box, type a filename over the temporary document name in the File Name text box. **(Figure 62)**
3. Click OK or press Enter.
4. If the Summary Info dialog box appears, enter as much information into the text boxes as you want and then click OK. Press Tab to move from text box to text box. Summary Info helps you find the file later. **(Figure 63)**

✔ Tips

- Saved files go into the default folder. To choose a different folder for saved files, double-click the folder on the display of folders.
- Each application has a way to set a default folder for your work. In the online help system, search for help on *default directories.*

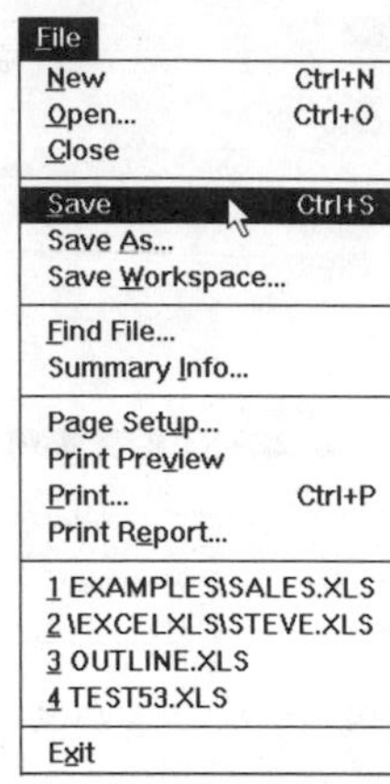

Figure 60. *The File menu.*

The Save button.

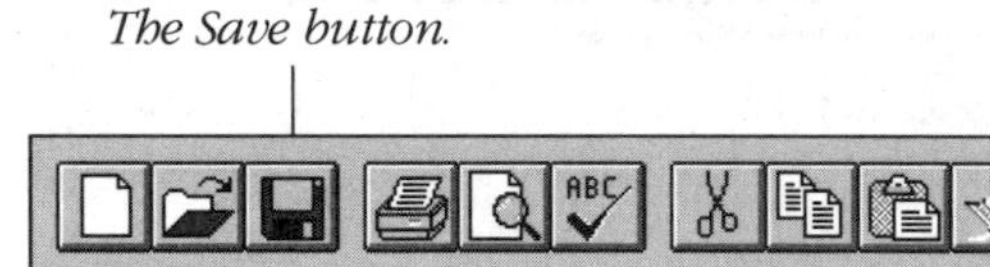

Figure 61. *The Save button.*

Enter a filename here.

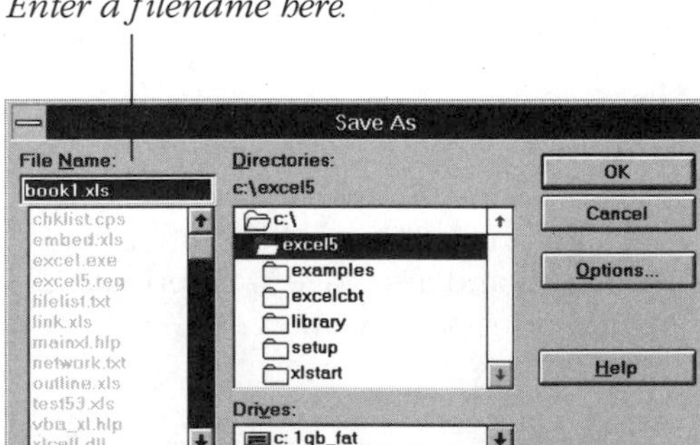

Figure 62. *The Save As dialog box.*

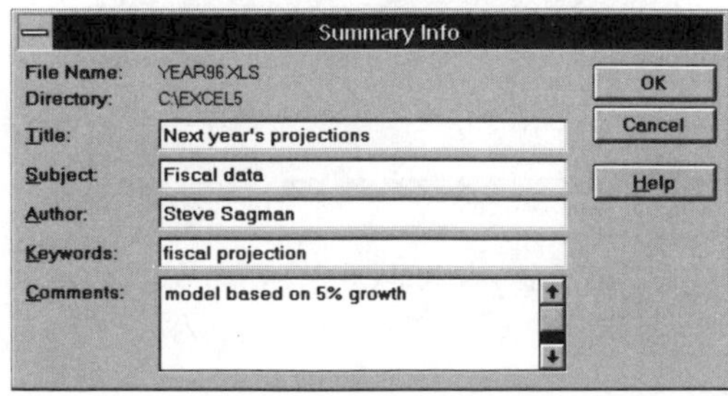

Figure 63. *The Summary Info dialog box.*

Figure 64. *The File menu.*

Reopening a Saved File

1. From the File menu, choose Open. **(Figure 64)**

   or

   Click the Open button. **(Figure 65)**

   or

   Press Ctrl+O.

2. On the Open dialog box, couble-click the filename to open. **(Figure 66)**

   or

   Click the filename and click OK.

✔ Tip

- You can use Find File to search for files based on the Summary Info information you entered when you saved the file.

The Open button..

Figure 65. *The Open button.*

Special Note on Folders:

Folders are the way Windows shows you the DOS directories available on your system. With the Windows File Manager, you can add or delete folders and create folders within folders. The File Manager also lets you manage (move, copy, rename, and delete) the folders and files you accumulate. You'll want to learn more about the File Manager to understand more about folders and files.

Double-click a filename.

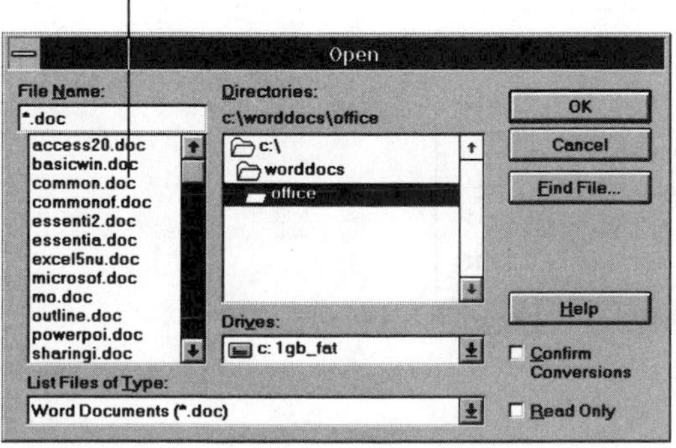

Figure 66. *Double-click a filename.*

Quitting an Office Application

Double-click the Control button at the left end of the application's title bar. **(Figure 67)**

or

From the File menu, choose Exit. **(Figure 68)**

or

Press Alt+F4.

✔ Tip

- Windows will not let you close an application without offering the chance to save any open documents that you have not yet saved.

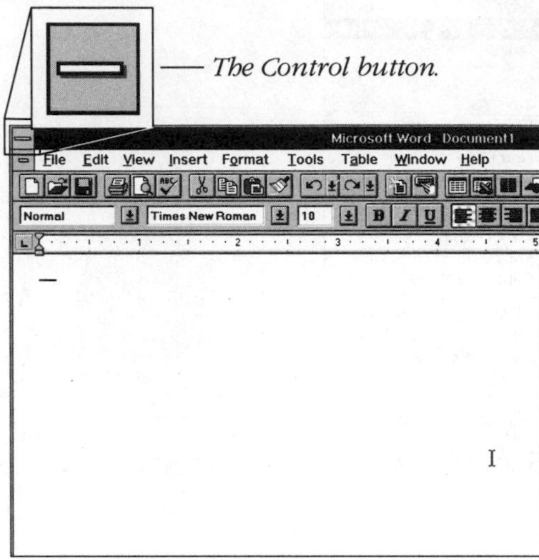

Figure 67. *The Control button.*

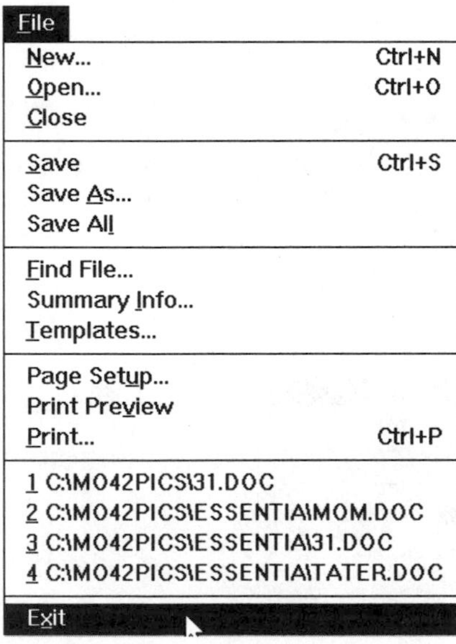

Figure 68. *The File menu.*

Word 6.0 Word Processing

Word 6.0 Word Processing

About Word 3

What is Word for Windows?

Word for Windows, the word processing component of the Microsoft Office suite, creates letters, memos, invoices, proposals, reports, forms, and just about any other printed document that you might want.

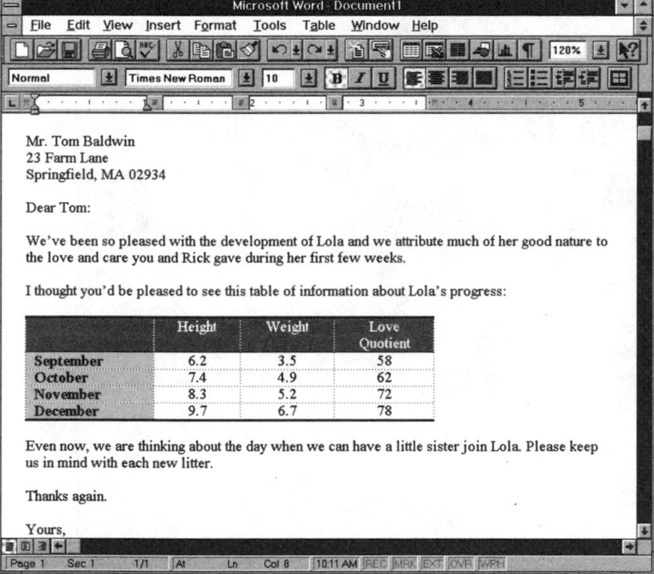

Mr. Tom Baldwin
23 Farm Lane
Springfield, MA 02934

Dear Tom:

We've been so pleased with the development of Lola and we attribute much of her good nature to the love and care you and Rick gave during her first few weeks.

I thought you'd be pleased to see this table of information about Lola's progress:

	Height	Weight	Love Quotient
September	6.2	3.5	58
October	7.4	4.9	62
November	8.3	5.2	72
December	9.7	6.7	78

Even now, we are thinking about the day when we can have a little sister join Lola. Please keep us in mind with each new litter.

Thanks again.

Yours,

You can type text into Word and insert drawings or scanned photos from other applications, then format the text and graphics into sophisticated documents, complete with running headers and footers, footnotes, cross-references, page numbering, tables of contents, and indexes. On the other hand, you might need only to create a simple text memo with Word's easy-to-use features.

Word's approach, as with other applications in the Office suite, is entirely visual. As you work in a document, you see all the text, graphics, and formatting exactly as they will appear when printed.

Word can easily work in concert with the other Office applications, too. It can display numbers from Excel or a presentation from PowerPoint. You can even use addresses from an Access database for a mail merge form letter in Word.

The Road to a Word Document

Entering and Editing the Text

Start a new document and type the text. Don't worry about formatting. You'll take care of that later with styles, or if you don't have styles, by manually formatting the characters and paragraphs. *Pages 47-54.*

Formatting the Characters

Select any words or paragraphs whose characters require a special look (a different font or font size, bold, italic, or underlined, or other special font effects) and "font format" them. If you've created styles that contain font formatting, you can apply the styles to save time, instead. *Pages 55-60.*

Formatting the Paragraphs

Select any paragraphs which need a unique look and "paragraph format" them. Change their indents, line spacing, centering, and tab settings in this step. Also add bullets or numbers, if necessary. If you've created styles that contain preset combinations of paragraph formatting options, this is the time to use them. *Pages 61-74.*

Formatting the Pages

With the text in shape, you can make any overall adjustments to the page that are required. You can change the page size, page shape, and the margins, set up multiple columns of text, and repaginate the text to fit the pages. You can also set up the elements that will appear on all pages, such as headers, footers, and page numbers. *Pages 75-82.*

Adding Tables or Objects from Other Applications

Word's built-in table tools make creating and revising tables of text or numbers quick and easy. If the table you need is a range of numbers from Excel, you can simply drag the range from the Excel window into your document. The range appears with all the data and formatting you applied in Excel. You may want to augment the document with information from other Office applications, too, such as a presentation or slide from PowerPoint. *Pages 83-94.*

Proofing the Document

Word's AutoCorrect can catch many typing errors on the fly as you type, but you'll still want to spell check the document to catch other possibly embarrassing typos. *Pages 95-106.*

Printing or Mailing the Document

Before you print, you can preview the document to find obvious formatting errors in advance. If you're ready for the "paperless office" you might want to attach the document to a Mail message instead, and send it to a recipient over your network.

Extras

Not in the everyday flow are these special features you'll learn about: printing envelopes, creating form letters, and using templates to create virtually automatic documents.

The Word 6 Window

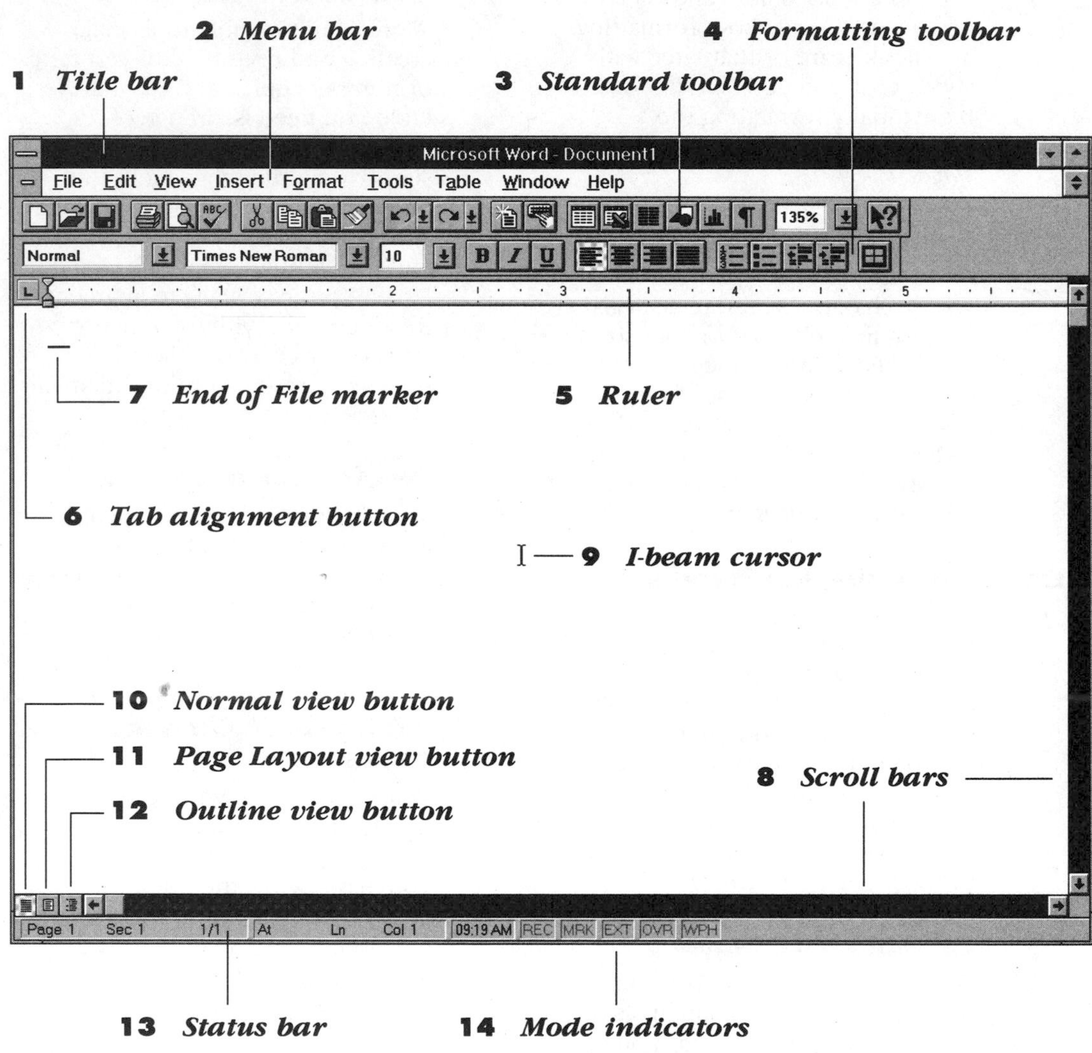
1 Title bar
2 Menu bar
3 Standard toolbar
4 Formatting toolbar
Microsoft Word - Document1
File Edit View Insert Format Tools Table Window Help
135%
Normal
Times New Roman
10
7 End of File marker
5 Ruler
6 Tab alignment button
9 I-beam cursor
10 Normal view button
11 Page Layout view button
12 Outline view button
8 Scroll bars
Page 1 Sec 1 1/1 At Ln Col 1 09:19 AM REC MRK EXT OVR WPH
13 Status bar
14 Mode indicators

Key to the Word 6 Window

1 *Title bar*

Displays the window name. Drag the title bar to move the window. Double-click the title bar to switch between maximized and restored window.

2 *Menu bar*

Click any name on the menu bar to pull down a menu, or press Alt+the underlined letter of the menu name.

3 *Standard toolbar*

Toolbar with buttons for standard file management and text editing and proofing commands.

4 *Formatting toolbar*

Toolbar with buttons for formatting characters and paragraphs

5 *Ruler*

Accurate horizontal ruler showing page width and position of tabs and indents.

6 *Tab alignment button*

Click this button before setting a tab to select a tab type.

7 *End of File marker*

Horizontal line showing the end of the current file. When you open a new document, the end of the file is at the top of the screen.

8 *Scroll bars*

Use these scroll bars to move the view of the document up or down or to quickly jump to a spot in the document. The length of the vertical scroll bar represents the length of the entire document. The position of the scroll button represents the position of the insertion point in the document.

9 *I-beam cursor*

The mouse pointer becomes an I-beam cursor when it is positioned on the text. Position the I-beam cursor and click the mouse button to place an insertion point. Drag the I-beam cursor across text to select the text.

10 *Normal view button*

Click this button to switch to a normal view of the document.

11 *Page Layout view button*

Click this button to switch to Page Layout view, which shows page borders, accurate margins, headers and footers and other elements exactly as they'll appear when printed.

12 *Outline view button*

Click this button to work with the document as an outline so you can develop the structure of a document.

13 *Status bar*

Shows the current page number and position of the insertion point in the document.

14 *Mode indicators*

Show special conditions that are in effect, such as a pressed Caps Lock key.

Starting Word

1. Double-click the Microsoft Word icon in the Program Manager. **(Figure 1)**

   or

   Click the Microsoft Word icon in the Microsoft Office Manager. **(Figure 2)**

✔ Tip

■ If Microsoft Word is already started, press Ctrl+Esc and choose Microsoft Word from the list of running applications. You can also press Alt+Tab repeatedly until the Microsoft Word icon appears. Then release the Alt key and the Word window will come to the front.

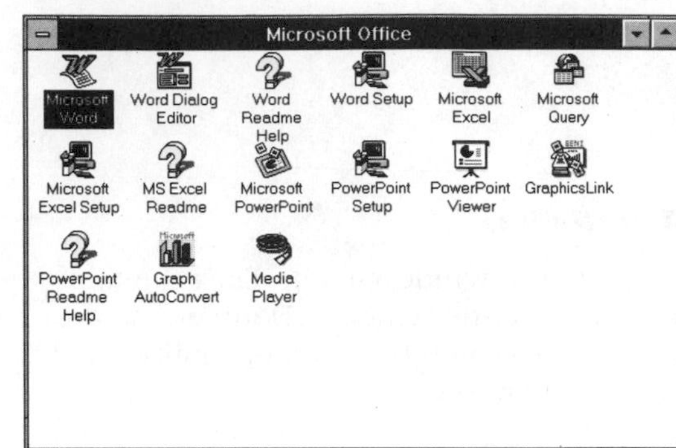

Figure 1. *The Microsoft Word icon in the Program Manager.*

Click here to start Word.

Figure 2. *The Microsoft Office Manager.*

Entering and Editing the Text

Starting a New Document

When Word starts, `Document1` is open and ready for you to type text. Documents are numbered sequentially and several can be open simultaneously. To start `Document2` follow these steps:

1. Click the New button to open a new document. **(Figure 1)**
   or
   Press Ctrl+N.
   or
   From the File menu, choose New **(Figure 2)** and then, in the New dialog box, click OK to use the default template named Normal. **(Figure 3)**
   To learn more about templates, see Saving a Document as a Template, page 101.

The New button.

Figure 1. *The New button.*

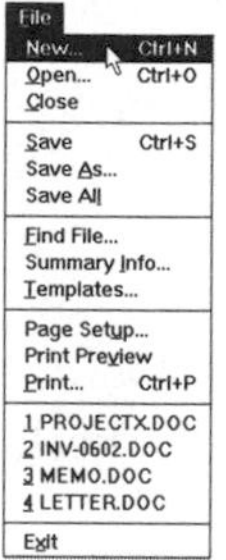

Figure 2. *The File menu.*

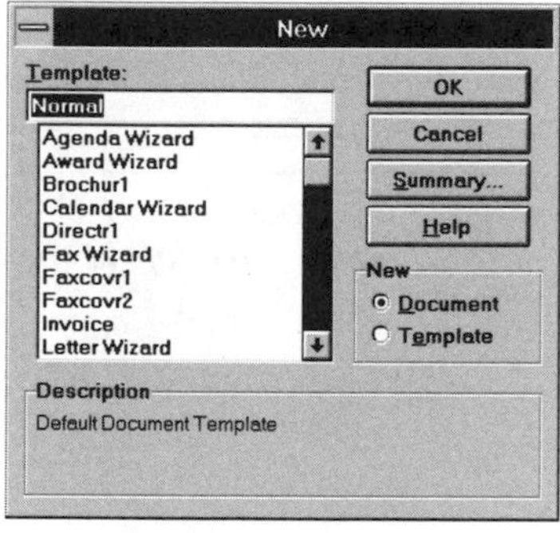

Figure 3. *The New dialog box.*

✔ **Tips**

- To switch from one open document to another, choose a document name from the list of open documents at the bottom of the Window menu. **(Figure 4)**
- A single document can be maximized within the Word window, or several documents can be arranged in their own windows within the Word window. *See Maximizing Windows, page 13.*

Figure 4. *The Window menu.*

Entering the Text

Typing in Word is just like typing with a typewriter except that you do **not** press Enter at the end of a line. When the insertion point (the cursor) reaches the right margin, it *wraps* automatically to the next line. Press Enter only to start a new paragraph. **(Figure 5)**

✔ Tips

- Press Backspace to back up and delete mistakes to the left of the insertion point. **(Figure 6)**
- Press Delete to delete characters to the right of the insertion point. **(Figure 7)**
- Word automatically corrects many common typos, such as forgetting to capitalize the first word in a sentence, or typing "teh" instead of "the." **(Figure 8)** *See Automatically Correcting Typos, page 95.*

MEMORANDUM
DATE: June 21, 1994
TO: Eric Weinberger
FROM: John White
RE: Project X
Our initial survey of the market for pet care products indicates that an overwhelming

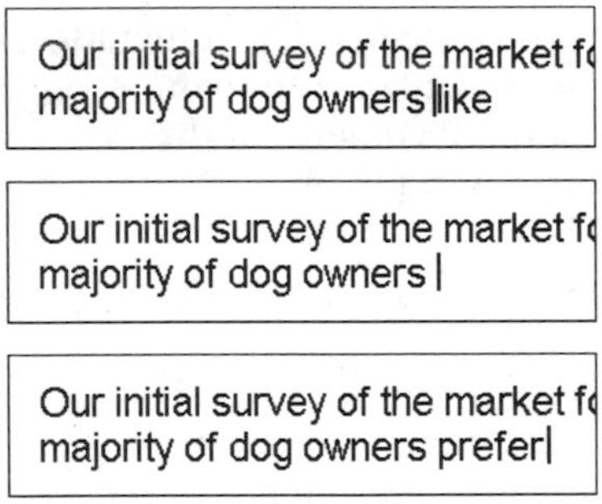

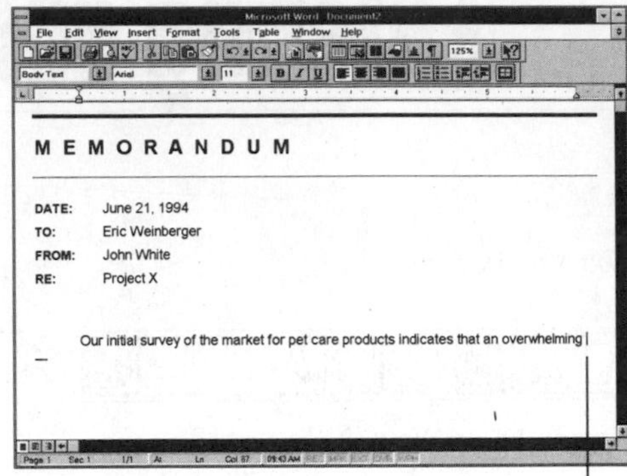

Figure 5. *Do not press Enter when you get here. Word will jump to the next line when no more text can fit on the current line.*

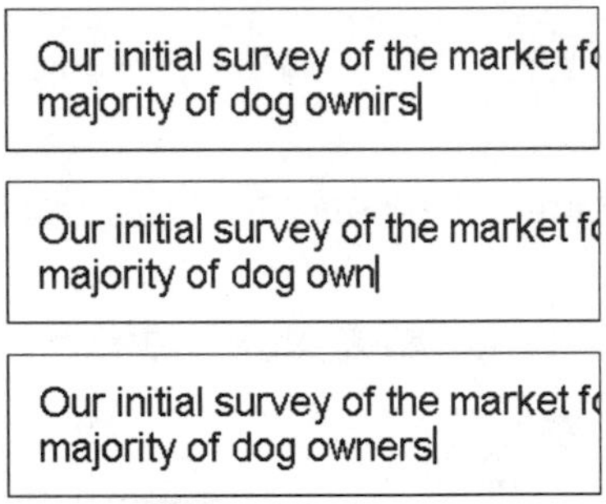

Our initial survey of the market f
majority of dog ownirs
Our initial survey of the market f
majority of dog own
Our initial survey of the market f
majority of dog owners

Figure 6. *Press Backspace to delete characters to the **left** of the insertion point.*

Our initial survey of the market f
majority of dog owners like
Our initial survey of the market f
majority of dog owners
Our initial survey of the market f
majority of dog owners prefer

Figure 7. *Press Delete to delete characters to the **right** of the insertion point.*

Our initial survey of the market for pe
majority of dog owners prefer teh
Our initial survey of the market for pe
majority of dog owners prefer the

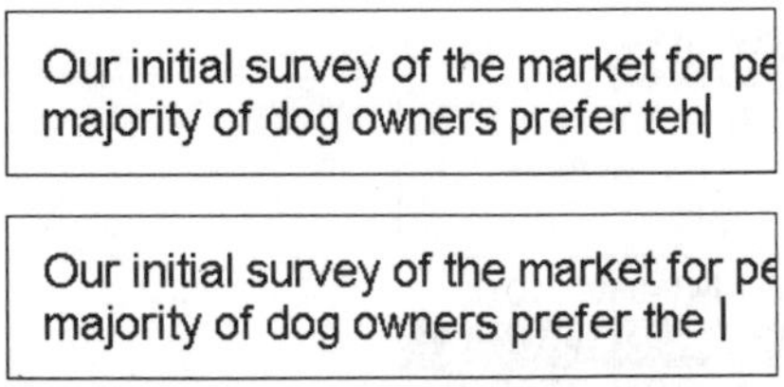

Figure 8. *Word automatically corrects typos when you finish a word.*

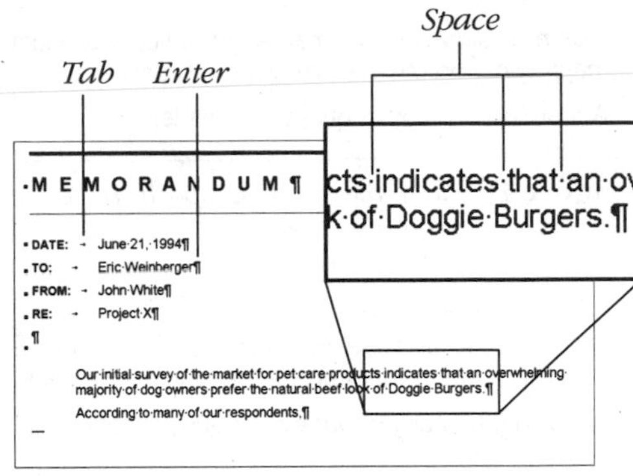

Figure 9. *Nonprinting characters.*

About the Paragraph Marks (Show/Hide ¶ button)

If nonprinting characters are turned on, you will see a ¶ at the end of each paragraph and a dot between each word to help you understand the formatting in your document. **(Figure 9)**

1. Click the Show/Hide ¶ button to turn on nonprinting characters. **(Figure 10)**

✔ Tip

- If nonprinting characters are already on, click the Show/Hide ¶ button again to turn them off.

Table 4-1. *The Nonprinting Characters.*

¶	End of paragraph
Dot	Space
→	Tab
↵	New line, same paragraph

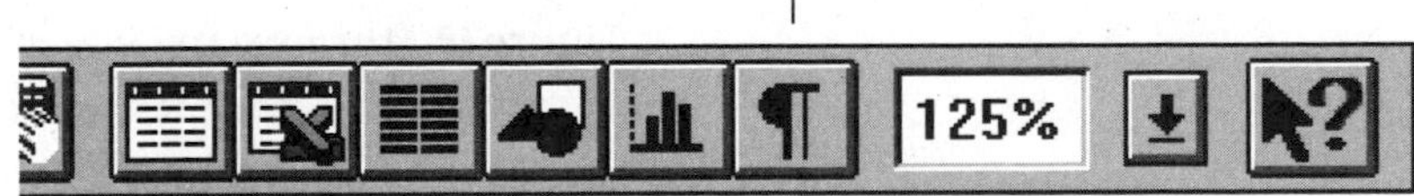

Figure 10. *The Show/Hide ¶ button.*

Text Editing

To insert new text, position the insertion point and then type new text at the insertion point. **(Figures 11-12)** *See Moving the Insertion Point, page 21.*

Press Backspace to delete characters to the left of the insertion point or press Delete to delete characters to the right of the insertion point.

To move or copy text, use Drag and Drop. *See Dragging and Dropping Text, page 27.*

To replace existing text, select the text, and then type new text in its place. **(Figure 13)** *See Selecting Text with the Mouse, pages 23-24; Selecting Text with the Keyboard, page 25; and Deleting and Replacing Text, page 26.*

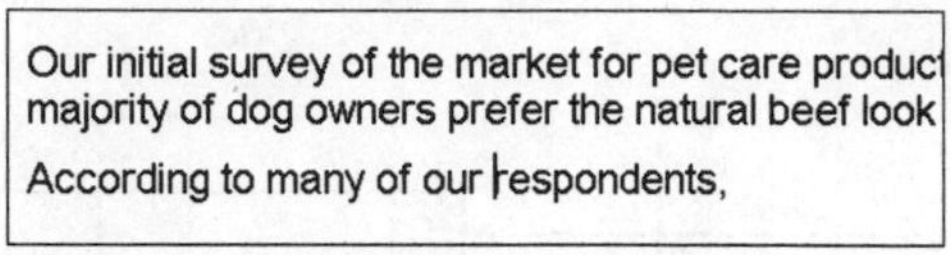

Our initial survey of the market for pet care produc
majority of dog owners prefer the natural beef look
According to many of our respondents,

Figure 11. *Place the insertion point at the location for the new text.*

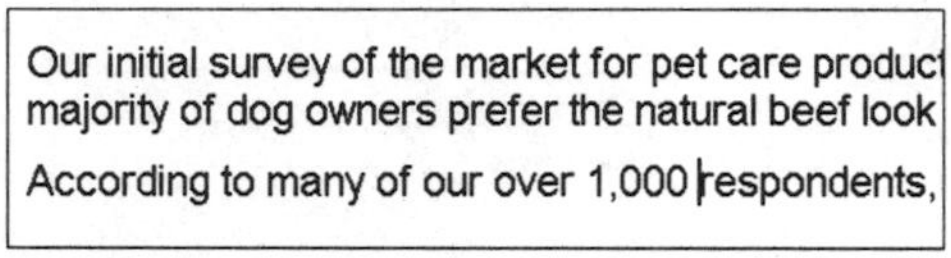

Our initial survey of the market for pet care produc
majority of dog owners prefer the natural beef look
According to many of our over 1,000 respondents,

Figure 12. *Anything you type is inserted at the insertion point.*

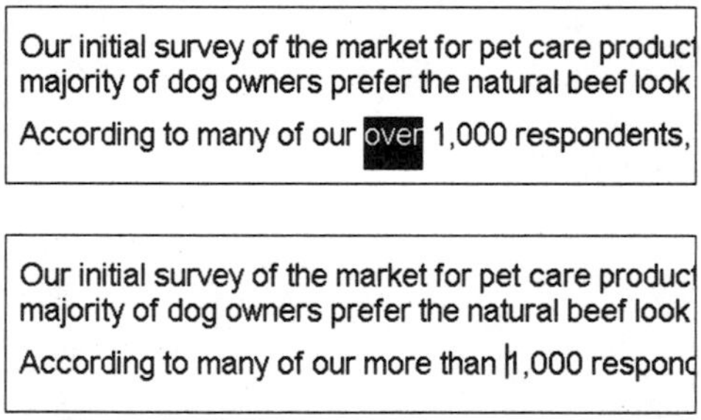

Our initial survey of the market for pet care produc
majority of dog owners prefer the natural beef look
According to many of our over 1,000 respondents,

Our initial survey of the market for pet care produc
majority of dog owners prefer the natural beef look
According to many of our more than 1,000 respond

Figure 13. *Anything you type while text is selected replaces the selected text.*

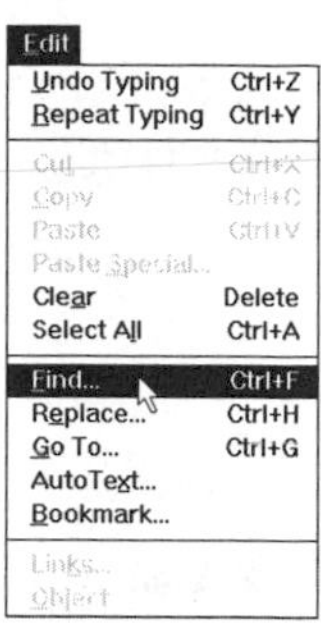

Figure 14. *The Find command.*

Type the text to find here.

Figure 15. *The Find dialog box.*

Click here.

Figure 16. *Click here to choose an earlier text item to find again.*

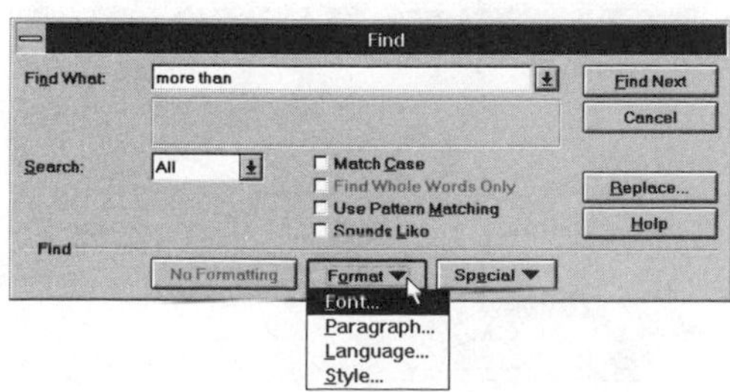

Figure 17. *Choose a format type here.*

Finding Text

1. From the Edit menu, choose Find. **(Figure 14)**

   or

   Press Ctrl+F.
2. In the Find dialog box, type text in the Find What text box. **(Figure 15)**
3. Click Find Next.

✓ Tips

- Click the pull-down button next to the Find What text box to view a list of text items you've already searched for. Choose from the list to repeat an earlier find. **(Figure 16)**
- To search for special formatting, click the Format button and then select a format on the subsequent menu and dialog boxes. **(Figure 17)**
- To search for special characters, click the Special button and then select the special character to find.

Table 4-2. ***Special Find Options***

Match Case	Finds words that contain the same combination of upper and lower case characters
Find Whole Words Only	Finds text when not part of a larger word. Ex: finds "art" but not "artistic."
Use Pattern Matching	Allows you to enter a code to specify a special character combination to find.
Sounds Like	Finds text that sounds like the Find What text.

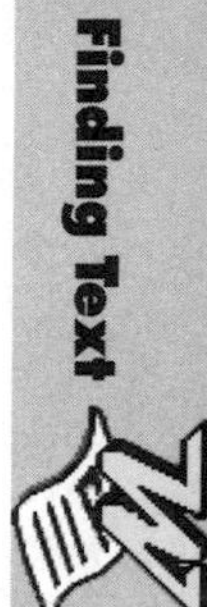

Word

Replacing Text

1. From the Edit menu, choose Replace. **(Figure 18)**

   or

   Press Ctrl+H.
2. In the Replace dialog box, type the text to find in the Find What text box. **(Figure 19)**
3. In the Replace With text box, type the replacement text.
4. Click the Find Next button.
5. Click Replace to replace the text or click Find Next to skip to the next occurrence of the Find What text.

   or

   Click Replace All to replace all occurrences of the Find What text in the entire document.

✔ Tips

- The Search pull-down list gives you the choice to search Up from the insertion point, Down from the insertion point, or All (through the entire document). **(Figure 20)**
- You can replace formatting as easily as you can replace text.

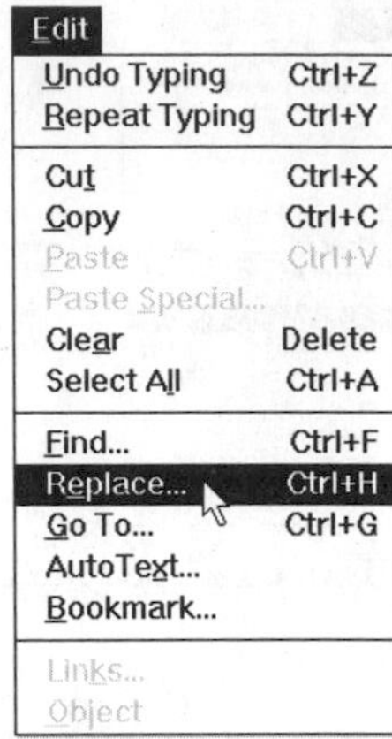

Figure 18. *The Edit menu.*

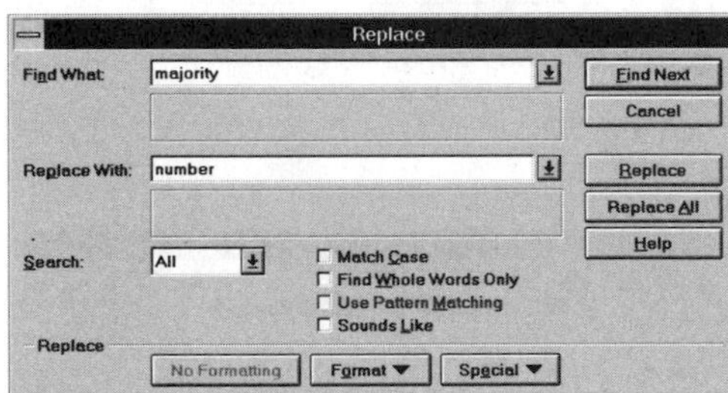

Figure 19. *The Replace dialog box.*

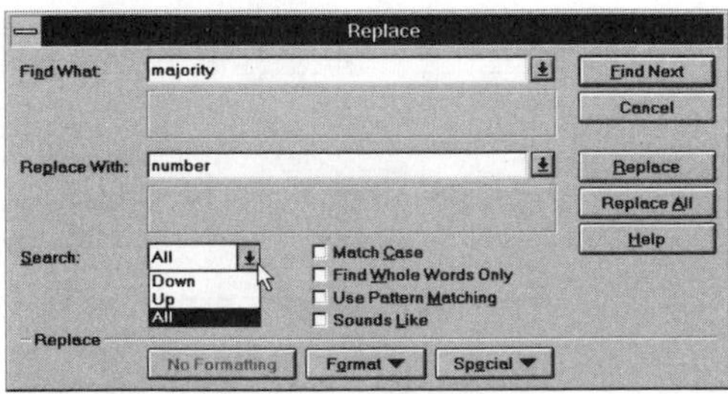

Figure 20. *The Search pull-down list.*

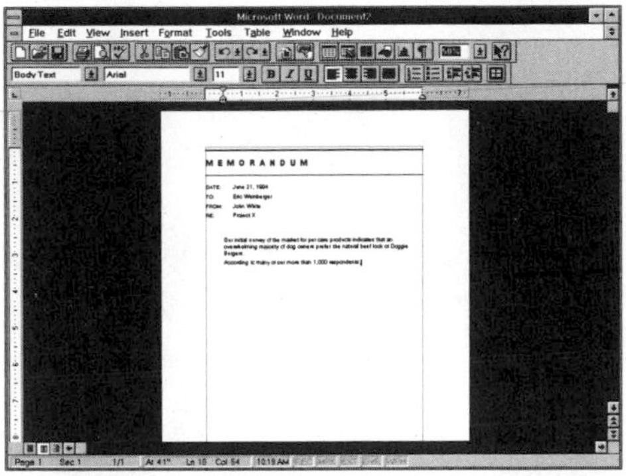

Figure 21. *Page Layout view*

Switching to Page Layout view

Switch to Page Layout view **(Figure 21)** to see the document as it will look when printed, including the accurate page borders, page margins, headers and footers, multiple columns, and frames that contain images.

1. Click the Page Layout View button. **(Figure 22)**

   or

   From the View menu, choose Page Layout.

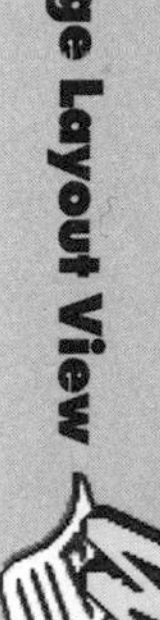

✔ Tips

- Page layout view is an actual working view of the document in which you can enter, edit, and format text.
- While in Page Layout view, turn from page to page by clicking the Next Page and Previous Page buttons. **(Figure 23)**
- While in Page Layout view, you can choose Whole Page from the Zoom Control list to see the entire page. **(Figure 24)** *See Zooming In and Out, page 33.*

The Page Layout View button.

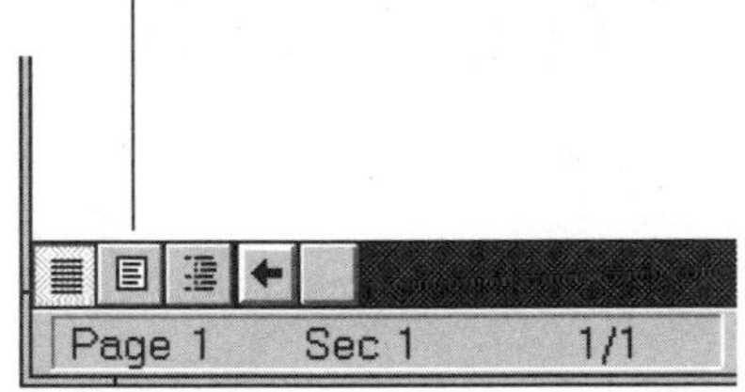

Figure 22. *The Page Layout View button.*

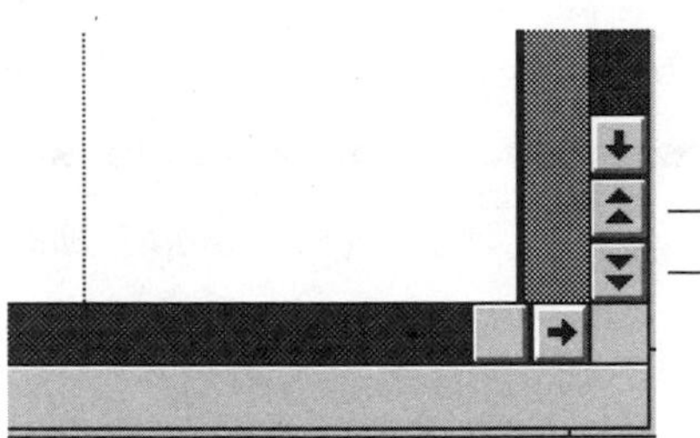

— *Previous Page button.*

— *Next Page button.*

Figure 23. *The Next Page and Previous Page buttons.*

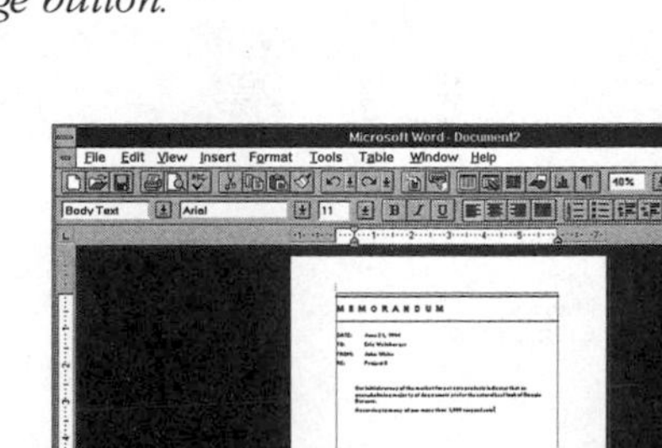

Figure 24. *Viewing the whole page in Page Layout view.*

The Other Views

In Outline view **(Figure 25)**, you can enter several levels of headings, type text underneath the headings, and rearrange both the headings and the text as you work out the structure of a document. To edit and rearrange the main headings, you can collapse any lower level headings underneath a heading at any level.

In Master Document view **(Figure 26)**, you form a compound document composed of individual documents. Any change made to one of the component documents shows up in the master document, and vice versa.

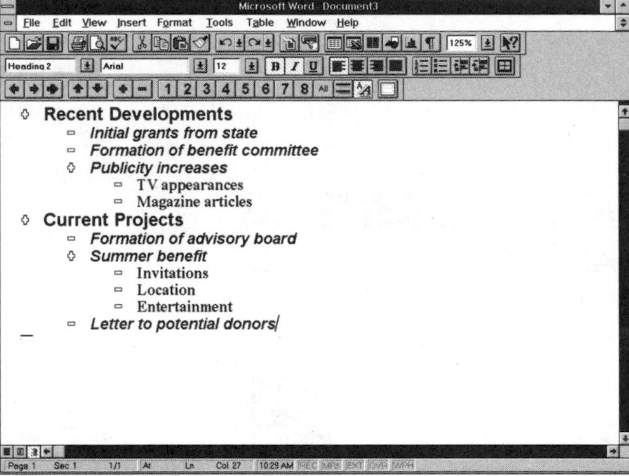

Figure 25. *Outline view.*

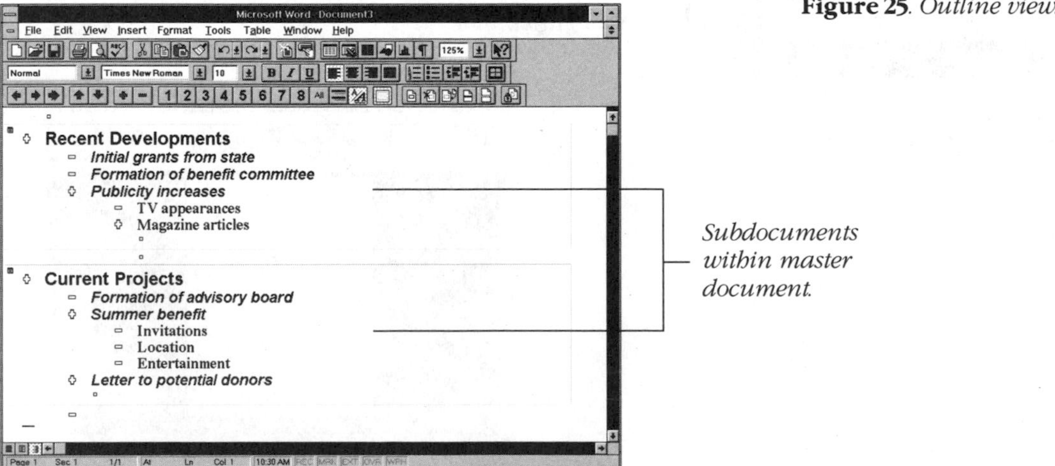

Figure 26: *Master Document view.*

Font Formatting 5

About Font Formatting

The look of the characters you type (letters, numbers, and punctuation) is automatically set when you begin typing, but you can change it by choosing different *font formatting*. **(Figure 1)**

As with any change, you must select the text to format **first** (an individual character, a word or two, a paragraph, or the entire document) and **then** select font formatting with a menu selection, a click of a toolbar button, or a special keyboard shortcut.

For speedy document formatting, font formatting can be part of the information you record in a *Style*. Applying a style you've created to a paragraph automatically character formats the entire paragraph. *See About Styles, page 71.*

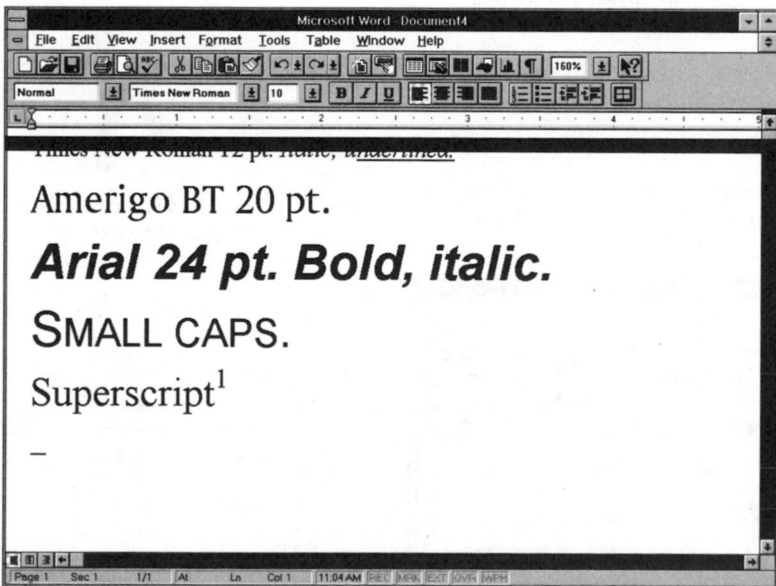

Figure 1. *Examples of different font formatting.*

Changing the Font and Font Size

1. Select the text to format. **(Figure 2)** *See Selecting Text, pages 23-25.*
2. Pull down the Font list on the Formatting toolbar and click a font name. **(Figure 3)**
3. Pull down the Font Size list and click a different size or double-click the current size and type a replacement. **(Figure 4)**

or

2. From the Format menu, choose Font and then, on the Font dialog box, select a font on the scrollable list under Font and a Font Size on the scrollable list under Size. **(Figure 5)**

✓ Tips

- To use the keyboard to change the font, press Ctrl+Shift+F, press the up or down arrow keys to select a font, and then press Enter.
- To return text to the standard font and size for the paragraph, select the text and press Ctrl+Spacebar or Ctrl+Shift+Z.
- To increase the font size of selected text, press Ctrl+Shift+>.
- To decrease the font size of selected text, press Ctrl+Shift+<.

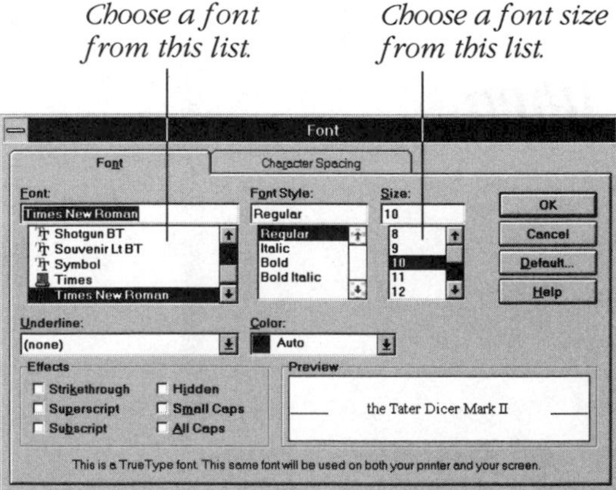

Figure 5. *The Font dialog box.*

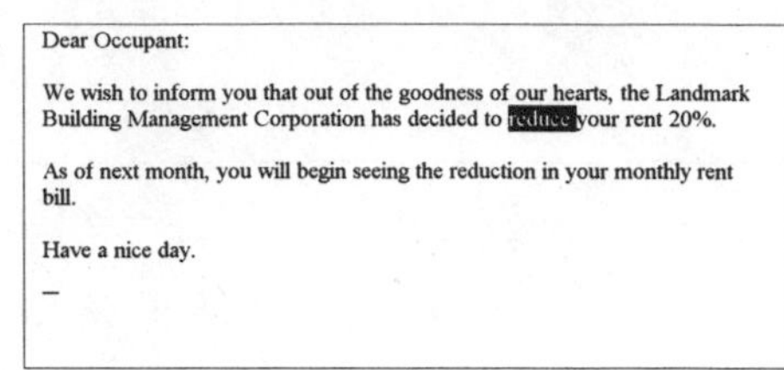

Figure 2. *Selected text.*

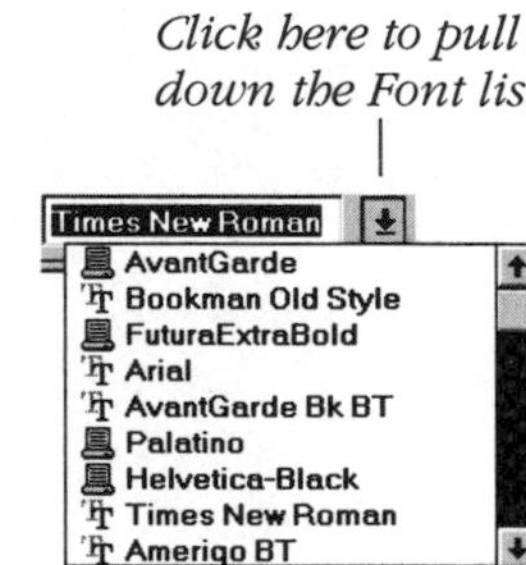

Figure 3. *The Font list.*

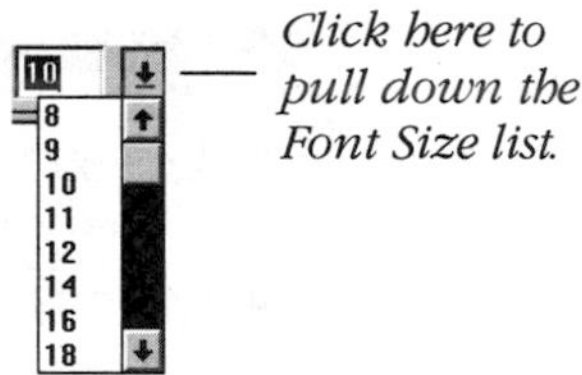

Figure 4. *The Font Size list.*

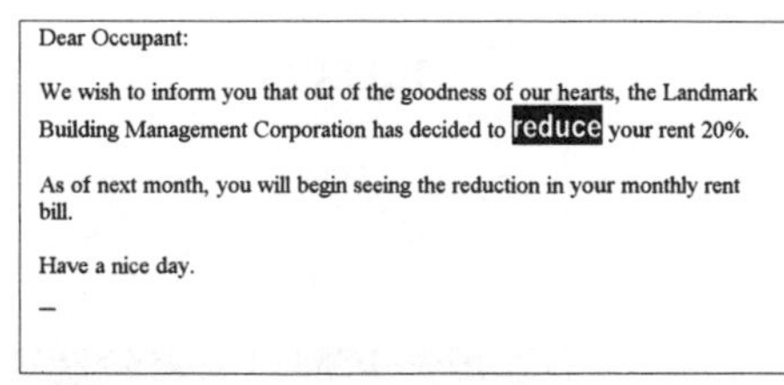

Figure 6. *Text with its new font and font size.*

As you know, your lease for office #200 in the East Coast Sales building will expire on December 31, 1994. Enclosed you will find a contract to extend your tenancy for an additional three years.

The contract includes a rental rate of $495.00 per month.

Figure 7. *Selected text.*

Figure 8. *The Bold, Italic, and Underline buttons.*

The Underline list.

The Font Style list.

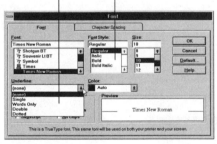

Figure 9. *The Font dialog box.*

As you know, your lease for office #200 in the East Coast Sales building will expire on **December 31, 1994**. Enclosed you will find a contract to extend your tenancy for an additional three years.

The contract includes a rental rate of $495.00 per month.

Figure 10. *Formatted text.*

Boldfacing, Italicizing and Underlining

1. Select the text to format. **(Figure 7)**
2. Click the Bold, Italic, or Underline buttons on the Formatting toolbar. **(Figure 8)**

   or

2. From the Format menu, choose Font and then, on the Font dialog box, click an item on the list under Font Style. To change underlining, click the pull-down button next to the Underline text box and then click an underline option on the list. **(Figures 9 and 11)**

✔ Tip

■ The Bold, Italic, and Underline buttons and keyboard shortcuts are toggles. Use them once to turn formatting on. Again to turn formatting off.

Table 5-1. *Keyboard Shortcuts*

Ctrl+b	Bold
Ctrl+i	Italic
Ctrl+u	Underline

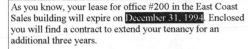

Single

Words Only

Double

Dotted

Figure 11. *Underline options.*

Expanding and Condensing Character Spacing

1. Select the text to format. **(Figure 12)**
2. From the Format menu, choose Font.
3. On the Character Spacing tab of the Font dialog box, click the up or down arrows next to the By text box to Expand or Condense the character spacing. **(Figure 13)**

✔ **Tip**

- To quickly return expanded or condensed text to normal, select the text and then press Ctrl+Spacebar or Ctrl+Shift+Z.

Figure 12. *Selected text.*

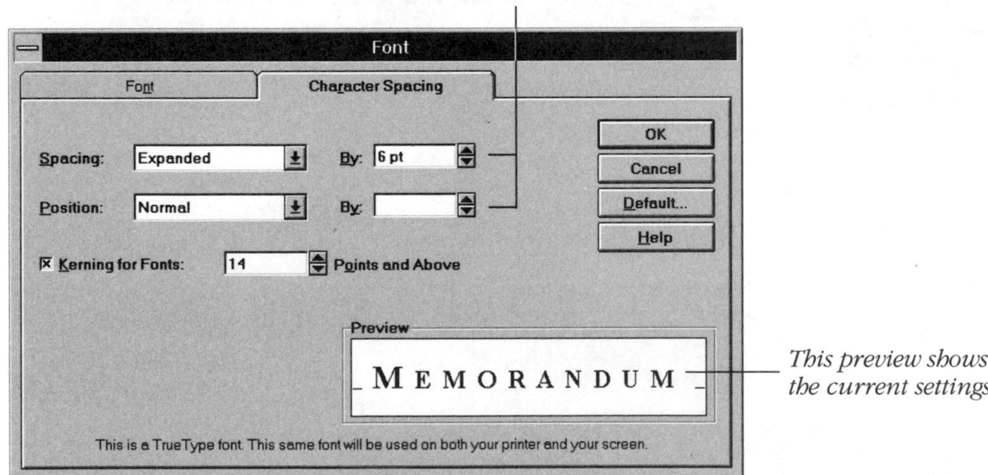

Figure 13. *The Character Spacing tab on the Font dialog box.*

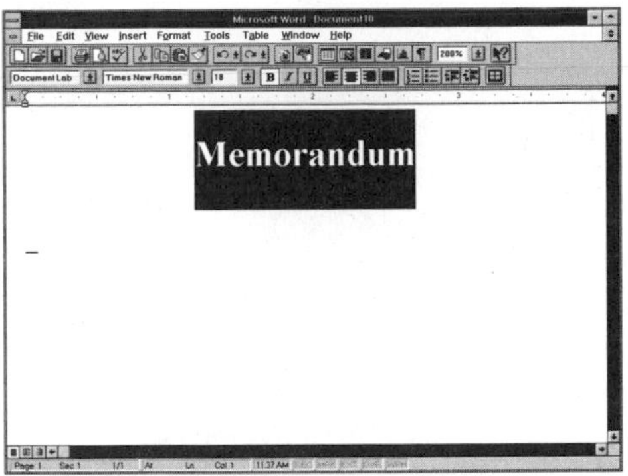

Figure 14. *Selected text.*

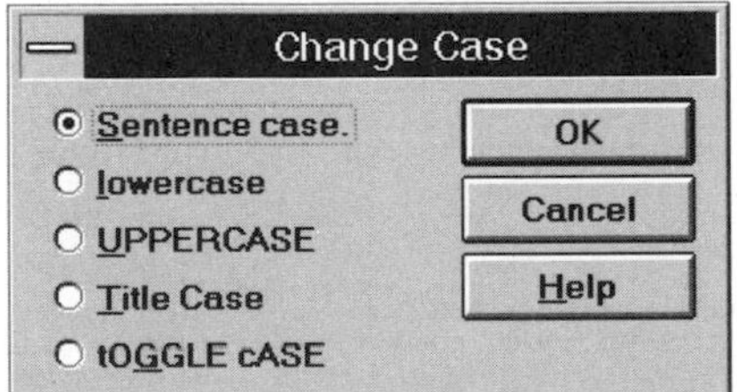

Figure 15. *The Change Case dialog box.*

Changing the Case of Characters

1. Select the text to format. **(Figure 14)**
2. Press Shift+F3 to toggle among Initial Caps, ALL CAPS, and all lower case.

   or

   From the Format menu, choose Change Case and select an option on the Change Case dialog box. **(Figure 15)**

   or

   From the Format menu, choose Font.
3. On the Font tab of the Font dialog box, click the Small Caps or All Caps checkboxes. Click either one again to clear it. **(Figure 16)**

Table 5-2. *Keyboard Shortcuts*

Shift+F3	Change the case of characters.
Ctrl+Shift+K	Small caps.
Ctrl+Shift+A	All caps.
Ctrl+Spacebar	Remove Small caps or All caps applied with keyboard shortcut.

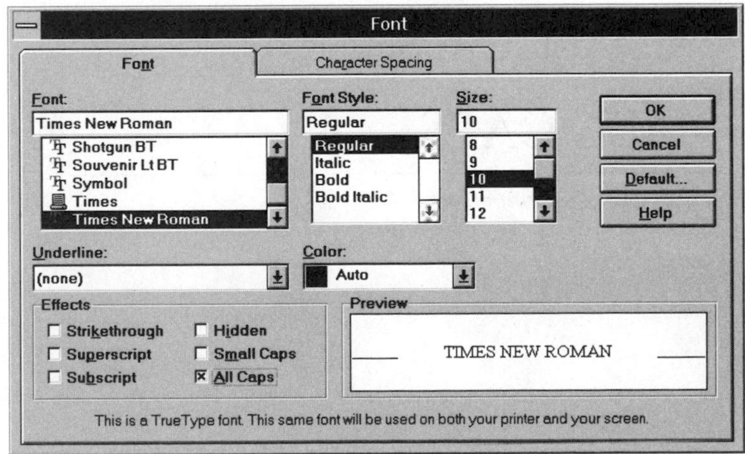

Figure 16. *The Font tab of the Font dialog box.*

Special Font Effects

On the Font tab of the Font dialog box, six checkboxes let you specify special effects for the selected text.

1. Select the text to format.
2. From the Format menu, choose Font.
3. On the Font tab of the Font dialog box, click as many effects as you'd like to apply to the selected text. **(Figure 17)**

~~Strikethrough~~

Text ^{Superscript}

Text $_{\text{Subscript}}$

Hidden

SMALL CAPS

ALL CAPS

Figure 17. *The Font effects.*

Paragraph Formatting 6

M E M O R A N D U M ¶

DATE: November 24, 1994¶
TO: George Washington¶
FROM: Abraham Lincoln¶

I hope this letter finds you in good health and good spirits.¶

I am writing now to solicit your advice on several issues of great importance to the state and our good people. Among my concerns is the continuing difficulties I have had with gathering support for my plans.¶

Figure 1. *Paragraph marks.*

About Paragraph Formatting

Paragraph formatting applies changes in appearance to entire paragraphs. The most popular paragraph formatting options include indenting, double spacing, centering, justifying, numbering, and adding bullets to paragraphs.

A paragraph can be any amount of text that ends in a paragraph mark **(Figure 1)**, from as little as a single word to multiple lines of text.

✔ Tip

- Use the Format Painter to copy paragraph formatting from one paragraph to others. *See Copying Formatting with the Format Painter, page 30.*

Selecting Paragraphs

To select a paragraph for paragraph formatting, click anywhere in the paragraph. The paragraph containing the insertion point will be formatted. **(Figure 2)**

To select multiple paragraphs, drag from anywhere in the first paragraph to format to anywhere in the last paragraph to format. If the selection extends into a paragraph, the paragraph will be formatted. **(Figure 3)**

✔ Tips

- You do not have to select an entire paragraph to apply paragraph formatting.
- To select multiple paragraphs quickly, drag down through the left margin next to the paragraphs.

Insertion point — *This paragraph will be formatted.*

I hope this letter finds you in good health and good spirits.¶

I am writing now to solicit your advice on several issues of great importance to the state and our good people. Among my concerns is the continuing difficulties I have had with gathering support for my plans.¶

Figure 2. *The paragraph containing the insertion point will be formatted.*

I hope this letter finds you in good health and good spirits.¶

I am writing now to solicit your advice on several issues of great importance to the state and our good people. Among my concerns is the continuing difficoulties I have had with gathering support for my plans.¶

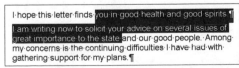

Figure 3. *Drag across multiple paragraphs to format.*

Indenting Paragraphs with the Ruler

1. Click in or select the paragraph or paragraphs to be formatted. **(Figure 4)**
2. Drag the left indent marker to set the left indent. **(Figures 5 and 7)**
   or
   Drag the rectangular button below the left indent marker to move the first line indent and the left indent markers simultaneously and maintain their relative positions. **(Figure 7)**
3. Drag the right indent marker to set the right indent. **(Figure 6)**

✔ Tips

- Click on a paragraph and then examine the indent markers on the ruler to check the indent settings for the paragraph.
- Click the Increase Indent button on the Formatting toolbar to increase the left indent one-half inch. **(Figure 8)**
- Click the Decrease Indent button to decrease the left indent one-half inch. **(Figure 8)**

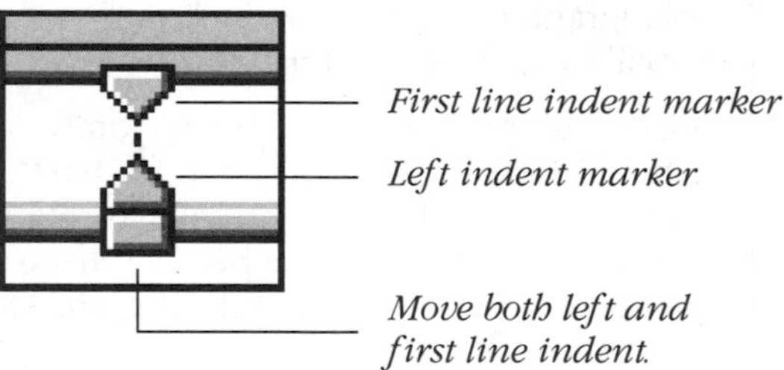

Figure 7. *The indent markers.*

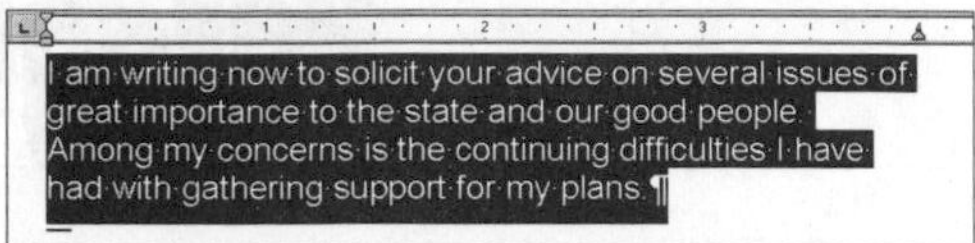

Figure 4. *Select a paragraph to format.*

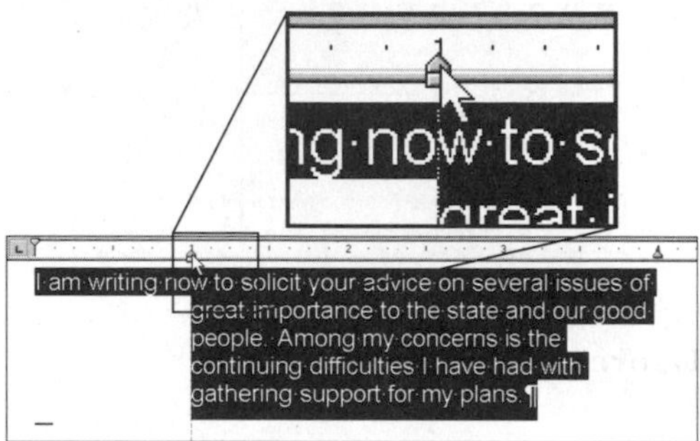

Figure 5. *The left indent marker.*

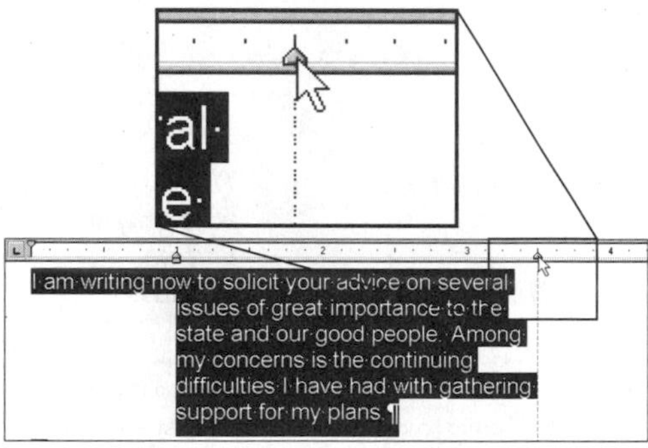

Figure 6. *The right indent marker.*

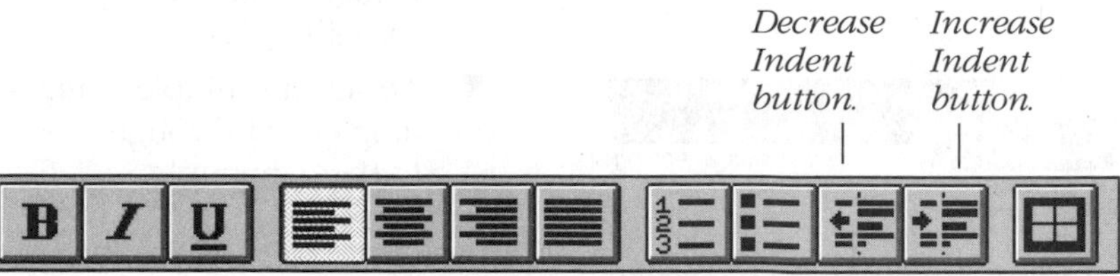

Figure 8. *The Increase Indent and Decrease Indent buttons.*

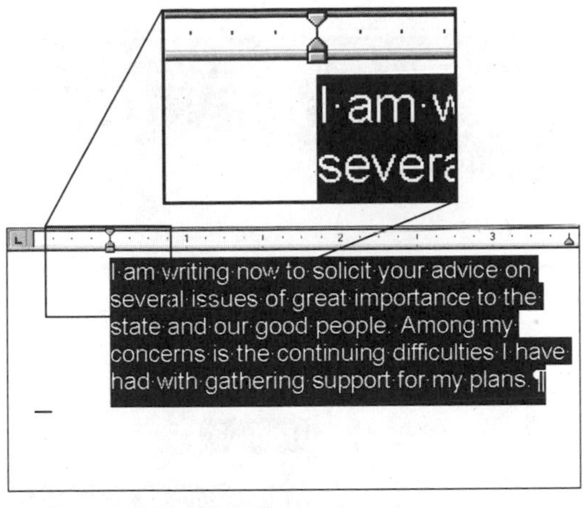

Figure 9. *Select a paragraph to format.*

Changing the First Line Indent

1. Select the paragraph or paragraphs to be formatted. **(Figure 9)**
2. Drag the first line indent marker to set the indent of the first line of a paragraph. **(Figure 10)**

✔ Tip

- Drag the first line indent to the left of the left indent marker to create a hanging indent. **(Figure 11)**

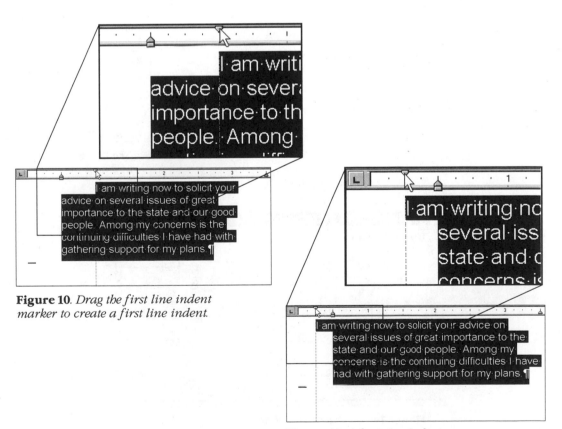

Figure 10. *Drag the first line indent marker to create a first line indent.*

Figure 11. *A hanging indent.*

Indenting with the Paragraph Dialog Box

1. Select the paragraph or paragraphs to be formatted. **(Figure 12)**
2. From the Format menu, choose Paragraph. **(Figure 13)**
3. On the Indents and Spacing tab of the Paragraph dialog box, change the left or right indent settings by clicking the increment/decrement buttons **(Figure 14)** or by double-clicking the current setting and typing a replacement.
4. If you want a hanging or first line indent, pull down the list under Special and choose either First Line or Hanging. Then, set the amount of the indent in the By text box.
5. Click OK.

✔ Tips

- Using the Paragraph Dialog box gives you the precision to enter exact measurements.
- Indents are measured from the left and right margins.

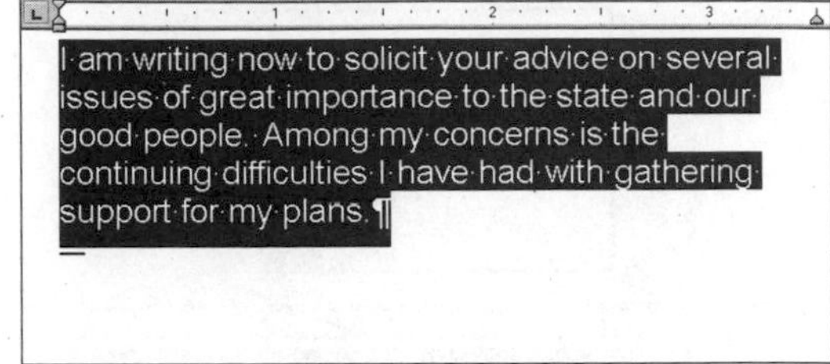

Figure 12. *Select a paragraph to format.*

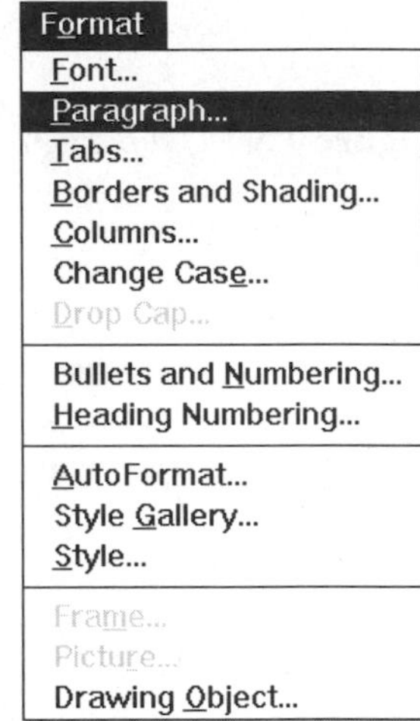

Figure 13. *The Format menu.*

The increment/decrement buttons.

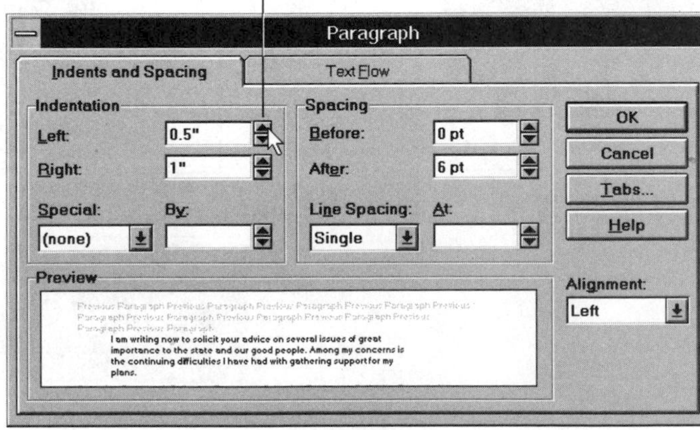

Figure 14. *The Paragraph dialog box.*

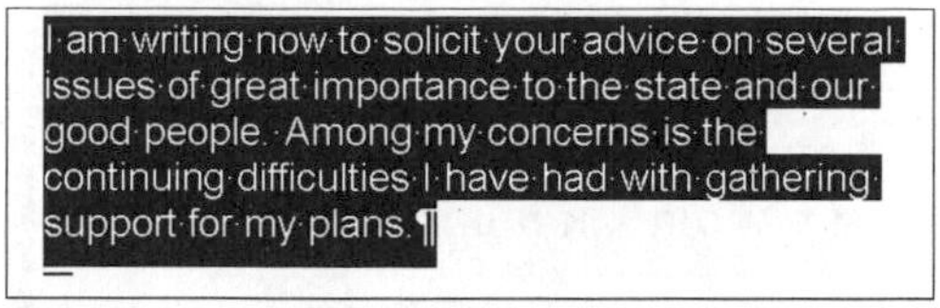

I am writing now to solicit your advice on several
issues of great importance to the state and our
good people. Among my concerns is the
continuing difficulties I have had with gathering
support for my plans.¶

Figure 15. *Select a paragraph to format.*

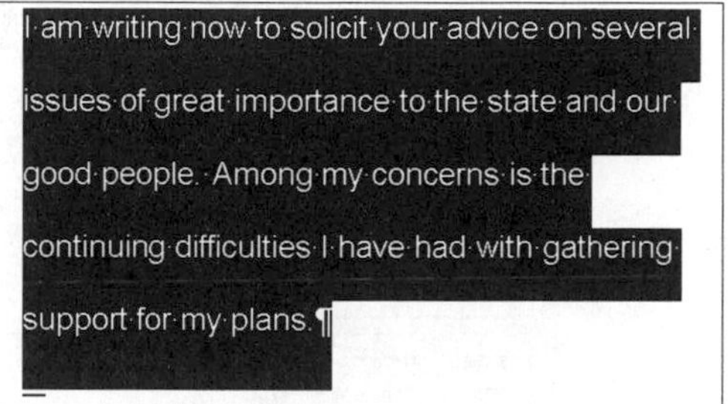

Figure 16. *Double-spaced paragraph.*

Double Spacing Paragraphs

1. Select the paragraph or paragraphs to be formatted. **(Figure 15)**
2. Press Ctrl+2. **(Figure 16)**

   or

   From the Format menu, choose Paragraph and choose Double from the Line Spacing drop-down list. Then click OK. **(Figure 17)**

✔ Tips

- Press Ctrl+1 to return a selected paragraph to single spacing.
- From the Line Spacing drop-down list on the Paragraph dialog box, you can also choose 1.5 lines, or set an exact line spacing by choosing Exactly and then selecting a measurement for At.

Choose an alternate line spacing here.

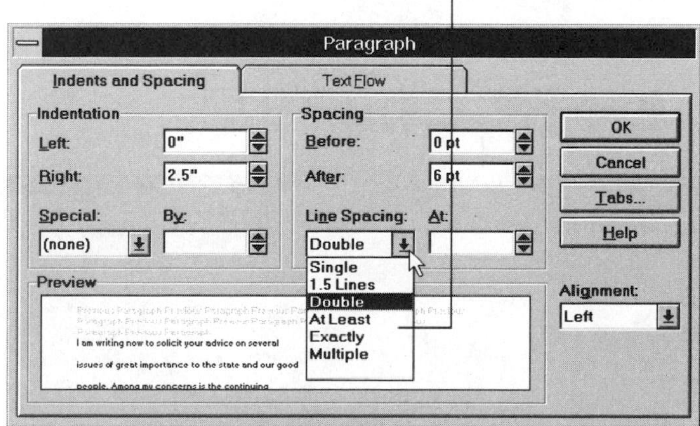

Figure 17. *The Line Spacing drop-down list.*

Centering and Justifying Paragraphs

Centered paragraphs are horizontally centered between the left and right margins. **(Figure 18)** The left and right sides of **justified** paragraphs are aligned with the left and right margins. **(Figure 19)**

1. Select the paragraph or paragraphs to be formatted.
2. Click the Center or Justify buttons on the Formatting toolbar. **(Figure 20)**

   or

   Press Ctrl+E to center or Ctrl+J to justify.

✔ Tips

- To return a paragraph to standard left alignment (aligned with the left margin and ragged right), click the Left button in the Formatting toolbar or press Ctrl+L.
- You can also select Paragraph from the Format menu and then, on the Paragraph dialog box, choose an option from the Alignment drop-down list. **(Figure 21)**
- Paragraphs that are indented will not be centered properly so be sure to remove the indents first.
- To align paragraphs with the right margin, click the Align Right button or press Ctrl+R.

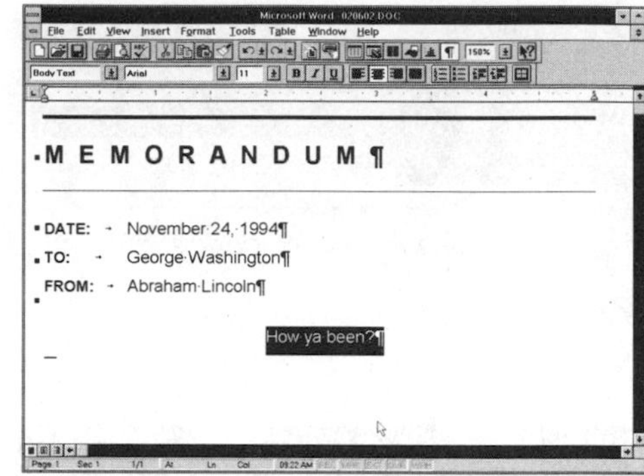

Figure 18. *Centered paragraph.*

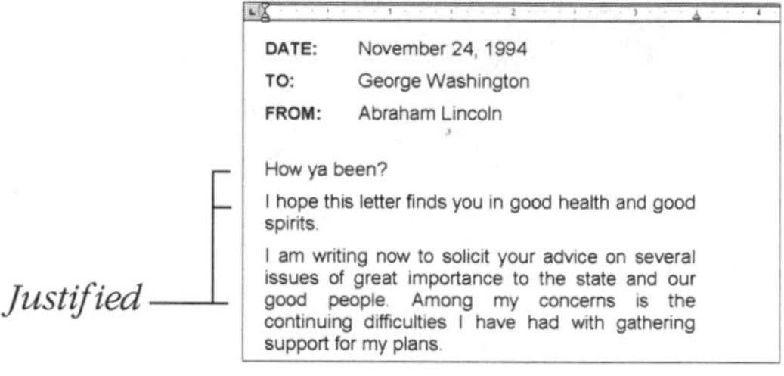

Figure 19. *Justified paragraph.*

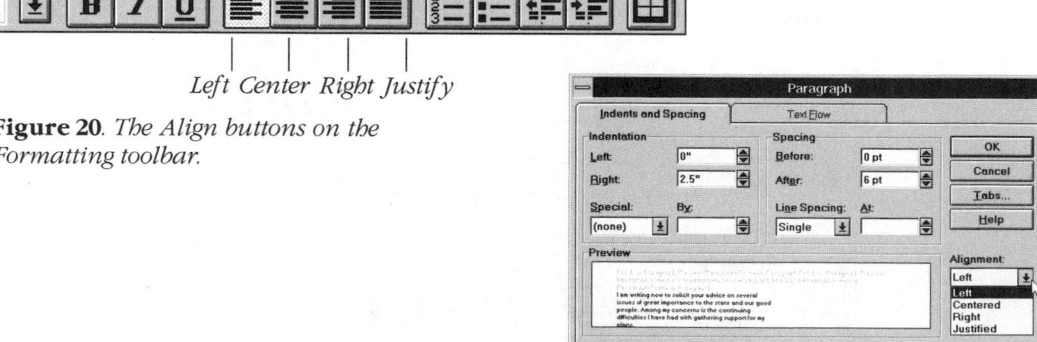

Figure 20. *The Align buttons on the Formatting toolbar.*

Figure 21. *The Alignment drop-down list.*

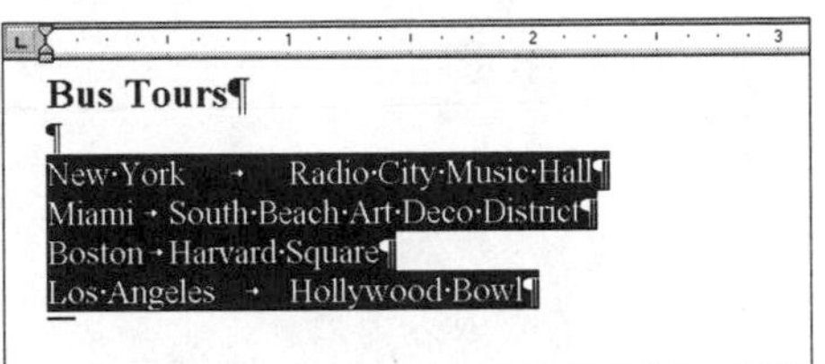

Figure 22. *Selected paragraphs.*

Tab alignment button.

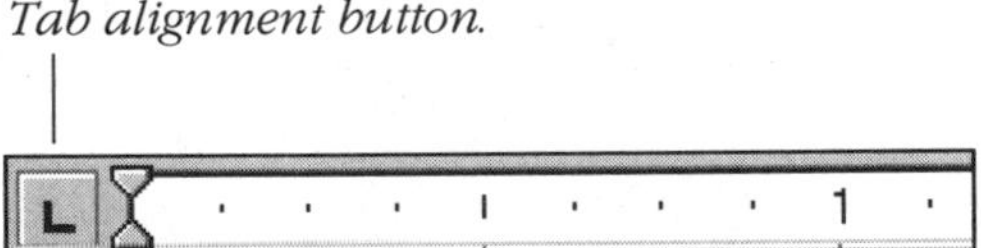

Figure 23. *The alignment marker.*

Click in the ruler to set a tab.

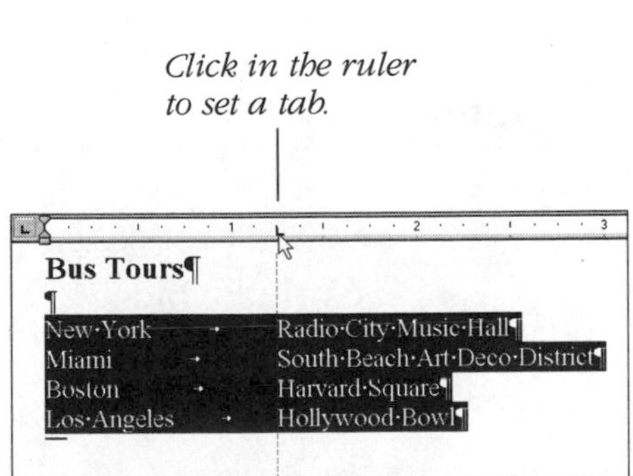

Figure 24. *Setting a tab.*

Setting Tabs

1. Select the paragraph or paragraphs to which you want to add tabs. **(Figure 22)**
2. Click the tab alignment button if you want to change the tab type. The default tab is left-aligned. **(Figure 23)**
3. Click in the ruler to set a tab of the type shown on the tab alignment button. **(Figure 24)**
4. Click again at a different spot in the ruler to set another tab of the same type.

   or

   Click the tab alignment button to select a different tab type before clicking in the ruler to set the tab.

✔ Tips

- To delete a tab, drag it up and off the ruler.
- To change tab settings, select the paragraphs to affect and then drag the tab markers left or right along the ruler.

Table 6-1. *Tab Alignment Settings*

Button	Setting
L	Left-aligned tab
⊥	Center-aligned tab
┘	Right-aligned tab
⊥.	Decimal-aligned tab

Adding Bullets to Paragraphs

1. Select the paragraph or paragraphs to be formatted. **(Figure 25)**

2. Click the Bullets button on the Formatting toolbar. **(Figure 26)**

or, to select a bullet shape and other bullet options:

2. From the Format menu, choose Bullets and Numbering.

or

Click the right mouse button and choose Bullets and Numbering from the shortcut menu.

3. On the Bulleted tab of the Bullets and Numbering dialog box, click one of the six large panes to select a bullet shape. **(Figure 27)**

4. Clear the Hanging Indent checkbox on the Bulleted tab only if you do not want the text to be aligned to the right of the bullet. **(Figure 27)**

✔ Tips

- To remove bullets, select the bulleted paragraphs and then click the Bullets button again.
- Bulleted paragraphs in a list have equal emphasis. To order the list, number the paragraphs instead. *See Numbering Paragraphs, page 69.*
- To set the bullet size, distance from text, and other options, click Modify on the Bulleted tab of the Bullets and Numbering dialog box.

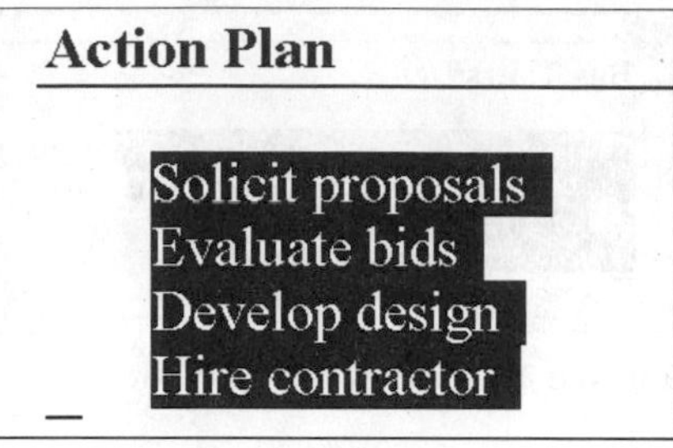

Figure 25. *Select a paragraph to format.*

The Bullets button.

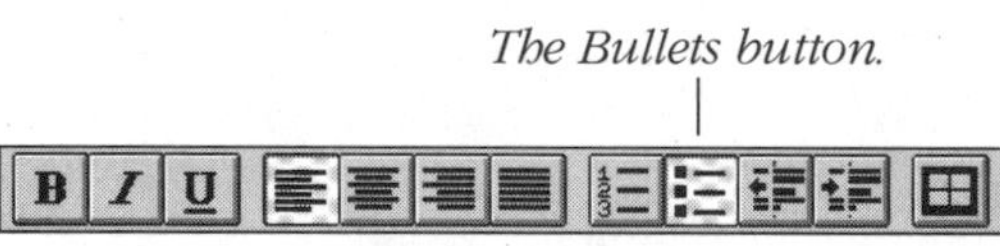

Figure 26. *The Formatting toolbar.*

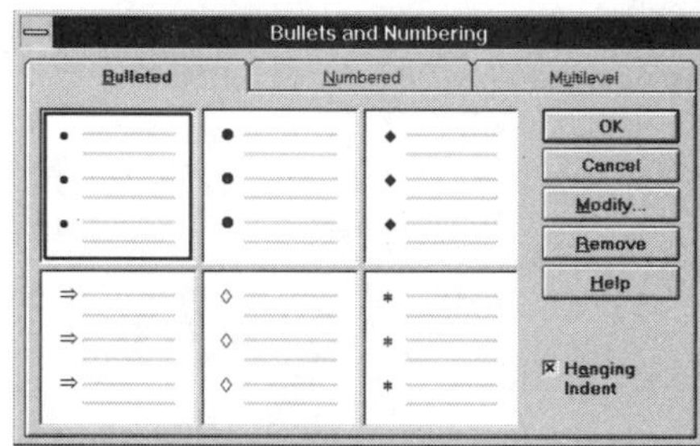

Figure 27. *The Bullets and Numbering dialog box.*

Action Plan

- Solicit proposals
- Evaluate bids
- Develop design
- Hire contractor

Figure 28. *The paragraphs with bullets.*

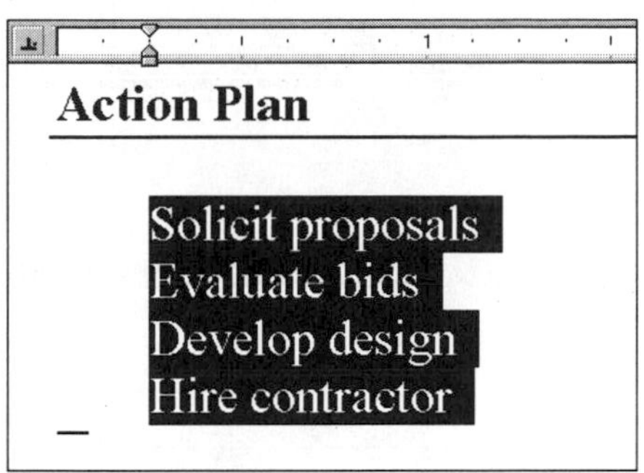

Figure 29. *Select a paragraph to format.*

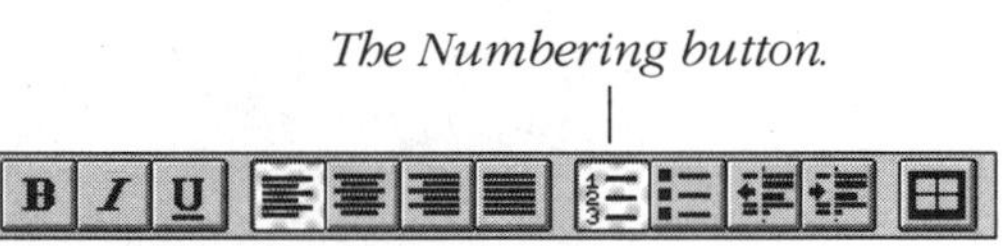

Figure 30. *The Formatting toolbar.*

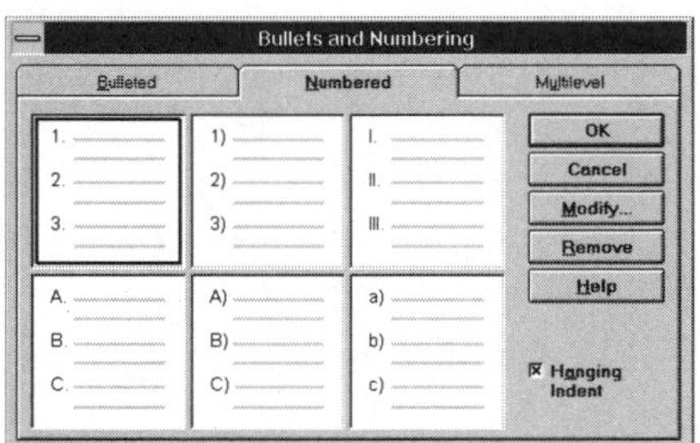

Figure 31. *The Bullets and Numbering dialog box.*

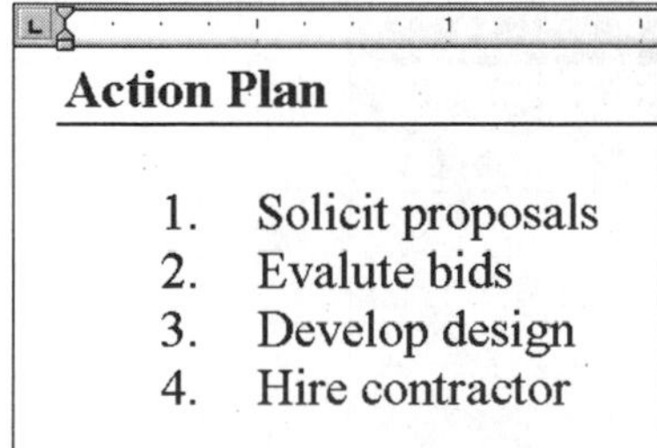

Figure 32. *The numbered list.*

Numbering Paragraphs

1. Select the paragraph or paragraphs to be formatted. **(Figure 29)**

2. Click the Numbering button on the Formatting toolbar. **(Figure 30)**

or, to select a numbering style and other numbering options

2. From the Format menu, choose Bullets and Numbering.

or

Click the right mouse button and choose Bullets and Numbering from the shortcut menu.

3. On the Numbered tab of the Bullets and Numbering dialog box, click one of the six large panes to select a numbering style. **(Figure 31)**

4. Clear the Hanging Indent checkbox only if you do not want the text to be aligned to the right of the numbers. **(Figure 32)**

✔ Tips

- To remove numbers, select the numbered paragraphs and then click the Numbering button again.
- To set the numbering style, distance from text, and other options, click Modify on the Numbered tab of the Bullets and Numbering dialog box.
- To stop numbering in a list of paragraphs or to skip over a paragraph in a list, select a paragraph in the list, click the right mouse button, and choose Skip Numbering or Stop Numbering.

Finding and Replacing Formatting

1. Press Ctrl+F to Find or Ctrl+H to replace text.

   or

   From the Edit menu, choose either Find or Replace. **(Figure 33)**
2. On the Find dialog box or the Replace dialog box, click the Format button to pull down a list of formats. **(Figure 34)**
3. Choose the formatting you want to find or replace. The formatting you choose will be described under the Find What text box. **(Figure 35)**
4. Click Find Next to find the formatting.

   or

   Click in the Replace With textbox, click the Format button, choose replacement formatting, and then click Find Next.

✔ Tips

- You can search for a style by clicking the Format button on the Find or Replace dialog box, clicking Style on the Format list, and then choosing a style. *To learn about styles, see Automatic Text Formatting, pages 71-74.*
- Type text into the Find What text box at Step 2 above to search for specific text with specific formatting.

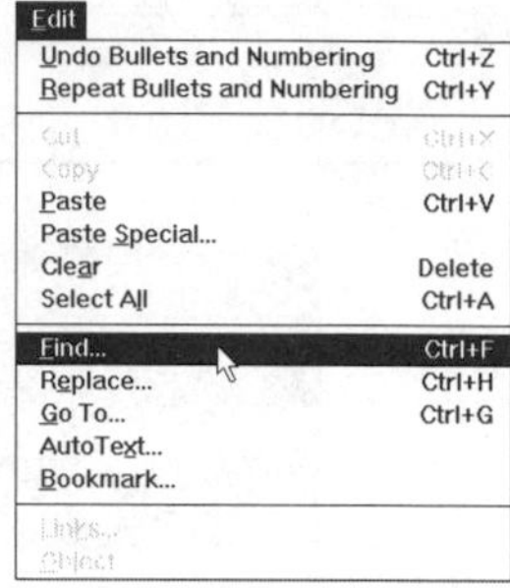

Figure 33. *The Edit menu.*

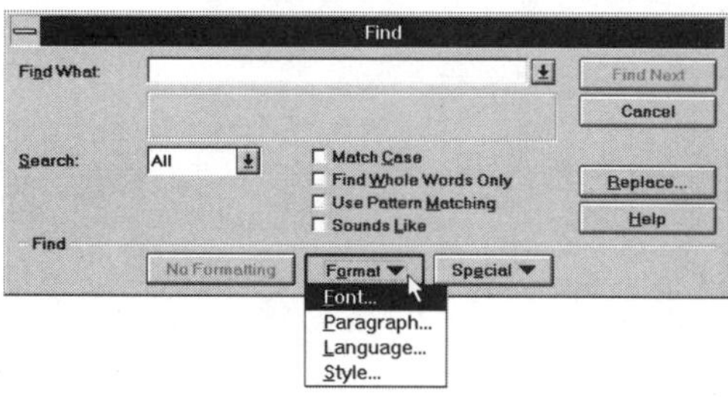

Figure 34. *The Format pull-down list.*

The formatting for which you are searching is described here.

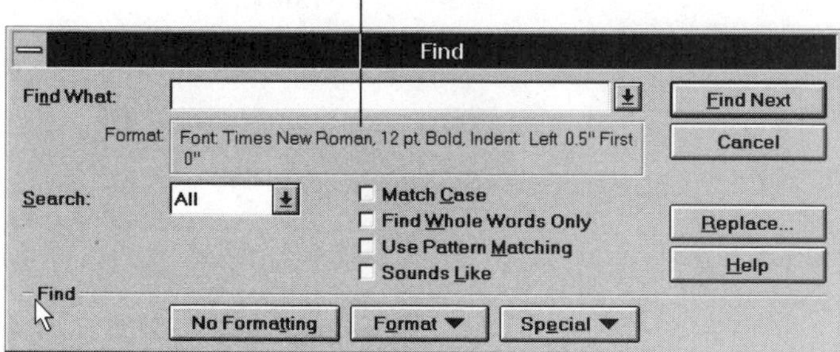

Figure 35. *The Find dialog box.*

Automatic Text Formatting 7

Before we complete the tour, I'd like to show you some superb English gardens:

24 Lily Pond Lane
117 Georgica St.
3 Heron Court
57 Hill Street

Figure 1. *Select the paragraphs to format.*

Click here to pull down the style list.

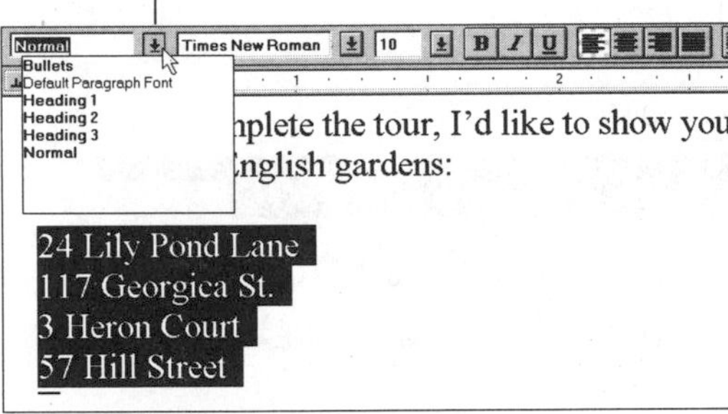

Figure 2. *The style list.*

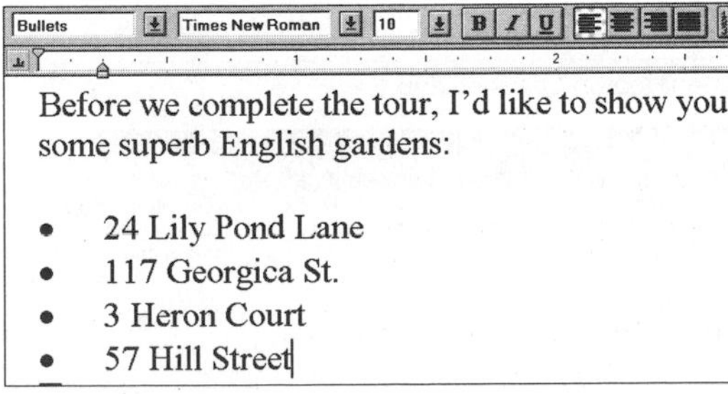

Figure 3. *Bullets style applied to selected paragraphs.*

About Styles

A *style*, which contains a complete set of formatting choices, is useful for applying a preset combination of formatting to characters or paragraphs quickly and easily. For example, a particular style can contain the formatting for headings. To format a heading, you'd select the heading and then choose the heading style from the Style list.

Character styles, applied only to text that you've selected first, contain font formatting. Paragraph styles, applied to entire paragraphs that you select, hold both font and paragraph formatting.

By default, paragraphs are given the Normal style and text is given the Default Paragraph Font style.

Choosing a Style from the Style List

1. Select the characters or paragraphs to format. **(Figure 1)**
2. On the Formatting toolbar, click the pull-down button next to the Style box to pull down the list of styles. **(Figure 2)**
3. Choose a style name on the list of styles.

✔ Tips

- Paragraph styles are bold on the style list. Character style names are not bold.
- You do not have to select an entire paragraph before you apply a style. Simply click anywhere in the paragraph.
- You can apply a style to several consecutive paragraphs by dragging from any point in the first paragraph to any point in the last paragraph and then selecting a paragraph style.

Word

Chapter 7

Creating a Paragraph Style

1. Apply font and paragraph formatting to a paragraph and then leave the paragraph selected. **(Figure 4)**
2. On the Formatting toolbar, double-click the current style name. **(Figure 5)**
3. Type the new style name in place of the old name and press Enter. **(Figure 6)**

✔ Tips

- You can also create a style by using the Style command on the Format menu. *See Creating a Character Style, page 74.*
- The styles you create are stored in the document. To use the styles in other documents, you must transfer them to a template.

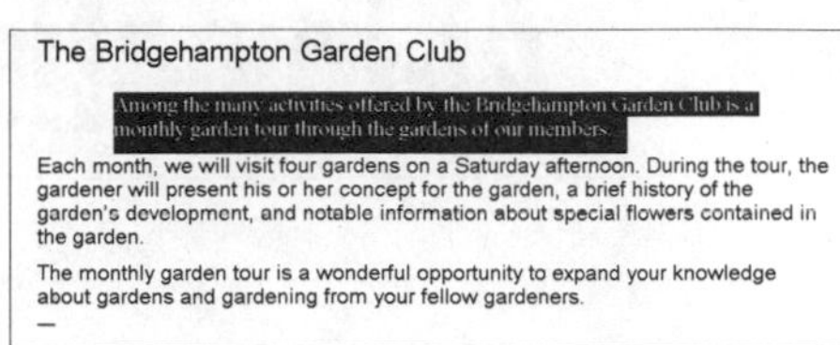

The Bridgehampton Garden Club

Among the many activities offered by the Bridgehampton Garden Club is a monthly garden tour through the gardens of our members.

Each month, we will visit four gardens on a Saturday afternoon. During the tour, the gardener will present his or her concept for the garden, a brief history of the garden's development, and notable information about special flowers contained in the garden.

The monthly garden tour is a wonderful opportunity to expand your knowledge about gardens and gardening from your fellow gardeners.

Figure 4. *Format a sample paragraph.*

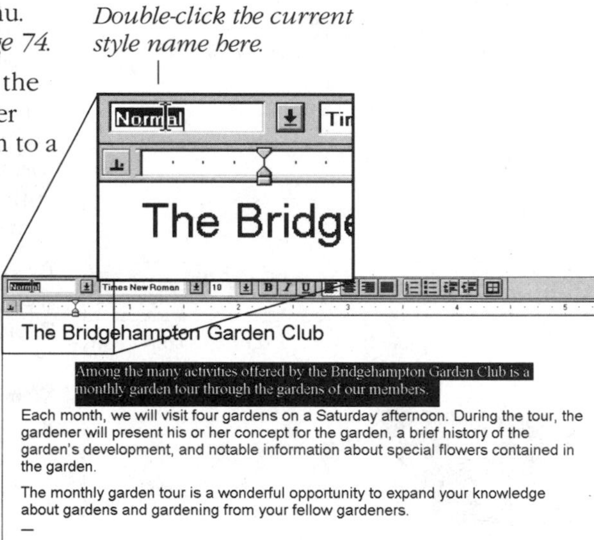

Figure 5. *Double-click the current style name.*

Type the new style name in place of the old name and press Enter.

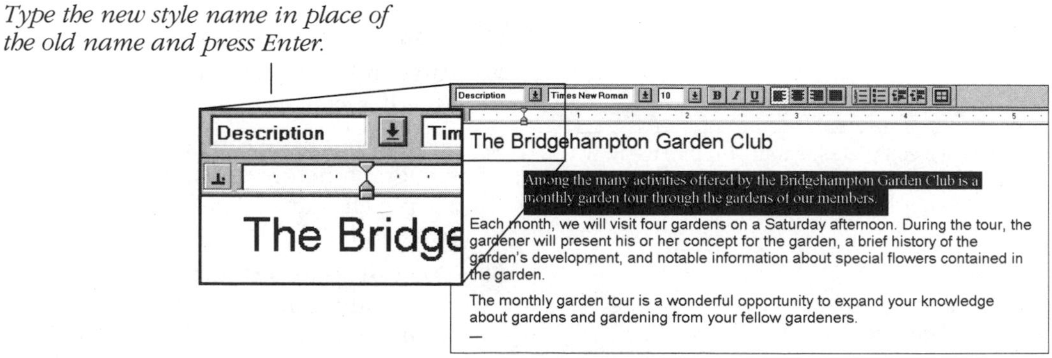

Figure 6. *Type the new style name.*

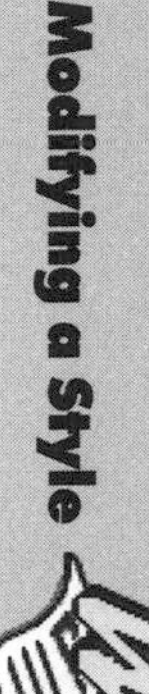

Word

Figure 7. *Make font and paragraph formatting changes.*

Figure 8. *Click the style name.*

Figure 9. *Click back on the modified text.*

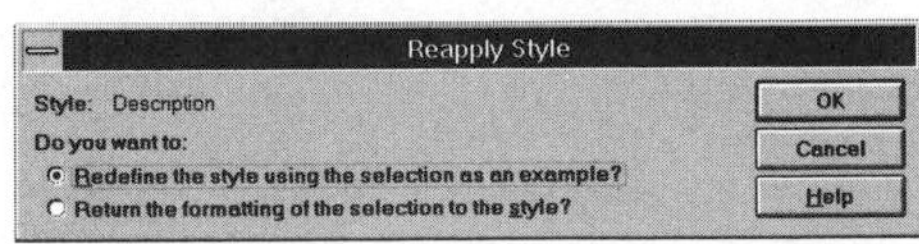

Figure 10. *The Reapply Style dialog box.*

Modifying a Paragraph Style

1. Make changes to the font or paragraph formatting of a paragraph that has been given the style that you want to modify. **(Figure 7)**
2. Click the current style name once. **(Figure 8)**
3. Click anywhere in the modified paragraph once. **(Figure 9)**
4. On the Reapply Style dialog box, make sure "Redefine the style using the selection as an example" is selected and click OK. **(Figure 10)** Every paragraph formatted by the modified style will be reformatted. **(Figure 11)**

✔ Tip

■ When you redefine a paragraph style, all paragraphs that are formatted with the style will be redefined.

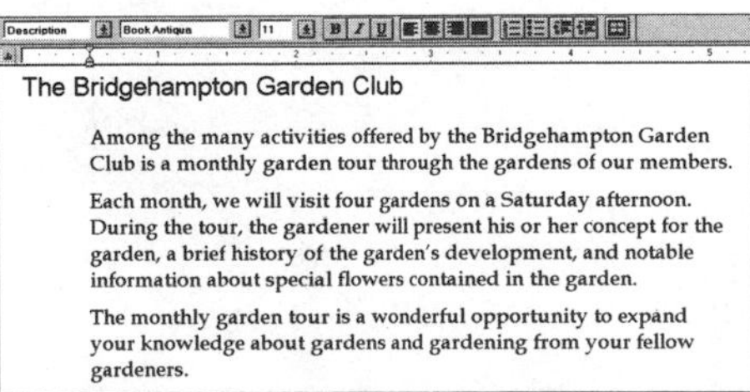

The Bridgehampton Garden Club

Among the many activities offered by the Bridgehampton Garden Club is a monthly garden tour through the gardens of our members.

Each month, we will visit four gardens on a Saturday afternoon. During the tour, the gardener will present his or her concept for the garden, a brief history of the garden's development, and notable information about special flowers contained in the garden.

The monthly garden tour is a wonderful opportunity to expand your knowledge about gardens and gardening from your fellow gardeners.

Figure 11. *All other paragraphs controlled by the modified style get the new formatting, too.*

Creating a Character Style

1. From the Format menu, select Style. **(Figure 12)**
2. On the Style dialog box, click New to create a new style. **(Figure 13)**
3. On the New Style dialog box, type a style name to replace the current, selected style name. **(Figure 14)**
4. Choose Character from the drop-down Style Type list.
5. Click the Format button and choose Font from the Format list. **(Figure 14)**
6. On the Font dialog box, select the formatting you'd like and then click OK. **(Figure 15)**
7. Click OK on the New Style dialog box.
8. Click Apply on the Style dialog box.

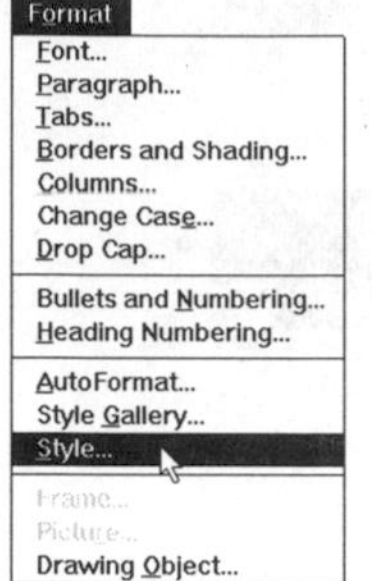

Figure 12. *The Format menu.*

Click here to create a new style.

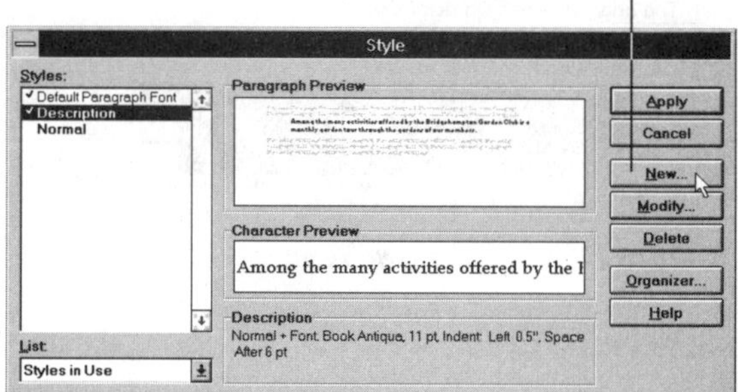

Figure 13. *The Style dialog box.*

Type a new style name here...

...then choose Character from the drop-down list.

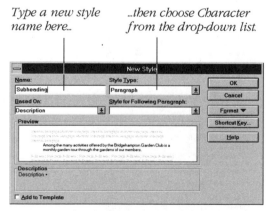

Figure 14. *The New Style dialog box.*

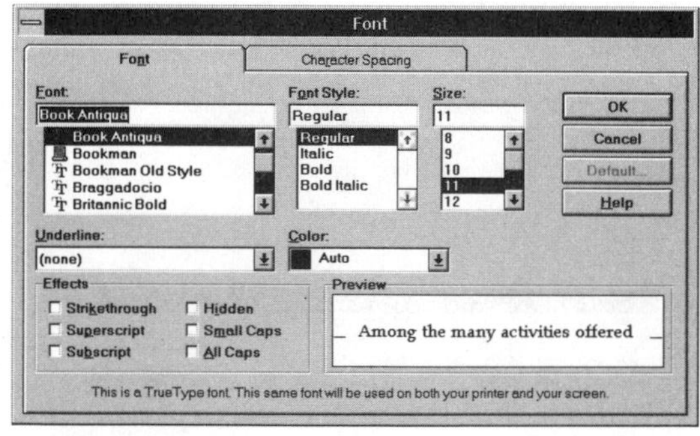

Figure 15. *The Font dialog box.*

Page Formatting 8

Word

File
New... Ctrl+N
Open... Ctrl+O
Close
Save Ctrl+S
Save As...
Save All
Find File...
Summary Info...
Templates...
Page Setup...
Print Preview
Print... Ctrl+P
1 MH.DOC
2 REPORT.DOC
3 PROJECTX.DOC
4 COVERLET.DOC
Exit

Figure 1. *The File menu.*

Click here to drop down the Paper Size list.

Page Setup
Margins | Paper Size | Paper Source | Layout
Paper Size: Letter 8½ x 11 in
Width: 8.5"
Height: 11"
Orientation
Portrait
Landscape
Preview
OK
Cancel
Default...
Help
Apply To: Whole Document

Figure 2. *The Paper Size tab of the Page Setup dialog box.*

About Page Formatting

Page formatting can be the first step in creating a new document or the last. In page formatting, you set the size and shape of the page, the size of the margins, and certain printer information that should be recorded with the document, such as whether the paper will be manually fed or taken from the printer's paper tray. Word will adjust the text on the page to fit the new page size and margins.

If you always print portrait, 8 1/2 x 11 pages with standard margins, you won't need to worry about page formatting.

Changing the Page Size and Shape

1. From the File menu, choose Page Setup. **(Figure 1)**
2. On the Paper Size tab of the Page Setup dialog box, choose one of the standard paper sizes from the drop-down Paper Size list. **(Figure 2)**

   or

   Enter a custom page size in the Width and Height text boxes.
3. Confirm that the Orientation setting you want for the page is selected: Portrait for vertical, or Landscape for horizontal.

✔ Tip

- The selections you make for paper size and orientation are for the current document only. New documents revert to the default settings.

Changing the Margins

The margins are the blank space at the top, bottom, left, or right edges of the page. To provide extra space for hole punching, you might want to increase the left margin, for example. **(Figure 3)**

1. From the File menu, choose Page Setup. **(Figure 4)**
2. On the Margins tab of the Page Setup dialog box, alter the Top, Bottom, Left, or Right settings. **(Figure 5)**
3. Alter the gutter width if you want to change the space between multiple columns on the page. *See Setting up Multiple Columns, page 81.*

✔ Tip

- To print a book with text on both sides of the page, click the Mirror Margins checkbox on the Margins tab of the Page Setup dialog box. The Left margin of a right page becomes the Inside margin and the Right margin becomes the Outside margin. On left pages, it's vice versa. To leave space for binding on the left side of the right page and the right side of the left page, you'd increase the Inside margin, for example.

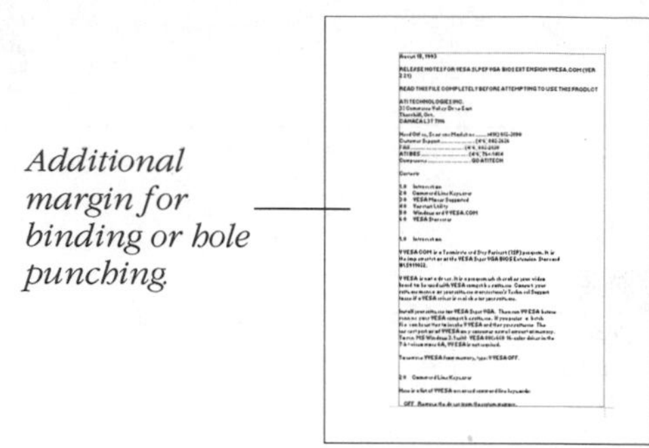

Figure 3. *Increase the left margin to provide space for hole punching.*

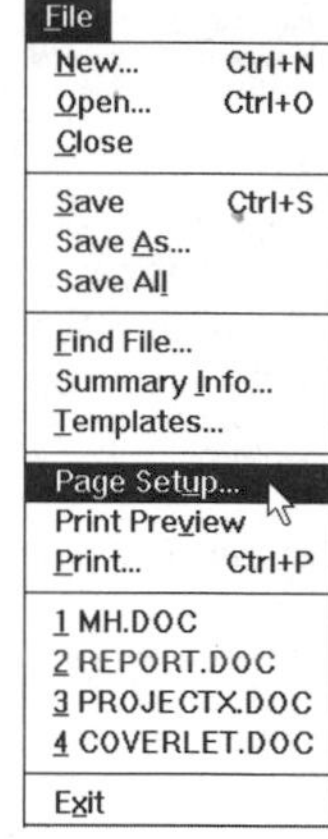

Figure 4. *The File menu.*

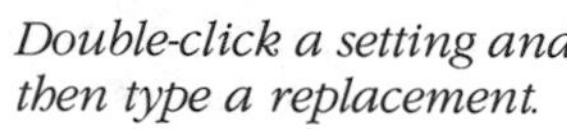

Double-click a setting and then type a replacement.

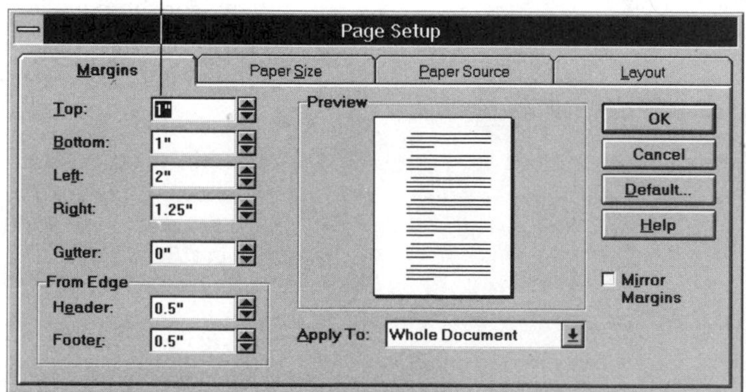

Figure 5. *The Margins tab of the Page Setup dialog box.*

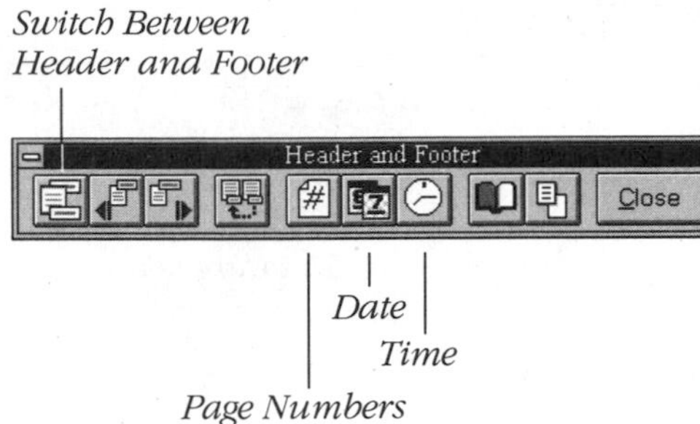

Figure 6. *The Header and Footer toolbar.*

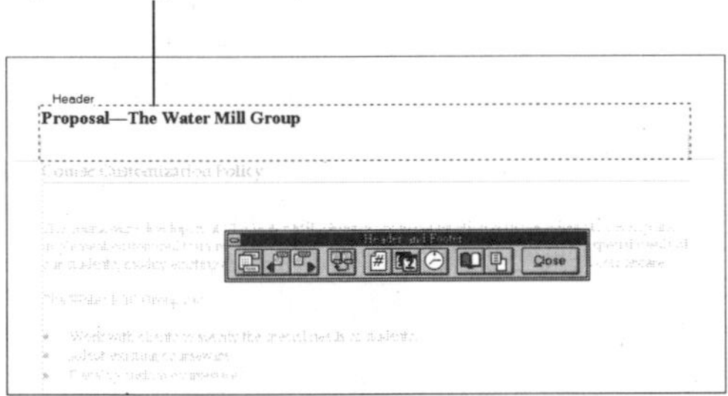

Figure 7. *Type text at the left side of the header or footer.*

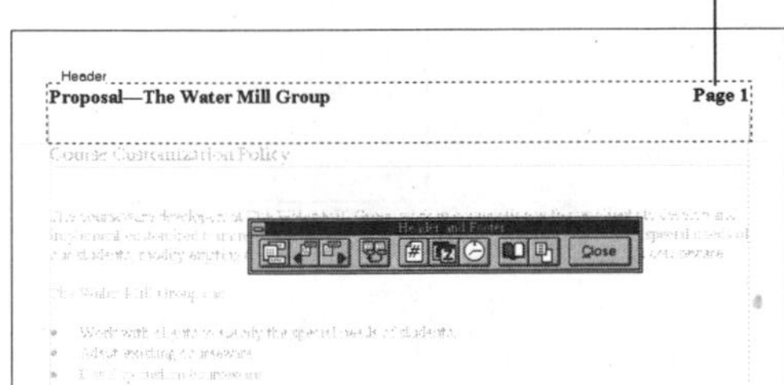

Figure 8. *Press Tab twice to skip to the right side of the header or footer.*

Setting up Headers and Footers

Headers are text that appears at the top of every page. Footers repeat at the bottom of every page.

1. From the View menu, choose Header and Footer. Word switches to Page Layout view, places the insertion point in the blank header space, and opens the Header and Footer toolbar. **(Figure 6)**
2. To edit the footer rather than the header, click the Switch Between Header and Footer button on the Header and Footer toolbar. **(Figure 6)**
3. Type text for the left side of the header or footer. **(Figure 7)**
4. Press Tab and type text for the center of the header or footer.

   or

   Press Tab again and type text for the right side of the header or footer. **(Figure 8)**
5. Click the Close button on the Header and Footer toolbar to finish editing the header or footer and return to the previous view.

✔ **Tips**

- You may want to change the Zoom setting to see the header or footer more clearly.
- Rather than type text, you can enter the page number, date, or time in the header or footer by clicking the appropriate buttons on the Header and Footer toolbar. **(Figure 6)**

Creating Multiple Sections

A document can contain multiple sections, each of which can have different page setup attributes: Different margins, page numbering, and headers and footers. A new document contains only one section until you insert a section break. Then, you can page format the new section independently.

1. Place the insertion point at the location for the start of the new section. **(Figure 9)**
2. From the Insert menu, choose Break. **(Figure 10)**
3. On the Break dialog box **(Figure 11)**, choose one of the four Section Breaks options. Word inserts a double dotted line marked with End of Section. **(Figure 12)**

✔ Tip

- Insert an Odd Page section break when you are printing left and right pages, you've started numbering on a right page (page 1), and you want each section to start on a new right page even if it means leaving a whole left page blank.

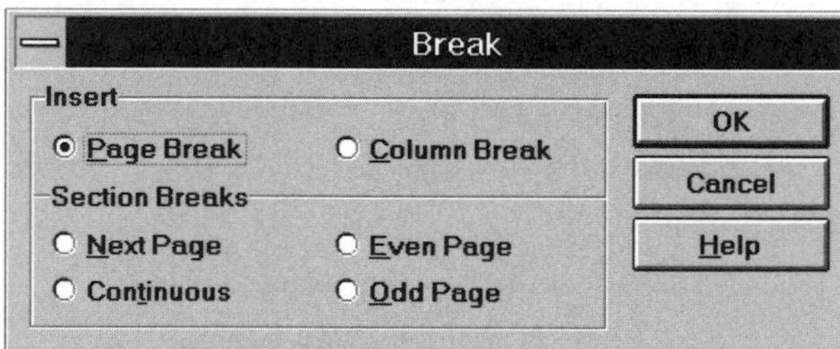

Figure 11. *The Break dialog box.*

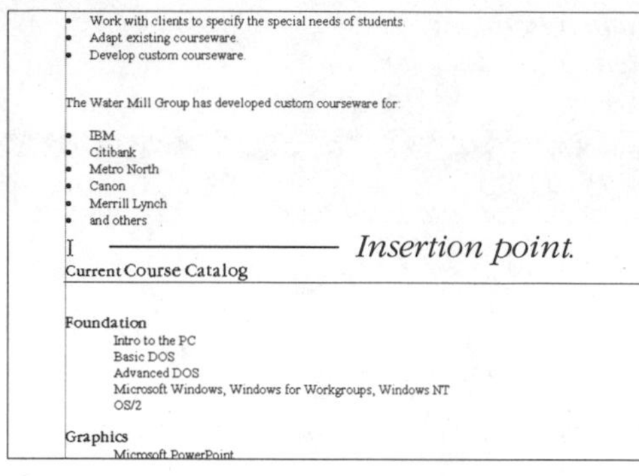

Figure 9. *Place the insertion point at the location for a section break.*

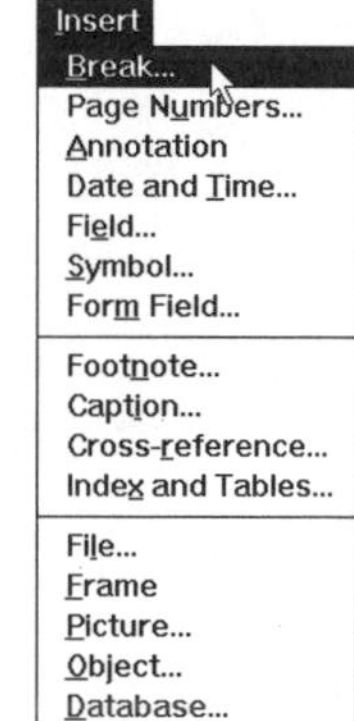

Figure 10. *The Insert menu.*

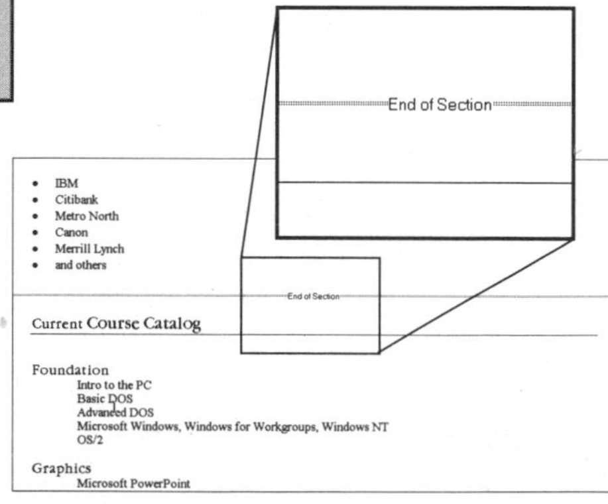

Figure 12. *A section break.*

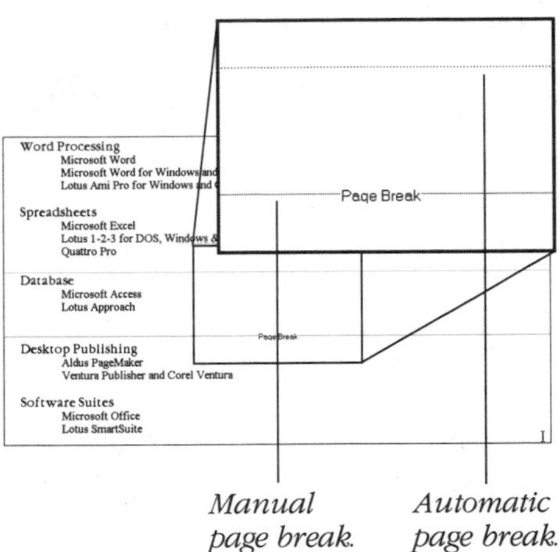

Figure 13. *Manual page break vs. Automatic page break.*

Table 8-1. *Section Breaks*

Next Page	Starts a new section at the top of the next page.
Continuous	Starts a new section without moving the text after the section break to a new page. If the previous section has multiple columns, Word evens out the bottoms of the columns.
Even Page	If the section break falls on an odd page, Word starts the new section on the next page. Otherwise, Word leaves the next odd page blank and starts the new section on the next even page.
Odd Page	If the section break falls on an even page, Word starts the new section on the next page. Otherwise, Word leaves the next page blank and starts the new section on the next odd page.

Paginating the Document

As you work in Normal view, Word enters an automatic page break (a dotted line across the page) whenever you fill a page. Whenever you pause while typing, Word readjusts the automatic page breaks, if necessary.

To start a new page earlier than the automatic page break, enter a manual page break. **(Figure 13)**

1. Position the insertion point on the line that should be the first line of the new page.

2. Press Ctrl+Enter.

or

2. From the Insert menu, choose Break.

3. Make sure Page Break is selected and then click OK.

✔ Tips

- To delete a manual page break, select the page break and press the Delete key.
- You **cannot** delete an automatic page break or move it down. Your only option is to insert a manual page break above the automatic page break.
- Word's Widow/Orphan Control ensures that Word does not break the page and leave a single line of text at the top or bottom of a page.
- By switching to Page Layout view or a Print Preview, you can see how the text falls on pages with the current page breaks. In Page Layout view, you can enter manual page breaks.

Numbering Pages

As you create a document's header or footer, you can always enter page numbering. *See Setting up Headers and Footers, page 77.* Another approach is more direct and it gives you the option to choose a number format and a starting number.

1. From the Insert menu, choose Page Numbers. **(Figure 14)**
2. On the Page Numbers dialog box, choose Top of Page or Bottom of Page from the Position drop-down list. **(Figure 15)**
3. Choose an Alignment from the Alignment drop-down list.
4. To show the page number on the first page, click the Show Number on First Page checkbox, otherwise the page numbers will first appear on page 2. **(Figure 15)**
5. Click the Format button and then, on the Page Number Format dialog box, choose a numbering style from the Number Format drop-down list. **(Figure 16)**

✔ Tip

■ While the Page Number Format dialog box is open, you can also enter a number in the Start At text box to start numbering at a number other than 1.

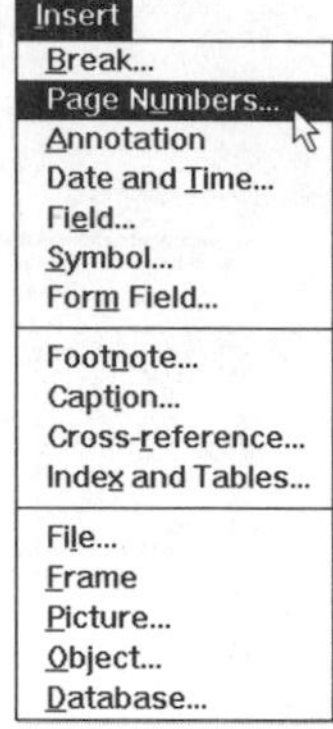

Figure 14. *The Insert menu.*

Position drop-down list box.

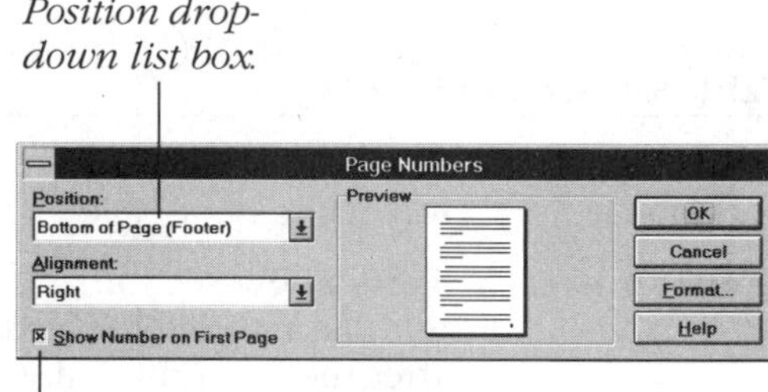

Click here to show page number on the first page of a document.

Figure 15. *The Page Numbers dialog box.*

Choose a numbering style here.

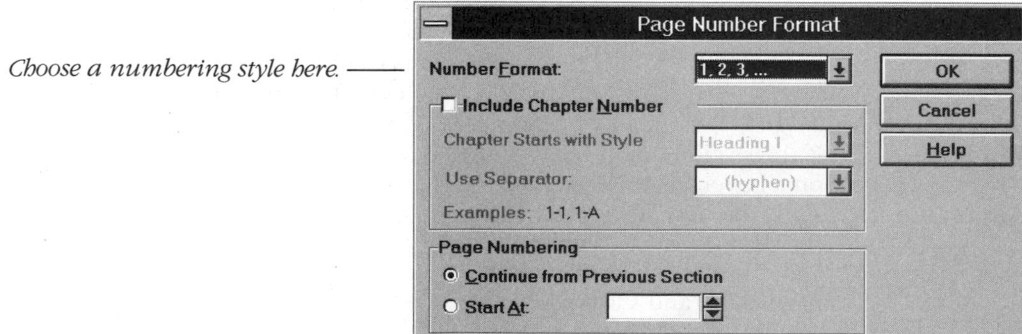

Figure 16. *The Page Number Format dialog box.*

The Columns button.

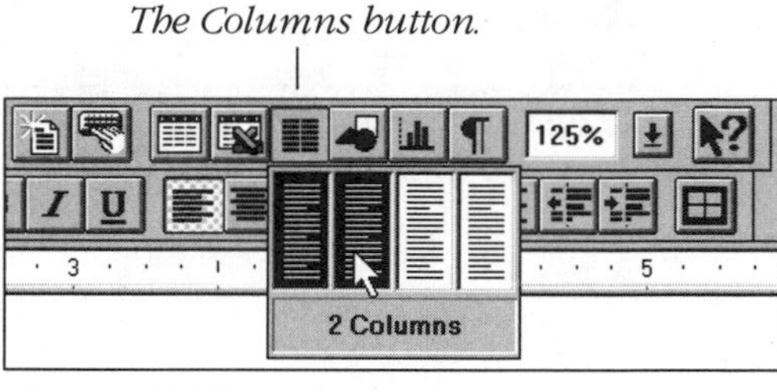

Figure 17. *The Columns button.*

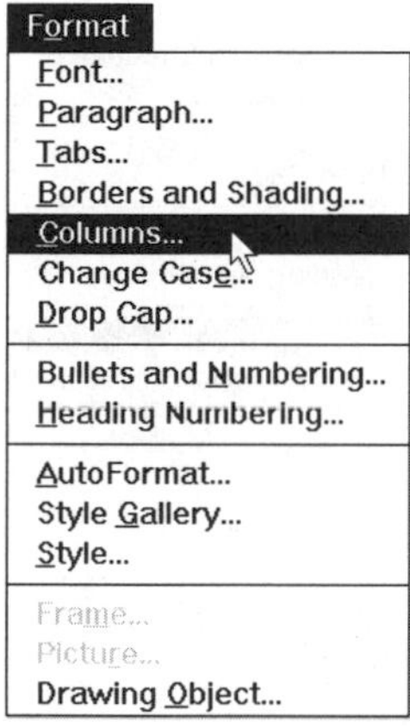

Figure 18. *The Format menu.*

Setting up Multiple Columns

1. Click the Columns button on the Standard toolbar and then drag across the number of columns you want. **(Figure 17)**

   or

1. From the Format menu, choose Columns. **(Figure 18)**
2. On the Columns dialog box, click one of the Presets or enter a number of columns in the Number of Columns text box. **(Figure 19)**
3. To obtain a vertical line between the columns, click the Line Between checkbox.

✔ Tips

- To vary the widths of columns, clear the Equal Column Width checkbox on the Columns dialog box and then use the Width and Spacing controls to modify the width and spacing for each column.
- The maximum number of columns on a page is 12.
- The gutter width on the Margins tab of the Page Setup dialog box determines the spacing between equal columns. *See Changing the Margins, page 76.*

Multiple Columns

Word

Click one of these panels to choose a number of columns.

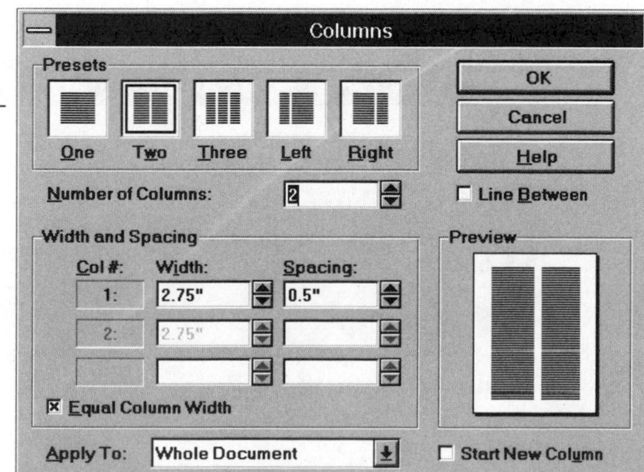

Figure 19. *The Columns dialog box.*

AutoFormatting a Document

AutoFormatting a document causes Word to analyze the document and apply styles to the text. AutoFormatting also removes extra paragraph marks, replaces indents created with spaces or tabs with paragraph indents, replaces asterisks or hyphens in bulleted lists with real bullets, and replaces (C), (R), and (TM) with copyright, registered trademark, and trademark symbols.

1. Click the AutoFormat button on the Standard toolbar. **(Figure 20)**

   or

1. From the Format menu, choose AutoFormat. **(Figure 21)**
2. On the AutoFormat dialog box, click OK. **(Figure 22)**

✔ Tip

- To change the way AutoFormat analyzes the document and to specify which of the standard actions it will carry out, click Options on the AutoFormat dialog box.

The AutoFormat button.

Figure 20. *The AutoFormat button.*

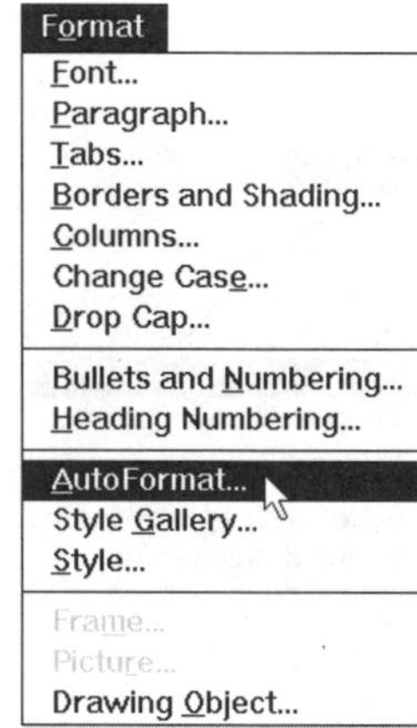

Figure 21. *The Format menu.*

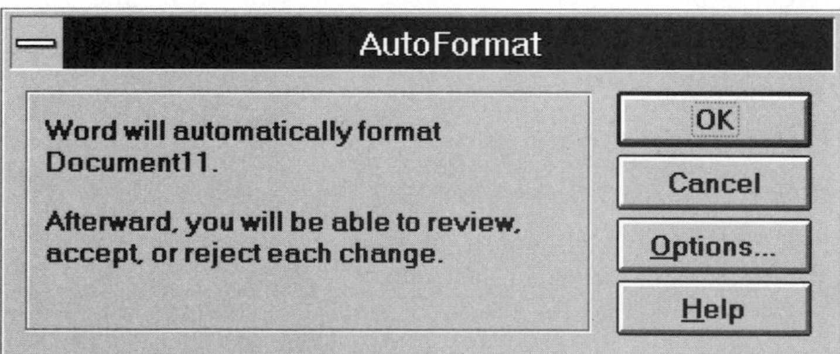

Figure 22. *The AutoFormat dialog box.*

Creating Tables 9

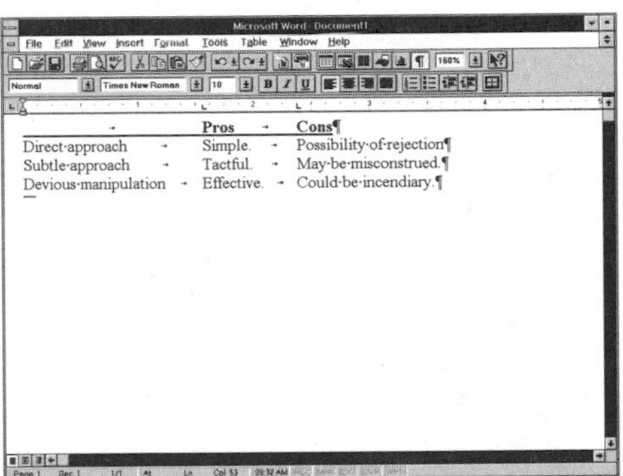

Figure 1. *Tabs used to align text in columns.*

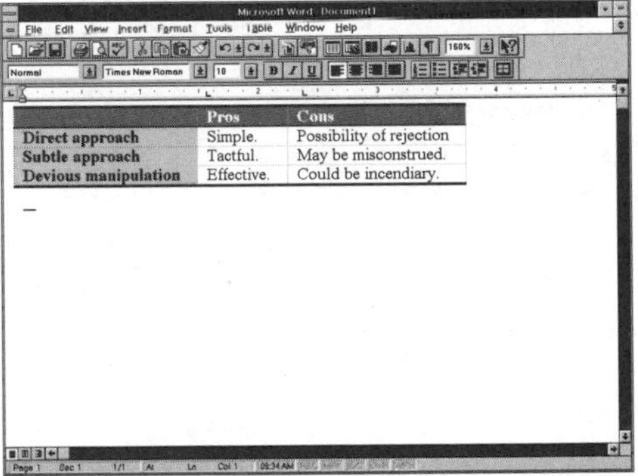

Figure 2. *A Word table.*

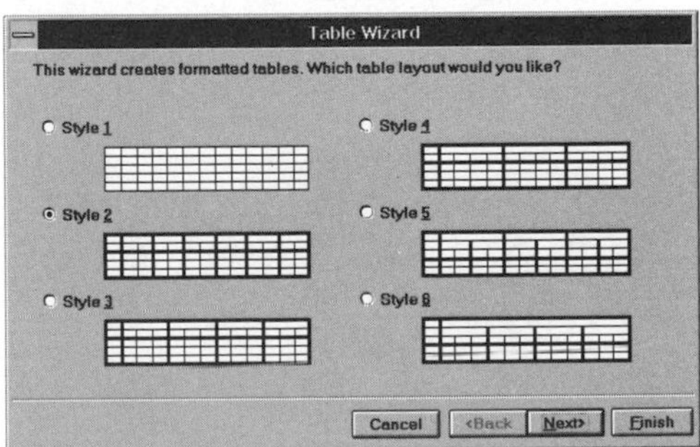

Figure 3. *Step 1 of The Table Wizard.*

About Tables

Old-fashioned word processors used tabs to align text and numbers in columns. **(Figure 1)** You can still use tabs in Word, but you're better off using Word's tables, which make it easy to both align data in columns and rows and to format the table so it looks professional. **(Figure 2)** Tables are so useful in Word that an entire chapter is devoted to them.

You can create a table manually or use the Table Wizard, which guides you step by step through the table making and formatting process. **(Figure 3)**

Starting a Table

Word provides two ways to start a table. The first method gives you the option to use the Table Wizard, which helps set up more complex tables and provides automatic table formatting options. The second method gives you a quick and dirty table that requires manual formatting.

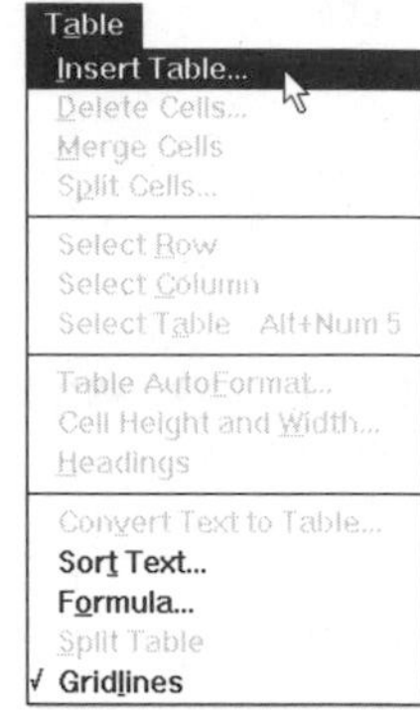

Figure 4. *The Table menu.*

Method 1:

1. Position the insertion point at the location for the table.
2. From the Table menu, choose Insert Table. **(Figure 4)**
3. On the Insert Table dialog box, choose the number of columns and rows. **(Figure 5)**

Optional steps:

- Click the Wizard button to use the Table Wizard to create the table. *See Using the Table Wizard, page 86.*
- Click the AutoFormat button to choose a format for the table so you can see the formatting as you create the table. **(Figure 6)**

---

4. Click OK to create the table.

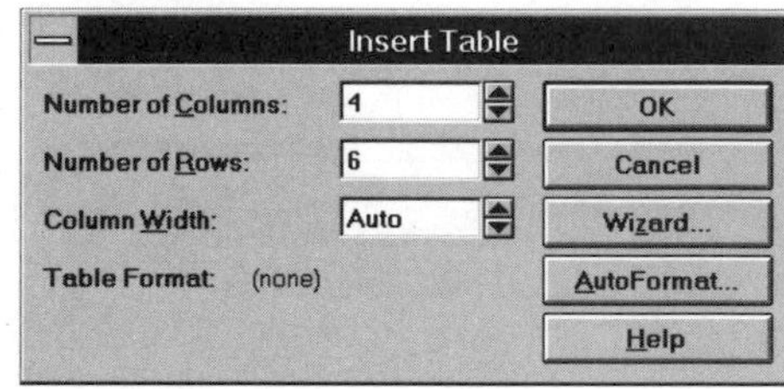

Figure 5. *The Insert Table dialog box.*

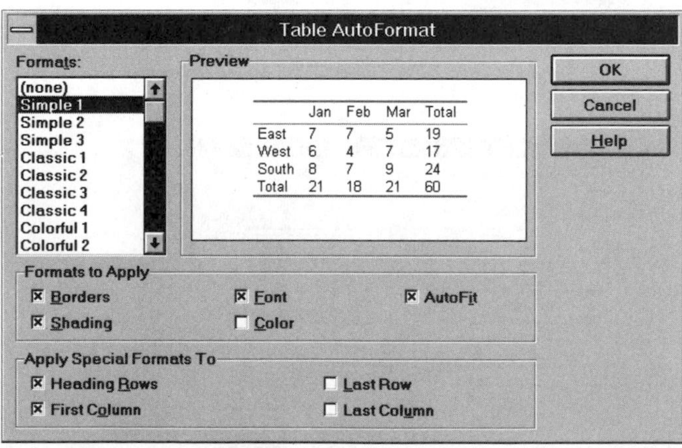

Figure 6. *The AutoFormat dialog box.*

Figure 7. *The Insert Table button.*

Method 2:

1. Position the insertion point at the location for the table.
2. Click the Insert Table button on the Standard toolbar. **(Figure 7)**
3. Drag across the number of columns and down the number of rows you want. **(Figure 8)** An unformatted table appears. **(Figure 9)**

✔ **Tip**

- You can apply an AutoFormat to a table or change the AutoFormat applied at any time by clicking anywhere in the table and then choosing Table AutoFormat from the Table menu.

Figure 8. *Drag across the grid to specify the table dimensions.*

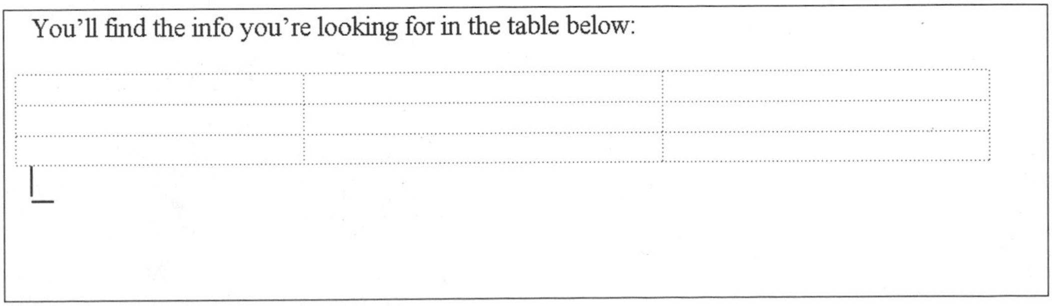

You'll find the info you're looking for in the table below:

Figure 9. *The new table.*

Using the Table Wizard

1. On the Insert Table dialog box, click Wizard. **(Figure 9)**
2. Make selections on the following series of Table Wizard dialog boxes. **(Figures 10-16)** After you make a selection, click **Next** to go to the next step, **Back** to return to the previous step, or **Finish** to skip the rest of the steps and accept the defaults.
3. On the Table AutoFormat dialog box, click on Format names on the Formats list and examine the previews shown in the dialog box. Click OK when you find the format you want. **(Figure 14)**

✓ Tips

- When you insert a table within a document, be sure to select the same direction for the table (portrait vs. landscape) as the rest of the document, otherwise Word will create a separate section for the table on a new page.
- The checkboxes on the Table AutoFormat dialog box allow you to select which aspects of the formatting in the AutoFormat to apply to your table.

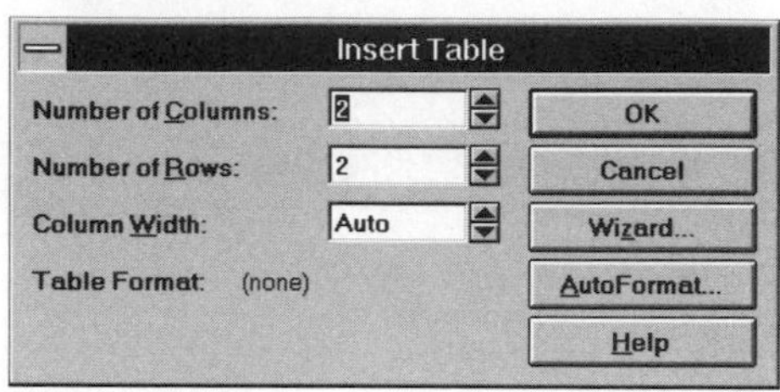

Figure 9. *The Insert Table dialog box.*

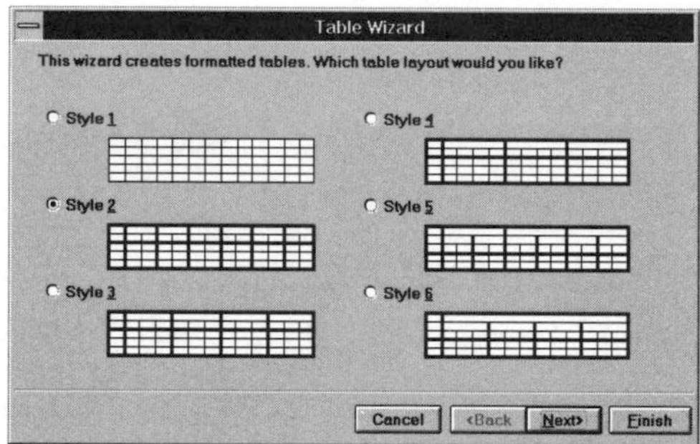

Figure 10. *Choose a table layout in the first step of the Table Wizard.*

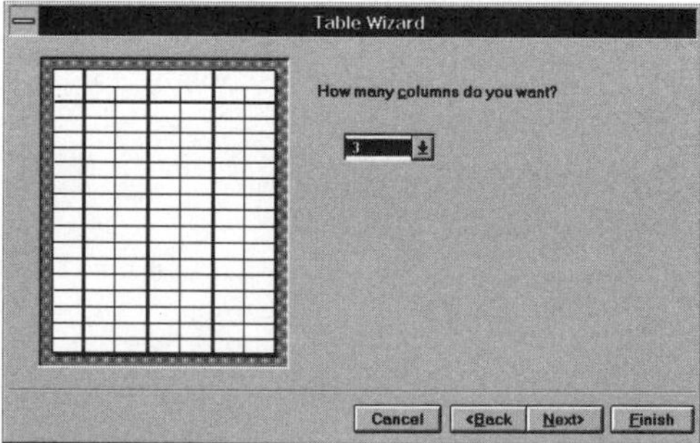

Figure 11. *Specify the number of columns in the second step of the Table Wizard.*

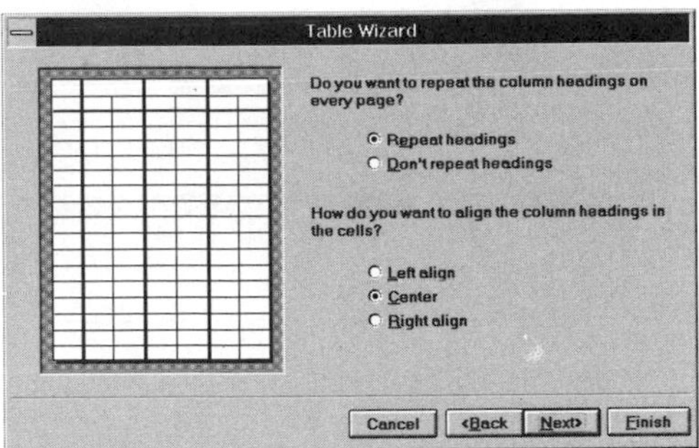

Figure 12. *Format the column headings in the third step of the Table Wizard.*

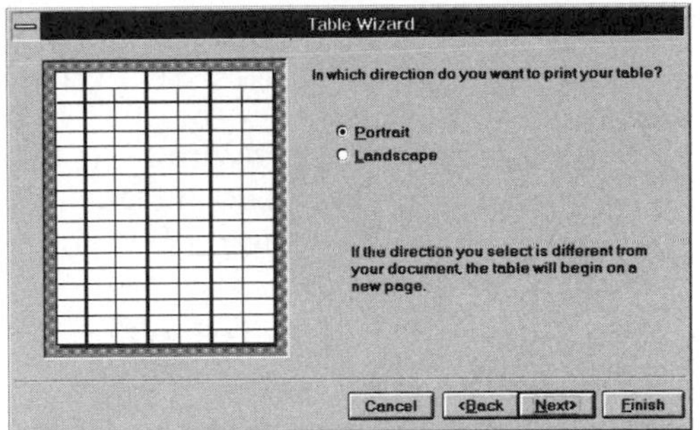

Figure 15. *Choose an orientation for the table in the sixth step of the Table Wizard.*

Figure 13. *Specify the row headings in the fourth step of the Table Wizard.*

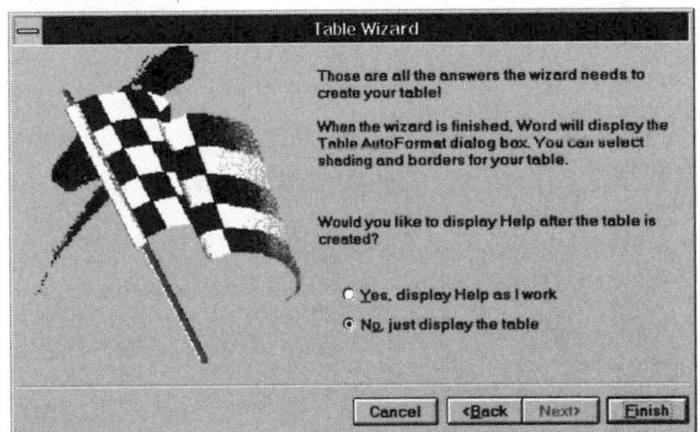

Figure 16. *The last step of the Table Wizard.*

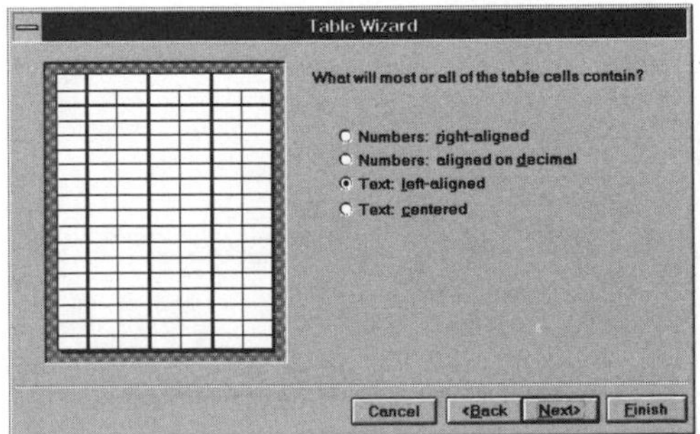

Figure 14. *Choose a default alignment for the cells in the fifth step of the Table Wizard.*

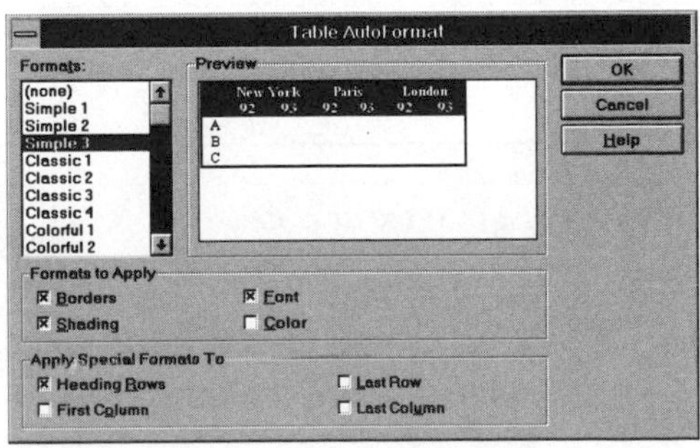

Figure 17. *The Table AutoFormat dialog box.*

Entering Data in the Table

1. Click in a cell and then type to insert data into the cell. As you type, the insertion point will wrap within the cell and the entire row will become taller to accommodate multiple lines of text, if necessary. **(Figure 15)**
2. Press Tab to move to the cell to the right. **(Figure 16)**
3. Type text into the next cell. **(Figure 17)**
4. Continue pressing Tab after you finish each cell. When you finish the last cell of the table, pressing Tab will create a new row.

✔ Tips

- When you reach the rightmost cell, pressing Tab moves the insertion point to the next line. **(Figure 18)**
- Press Shift+Tab to move back a cell.
- If there is already text in a cell, pressing Tab to move to the cell both moves to the cell and selects the text.

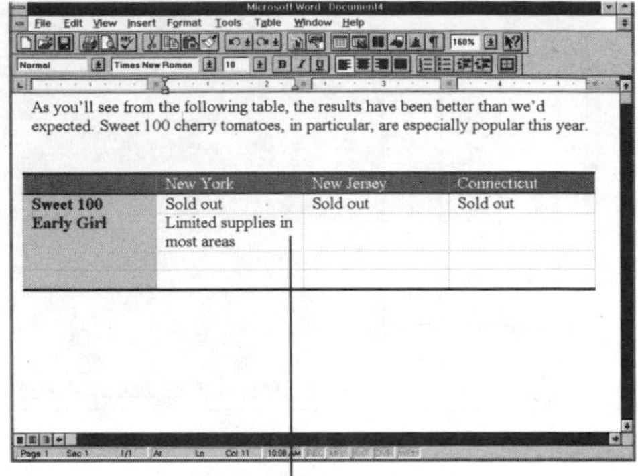

As you'll see from the following table, the results have been better than we'd expected. Sweet 100 cherry tomatoes, in particular, are especially popular this year.

	New York	New Jersey	Connecticut
Sweet 100	Sold out	Sold out	Sold out
Early Girl	Limited supplies in most areas		

Figure 15. *Rows grow in height to accommodate the largest entry.*

	New York	New Jersey	Connecticut
Sweet 100	Sold out	Sold out	Sold out
Early Girl	Limited supplies in most areas		

Figure 16. *Press Tab to move to the next cell.*

	New York	New Jersey	Connecticut
Sweet 100	Sold out	Sold out	Sold out
Early Girl	Limited supplies in most areas	In stock	

Figure 17. *Type into the next cell.*

	New York	New Jersey	Connecticut
Sweet 100	Sold out	Sold out	Sold out
Early Girl	Limited supplies in most areas	In stock	In stock

Figure 18. *Press Tab at the rightmost cell to move to the next line.*

	New York	New Jersey	Connecticut
Sweet 100	Sold out	Sold out	Sold out
Early Girl	Limited supplies in most areas	In stock	In stock
Plum	Limited supplies	In stock	Limited supplies
Big Boy	In stock	In stock	Limited supplies

Figure 20. *Drag across a row...*

	New York	New Jersey	Connecticut
Sweet 100	Sold out	Sold out	Sold out
Early Girl	Limited supplies in most areas	In stock	In stock
Plum	Limited supplies	In stock	Limited supplies
Big Boy	In stock	In stock	Limited supplies

Figure 21. *...or drag down a column.*

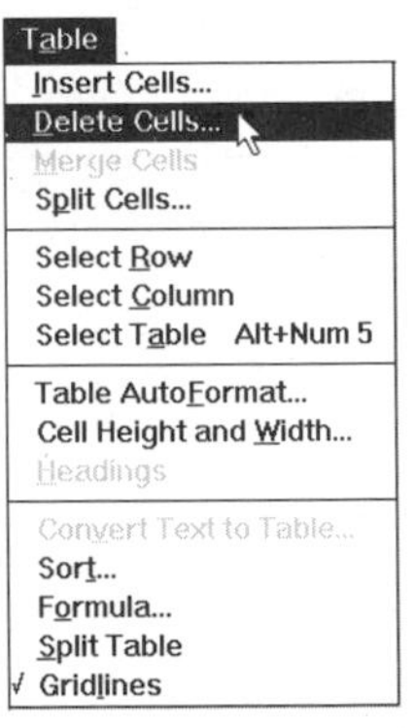

Figure 22. *The Table menu.*

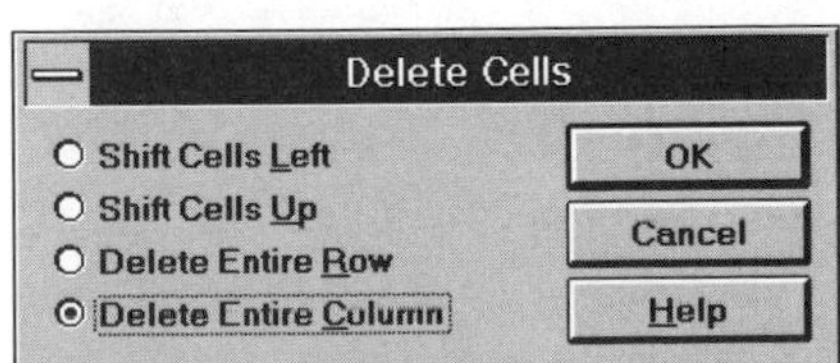

Figure 23. *The Delete Cells dialog box.*

Deleting Columns or Rows

1. Drag across any cells in the rows or the columns to delete. **(Figures 20-21)**
2. From the Table menu, choose Delete Cells. **(Figure 22)**
3. On the Delete Cells dialog box, choose Delete Entire Row or Delete Entire Column. **(Figure 23)**

✔ Tip

■ To delete an entire table, drag across all the columns and choose Delete Entire Column or drag down all the rows and choose Delete Entire Row.

Deleting Columns/Rows

Word

Inserting a Column or Row

To insert a row:

1. Click in a cell at the location for the new, blank row. **(Figure 23)**
2. From the Table menu, choose Insert Rows. **(Figure 24)**

To insert a column:

1. Position the mouse pointer at the top of the column at the location for the new column. A large, down arrow appears. **(Figure 25)**
2. Click while the down arrow is visible to select the column. **(Figure 26)**
3. From the Table menu, choose Insert Columns. **(Figure 27)**

	New York	New Jersey	Connecticut
Sweet 100	Sold out	Sold out	Sold out
Early Girl	Limited supplies in most areas	In stock	In stock
Plum	Limited supplies	In stock	Limited supplies
Big Boy	In stock	In stock	Limited supplies

Figure 23. *Click at the destination of the new row.*

Table
Insert Rows
Delete Cells...
Merge Cells
Split Cells...
Select Row
Select Column
Select Table Alt+Num 5
Table AutoFormat...
Cell Height and Width...
Headings
Convert Text to Table...
Sort...
Formula...
Split Table
√ Gridlines

Figure 24. *The Table menu.*

	New York	New Jersey	Connecticut
Sweet 100	Sold out	Sold out	Sold out
Early Girl	Limited supplies in most areas	In stock	In stock
Plum	Limited supplies	In stock	Limited supplies
Big Boy	In stock	In stock	Limited supplies

Figure 25. *Position the mouse pointer at the top of a column.*

	New York	New Jersey	Connecticut
Sweet 100	Sold out	Sold out	Sold out
Early Girl	Limited supplies in most areas	In stock	In stock
Plum	Limited supplies	In stock	Limited supplies
Big Boy	In stock	In stock	Limited supplies

Figure 26. *Click to select the entire column.*

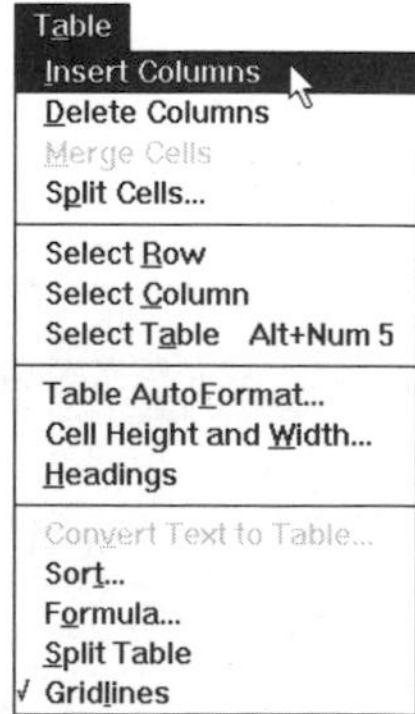

Figure 27. *The Table menu.*

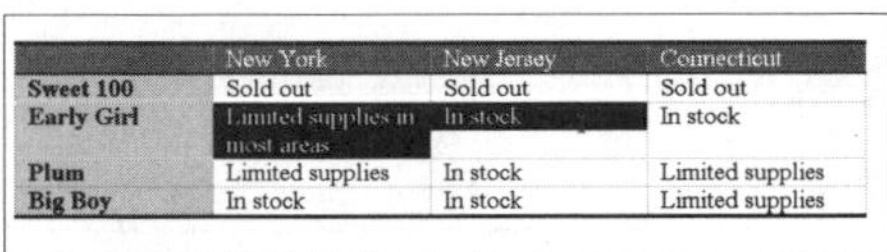

	New York	New Jersey	Connecticut
Sweet 100	Sold out	Sold out	Sold out
Early Girl	Limited supplies in most areas	In stock	In stock
Plum	Limited supplies	In stock	Limited supplies
Big Boy	In stock	In stock	Limited supplies

Figure 28. *Drag across the number of columns to insert.*

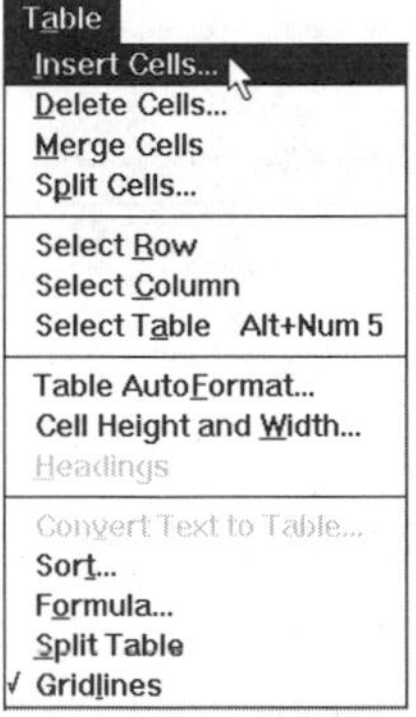

Figure 29. *The Table menu.*

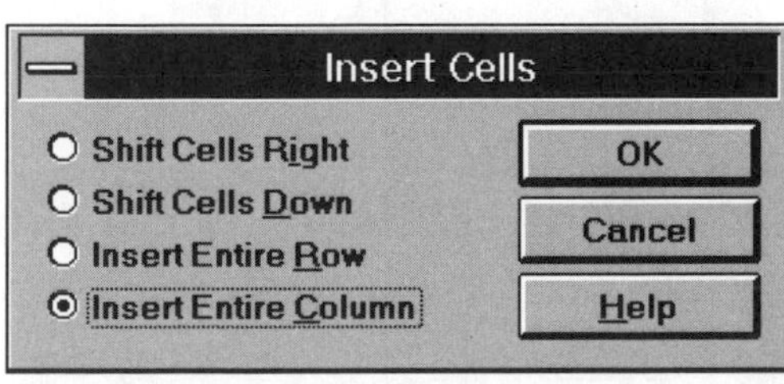

Figure 30. *The Insert Cells dialog box.*

Inserting Multiple Columns or Rows

1. Drag across the number of columns to insert or drag down the number of rows to insert. **(Figure 28)**
2. From the Table menu, choose Insert Cells. **(Figure 29)**
3. On the Insert Cells dialog box, choose either Insert Entire Row or Insert Entire Column. **(Figure 30)**

✔ **Tip**

■ The new columns or rows will be inserted before the existing columns or rows.

Changing Column Width and Row Height

To change the column width by dragging:

1. Place the mouse pointer on the vertical border at the right edge of the column to widen.
2. Drag the border to the right. **(Figure 31)**

	New York	New Jersey	Connecticut
Sweet 100	Sold out	Sold out	Sold out
Early Girl	Limited supplies in most areas	In stock	In stock
Plum	Limited supplies	In stock	Limited supplies
Big Boy	In stock	In stock	Limited supplies

Figure 31. *Drag the right border of a column to widen the column.*

To change the height of a row:

1. Select any cells in the rows to heighten. **(Figure 32)**
2. From the Table menu, choose Cell Height and Width. **(Figure 33)**
3. On the Rows tab of the Cell Height and Width dialog box, modify the At setting. **(Figure 34)**

	New York	New Jersey	Connecticut
Sweet 100	Sold out	Sold out	Sold out
Early Girl	Limited supplies in most areas	In stock	In stock
Plum	Limited supplies	In stock	Limited supplies
Big Boy	In stock	In stock	Limited supplies

Figure 32. *Select cells.*

✔ Tips

- Select cells in columns and then use the controls on the Column tab of the Cell Height and Width dialog box to set exact column widths.
- On the Column tab, you can also add more space between columns.
- You can drag the right edge of the table to widen the last column.

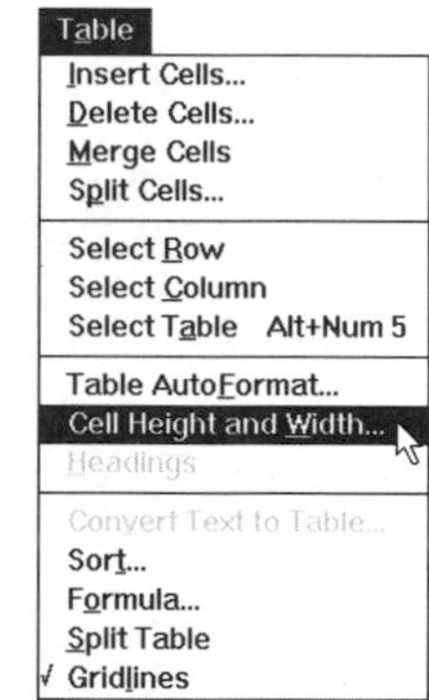

Figure 33. *The Table menu.*

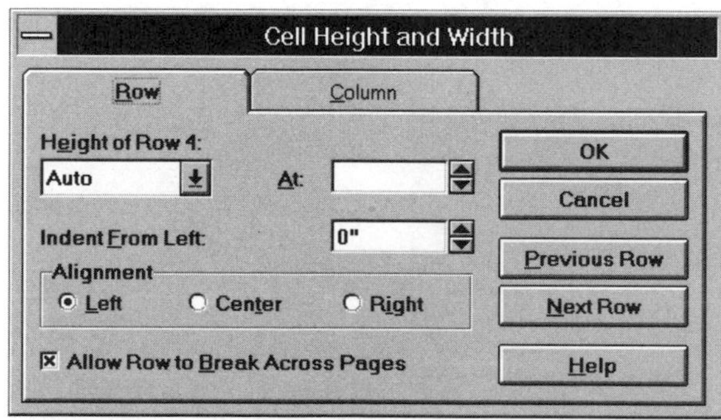

Figure 34. *The Cell Height and Width dialog box.*

	New York	New Jersey	Connecticut
Sweet 100	Sold out	Sold out	Sold out
Early Girl	Limited supplies in most areas	In stock	In stock
Plum	Limited supplies	In stock	Limited supplies
Big Boy	In stock	In stock	Limited supplies

Figure 35. *Select cells first.*

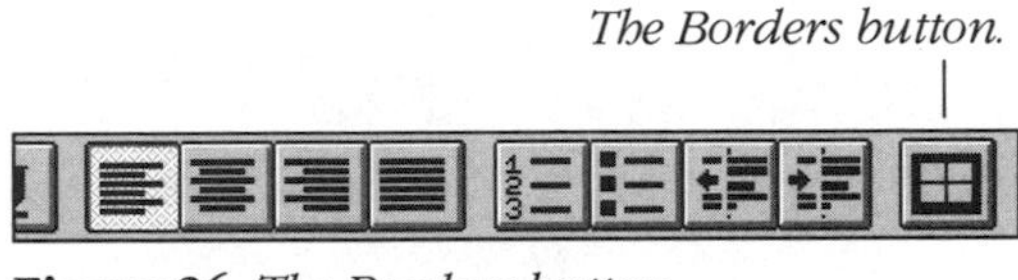

Figure 36. *The Borders button.*

Turning on Borders and Shading

Borders are lines surrounding the cells. Shading is a fill within the cells.

1. Select the cells for which you want to modify the borders or add shading. **(Figure 35)**
2. Click the Borders button on the Formatting toolbar. **(Figure 36)**
3. On the Borders toolbar, select a line style and thickness from the Line Style drop-down list. **(Figure 37)**
4. On the Borders toolbar, click the appropriate Border button to apply borders to the top, bottom, left, right, inside, or outside of the selected cells.
5. To apply a shading to the selected cells, select a shading from the Shading drop-down list.

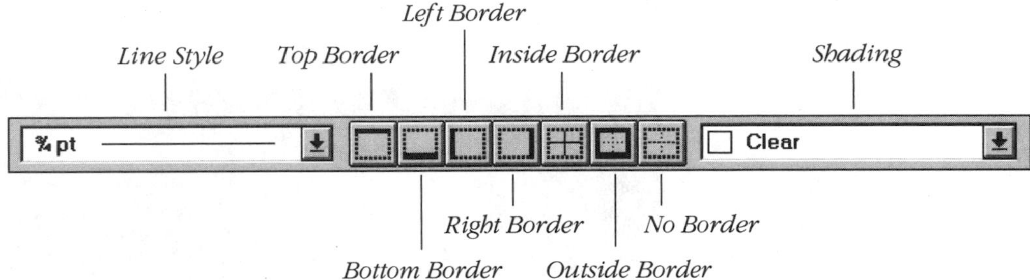

Figure 37. *The Borders toolbar.*

	New York	New Jersey	Connecticut
Sweet 100	Sold out	Sold out	Sold out
Early Girl	Limited supplies in most areas	In stock	In stock
Plum	Limited supplies	In stock	Limited supplies
Big Boy	In stock	In stock	Limited supplies

Figure 38. *Shaded cells.*

Converting Text to a Table

When somebody else has created a table in a document with plain old tabs, you can easily convert the tab table to a standard Word table that can be more easily modified and formatted.

1. Select all the lines of the existing tab table. **(Figure 39)**
2. Click the Insert Table button on the Standard toolbar.

   or

   From the Table menu, choose Convert Text to Table. **(Figure 40)**
3. On the Convert Text to Table dialog box, click AutoFormat to select a format for the table if you want and then click OK. **(Figures 41–42)**

✔ Tip

■ By using the Convert Text to Table command on the Table menu, you can convert a list of paragraphs to a table by choosing Paragraphs for Separate Text At.

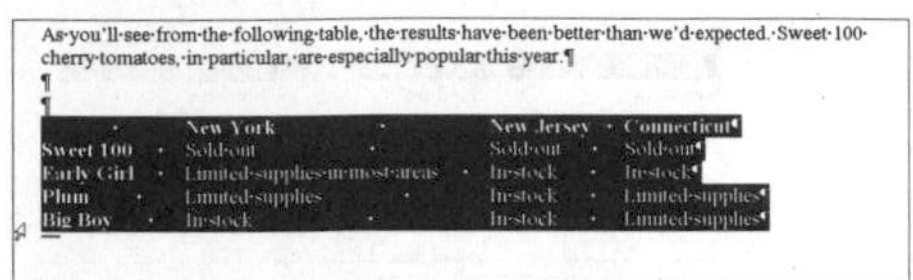

As you'll see from the following table, the results have been better than we'd expected. Sweet 100 cherry tomatoes, in particular, are especially popular this year.

	New York	New Jersey	Connecticut
Sweet 100	Sold out	Sold out	Sold out
Early Girl	Limited supplies in most areas	In stock	In stock
Plum	Limited supplies	In stock	Limited supplies
Big Boy	In stock	In stock	Limited supplies

Figure 39. *Select the existing table.*

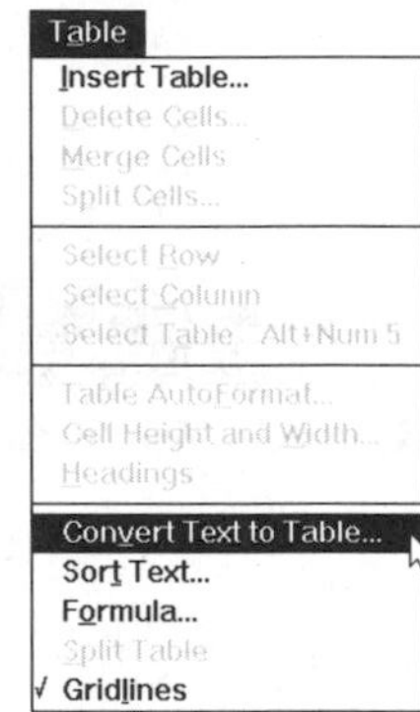

Figure 40. *The Table menu.*

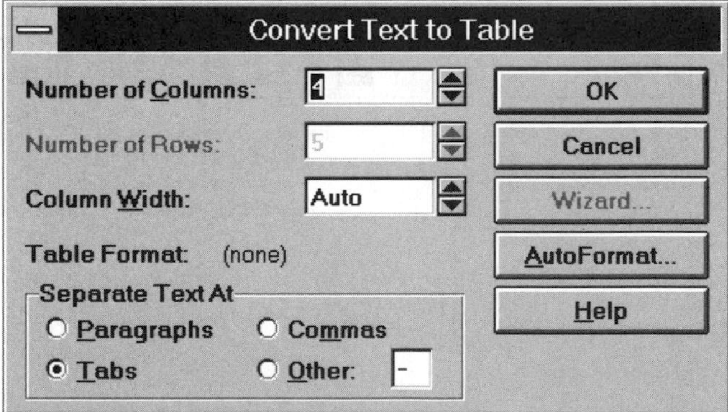

Figure 41. *The Convert Text to Table dialog box.*

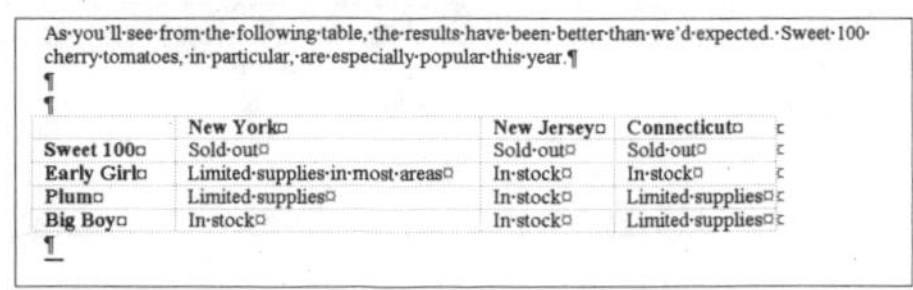

As you'll see from the following table, the results have been better than we'd expected. Sweet 100 cherry tomatoes, in particular, are especially popular this year.

	New York	New Jersey	Connecticut
Sweet 100	Sold out	Sold out	Sold out
Early Girl	Limited supplies in most areas	In stock	In stock
Plum	Limited supplies	In stock	Limited supplies
Big Boy	In stock	In stock	Limited supplies

Figure 42. *The unformatted table.*

Special Word Techniques 10

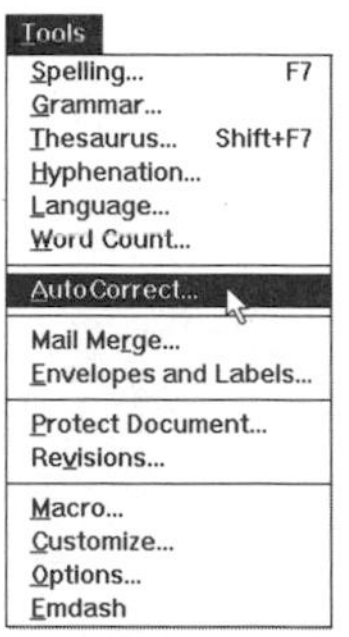

Figure 1. *The Tools menu.*

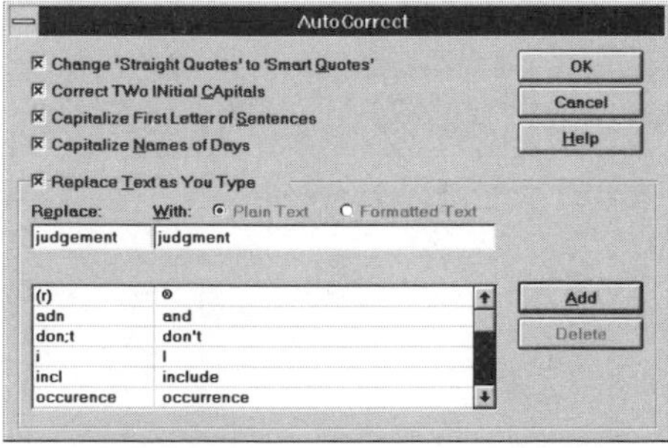

Figure 2. *The AutoCorrect dialog box.*

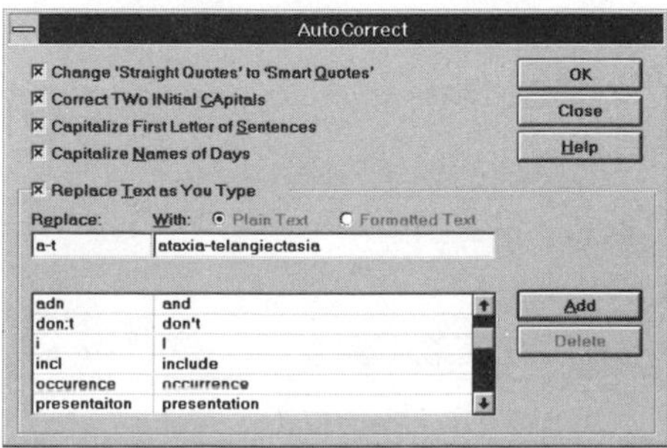

Figure 3. *You can use AutoCorrect to expand abbreviations.*

Automatically Correcting Typos

Word's AutoCorrect works quietly behind the scenes, automatically correcting many common typos as you type. It has its own short list of common typos and their corrections but you can add your own most frequent typos and the corresponding corrections to the list.

AutoCorrect also automatically capitalizes the first word in a sentence if you forget, removes instances of TWo capitals at the beginning of a word, and capitalizes the names of days for you.

To add typos and corrections to the AutoCorrect list:

1. From the Tools menu, choose AutoCorrect. **(Figure 1)**
2. Type the typo in the Replace text box.
3. Type the correction in the With text box. **(Figure 2)**
4. Click the Add button.

✔ Tips

- To insert text with a special font formatting, type the correction and format it in a document, then copy the correction and paste it into the With text box on the AutoCorrect dialog box. Be sure to click Formatted Text before you click Add.
- You can enter an abbreviation as the Replace term and the full technical, medical, or legal term as the With item and then have AutoCorrect enter long, complex terms for you whenever you type the abbreviation. **(Figure 3)**

Word

Automatically Entering Text

AutoText saves you from repetitively typing text that you need frequently. With AutoText, you can insert any amount of text in a document, from a single word to multiple paragraphs. Assembling boilerplate documents from standard passages, such as putting together contracts by combining standard clauses, is an ideal task for AutoText.

To use AutoText, you type a passage of text once and then save it as an AutoText entry, giving it a name in the process, such as "closing." Then to recall an AutoText entry, you type the name and press F3. In previous versions of Word, AutoText was called the Gallery.

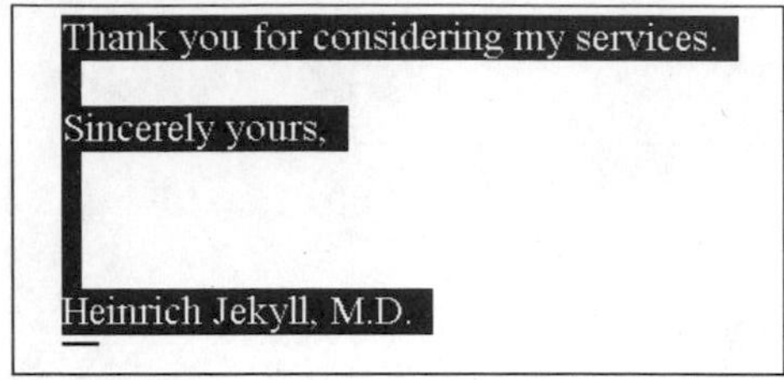

Figure 3. *Type and then select the AutoText entry.*

To create an AutoText entry:

1. Type the text to save and select it. **(Figure 3)**
2. Click the Edit AutoText button. **(Figure 4)**
   or
   Choose AutoText from the Edit menu.
3. In the Name text box, replace the suggested name that is highlighted with a name of your own. **(Figure 5)**
4. Click Add to add the text to the list of available AutoText entries.

The Edit AutoText Button.

Figure 4. *The Edit AutoText button.*

Enter a name for the Autotext entry here.

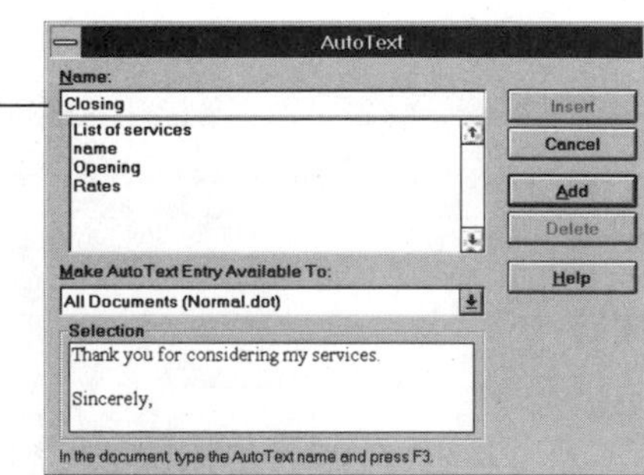

Figure 5. *The AutoText dialog box.*

Mr. John Hyde
24 Barkley Place
London, England

Dear Mr. Hyde.

I should like to inform you that I will be opening a modest office in your neighborhood at which I will perform all manor of medical procedures.

If any such needs arise, I would be most grateful if you did call.

Closing

Figure 6. *Type the name of the AutoText entry.*

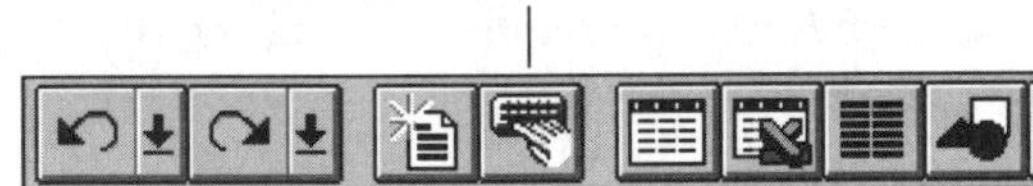

Figure 7. *The Insert AutoText button.*

Dear Mr. Hyde.

I should like to inform you that I will be opening a modest office in your neighborhood at which I will perform all manor of medical procedures.

If any such needs arise, I would be most grateful if you did call.

Thank you for considering my services.

Sincerely,

Dr. Heinrich Jekyll

Figure 8. *The AutoText is inserted.*

To insert an AutoText entry:

1. Type the name of the AutoText entry. **(Figure 6)**
2. Click the Insert AutoText button. **(Figure 7)**

   or

   Press F3.

   or

   From the Edit menu, choose AutoText. Select the name of the AutoText entry from the list, and click Insert.

✔ **Tips**

- You can include graphics in an AutoText entry to automatically insert a logo in a document.
- You can use AutoText to automatically enter long medical, legal, or technical terms.
- To save a formatted paragraph as an AutoText entry, select the paragraph mark at the end of the paragraph in Step 2. Otherwise, the text will be inserted as plain text.
- The Insert AutoText button becomes the Edit AutoText button when you select newly typed text.

Inserting Symbols from the Wingdings Font

The Wingdings font contains dozens of useful and fun pictures that you can embed in a document. Word provides an automatic method of inserting symbols into a document.

1. Position the insertion point at the destination for the symbol. **(Figure 9)**
2. From the Insert menu, choose Symbol. **(Figure 10)**
3. On the Symbols tab of the Symbol dialog box, pull-down the list of Fonts and choose Wingdings. **(Figure 11)**
4. Click on any symbol to magnify it. **(Figure 12)**
5. Click the symbol you want and then click Insert.
6. Click Cancel to close the Symbol dialog box.

✔ Tips

- You can select symbols from other fonts, too.
- On the Special Characters tab of the Symbol dialog box, you'll find frequently used characters that you can select and insert in any document.

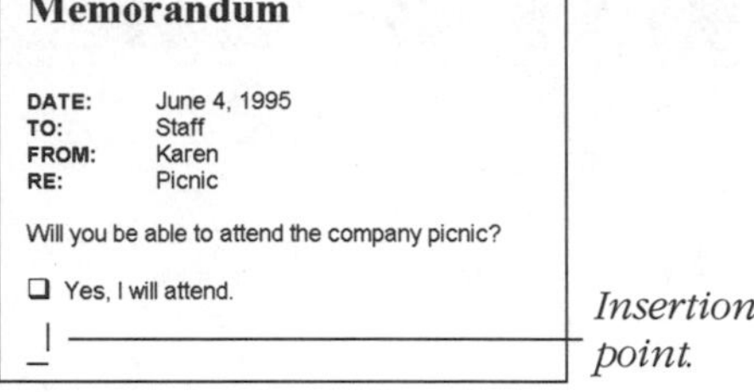

Figure 9. *Position the insertion point in the document.*

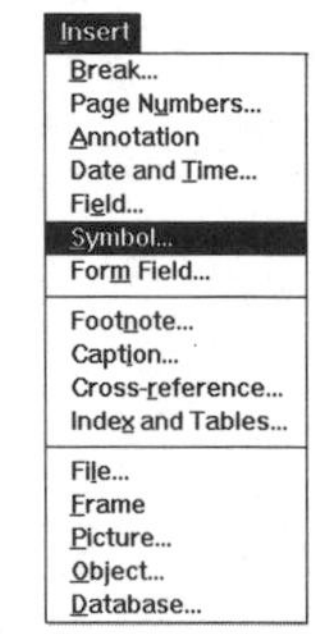

Figure 10. *The Insert menu.*

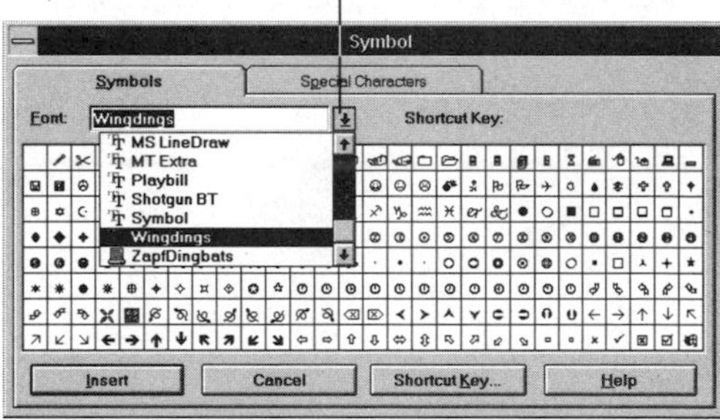

Figure 11. *The Font pull-down list.*

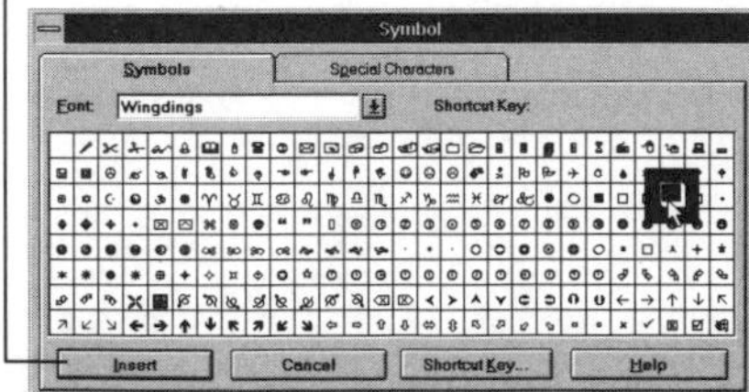

Figure 12. *Magnify a symbol by clicking on it.*

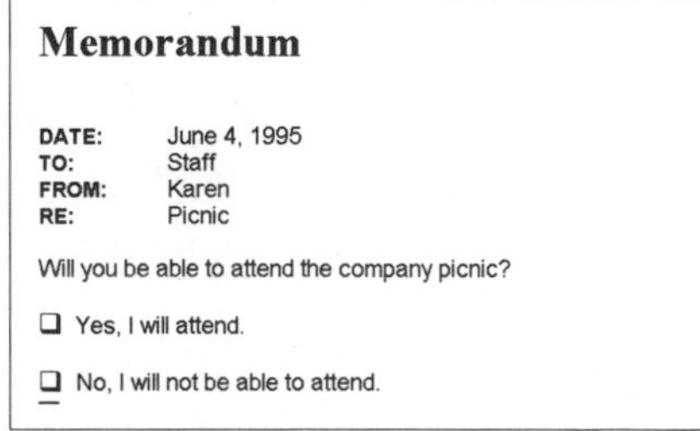

Figure 13. *The symbol inserted.*

Tools
Spelling... F7
Grammar...
Thesaurus... Shift+F7
Hyphenation...
Language...
Word Count...
AutoCorrect...
Mail Merge...
Envelopes and Labels...
Protect Document...
Revisions...
Macro...
Customize...
Options...
Emdash

Figure 13. *The Tools menu.*

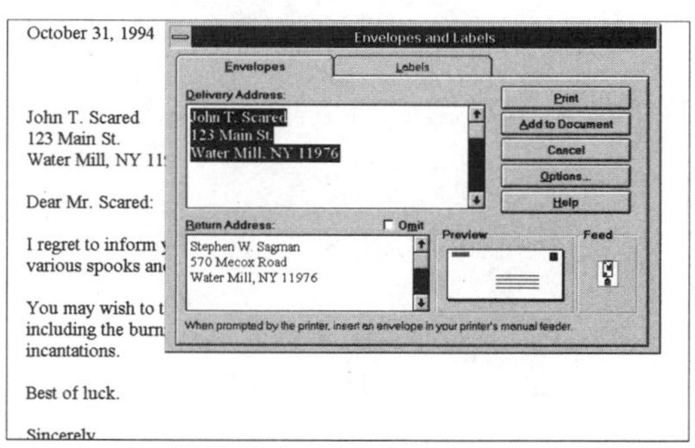

Figure 14. *Envelopes tab of the Envelopes and Labels dialog box.*

Printing Envelopes

Word can extract the mailing address from a letter and automatically format and print an envelope.

1. From the Tools menu, select Envelopes and Labels. **(Figure 13)**

   or, if the document contains more than one address, select the proper address before you select Envelopes and Labels.

2. If the address and return address are correct on the Envelopes tab of the Envelopes and Labels dialog box, click the Print button. **(Figure 14)**

   or

   Make any necessary modifications to the address and return address before clicking the Print button.

✔ Tips

- If your envelopes have a pre-printed return address, make sure the Omit checkbox is checked to omit the return address before clicking the Print button.
- To choose a different envelope size, or change the font and location of the addresses on the envelopes, click the Options button on the Envelopes and Labels dialog box to get to the Envelope Options dialog box. *See Envelope Printing Options, page 100.*

Envelope Printing Options

Before you print the envelopes, you can examine the Envelope Printing Options and change the way envelopes will print, if necessary.

1. On the Envelopes and Labels dialog box, click the Options button. **(Figure 15)**
2. On the Envelope Options tab of the Envelope Options dialog box, change the envelope size and font and location of the addresses. **(Figure 16)**
3. On the Printing Options tab of the Envelope Options dialog box choose the envelope feed direction that matches the way your printer works. **(Figure 17)**
4. If your printer has an envelope feeder, select the envelope tray from the Feed From drop-down list.

✔ Tips

- Word chooses the best options based on the current selected printer.
- The Delivery Point Bar Code option prints a machine-readable version of the zip code on the envelope.
- If you are printing Reply envelopes, you can also have word print a FIM code. FIMs are only necessary with Business Reply mail. Check with your post office for more information about FIMs.

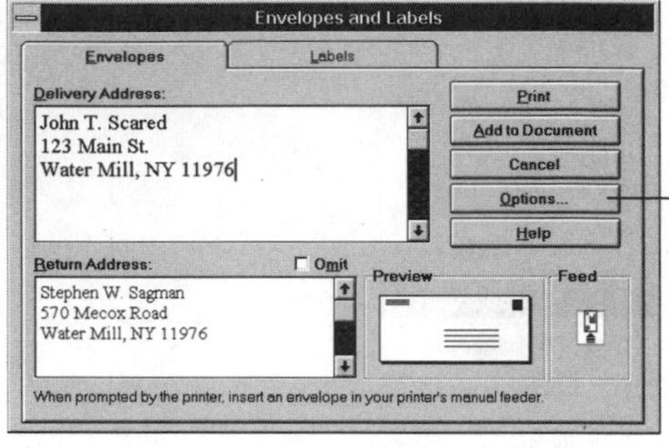

Figure 15. *The Options button on the Envelopes and Labels dialog box.*

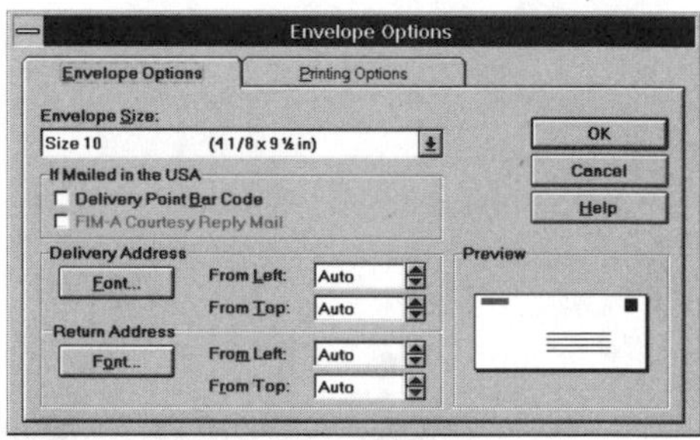

Figure 16. *The Envelope Options tab of the Envelope dialog box.*

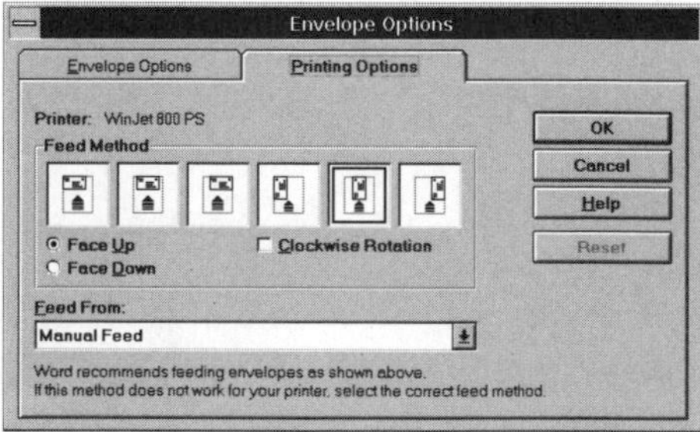

Figure 17. *The Printing Options tab of the Envelope Options dialog box.*

Word

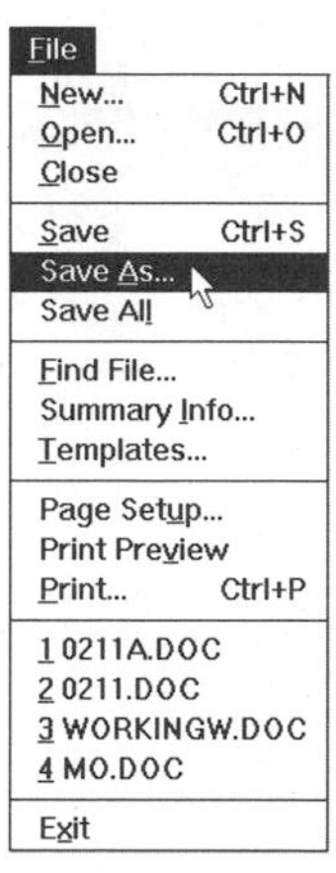

Figure 19. *The File menu.*

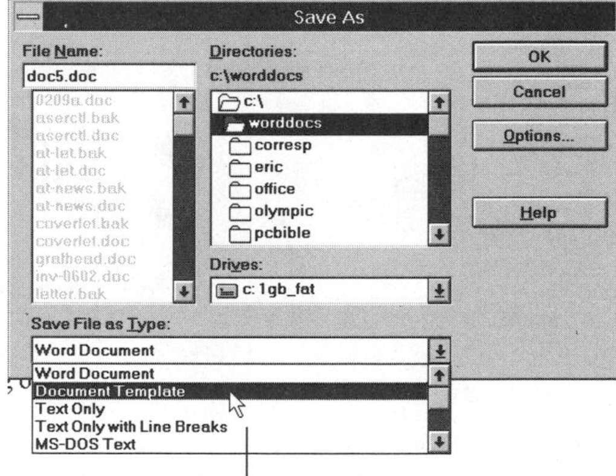

Choose Document Template here.

Figure 20. *Save As dialog box.*

Saving a Document as a Template

Templates contain entire document designs, possibly even including some of the text. When you start a new document with the New command on the File menu, you get the option to choose one of the preformatted templates that come with Word. These include templates for many popular business and professional documents. If none of the templates exactly suits your needs, you can modify them or save your own document designs as templates. Then, you can easily create many other documents based on the same design.

1. Create a sample document and format it by creating and applying a set of styles. *See Creating a Paragraph Style, page 72 and Choosing a Style from the Style List, page 71.*
2. Delete any text that you do not want saved as part of the template. To save only the styles and page formatting, delete all the text, for example.
3. From the File menu, choose Save As. **(Figure 19)**
4. From the Save File as Type pull-down list, choose Document Template. **(Figure 20)**
5. Type a name for the template in the File Name text box.
6. Click OK.

✔ Tips

- Document Templates are automatically stored with all the other templates.
- AutoText entries, macros, and custom toolbars are saved in the template, so you may want to create AutoText entries and modify the toolbars before saving the document as a template. *See Automatically Entering Text, page 96, and Selecting Toolbars, page 31.*

Modifying an Existing Template

1. From the File menu, choose Open. **(Figure 21)**
   or
   Press Ctrl+O.
2. On the Open dialog box, choose Document Template from the List Files of Types drop-down list. **(Figure 22)**
3. Double-click a template name on the list to open the template.
4. Make editing and formatting changes to the template.
5. From the File menu, choose Save. **(Figure 23)**

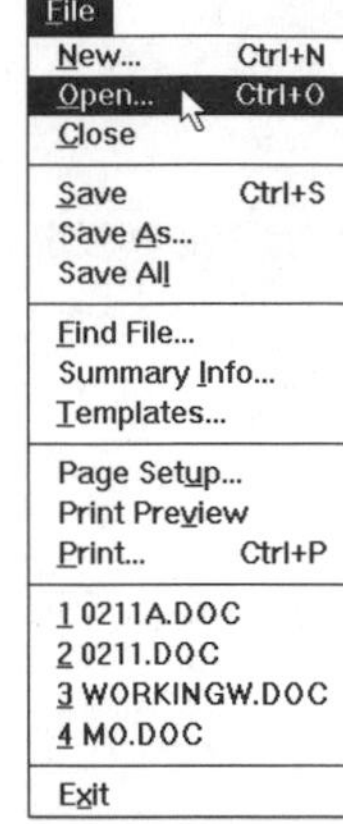

Figure 21. *The File menu.*

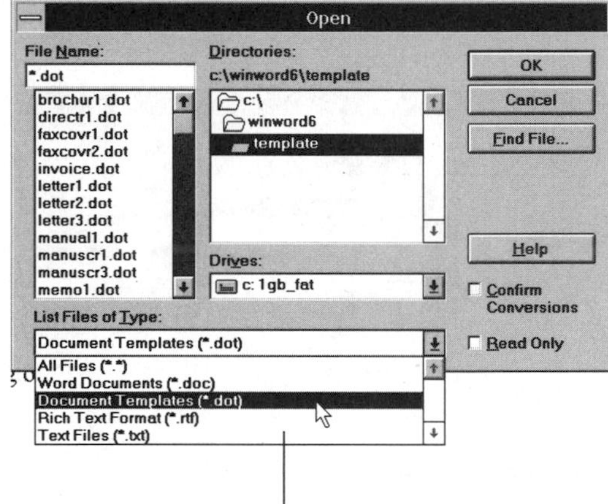

Figure 22. *Choose Document Template here.*

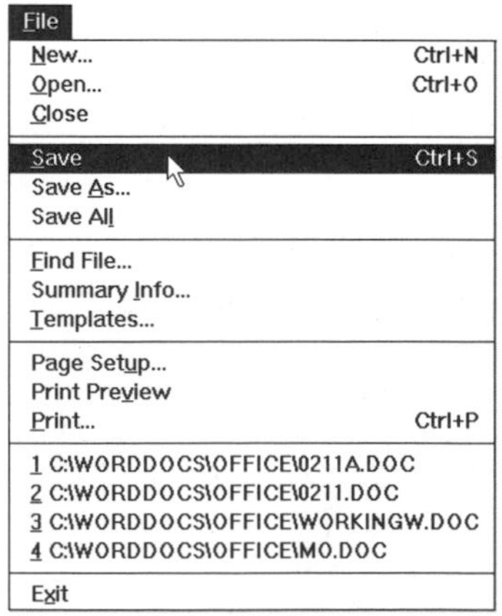

Figure 23. *The File menu.*

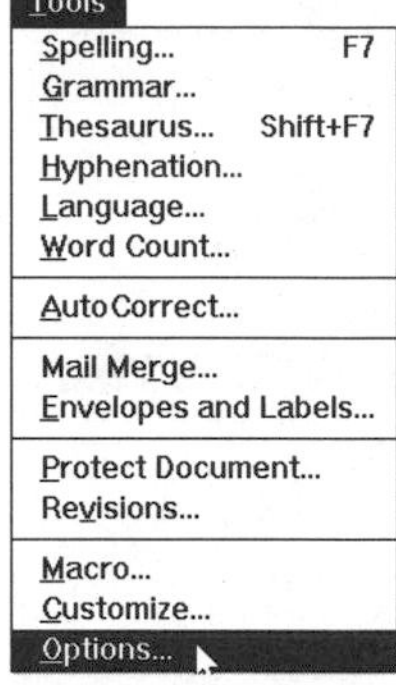

Figure 24. *The Tools menu.*

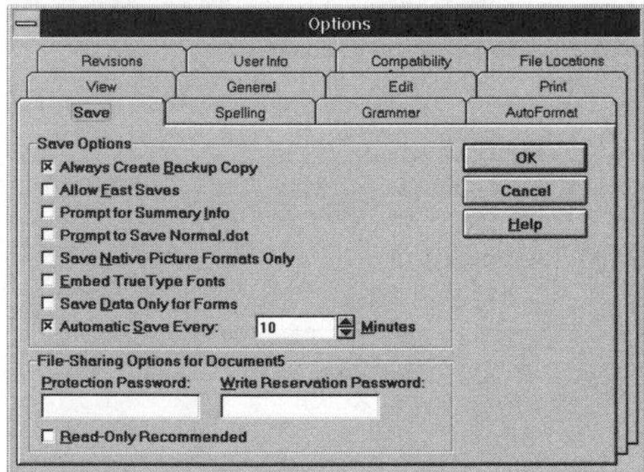

Figure 25. *The Options dialog box.*

Using Automatic Saves

You can have Word automatically save your document at preset intervals. You'll want to turn this feature on as it gives you protection in case of a power loss or other calamity, and the saving process occurs very quickly and will not disturb your work.

1. From the Tools menu, select Options. **(Figure 24)**
2. Click the Save tab of the Options dialog box. **(Figure 25)**
3. Make sure Automatic Save Every __ Minutes is turned on.
4. Change the number of minutes if you wish.
5. Click OK.

✔ Tips

- Even though Word can automatically save your work, you must still save your work in a file as usual when you finish a document. Word's automatic saving simply creates a special file on disk so Word can restore the file if your typing session is interrupted before you perform a normal save.
- If the power fails or disaster strikes while you're working, Word will display a list of automatically saved documents when you next start Word. Simply select your work in progress from the list.

Creating Form Letters with Mail Merge

Word provides built-in, guided help for performing the three major steps in creating mail merged letters, labels, or envelopes: **1.** Creating the merge letter; **2.** Creating or opening the data source; and **3.** Printing the mail merge.

Word will have you create a merge document, prepare or open a data source, and then return to the merge document where you will create the merge

1. From the Tools menu, select Mail Merge. **(Figure 27)**
2. On the Mail Merge Helper, click each option and then follow the onscreen instructions. Before Word helps you create the actual merge letter, it helps you create or open the data source for the database. Then, it returns to the merge document and displays the Mail Merge toolbar. **(Figure 28)**
3. Type the text of the merge document, clicking the Insert Merge Field button whenever you want to include information from the data source.
4. When the merge document is complete, click the Check for Errors button and then click the Merge to Printer button or the Merge to New Document button to create a document you can print later.

✔ Tips

- Click the Mail Merge button on the Mail Merge toolbar to choose a destination for the merge and to select data for the merge.
- Merging data from Access is easy. *See Access to Word: Sending Data to a Mail Merge, page 321 for details.*

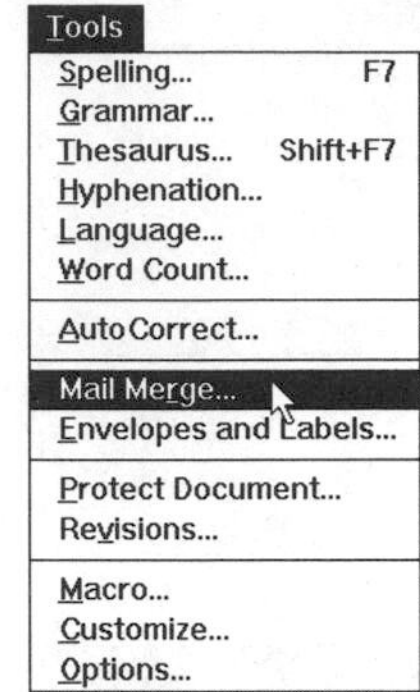

Figure 27. *The Tools menu.*

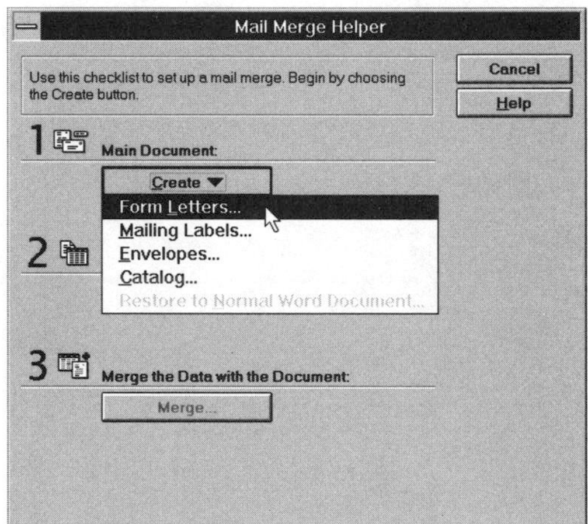

Figure 28. *The Mail Merge Helper.*

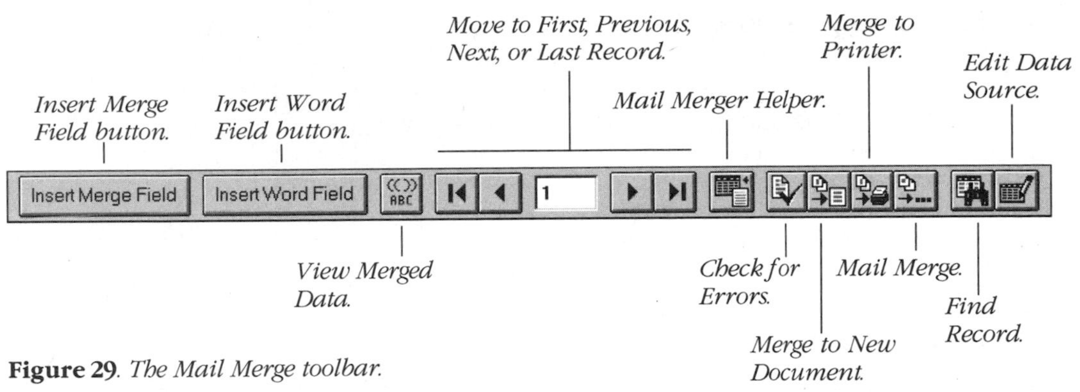

Figure 29. *The Mail Merge toolbar.*

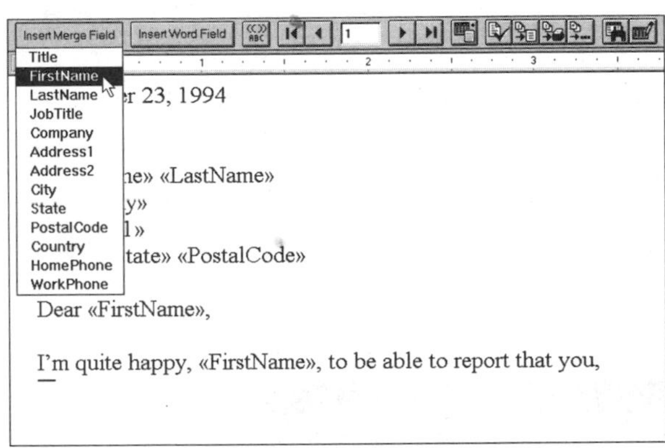

Figure 30. *Choose field names from the Insert Merge Field list as you type the mail merge letter.*

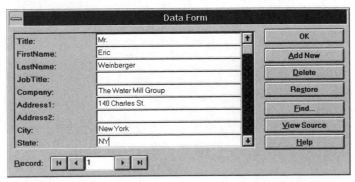

Data Form

Title:	Mr.
FirstName:	Eric
LastName:	Weinberger
JobTitle:	
Company:	The Water Mill Group
Address1:	140 Charles St.
Address2:	
City:	New York
State:	NY

OK
Add New
Delete
Restore
Find...
View Source
Help

Record: 1

Figure 31. *You can use the Data Form provided by the Mail Merge helper to enter the data.*

Changing the Appearance of the Word Window

You can choose whether to display the status bar, the scroll bars, and the toolbars, or whether to keep a minimalist view devoted to the text. You can also decide which of the nonprinting characters to display. *See About the Paragraph Marks, page 49.*

1. From the Tools menu, choose Options. **(Figure 29)**
2. On the View tab of the Options dialog box, use the checkboxes in the Window and Nonprinting Characters areas to decide which elements to display. **(Figure 30)**
3. On the View tab you can also turn on Wrap to Window to keep all the text in view even when you reduce the size of the Word window or increase the Zoom factor. When Wrap to Window is on, the arrangement of words onscreen may not match the arrangement on the printed page.

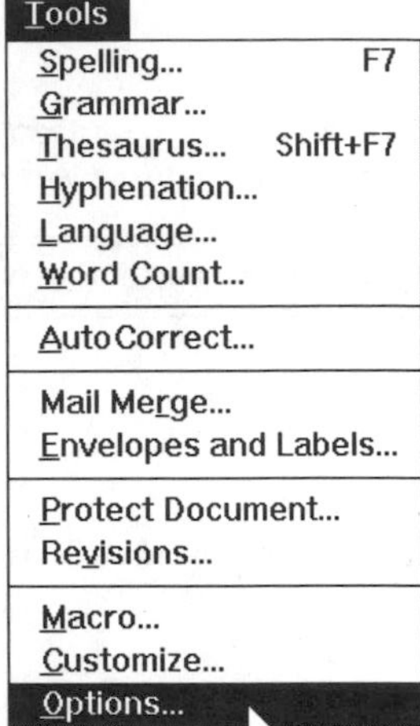

Figure 29. *The Tools menu.*

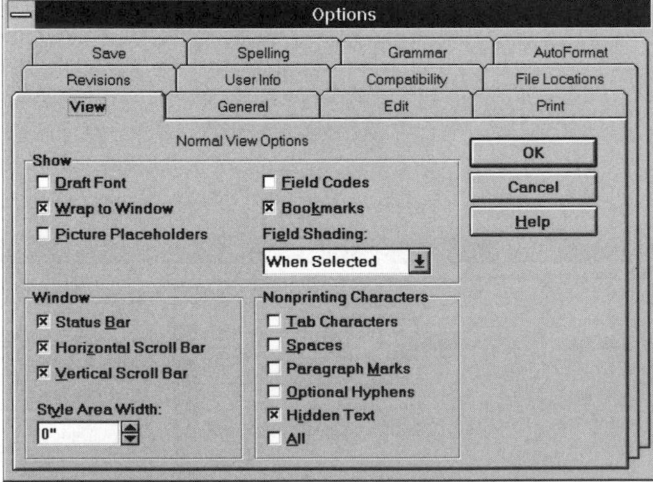

Figure 30. *The View tab of the Options dialog box.*

Excel 5.0 Number Crunching

Excel 5.0 Number Crunching

About Excel

What is Excel?

Excel, the spreadsheet of the Microsoft Office suite, tracks numbers, calculates and analyzes numbers, and creates charts to depict them visually.

After you type numbers into a grid of cells on an Excel sheet, you can enter formulas into adjacent cells that total, subtract, multiple, or divide the numbers. You can also enter functions (special Excel formulas) that perform dozens of more complex calculations on the numbers, ranging from simple averaging, through sophisticated financial calculations such as Net Present Value, to highly involved statistical computations, such as the inverse of the one-tailed probability of the chi-squared distribution.

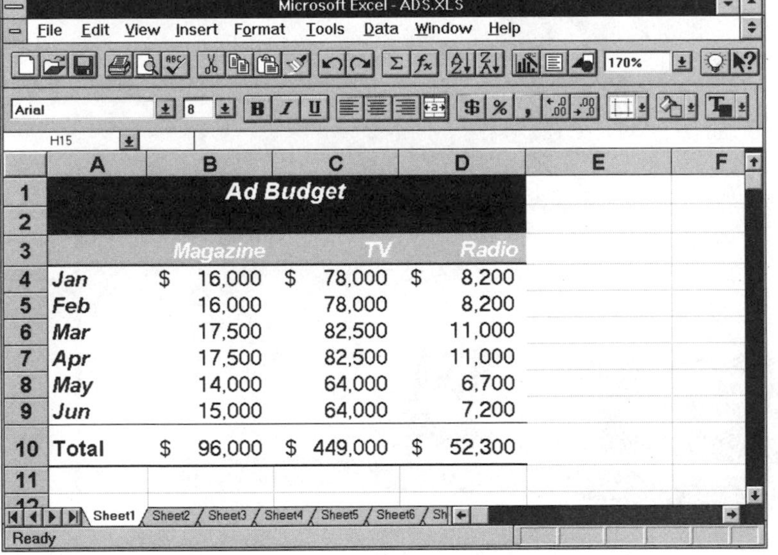

Excel also offers simple database capabilities. You can accumulate records of information that are both textual and numeric, and sort, search through, and extract data from the database. For relational database capabilities, or if you have a lot of data to store, you'll want to use Microsoft Access, instead.

To view your numbers graphically, you can have Excel create a chart. Excel uses the same charting program as PowerPoint so its charts are professional and presentable.

The Road to an Excel Sheet

The Bridgehampton Garden Club

Sheet1

Fund Raising Events	Spring	Summer	Fall
Garden Tour	240	310	120
Bulb Planting	350	-	510
Cuttings Club	100	465	275
Plant Auction	580	-	430
Flower Festival	335	250	145
	S 1,605	S 1,025	S 1,480

Fill Cells with Row and Column Headings and Data

Into the worksheet grid of cells, enter the row and column headings and the numbers that go underneath. Use AutoFill, if you can, to enter sequences like month names. *Pages 115-120.*

Enter the Calculations

Into cells that are adjacent to the data, enter the formulas that will calculate the results you need. Summing a column is the most familiar formula, but Excel provides dozens of special "functions" that can perform sophisticated calculations on your data. *Pages 121-130.*

Changing the Sheet Structure

With the numbers and calculations in place, you can structure the sheet to make it easy to interpret. You might widen a column, lock the headings so they remain on the screen at all times, or split the sheet into panes you can use to view or edit different areas of a sheet simultaneously. *Pages 131-136.*

Formatting the Sheet

AutoFormatting a sheet can enhance the sheet's appearance and make it more presentable or easier to understand. Excel's dozens of AutoFormat designs make designing the sheet a simple menu pick. Then, to refine the sheet, you can further format sheet elements. You can format the text or numbers, add borders and shading to cells, or use styles to apply formatting automatically. *Pages 137-144.*

Annotating and Auditing the Sheet

Add notes to cells to attach text messages or even voice annotations. Name the sheets in a workbook to make them easier to understand. And, before you stake your reputation on the accuracy of the sheet, use Excel's built-in auditing tools to check the formulas. *Pages 149-151.*

Printing or Mailing the Sheet

Excel's print preview gives you a bird's eye view of your work before you commit it to paper. To send a sheet to a colleague, you can attach it to a Microsoft Mail note, instead.

Extras

Excel also includes sophisticated charting and database capabilities so you can graphically represent numeric data or collect and store large quantities of information. For the charting, you may prefer to use PowerPoint, and for the database, Access is your better bet. *Pages 152-160.*

The Excel 5 Window

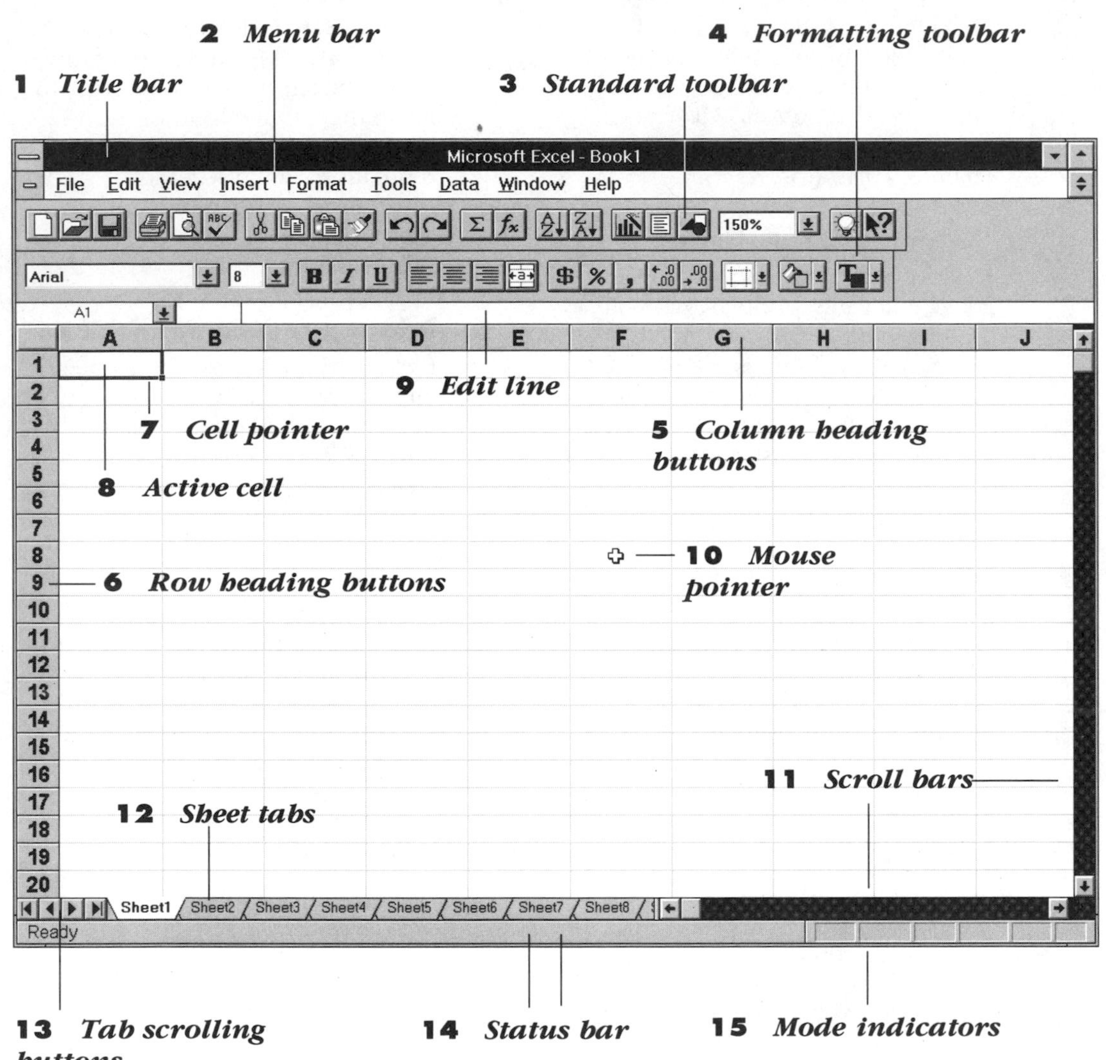
1 Title bar
2 Menu bar
3 Standard toolbar
4 Formatting toolbar
Microsoft Excel - Book1
File Edit View Insert Format Tools Data Window Help
150%
Arial
8
A1
A B C D E F G H I J
9 Edit line
7 Cell pointer
5 Column heading buttons
8 Active cell
10 Mouse pointer
6 Row heading buttons
11 Scroll bars
12 Sheet tabs
Sheet1 Sheet2 Sheet3 Sheet4 Sheet5 Sheet6 Sheet7 Sheet8
Ready
13 Tab scrolling buttons
14 Status bar
15 Mode indicators

Key to the Excel 5 Window

1 ***Title bar***

Displays the window name. Drag the title bar to move the window. Double-click the title bar to switch between maximized and restored window.

2 ***Menu bar***

Click any name on the menu bar to pull down a menu, or press Alt+the underlined letter of the menu name.

3 ***Standard toolbar***

Toolbar with buttons for standard file management and text editing and proofing commands.

4 ***Formatting toolbar***

Toolbar with buttons for formatting cells and the contents of cells.

5 ***Column heading buttons***

Label the columns. Click a column heading button to select a column. Drag across column heading buttons to select multiple columns.

6 ***Row heading buttons***

Label the rows. Click a row heading button to select a row. Drag across row heading buttons to select multiple rows.

7 ***Cell pointer***

The cell pointer surrounds the currently selected cell. Click a different cell to move the cell pointer or press the arrow keys.

8 ***Active cell***

The cell into which data enters when you start to type. When you select a range, the active cell is the only cell that remains unhighlighted.

9 ***Edit line***

Displays the contents of the selected cell. You can edit the contents here or within the cell.

10 ***Mouse pointer***

The mouse pointer appears as a large plus sign when it is on a cell. Click the mouse to select the cell.

11 ***Scroll bars***

Use these scroll bars to move the view of the document up or down or to quickly jump to a spot in the document. The length of the vertical scroll bar represents the length of the entire document. The position of the scroll button represents the position of the insertion point in the document.

12 ***Sheet tabs***

Click these tabs to switch from sheet to sheet. Double-click a tab to rename a sheet.

13 ***Tab scrolling buttons***

Use these buttons to scroll forward or back a sheet or to jump to the first or last sheet.

14 ***Status bar***

Provides information about the current sheet or the current operation.

15 ***Mode indicators***

Show special conditions that are in effect, such as a pressed Caps Lock key.

Starting Excel

1. Double-click the Microsoft Excel icon in the Program Manager. **(Figure 1)**

   or

   Click the Microsoft Excel icon in the Microsoft Office Manager. **(Figure 2)**

✔ Tip

- If Microsoft Excel is already started, press Ctrl+Esc and choose Microsoft Excel from the list of running applications on the Task List. You can also press Alt+Tab repeatedly until the Microsoft Excel icon appears. Then release the Alt key and the Excel window will come to the front.

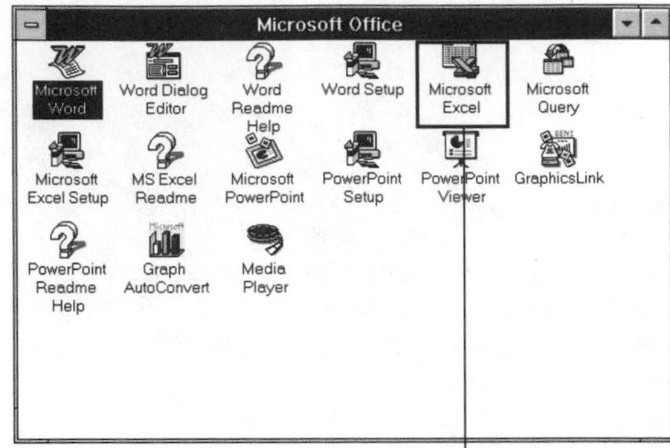

Figure 1. *The Microsoft Excel icon in the Program Manager.*

Click here to start Excel.

Figure 2. *The Microsoft Office Manager.*

Entering Headings and Data

Planning the Worksheet

Most worksheets conform to a standard design, with rows and columns of data, headings at the tops of columns and left of rows, and calculations at the bottoms of columns and/or the ends of rows. **(Figure 1)**

Because everyone is familiar with this basic structure, your worksheet will be universally understood.

Excel is a blank slate, though, onto which you can write any worksheet design. The 256 columns and 16,384 rows should give you ample space to be creative.

Microsoft Excel - Book1

File Edit View Insert Format Tools Data Window Help

	A	B	C	D	E	F	G
1			Ad Budget				
2							
3			Magazine	TV	Radio		
4		Jan	$ 16,000	$ 78,000	$ 8,200		
5		Feb	$ 16,000	$ 78,000	$ 8,200		
6		Mar	$ 17,500	$ 82,500	$ 11,000		
7		Apr	$ 17,500	$ 82,500	$ 11,000		
8		May	$ 14,000	$ 64,000	$ 6,700		
9		Jun	$ 15,000	$ 64,000	$ 7,200		
10		Total	$ 96,000	$ 449,000	$ 52,300		

Sheet1 / Sheet2 / Sheet3 / Sheet4 / Sheet5 / Sheet6 / Sheet7 / Sheet8

Ready

Figure 1. *The most common worksheet structure.*

Moving Within a Sheet

To enter data into a cell, you must move to the cell first.

1. Click in the cell. **(Figure 2)**

   or

   Press the arrow keys to move the cell pointer to the cell.

   or

   Click the current cell address on the edit line and type the new cell address to jump to. **(Figure 3)**

✔ Tips

- The cell surrounded by the cell pointer is called the *active cell.*
- You can use the scroll bars to scroll through the document without changing the active cell.

Table 12-1. ***Keyboard Shortcuts for Moving Within a Worksheet***

Arrow key	Move to the adjacent cell up, down, left, or right.
PgUp or **PgDn**	Move up or down one screenful.
Alt+PgUp or **Alt+PgDn**	Move left or right one screenful.
Tab	Move right one screenful.
Shift+Tab	Move left one screenful.
Ctrl+Home	Move to cell A1.
Home	Move to first cell of the row.
Ctrl+End	Move to last cell of last row that contains data.

The address of the active cell.

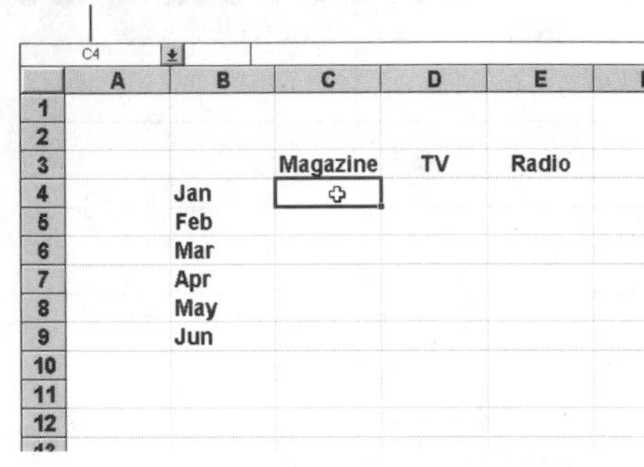

Figure 2. *Move the cell pointer to the cell into which you want to enter data and then click.*

Click here and then type a replacement address.

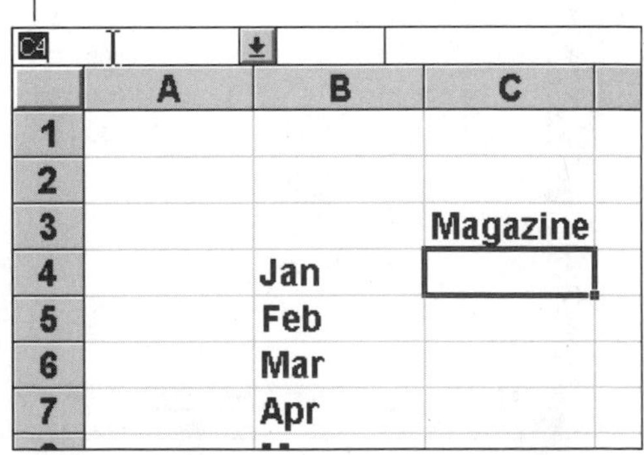

Figure 3. *Editing the current cell address.*

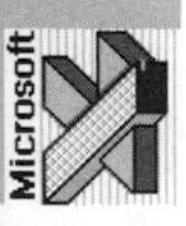

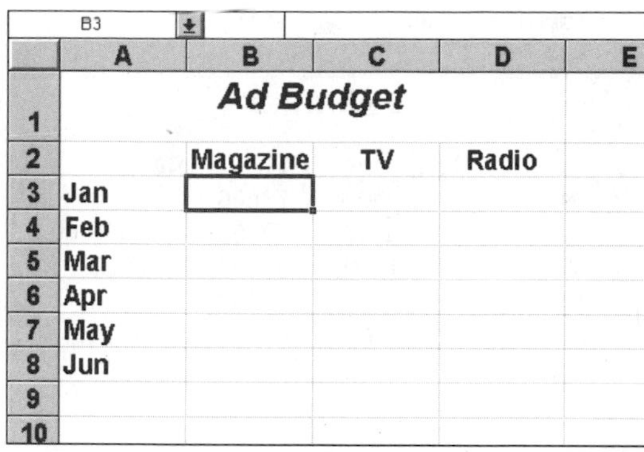

Figure 4. *Select the cell.*

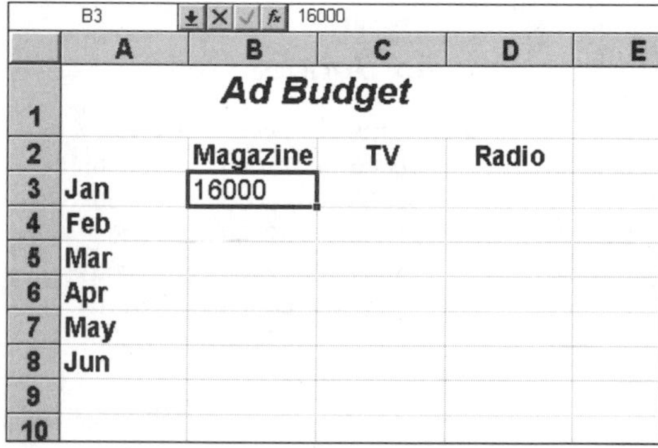

Figure 5. *Type the entry.*

Text is left-aligned.

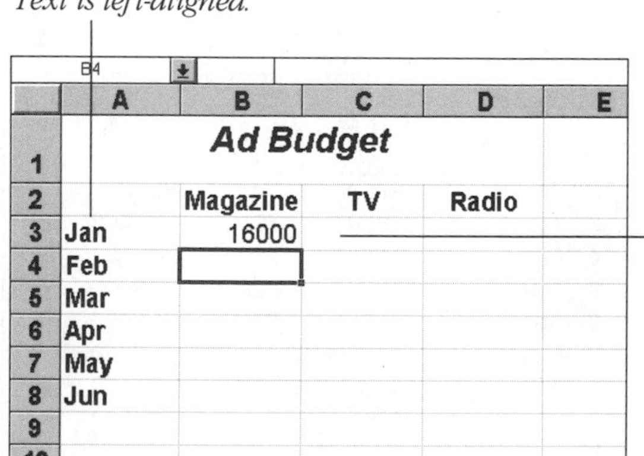

Numbers are right-aligned.

Figure 6. *Move to the next cell.*

Typing Data into a Cell

1. Select the cell. **(Figure 4)** *See Moving Within a Sheet, page 116.*
2. Type text, a number, or a formula. **(Figure 5)**
3. Move to the next cell. The data is entered in the previous cell automatically. **(Figure 6)**

✔ Tips

- You don't have to press Enter after you type the contents of a cell. You can simply press an arrow key to move to the next cell.
- Text is automatically left-aligned in cells. Numbers are right-aligned. **(Figure 6)**
- If you need a series of consecutive dates or numbers for column or row headings (month names, for example), use AutoFill to enter them automatically. *See AutoFilling a Range, page 120.*

Editing Cells

The easiest way to change the text or number in a cell is to click the cell and then type right over the contents. But if you have a formula in the cell, you may want to edit the formula instead, so you don't have to retype the whole entry.

1. Click on the cell and then type over the contents. **(Figure 7)**

   or

1. Double-click the cell to place an insertion point in the contents.
2. Edit the contents as though you were editing text in **Word**. *See Text Editing, page 50.*
3. Press Enter to enter the revision into the cell. **(Figure 8)**

✔ Tips

- When you click a cell, the cell contents appears on the edit line also. **(Figure 9)** You can click on the edit line and edit the cell contents there.
- To abandon any revisions you've made, press Esc to leave the original contents of a cell intact before you press Enter to enter the revisions.

B3 | 10000

	A	B	C	D	E
1		Ad Budget			
2		Magazine	TV	Radio	
3	Jan	10000	78000	11500	
4	Feb	16000	78000	11500	
5	Mar	21500	82500	9000	
6	Apr	21500	82500	9000	
7	May	14000	64000	6500	
8	Jun	14000	64000	6500	
9					
10					

Figure 7. *Select a cell and then type to replace the cell's contents.*

G13

	A	B	C	D	E
1		Ad Budget			
2		Magazine	TV	Radio	
3	Jan	18000	78000	11500	
4	Feb	16000	78000	11500	
5	Mar	21500	82500	9000	
6	Apr	21500	82500	9000	
7	May	14000	64000	6500	
8	Jun	14000	64000	6500	
9					
10					

Figure 8. *The revised entry.*

The contents of the cell you select appears here.

B2 | Magazine

	A	B	C	D	E
1		Ad Budget			
2		Magazine	TV	Radio	
3	Jan	18000	78000	11500	
4	Feb	16000	78000	11500	
5	Mar	21500	82500	9000	
6	Apr	21500	82500	9000	
7	May	14000	64000	6500	
8	Jun	14000	64000	6500	
9					
10					

Figure 9. *The contents of the currently selected cell appears on the edit line.*

	A	B	C	D	E
1		Ad Budget			
2		Magazine	TV	Radio	
3	Jan				
4	Feb				
5	Mar				
6	Apr				
7	May				
8	Jun				
9					
10					

Figure 10. *Place the mouse pointer at the first cell for the range.*

	A	B	C	D	E
1		Ad Budget			
2		Magazine	TV	Radio	
3	Jan				
4	Feb				
5	Mar				
6	Apr				
7	May				
8	Jun				
9					
10					

Figure 11. *Drag to the last cell.*

Filling an Entry Range

To quickly enter data into a rectangular range of cells, create an entry range.

1. Place the mouse pointer on the upper left corner cell of the range. **(Figure 10)**
2. Click and drag to the lower right corner cell of the range. **(Figure 11)** The active cell is the cell at the upper left corner of the entry range.
3. Type data into each cell and then press Enter. The cell pointer moves down each column from cell to cell automatically. When it reaches the bottom of a column, it jumps to the top of the next column within the entry range. **(Figures 12–13)**

	A	B	C	D	E
1		Ad Budget			
2		Magazine	TV	Radio	
3	Jan	18000			
4	Feb	16000			
5	Mar	21500			
6	Apr	21500			
7	May	14000			
8	Jun	14000			
9					
10					

Figure 12. *Press Enter at the bottom of a column to continue at the top of the next column.*

	A	B	C	D	E
1		Ad Budget			
2		Magazine	TV	Radio	
3	Jan				
4					
5					
6					
7					
8					
9					
10					

Figure 13. *Press Enter after typing a value into a cell to move to the cell below.*

AutoFilling a Range

When a range of cells needs to be filled with consecutive numbers, numbers that follow a specific pattern, dates, or dates that follow a specific pattern, such as every Monday, use AutoFill as a quick and convenient method to automatically enter the sequence.

1. Into the first cell of the sequence, type the first number or date. **(Figure 14)**
2. Into an adjacent cell, type the next number or date. **(Figure 15)**
3. Select the two cells. **(Figure 16)**
4. Carefully place the mouse pointer on the Fill handle at the lower right corner of the border surrounding the two cells.
5. Drag the Fill handle to extend the sequence. **(Figure 17)**
6. Release the mouse button when the sequence is complete. **(Figure 18)**

✔ **Tip**

■ As you drag to extend the sequence, the current value appears at the left end of the edit line.

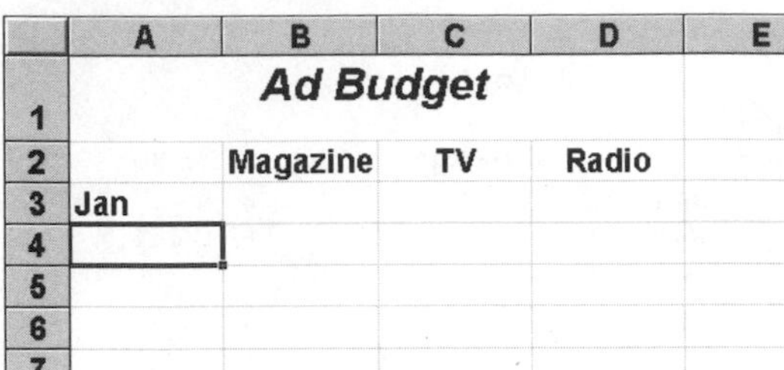

	A	B	C	D	E
1		Ad Budget			
2		Magazine	TV	Radio	
3	Jan				
4					
5					
6					
7					

Figure 14. *Enter the first number or date.*

	A	B	C	D	E
1		Ad Budget			
2		Magazine	TV	Radio	
3	Jan				
4	Feb				
5					
6					
7					

Figure 15. *Type the next number or date in an adjacent cell.*

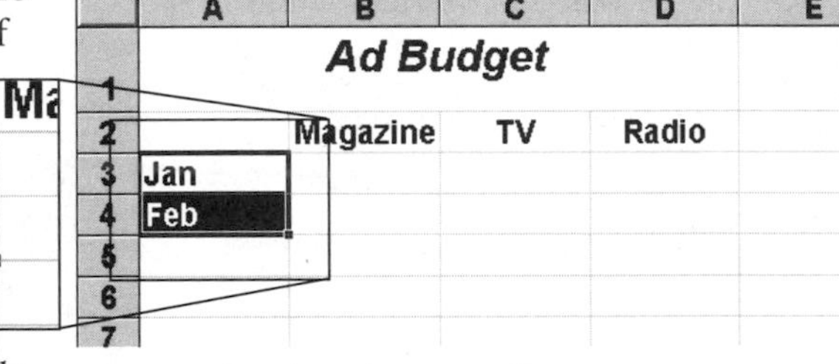

	A	B	C	D	E
1		Ad Budget			
2		Magazine	TV	Radio	
3	Jan				
4	Feb				
5					
6					
7					

The Fill handle.

Figure 16. *Select the two cells.*

	A	B	C	D	E
1		Ad Budget			
2		Magazine	TV	Radio	
3	Jan				
4	Feb				
5					
6					
7					
8					
9					
10					

Figure 17. *Drag the Fill handle to extend the pattern established in the first two cells.*

	A	B	C	D	E
1		Ad Budget			
2		Magazine	TV	Radio	
3	Jan				
4	Feb				
5	Mar				
6	Apr				
7	May				
8	Jun				
9					
10					

Figure 18. *Release the mouse button to complete the sequence.*

Entering the Calculations

Entering Simple Calculations

A calculation can be simple (a sum of a column of numbers) or complex (a financial, statistical, or scientific computation) but it is always entered as a *formula* that begins with an equal sign (=).

To sum two numbers in a cell, you could type =23+46, for example. To sum the contents of two cells, you would include their cell addresses in the formula, such as =B3+C3. The cell into which you type the formula displays the result of the calculation. **(Figure 1)**

If any numbers change in the cells that supply values to the formula, the result of the calculation changes immediately. This immediate recalculation lets you perform what-if analyses; You can see the change in the bottom line immediately when you change any of the contributing numbers.

	A	B	C	D
1	Simple calculation	Sum a column	Mortgage Payment	
2				
3		23	Interest/month	0.71%
4		43	# of payments	360
5		54	Mortgage amt.	167,000
6	101	120	Monthly payment	($1,284.09)
7				

=26+75　　=SUM(B3:B5)　　=PMT(D3,D4,D5)

Figure 1. *Some typical calculations.*

Building a Simple Formula

1. Click the destination cell for the formula. **(Figure 2)**
2. Type an equal sign (press the equal sign key.) **(Figure 3)**
3. Click in the first cell whose address you want in the formula. **(Figure 4)**
4. Type an operator. *See Table 13-1. Table of Operators, this page.* **(Figure 5)**
5. Click the next cell whose address should appear in the formula. **(Figure 6)**
6. Type another operator to continue the formula if you want.

   or
7. Press Enter to enter the formula into the cell and display the result of the calculation.

✔ Tips

- If adjacent cells require a similar formula, you can copy the formula from cell to cell. *See Copying Formulas to Adjacent Cells, page 125.*
- You can enter a combination of typed numbers and cell addresses in formulas, such as =C2*2.5 (the contents of cell C2 multiplied by 2.5).

Table 13-1. *Common Operators*

+	Plus
–	Minus
*	Multiply (asterisk)
/	Divide

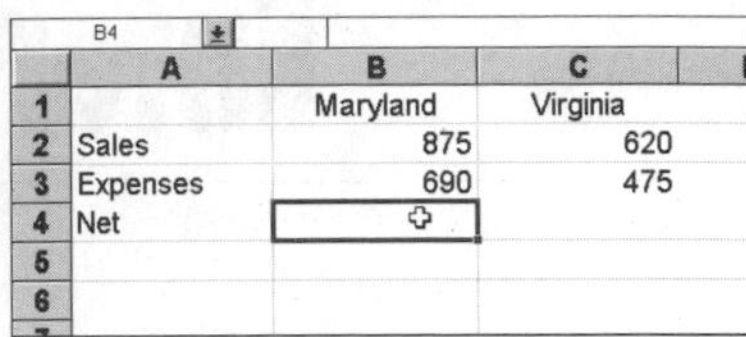

Figure 2. *Click at the destination for the formula.*

Figure 3. *The formula builds both in the cell and on the edit line.*

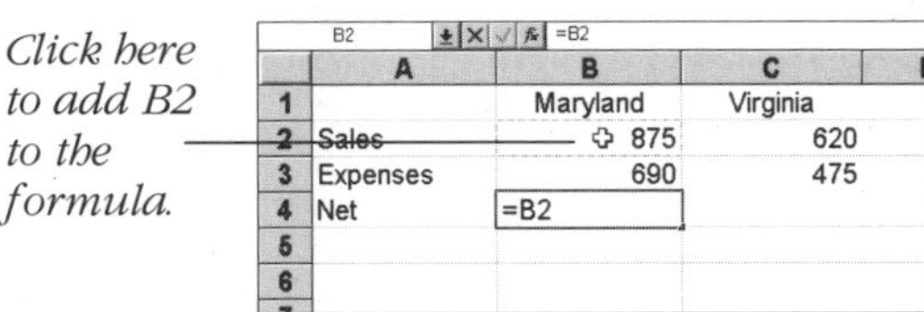

Figure 4. *Click on a cell.*

Figure 5. *Type an operator.*

Figure 6. *The address of each cell you click adds to the formula.*

B7				
	A	B	C	D
1		Jimmy	Pete	
2	Mon	17.50	12.00	
3	Tue	14.25	13.50	
4	Wed	16.50	12.75	
5	Thu	16.00	14.00	
6	Fri	18.00	14.50	
7				
8				
9				
10				
11				

Figure 7. *Click at the destination for the sum.*

The AutoSum button.

Figure 8. *The AutoSum button. Excel creates the formula for you.*

Summing Columns or Rows

Excel includes special help for summing a column or row.

1. Click in the empty cell below the last entry in the column or to the right of the last entry in the row. **(Figure 7)**
2. Click the AutoSum button. **(Figure 8)**
3. Press Enter to enter the formula that has automatically appeared in the cell. **(Figure 9)**

✔ Tips

- Excel looks for a range of numbers it can sum that is above the cell you've selected for the total. If it does not find a range of numbers or if it finds text, it looks to the left for a range of numbers.
- To quickly enter sums below a number of adjacent columns, select the empty cells at the bottoms of all the columns before clicking the AutoSum button. Excel will insert a sum in each selected cell. **(Figure 10)**

Summing Columns/Rows

Excel

B2	=SUM(B2:B6)			
	A	B	C	D
1		Jimmy	Pete	
2	Mon	17.50	12.00	
3	Tue	14.25	13.50	
4	Wed	16.50	12.75	
5	Thu	16.00	14.00	
6	Fri	18.00	14.50	
7		=SUM(B2:B6)		
8				
9				
10				
11				

Figure 9. *Excel has created the formula for you.*

B7				
	A	B	C	D
1		Jimmy	Pete	Tommy
2	Mon	17.50	12.00	9.0
3	Tue	14.25	13.50	9.8
4	Wed	16.50	12.75	11.0
5	Thu	16.00	14.00	12.8
6	Fri	18.00	14.50	15.0
7				
8				

Figure 10. *You can select the cells below any number of adjacent columns before clicking the AutoSum button.*

Totaling a Column with the Sum Function

1. Click in the destination cell for the formula. **(Figure 11)**
2. Enter an equal sign to start the formula. **(Figure 12)**
3. Type the word SUM. **(Figure 13)**
4. Enter a left parenthesis (Shift-9). **(Figure 14)**
5. Drag across the range of numbers to sum. **(Figure 15)**
6. Press Enter. **(Figure 16)**

✔ Tips

- You don't need to close the parentheses before pressing Enter. Excel will do it for you.
- The word SUM is an example of an Excel *function*. Excel contains hundreds of functions for common and uncommon math, statistical, financial, date, time, and other calculations. *See Using Functions, page 128.*

B7

	A	B	C	D
1		Jimmy	Pete	
2	Mon	17.50	12.00	
3	Tue	14.25	13.50	
4	Wed	16.50	12.75	
5	Thu	16.00	14.00	
6	Fri	18.00	14.50	
7				
8				

Figure 11. *Click at the destination for the formula.*

B7 =

	A	B	C	D
1		Jimmy	Pete	
2	Mon	17.50	12.00	
3	Tue	14.25	13.50	
4	Wed	16.50	12.75	
5	Thu	16.00	14.00	
6	Fri	18.00	14.50	
7		=		
8				

Figure 12. *Start a formula with an equals sign.*

=sum

Figure 13. *Type "sum."*

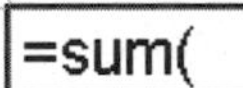

Figure 14. *Type a left parenthesis.*

5R x 1C =sum(B2:B6

	A	B	C	D
1		Jimmy	Pete	
2	Mon	17.50	12.00	
3	Tue	14.25	13.50	
4	Wed	16.50	12.75	
5	Thu	16.00	14.00	
6	Fri	18.00	14.50	
7		=sum(B2:B6		
8				

Figure 15. *Drag across the range of numbers to sum. In this case, from B2 to B6.*

B7 =SUM(B2:B6)

	A	B	C	D
1		Jimmy	Pete	
2	Mon	17.50	12.00	
3	Tue	14.25	13.50	
4	Wed	16.50	12.75	
5	Thu	16.00	14.00	
6	Fri	18.00	14.50	
7		82.25		
8				

Figure 16. *The sum.*

B7 | =SUM(B2:B6)

	A	B	C	D
1		Jimmy	Pete	Tommy
2	Mon	17.50	12.00	9.0
3	Tue	14.25	13.50	9.8
4	Wed	16.50	12.75	11.0
5	Thu	16.00	14.00	12.8
6	Fri	18.00	14.50	15.0
7		82.25		
8				

The Fill handle.

Figure 17. *Click on the cell with the formula.*

Copying Formulas to Adjacent Cells

Rather than retype the formula in adjacent cells, copy it across. Excel will adjust the formula in the direction of the copy.

1. Click on the cell containing the formula. **(Figure 17)**
2. Drag the Fill handle at the lower right corner of the cell across the adjacent cells to which you want to copy the formula. **(Figure 18)**

✔ **Tip**

■ When the mouse pointer is positioned properly on the Fill handle, the pointer becomes a small plus sign. Otherwise, the mouse pointer is a large, heavy plus sign.

=SUM(B2:B6)

	A	B	C	D
1		Jimmy	Pete	Tommy
2	Mon	17.50	12.00	9.0
3	Tue	14.25	13.50	9.8
4	Wed	16.50	12.75	11.0
5	Thu	16.00	14.00	12.8
6	Fri	18.00	14.50	15.0
7		82.25		
8				

Figure 18. *Drag the Fill handle across adjacent cells.*

Excel adjusts the formula as it copies the formula across to column D so the formula in column D refers to other cells in Column D.

D7 | =SUM(D2:D6)

	A	B	C	D
1		Jimmy	Pete	Tommy
2	Mon	17.50	12.00	9.0
3	Tue	14.25	13.50	9.8
4	Wed	16.50	12.75	11.0
5	Thu	16.00	14.00	12.8
6	Fri	18.00	14.50	15.0
7		82.25	66.75	57.50
8				

Figure 19. *The formula copied to adjacent cells.*

Another Example of a Function: Averaging Numbers

1. Click in the destination cell for the formula that will calculate the average. **(Figure 20)**
2. Enter an equal sign.
3. Type the word AVERAGE. **(Figure 21)**
4. Enter a left parenthesis. (Shift-9)
5. Drag across the cells to average. **(Figure 22)**
6. Press Enter. **(Figure 23)**

E2

	A	B	C	D	E
1		Jimmy	Pete	Tommy	Average
2	Mon	17.50	12.00	9.00	
3	Tue	14.25	13.50	9.75	
4	Wed	16.50	12.75	11.00	
5	Thu	16.00	14.00	12.75	
6	Fri	18.00	14.50	15.00	
7		82.25	66.75	57.50	
8					

Figure 20. *Click at the destination for the formula.*

E2 =average(

	A	B	C	D	E
1		Jimmy	Pete	Tommy	Average
2	Mon	17.50	12.00	9.00	=average(
3	Tue	14.25	13.50	9.75	
4	Wed	16.50	12.75	11.00	
5	Thu	16.00	14.00	12.75	
6	Fri	18.00	14.50	15.00	
7		82.25	66.75	57.50	
8					

Figure 21. *Type the formula.*

1R x 3C =average(B2:D2

	A	B	C	D	E
1		Jimmy	Pete	Tommy	Average
2	Mon	17.50	12.00	9.00	=average(B2:D2
3	Tue	14.25	13.50	9.75	
4	Wed	16.50	12.75	11.00	
5	Thu	16.00	14.00	12.75	
6	Fri	18.00	14.50	15.00	
7		82.25	66.75	57.50	
8					

Figure 22. *Drag across the cells to average.*

E3

	A	B	C	D	E
1		Jimmy	Pete	Tommy	Average
2	Mon	17.50	12.00	9.00	12.83
3	Tue	14.25	13.50	9.75	
4	Wed	16.50	12.75	11.00	
5	Thu	16.00	14.00	12.75	
6	Fri	18.00	14.50	15.00	
7		82.25	66.75	57.50	
8					

Figure 23. *The cell displays the result of the formula.*

D9

	A	B	C	D	E
1		Jimmy	Pete	Tommy	Averag
2	Mon	17.50	12.00	9.00	12
3	Tue	14.25	13.50	9.75	12
4	Wed	16.50	12.75	11.00	13
5	Thu	16.00	14.00	12.75	14
6	Fri	18.00	14.50	15.00	15
7		82.25	66.75	57.50	
8					
9	Total of Jimmy and Tommy				
10					

Figure 24. *Click at the destination for the formula.*

D9 =sum(

	A	B	C	D	E
1		Jimmy	Pete	Tommy	Averag
2	Mon	17.50	12.00	9.00	12
3	Tue	14.25	13.50	9.75	12
4	Wed	16.50	12.75	11.00	13
5	Thu	16.00	14.00	12.75	14
6	Fri	18.00	14.50	15.00	15
7		82.25	66.75	57.50	
8					
9	Total of Jimmy and Tommy			=sum(	
10					

Figure 25. *Enter the function.*

Calculating Numbers in Non-Adjacent Cells

1. Click on the destination cell for the formula. **(Figure 24)**
2. Start the formula as usual with an equal sign.
3. Enter a function followed by the left parenthesis. **(Figure 25)**
4. Click on the first cell to include. **(Figure 26)**
5. Type a comma.
6. Click on the next cell to include. **(Figure 27)**
7. Repeat Steps 5-6 until you have included as many cells as necessary.
8. Press Enter to enter the formula.

✔ Tip

- A formula can contain a combination of discrete cells and ranges, such as =SUM(B2,B4,B9:B11). This formula will add the contents of B2, B4, and B9 through B11.

Non-adjacent Cells

Microsoft Excel

B7 =sum(B7

	A	B	C	D	E
1		Jimmy	Pete	Tommy	Averag
2	Mon	17.50	12.00	9.00	12
3	Tue	14.25	13.50	9.75	12
4	Wed	16.50	12.75	11.00	13
5	Thu	16.00	14.00	12.75	14
6	Fri	18.00	14.50	15.00	15
7		82.25	66.75	57.50	
8					
9	Total of Jimmy and Tommy			=sum(B7	
10					

Figure 26. *Click on a cell to include.*

D7 =sum(B7,D7

	A	B	C	D	E
1		Jimmy	Pete	Tommy	Averag
2	Mon	17.50	12.00	9.00	12
3	Tue	14.25	13.50	9.75	12
4	Wed	16.50	12.75	11.00	13
5	Thu	16.00	14.00	12.75	14
6	Fri	18.00	14.50	15.00	15
7		82.25	66.75	57.50	
8					
9	Total of Jimmy and Tommy			=sum(B7,D7	
10					

Figure 27. *Type a comma and then click on the next cell to include.*

Using Functions

SUM and AVERAGE are only two of the dozens of functions that are included in Excel. To find others, click the Function Wizard button on the edit line **(Figure 1)** as you are building the formula. The Function Wizard will take you through the steps of building a formula. **(Figures 29-34)**

Function Wizard button.

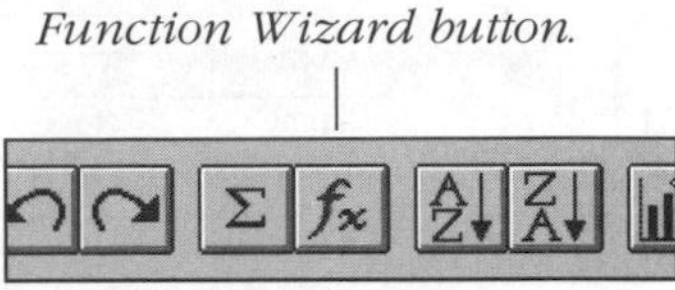

Figure 28. *The Function Wizard button.*

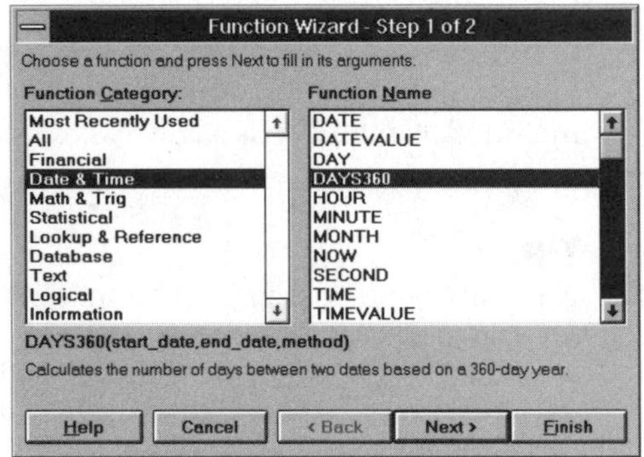

Figure 29. *Selecting the function that calculates the number of days between two dates.*

Function Wizard button.

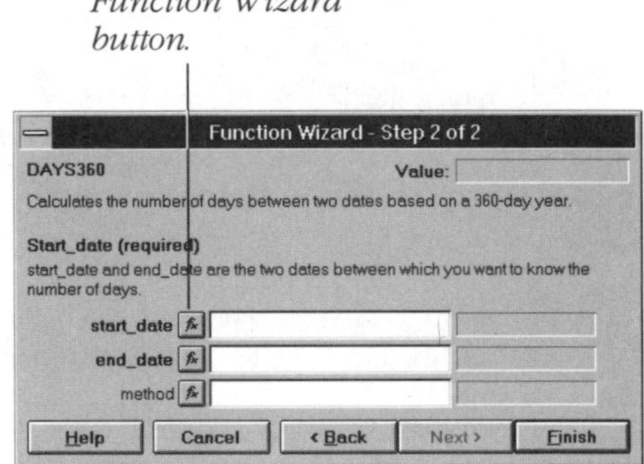

Figure 30. *Step 2 asks you to enter the numbers of the start and end dates. To use the DATE function to calculate the date numbers, you can click the Function Wizard button next to the entry.*

"Nested" indicates that you are running the Function Wizard from within a function you are building.

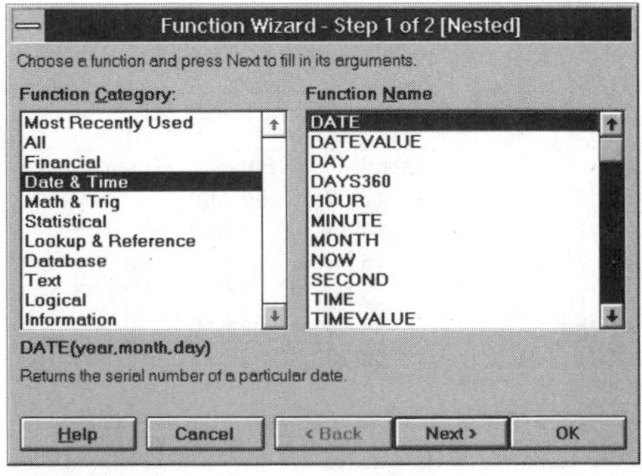

Figure 31. *Select the DATE function on Step 1 of the Function Wizard.*

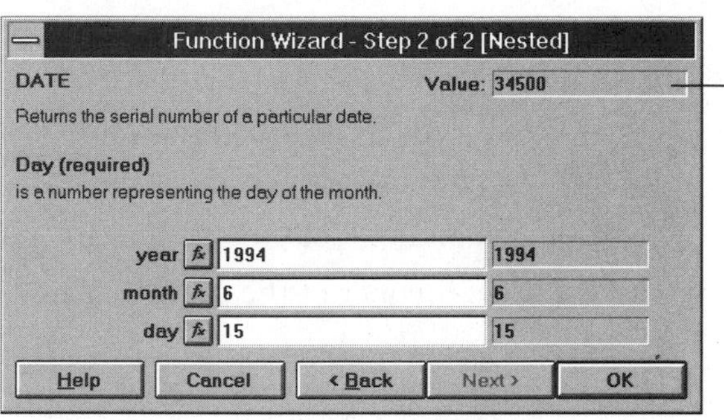

The date number.

Figure 32. *Enter the year, month, and day to obtain the date number and click OK.*

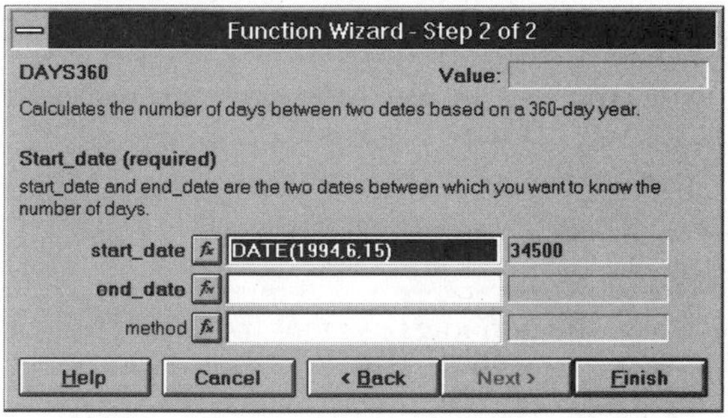

Function Wizard - Step 2 of 2
DAYS360
Value:
Calculates the number of days between two dates based on a 360-day year.
Start_date (required)
start_date and end_date are the two dates between which you want to know the number of days.
start_date DATE(1994,6,15) 34500
end_date
method
Help
Cancel
< Back
Next >
Finish

Figure 33. *The DATE function is entered into the start_date text box automatically.*

Figure 34. *Complete the end_date entry and then click Finish to end the Wizard.*

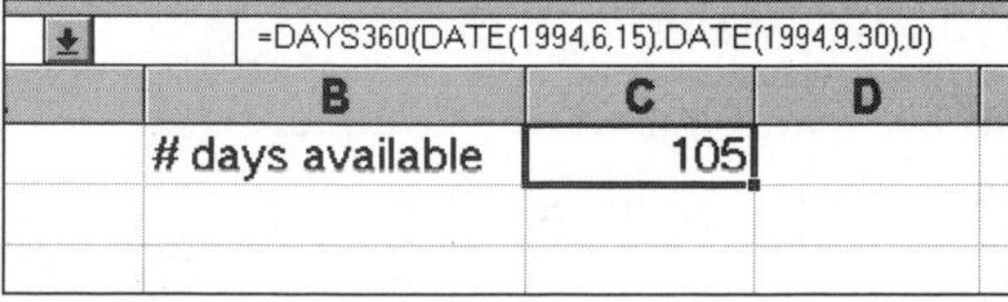

Figure 35. *The completed function.*

Some Useful Functions

DATE(year, month, day)	Provides the serial number of a particular date.
DAYS360(start_date, end_date, method)	Calculates the number of days between two dates based on a 360-day year.
TODAY( )	Provides the serial number of today's date.
NOW( )	Provides the serial number of the current date and time.
DDB(cost, salvage, life, period, factor)	Provides the depreciation of an asset for a spcified period using the double-declining balance method or some other method you specify.
FV(rate, nper, pmt, pv, type)	Calculates the future value of an investment.
IRR(values, guess)	Provides the internal rate of return for a series of cash flows.
NPV(rate, value1, value2, ...)	Calculates the net present value of an investment based on a series of periodic cash flows and a discount rate
PMT(rate, nper, pv, fv, type)	Calculates the periodic payment for an annuity or loan.
PV(rate, nper, pmt, fv, type)	Calculates the present value of an investment
ROUND(number, num_digits)	Rounds a number to a specified number of digits.
SUM(number1, number2, ...)	Calculates the sum of all the numbers in the list of arguments.*
AVERAGE(number1, number2, ...)	Calculates the average (arithmetic mean) of the arguments.*
MAX(number1, number2, ...)	Calculates the maximum value in a list of arguments.*
MEDIAN(number1, number2, ...)	Calculates the median of the given numbers.*
MIN(number1, number2, ...)	Calculates the smallest number in the list of arguments.*
STDEV(number1,number2,...)	Estimates standard deviation based on a sample. The standard deviation is a measure of how widely values are dispersed from the average value (the mean).*
VAR(number1, number2, ...)	Estimates variance based on a sample.*
VALUE(text)	Converts text to a number.

*(number1, number 2, ...) can also be specified as a range (C25:C47).

Changing the Sheet's Structure

	A	B	C	
1		Q1 94	Q2 94	Q
2	Income			
3	Beans	12400	13200	
4	T-Shirts	2600	2800	
5	Baked Goods	8800	9000	
6	Coffeemakers	1900	2100	
7	Gelato	5600	6700	

Figure 1. *The mouse pointer changes to a double arrow.*

	A	B	C	
1		Q1 94	Q2 94	Q
2	Income			
3	Beans	12400	13200	
4	T-Shirts	2600	2800	
5	Baked Goods	8800	9000	
6	Coffeemakers	1900	2100	
7	Gelato	5600	6700	

Figure 2. *Drag right or left to widen or narrow the column below.*

	A	B	C
1		Q1 94	Q2 94
2	Income		
3	Beans	12400	1320
4	T-Shirts	2600	280
5	Baked Goods	8800	900
6	Coffeemakers	1900	210
7	Gelato	5600	670

Figure 3. *The newly widened column.*

	A	B
1		Q1 94
2	Income	
3	Beans	12
4	T-Shirts	2
5	Baked Goods	8

Figure 4. *The mouse pointer changes to a double arrow.*

Widening Columns and Rows

To change the width of a column:

1. Place the mouse pointer on the right edge of the gray column heading button for the column to widen. **(Figure 1)**
2. When the mouse pointer changes to a double arrow, drag right or left. **(Figures 2–3)**

To change the height of a row:

1. Place the mouse pointer on the bottom edge of the gray row heading button for the row to heighten. **(Figure 4)**
2. When the mouse pointer changes to a double arrow, drag up or down.

✔ Tips

- To change the width of multiple columns or rows, select the columns or rows by dragging across their column heading or row heading buttons. Then drag the edge of any column heading or row heading button that is selected. All the selected columns or rows will change uniformly.
- You can also select Column or Row on the Format menu and then choose Width or Height on the submenu to get to the Column Width or Row Height dialog boxes. On these dialog boxes, you can choose an exact setting.

Inserting and Deleting Rows and Columns

1. Click in any cell of the row or column where you'd like the new blank row or column. The remaining rows or columns will be pushed down or to the right. **(Figure 5)**
2. From the Insert menu choose Rows or Columns. **(Figures 6-7)**

✔ Tips

- To insert multiple columns, drag across the column heading buttons (labeled A, B, C, and so on) to highlight the locations of the new columns instead of Step 1 above. To insert multiple rows, drag across row heading buttons, instead. **(Figure 8)**
- You can also click a column or row heading button to select the destination for a new column or row or the column or row to be deleted. Next, click the right mouse button and choose Insert or Delete from the shortcut menu.

	A	B	C	D	
1		Q1 94	Q2 94	Q3 94	Q4
2	Income				
3	Beans	12400	13200	15000	
4	T-Shirts	2600	2800	3100	
5	Baked Goods	8800	9000	10100	
6	Coffeemakers	1900	2100	2400	
7	Gelato	5600	6700	11200	
8					
9	Expenses				
10	Personnel	6200	6500	6900	
11	Overhead	4100	4100	4300	
12	Taxes	1900	1900	1900	
13	Services	950	990	1100	
14					

Figure 5. *Click in a cell in the column where you'd like a new column inserted.*

Insert
- Cells
- Rows
- Columns
- Worksheet
- Chart ▸
- Macro ▸
- Page Break
- Function...
- Name ▸
- Note...
- Picture...
- Object...

Figure 6. *The Insert menu.*

	A	B	C	D	
1		Q1 94	Q2 94	Q3 94	Q4
2	Income				
3	Beans	12400	13200	15000	
4	T-Shirts	2600	2800	3100	
5	Baked Goods	8800	9000	10100	
6	Coffeemakers	1900	2100	2400	
7	Gelato	5600	6700	11200	
8					
9					
10	Expenses				
11	Personnel	6200	6500	6900	
12	Overhead	4100	4100	4300	
13	Taxes	1900	1900	1900	
14	Services	950	990	1100	

Figure 7. *New blank row.*

	A	B	C	D
1		Q1 94	Q2 94	Q3 94
✣	Income			
3	Beans	12400	13200	15
4	T-Shirts	2600	2800	3
5	Baked Goods	8800	9000	10
6	Coffeemakers	1900	2100	2
7	Gelato	5600	6700	11
8				

Figure 8. *Drag across two row heading buttons to specify two rows for insertion.*

	A	B	C	D	E
1		Q1 94	Q2 94	Q3 94	Q4 94
2	Income				
3	Beans	12400	13200	15000	16900
4	T-Shirts	2600	2800	3100	4700
5	Baked Goods	8800	9000	10100	11500
6	Coffeemakers	1900	2100	2400	2600
7	Gelato	5600	6700	11200	9400
8	Grinders	2200	2400	2800	
9					

Figure 9. *Click a cell.*

Inserting and Deleting Cells

When you tell Excel to insert or delete a cell within a range of data, Excel needs to know how to move the data that's in adjacent cells. You specify your choice on the Insert or Delete dialog box.

1. Click at the destination for the new, blank cell. **(Figure 9)**

   or

   Click on the cell you want to delete.
2. To insert a cell, choose Cells from the Insert menu **(Figure 10)** or click the right mouse button and choose Insert from the shortcut menu.

   or

   To delete a cell, choose Delete from the Edit menu **(Figure 11)** or click the right mouse button and choose Delete from the shortcut menu.
3. On the Insert dialog box, select either Shift Cells Right or Shift Cells Down. **(Figure 12)**

   or

   On the Delete dialog box, select either Shift Cells Left or Shift Cells Up. **(Figure 13)**

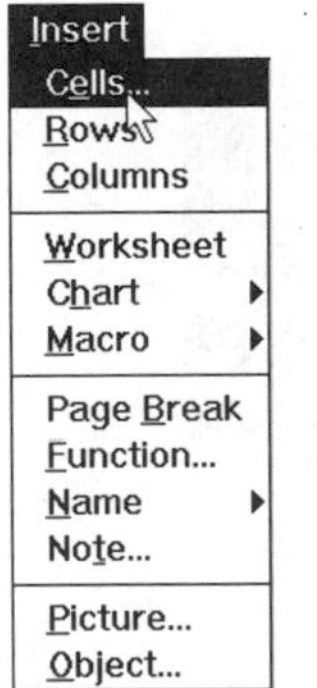

Figure 10. *The Insert menu.*

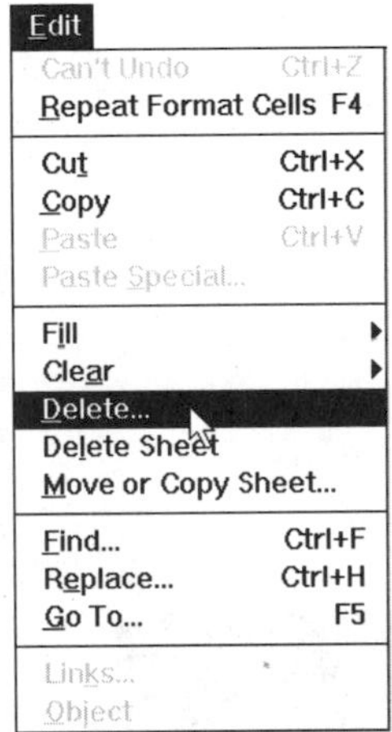

Figure 11. *The Edit menu.*

Figure 12. *The Insert dialog box.*

Figure 13. *The Delete dialog box.*

	A	B	C	D	E
1		Q1 94	Q2 94	Q3 94	Q4 94
2	Income				
3	Beans	12400	13200	15000	16900
4	T-Shirts	2600	2800	3100	4700
5	Baked Goods	8800	9000	10100	11500
6	Coffeemakers	1900	2100	2400	2600
7	Gelato	5600	6700	11200	9400
8	Grinders		2200	2400	2800

Cells shifted to the right.

Figure 14. *Inserted cell.*

Moving and Copying Data

Excel's drag and drop makes moving and copying data especially easy.

1. Select the range of cells to move or copy. **(Figure 15)**
2. Place the mouse pointer on the border of the range so the pointer becomes an arrow. **(Figure 16)**
3. To move the cells, drag the border of the range to move the range to a new location. **(Figure 17)**

   or

   To copy the cells, press and hold Ctrl while you drag the border of the range. A small plus appears next to the mouse pointer to indicate that you are copying rather than moving. **(Figure 18)**
4. Release the mouse button to drop the range at the new location. **(Figure 19)**

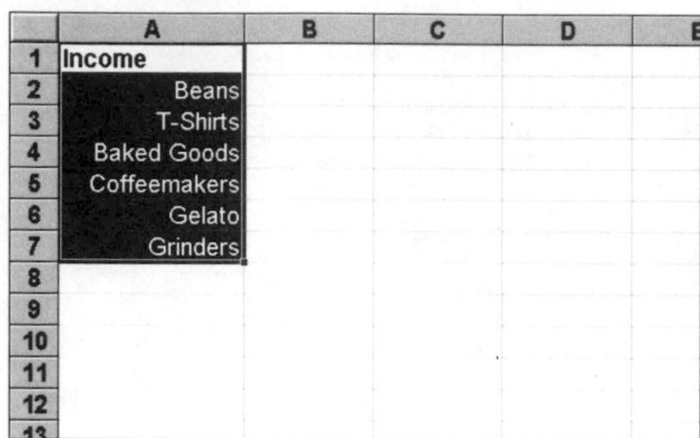

Figure 15. *Select a range of cells.*

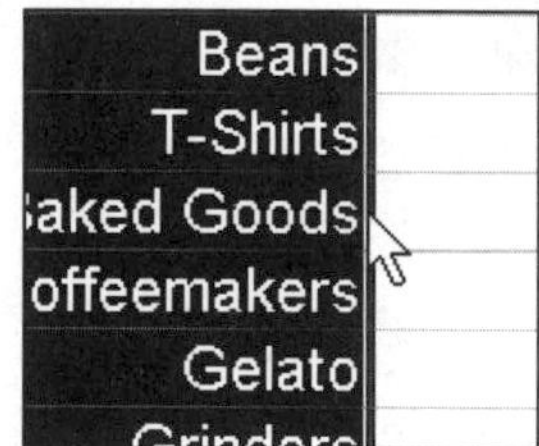

Figure 16. *The mouse pointer on the range border.*

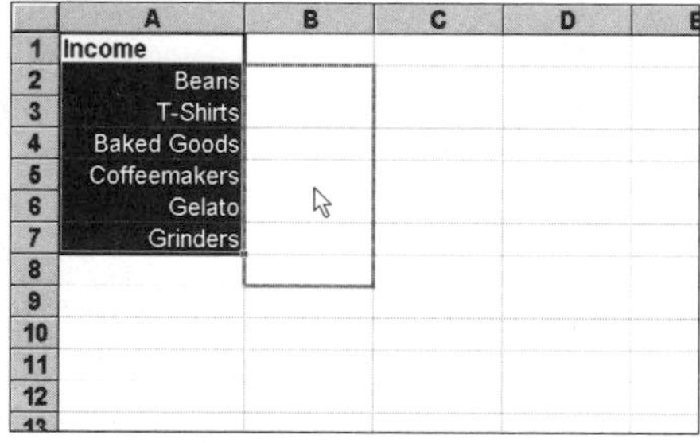

Figure 17. *Drag the border of the range to move the range.*

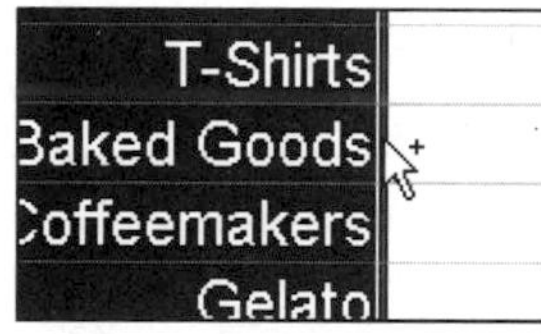

Figure 18. *The small plus sign next to the mouse pointer shows that a copy is in progress.*

	A	B	C
1			
2		Income	
3		Beans	
4		T-Shirts	
5		Baked Goods	
6		Coffeemakers	
7		Gelato	
8		Grinders	
9			

Figure 19. *The range moved to its new location.*

	A	B	C	D	E	F
1		Q1 94	Q2 94	Q3 94	Q4 94	
2	Income					
3	Beans	12400	13200	15000	16900	
4	T-Shirts	2600	2800	3100	4700	
5	Baked Goods	8800	9000	10100	11500	
6	Coffeemakers	1900	2100	2400	2600	
7	Gelato	5600	6700	11200	9400	
8	Grinders	2100	2200	2400	2800	
9						
10	Expenses					
11	Personnel	6200	6500	6900	7200	
12	Supplies	4100	4100	4300	4500	
13	Utilities	820	840	840	880	
14	Packaging	1100	1200	1400	1500	
15	L&P	2000	0	1200	0	
16	Accounting	620	740	750	1000	
17	Taxes	1900	1900	1900	1900	
18	Other Services	950	990	1100	1150	
19						
20	Net	13610	17530	23410	26970	

Sheet1 / Sheet2 / Sheet3 / Sheet4 / Sheet5 / Sheet6 / Sheet7 / Sheet8

Figure 20. *Click at the upper left corner of the data range.*

Figure 21. *The Window menu.*

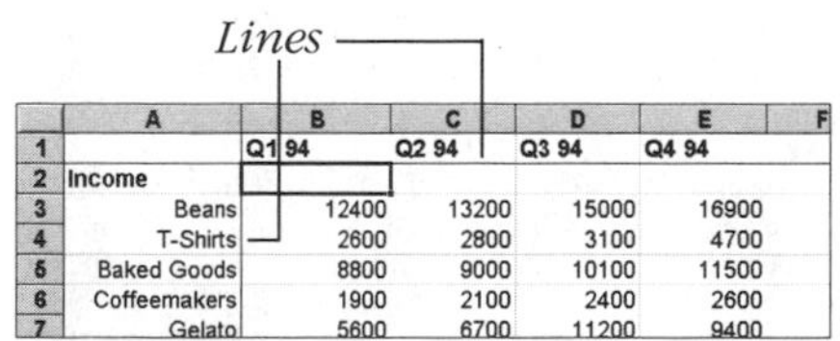

	A	B	C	D	E	F
1		Q1 94	Q2 94	Q3 94	Q4 94	
2	Income					
3	Beans	12400	13200	15000	16900	
4	T-Shirts	2600	2800	3100	4700	
5	Baked Goods	8800	9000	10100	11500	
6	Coffeemakers	1900	2100	2400	2600	
7	Gelato	5600	6700	11200	9400	

Figure 22. *Lines appear to indicate which areas of the sheet are frozen.*

Freezing the Headings

To keep the column and row headings from scrolling off the screen while you scroll through a large worksheet, you can *freeze* the headings.

1. Click on the cell at the upper left corner of the region that contains the data. **(Figure 20)**
2. From the Window menu, choose Freeze Panes. **(Figures 21-22)**

✔ Tips

- Pressing Ctrl+Home now moves the cell pointer to the upper left corner of the data range.
- To unfreeze the panes, choose Unfreeze Panes from the Window menu.

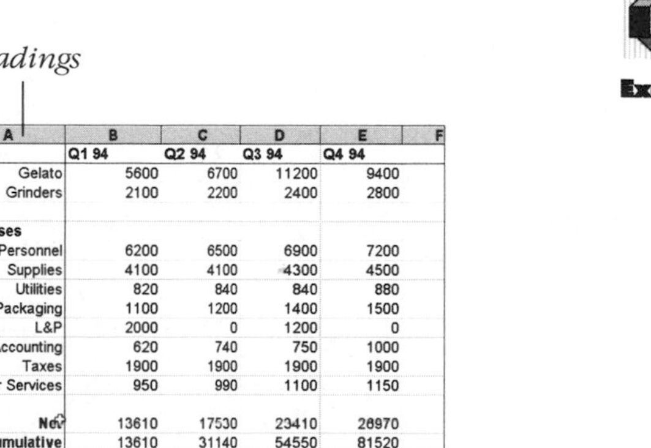

	A	B	C	D	E	F
1		Q1 94	Q2 94	Q3 94	Q4 94	
7	Gelato	5600	6700	11200	9400	
8	Grinders	2100	2200	2400	2800	
9						
10	Expenses					
11	Personnel	6200	6500	6900	7200	
12	Supplies	4100	4100	4300	4500	
13	Utilities	820	840	840	880	
14	Packaging	1100	1200	1400	1500	
15	L&P	2000	0	1200	0	
16	Accounting	620	740	750	1000	
17	Taxes	1900	1900	1900	1900	
18	Other Services	950	990	1100	1150	
19						
20	Net	13610	17530	23410	26970	
21	Cumulative	13610	31140	54550	81520	
22						
23						
24						
25						

Sheet1 / Sheet2 / Sheet3 / Sheet4 / Sheet5 / Sheet6 / Sheet7 / Sheet8

Figure 23. *The headings stay frozen when you scroll through the data.*

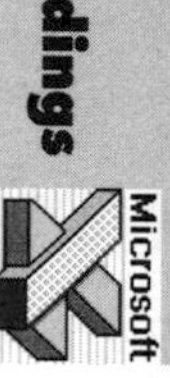

Splitting a Sheet

Splitting a sheet lets you display and scroll through four different regions of the sheet independently.

1. Click in the cell that you want to become the upper left corner of the bottom right pane. **(Figure 24)**
2. From the Window menu, choose Split. **(Figure 25)**

✔ **Tips**

- To remove the split, choose Remove Split from the Window menu.
- You can drag the thick split lines to change the relative sizes of the panes. **(Figure 26)**

	A	B	C	D	E
1		Q1 94	Q2 94	Q3 94	Q4 94
2	Income				
3	Beans	12400	13200	15000	16900
4	T-Shirts	2600	2800	3100	4700
5	Baked Goods	8800	9000	10100	11500
6	Coffeemakers	1900	2100	2400	2600
7	Gelato	5600	6700	11200	9400
8	Grinders	2100	2200	2400	2800
9					
10	Expenses				
11	Personnel	6200	6500	6900	7200
12	Supplies	4100	4100	4300	4500
13	Utilities	820	840	840	880
14	Packaging	1100	1200	1400	1500
15	L&P	2000	0	1200	0
16	Accounting	620	740	750	1000
17	Taxes	1900	1900	1900	1900
18	Other Services	950	990	1100	1150
19					
20	Net	13610	17530	23410	26970

Figure 24. *Click on a cell.*

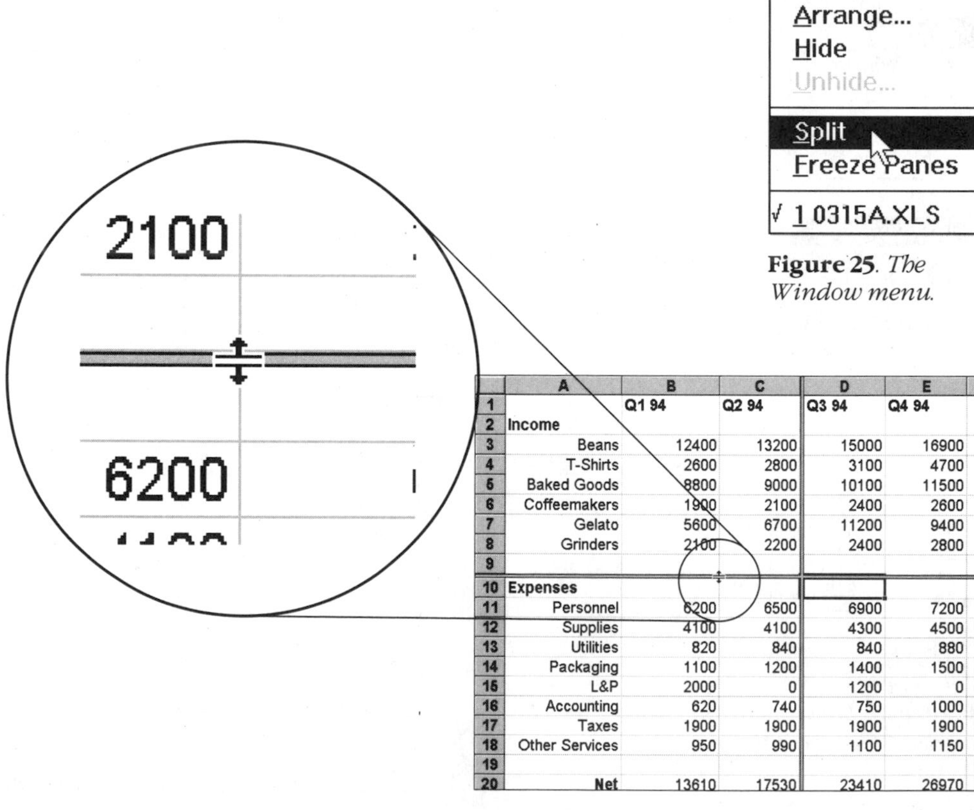

Figure 25. *The Window menu.*

	A	B	C	D	E
1		Q1 94	Q2 94	Q3 94	Q4 94
2	Income				
3	Beans	12400	13200	15000	16900
4	T-Shirts	2600	2800	3100	4700
5	Baked Goods	8800	9000	10100	11500
6	Coffeemakers	1900	2100	2400	2600
7	Gelato	5600	6700	11200	9400
8	Grinders	2100	2200	2400	2800
9					
10	Expenses				
11	Personnel	6200	6500	6900	7200
12	Supplies	4100	4100	4300	4500
13	Utilities	820	840	840	880
14	Packaging	1100	1200	1400	1500
15	L&P	2000	0	1200	0
16	Accounting	620	740	750	1000
17	Taxes	1900	1900	1900	1900
18	Other Services	950	990	1100	1150
19					
20	Net	13610	17530	23410	26970

Figure 26. *Click and drag here to change the sizes of the panes.*

Formatting the Sheet

	A	B	C	D	E
1	Book Sales				
2					
3		Hardcover	Paperback	Total	
4	Jan	160	535	695	
5	Feb	158	570	728	
6	Mar	173	595	768	
7	Apr	156	547	703	
8	May	190	580	770	
9	Jun	210	595	805	
10	1st Half	1,047	3,422	4,469	
11	Jul	225	620	845	
12	Aug	230	816	1,046	
13	Sep	189	585	774	
14	Oct	202	612	814	
15	Nov	212	690	902	
16	Dec	525	1139	1,664	
17	2nd Half	1,583	4,462	6,045	
18	Total	2,630	7,884	10,514	

Figure 1. *Click on a cell in the range to format.*

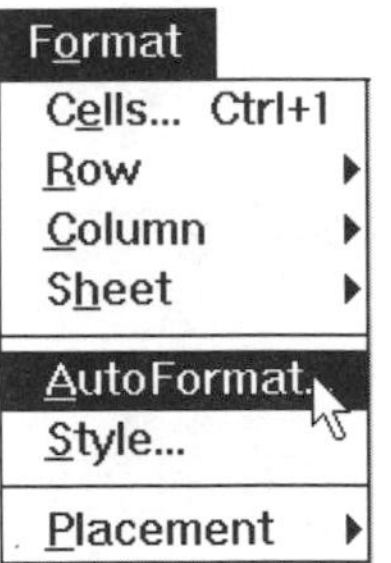

Figure 2. *The Format menu.*

Choosing an AutoFormat

The fastest and easiest way to make a sheet presentable is to give it an AutoFormat. An AutoFormat contains a complete look for a range of data by changing the font, text alignment, number formatting, borders, patterns, colors, column widths, and row heights. Excel provides a selection of AutoFormats, each with a different look.

1. Click any cell in the range to format. **(Figure 1)**
   or
   Select the range to format.
2. From the Format menu, choose AutoFormat. **(Figure 2)**
3. On the AutoFormat dialog box, select an AutoFormat from the list and then click OK. **(Figures 3-4)**

✔ Tips

- To remove an AutoFormat immediately after applying it, use Undo.
- To remove an AutoFormat later, select the range, follow Steps 2 and 3 above, and then choose None from the list of AutoFormats.

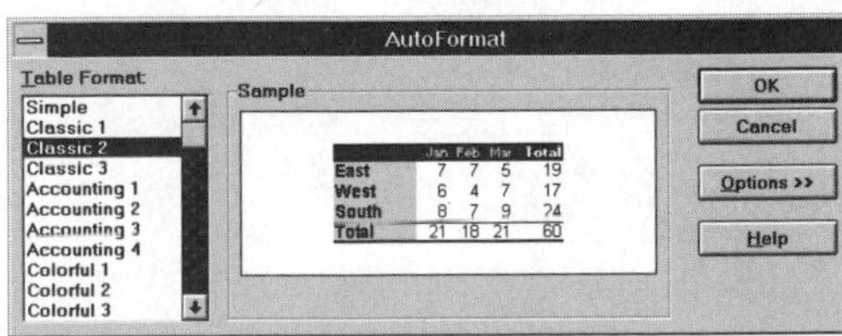

Figure 3. *The AutoFormat dialog box.*

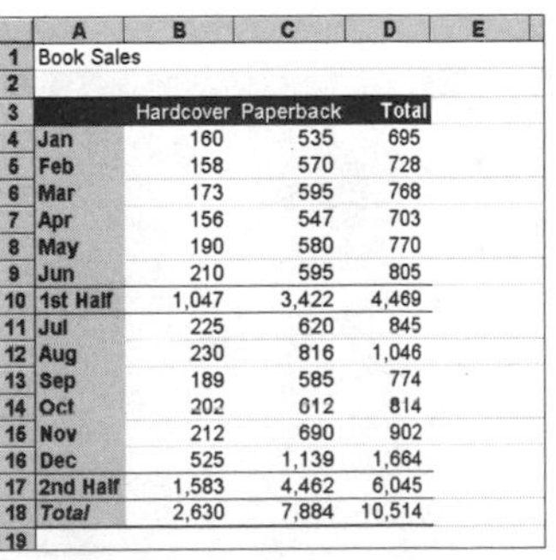

	A	B	C	D	E
1	Book Sales				
2					
3		Hardcover	Paperback	Total	
4	Jan	160	535	695	
5	Feb	158	570	728	
6	Mar	173	595	768	
7	Apr	156	547	703	
8	May	190	580	770	
9	Jun	210	595	805	
10	1st Half	1,047	3,422	4,469	
11	Jul	225	620	845	
12	Aug	230	816	1,046	
13	Sep	189	585	774	
14	Oct	202	612	814	
15	Nov	212	690	902	
16	Dec	525	1,139	1,664	
17	2nd Half	1,583	4,462	6,045	
18	*Total*	2,630	7,884	10,514	
19					

Figure 4. *The AutoFormatted range.*

Text Formatting

1. Select the cell or cells that contain the text to format. **(Figure 5)**
2. Choose formatting options by clicking the text formatting buttons on the Formatting toolbar. **(Figure 6)**

or

1. Select the cell or cells that contain the text to format.
2. From the Format menu, choose Cells or click the right mouse button and choose Format Cells from the shortcut menu.
3. On the Format Cells dialog box, change options on the Alignment and Font tabs. **(Figures 7-8)**

	A	B	C
1	Book Sales		
2			
3		Hardcover	Pape
4	Jan	160	
5	Feb	158	
6	Mar	172	

Figure 5. *Select the cells with the text to format.*

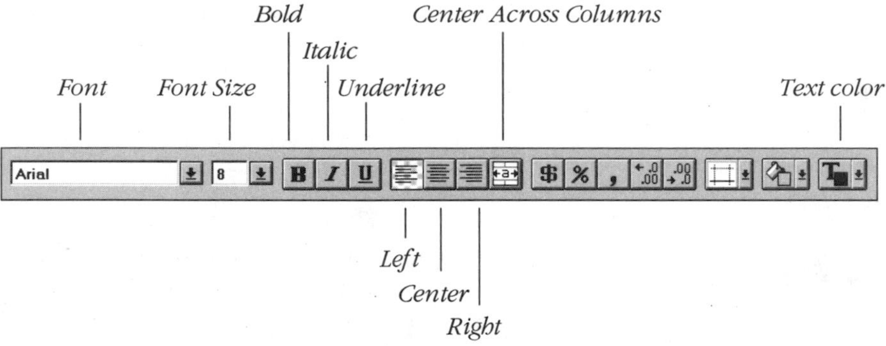

Figure 6. *The text formatting buttons on the Formatting toolbar.*

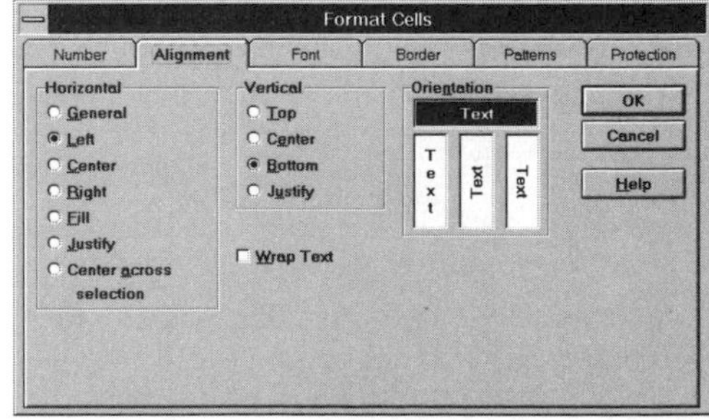

Figures 7. *The Alignment tab.*

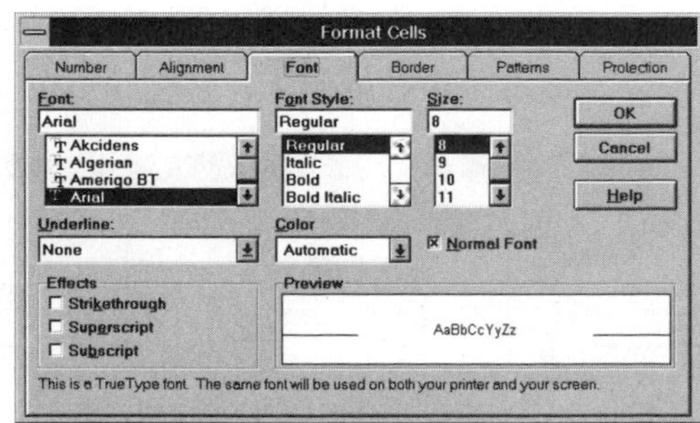

Figure 8. *The Font tab.*

	A	B	C	D
1	*Book Sales*			
2				
3		Hardcover	Paperback	Total
4	Jan	160	535	695
5	Feb	158	570	728
6	Mar	173	595	768
7	Apr	156	547	703
8	May	190	580	770

Figure 9. *Enter the title in the leftmost cell above the range.*

Centering a Title Above a Range

1. Type the title into the leftmost cell above the range. **(Figure 9)**
2. Select the cells above the range. **(Figure 10)**
3. Click the Center Across Columns button. **(Figure 11)**

   or

   From the Format menu, choose Cells. Then choose Center Across Selection on the Alignment tab of the Format Cells dialog box. **(Figure 12)**

✔ Tip

- Click the Center Across Columns button again to return the text to left aligned.

	A	B	C	D
1	*Book Sales*			
2				
3		Hardcover	Paperback	Total
4	Jan	160	535	695
5	Feb	158	570	728
6	Mar	173	595	768
7	Apr	156	547	703
8	May	190	580	770

Figure 10. *Select the cells above the range.*

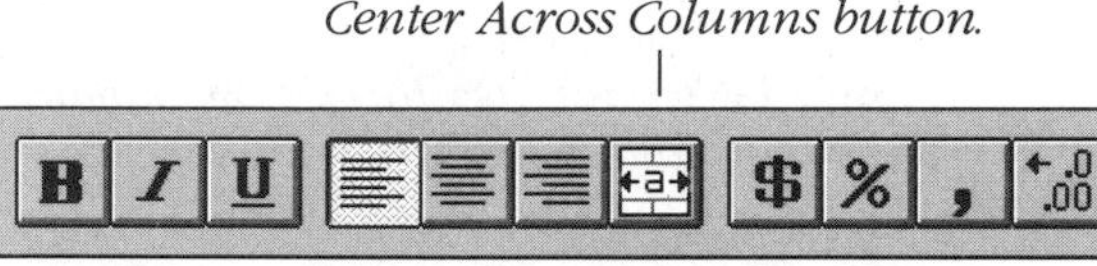

Figure 11. *The Center Across Columns button.*

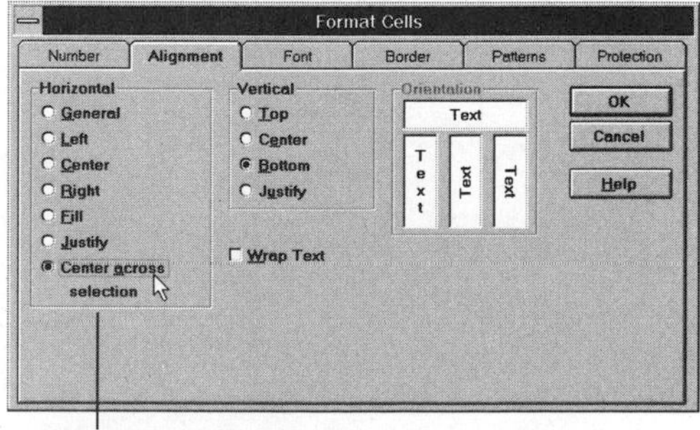

Figure 12. *Click here to center the text across the selected cells.*

	A	B	C	D
1		*Book Sales*		
2				
3		Hardcover	Paperback	Total
4	Jan	160	535	695
5	Feb	158	570	728
6	Mar	173	595	768
7	Apr	156	547	703
8	May	190	580	770

Figure 13. *The centered title.*

Number Formatting

1. Select the numbers to format. **(Figure 14)**
2. Click the appropriate number formatting button on the Formatting toolbar. **(Figure 15)**

   or

   From the Format menu, choose Cells and then, on the Number tab of the Format Cells dialog box, choose a Category and Formatting Code. **(Figure 16)**

✔ Tips

- Until you choose a special number format, numbers are formatted with the General number format (right aligned, up to 11 decimal places).
- If you enter numbers preceded by a dollar sign, Excel automatically applies Currency formatting. If you enter numbers followed by a percent sign, Excel automatically applies Percentage formatting.
- Number formatting can be saved as a style. *See Creating Styles, page 144.*

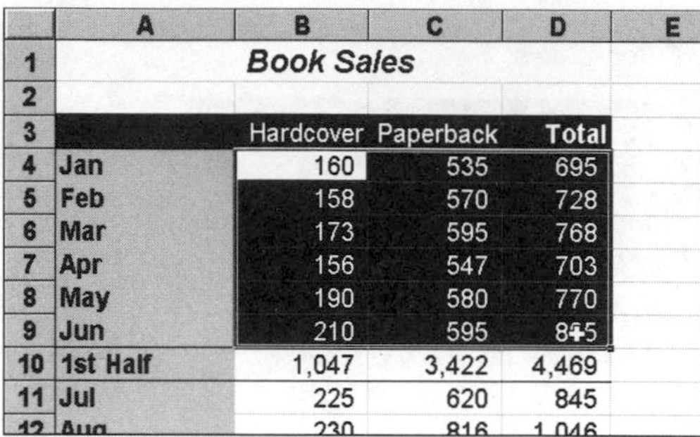

	A	B	C	D	E
1		Book Sales			
2					
3		Hardcover	Paperback	Total	
4	Jan	160	535	695	
5	Feb	158	570	728	
6	Mar	173	595	768	
7	Apr	156	547	703	
8	May	190	580	770	
9	Jun	210	595	805	
10	1st Half	1,047	3,422	4,469	
11	Jul	225	620	845	
12	Aug	230	816	1,046	

Figure 14. *Select the numbers to format.*

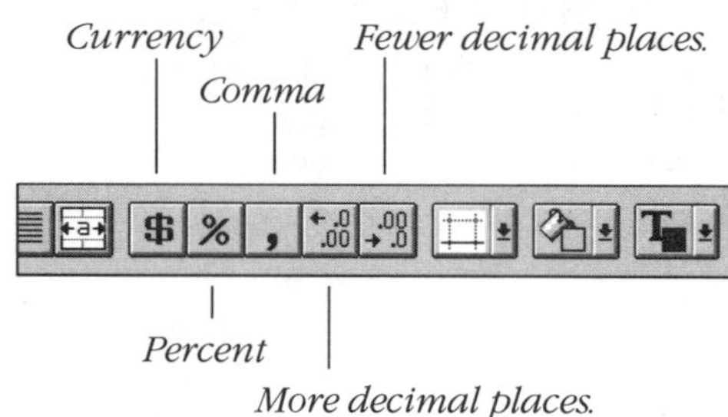

Figure 15. *The number formatting buttons on the Formatting toolbar.*

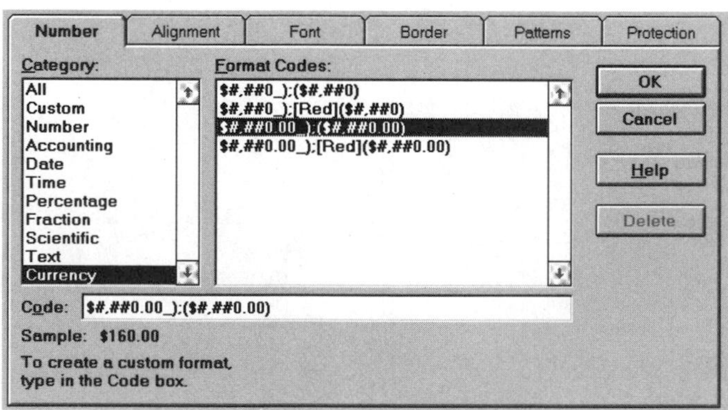

Figure 16. *The Number tab of the Format Cells dialog box.*

	A	B	C	D
1		Book Sales		
2				
3		Hardcover	Paperback	Total
4	Jan	160	535	695
5	Feb	158	570	728
6	Mar	173	595	768
7	Apr	156	547	703
8	May	190	580	770

Figure 17. *Select the range first.*

Borders button.

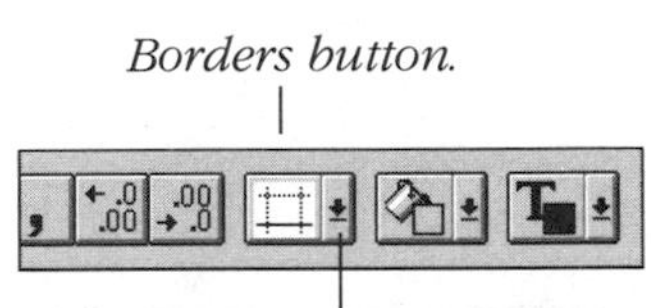

Figure 18. *Click here to see the available borders.*

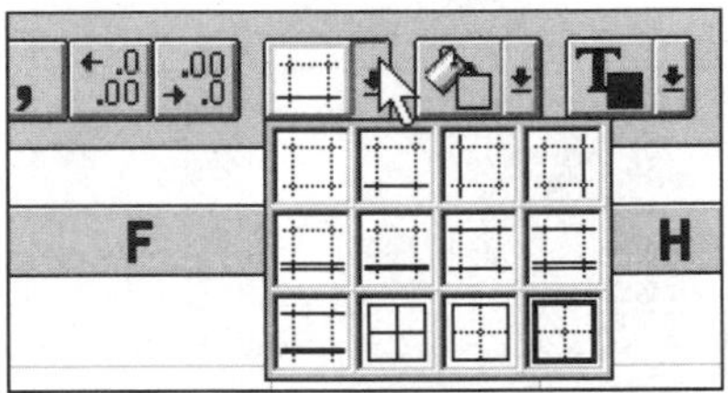

Figure 19. *Click one of these panes to select the border it displays.*

	A	B	C	D
1		Book Sales		
2				
3		Hardcover	Paperback	Total
4	Jan	160	535	695
5	Feb	158	570	728
6	Mar	173	595	768
7	Apr	156	547	703
8	May	190	580	770

Figure 20. *A border added to the range.*

Adding Borders to a Range

A border is a line at the edge of a cell. You can use borders to divide the information on the sheet into logical regions. Borders both appear on the screen and print out when you print the sheet.

1. Select the range to which you'd like to apply a border. **(Figure 17)**
2. Click the pull down button next to the Borders button to see the full range of borders. **(Figure 18)**
3. Click the pane on the display of borders that matches the border you want for the range. **(Figures 19-20)**

or

1. Select the range to which you'd like to apply a border.
2. From the Format menu, choose Cells or click the right mouse button and choose Format Cells from the shortcut menu.
3. On the Border tab of the Format Cells dialog box, choose a border, a border style, and a color. **(Figure 21)**

✔ Tips

- To choose the most recently used border, you can click the Borders button.
- To remove the borders around a range, select the range, pull down the display of borders and choose the pane at the upper left corner.

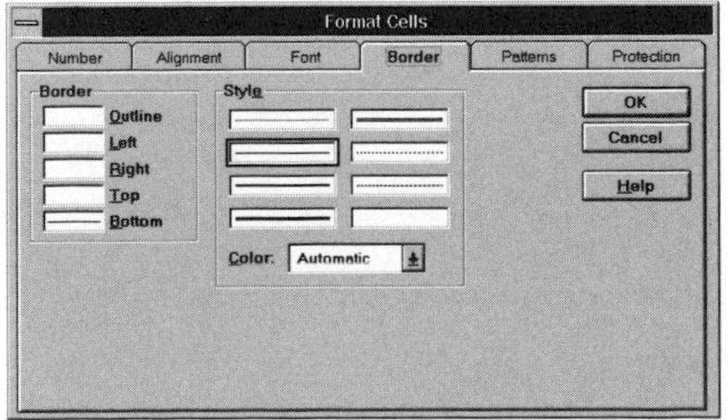

Figure 21. *The Border tab of the Format Cells dialog box.*

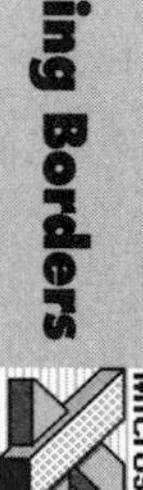

Excel

Adding Shading to a Range

1. Select the range to which you'd like to add shading. **(Figure 22)**
2. From the Format menu, choose Cells, or click the right mouse button and choose Format Cells from the shortcut menu.
3. On the Patterns tab of the Format Cells dialog box, choose a color if you want the shading to be other than gray. Otherwise, pull down the list of patterns and choose one of the shades of gray at the top of the display of patterns. **(Figures 23-24)**

✔ **Tip**

- Shading is often applied automatically to parts of a range when you select an AutoFormat.

	A	B	C	D
1	Book Sales			
2				
3		Hardcover	Paperback	Total
4	Jan	160	535	695
5	Feb	158	570	728
6	Mar	173	595	768
7	Apr	156	547	703
8	May	190	580	770
9	Jun	210	595	805
10	1st Half	1,047	3,422	4,469
11	Jul	225	620	845

Figure 22. *Select the range to shade.*

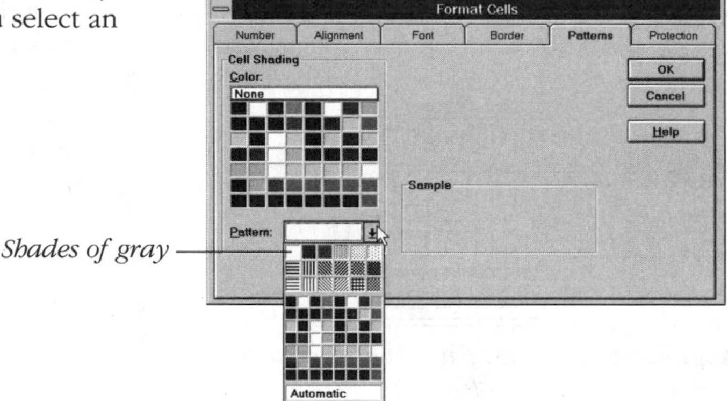

Figure 23. *Choose one of these patterns to shade the selected cells.*

	A	B	C	D
1	Book Sales			
2				
3		Hardcover	Paperback	Total
4	Jan	160	535	695
5	Feb	158	570	728
6	Mar	173	595	768
7	Apr	156	547	703
8	May	190	580	770
9	Jun	210	595	805
10	1st Half	1,047	3,422	4,469
11	Jul	225	620	845

Figure 24. *The shaded cells.*

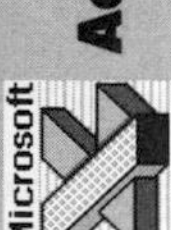

	A	B	C	D
1		Book Sales		
2				
3		Hardcover	Paperback	Total
4	Jan	160	535	695
5	Feb	158	570	728
6	Mar	173	595	768
7	Apr	156	547	703
8	May	190	580	770
9	Jun	210	595	805
10	1st Half	1,047	3,422	4,469
11	Jul	225	620	845
12	Aug	230	816	1,046
13	Sep	189	585	774
14	Oct	202	612	814
15	Nov	212	690	902
16	Dec	525	1,139	1,664
17	2nd Half	1,583	4,462	6,045
18	Total	2,630	7,884	10,514
19				

Figure 25. *Select the cells to format.*

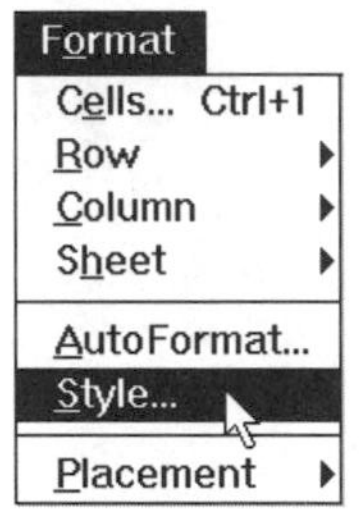

Figure 26. *The Format menu.*

Selecting Styles

A style is a preset combination of formatting. You can choose one of the existing styles or create your own.

1. Select the cells to format. **(Figure 25)**
2. From the Format menu, choose Style. **(Figure 26)**

   or

   Press Alt+apostrophe.
3. On the Style dialog box, choose a style from the drop-down list. **(Figure 27)**
4. Make sure the checkboxes for the formatting aspects that you'd like the style to apply are checked on the Style dialog box.

✔ Tips

- Styles on the style list that are followed with a (0) are formatted to zero decimal places.
- Cells are given the Normal style unless you specify a different style.
- To change the default cell formatting, modify the Normal style. *See Creating Styles, page 144.*

Choose a style here.

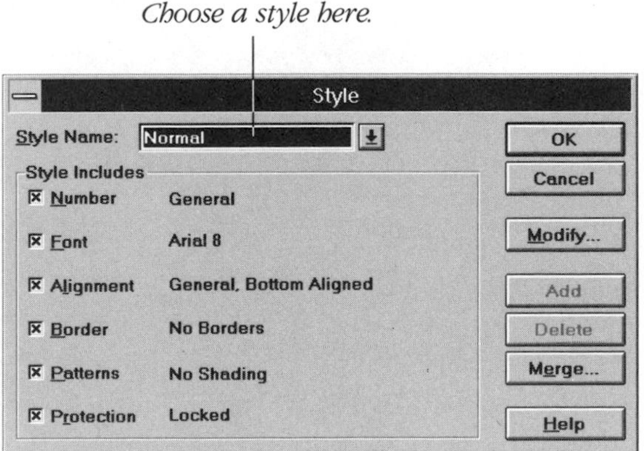

Figure 27. *The Style dialog box.*

Creating Styles

1. Format a cell with all the formatting you want. **(Figure 28)** *See Text Formatting, page 138, and Number Formatting, page 140.*
2. From the Format menu, choose Style. **(Figure 29)**

   or

   Press Alt+apostrophe
3. Type a new style name into the Style text box. **(Figure 30)**
4. Click OK.

✔ Tip

- By clicking the Merge button on the Style dialog box, you can copy the styles from another open workbook.

12	Aug	230	816	1,046
13	Sep	189	585	774
14	Oct	202	612	814
15	Nov	212	690	902
16	Dec	525	1,139	1,664
17	2nd Half	1,583	4,462	6,045
18	Total	$ 2,630	7,884	10,514
19				
20				

Figure 28. *Format a sample cell.*

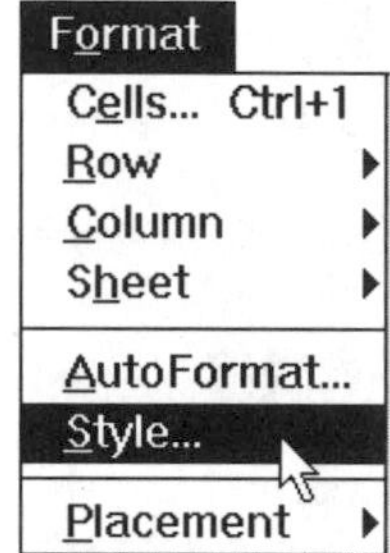

Figure 29. *The Format menu.*

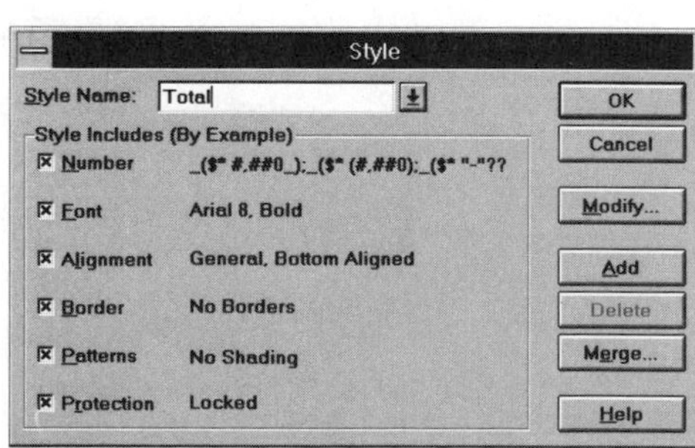

Figure 30. *Type a new style name into the Style text box.*

Working with Multiple Sheets 16

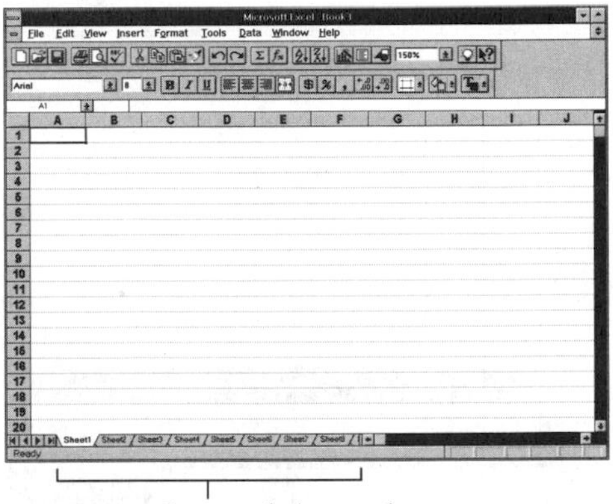

Figure 1. *The Worksheet tabs.*

About Using Multiple Sheets

Each Excel workbook contains 16 worksheets. You may use only the first worksheet for all your data and calculations. But you also might want to organize your information by placing certain data on each worksheet and then consolidating the results on a grand total worksheet.

The worksheet tabs that are visible below the current sheet let you switch easily from sheet to sheet. **(Figure 1)**

Changing to Another Sheet

1. Click the tab of thc sheet to display. **(Figure 2)**

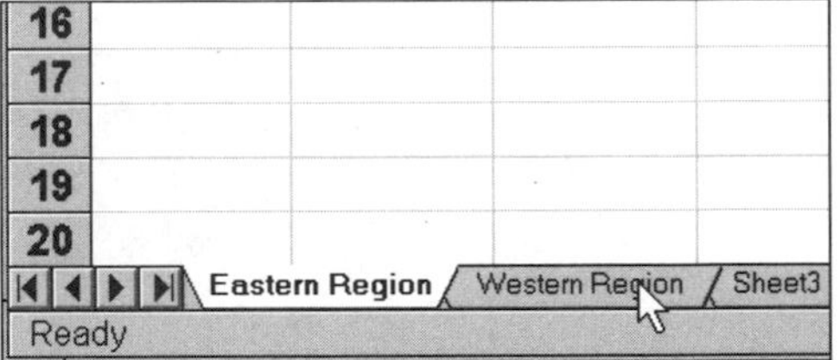

Figure 2. *To bring a worksheet to the front, click its tab.*

✔ Tips

- If the tab is not visible, use the Tab scrolling buttons to scroll through the tabs. **(Figure 3)**
- You can rearrange the order of sheets by dragging their tabs to the left or right.

Changing Sheets

Excel

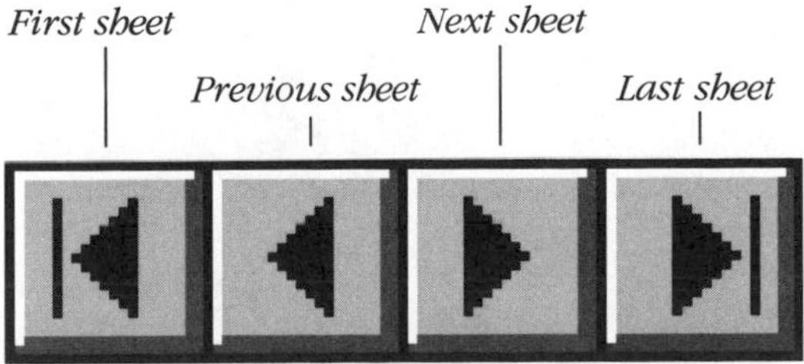

Figure 3. *The Tab scrolling buttons.*

Naming Sheets

Naming the sheets you use replaces the default names (Sheet1, Sheet2, and so on) with useful, informative names (Marketing, Manufacturing, Personnel, for example).

1. Double-click the tab of the sheet to rename. **(Figure 4)**
2. On the Rename Sheet dialog box, type the new name over the current name in the Name text box. **(Figure 5)**
3. Click OK. **(Figure 6)**

✔ Tips

- You can also choose Sheet Rename from the Format menu to get to the Rename Sheet dialog box.
- Sheet names can be up to 31 characters long and can include spaces.

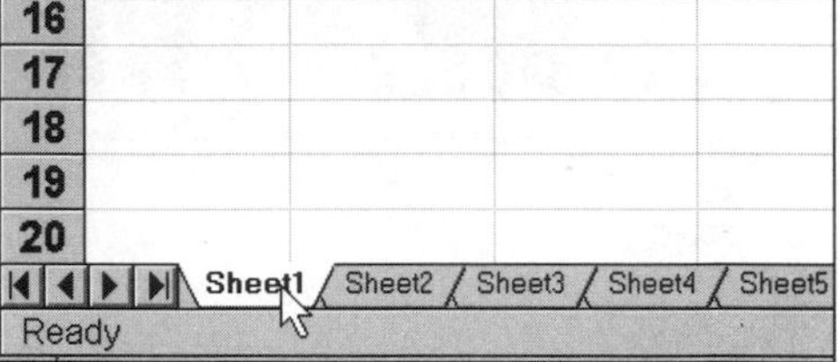

Figure 4. *Double-click a tab to rename the sheet.*

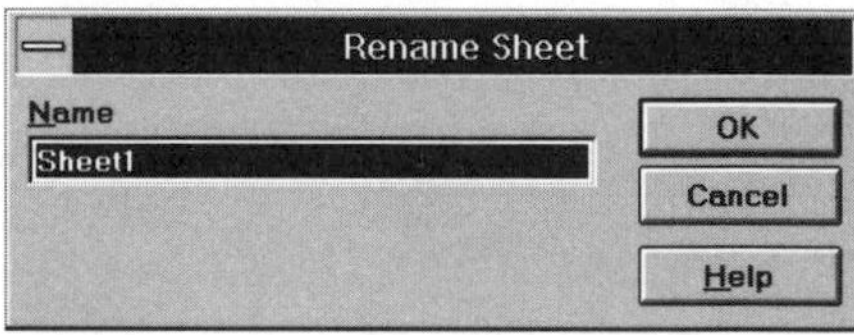

Figure 5. *The Rename Sheet dialog box.*

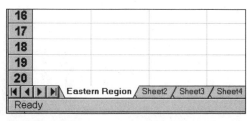

Figure 6. *The new name appears on the tab.*

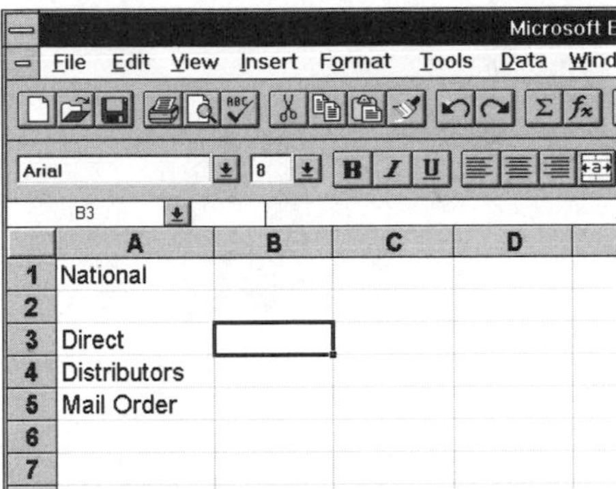

Figure 7. *Start the formula.*

Referring to Data from Other Sheets in Formulas

While building a formula, you can include data from another sheet.

1. Click in the destination cell for the formula. **(Figure 7)**
2. Start the formula as usual by entering an equals sign.
3. Refer to cells on other sheets by switching to the sheets and then selecting the cell or cells. **(Figure 8)**
4. Press Enter when you finish building the formula. You will be returned to the sheet where you started the formula. **(Figure 9)**

✔ Tip

- If you've named ranges in other sheets, you can enter the range names in the formula without worrying about which sheet the data is on. Excel will find the range on any sheet in the workbook.

	A	B
1	Western Region	
2		
3	Direct	32,000
4	Distributors	51,000
5	Mail Order	24,000
6		107,000

Figure 8. *Switch to another sheet and select the cells to include in the formula.*

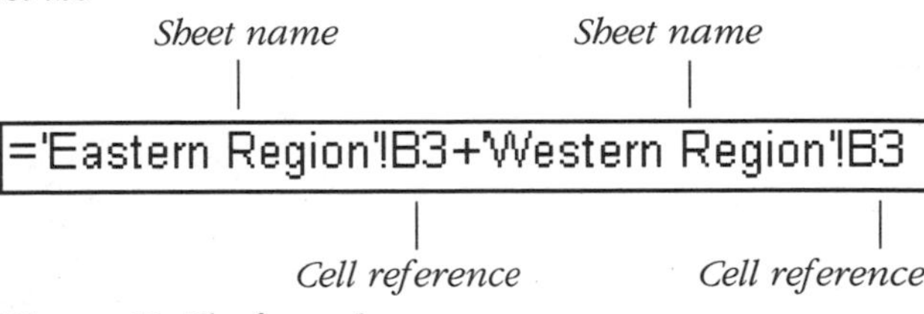

Figure 10. *The formula.*

	A	B
1	National	
2		
3	Direct	69,000
4	Distributors	
5	Mail Order	

Figure 9. *Press Enter to complete the formula.*

Consolidating to a Sheet

When successive sheets of a workbook contain the exact same arrangement of data, you can sum ranges that extend "down" from sheet to sheet data rather than across a single sheet. This is called 3-D referencing. **(Figure 11)**

1. On the consolidation sheet, click in the destination cell for the formula. **(Figure 12)**
2. Start the formula by entering an equals sign followed by the function or operator, such as SUM, and the left parenthesis. **(Figure 13)**
3. Select the range on the first sheet in the range of sheets. **(Figure 14)**
4. Press and hold the Shift key on the keyboard.
5. Click the tab of the last sheet in the range. **(Figure 15)**
6. Press Enter. **(Figure 16)**

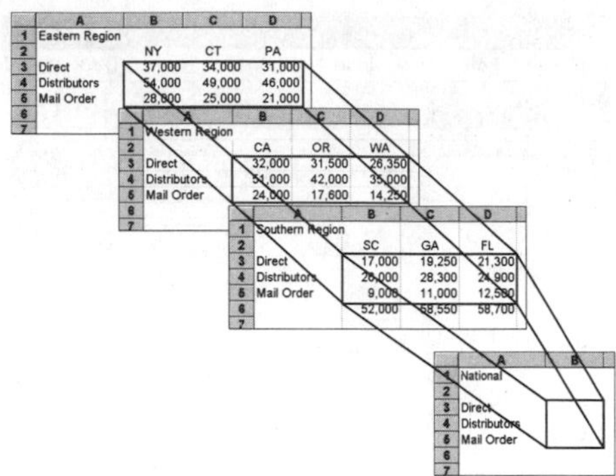

Figure 11. *3-D referencing.*

	A	B
1	National	
2		
3	Direct	
4	Distributors	
5	Mail Order	
6		

Figure 12. *Click at the destination for the formula. (B3, in this case)*

	A	B
1	National	
2		
3	Direct	=sum(
4	Distributors	
5	Mail Order	
6		

Figure 13. *Start the formula as usual.*

B3 =sum('Eastern Region'!B3:D3

	A	B	C	D
1	Eastern Region			
2		NY	CT	PA
3	Direct	37,000	34,000	31,000
4	Distributors	54,000	49,000	46,000
5	Mail Order	28,000	25,000	21,000
6		119,000	108,000	98,000
7				

Figure 14. *Select the range on the first sheet.*

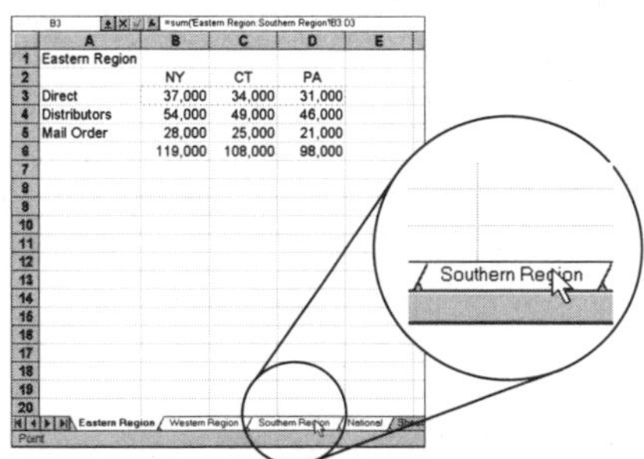

Figure 15. *While holding the Shift key, click the tab on the last range.*

The reference in the formula contains both a range of sheets and a range of cells.

B3 =SUM('Eastern Region:Southern Region'!B3:D3)

	A	B	C	D
1	National			
2				
3	Direct	249,400		
4	Distributors			
5	Mail Order			
6				

Figure 16. *The formula.*

Special Excel Techniques

	A	B	C	D	E
1	**Fundraiser Projected Revenue**				
2		*Week 1*	*Week 2*	*Week 3*	*Week 4*
3	Personal invitations	$ 2,600	$ 3,120	$ 2,470	$ 2,130
4	Mailing lists	650	1,300	1,560	1,040
5	Radio sales	1,105	1,235	780	260
6	Association list	2,340	4,030	1,820	1,235
7	Donations	390	650	520	325
8		$ 7,085	$ 10,335	$ 7,150	$ 4,990
9					
10					
11					

Figure 1. *Select a cell.*

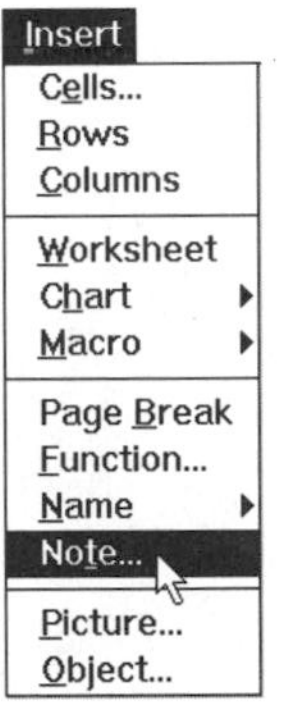

Figure 2. *The Insert menu.*

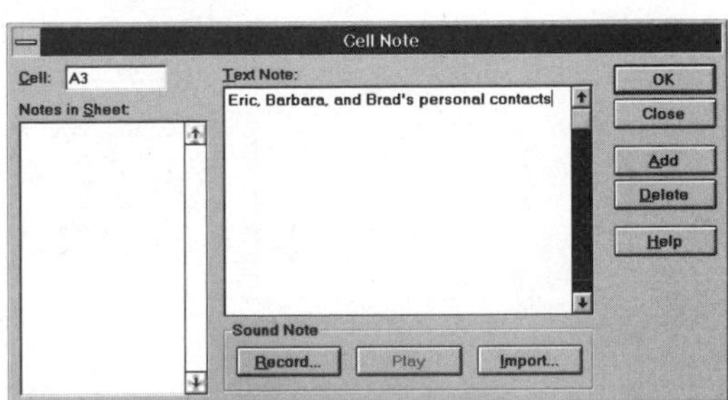

Figure 3. *The Cell Note dialog box.*

Inserting Notes in Cells

A note is an annotation that you attach to a cell to provide information about the cell's contents. Notes can be text or sound (if you have sound hardware in your PC). To view a note, double-click the cell to which the note is attached.

1. Select the cell to which you want to attach a note. **(Figure 1)**
2. From the Insert menu, choose Note. **(Figure 2)**
3. On the Cell Note dialog box, type the text for the note into the Text Note box. **(Figure 3)**
4. Click OK.

✔ Tips

- A note is indicated by a note marker at the upper right corner of the cell (a small red dot). **(Figure 4)**
- To remove a note, double-click the cell containing the note, select the note on the Cell Note dialog box, and then click the Delete button on the dialog box.

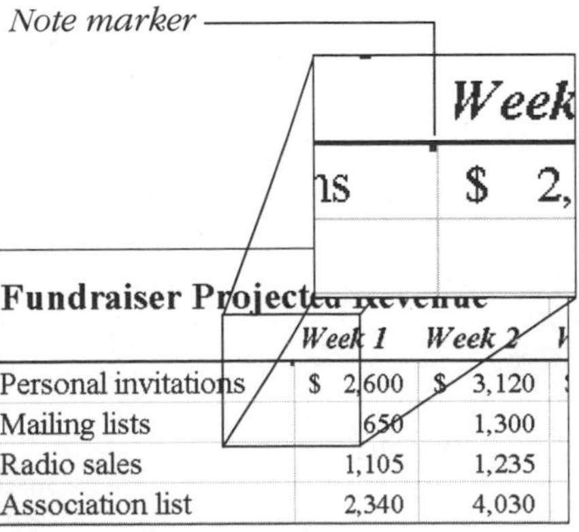

Figure 4. *Note marker.*

Naming Ranges

When you give a range a name, you can use the name in formulas rather than the range address. **(Figure 5)** Range names make it easier to refer to data and easier to understand formulas.

1. Select the range that you want to name. **(Figure 6)**
2. From the Insert menu, choose Name. **(Figure 7)**
3. On the Name submenu, choose Define.
4. Enter the name into the Define Name dialog box. **(Figure 8)**
5. Click OK.

✔ **Tip**

- You can give a name to an individual cell or a range of cells.

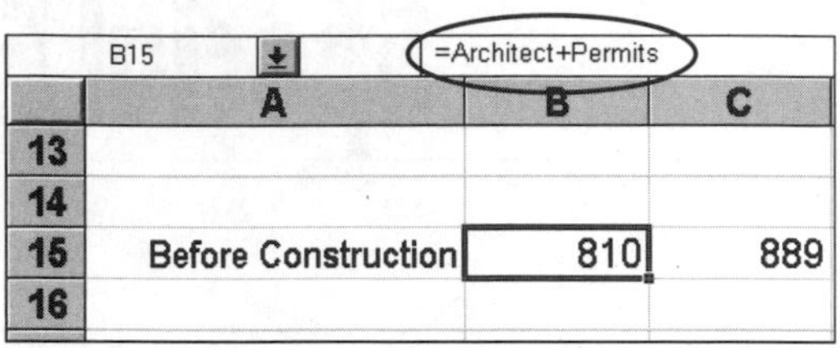

Figure 5. *Using range names in a formula.*

	A	B	C	D	E
1					
2	Construction Expenses	*Week 1*	*Week 2*	*Week 3*	*Total*
3	Lumber	1,200	1,600	600	3,400
4	Sheetrock	750	690	200	1,640
5	Nails	130	-	-	130
6	Misc Hardware	640	480	275	1,395
7	*Total*	2,720	2,770	1,075	6,565
8					

Figure 6. *Select the range to name.*

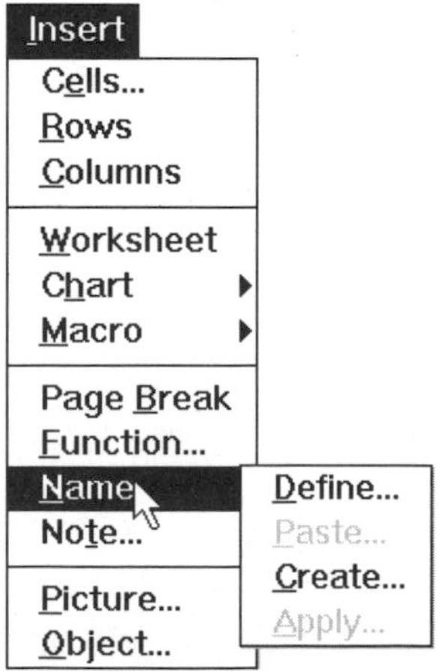

Figure 7. *The Insert menu.*

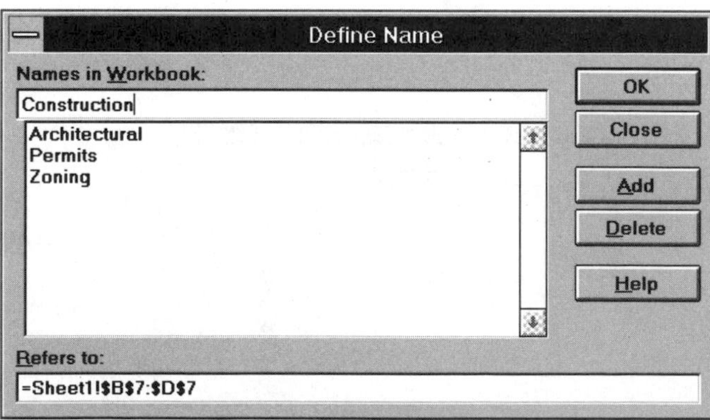

Figure 8. *The Define Name dialog box.*

	A	B	C	D	E
7	Construction Expenses	Week 1	Week 2	Week 3	Total
8	Lumber	1,200	1,600	600	3,400
9	Sheetrock	750	690	200	1,640
10	Nails	130	-	-	130
11	Misc Hardware	640	480	275	1,395
12	Total	2,720	2,770	1,075	6,565

Figure 9. *Select the formula or formulas to trace.*

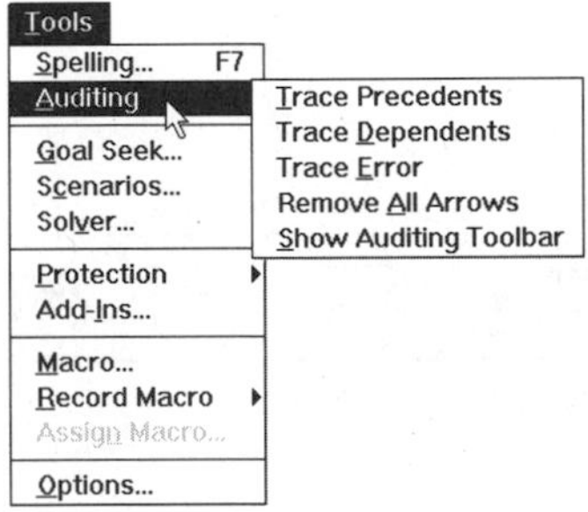

Figure 10. *The Tools menu.*

Auditing a Worksheet

To avoid bogus results from incorrect formulas, you can have Excel show you which cells have supplied data for a formula.

1. Select the cell or cells that contain the formulas. **(Figure 9)**
2. From the Tools menu, choose Auditing. **(Figure 10)**
3. On the Auditing submenu, choose Trace Precedents.
4. Choose Trace Precedents again to see an additional level of precedents, if it exists.

✔ Tips

- To clear the arrows, choose Remove All Arrows from the Auditing submenu.
- The Auditing toolbar contains Trace Precedents and Remove All Arrows buttons. **(Figure 12)** *See Selecting Toolbars, page 31.*

Auditing a Worksheet

Excel

	A	B	C	D	E
7	Construction Expenses	Week 1	Week 2	Week 3	Total
8	Lumber	1,200	1,600	600	3,400
9	Sheetrock	750	690	200	1,640
10	Nails	130	-	-	130
11	Misc Hardware	640	480	275	1,395
12	Total	2,720	2,770	1,075	6,565

Figure 11. *Arrows show the links between a formula and the cells that have supplied data to it.*

Trace Precedents button. *Remove All Arrows.*

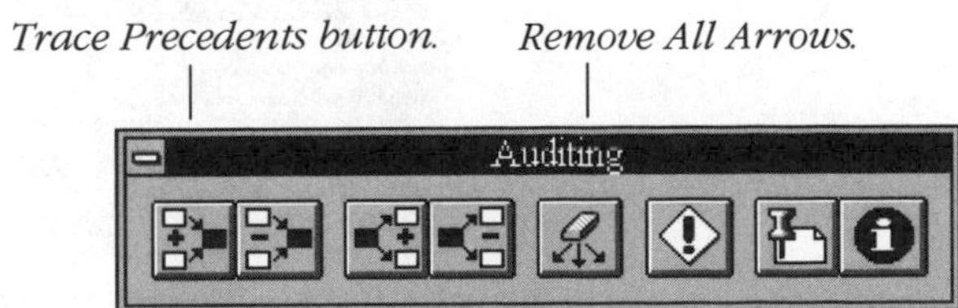

Figure 12. *The Auditing toolbar.*

Creating a Chart with the Chart Wizard

1. Select the data to chart. **(Figure 13)**
2. Click the ChartWizard button in the Standard toolbar. **(Figure 14)**
3. Drag out a box that marks the location for the chart on a clear area of the worksheet. **(Figure 15)**
4. Follow the instructions and make selections on the series of steps in the Chart Wizard dialog boxes that follow. **(Figures 16-20)**

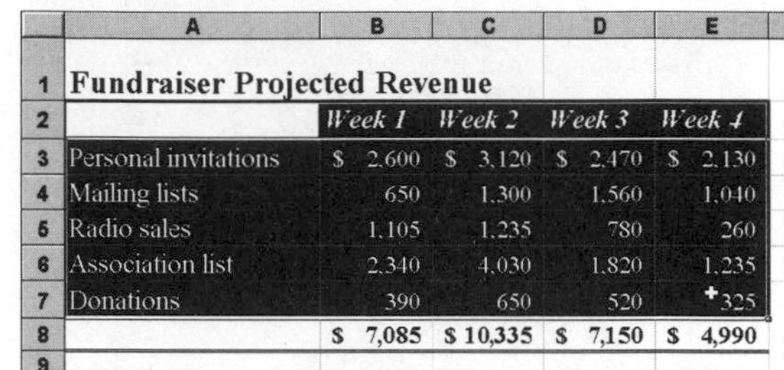

	A	B	C	D	E
1	Fundraiser Projected Revenue				
2		*Week 1*	*Week 2*	*Week 3*	*Week 4*
3	Personal invitations	$ 2,600	$ 3,120	$ 2,470	$ 2,130
4	Mailing lists	650	1,300	1,560	1,040
5	Radio sales	1,105	1,235	780	260
6	Association list	2,340	4,030	1,820	1,235
7	Donations	390	650	520	325
8		$ 7,085	$ 10,335	$ 7,150	$ 4,990

Figure 13. *Select the data to chart.*

The ChartWizard button.

Figure 14. *The ChartWizard button.*

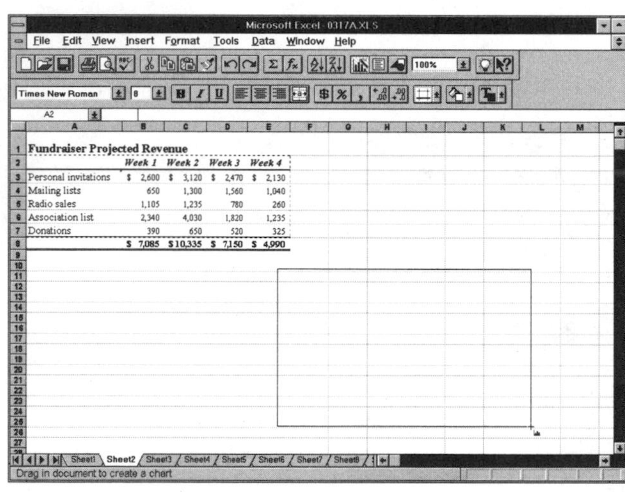

Figure 15. *Drag out a box.*

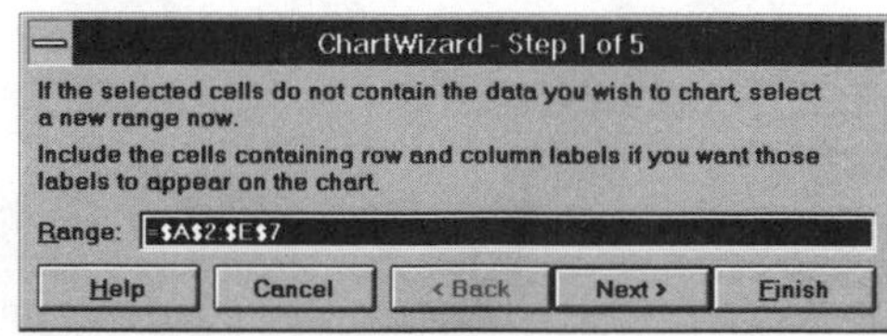

Figures 16. *Confirm the range to chart in ChartWizard Step 1.*

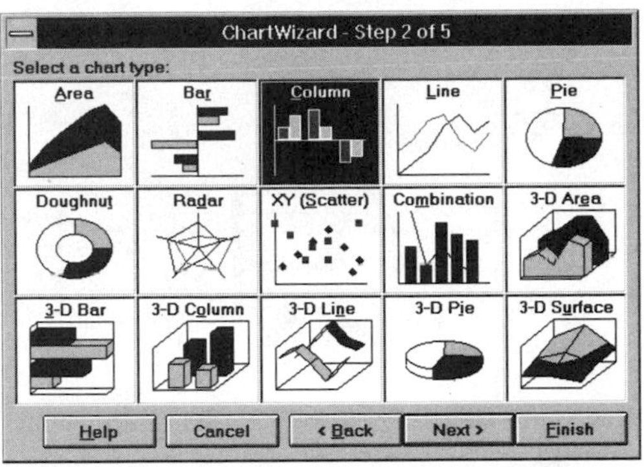

Figure 17. *Select a chart type in ChartWizard Step 2.*

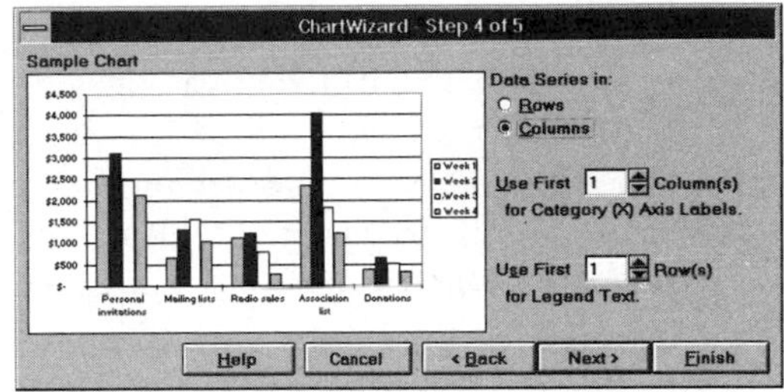

Figure 19. *Confirm the structure of the chart in ChartWizard Step 4.*

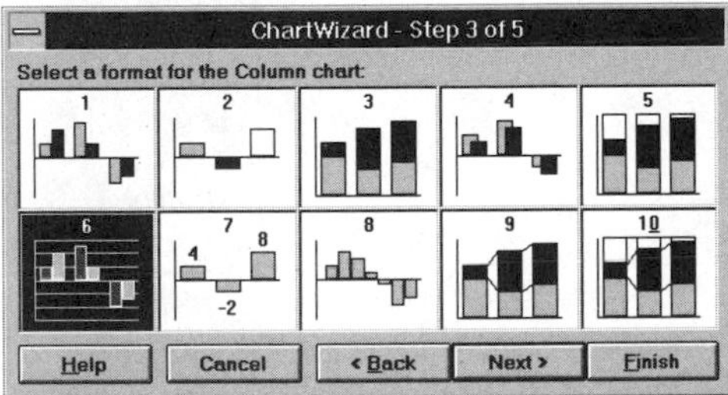

Figure 18. *Select a chart format in ChartWizard Step 3.*

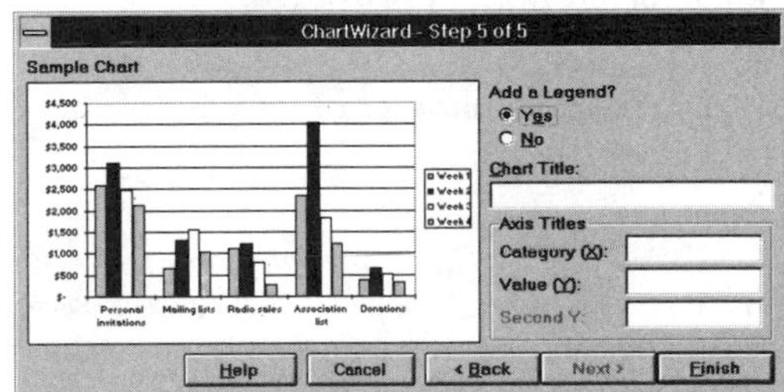

Figure 20. *Title the chart in ChartWizard Step 5, then click Finish.*

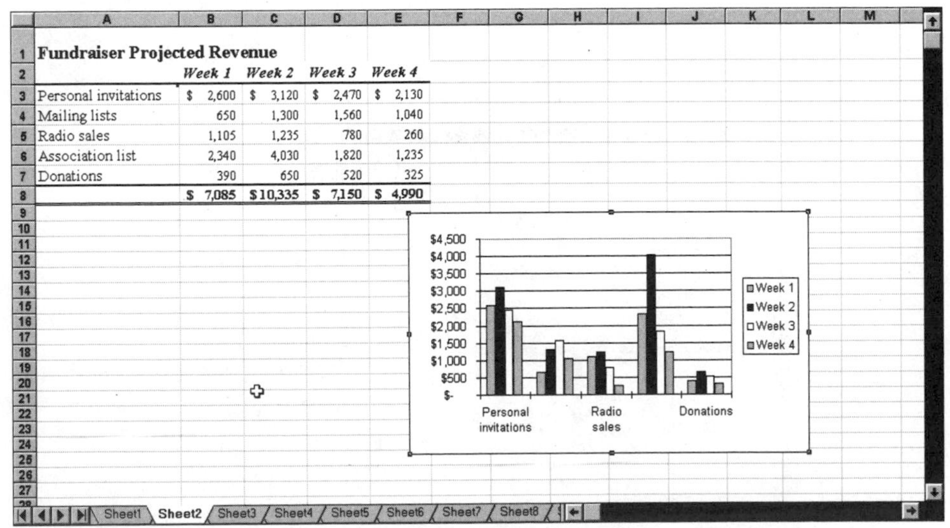

	A	B	C	D	E
1	**Fundraiser Projected Revenue**				
2		***Week 1***	***Week 2***	***Week 3***	***Week 4***
3	Personal invitations	$ 2,600	$ 3,120	$ 2,470	$ 2,130
4	Mailing lists	650	1,300	1,560	1,040
5	Radio sales	1,105	1,235	780	260
6	Association list	2,340	4,030	1,820	1,235
7	Donations	390	650	520	325
8		$ 7,085	$10,335	$ 7,150	$ 4,990

Figure 21. *Completed chart.*

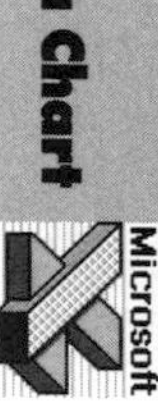

Modifying a Chart

1. Double-click a chart to activate it. **(Figure 22)**
2. Use commands on the Insert and Format menus to change the design of the chart. **(Figure 23)**
3. Click outside the border surrounding the chart to finish modifying the chart.

✔ Tips

- While a chart is active, you can click any part of the chart once to select it and then double-click to obtain a dialog box that contains options for the selected part. **(Figure 24)**
- Drag the chart to move it on the sheet or drag the handles of its window to resize the chart.

Note: *You'll find far more detail about modifying charts on pages 189-196, which cover creating graphs in PowerPoint. Charting is identical in both Excel 5 and PowerPoint 4.*

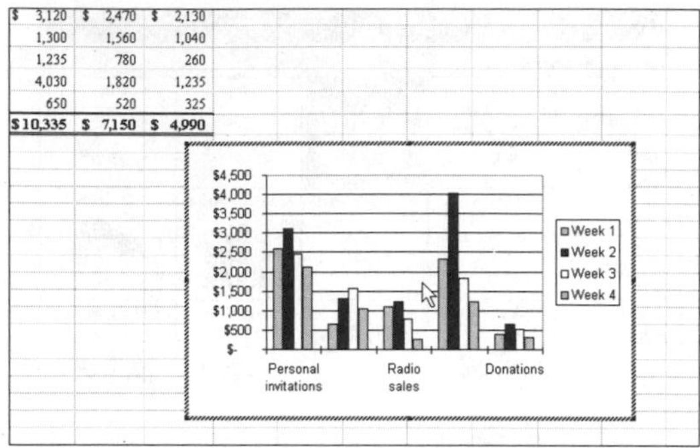

Figure 22. *A thick gray border appears around a chart when you double-click it.*

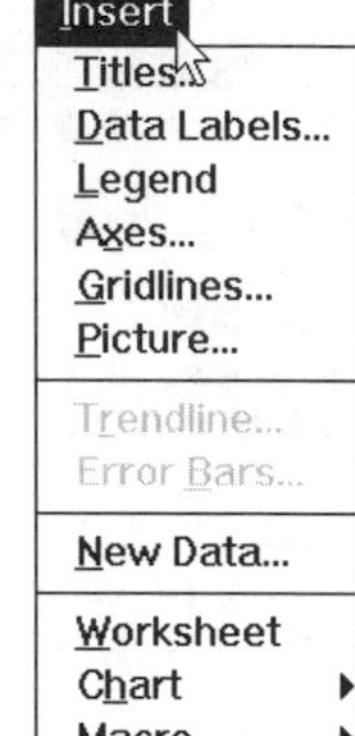

Figure 23. *While a chart is activated, the Insert menu displays chart commands and options.*

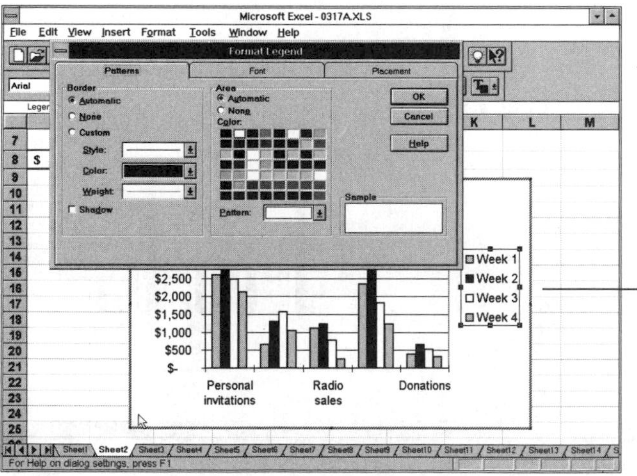

Double-click the legend to summon the Format Legend dialog box.

Figure 24. *Double-click any chart part to change its options.*

Excel Database Techniques

	A	B	C	D	E
1	Fname	Lname	Employee no.	Total vacation days	Vacation days used
2	Eric	Weinberger	2394	15	5
3	Audrey	Marr	2089	20	12
4	David	Lawrence	3132	20	14
5	Thomas	Speeches	3082	50	28
6	Robert	Westover	2965	20	12
7	Cohen	Susan	2075	10	5
8	Cohen	Aaron	2104	10	5
9					

Figure 1. *Each* **record** *of information occupies a row. Each column is a* **field**.

About Excel's Database Capabilities

Unless you work with extremely large databases (thousands and thousands of sets of data) Excel can provide all the database power you'll need.

In Excel, you enter data in rows. Each row is a *record* (one complete set of information). **(Figure 1)** Each column in the row, called a *field*, contains one particular type of information in the record.

Rather than enter information directly into the cells of a sheet, you can also create a fill-in-the-blanks data *form* to make it easier to enter, edit, delete and search through information. **(Figure 2)**

After you enter the data, you can search through it, sort it, and pull out only the information that matches particular criteria.

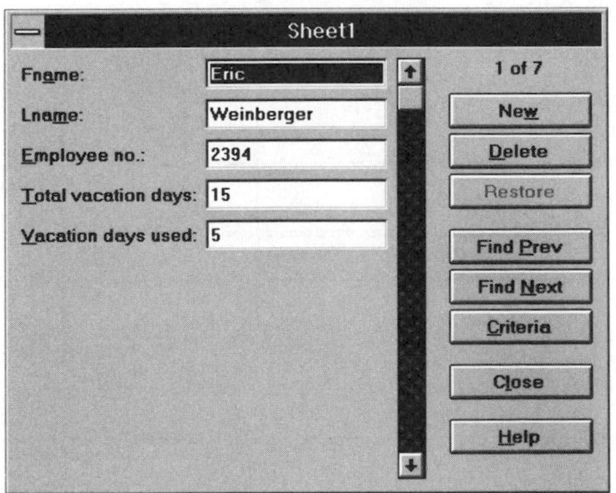

Figure 2. *A data form.*

Setting up the Database

1. Enter the field names at the tops of a group of adjacent columns. **(Figure 3)**
2. Enter the data into rows below the field names. **(Figure 4)**

✔ Tips

- Press Tab when you complete a cell to move to the next cell to the right.
- Press Enter when you complete a cell to move to the next cell below.

	A	B	C	D	E
1	Fname	Lname	Employee no.	Total vacation days	Vacation days used
2					
3					
4					
5					
6					

Figure 3. *The field names.*

One field.

One record.

	A	B	C	D	E
1	Fname	Lname	Employee no.	Total vacation days	Vacation days used
2	Eric	Weinberger	2394	15	5
3	Audrey	Marr	2089	20	12
4					
5					
6					

Figure 4. *Data entered below the field names.*

Creating a Form

1. Click any cell that contains data. **(Figure 5)**
2. From the Data menu, choose Form. **(Figures 6-7)**

✓ Tips

- To put away the form, click Close.
- Press Tab to move from field to field on a form.
- Press Shift+Tab to return to the previous field on a form.

	A	B	C	D	E
1	Fname	Lname	Employee no.	Total vacation days	Vacation days used
2	Eric	Weinberger	2394	15	5
3	Audrey	Marr	2089	20	12
4	David	Lawrence	3132	20	14
5	Thomas	Speeches	3082	50	28
6	Robert	Westover	2965	20	12

Figure 5. *Click a cell in the database.*

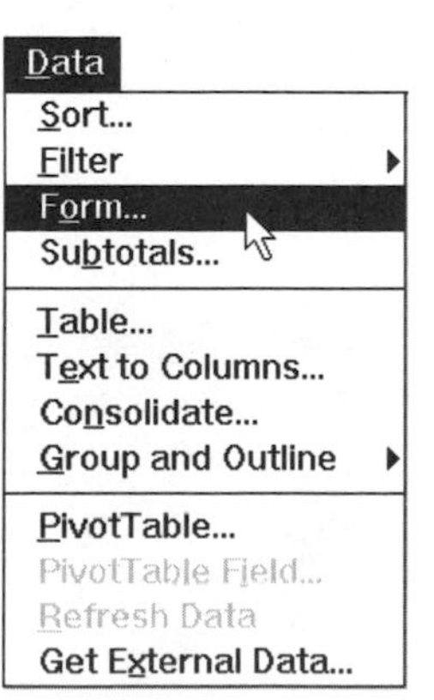

Figure 6. *The Data menu.*

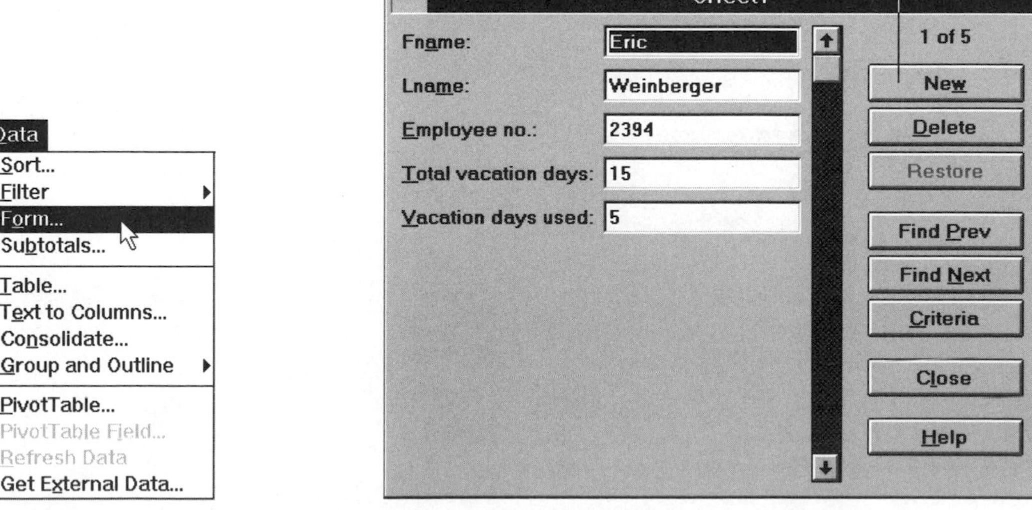

Figure 7. *The data form.*

Sorting the Database

1. Click any cell in the database. **(Figure 8)**
2. From the Data menu, choose Sort. **(Figure 9)**
3. On the Sort dialog box, choose a field name from the Sort By drop-down list. **(Figure 10)**
4. To perform secondary and tertiary sorts on the data, choose additional fields from the two Then By drop-down lists also on the Sort dialog box.
5. To sort from smallest to largest or earliest to latest, choose Ascending. To sort from largest to smallest or latest to earliest, choose Descending.
6. Click OK. **(Figure 11)**

	A	B	C	D	E
1	Fname	Lname	Employee no.	Total vacation days	Vacation days used
2	Eric	Weinberger	2394	15	5
3	Audrey	Marr	2089	20	12
4	David	Lawrence	3132	20	14
5	Thomas	Speeches	3082	50	28
6	Robert	Westover	2965	20	12
7					
8					

Figure 8. *Click a cell in the database.*

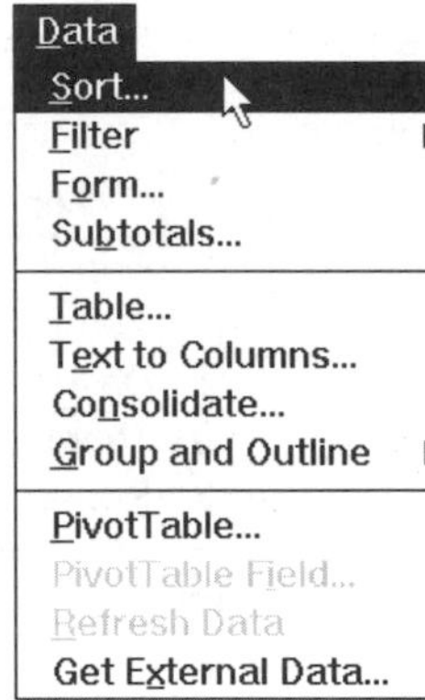

Figure 9. *The Data menu.*

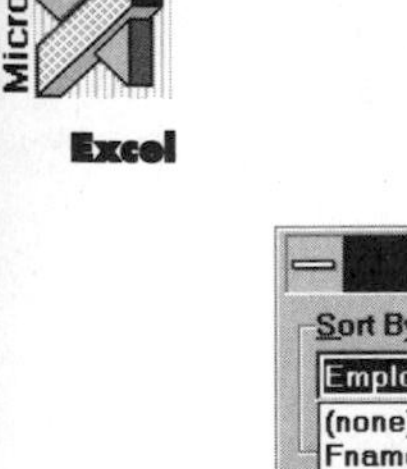

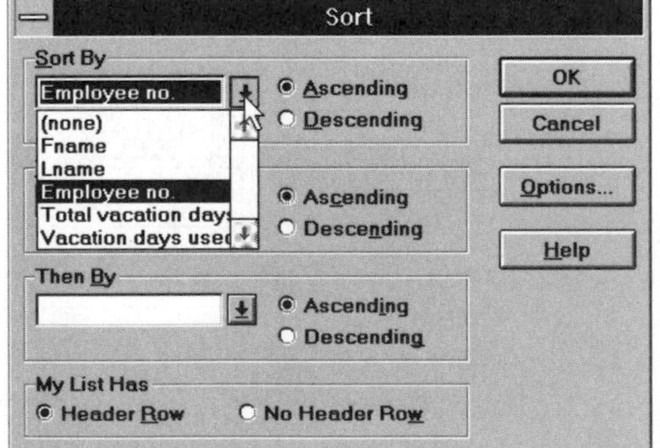

Figure 10. *The Sort dialog box.*

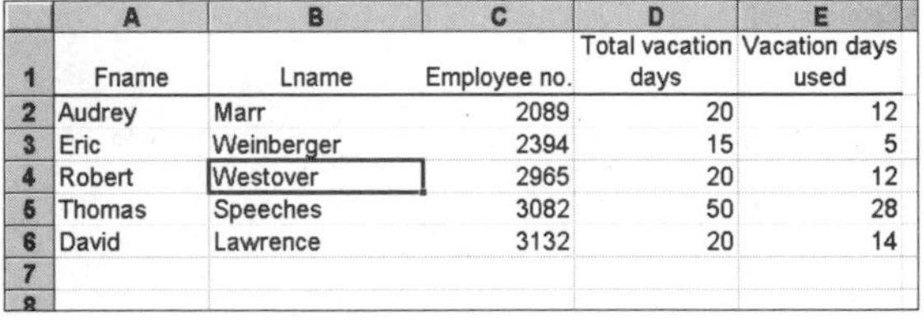

	A	B	C	D	E
1	Fname	Lname	Employee no.	Total vacation days	Vacation days used
2	Audrey	Marr	2089	20	12
3	Eric	Weinberger	2394	15	5
4	Robert	Westover	2965	20	12
5	Thomas	Speeches	3082	50	28
6	David	Lawrence	3132	20	14
7					
8					

Figure 11. *The sorted data.*

	A	B	C	D	E	F
1	Fname	Lname	Employee no.	Status	Total vacation days	Vacation days used
2	Audrey	Marr	2089	Permanent	20	12
3	Eric	Weinberger	2394	Permanent	15	5
4	Robert	Westover	2965	Temporary	20	12
5	Thomas	Speeches	3082	Temporary	50	28
6	David	Lawrence	3132	Temporary	20	14
7						

Figure 12. *Click on any cell in the database.*

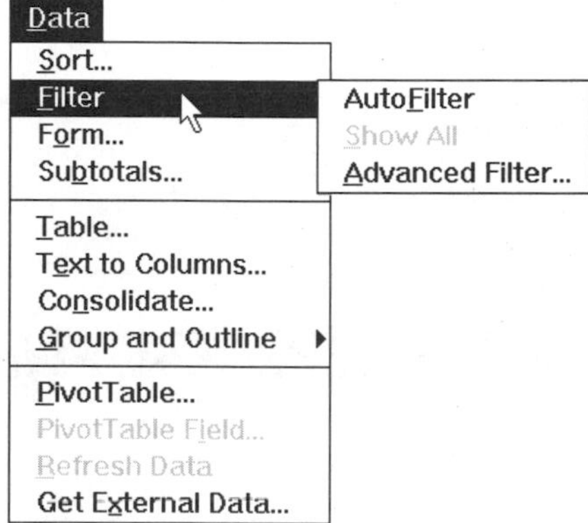

Figure 13. *The Data menu.*

Extracting Data

1. Click any cell in the database. **(Figure 12)**
2. From the Data menu, choose Filter. **(Figure 13)**
3. On the Filter submenu, choose AutoFilter.
4. Click any of the pull-down buttons next to the field names to see a list of the entries in that field. **(Figure 14)**
5. Choose an entry on the list to view only those records that match the entry. **(Figure 15)**

✔ Tips

- Click a cell outside the database and then choose AutoFilter from the Filter submenu again to display the entire database.
- When the data is filtered, the row headings of the extracted data are blue.
- The field upon which the data is filtered shows a blue drop-down button.

Extracting Data

Excel

	A	B	C	D	E	F
1	Fname	Lname	Employee n	Status	Total vacation days	Vacation days used
2	Audrey	Marr	2089	(All)	20	12
3	Eric	Weinberger	2394	(Custom...)	15	5
4	Robert	Westover	2965	Permanent	20	12
5	Thomas	Speeches	3082	Temporary	50	28
6	David	Lawrence	3132	(Blanks)	20	14
7				(NonBlanks)		

Figure 14. *Select an entry from one of the pull-down lists.*

	A	B	C	D	E	F
1	Fname	Lname	Employee n	Status	Total vacation days	Vacation days used
2	Audrey	Marr	2089	Permanent	20	12
3	Eric	Weinberger	2394	Permanent	15	5
7						
8						
9						
10						

Figure 15. *Only records that match the selected entry appear.*

Totaling Numeric Data in a Database

1. Select any cell in the database.
2. From the Data menu, choose Subtotals. **(Figure 16)**
3. On the Subtotals dialog box, select a field from the At Each Change in drop-down list. A subtotal will appear each time this field changes value. A grand total appears at the bottom of the list. **(Figures 17-18)**

✔ Tip

- Use the controls to the left of the database to show only the subtotals. **(Figure 18)**

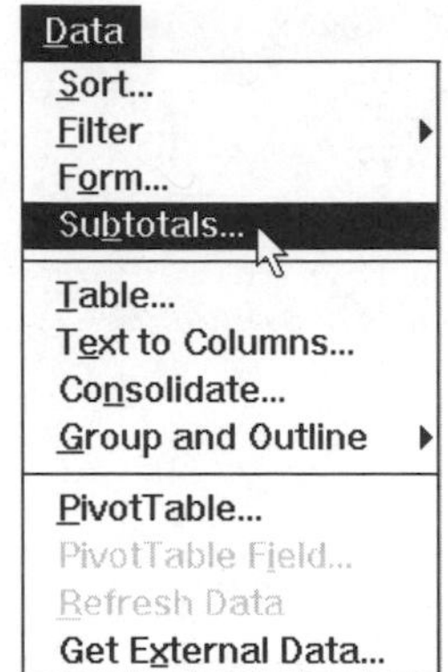

Figure 16. *The Data menu.*

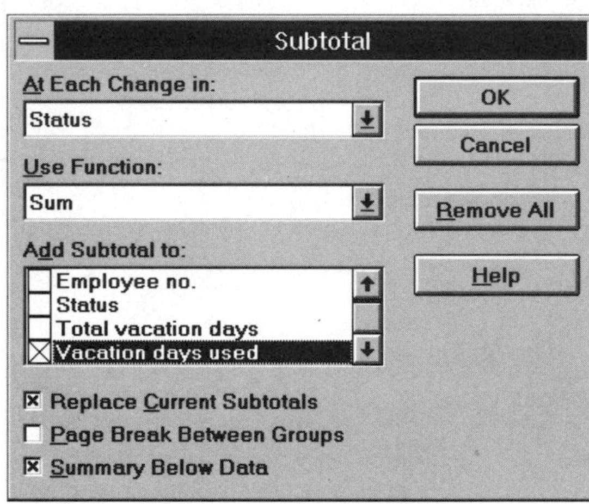

Figure 17. *The Subtotals dialog box.*

Click the minus buttons to hide detail and show only the totals.

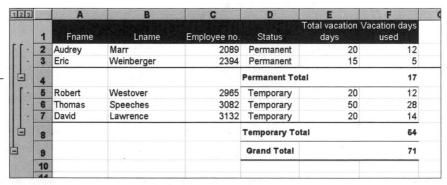

	A	B	C	D	E	F
1	Fname	Lname	Employee no.	Status	Total vacation days	Vacation days used
2	Audrey	Marr	2089	Permanent	20	12
3	Eric	Weinberger	2394	Permanent	15	5
4				**Permanent Total**		**17**
5	Robert	Westover	2965	Temporary	20	12
6	Thomas	Speeches	3082	Temporary	50	28
7	David	Lawrence	3132	Temporary	20	14
8				**Temporary Total**		**64**
9				**Grand Total**		**71**
10						

Figure 18. *Use these controls to show only the totals.*

PowerPoint 4.0 Presenting

PowerPoint 4.0 Presenting

About PowerPoint

What is PowerPoint?

PowerPoint is the presentation graphics component of the Microsoft Office suite. It creates charts and graphs, slides, handouts, overheads, and any other presentation materials you might use during a stand-up, dog and pony show. PowerPoint even creates slide shows, which are electronic presentations that you can run on your computer screen or on a projection in front of an audience.

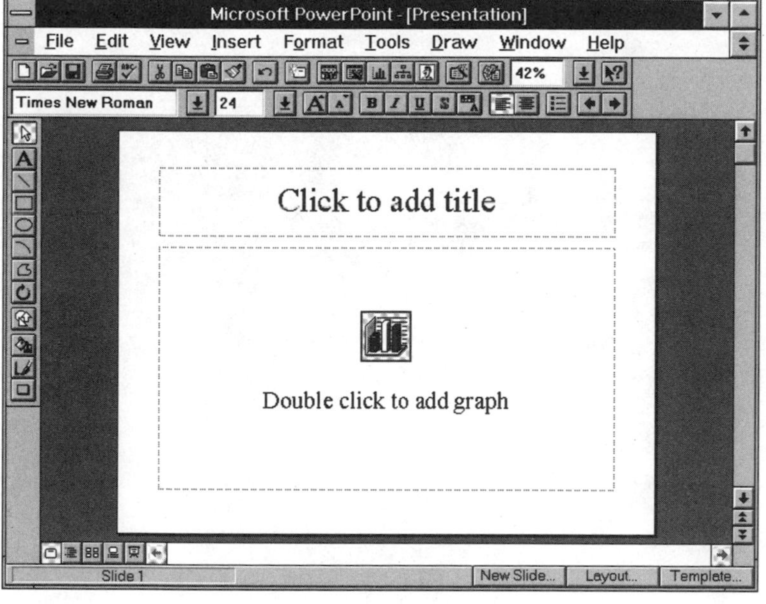

PowerPoint comes with dozens of professionally designed templates that take care of the look of a presentation so you can focus on the message. It even comes with a selection of sample presentation outlines from which you can choose to get a start on the presentation content.

Bulleted text slides, graphs, tables, organization charts, clip art, and drawing tools are all elements of PowerPoint's powerful arsenal.

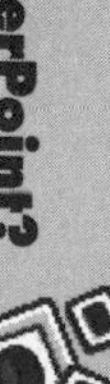

The Road to a PowerPoint Presentation

The Bridgehampton Garden Club

Why Join?

- Associate with Other Gardeners
- Learn From the Experts
- Monthly Garden Tours
- Discounts at Local Nurseries

Starting the Presentation

PowerPoint offers not one, but several different ways to start a presentaton, including using the Pick a Look Wizard to choose a design first, or the AutoContent Wizard to choose a presentation outline first. *Pages 169-176.*

Creating the Text Slides

You may prefer to develop the text in Outline view, where you can see all the text in one place. Or, you can generate slides one at a time, typing text directly into the special text placeholders on the slides as you go. Creating slides with PowerPoint is no more difficult than filling in the blanks. If you've outlined the presentation in Word, you can even transfer the outline to a new PowerPoint presentation automatically. *Pages 177-188.*

Creating Graphs and Tables

If the information you need to get across is numeric, you might want to consider a graph slide. PowerPoint also makes organization charts and tables to depict other sorts of information visually. *Pages 189-210.*

Customizing the Presentation

In Slide Sorter view, you get a bird's eye view of the entire presentation. You can rearrange slides, change the overall design, and delete extraneous slides. In Slide view, you can add a logo to or change the color or design of the background, change the font and color schemes, or change the template, which governs the overall look of the presentation. *Pages 211-214.*

Adding Special Graphics

PowerPoint's sophisticated drawing tools and commands make it easy to embellish slides with special graphics. You can even import a scanned photograph or a graphic from another application. *Pages 221-224.*

Creating a Slide Show

The big payoff comes when you're ready to present the presentation. You can generate 35mm slides and handouts just as you'd expect, but you can also create an onscreen, electronic presentation complete with TV-like special effects and transitions, and sound and music. Then, you can even send the slide show, along with the special PowerPoint Viewer module, to another computer user who is not fortunate enough to have PowerPoint. *Pages 225-228.*

The PowerPoint 4 Window

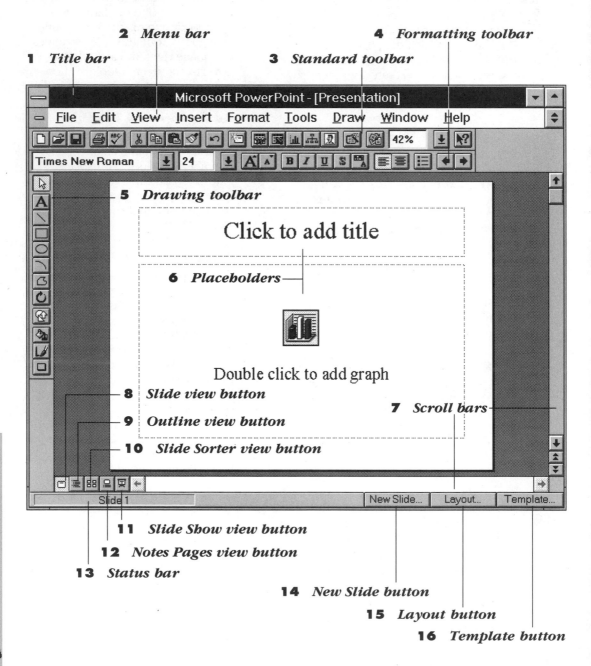

1 *Title bar*

2 *Menu bar*

3 *Standard toolbar*

4 *Formatting toolbar*

5 *Drawing toolbar*

6 *Placeholders*

7 *Scroll bars*

8 *Slide view button*

9 *Outline view button*

10 *Slide Sorter view button*

11 *Slide Show view button*

12 *Notes Pages view button*

13 *Status bar*

14 *New Slide button*

15 *Layout button*

16 *Template button*

Key to the PowerPoint 4 Window

1 *Title bar*

Displays the window name. Drag the title bar to move the window. Double-click the title bar to switch between maximized and restored window.

2 *Menu bar*

Click any name on the menu bar to pull down a menu, or press Alt+the underlined letter of the menu name.

3 *Standard toolbar*

Toolbar with buttons for file management, editing, and proofing commands.

4 *Formatting toolbar*

Toolbar with buttons for formatting text.

5 *Drawing toolbar*

Toolbar with buttons for adding graphic objects to slides.

6 *Placeholders*

Double-click these placeholders to add elements to slides.

7 *Scroll bars*

Use these scroll bars to move the view of the document up or down or to quickly jump to a spot in the document. The length of the vertical scroll bar represents the length of the entire document. The position of the scroll button represents the position of the insertion point in the document.

8 *Slide view button*

Click this button to switch to Slide view which shows a single slide.

9 *Outline view button*

Click this button to switch to Outline view, which shows the text of the presentation in outline form.

10 *Slide Sorter view button*

Click this button to switch to Slide Sorter view, which shows miniatures of slides arranged in a grid.

11 *Slide Show view button*

Click this button to view the slides of the presentation in sequence, as a slide show.

12 *Notes Pages view button*

Click this button to view a slides and notes you've typed about the slide for the presenter.

13 *Status bar*

Shows the current slide number.

14 *New Slide button*

Click this button to start a new slide.

15 *Layout button*

Click this button to summon the dialog box that shows sample layouts for the slide.

16 *Template button*

Click this button to choose a different template to redesign the appearance of the presentation.

Starting PowerPoint

1. Double-click the Microsoft PowerPoint icon in the Program Manager. **(Figure 1)**

   or

   Click the Microsoft PowerPoint icon in the Microsoft Office Manager. **(Figure 2)**

✔ Tip

- If PowerPoint is already started, press Ctrl+Esc and choose Microsoft PowerPoint from the list of running applications on the Task List. You can also press Alt+Tab repeated until the Microsoft PowerPoint icon appears. Then release the Alt key and the PowerPoint window will come to the front.

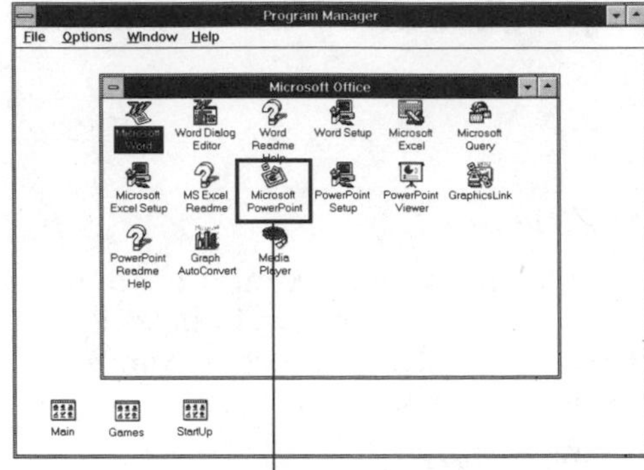

Figure 1. *The Microsoft PowerPoint icon in the Program Manager.*

Click here to start PowerPoint.

Figure 2. *The Microsoft Office Manager.*

Starting a Presentation 20

The New button.

Figure 1. *The New button.*

Figure 2. *The File menu.*

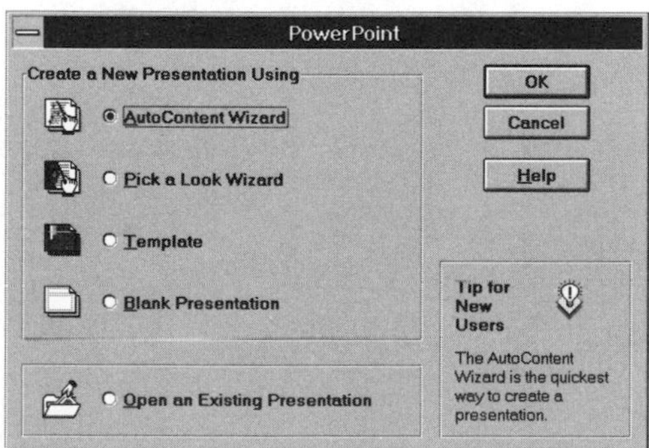

Figure 3. *The PowerPoint dialog box.*

About Starting a Presentation

Whenever you start a new presentation, PowerPoint offers several choices on the PowerPoint dialog box. To concentrate on content first, choose one of the suggested presentation outlines offered by the AutoContent Wizard. To concentrate on appearance first, use the Pick a Look Wizard.

1. Click the New button on the Standard toolbar. **(Figure 1)**

   or

   Press Ctrl+N.

   or

   From the File menu, choose New. **(Figure 2)**

2. On the PowerPoint dialog box, double-click AutoContent Wizard or Pick a Look Wizard. **(Figure 3)**

✔ Tips

- If you've already created a presentation during the current PowerPoint session, the PowerPoint dialog box is named the New Presentation dialog box, instead.
- To choose a presentation look by filename, double-click Template on the PowerPoint dialog box.
- To start with a blank presentation and then add formatting later, double-click Blank Presentation on the PowerPoint dialog box.

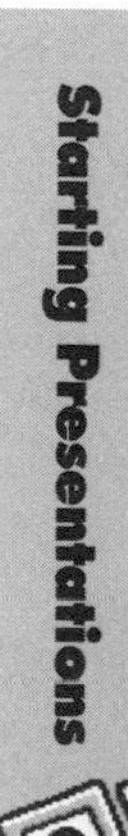

Using the AutoContent Wizard

The AutoContent Wizard offers a choice of sample presentation outlines, then drops you off in Outline view, where you can replace the sample outline text provided by the Wizard with your own.

1. Click Next on the Step 1 screen of the AutoContent Wizard. **(Figure 4)**
2. In Step 2, enter a presentation title and other information for the opening slide and then click Next. **(Figure 5)**
3. In Step 3, select an outline by name and click Next. **(Figure 6)**
4. In Step 4, click the Finish button. **(Figures 7-8)**

✔ Tips

- To return to a previous step, click Back on any Wizard dialog box.
- To skip the following steps and accept their default choices, click Finish.
- Each outline generates a presentation with a preset look. You can change the look by choosing a different template. *See Selecting a New Design, page 215.*
- The Cue Cards window may open on top of the outline to offer onscreen help. You can close the Cue Cards window just as you can any other window.

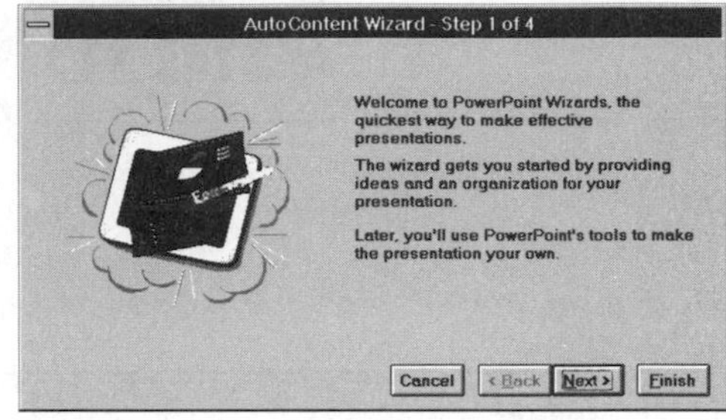

Figure 4. *Step 1 of the AutoContent Wizard.*

Type as much text as you want into these text boxes.

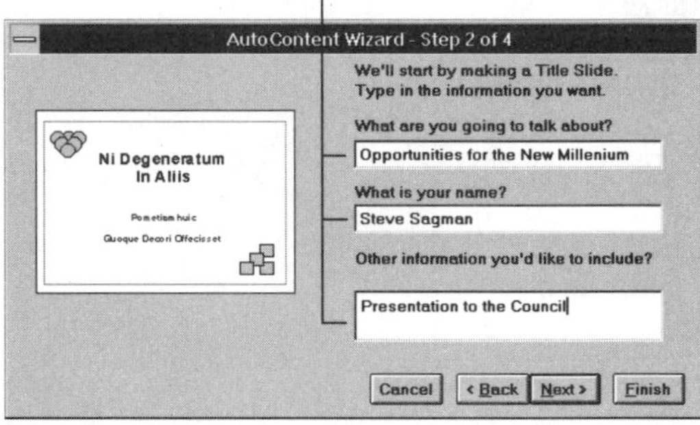

Figure 5. *Step 2 of the AutoContent Wizard.*

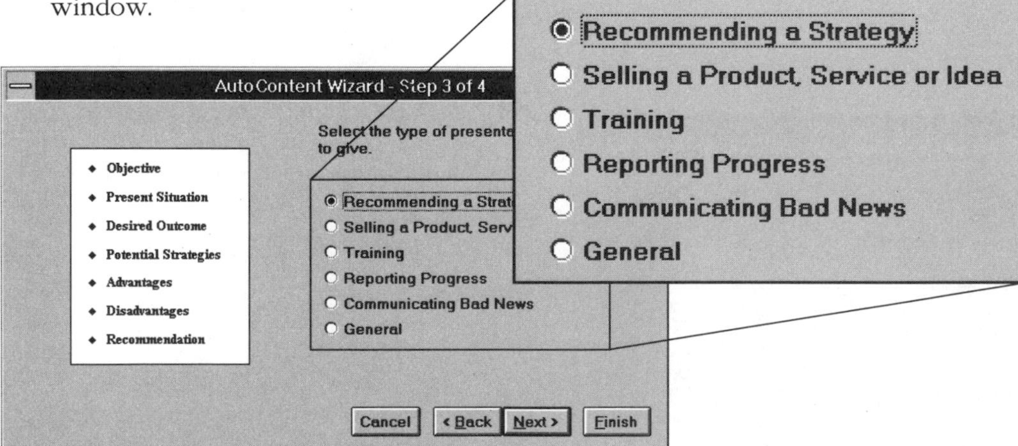

Figure 6. *Step 3 of the AutoContent Wizard.*

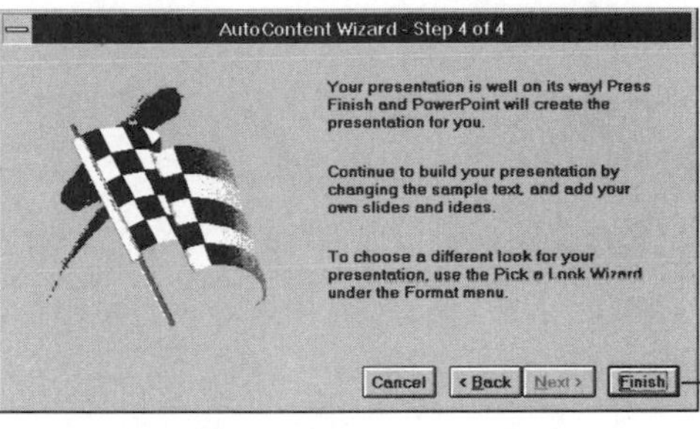

Click here to finish using the Wizard.

Figure 7. *Step 4 of the AutoContent Wizard.*

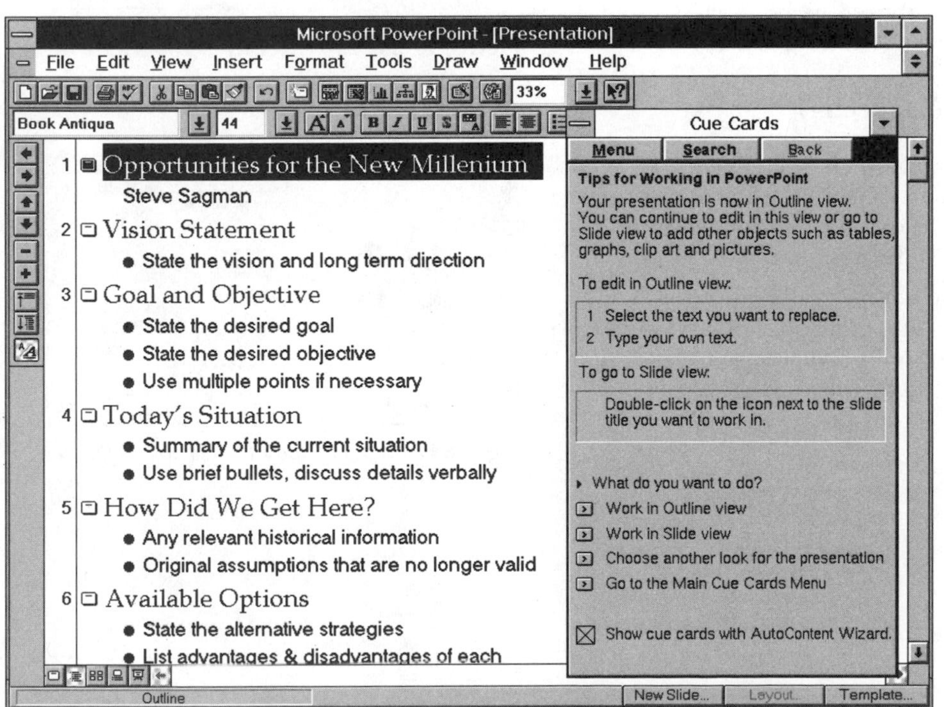

Figure 8. *The sample outline provided by the "Recommending a Strategy" option.*

Using the Pick a Look Wizard

The Pick a Look Wizard guides you in selecting a template that will govern the appearance of a presentation and in choosing a format for the presentation output.

1. In Step 1 of the Wizard, click Next. **(Figure 9)**
2. In Step 2, choose an output format for the presentation by clicking one of the four radio buttons, and click Next. **(Figure 10)**
3. In Step 3, choose one of the four templates shown, or click More to choose from the full list of templates, and then click Next. **(Figure 11)**
4. In Step 4, choose the output formats you'll use and click Next. **(Figure 12)**
5. In the next several steps, enter the special text that will appear on each output option selected in Step 4, and then click Next. **(Figure 13)**
6. When you reach the final step, click Finish. **(Figure 14)**

✔ Tips

- The Pick a Look Wizard drops you off in Slide View, where you can begin adding slides. **(Figure 15)**
- You can change the look of the presentation at any time by choosing a different template. *See Selecting a New Design, page 215.*

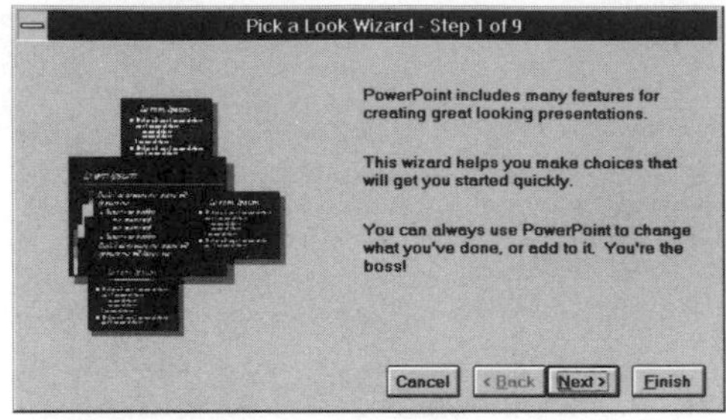

Figure 9. *Step 1 of the Pick a Look Wizard.*

Figure 10. *Step 2 of the Pick a Look Wizard.*

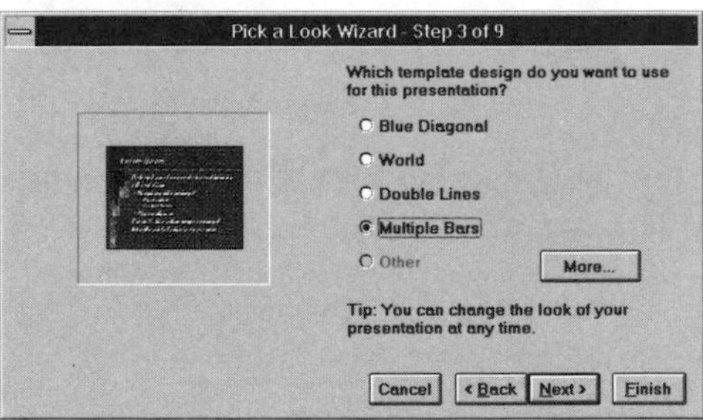

Figure 11. *Step 3 of the Pick a Look Wizard.*

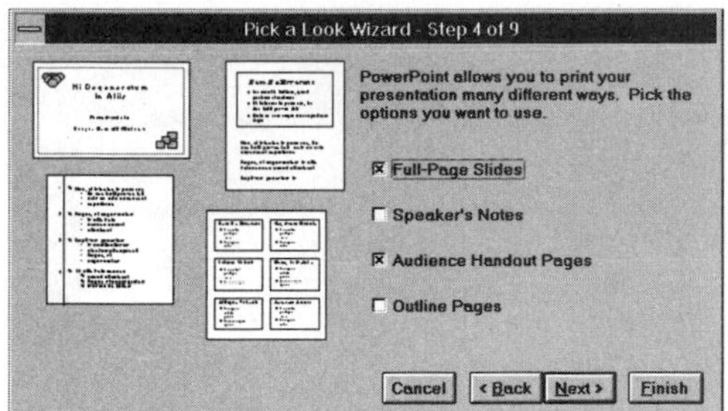

Figure 12. *Step 4 of the Pick a Look Wizard.*

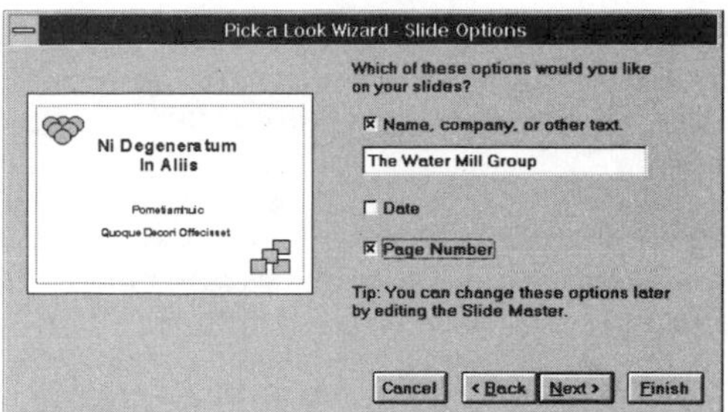

Figure 13. *Step 5 of the Pick a Look Wizard.*

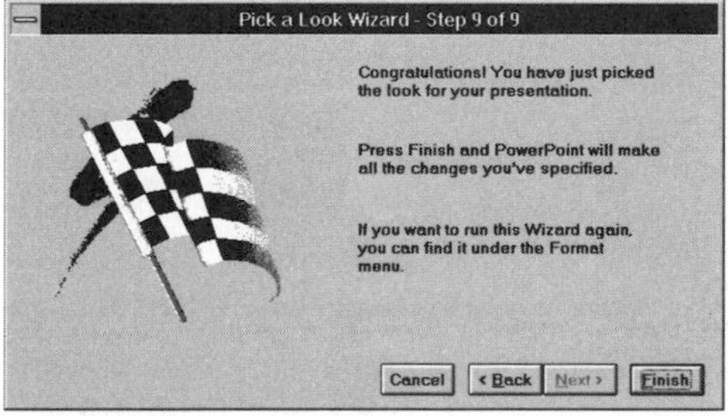

Figure 14. *The final step of the Pick a Look Wizard.*

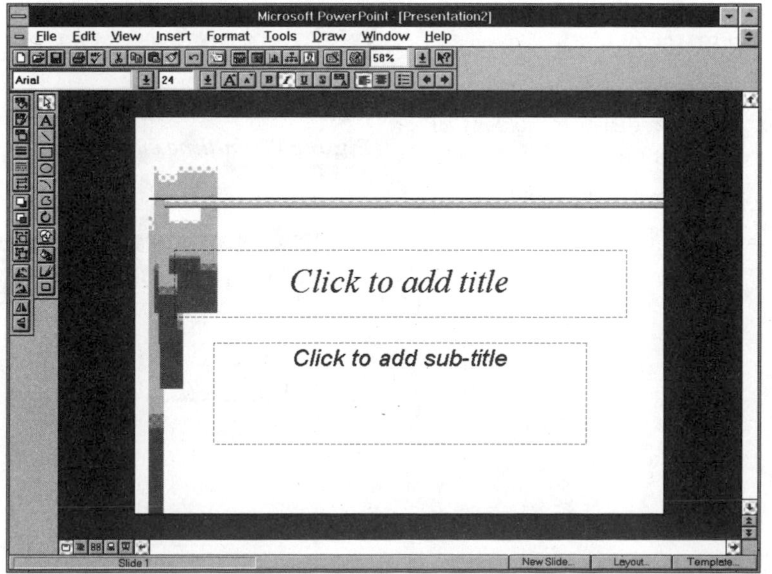

Figure 15. *The PowerPoint window after the completion of the Pick a Look Wizard.*

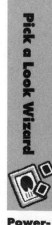

Changing Views

Slide View displays one slide at a time so you can enter text and graphics. **(Figure 16)**

Outline view displays only the text of the presentation in outline form so you can work easily with the content. **(Figure 17)**

Slide Sorter View displays miniatures of multiple slides so you can reorganize the slides and change the overall look of the presentation. Here you can also add and edit the transition effects for the slide show. **(Figure 18)**

Notes Pages View lets you enter and edit speaker's notes for the presenter. **(Figure 19)**

Slide Show View displays the presentation one slide after another in sequence as an automatic slide show (electronic presentation).

1. Click the appropriate button at the lower left corner of the presentation window. **(Figure 19-20)**

   or

   From the View menu, choose the view you want. **(Figure 21)**

✔ Tips

- Each view shows a different aspect of the same presentation.
- You can switch from one view to another at any time.

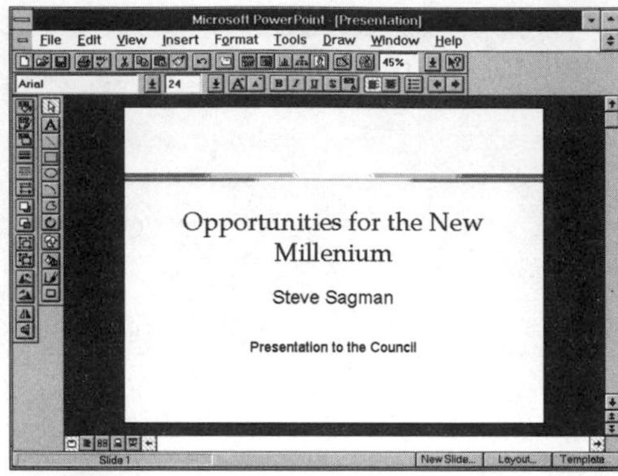

Figure 16. *Slide view.*

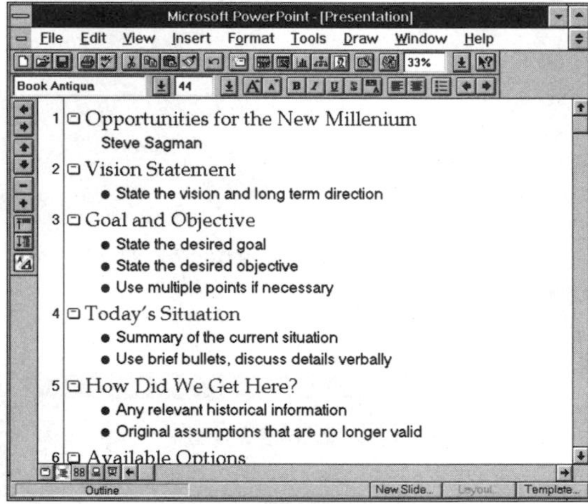

Figure 17. *Outline view.*

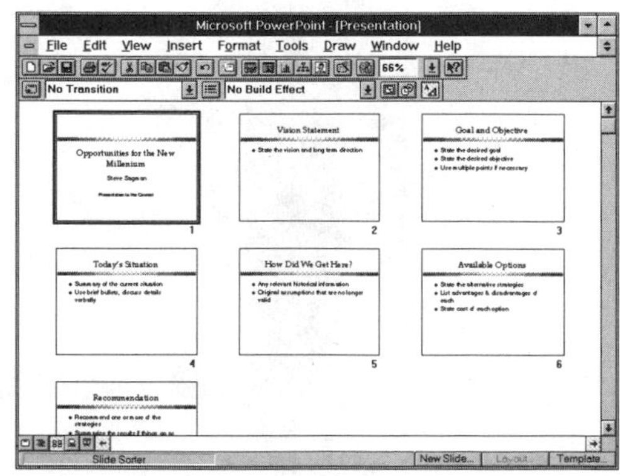

Figure 18. *Slide Sorter view.*

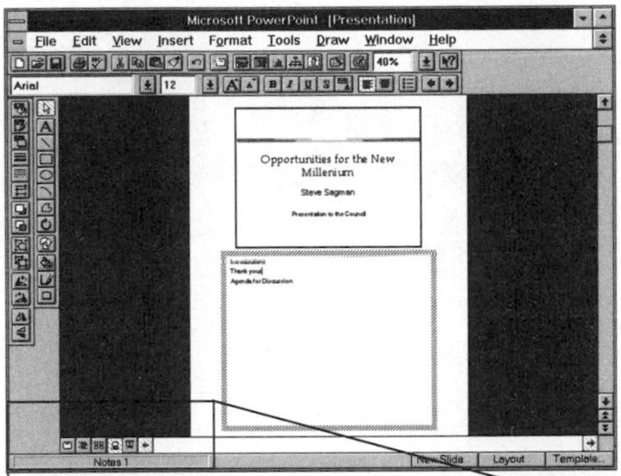

Figure 19. *Notes Pages view.*

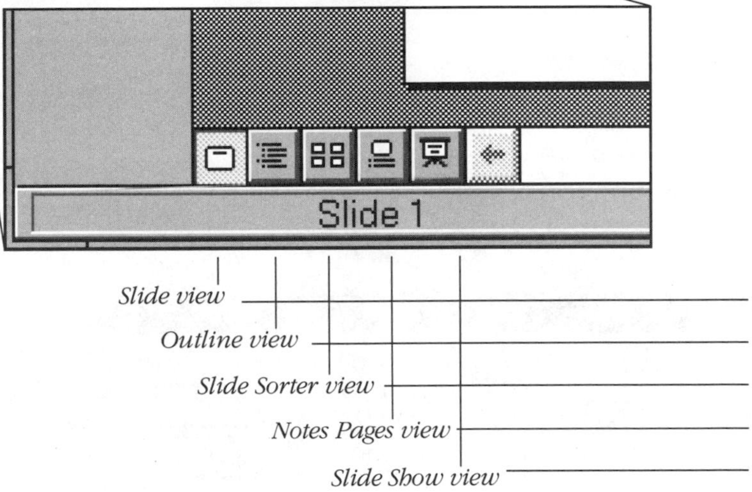

Slide view

Outline view

Slide Sorter view

Notes Pages view

Slide Show view

Figure 20. *The View buttons.*

View
• Slides
Outline
Slide Sorter
Notes Pages
Slide Show...
Master
Toolbars...
Ruler
Guides
Zoom...

Figure 21. *The View menu.*

Adding Slides

1. Click the New Slide button. **(Figure 22)**
   or
   Press Ctrl+M.
2. On the New Slide dialog box, double-click a slide layout. **(Figure 23)**

✔ Tips

- If Show New Slide Dialog is turned off on the Options dialog box, a Bulleted List slide will appear each time you click the New Slide button.
- If you choose the wrong slide layout, click the Layout button and then choose the correct layout on the Slide Layout dialog box.

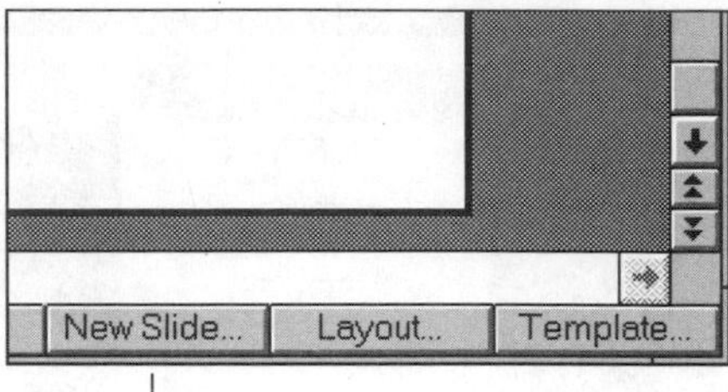

Figure 22. *The New Slide button.*

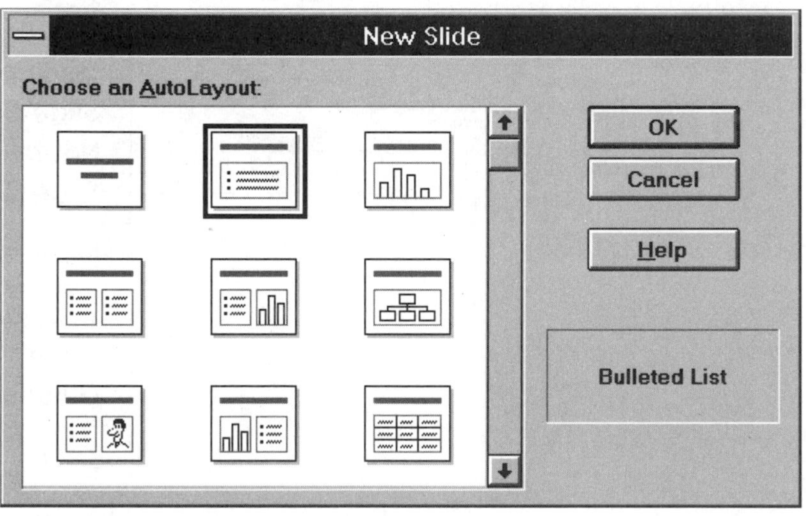

Figure 23. *The New Slide dialog box.*

21 Outlining the Presentation

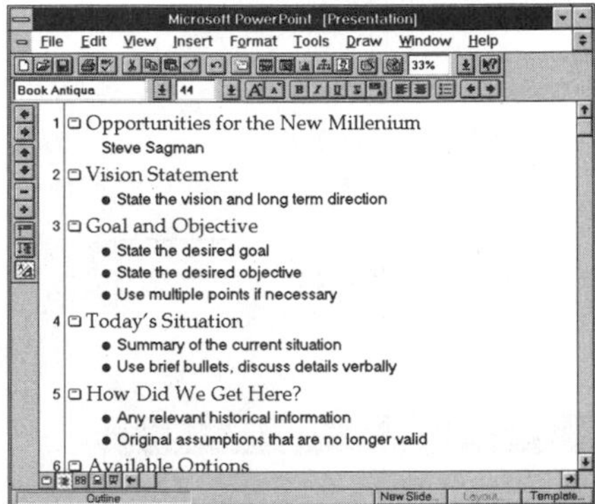

Figure 1. *Outline view.*

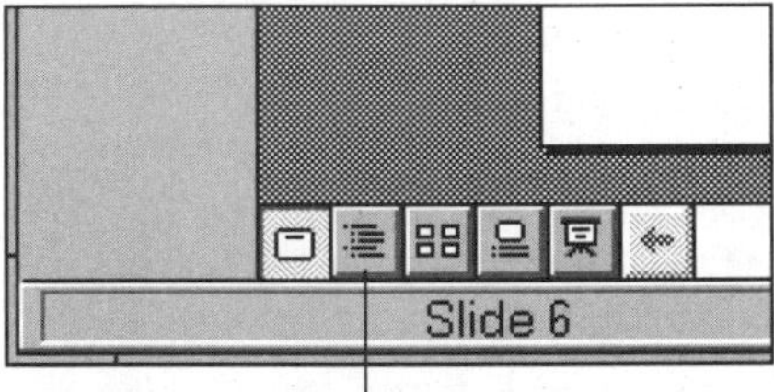

Figure 2. *The Outline view button.*

Figure 3. *The View menu.*

About Outlining

Outline view shows only the presentation text in outline form so you can focus exclusively on the content. **(Figure 1)** In Outline view, you see the text of the presentation on one screen so you can rearrange the flow, add or delete topics, and refine the wording of slides.

The AutoContent Wizard drops you off in Outline view automatically so you can modify the sample presentation outline it provides. You can also start in Outline view and enter the text of a presentation before switching to Slide view to add charts and graphs, tables, drawings, and other elements to individual slides. Even if you've already created a full presentation in Slide view, you can still switch to Outline view temporarily to focus on the text.

Switching to Outline View

1. Click the Outline view button. **(Figure 2)**

   or

2. From the View menu, choose Outline. **(Figure 3)**

Entering the Text

1. Type the title for a slide next to the slide icon and press Enter. **(Figure 4)**
2. Type the title of the next slide and press Enter. **(Figure 5)**

   or

   Press Tab, type the first bulleted text line for the current slide, and press Enter. **(Figure 6)**
3. Type any more bulleted text items, pressing Enter after each.

   or

   Press Shift+Tab to start a new slide. **(Figure 7)**
4. Continue as above to create new slides or add bulleted text points to the current slide.

✔ Tip

- To create a slide for a graph, organization chart, table, or drawing, simple type a slide title without entering bulleted text items underneath.

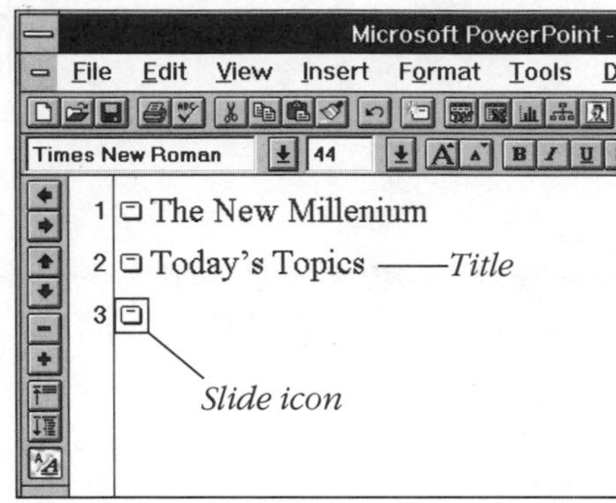

Figure 4. *Type the slide title.*

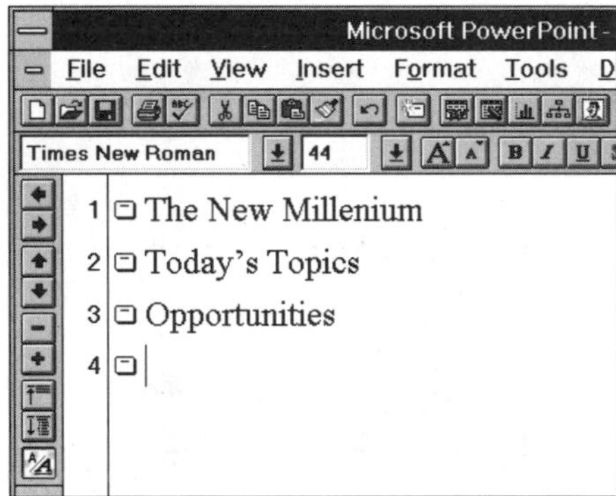

Figure 5. *Press Enter to begin a new slide.*

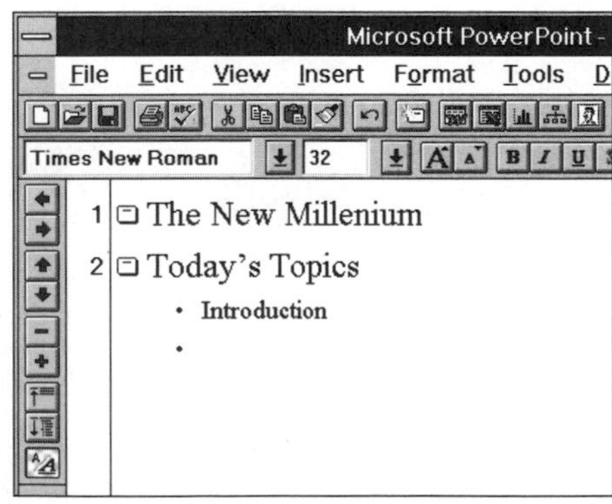

Figure 6. *Press Tab to begin typing bulleted items.*

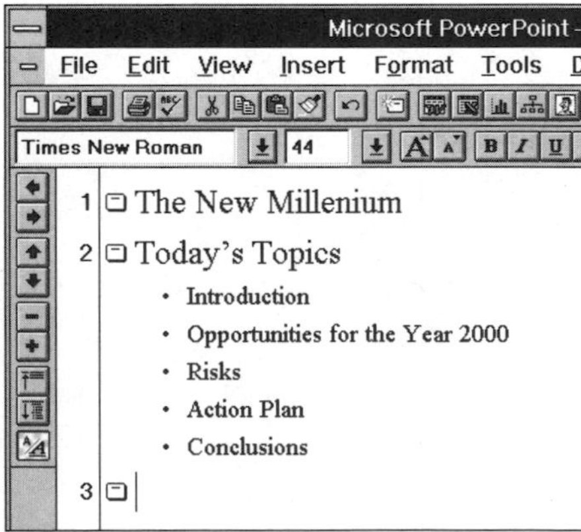

Figure 7. *Press Shift+Tab to type the next slide's title.*

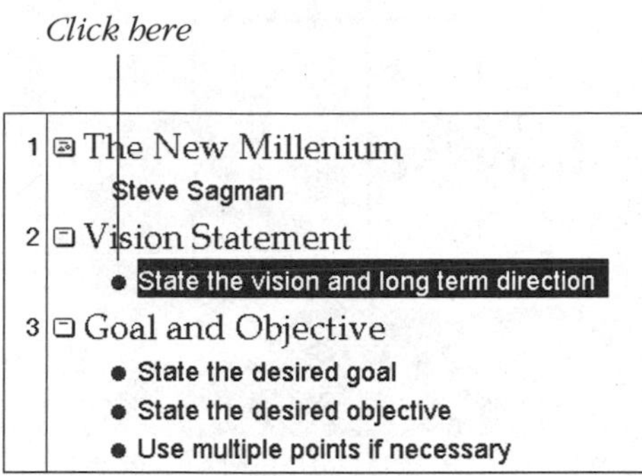
Click here
1 The New Millenium
Steve Sagman
2 Vision Statement
State the vision and long term direction
3 Goal and Objective
State the desired goal
State the desired objective
Use multiple points if necessary

Figure 8. *Click a bullet.*

1 The New Millenium

Steve Sagman

2 Vision Statement

- To meet the challenges of a new era.

3 Goal and Objective

- State the desired goal
- State the desired objective
- Use multiple points if necessary

Figure 9. *Type a replacement.*

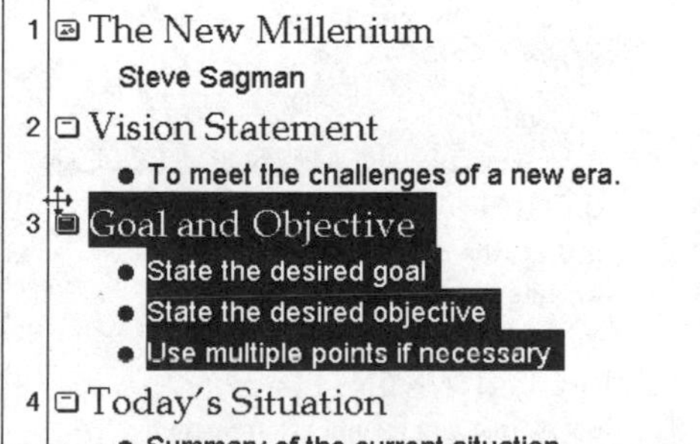
1 The New Millenium
Steve Sagman
2 Vision Statement
To meet the challenges of a new era.
3 Goal and Objective
State the desired goal
State the desired objective
Use multiple points if necessary
4 Today's Situation

Figure 10. *Click a slide icon to select all the text on the slide.*

Replacing Existing Text

If you use the AutoContent Wizard to obtain one of the sample outlines, you must replace the sample text with your own.

1. Click a bullet to select a bulleted text line. **(Figure 8)**

   or

   Triple-click anywhere on a bulleted text line.

2. Type replacement text. **(Figure 9)**

✔ Tip

- Click a slide icon to select all the text on a slide. Then type replacement text, slide title and all. **(Figure 10)**

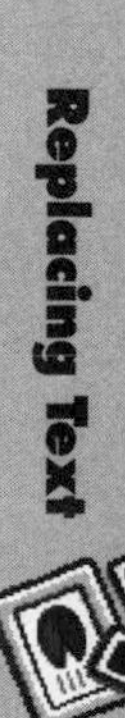
Replacing Text

Reorganizing the Slides

1. Click a slide icon. **(Figure 11)**
2. Drag the icon up or down in the outline. **(Figure 12)**

   or

   Click the Move Up or Move Down buttons on the Outlining toolbar. **(Figure 13)**
3. Release the mouse button to drop the slide at its new position. **(Figure 14)**

✔ Tip

- You can click the bullet at the beginning of a text item and then click the Move Up or Move Down buttons to move an individual line on a single slide.

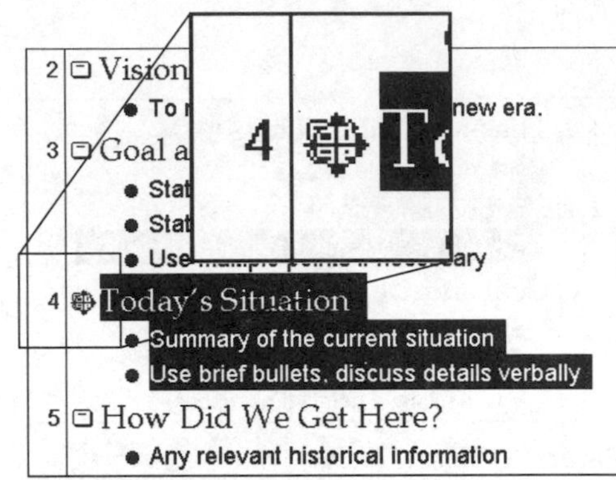

2 Vision
To r
new era.
3 Goal a
4
Stat
Stat
Use
ary
4 Today's Situation
Summary of the current situation
Use brief bullets, discuss details verbally
5 How Did We Get Here?
Any relevant historical information

Figure 11. *Click a slide icon.*

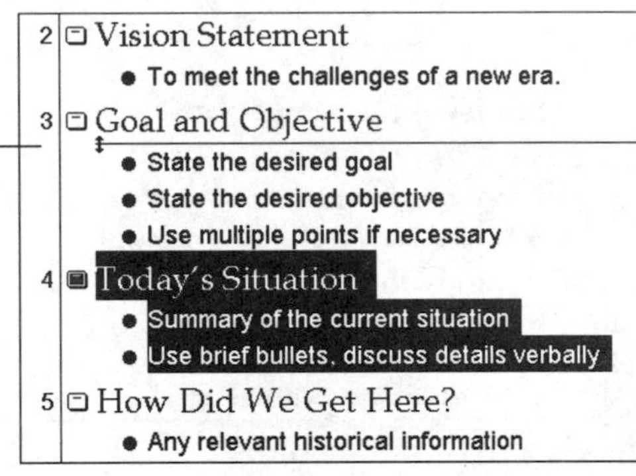

2 Vision Statement
To meet the challenges of a new era.
3 Goal and Objective
State the desired goal
State the desired objective
Use multiple points if necessary
4 Today's Situation
Summary of the current situation
Use brief bullets, discuss details verbally
5 How Did We Get Here?
Any relevant historical information

The double-arrow mouse pointer and line show the proposed destination.

Figure 12. *A horizontal line indicates the new position for the slide.*

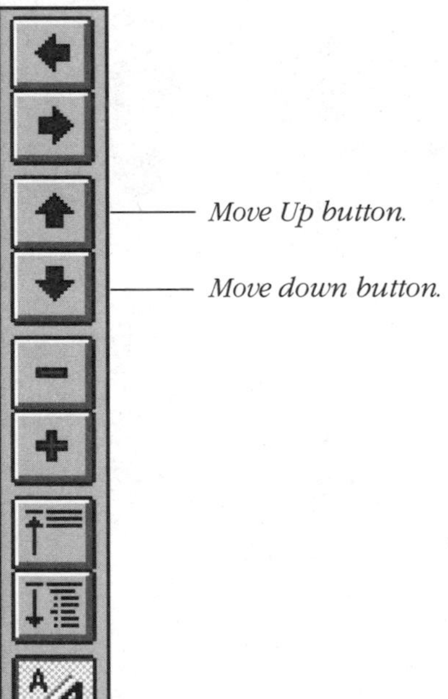

Move Up button.
Move down button.

Figure 13. *The Move Up and Move Down buttons.*

2 Vision Statement
- To meet the challenges of a new era.

3 Today's Situation
- Summary of the current situation
- Use brief bullets, discuss details verbally

4 Goal and Objective
- State the desired goal
- State the desired objective
- Use multiple points if necessary

5 How Did We Get Here?
- Any relevant historical information

Figure 14. *Release the mouse button to drop the slide text.*

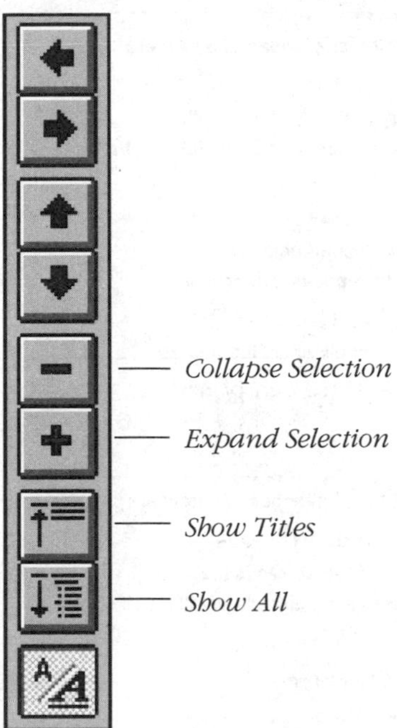
Collapse Selection
Expand Selection
Show Titles
Show All

Figure 15. *The Outlining toolbar.*

Showing Only the Slide Titles

Show only the slide titles to temporarily disregard the detail in an outline.

1. Click the Show Titles button on the Outlining toolbar. **(Figure 15)**

✔ **Tips**

- To once again reveal the text on the slides, click the Show All button on the Outlining toolbar. **(Figure 15)**
- To hide or reveal text on a single slide, click the slide icon and then click the Collapse Selection button on the Outlining toolbar. **(Figure 17)** To see the text again, click the Expand Selection button.

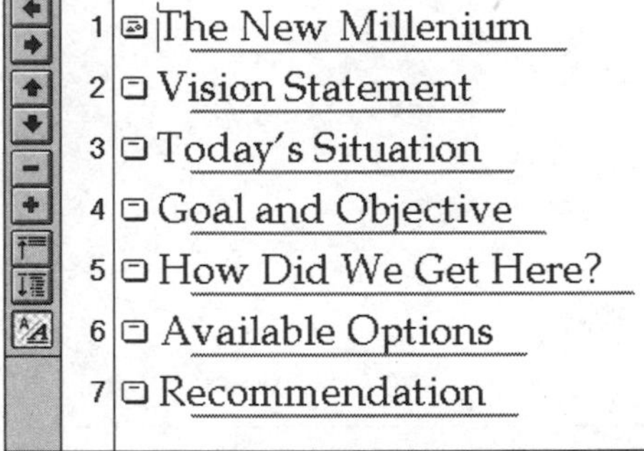
1 The New Millenium
2 Vision Statement
3 Today's Situation
4 Goal and Objective
5 How Did We Get Here?
6 Available Options
7 Recommendation

Figure 16. *Lines under the slide titles indicate that text is collapsed underneath.*

3 Today's Situation
• Summary of the current situation
• Use brief bullets, discuss details verbally
4 Goal and Objective
• State the desired goal
• State the desired objective
• Use multiple points if necessary
5 How Did We Get Here?
• Any relevant historical information
3 Today's Situation
• Summary of the current situation
• Use brief bullets, discuss details verbally
4 Goal and Objective
5 How Did We Get Here?
• Any relevant historical information
• Original assumptions that are no longer va
6 Available Options

Figure 17. *Before and After: Collapsing the Goal and Objective text.*

Showing Only Titles

Inserting Slides

1. Click at the end of the last line of a slide. **(Figure 18)**
2. Click the New Slide button. **(Figure 19)**

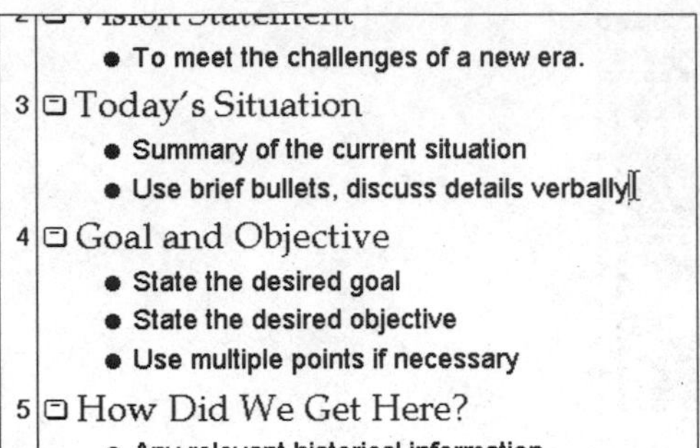
To meet the challenges of a new era.
3 Today's Situation
Summary of the current situation
Use brief bullets, discuss details verbally
4 Goal and Objective
State the desired goal
State the desired objective
Use multiple points if necessary
5 How Did We Get Here?

Figure 18. *Click at the end of a slide.*

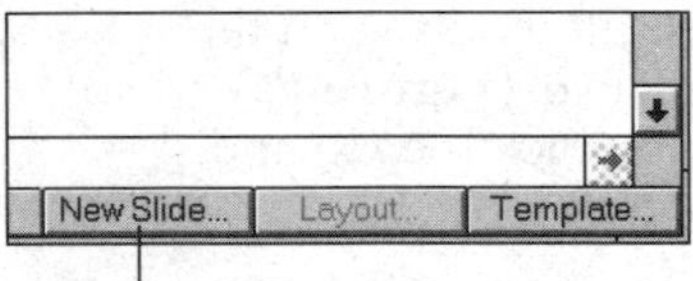
New Slide...
Layout...
Template...

Figure 19. *The New Slide button.*

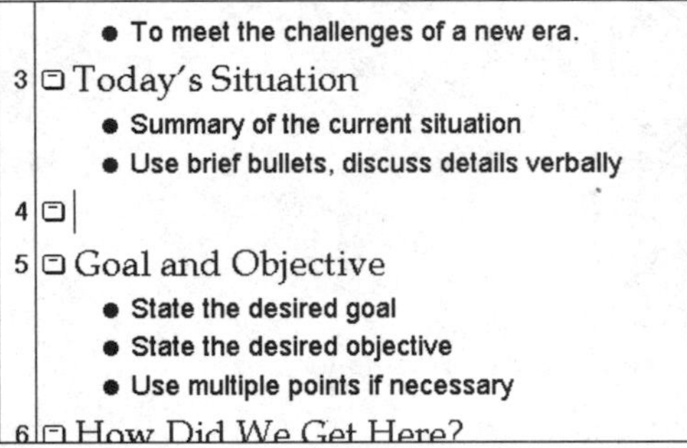
To meet the challenges of a new era.
3 Today's Situation
Summary of the current situation
Use brief bullets, discuss details verbally
4
5 Goal and Objective
State the desired goal
State the desired objective
Use multiple points if necessary

Figure 20. *The new, blank slide appears.*

Deleting Slides

1. Click a slide icon to select an entire slide. **(Figure 21)**
2. Press the Delete key on the keyboard. **(Figure 22)**

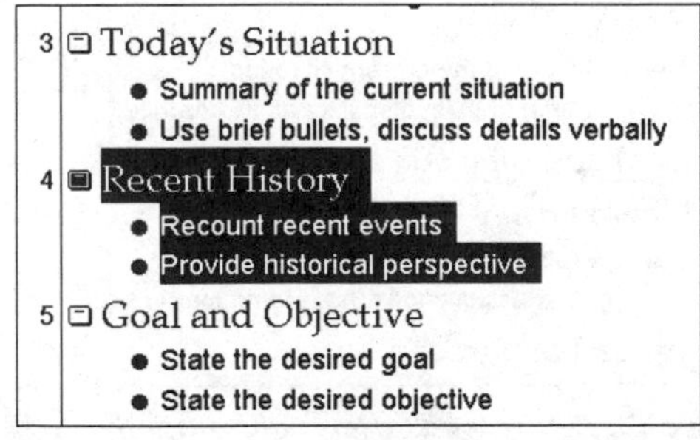
3 Today's Situation
Summary of the current situation
Use brief bullets, discuss details verbally
4 Recent History
Recount recent events
Provide historical perspective
5 Goal and Objective
State the desired goal
State the desired objective

Figure 21. *Click a slide icon and press Delete.*

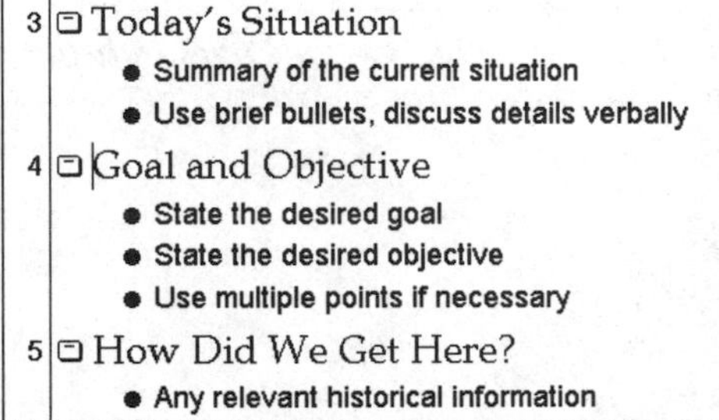
3 Today's Situation
Summary of the current situation
Use brief bullets, discuss details verbally
4 Goal and Objective
State the desired goal
State the desired objective
Use multiple points if necessary
5 How Did We Get Here?
Any relevant historical information

Figure 22. *The slide is deleted.*

Creating Text Slides 22

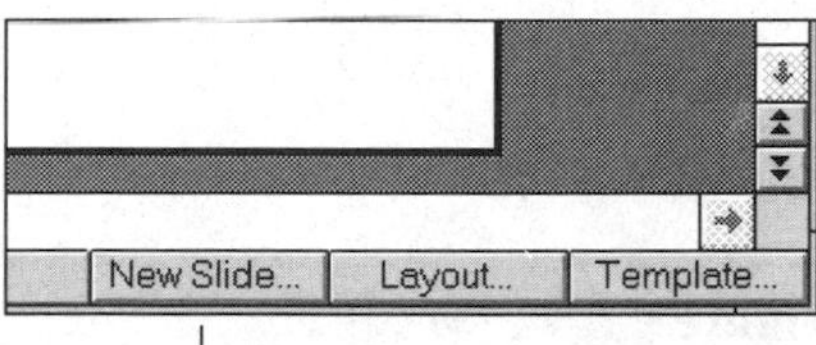

Figure 1. *The New Slide button.*

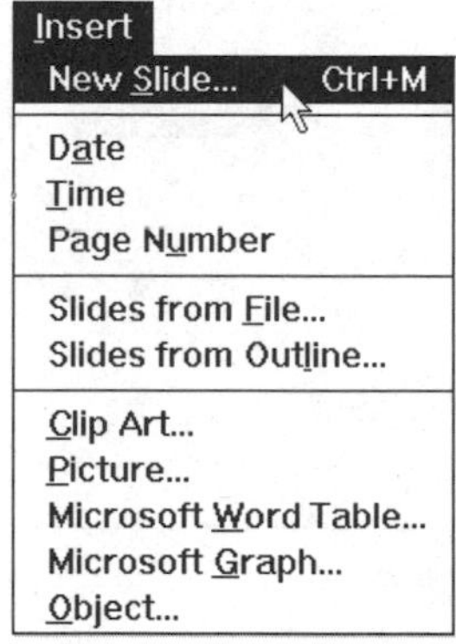

Figure 2. *The Insert menu.*

Starting a Text Slide

If you don't use Outline view to enter the text of slides, you can create text slides in Slide view.

1. In Slide view, click the New Slide button. **(Figure 1)**

   or

   From the Insert menu, choose New Slide. **(Figure 2)**

   or

   Press Ctrl+M.

2. On the New Slide dialog box, choose the second layout, Bulleted List, and then click OK. **(Figures 3–4)**

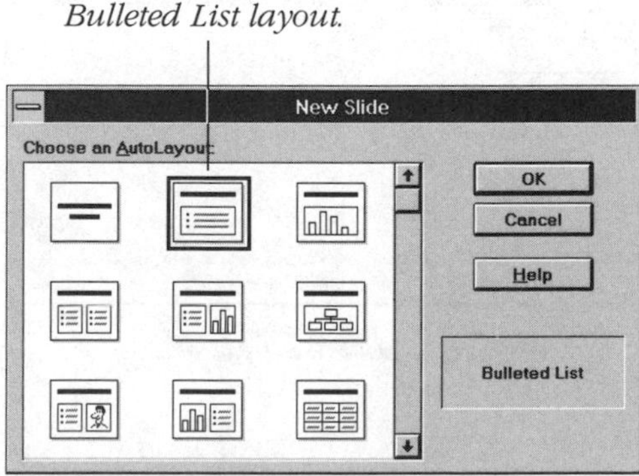

Figure 3. *The New Slide dialog box.*

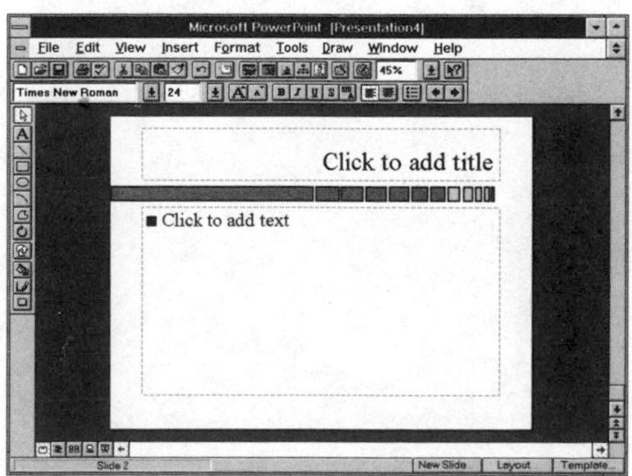

Figure 4. *The Bulleted List layout.*

Filling in Text Placeholders

1. Click a "Click to add title" or "Click to add text" placeholder. **(Figure 5)**
2. Type text. **(Figure 6)**
3. Click the next placeholder and type the next text. **(Figure 7)**

✔ Tips

- When you finish typing text into a placeholder, press Ctrl+Enter to jump to the next placeholder.
- When you finish the text in the last placeholder on the page, you can press Ctrl+Enter to add a new bulleted list slide.

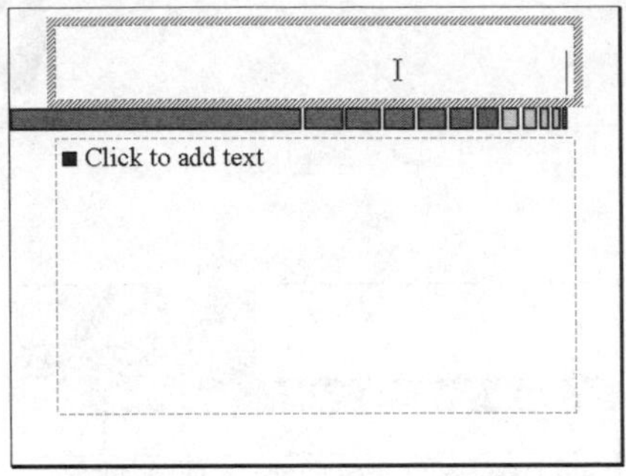

Figure 5. *Click the "Click to add title" placeholder.*

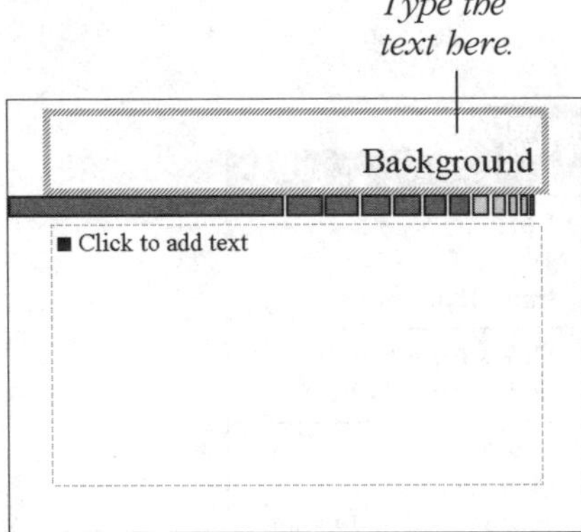

Figure 6. *Type text.*

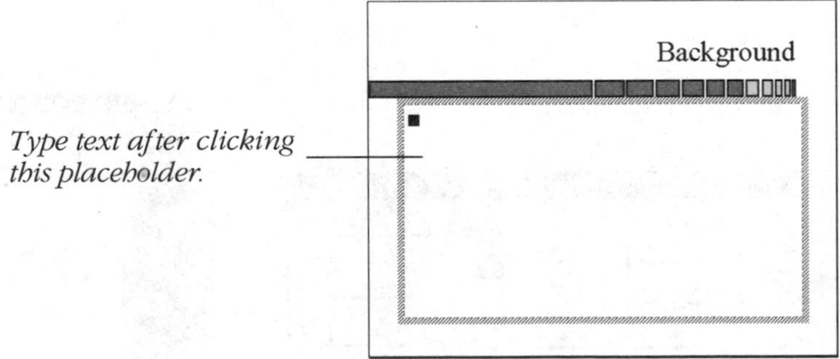

Figure 7. *Click the next text placeholder.*

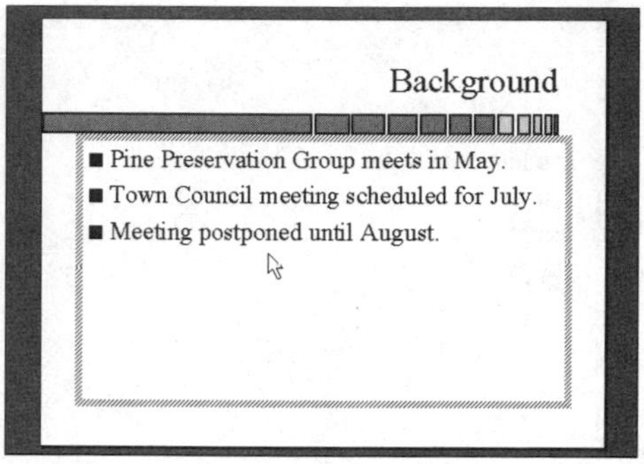

Figure 8. *Click on the text block.*

Selecting Text Blocks

Selecting characters, words, or paragraphs within a text block is just like selecting them in a **Word** document. *See Selecting Text, page 23-25.*

To move or format an entire text block, though, PowerPoint makes it easy to select the entire text block.

1. Click anywhere on a text block. **(Figure 8)**
2. Click on the border surrounding the text block. Handles appear. **(Figures 9-10)**

✔ Tips

- Click within a selected text block to select text within the block.
- To select a bulleted item in a text block, click the bullet.

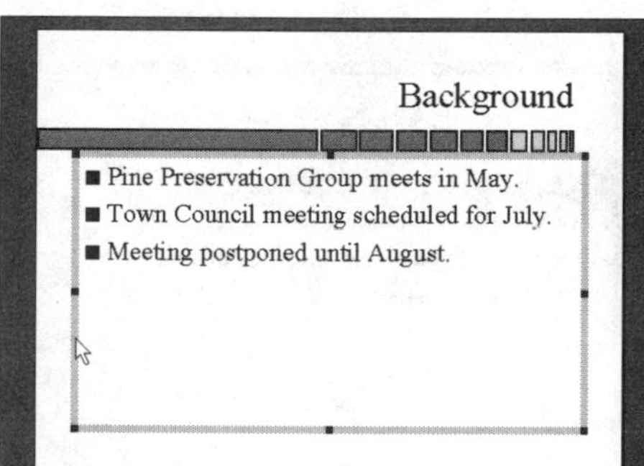

Figure 9. *Click on a border.*

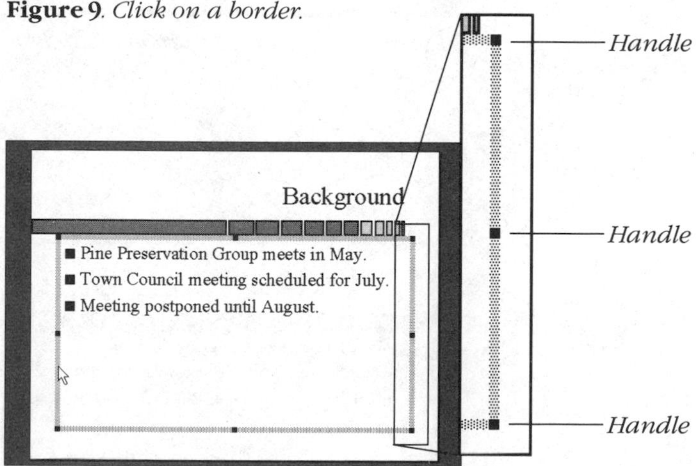

Figure 10. *Handles appear.*

Moving and Resizing Text Blocks

1. To move a selected text block, place the pointer on the border surrounding a selected text block. **(Figure 11)** *See Selecting Text Blocks, page 185.*

   or

   To resize a text block, place the pointer on a handle. **(Figure 12)**
2. Hold down the mouse button and drag the mouse. **(Figure 13)**

✔ Tips

- The text inside a text block re-wraps to fit within the new size of the block.
- Hold down the Ctrl key as you resize a text block to resize the block about its center.

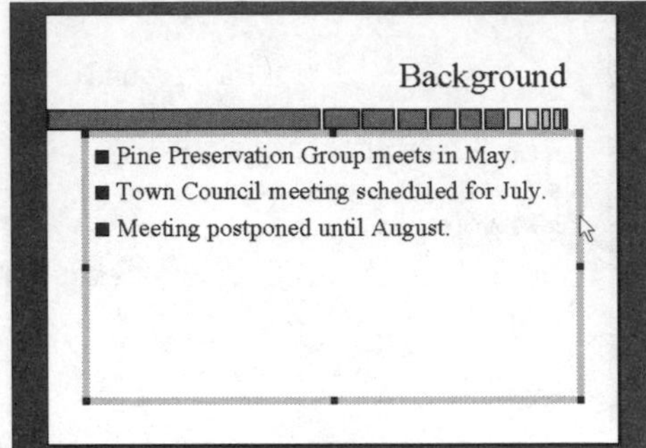

Figure 11. *Place the pointer on the border.*

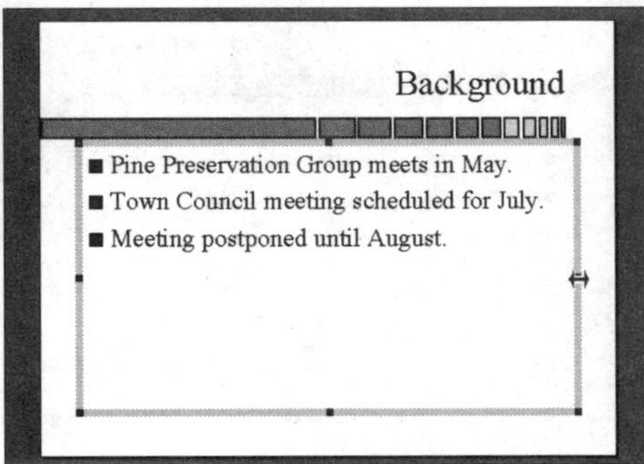

Figure 12. *Place the pointer on a handle.*

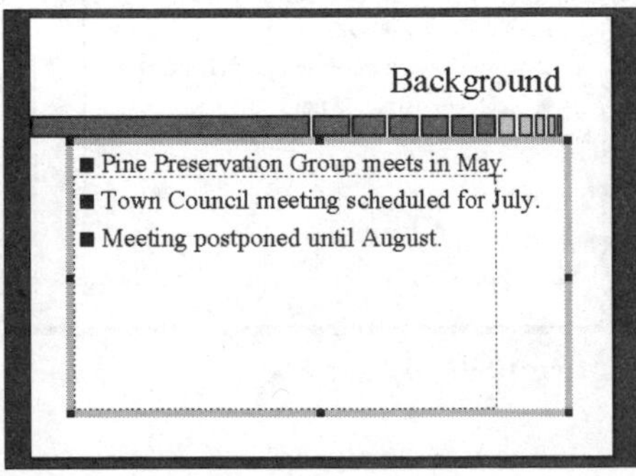

Figure 13. *Drag the handle to resize a text block.*

Formatting Text

1. Select the text within a text block to format. **(Figure 14)**
   or
   Select the text block to format.
2. Click a text formatting button on the Formatting toolbar. **(Figure 15)** *See Font Formatting, pages 55-60.*
   or
   From the Format menu, choose Font, Bullet, Alignment, Line Spacing, or Change Case and make selections on the next dialog box to appear. **(Figure 16)**
   or
   Click the right mouse button and choose Font or Bullet from the shortcut menu. Then make selections on the Font or Bullet dialog box. **(Figures 17-18)**

✔ Tips

- Any text formatting changes you make are preserved when you choose a different template to change the overall design of the presentation.
- To quickly add periods to the ends of all bulleted lines in a text block, select the block and choose Periods from the Format menu. Then select Add Periods or Remove Periods from the Periods dialog box.

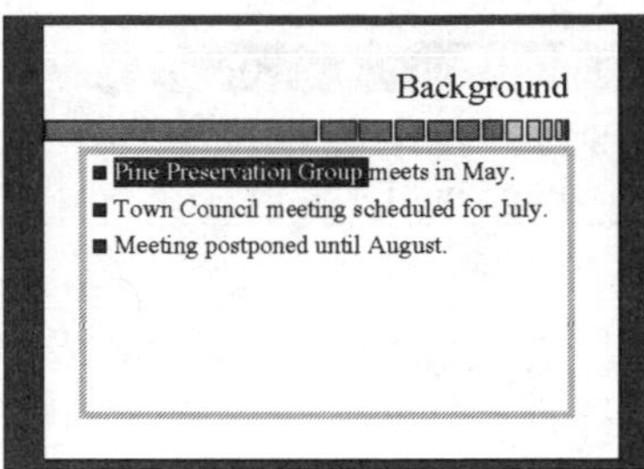

Figure 14. *Select text to format.*

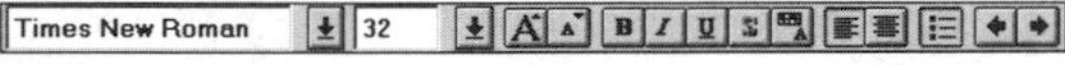

Figure 15. *The Formatting toolbar.*

Figure 16. *The Format menu.*

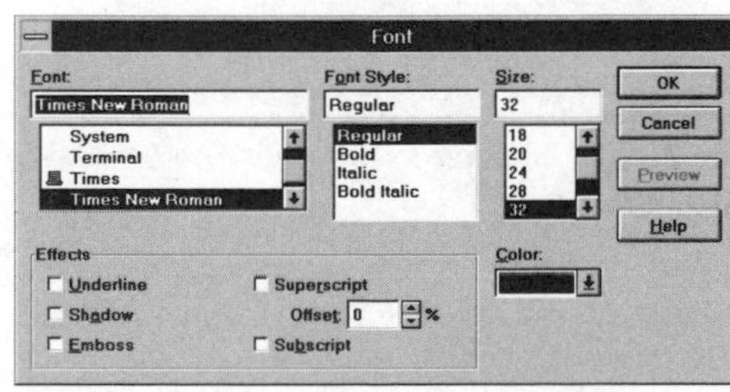

Figure 17. *The Font dialog box.*

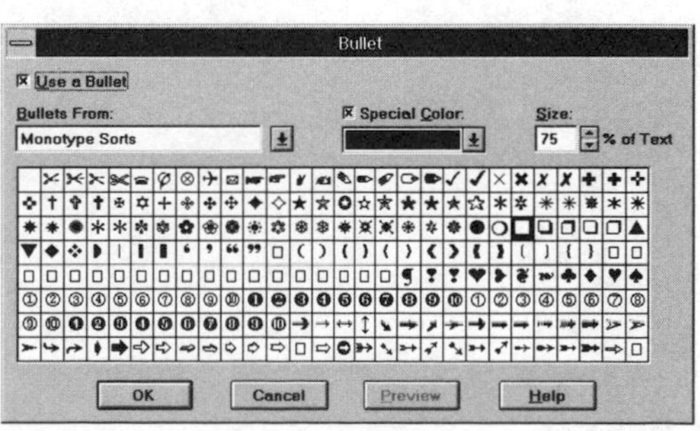

Figure 18. *The Bullet dialog box.*

Rearranging Text in a Block

1. Drag the bullet at the beginning of a text item up, down, left, or right to change the position of the text item within the block. **(Figures 19-20)**

   or

   Click on a bulleted text item and press Alt+Shift+Arrow key to move the text item up, down, left, or right.

✔ Tips

- When you move a text item to the right, it appears to be indented under the previous text item. **(Figure 21)**
- When you move a text item to the left or right, you move the text item to a different level. Each level may have a different default text format and bullet style.

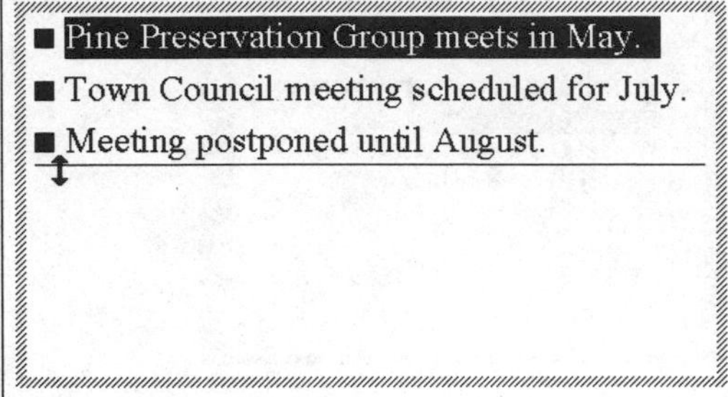

Figure 19. *Drag the bullet at the beginning of a text item.*

■ Town Council meeting scheduled for July.
■ Meeting postponed until August.
■ Pine Preservation Group meets in May.

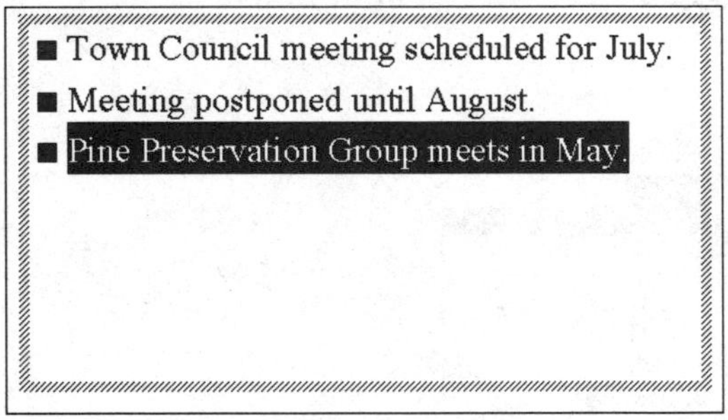

Figure 20. *The text dragged to its new location.*

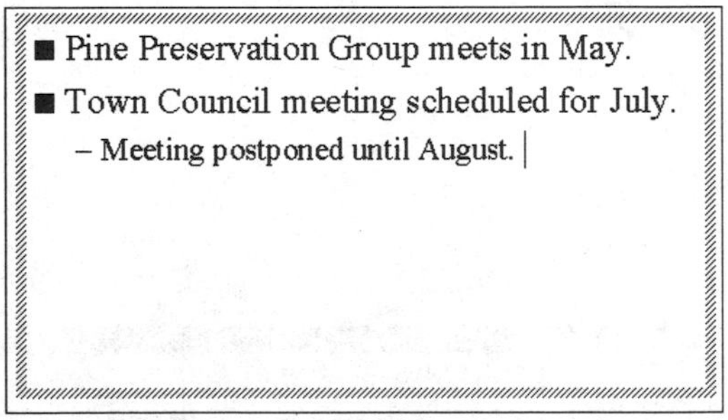

■ Pine Preservation Group meets in May.
■ Town Council meeting scheduled for July.
– Meeting postponed until August.

Figure 21. *Text moved to the right one level appears indented.*

Creating Graph Slides 23

Choose one of these three layouts.

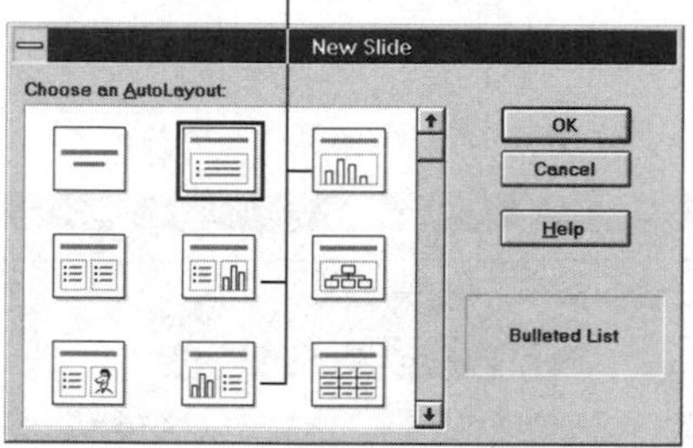

Figure 1. *The New Slide dialog box.*

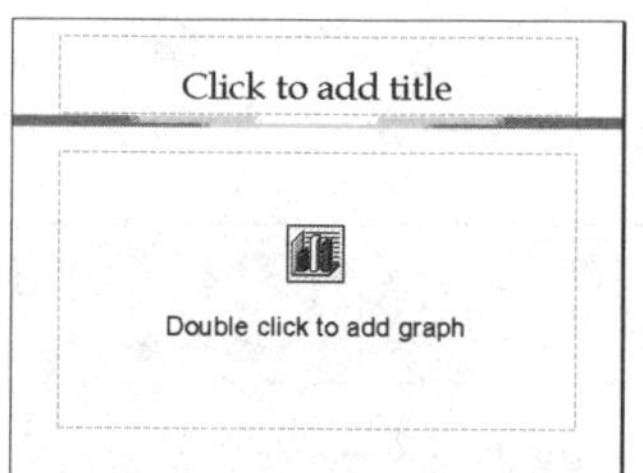

Figure 2. *Double click a graph placeholder.*

Insert Graph button.

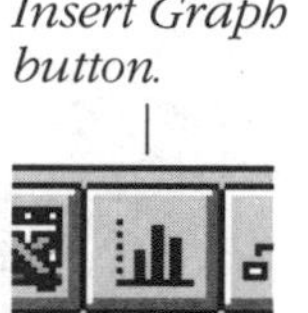

Figure 3. *The Insert Graph button.*

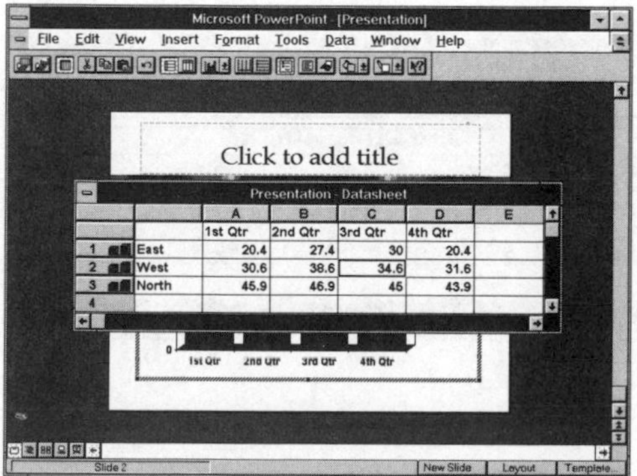

Figure 4. *A sample graph and datasheet appear within a border on the current slide.*

About Graphing

When chosen wisely, a graph can make even complex numeric information visual and therefore easy to interpret and communicate.

To create or edit a graph, PowerPoint uses Graph 5, the same graphing module used by Excel. Graph 5 creates a *chart*, and while doing so commandeers the PowerPoint window, replacing PowerPoint's menus and toolbars with its own. When you click outside the border of the completed chart, the PowerPoint menus and toolbars reappear.

Starting a Chart

1. Click the New Slide button.
2. On the New Slide dialog box, choose one of the three layouts that includes a graph placeholder (Graph, Text & Graph, Graph & Text.) **(Figure 1)**
3. Double-click the "Double click to add graph" placeholder. **(Figure 2)**

   or

1. Turn to the slide to which you'd like to add a graph.
2. Click the Insert Graph button on the Standard toolbar. **(Figure 3)**

   or

   From the Insert menu, choose Microsoft Graph.

Replacing the Sample Data on the Data Sheet

1. Click any cell in the Excel-like grid and type over its contents. **(Figure 5)**

   or

   Select all the cells that contain data and begin typing new data in columns. Press Enter after typing each new heading or number. When the cell pointer reaches the bottom of a column, it jumps to the top of the next column automatically. **(Figure 6)**

2. Click the View Datasheet button in the Graph toolbar to close the datasheet and view the graph. **(Figure 7)**

   or

   Click any part of the graph that is visible.

✓ Tip

- To exclude a row or column of data from the graph, double-click the row or column heading button. **(Figure 8)**

Presentation - Datasheet

		A	B	C	D	E
		1st Qtr	2nd Qtr	3rd Qtr	4th Qtr	
1	East	20.4	27.4	30	20.4	
2	West	30.6	38.6	34.6	31.6	
3	North	45.9	46.9	45	43.9	
4						

Figure 5. *The data sheet.*

The cell pointer.

Presentation - Datasheet

		A	B	C	D	E
		1st Qtr	2nd Qtr	3rd Qtr	4th Qtr	
1	East	20.4	27.4	30	20.4	
2	West	30.6	38.6	34.6	31.6	
3	North	45.9	46.9	45	43.9	
4						

Figure 6. *Select the cells that contain data to replace.*

The View Datasheet button.

Figure 7. *The View Datasheet button.*

Column heading buttons.

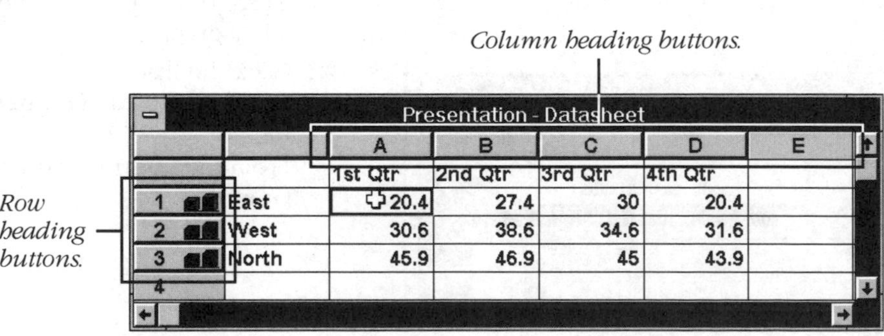

		A	B	C	D	E
		1st Qtr	2nd Qtr	3rd Qtr	4th Qtr	
1	East	20.4	27.4	30	20.4	
2	West	30.6	38.6	34.6	31.6	
3	North	45.9	46.9	45	43.9	
4						

Figure 8. *The row and column heading buttons.*

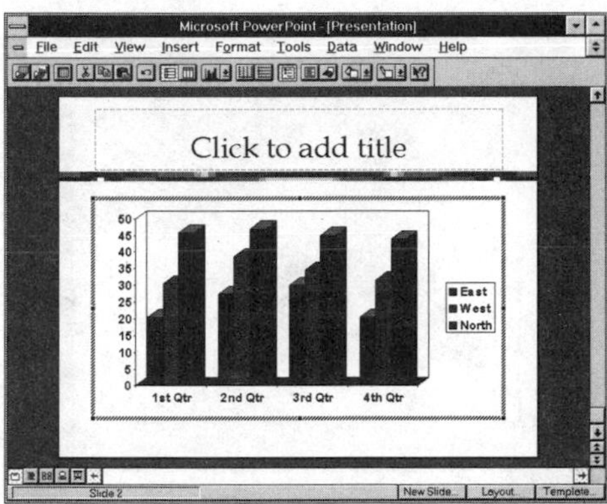

Figure 9. *Double-click the chart to format.*

The Chart Type button.

Chart type pane.

Figure 10. *The Chart Type button.*

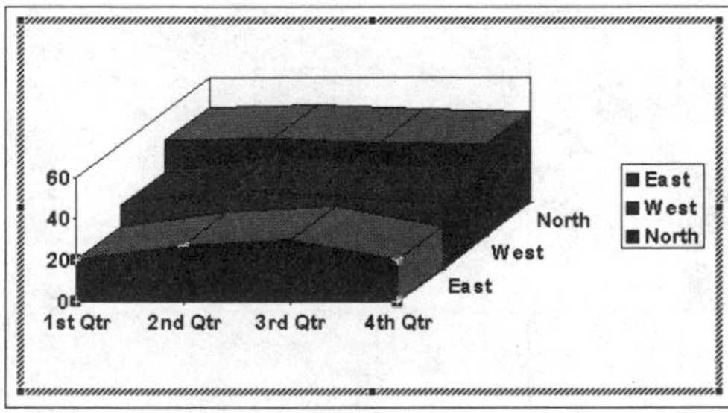

Figure 11. *The modified chart.*

Changing the Chart Type

The most basic commands to format a new chart are available as buttons on the Graph toolbar.

1. Double-click the chart if necessary to make it active (surrounded by a thick border). **(Figure 9)**
2. Click the pull-down button next to the the Chart Type button on the Graph toolbar. **(Figure 10)**
3. Click on a chart type pane to change the chart type of the chart.

✔ Tips

- Choosing an AutoFormat for the chart gives you many more chart type options. *See Choosing an AutoFormat, on the next page.*
- You can create a Chart Type toolbar by positioning the pointer on the pull-down Chart Type button, holding down the mouse button, and then dragging to another point on the screen.

Choosing an AutoFormat

Choosing an AutoFormat for a chart is a shortcut for formatting the chart. An AutoFormat specifies a chart type and sets many chart formatting options automatically.

1. Double-click the chart if necessary to make it active. **(Figure 12)**
2. From the Format menu, choose AutoFormat. **(Figure 13)**
3. Select a chart type from the Galleries list. **(Figure 14)**
4. Double-click on one of the numbered panes which display charts with various option settings. **(Figure 14)**

✓ Tips

- Click User-Defined on the AutoFormat dialog box to choose one of the special chart formats you've created and added to the selection.
- To add a chart format, format a chart manually and select the chart. Then, on the AutoFormat dialog box, choose User-Defined and click the Add button.

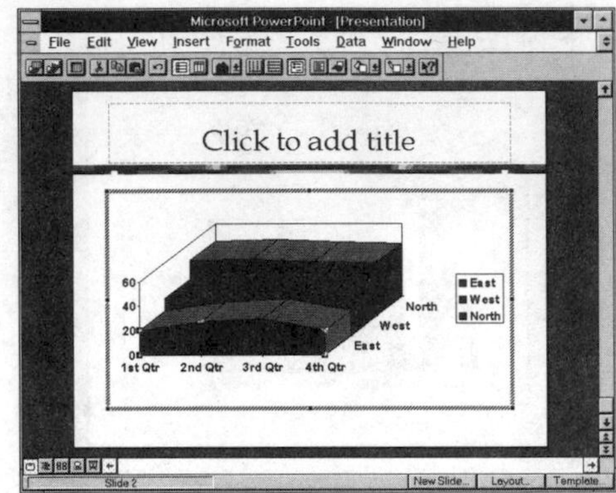

Figure 12. *Double-click the chart to format.*

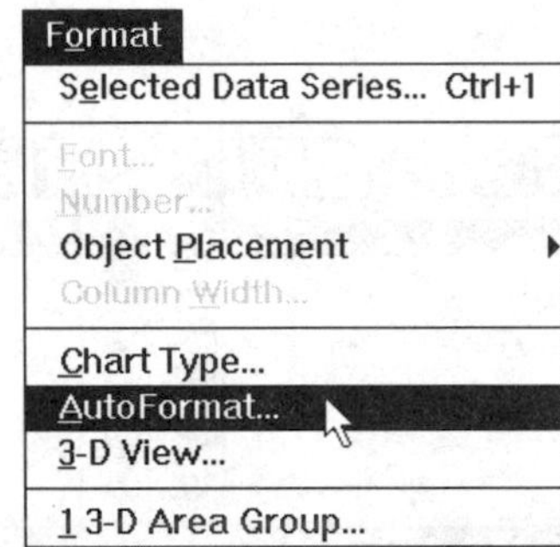

Figure 13. *The Format menu.*

...and select a format here.

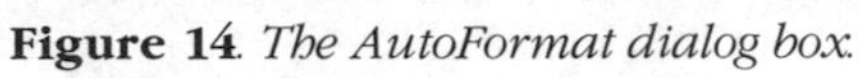

Figure 14. *The AutoFormat dialog box.*

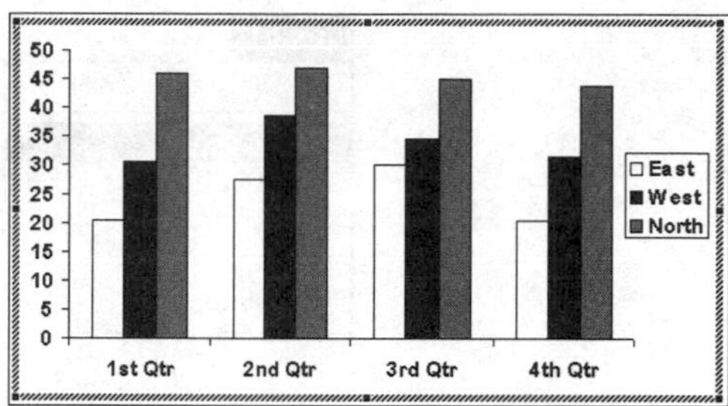

Figure 15. *Double-click the chart to format.*

Displaying a Legend and Grid Lines

1. Double-click the chart to make it active, if necessary. **(Figure 15)**
2. To turn the legend on or off, click the Legend button on the Graph toolbar. **(Figure 16)**

   or

   To turn the grid lines on or off, click the Vertical Gridlines and/or Horizontal Gridlines buttons on the Graph toolbar. **(Figure 16)**

✔ Tips

- You can also add a legend or gridlines by selecting Legend or Gridlines from the Insert menu.
- When you add gridlines from the Insert menu, you can choose Major Gridlines or Minor Gridlines for each axis. **(Figure 17)**

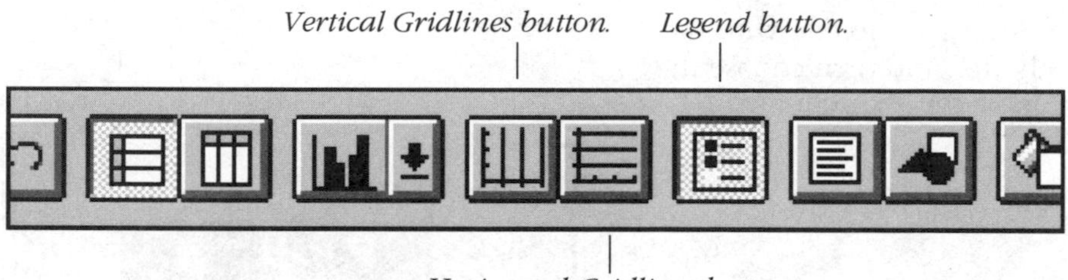

Figure 16. *The Graph toolbar.*

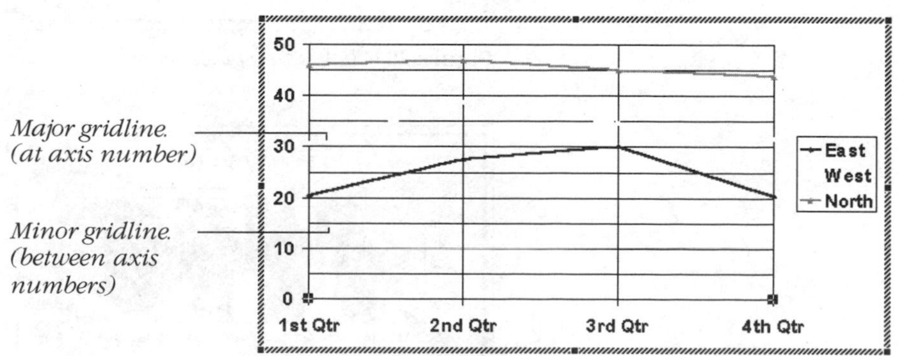

Figure 17. *Major vs. Minor Gridlines.*

Adding Chart Titles

1. Double-click the chart to make it active, if necessary.
2. From the Insert menu, choose Titles. **(Figure 18)**
   or
   Click within the chart border with the right mouse button and choose Insert Titles from the shortcut menu.
3. On the Titles dialog box, click the checkboxes for the titles you'd like to add. **(Figure 19)**
4. On the chart, click a title placeholder and then type the new title. **(Figures 20–21)**

✔ Tips

- To remove a title, choose Titles from the Insert menu again and then, on the Titles dialog box, clear the checkbox for the title to remove.
- To format a title, click the title with the right mouse button and then choose the Format option on the shortcut menu.

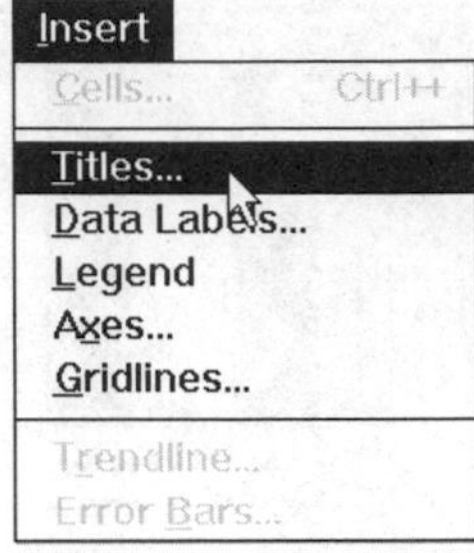

Figure 18. *The Insert menu.*

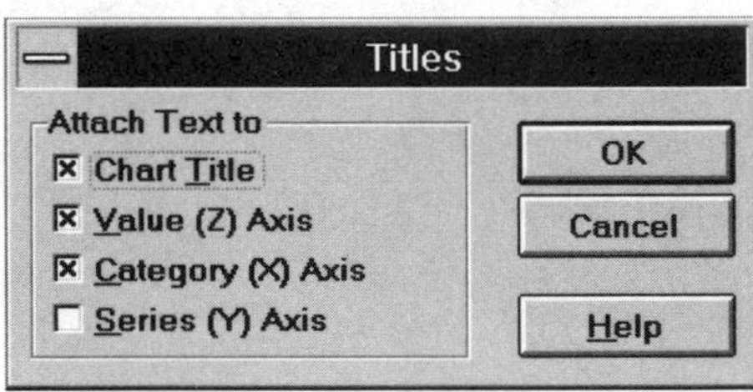

Figure 19. *The Titles dialog box.*

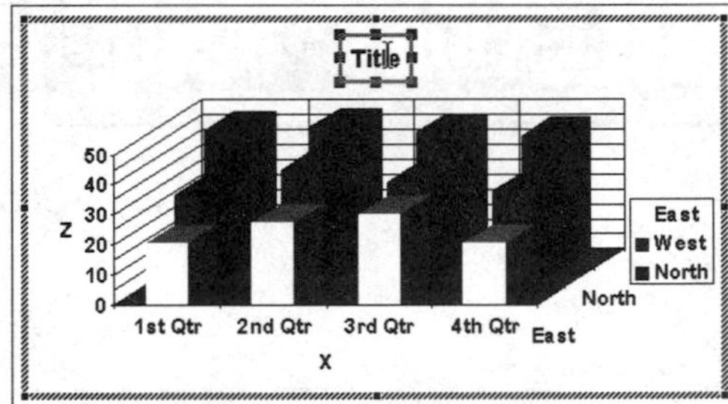

Figure 20. *Click a title placeholder...*

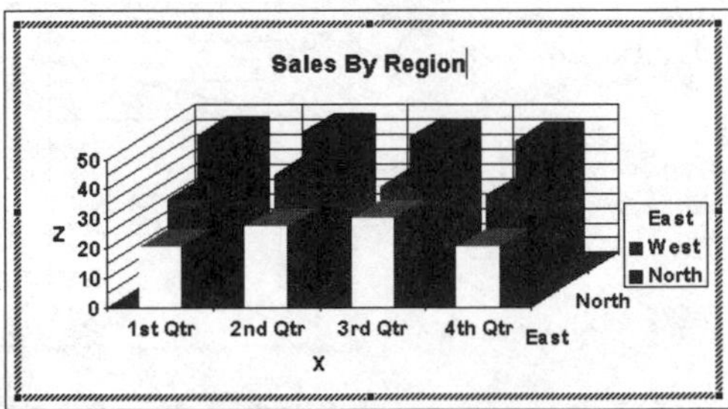

Figure 21. *...and then type the new title.*

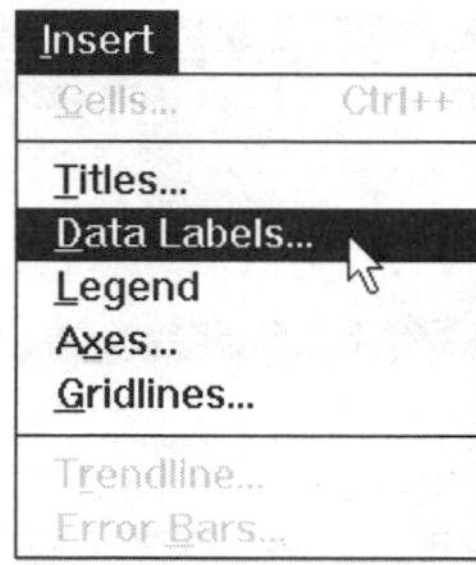

Figure 22. *The Insert menu.*

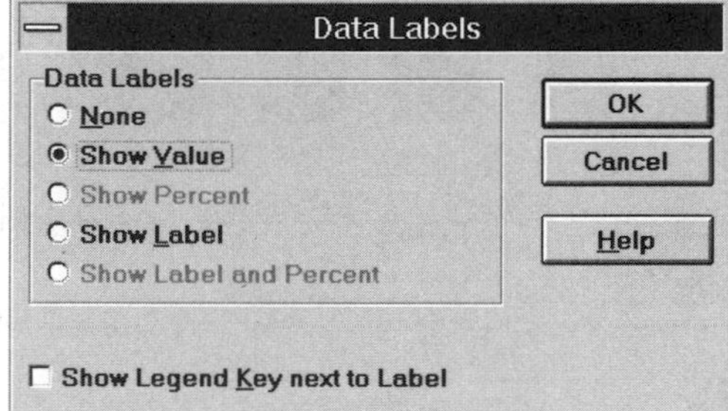

Figure 23. *The Data Labels dialog box.*

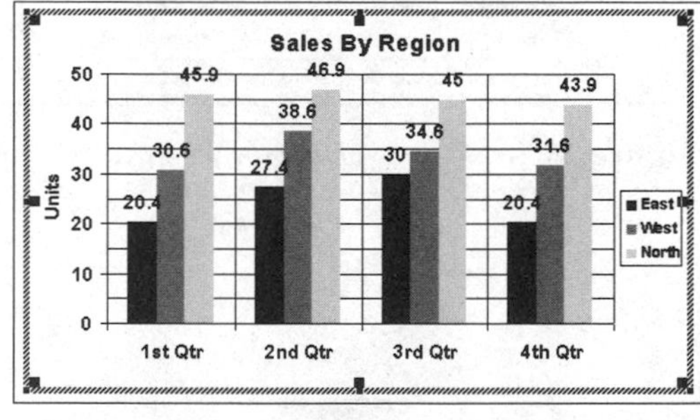

Figure 24. *Data Labels on all series.*

Adding Data Labels

To turn on data labels for every series in the chart:

1. Double-click the chart if necessary to make it active.
2. From the Insert menu, choose Data Labels. **(Figure 22)**

   or

   Click within the chart border with the right mouse button and choose Insert Data Labels from the shortcut menu.
3. On the Data Labels dialog box, choose one of the options other than None and click OK. **(Figures 23-24)**

To turn on data labels for a single series:

1. Click one set of bars, one line, one pie slice, or similar chart element. **(Figure 25)**
2. Follow Steps 2 and 3 above.

✔ **Tips**

- To remove data labels, choose None on the Data Labels dialog box.
- To format data labels, double-click the series to which they are attached and then make changes on the Data Labels tab of the Format Data Series dialog box.

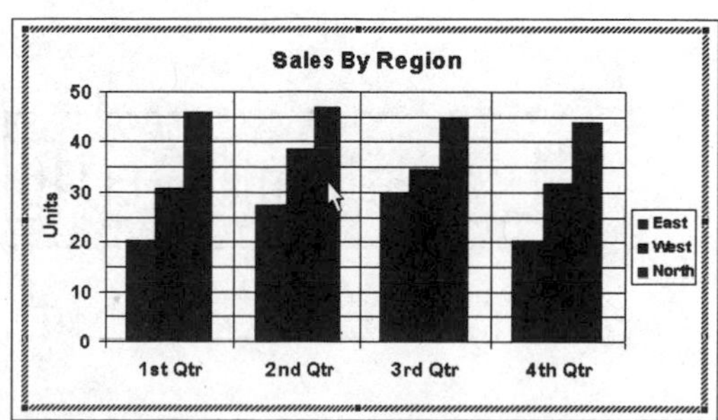

Figure 25. *Select one series before turning on data labels.*

By Rows vs. By Columns

The sets of data that you need to chart are arranged either in rows or in columns on the data sheet. **(Figures 26-28)** To inform Graph how your data is arranged, click the By Rows or By Columns button.

1. Double-click the chart if necessary to make it active.
2. Click the By Columns or By Rows button. **(Figure 29)**

   or

   From the Data menu, choose Series in Rows or Series in Columns. **(Figure 30)**

✔ Tip

- Choosing an alternate view of the data (By Rows rather than By Columns, or vice versa) is legitimate only when both the columns and rows of the datasheet hold related series of data.

Presentation - Datasheet

		A	B	C	D	E
		1st Qtr	2nd Qtr	3rd Qtr	4th Qtr	
1	East	20.4	27.4	30	20.4	
2	West	30.6	38.6	34.6	31.6	
3	North	45.9	46.9	45	43.9	
4						

Figure 26. *The datasheet.*

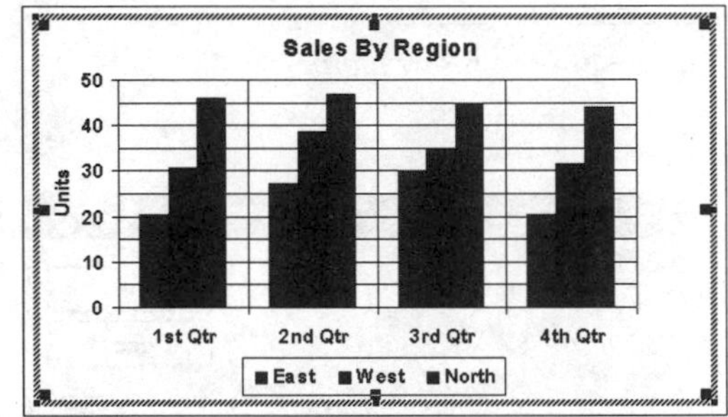

Figure 27. *Data charted by rows.*

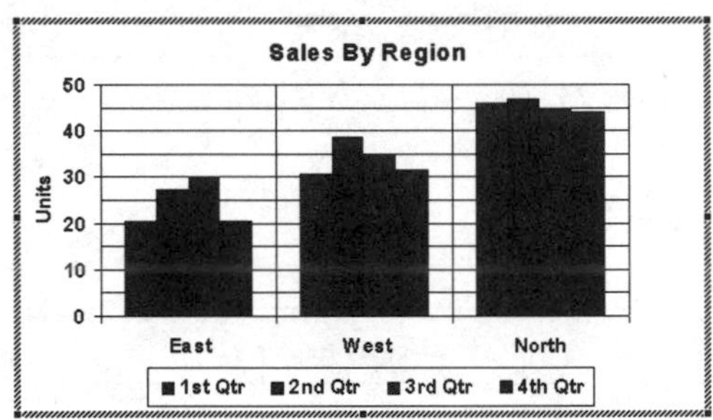

Figure 28. *Same data charted by columns.*

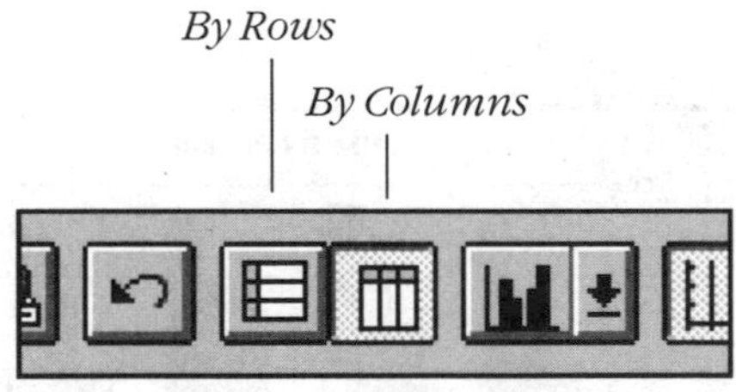

Figure 29. *The By Columns and By Rows buttons.*

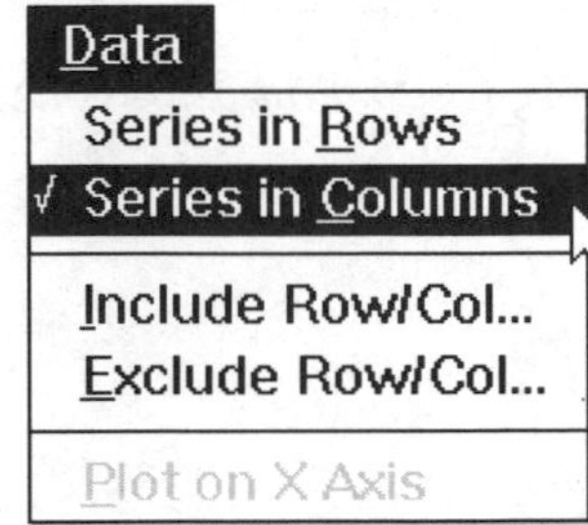

Figure 30. *The Data menu.*

By Rows vs By Columns

Power-Point

Formatting Charts

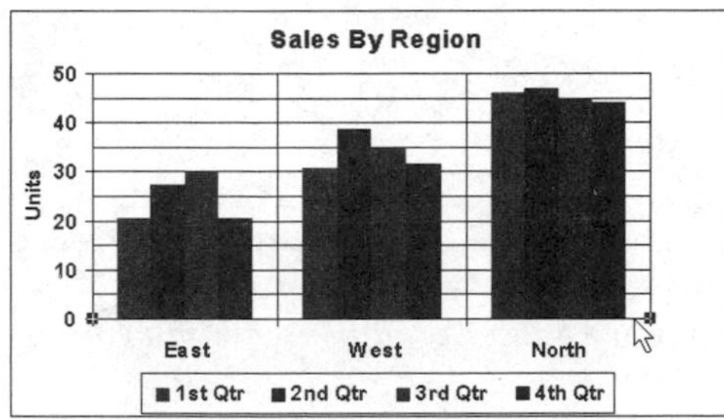

Figure 1. *Double-click an axis to format the axis.*

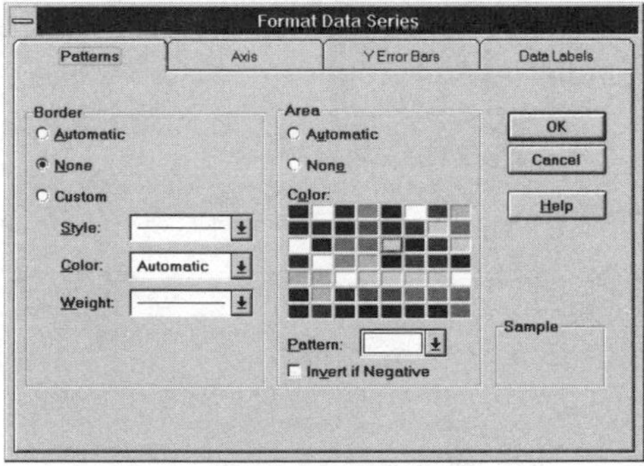

Figure 2. *The Format Data Series dialog box has four tabs of settings.*

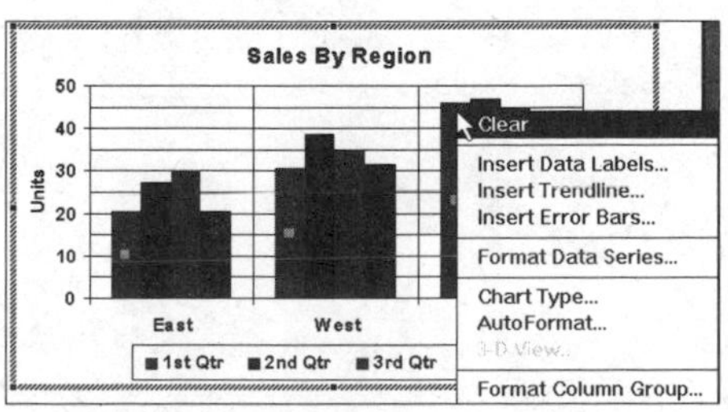

Figure 3. *The shortcut menu.*

About Chart Formatting

The easiest way to change the overall appearance of a chart is to choose a different AutoFormat. *See Choosing an AutoFormat, page 192.* You can also format the appearance of an individual element of the chart (one set of bars, one line, an axis, etc.) or change the style of the series in the chart by formatting a *series group*.

Formatting a Chart Element

1. Double-click the chart if necessary to make it active.
2. Double-click the chart element to format. **(Figure 1)**
3. On the Format dialog box, choose formatting settings on the appropriate tab or tabs. **(Figure 2)**

or

1. Select a chart element by clicking it.
2. Click the right mouse button to summon the shortcut menu. **(Figure 3)**
3. Choose the Format command that will format the chart element you've selected.
4. On the Format dialog box, choose formatting settings on the appropriate tab or tabs.

✔ Tips

- You can also select a chart element and then press Ctrl+1 or choose the first command on the Format menu, which reads "Selected *Chart Element*."
- After you format one chart element, you can double-click a different chart element to format.

Formatting a Group

1. Double-click the chart to make it active, if necessary.
2. At the bottom of the Format menu, choose the Format Group command. **(Figure 4)**

   or

   Click the chart with the right mouse button and choose the Format Group command at the bottom of the shortcut menu. **(Figure 5)**
3. On the Subtype tab of the Format Group dialog box, click the pane that displays the subtype you want. **(Figure 6)**

   or

   Change the settings on the other tabs in the Format Group dialog box.
4. Click OK.

✔ Tip

■ The sample on the Format Group dialog box previews the effect of any setting change.

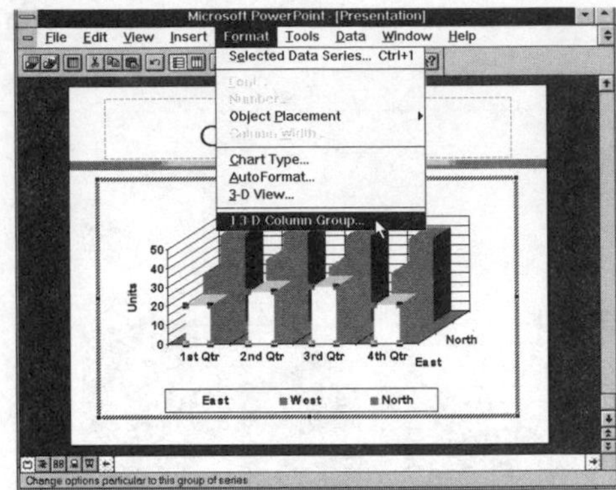

Figure 4. *The Format 3-D Column Group command.*

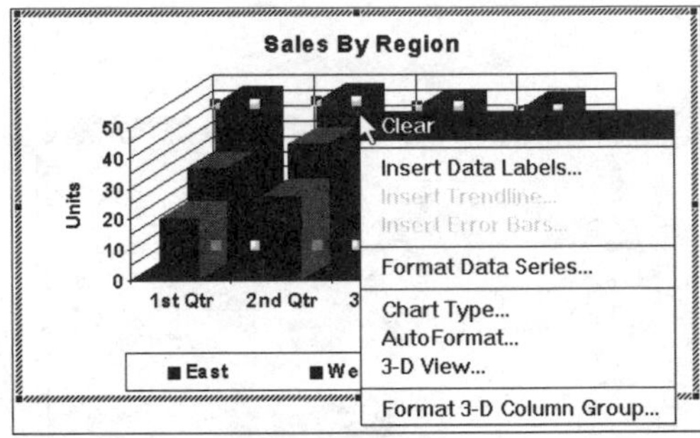

Figure 5. *The shortcut menu.*

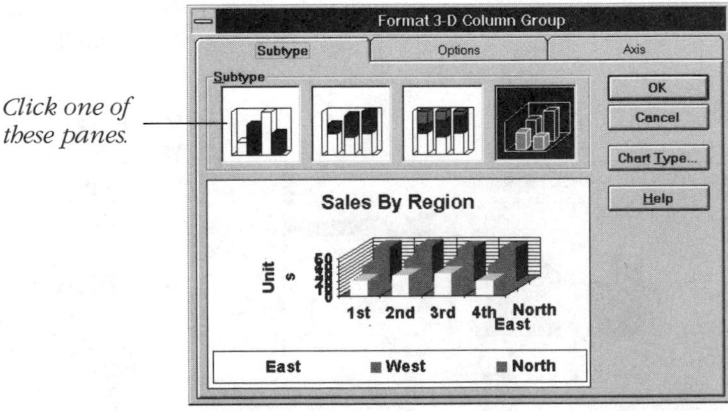

Figure 6. *The Subtype tab for a 3-D Column chart.*

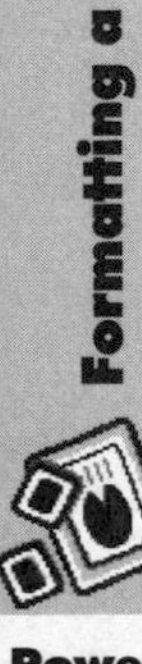

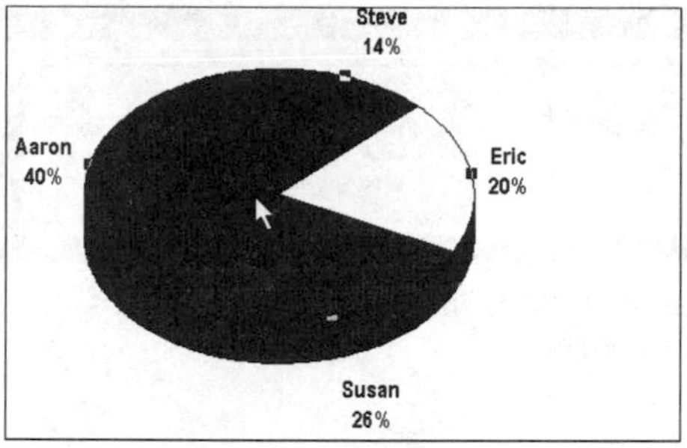

Steve
14%
Aaron
40%
Eric
20%
Susan
26%

Figure 7. *Click the pie.*

Cutting a Pie Chart Slice

1. Double-click the chart to make it active, if necessary.
2. Click the pie once to select the entire pie. **(Figure 7)**
3. Click the slice to cut. **(Figure 8)**
4. Drag the slice away from the pie. **(Figures 9–10)**

✔ Tip

■ To rejoin the slice with the pie, drag the slice back toward the center of the pie.

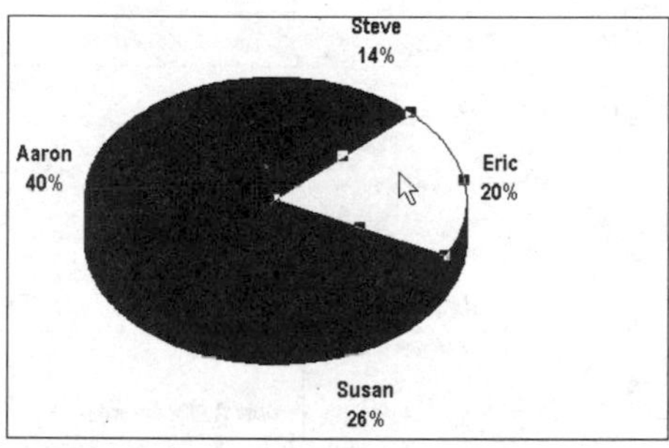

Figure 8. *Click the slice to cut.*

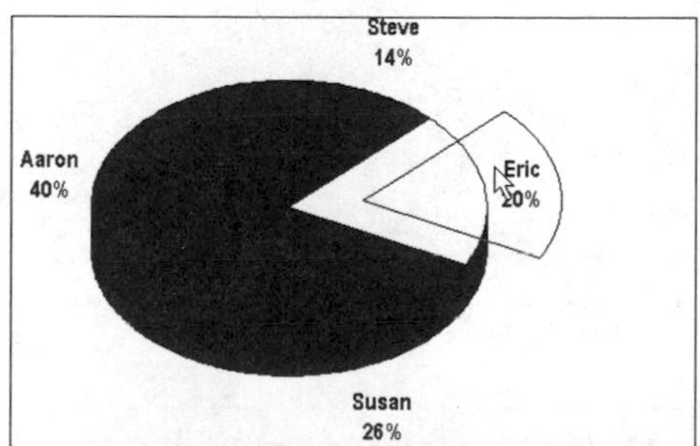

Figure 9. *Drag the slice away from the pie.*

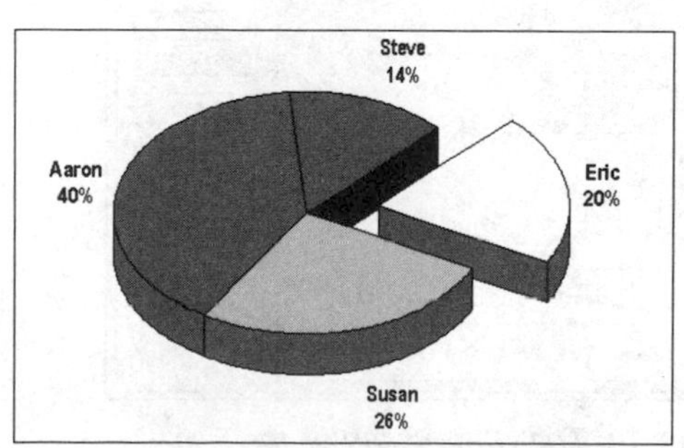

Figure 10. *The cut slice.*

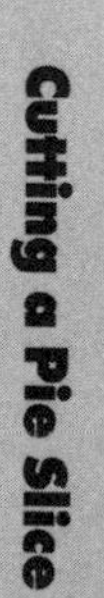

Creating High-Low-Close Charts

1. Double-click the chart to make it active, if necessary.
2. On the datasheet, make sure the data is ordered either High-Low-Close or Open-High-Low-Close. **(Figure 11)**
3. Choose the 2-D Line chart type. **(Figure 12)**
4. From the Format menu, choose Line Group. **(Figure 13)**
5. On the Options tab of the Format Line Group dialog box, turn on Up-Down Bars and High-Low Lines. **(Figure 14)**
6. If you want, double-click each line and then, on the Format Data Series dialog box, set Line to None on the Patterns tab.

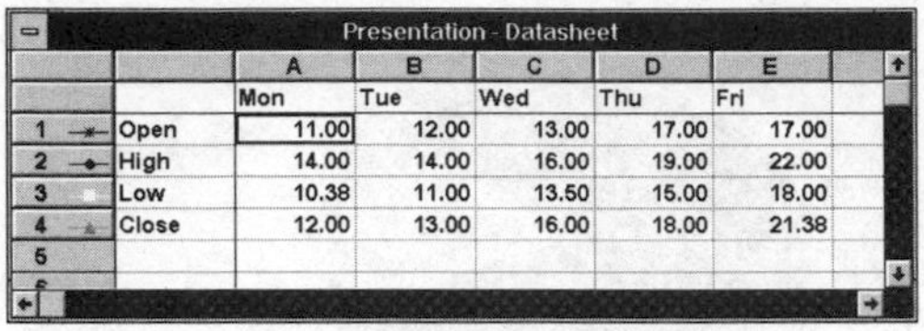

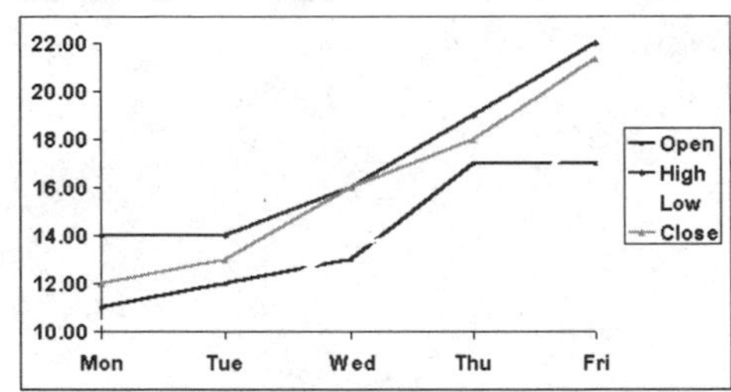

Presentation - Datasheet

		A	B	C	D	E
		Mon	Tue	Wed	Thu	Fri
1	Open	11.00	12.00	13.00	17.00	17.00
2	High	14.00	14.00	16.00	19.00	22.00
3	Low	10.38	11.00	13.50	15.00	18.00
4	Close	12.00	13.00	16.00	18.00	21.38
5						

Figure 11. *The datasheet for a High-Low-Close chart.*

Figure 12. *The 2-D Line chart type.*

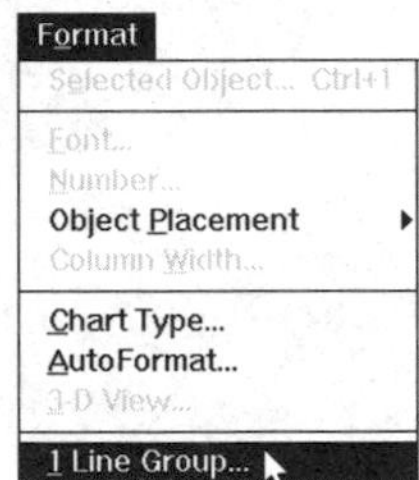

Figure 13. *The Format menu.*

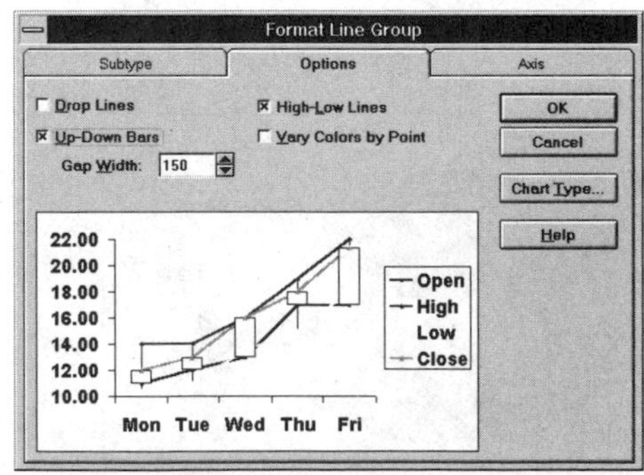

Figure 14. *The Options tab of the Format Line Group dialog box.*

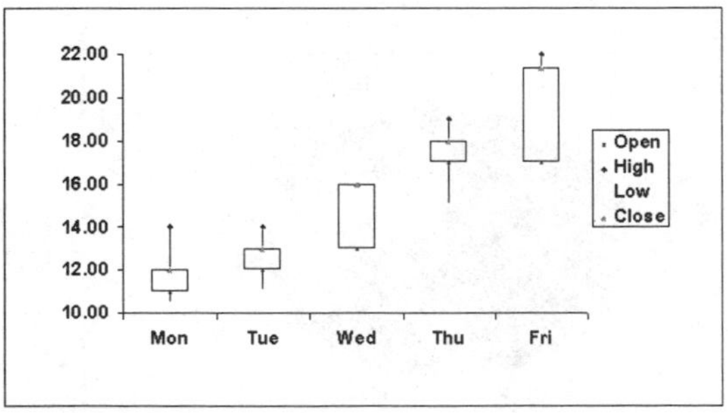

Figure 15. *The High-Low-Close chart.*

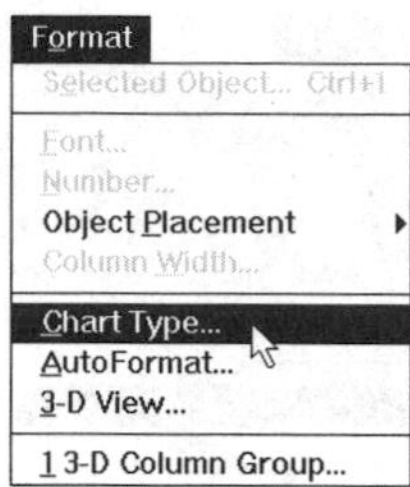

Figure 16. *The Format menu.*

Switching Between 3-D and 2-D Chart Types

1. Double-click the chart to make it active, if necessary.
2. From the Format menu or the shortcut menu, choose Chart Type. **(Figure 16)**
3. On the Chart Type dialog box, click the appropriate Dimension setting, either 2-D or 3-D. **(Figure 17)**
4. Click OK. **(Figure 18)**

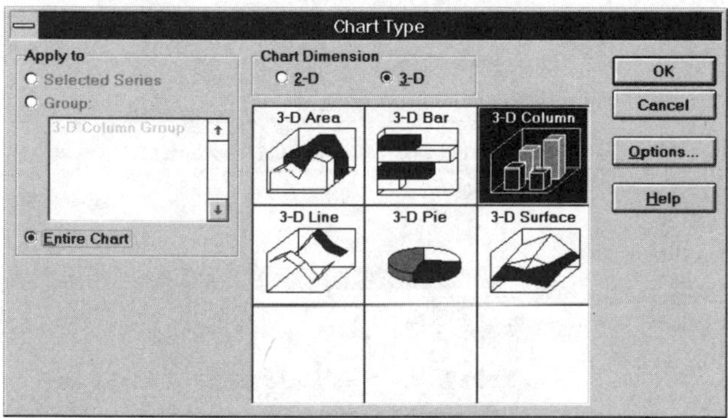

Figure 17. *The Chart Type dialog box.*

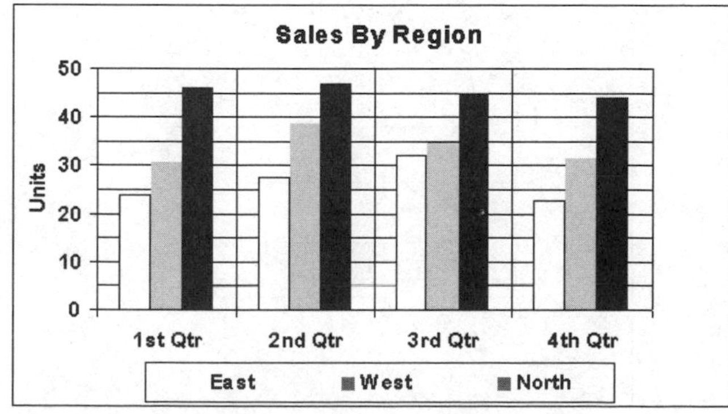

Figure 18. *The 2-D Chart.*

Changing the View of 3D Charts

1. Double-click the chart to make it active, if necessary.
2. From the Format or shortcut menus, choose 3-D View. **(Figure 19)**
3. Click the large buttons on the 3-D View dialog box to rotate the 3-D wireframe model shown on the dialog box. **(Figure 20)**
4. To add perspective, clear the Right Angle Axes checkbox and then click the Perspective buttons to increase or decrease the perspective. **(Figure 21)**
5. Click Apply to apply the 3-D view of the model to your chart.

✔ Tips

- To change the proportions of the chart, clear the Auto Scaling checkbox and change the Height of Base percentage.
- You may prefer to change the 3-D view of a graph by dragging a corner handle of the graph. Release the corner handle when the wireframe representation of the graph is positioned to your liking. **(Figure 22)**

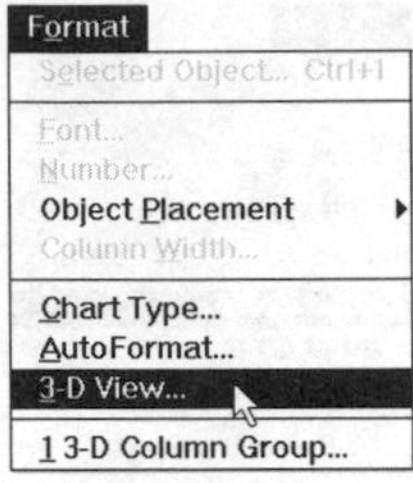

Figure 19. *The Format menu.*

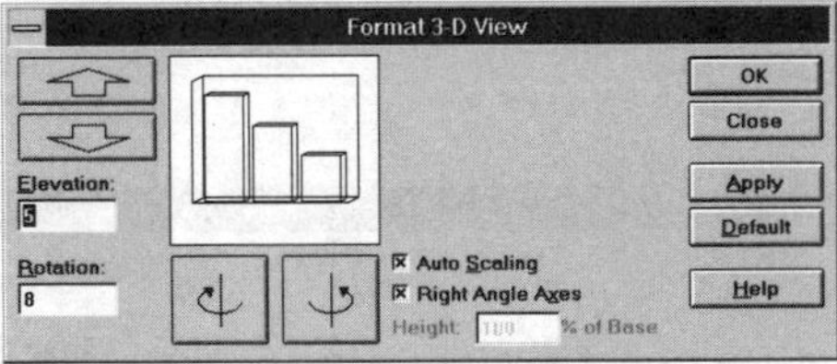

Figure 20. *The Format 3-D View dialog box.*

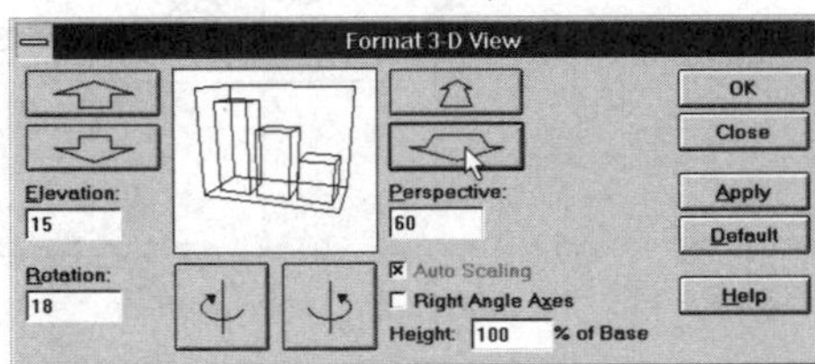

Figure 21. *Adding Perspective.*

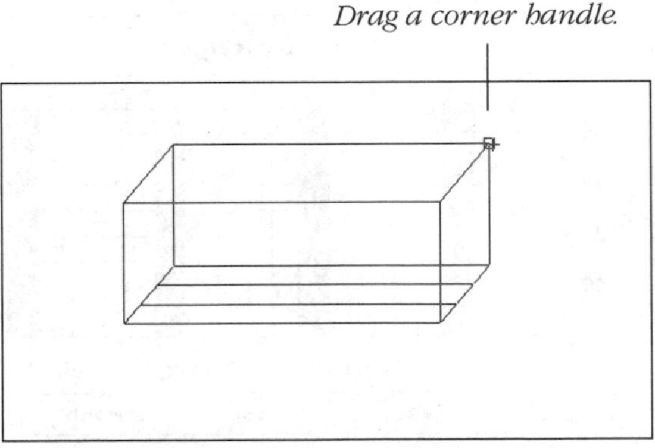

Figure 22. *Dragging a corner handle to rotate a wireframe representation of a 3-D graph.*

Changing the 3-D View

Power-Point

Organization Charts and Tables 25

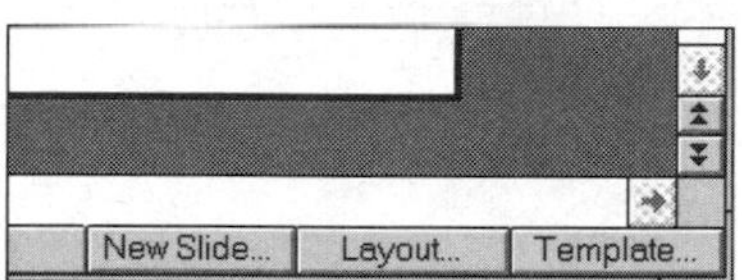

Figure 1. *The New Slide button.*

Double-click the Org Chart layout.

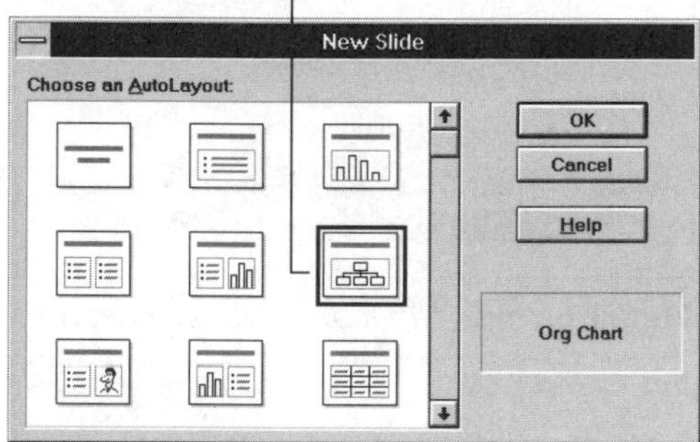

Figure 2. *The New Slide dialog box.*

Insert Org Chart button.

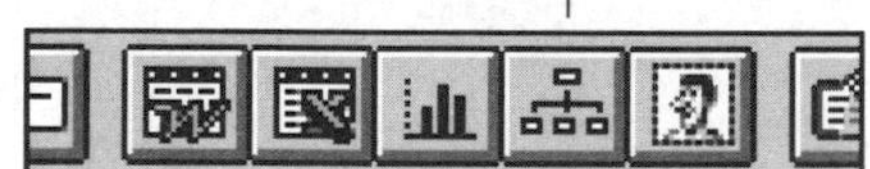

Figure 3. *The Insert Org Chart button.*

Starting an Org Chart

1. Click the New Slide button to start a new slide. **(Figure 1)**
2. On the New Slide dialog box, double-click the Org Chart layout. **(Figure 2)**
3. On the new slide, double-click the "Double click to add org chart" placeholder.

or, to add an org chart to an existing slide

1. Turn to the slide to which you want to add an org chart.
2. Click the Insert Org Chart button on the Standard toolbar. **(Figure 3)**

✔ Tip

- Org charts are created by a module called Microsoft Organization Chart, which appears in a separate window. **(Figure 4)** When you finish the org chart, the chart will be placed on the current slide.

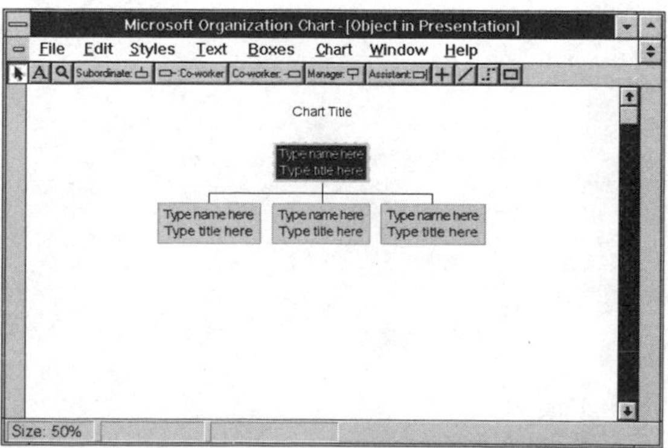

Figure 4. *The Microsoft Organization Chart window.*

Entering Org Members

1. Into the box at the top of the hierarchy, type the head of the hierarchy's name. **(Figure 5)**
2. Press Tab to highlight the next line within the same box and type the organization member's title. **(Figure 6)**

   or

   Click in a different box and enter a name. **(Figure 7)**

   or

   Press Ctrl+Down arrow to move to the box below and enter a name.
3. If you want to enter additional information in the same box, press Tab to highlight each successive line and then type over the prompt text.

✔ Tip

- To edit the information in a box, click the box, pause briefly, and then click again to place an insertion point in the box. If you double-click without pausing between the clicks, the program thinks that you intend to select the box and others at the same level.

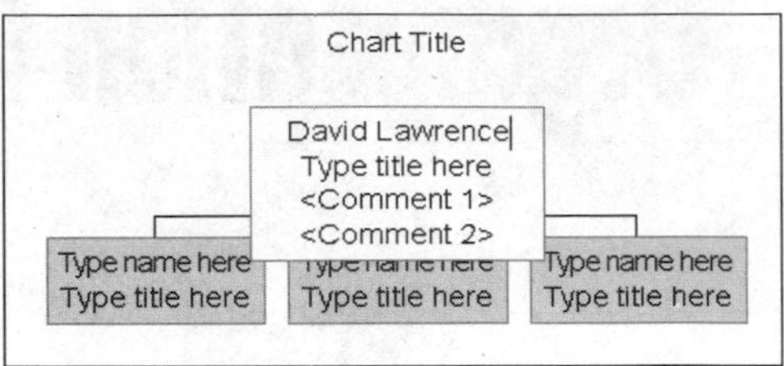

Figure 5. *Type the name of the head of the hierarchy.*

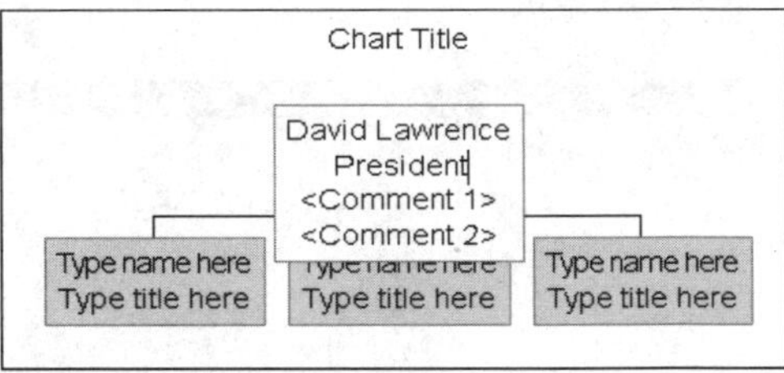

Figure 6. *Press Tab to move to the next line.*

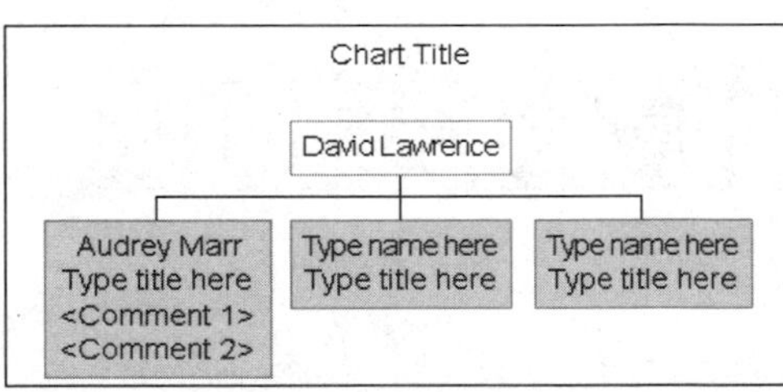

Figure 7. *Click in a different box to fill.*

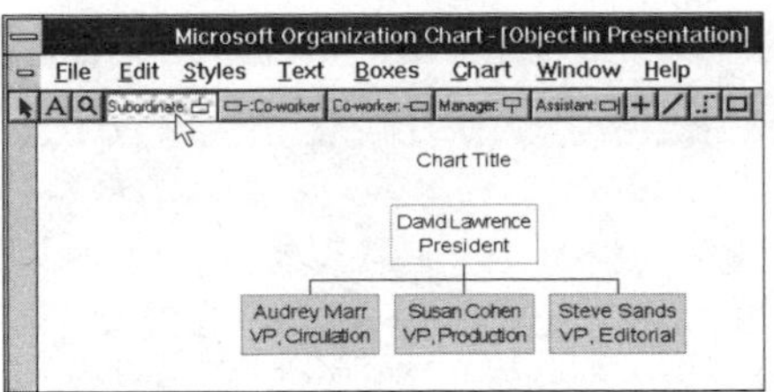

Figure 8. *Click the subordinate button.*

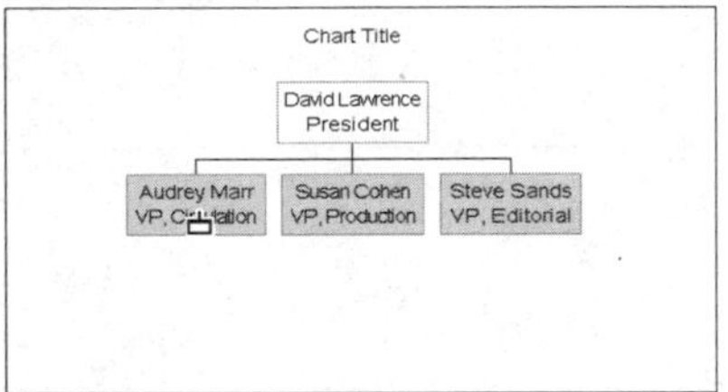

Figure 9. *Place the mouse pointer on a box.*

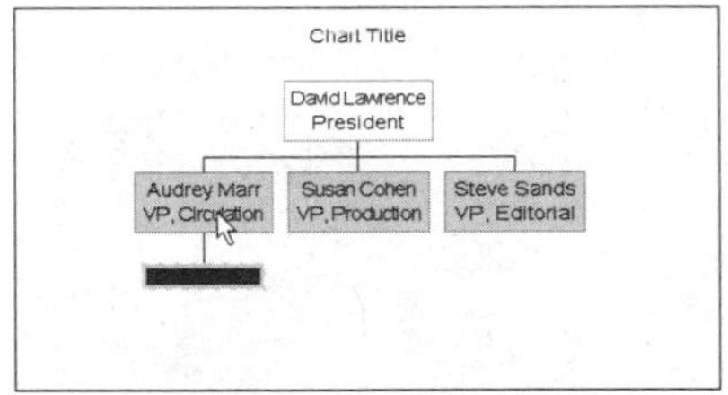

Figure 10. *Click to add a subordinate.*

Adding Subordinates

The initial structure contains only four organization members, a manager and three subordinates. To build a more complete structure, you will need to add more subordinates.

1. Click the Subordinate button. **(Figure 8)**
2. Place the mouse pointer on a box that requires a subordinate. **(Figure 9)**
3. Click to add a subordinate. **(Figure 10)**

✔ Tips

- To add multiple subordinates, click the Subordinate button several times (once for each subordinate to add) and **then** click an organization member.
- To add a coworker beside a box, click one of the Co-worker buttons and then click a box. **(Figures 11-12)**
- To **move** a subordinate to another organization member, drag thc subordinate on top of the other member's box and then release the mouse button.

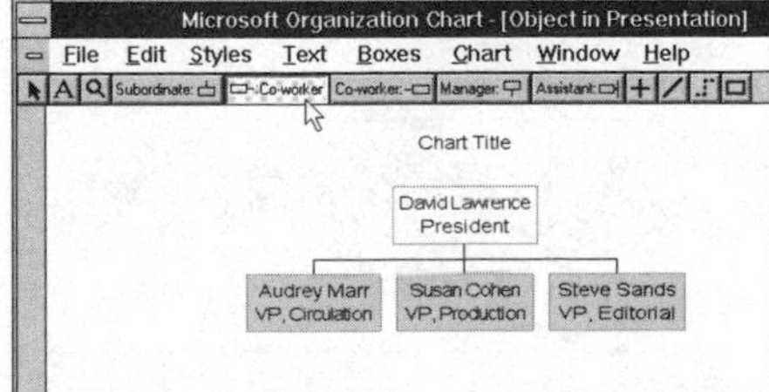

Figures 11. *The Co-worker buttons.*

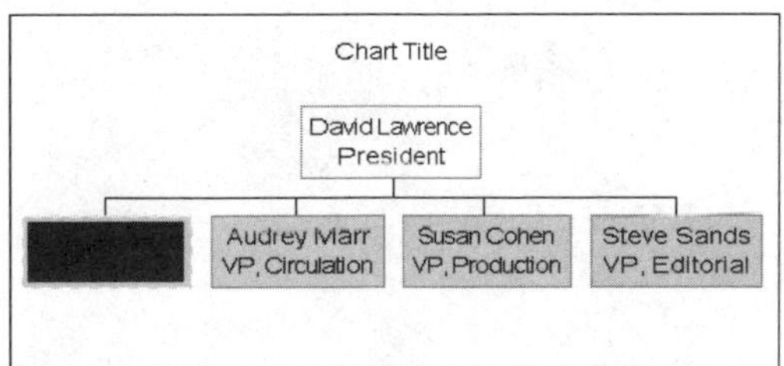

Figure 12. *A Co-worker added to a box.*

Adding an Assistant

1. Click the Assistant button. **(Figure 13)**
2. Click the box for the member who is to receive an assistant. **(Figures 14-15)**

✔ Tips

- You can add several assistants to a single organization member.
- To delete an assistant, click the box and then press the Delete key.

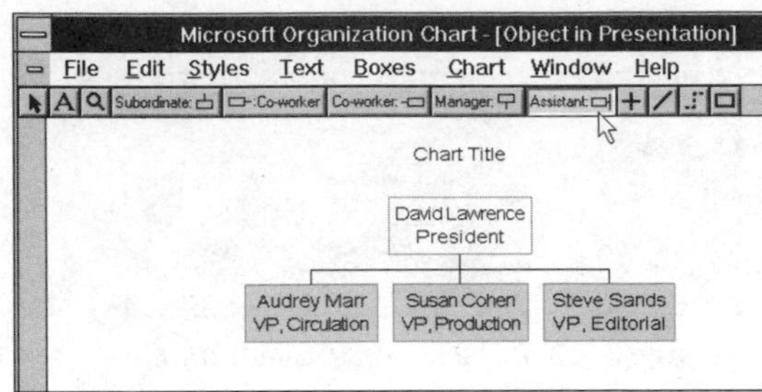

Figure 13. *The Assistant button.*

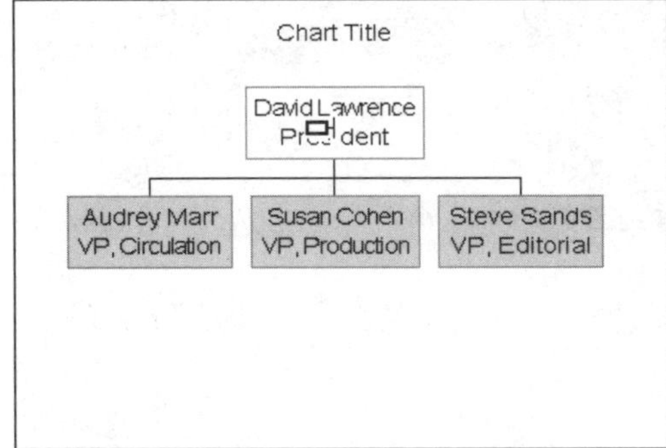

Figure 14. *Position the mouse pointer on the box for the member who is to receive the assistant.*

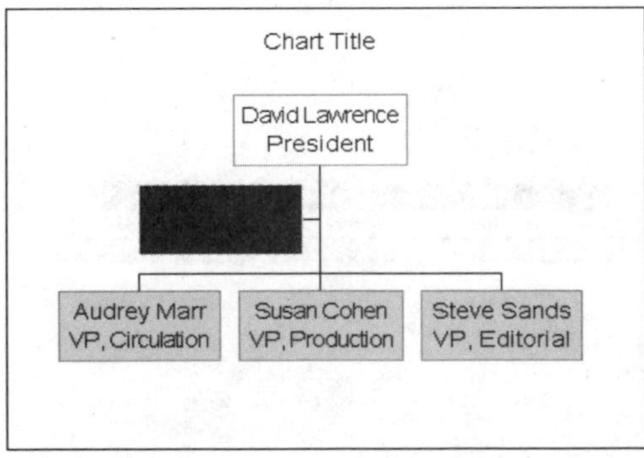

Figure 15. *Click the box to add the assistant.*

Figure 16. *Dragging a selection box.*

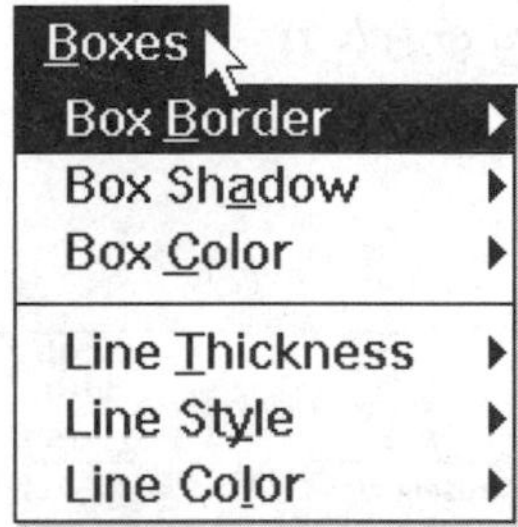

Figures 17. *The Boxes menu.*

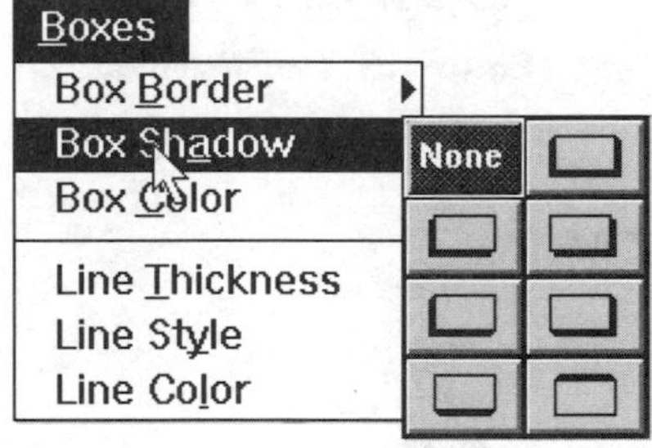

Figure 18. *Choose an option from the submenu.*

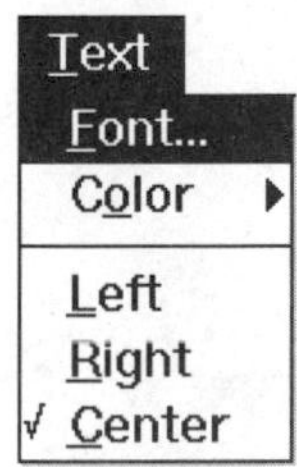

Figure 19. *The Text menu.*

Formatting the Boxes, Text, and Lines

1. Click a box or line.

   or

   Drag a selection box that encloses multiple boxes or lines to format. **(Figure 16)**

2. To format a box, choose one of the Box options on the Boxes menu and choose a setting from the submenu that appears. **(Figures 17-18)**

   or, to format the text

   Choose an option on the Text menu and then choose a setting for the option. **(Figure 19)**

   or, to format the connecting lines

   Choose one of the Line options on the Boxes menu. **(Figure 17)**

✔ Tips

- To select multiple boxes, you can also hold down the Shift key while clicking each box.
- Double-click a box to select all boxes at the same level **(Figure 20)**
- The shadow color of boxes is set by the Line color.

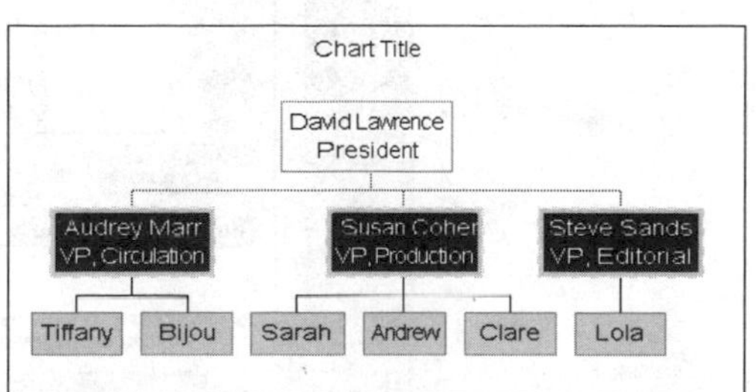

Figure 20. *Double-click any box to select all the boxes at the same level.*

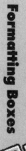

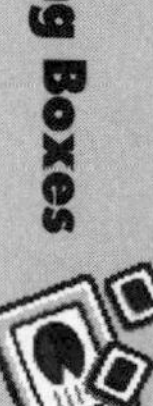

Finishing the Chart and Leaving Microsoft Organization Chart

1. Complete the chart. **(Figure 21)**
2. From the File menu, choose the Update command. **(Figure 22)**
3. From the File menu, choose the Exit and Return to command. **(Figure 23)**
4. Drag the chart or drag the chart's handles to move or resize the chart on the PowerPoint slide as necessary. **(Figure 24)**

✔ **Tip**

■ Anytime you want to edit an existing chart, double-click the chart.

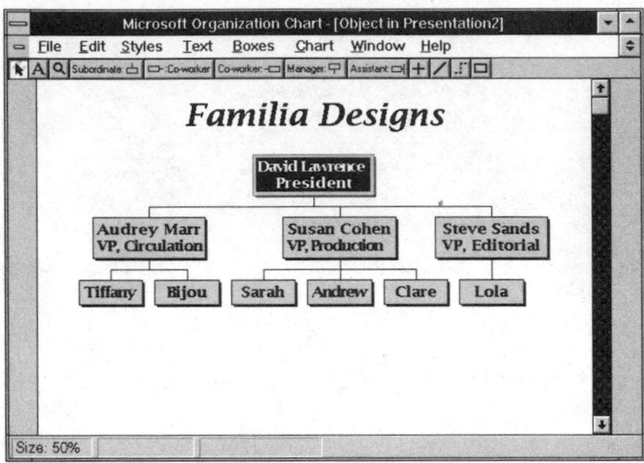

Figure 21. *The completed org chart.*

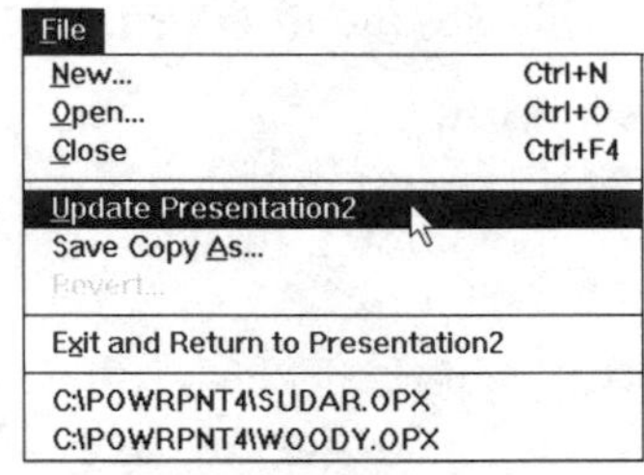

Figure 22. *The File menu.*

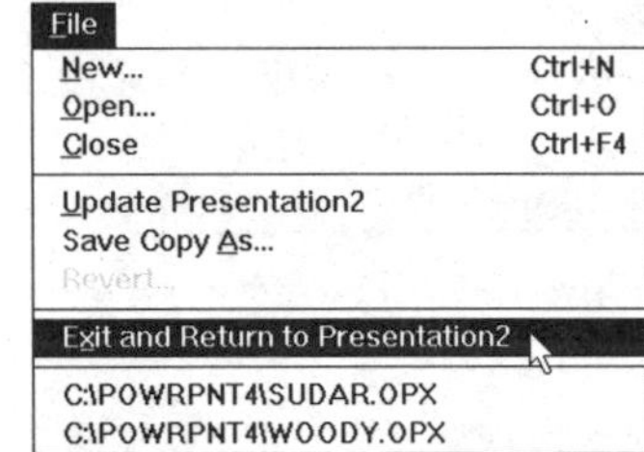

Figure 23. *The File menu.*

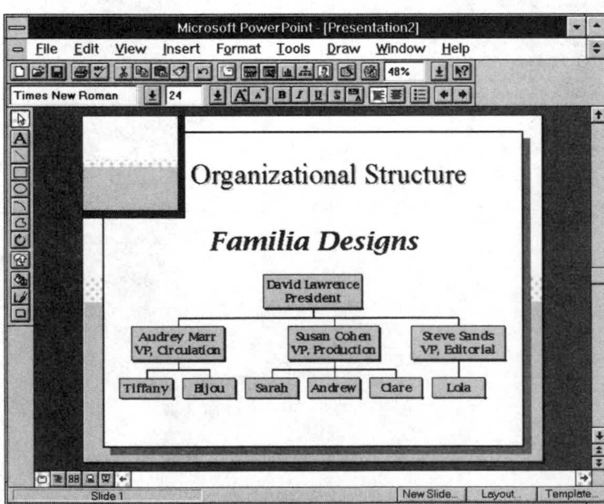

Figure 24. *The organization chart on the PowerPoint slide.*

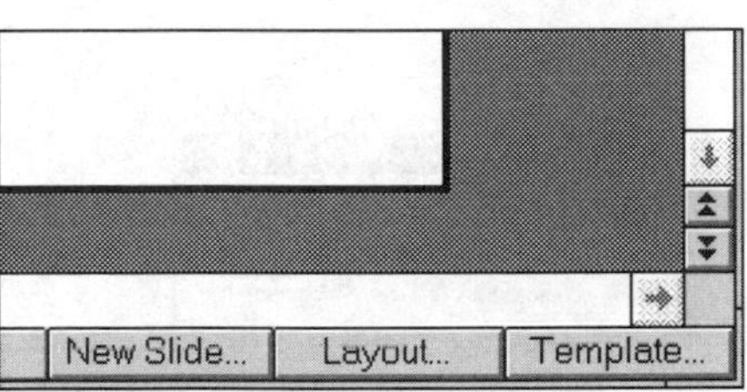

Figure 25. *The New Slide button.*

Starting a Table

1. Click the New Slide button to start a new slide. **(Figure 25)**
2. On the New Slide dialog box, double-click the Table layout. **(Figure 26)**
3. Double click the "Double click to add table" placeholder on the new slide.
4. On the Insert Word Table dialog box, set the number of columns and number of rows. Then click OK. **(Figure 27)**

or, to add a table to an existing slide:

1. Turn to the slide to which you want to add a table.
2. Click the Insert Microsoft Word Table button in the Standard toolbar and drag across the number of rows and columns you want in the new table. **(Figure 28)**

   or

   Choose Microsoft Word Table from the Insert menu.

Double-click the Table layout.

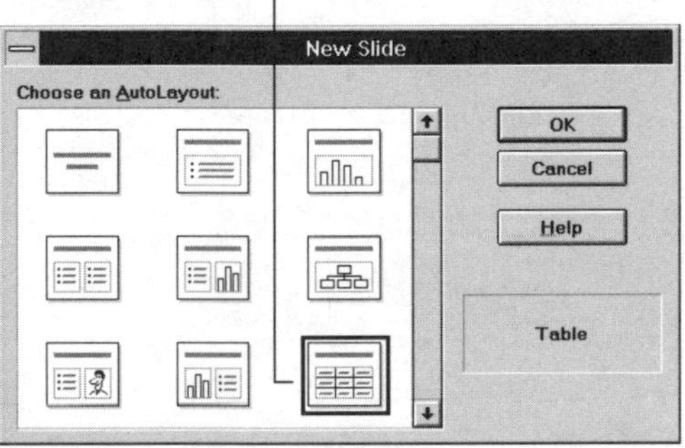

Figure 26. *The New Slide dialog box.*

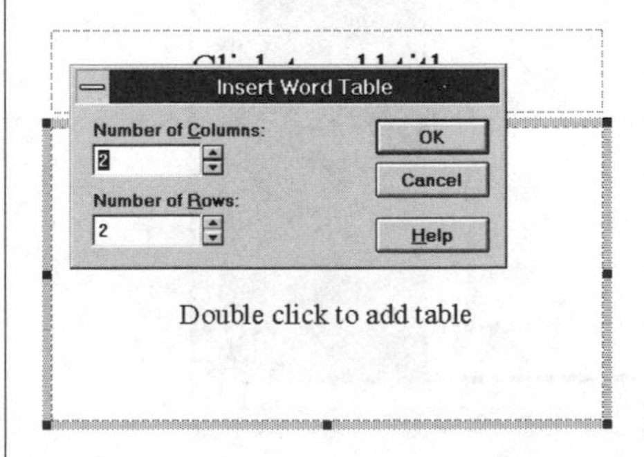

Figure 27. *The Insert Word Table dialog box.*

Figure 28. *Drag across the number of rows and columns you want.*

Entering the Data and Formatting the Table

PowerPoint uses the **Microsoft Word** table module to create and format tables. Therefore, creating a table in PowerPoint is just like creating a table in **Word**. In fact, if you double-click the "Double click to add table" placeholder in **PowerPoint**, the Insert *Word* Table dialog box appears to request the number of columns and rows you want in the table. **(Figure 29)**

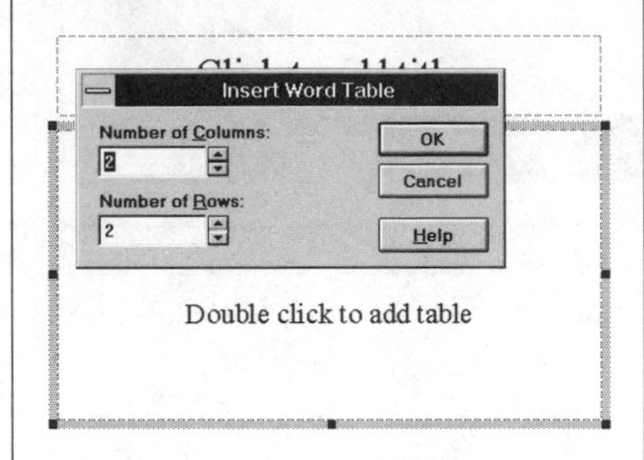

Figure 29. *The Insert Word Table dialog box.*

While you are creating or editing the table, **Microsoft Word's** menus and toolbars occupy the **PowerPoint** window and the table is surrounded by a heavy gray frame. **(Figure 30)**

When you finish the table, click outside the frame and **PowerPoint's** menus and toolbars regain the screen.

To edit an existing table, double-click the table. The familiar gray frame will reappear around the table and **Word's** menus and toolbars reemerge.

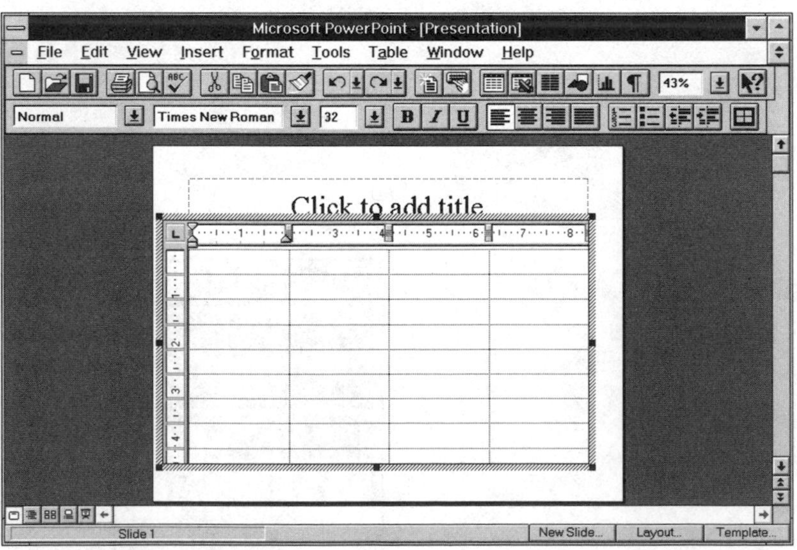

Figure 30. *Editing a table.*

Using the Slide Sorter

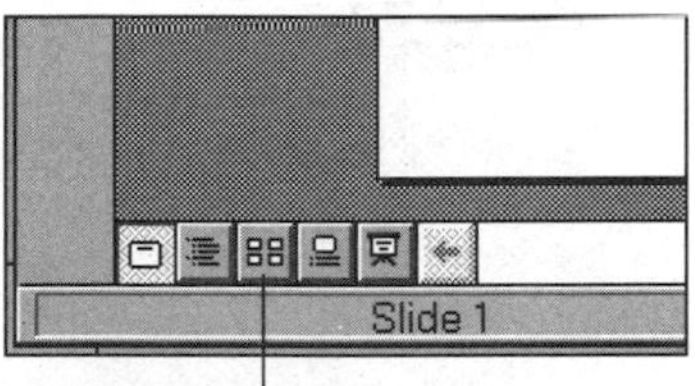

Slide Sorter View button.

Figure 1. *The Slide Sorter View button.*

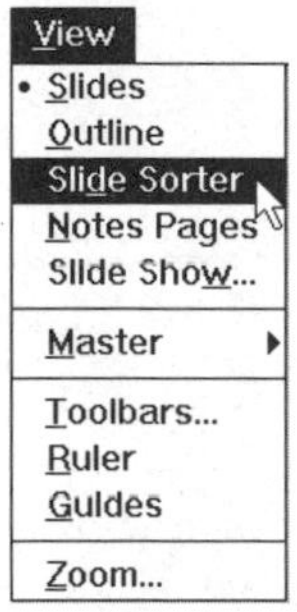

Figure 2. *The View menu.*

About the Slide Sorter

Slide Sorter view is just another of PowerPoint's views of a presentation. It displays rows of slides in miniature the way you place 35mm slides in rows on a light table to get an overview of the presentation. In Slide Sorter view, you can rearrange slides, delete or duplicate slides, and change the template to change the overall look of the presentation.

Switching to Slide Sorter View

1. Click the Slide Sorter View button. **(Figure 1)**

or

From the View menu, choose Slide Sorter. **(Figure 2)**

✔ Tip

■ To switch to a view of a single slide, double-click the slide or click the slide and then click the Slide View button.

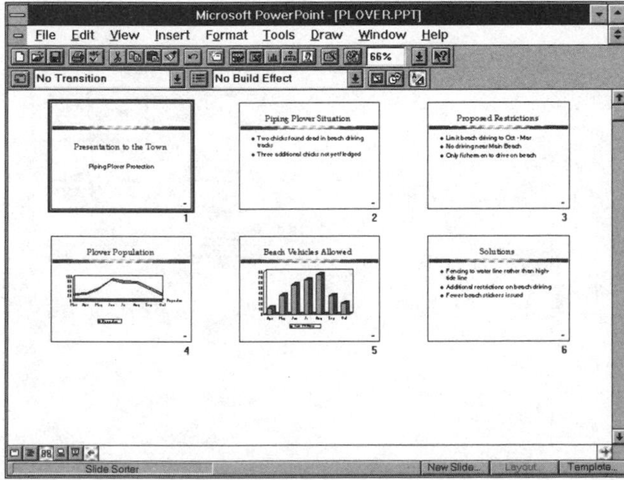

Figure 3. *Slide Sorter view.*

Reordering Slides

1. Place the mouse pointer on the slide to reposition in the presentation. **(Figure 4)**
2. Hold down the mouse button and drag the slide to a new position. A vertical line appears to indicate where the slide will drop when you release the mouse button. **(Figure 5)**
3. Release the mouse button to drop the slide. **(Figure 6)**

✔ Tips

- You can select several slides to move by drawing a selection box around the group of slides then dragging the group to the new position. **(Figure 7)**
- To gather slides from different parts of a presentation, hold down the Shift key as you click each slide. Then drag any one slide to a new point in the presentation. All the selected slides will appear in sequence and in the same relative order at the new position.

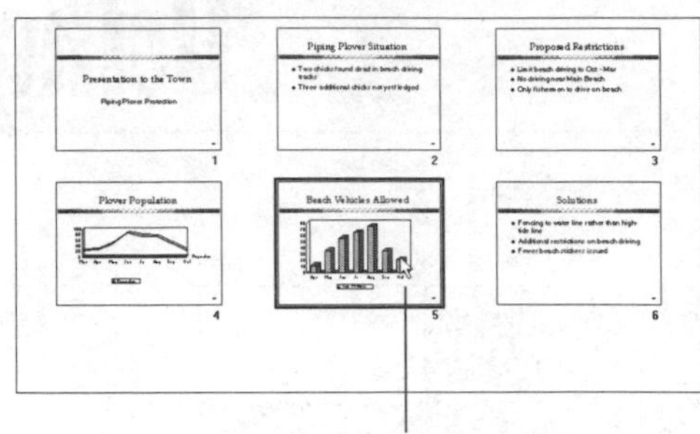

Figure 4. *Place the mouse pointer on a slide.*

The slide will drop here if you release the mouse button.

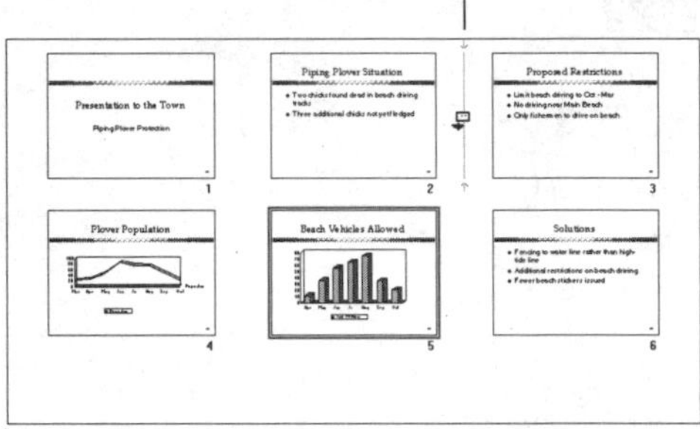

Figure 5. *A line indicates the position at which the slide will drop.*

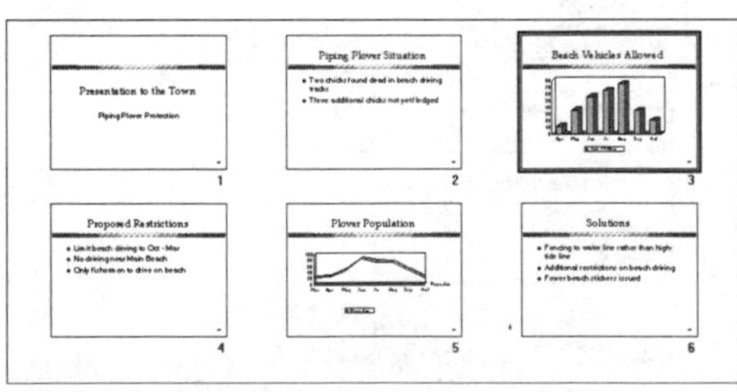

Figure 6. *The slide appears at the new position.*

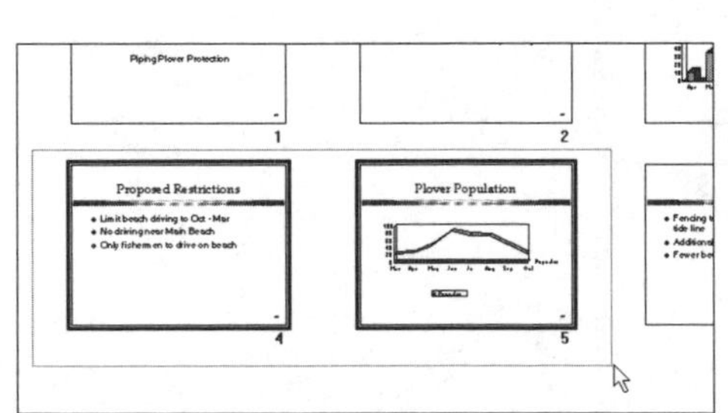

Figure 7. *Drag a selection box around several slides to select the slides.*

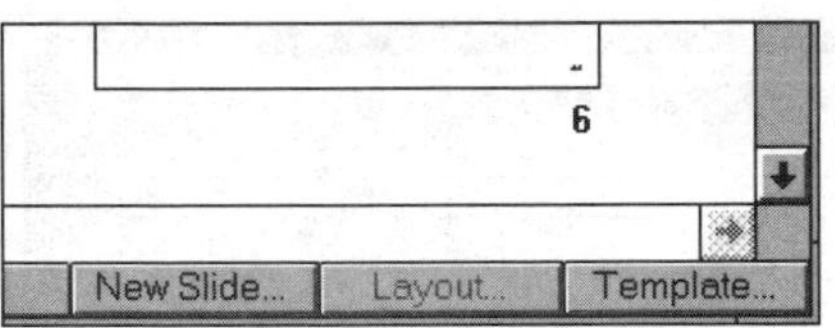

The Template button.

Figure 8. *The Template button.*

Changing the Overall Design in Slide Sorter View

1. Click the Template button. **(Figure 8)**

or

From the Format menu, choose Presentation Template.

2. On the Presentation Template dialog box, select a template from the list of templates at the left. **(Figure 9)**

or

Double-click the template directory icon (yellow folder) in the Directories box and then double-click a different category of templates before selecting a template from the list at the left. *For more on templates, see Selecting a New Design, page 215.*

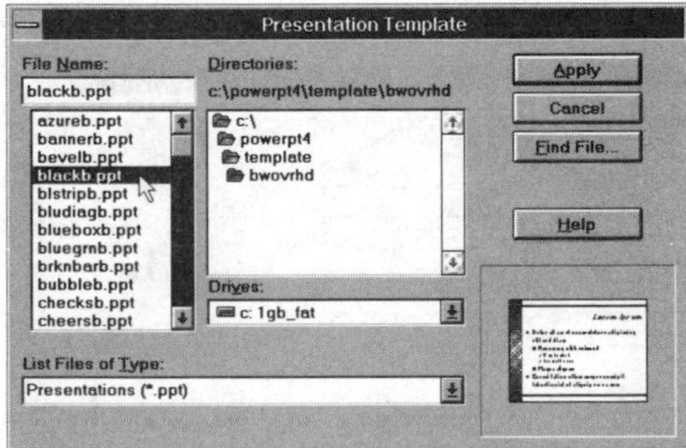

Figure 9. *The Presentation Template dialog box.*

✔ Tip

- To change the appearance of one segment of the presentation, you can select certain slides in the Slide Sorter, choose Slide Background from the Format menu, and choose a different background color or design.

Table 26-1. ***Template Categories***

BWOVRHD	Black and white templates.
CLROVRHD	Color printer templates (lighter colors, suitable for printing and 35mm slides).
SLDSHOW	Slide show templates (vivid colors suitable for display on the screen).

Duplicating and Deleting Slides

1. Select the slide or slides to delete or duplicate. **(Figure 10)**
2. Press Ctrl+D to duplicate the slide. **(Figure 11)**

   or

   Press Delete to delete the slide. **(Figure 12)**

✔ Tips

- To delete a slide, you can also choose Delete Slide from the Edit menu.
- To duplicate a slide, you can also choose Duplicate from the Edit menu.

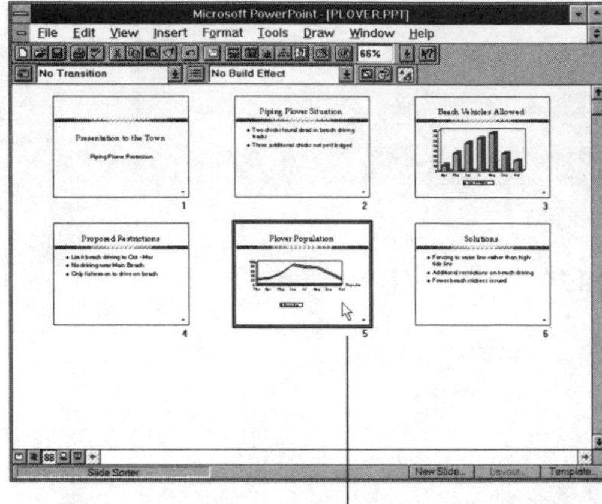

Figure 10. *Select the slide to duplicate or delete.*

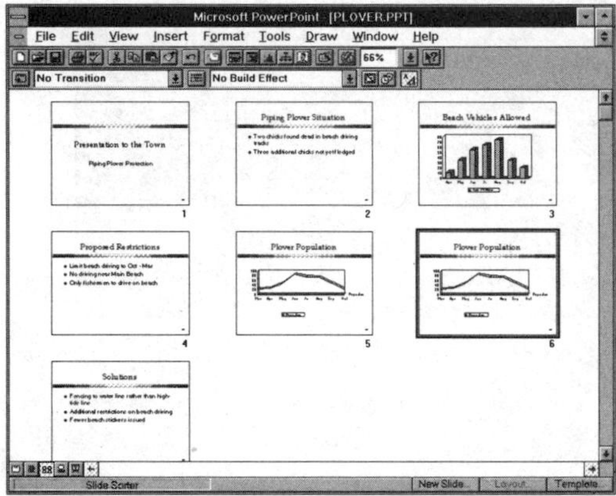

Figure 11. *The slide is duplicated.*

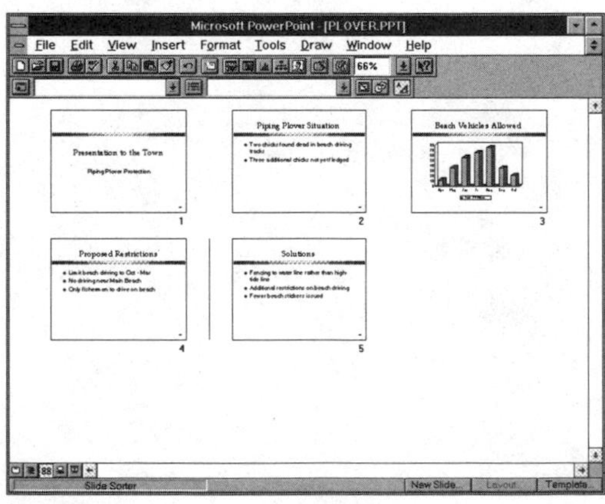

Figure 12. *The slide is deleted.*

Customizing a Presentation

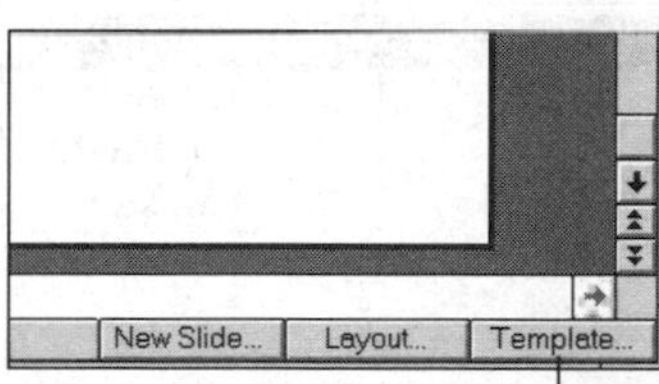

Figure 1. *The Template button.*

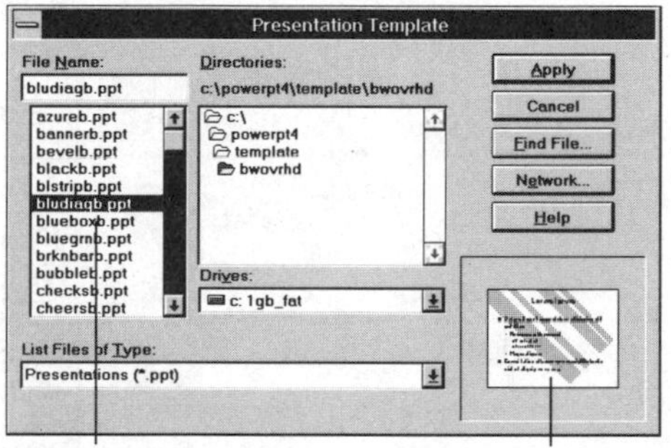

Click any template name once... *...to see a preview of the design here.*

Figure 2. *The Presentation Template dialog box.*

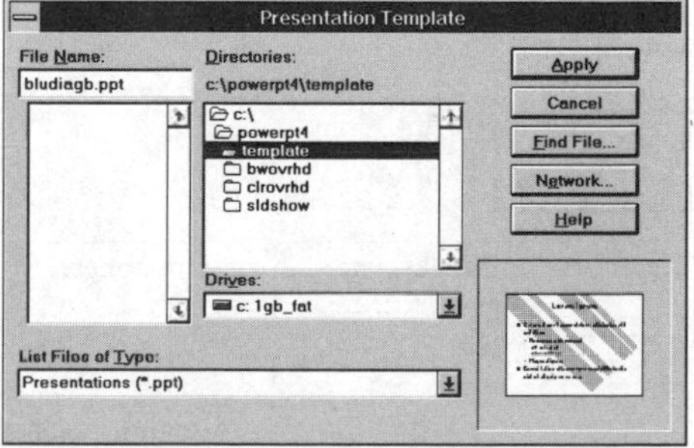

Figure 3. *Double-click the template directory to see the template subdirectories inside.*

Selecting a New Design

Changing a presentation's *template* can give a presentation an entirely new look, perhaps for a different audience. If you'll be printing black & white handouts on a laser printer, you might want to apply a black & white template to a color presentation.

A template contains a color scheme (a combination of colors used for text and other foreground presentation elements) and a slide master design (a background color, a selection of text fonts and formatting, and a background graphic design).

1. In any view, click the Template button. **(Figure 1)**

   or

   From the Format menu, choose Presentation Template.

2. On the Presentation Template dialog box, select a template from the list of templates at the left. **(Figure 2)**

   or

   Double-click the template directory icon (the yellow folder labeled "template") in the Directories box and then double-click a different category of templates. Then double-click a template name on the list at the left. **(Figure 3)**

Adding a Logo to the Background

Your company's or client's logo can give a stock presentation an important made-to-order look.

1. From the View menu, choose Master and then choose Slide Master from the submenu. **(Figure 4)**
   or
   Hold down the Shift key as you click the Slide View button.
2. With PowerPoint's drawing tools on the Drawing toolbar, modify the existing background graphic objects or add new objects. **(Figure 5)** *See Drawing Shapes, page 221.*
   or, to insert a logo stored in a graphic file:
   From the Insert menu, choose Picture and then select a graphic file on the Insert Picture dialog box.
3. Click one of the View buttons to leave Slide Master view and see the effect of the changes you've made. **(Figure 6)**

✔ Tips

- You can copy and paste a graphic image from another Windows program onto the slide master, or copy and paste graphics from the slide master of another presentation onto the slide master of the current presentation.
- Any graphics that are already on the slide master as part of the template background must be ungrouped before you can modify them. *See Grouping and Ungrouping Shapes, page 222.*
- Click the Drawing toolbar with the right mouse button and then click Drawing+ on the list of toolbars to add a special toolbar with advanced drawing commands.

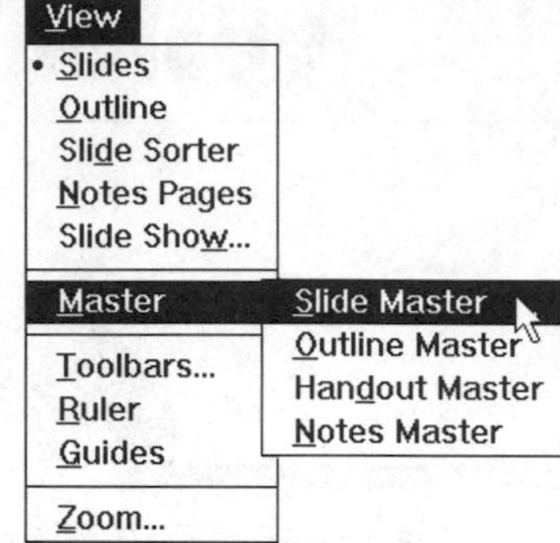

Figure 4. *The View menu.*

Figure 5. *The Drawing toolbar.*

The logo.

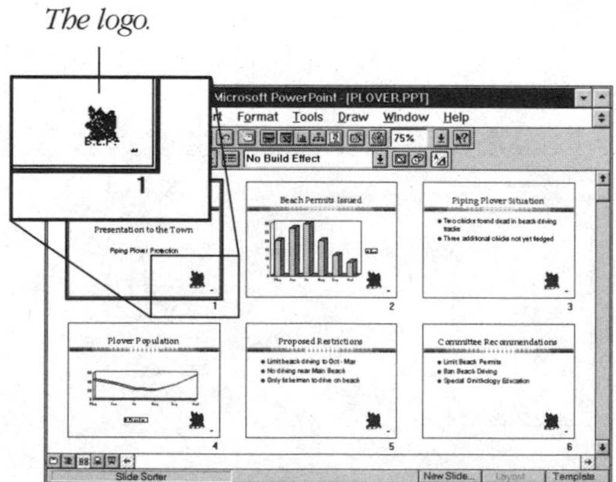

Figure 6. *An inserted logo on every slide in Slide View.*

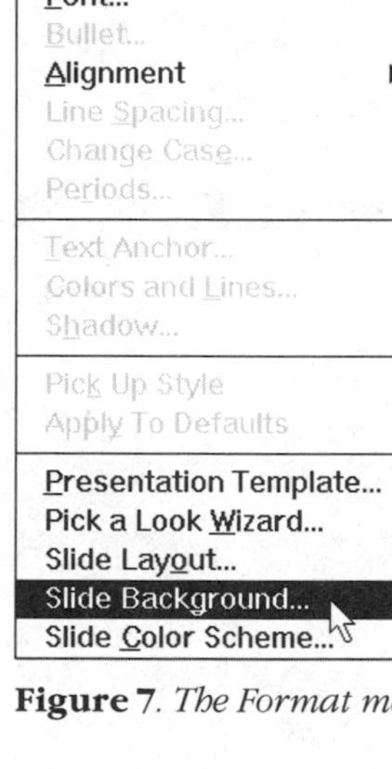

Figure 7. *The Format menu.*

Choose a shade style... *...and a variant...*

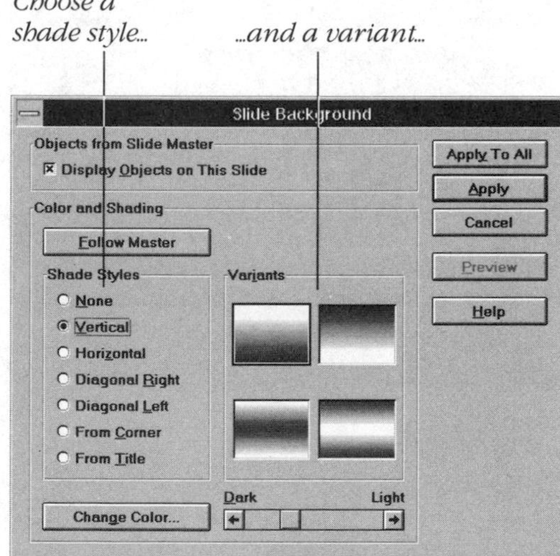

...then click one of these buttons.

Figure 8. *The Slide Background dialog box.*

Changing the Background Color and Shading

1. In Slide view or Slide Master view, choose Slide Background from the Format menu. **(Figure 7)**
2. On the Slide Background dialog box, choose a Shade Style and a Variant. **(Figure 8)**
3. To modify the background color, click Change Color on the Slide Background dialog box and use the Dark to Light scroll bar to change the darkness of the shading, if necessary.
4. Click Apply to All to apply the changes to all the slides. **(Figure 9)**

   or

   Click Apply to change the background of the current slide only.

✔ Tip

- To see the new background shading while the Slide Background dialog box is still open, click the Preview button and then move the dialog box to the side.

Figure 9. *The new shading on a slide.*

Changing the Text Fonts

1. From the View menu, choose Master and then choose Slide Master from the submenu. **(Figure 10)**

or

Hold down the Shift key as you click the Slide View button.

2. Select the text in the Title Area or the text in the Object Area on the Slide Master and then change the text formatting as you would text on any slide. **(Figure 11)** *See Formatting the Text, page 187.*

or, to format the text at a particular bullet level on bullet slides

Select the text in the Object area at the bullet level to format and then make formatting changes. **(Figure 12)**

3. Click any View button to switch to another view. **(Figure 13)**

✔ Tips

- To change the bullet style at a bullet level, select the text at that level, choose Bullet from the Format menu and then choose a different bullet style, size, and color on the Bullet dialog box.
- The color of the text is determined by the color scheme, but changing the color of text on the slide master overrides the color scheme.

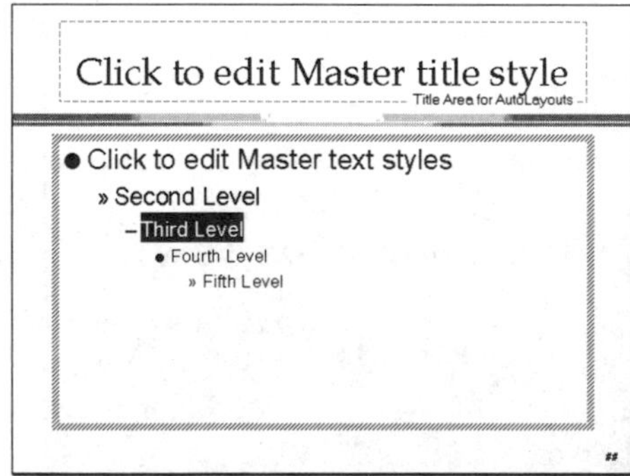

Figure 12. *Select the text at a particular bullet level to change text formatting at that level throughout the presentation.*

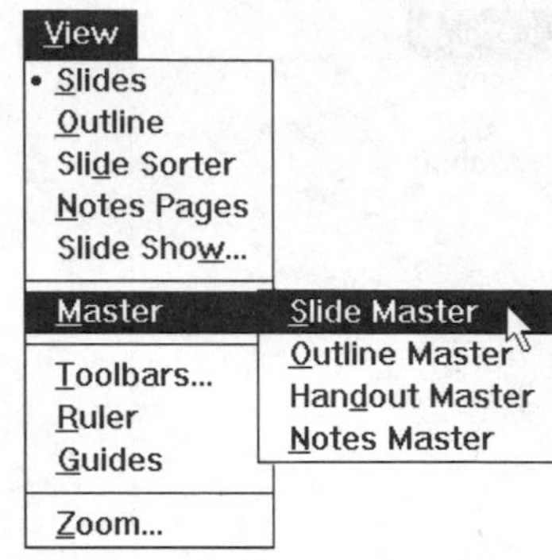

Figure 10. *The View menu.*

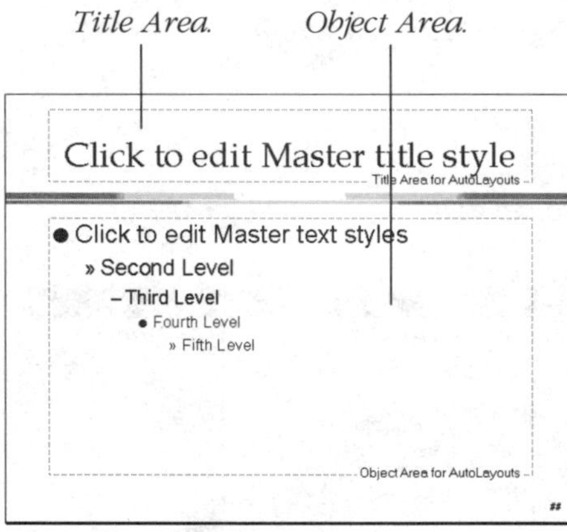

Figure 11. *The Slide Master.*

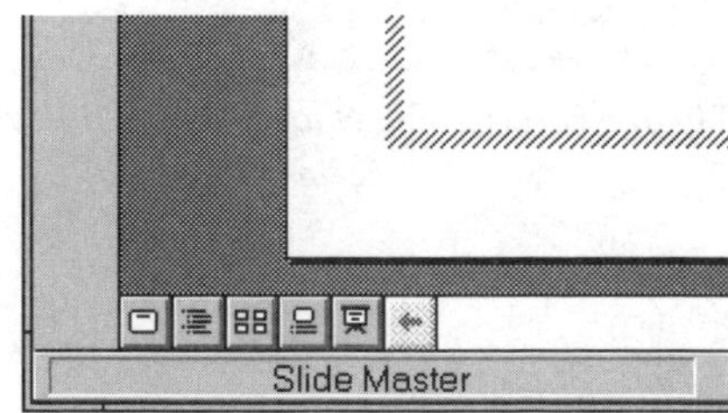

Figure 13. *Click any View button.*

Changing the Text Fonts

Power-Point

Format
- Font...
- Bullet...
- Alignment
- Line Spacing...
- Change Case...
- Periods...
- Text Anchor...
- Colors and Lines...
- Shadow...
- Pick Up Text Style
- Apply Style
- Presentation Template...
- Pick a Look Wizard...
- Master Layout...
- Slide Background...
- Slide Color Scheme...

Figure 14. *The Format menu.*

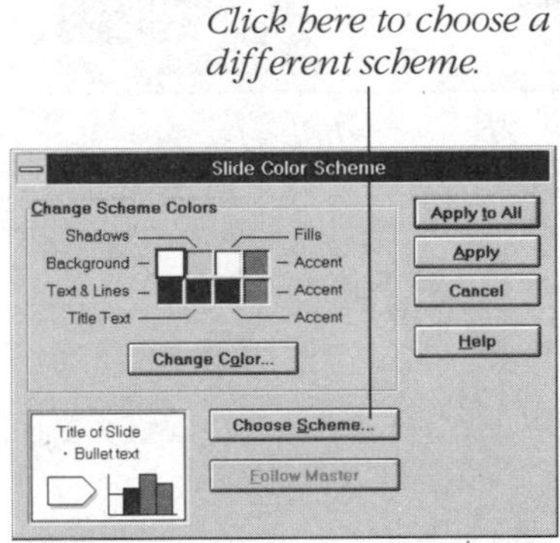

Figure 15. *The Color Scheme dialog box.*

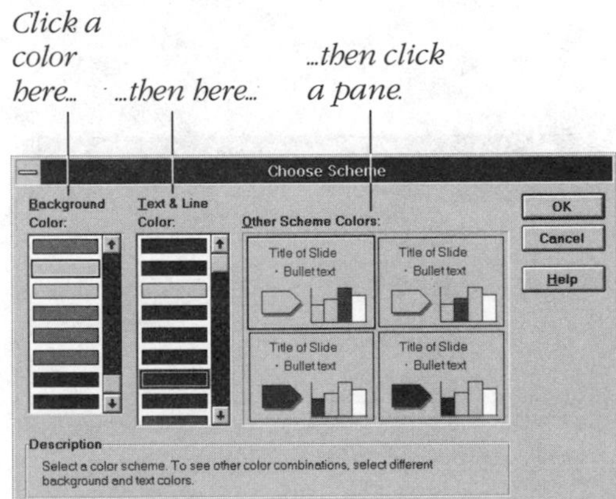

Figure 16. *Choose a Background color and then a Text & Line color.*

Changing the Color Scheme

The eight colors of the *color scheme* are the colors used by all the elements on slides unless you change the color of a specific element. The color scheme is stored in a template, so when you switch templates, you end up switching color schemes, too.

You can select predefined color schemes or create your own.

1. From the Format menu, choose Slide Color Scheme. **(Figure 14)**
2. On the Color Scheme dialog box, click the Choose Scheme button. **(Figure 15)**
3. On the Choose Scheme dialog box, click a Background color, then click one of the coordinating Text & Line colors that appears. **(Figure 16)**
4. Click one of the large panes that displays other scheme colors and click OK.
5. On the Slide Color Scheme dialog box, click Apply to All.

✔ Tips

- To change a color in the color scheme, double-click the color or click the color and click the Change Color button. Then choose a color on the Color dialog box that appears. **(Figure 17)**
- To return to the original color scheme in the template, click the Follow Master button on the Slide Color Scheme dialog box.

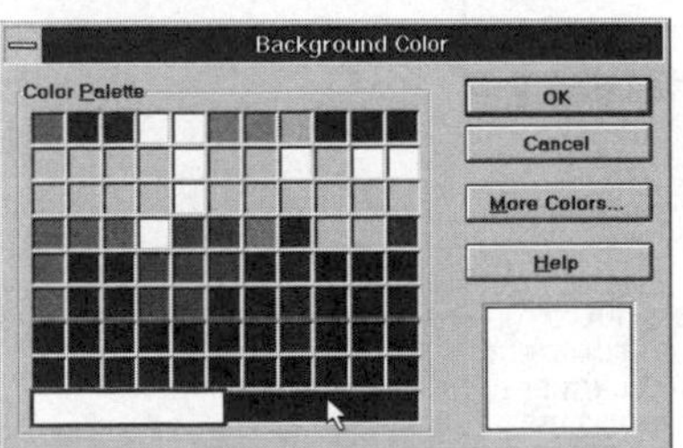

Figure 17. *The Background Color dialog box.*

Saving a Custom Design

Simply by saving a specially formatted presentation, you've created a design you can apply to other presentations later. Simply open the presentation, start a new presentation, and choose Current Presentation Format on the New Presentation dialog box.

You can also open a template, make any or all of the changes detailed in this chapter, and then save the custom template for use with future presentations.

1. Click the Open button on the Standard toolbar. **(Figure 18)**
2. On the Open dialog box, select one of the three directories under the template directory (BWOVRHD, CLROVRHD, or SLDSHOW). **(Figure 19)**
3. Double-click the template to edit.
4. Make formatting changes to the color scheme and slide master.
5. From the File menu, choose Save As. **(Figure 20)**
6. Save the template with a new name. **(Figure 21)**

✔ Tip

- You do not need to specify that you want to save a design as a template. Simply save the presentation. You'll use it as a template later.

Figure 18. *The Open button.*

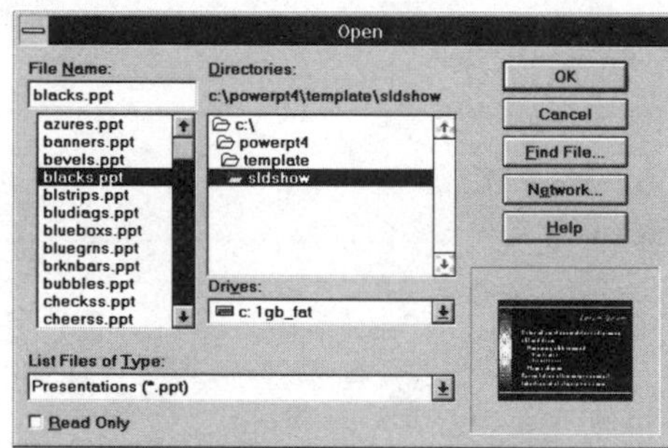

Figure 19. *The Open dialog box.*

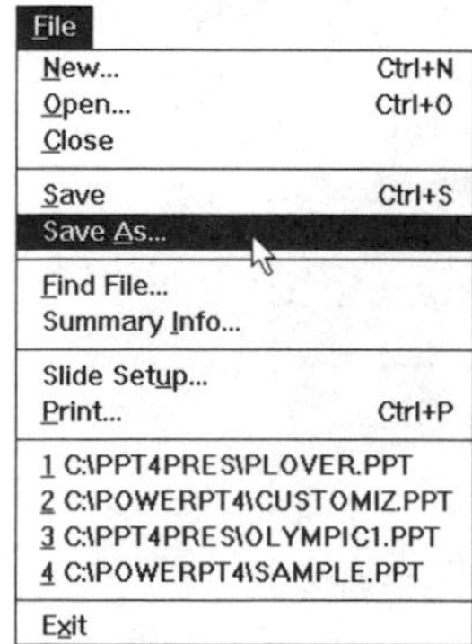

Figure 20. *The File menu.*

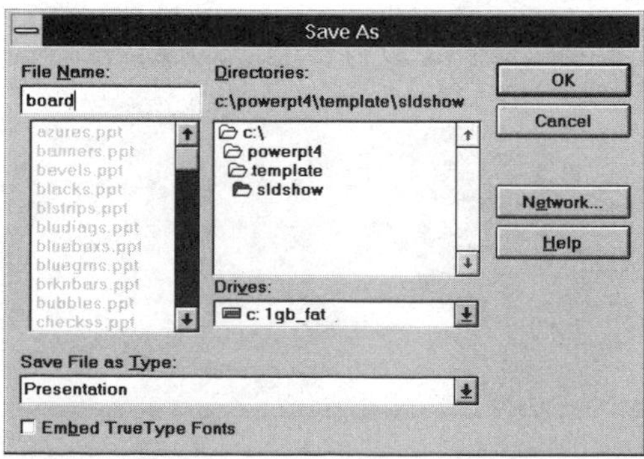

Figure 21. *The Save As dialog box.*

Drawing on Slides 28

Figure 1. *The Drawing toolbar.*

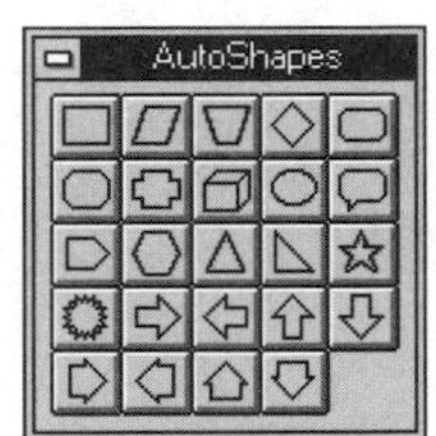

Figure 2. *The AutoShapes toolbar.*

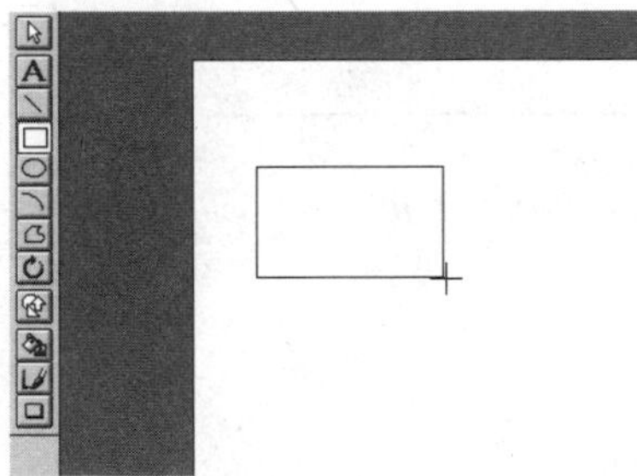

Figure 3. *Drag to create the shape.*

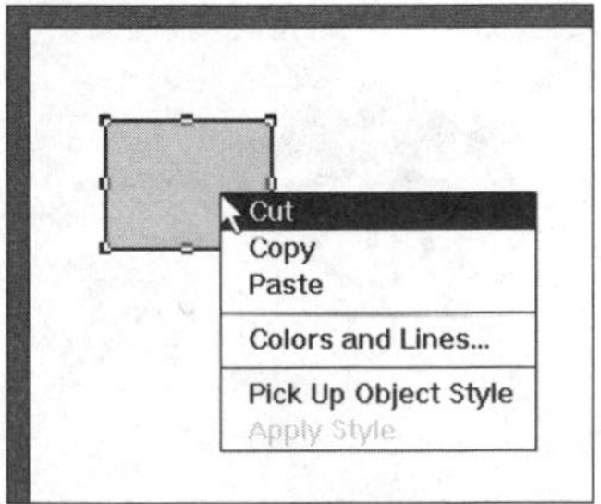

Figure 4. *The shortcut menu.*

Drawing Shapes

1. In Slide view, click one of the drawing tools on the Drawing or AutoShapes toolbars. **(Figures 1-2)**
2. Drag with the mouse pointer to create the shape. **(Figure 3)**
3. Click the shape with the right mouse button and choose Colors and Lines from the shortcut menu. **(Figure 4)**
4. On the Colors and Lines dialog box, choose a fill color, line color, and line style. **(Figure 5)**

✔ Tips

- Click the AutoShapes button to summon the AutoShapes toolbar. Then select any AutoShape and drag across the slide to create the shape. Click the AutoShapes button again to put away the AutoShapes toolbar. **(Figure 2)**
- To add or remove the fill color, the surrounding line, or a shadow, click the Fill On/Off, Line On/Off, or Shadow On/Off buttons.
- To add text to the center of any shape, click the shape and then begin typing.

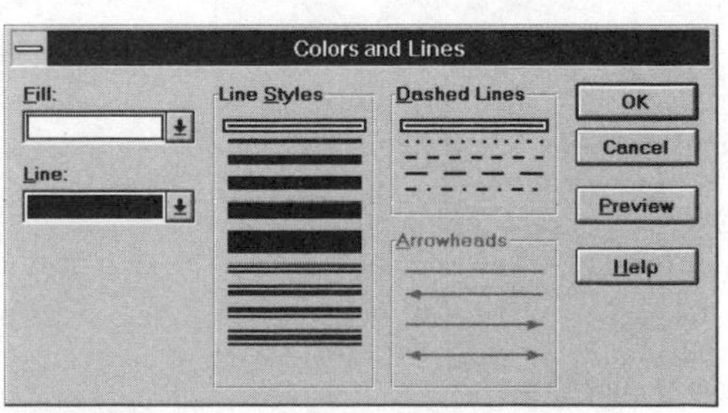

Figure 5. *The Colors and Lines dialog box.*

Grouping and Ungrouping Shapes

By grouping several objects, you can treat them as a single object. Simply select and then move, copy, or format the group.

1. Hold down the Shift key as you click each object for the group. **(Figure 6)**

   or

   With the Selection Tool, draw a selection box that entirely encloses only the objects to group. **(Figure 7)**
2. From the Draw or shortcut menus, choose Group. A single set of handles surrounds the objects in the group. **(Figures 8-9)**

✔ Tips

- To ungroup objects, select the group and then choose Ungroup from the Draw or shortcut menus.
- The Regroup command reestablishes the last group that was ungrouped.

Figures 6. *Hold down Shift as you click objects one after another.*

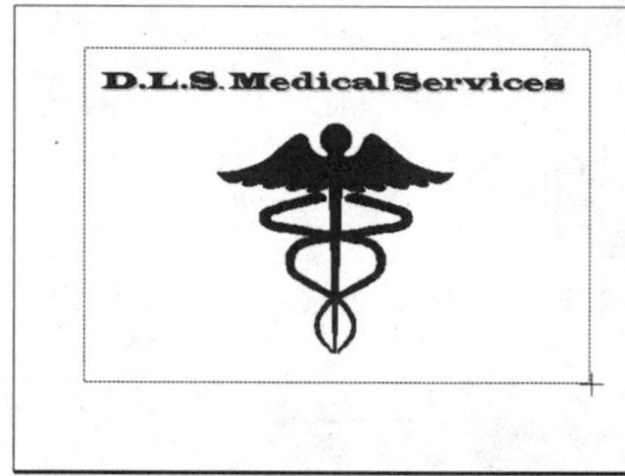

Figure 7. *Draw a selection box around objects to group with the Selection Tool.*

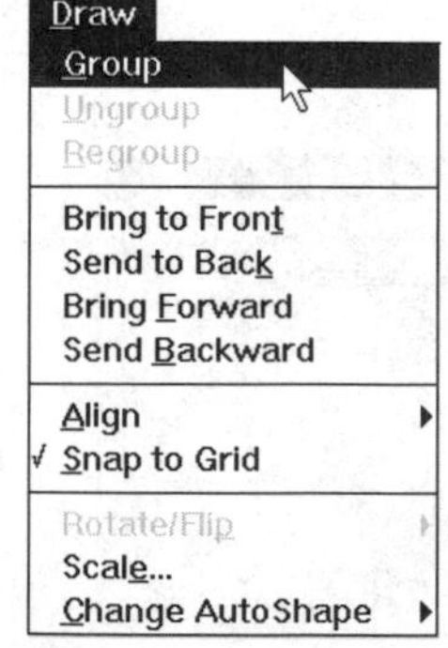

Figures 8. *The Draw menu.*

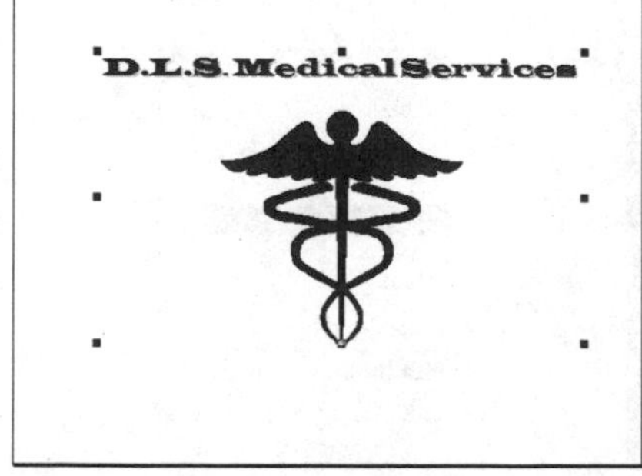

Figure 9. *Handles surround the group.*

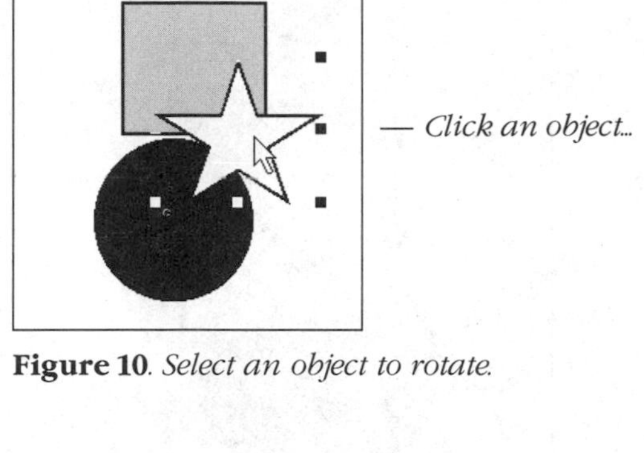

Figure 10. *Select an object to rotate.*

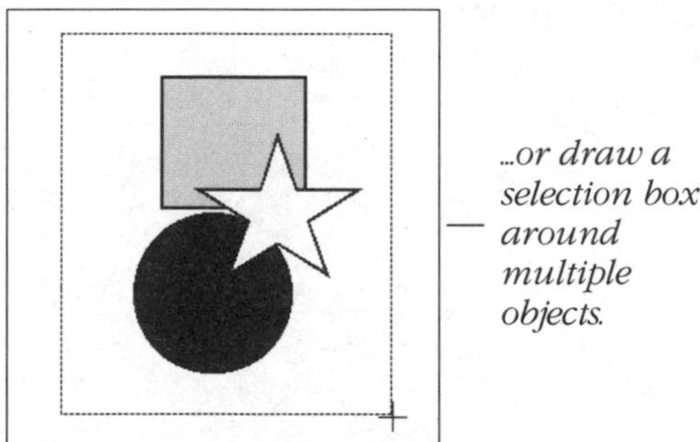

Figure 11. *Select the objects to align.*

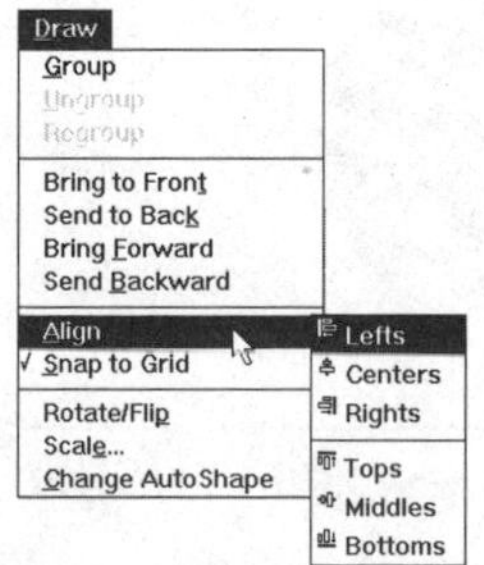

Figure 12. *The Align submenu.*

Aligning and Rotating Shapes

1. Select the object to rotate or the objects to align. **(Figures 10-11)**
2. From the Draw menu, choose Align and then choose an option on the submenu. **(Figure 12)**

   or

   From the Draw menu, choose Rotate/Flip and choose an option on the submenu. **(Figure 13)**

✔ Tips

- Objects align with the object that extends farthest from the center of all the objects.
- If you choose Free Rotate, place the pointer on a corner handle and drag around the center of the object to the desired angle. **(Figure 14)**

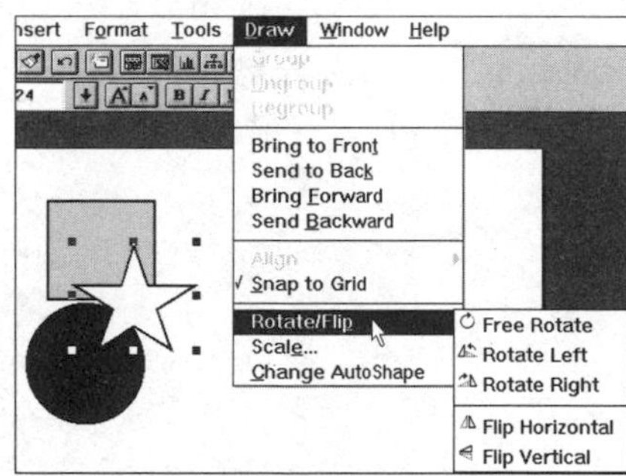

Figure 13. *The Rotate/Flip submenu.*

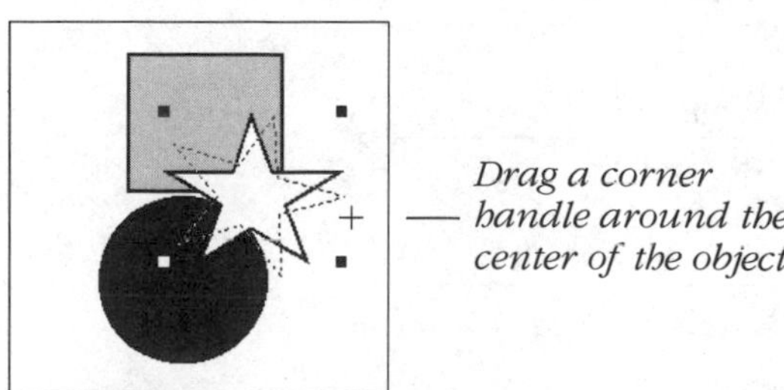

Figure 14. *Free Rotating an object.*

Overlapping Shapes

1. Select an object to move above or below other overlapping objects. **(Figure 15)**
2. From the Draw menu, choose Send to Back, Send to Front, Bring Forward (one level) or Send Backward (one level). **(Figures 16-17)**

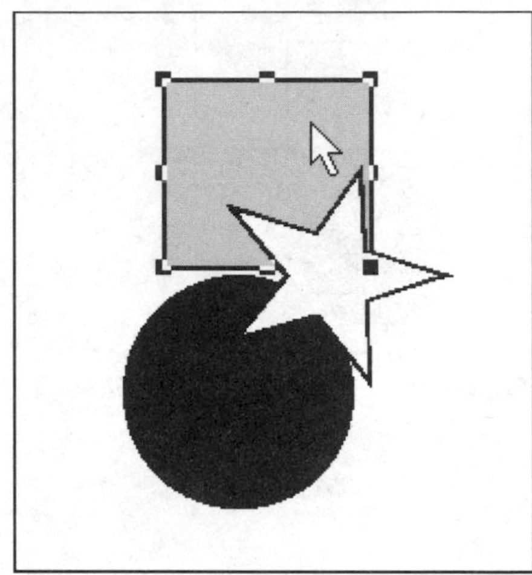

Figure 15. *Select an object to shift in the overlapping pile.*

Table 28-1. *Overlap Options*

Send to Back	Moves an object to the bottom of an overlapping pile.
Bring to Front	Moves an object to the top of an overlapping pile.
Bring Forward	Moves an object one layer closer in the pile.
Send Backward	Moves an object one layer farther down in the pile.

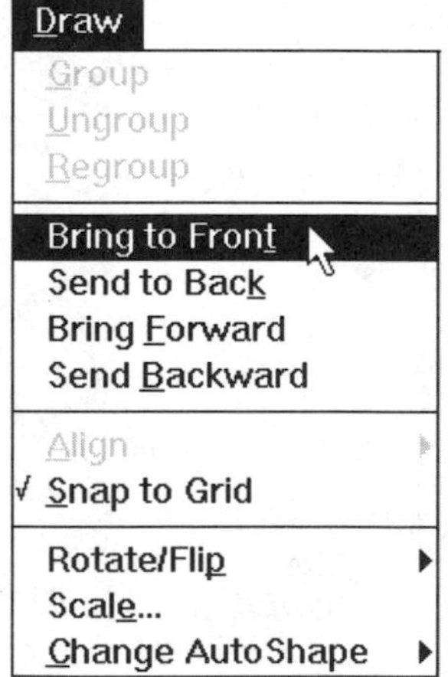

Figure 16. *The Draw menu.*

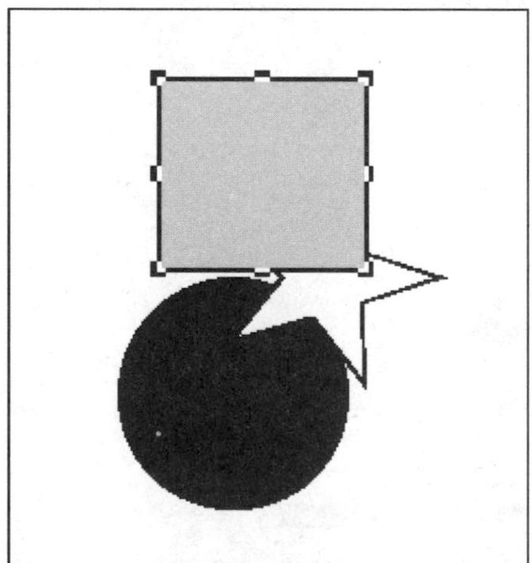

Figure 17. *The object after it is brought to the front.*

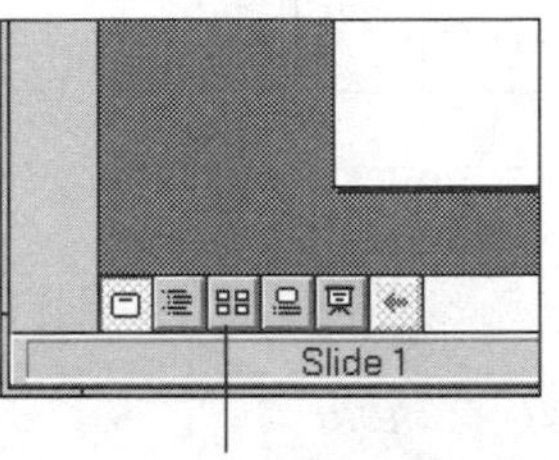

Figure 1. *Slide Sorter View button.*

Transition button. *Transition Effects box.*

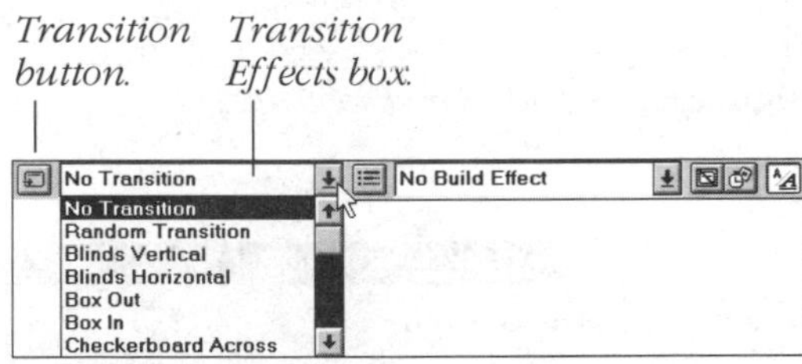

Figure 2. *The Slide Sorter toolbar.*

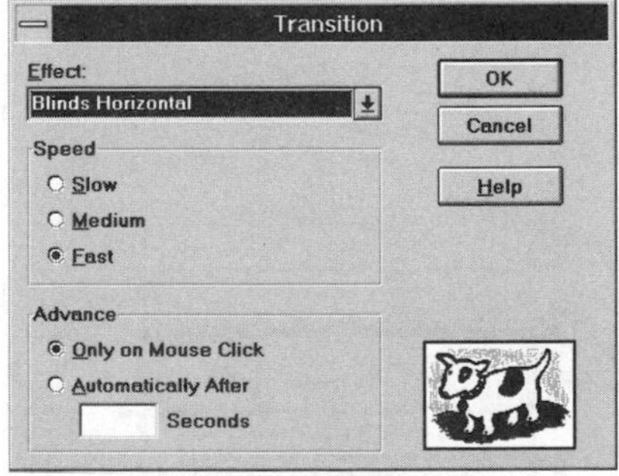

Figure 3. *The Transition dialog box.*

Adding Transition Effects

Transition effects are the dissolves, splits, wipes, and other TV-like effects that a slide show can use to bring each new slide into view.

1. Click the Slide Sorter View button to switch to the Slide Sorter. **(Figure 1)**
2. Click the slide for which you want to change the transition effect.
3. Click the pull-down button next to the Transition Effects box on the Slide Sorter toolbar and select a transition effect from the list. **(Figure 2)**

   or

   Click the Transition button and choose a transition Effect, Speed, and Advance option on the Transition dialog box. **(Figure 3)**

✔ Tips

- To apply the same transition effect to multiple slides, hold down the Shift key and click the slides and then choose a transition effect.
- To preview the transition effect in Slide Sorter view, click the transition icon that appears below each slide that has a transition effect. **(Figure 4)**

The transition icon.

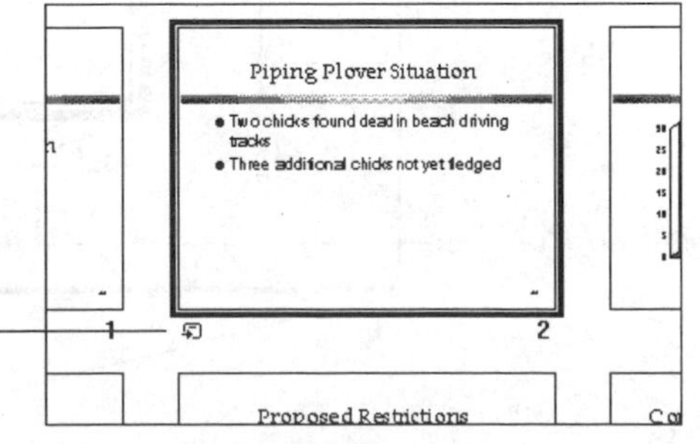

Figure 4. *The transition icon.*

Adding Build Effects

A build effect brings each bullet on a bullet slide into view with a special effect.

1. In Slide Sorter view, click the bullet slide that requires a build effect. **(Figure 5)**
2. Click the pull down button next to the Build Effects box on the Slide Sorter toolbar and select a build effect from the list. **(Figure 6)**

   or

   Click the Build button and, on the Build dialog box, choose whether to dim previous bullets, select the color of dimmed bullets, and choose a build effect. **(Figure 7)**

✔ Tips

- To apply the same build effect to multiple slides, hold down the Shift key and click the slides and then choose a build effect.
- A slide with a build effect shows a build icon at the lower left corner. Unlike the transition icon, you cannot click the build icon to preview the build. **(Figure 8)**

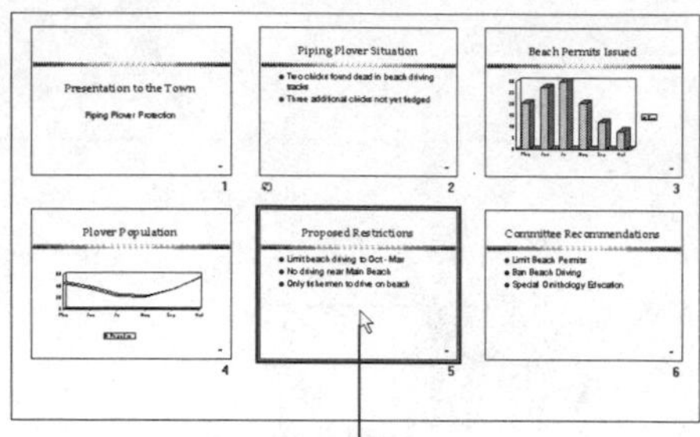

Figure 5. *Select the bullet slide.*

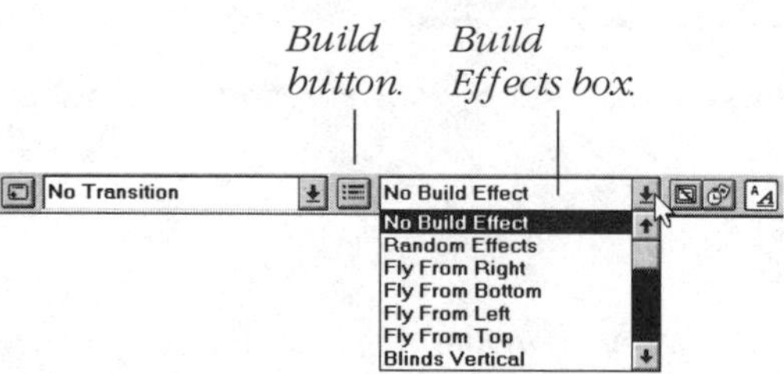

Figure 6. *The Slide Sorter toolbar.*

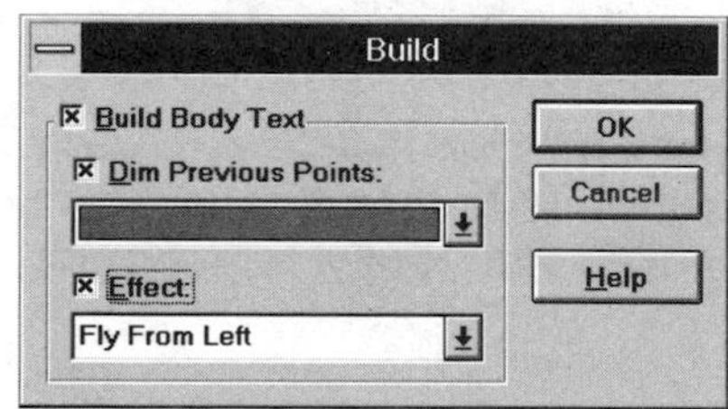

Figure 7. *The Build dialog box.*

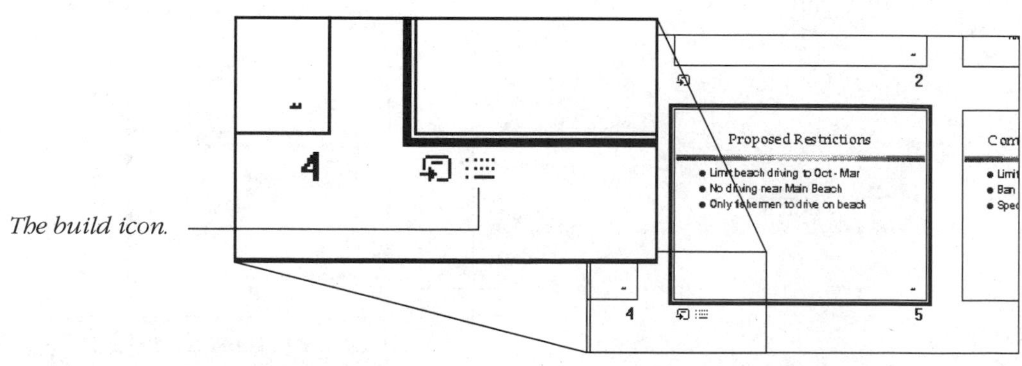

Figure 8. *The build icon.*

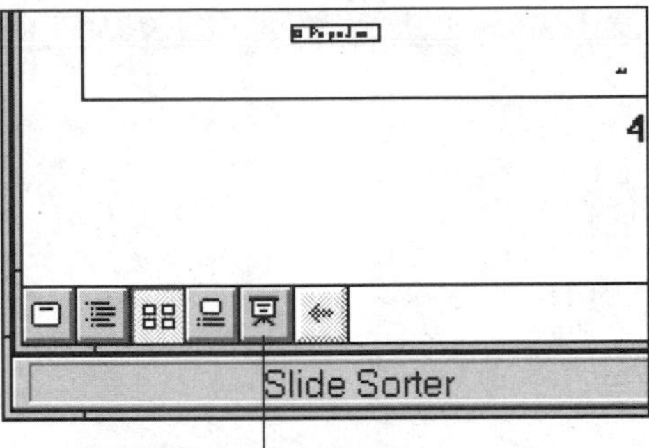

Slide Show view button.

Figure 9. *The Slide Show view button.*

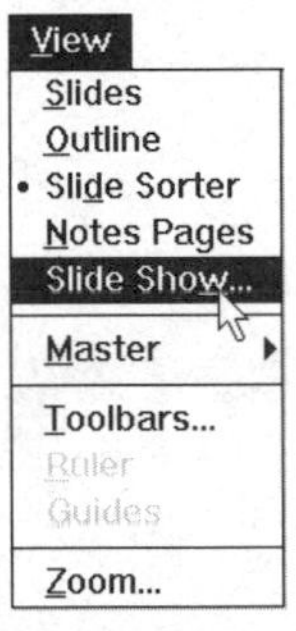

Figure 10. *The View menu.*

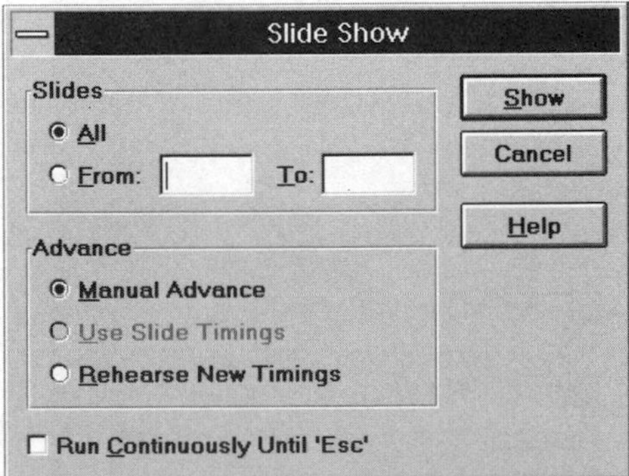

Figure 11. *The Slide Show dialog box.*

Displaying the Show

1. In Slide Sorter view, click on the first slide to view in the show and then click the Slide Show view button. **(Figure 9)**

   or

1. From the View menu, choose Slide Show. **(Figure 10)**
2. On the Slide Show dialog box, choose All and click Show or enter From and To slide numbers and click Show to display only a segment of the show. **(Figure 11)**

✔ Tips

■ Choose Rehearse New Timings on the Slide Show dialog box or click the Rehearse Timings button on the Slide Sorter toolbar to practice the show and record the overall length of the show and the duration of each slide as you advance the show manually. To use the slide timings you recorded during rehearsal, choose Use Slide Timings on the Slide Show dialog box.

Table 29-1. ***Slide Show Keystrokes and Mouse Clicks.***

Advance to the next slide	Left mouse button, Spacebar, Right arrow, Down arrow, PgDn, or N.
Back up to previous slide	Right mouse button, Backspace, Left arrow, Up arrow, PgUp, or P
Go to slide number	Slide number+Enter
Pause/Resume automatic show	S or + on the numeric keypad
Switch to temporary black screen	B or period. B or period again to resume.

Using the PowerPoint Viewer

The PowerPoint Viewer can display a slide show without the rest of the PowerPoint program installed. You can send the slide show file and PowerPoint Viewer to another user without PowerPoint so they can view your presentation.

1. Create the show, add the transition and build effects, and rehearse the show to set the slide timings.
2. Make sure Use Slide Timings is set on the Slide Show dialog box.
3. Save the presentation in a file.
4. Start the PowerPoint viewer by double-clicking the PowerPoint Viewer icon in the Windows Program Manager. **(Figure 12)**
5. In the Microsoft PowerPoint Viewer window, select the presentation and click Show. **(Figure 13)**

✔ Tips

- Click Run Continuously Until 'Esc' to run the presentation unattended.
- Click Use Automatic Timings to use the automatic timings you recorded during rehearsal.
- To send a slide show and the PowerPoint Viewer to someone else, copy the PowerPoint Viewer disk and then instruct the recipient to run VSETUP.EXE to install the Viewer on his or her system.

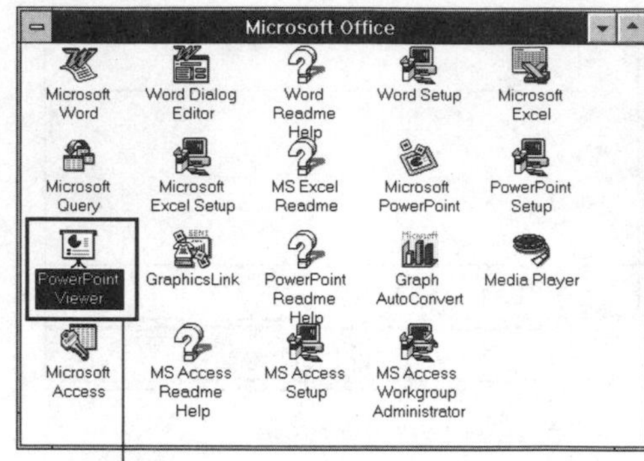

Figure 12. *The PowerPoint Viewer icon.*

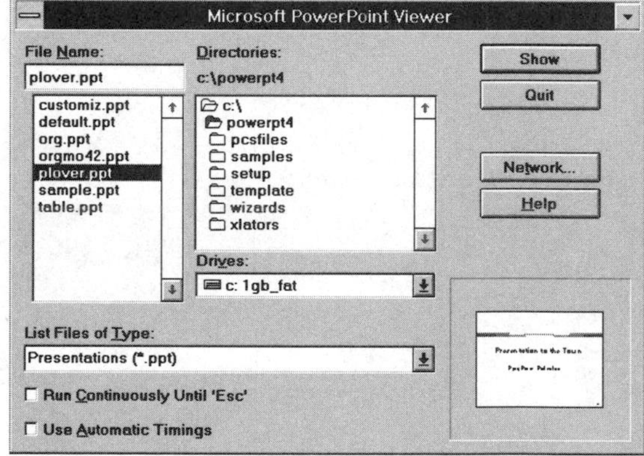

Figure 13. *The Microsoft PowerPoint Viewer window.*

Access 2.0 Database Management

Access 2.0 Database Management

About Access 30

What is Access?

Access 2.0 is the database management system within the Microsoft Office Professional suite. Access is not included in the Standard version of the Microsoft Office suite, but may be purchased separately and then added to the suite.

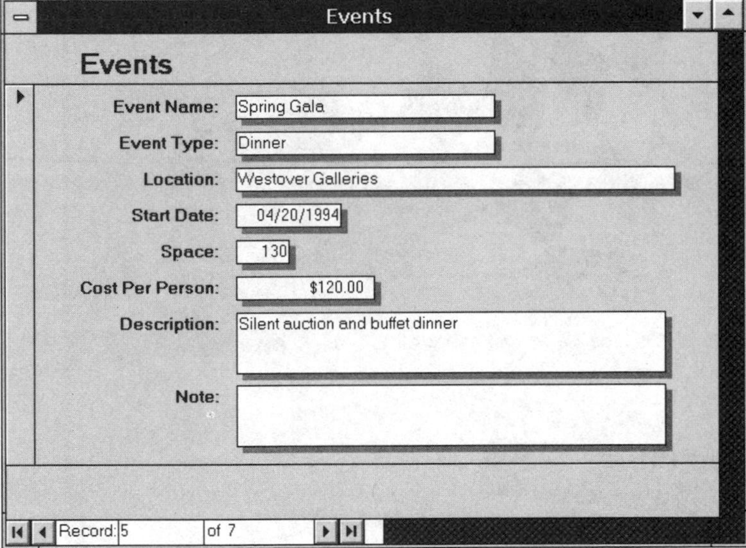

Access

Access allows you to store and manage large quantities of data. The data is organized in units called records. An Access database contains tables, which hold the records; forms, which display the records in the tables one by one; reports, which print batches of records; and queries, which locate specific information.

Access Wizards make it especially easy to set up tables, forms, reports, and queries.

An Access database can feed information to a Word mail merge so you can send a form letter to selected addresses in a database.

Excel also provides database capabilities, but its storage capacities are limited. Access can hold a virtually unlimited amount of data.

Access is also a relational database, which means you can establish relationships between records which share information.

The Road to an Access Database

Setting Up a Table

All the data in a database is stored in tables, so you must design the tables first. Access helps create tables with the TableWizard, which offers you dozens of common fields for storing the individual bits of information in each record. Mix and match the fields to create the table. *Pages 237-246.*

Creating a Form

You can type your data directly into a table, but it's much easier to type it into a form, which displays a single record and fill-in blanks. Once again, an Access Wizard helps you create a form with all the controls (fill-in blanks, checkboxes, and other items) that you'll need. *Pages 247-254.*

Entering and Editing the Data

With the form all set up, you can easily begin entering the records of the database. The form can also help you view records that are already in the database. *Pages 255-258.*

Finding, Sorting, & Filtering the Information

Retrieving the information you need from a database is as easy as entering it. You can simply search for matching text in a field, create a filter to display only selected records, sort the data, or create a complex query, which can pull out information according to special criteria. *Pages 259-268.*

Creating a Report

The Report Wizard helps you organize database information into presentable pages. It also helps you categorize related information into groups and total numeric information. *Pages 269-274.*

Extras

You might want to use Access as the source of names and address for a Word mail merge. *Page 321.*

The Access 2 Window

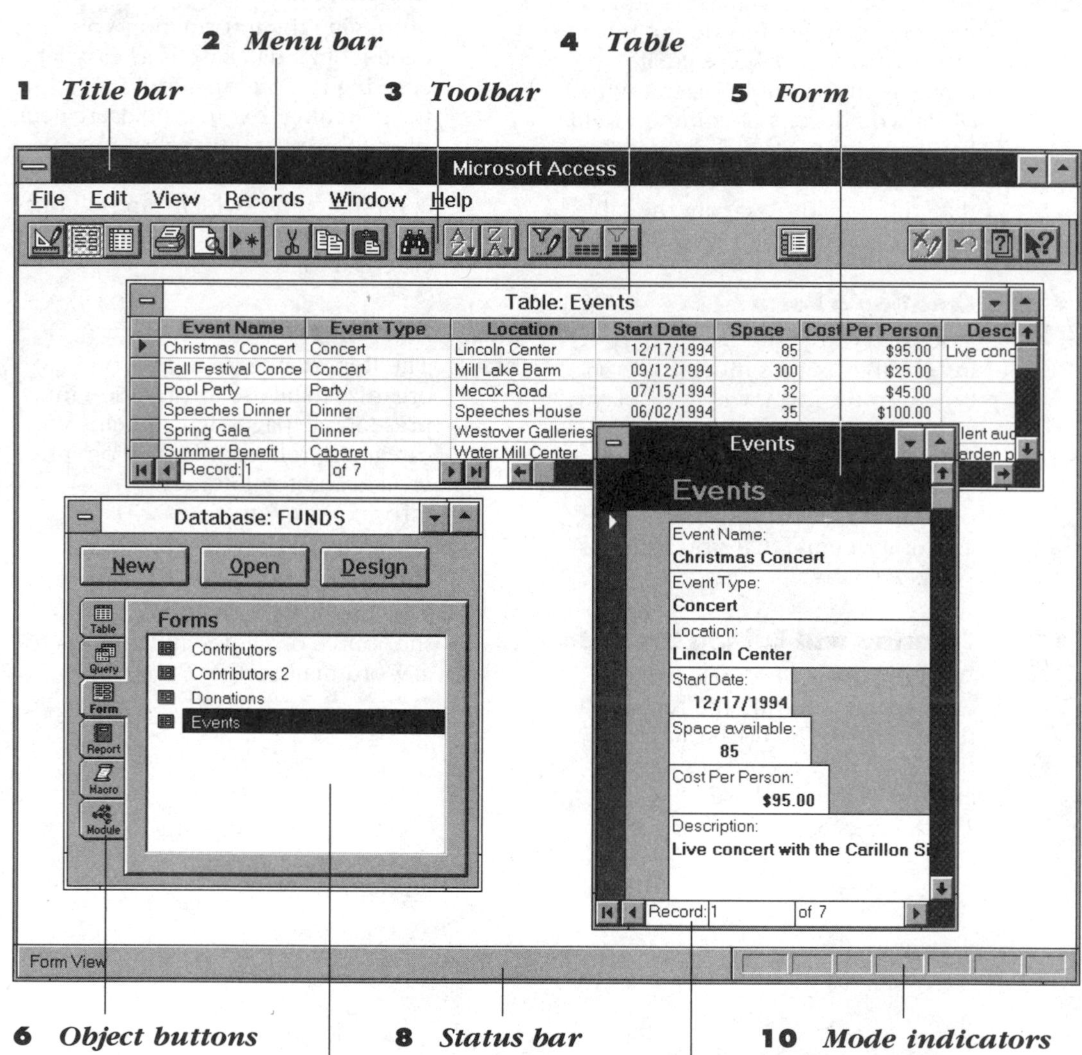

Key to the Access 2 Window

1 *Title bar*

Displays the window name. Drag the title bar to move the window. Double-click the title bar to switch between maximized and restored window.

2 *Menu bar*

Click any name on the menu bar to pull down a menu, or press Alt+the underlined letter of the menu name.

3 *Toolbar*

Toolbar with buttons for the most frequently needed commands. Access provides the different toolbars at different times as you work in Access with buttons appropriate for the current task.

4 *Table*

Tables hold the information in a database. A single database can contain many different tables, each holding a different set of related records.

5 *Form*

A fill-in-the-blanks form used to enter, edit, and view the information in a table one record at a time. A single database can contain many different forms, perhaps even more than one for each database.

6 *Object buttons*

Click these buttons to change to the tab that shows the object type you want to work with. Objects in a database are tables, forms, reports, queries, macros, and modules.

7 *Database window*

Displays lists of the objects in a database. The Database window contains tabs that show objects of a certain type. Click a tab, click an object, and then click one of the buttons in the Database window to work with the database.

8 *Status bar*

Shows current status information about the current task.

8 *Record navigation buttons*

These controls move from record to record in the database. On a form and the table, they display the first, next, previous, or last record. They also display the current record number and the total number of records in the database.

10 *Mode indicators*

Show special conditions that are in effect, such as a pressed Caps Lock key.

Starting Access

1. Double-click the Microsoft Access icon in the Program Manager. **(Figure 1)**

   or

   Click the Microsoft Access icon in the Microsoft Office Manager. **(Figure 2)**

✔ Tip

- If Microsoft Access is already started, press Ctrl+Esc and choose Microsoft Access from the list of running applications on the Task List. You can also press Alt+Tab repeatedly until the Microsoft Access icon appears. Then release the Alt key and the Access window will come to the front.

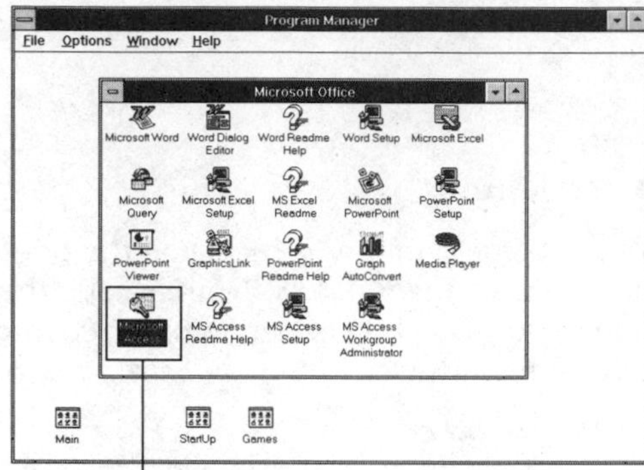

Microsoft Access icon.

Figure 1. *The Windows Program Manager.*

Figure 2. *The Microsoft Office Manager.*

Setting Up a Table

New Database button.

Figure 1. *The New Database button.*

Enter a filename for the new database here.

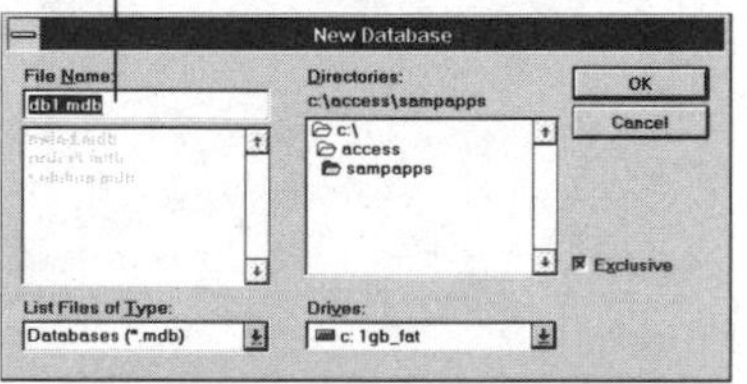

Figure 2. *The New Database dialog box.*

Figure 3. *The Database window.*

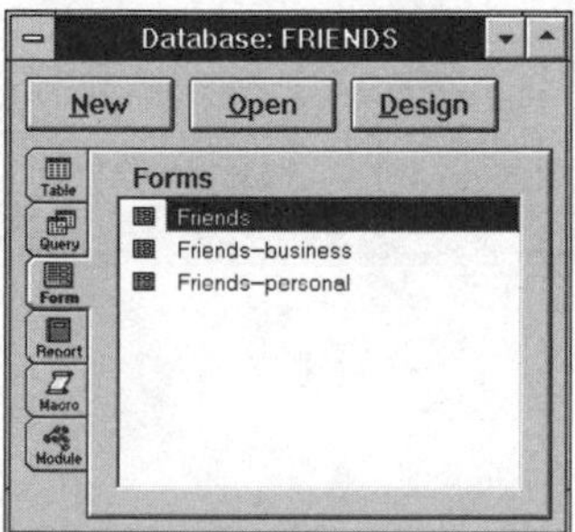

Figure 4. *The Form tab.*

Creating a New Database

1. Click the New Database button on the Database toolbar. **(Figure 1)**

   or

   From the File menu, choose New Database.
2. Enter a filename for the database into the New Database dialog box. **(Figure 2)**

Access

About the Database Window

The Database window displays lists of the components (tables, forms, reports, and other items) that constitute a database. It also provides buttons you use to create a new component, open an existing component, or modify the design of an existing component. Components are officially called *objects*. When the Database window first opens, the Table tab displays any table objects that are in the database. **(Figure 3)** To see a list of objects of a different type, click one of the tabs to the left of the list, such as the Form tab. **(Figure 4)**

Saving the Database

You don't need to save the data you add to a database file. Every change to the data in the database is saved on disk automatically. But you do need to save each of the objects that you create within the database (tables, queries, forms, reports, etc.) Lists of these objects are shown in the Database window. **(Figures 3-4)**

About Tables and Other Database Objects

A table is a complete collection of data displayed in rows and columns. Each row is one set of information, called a ***record***. Each column in the row, called a ***field***, is one part of the information in the record. **(Figure 5, below)**

You can display, edit, or print the data in a table, but you will want to create a ***form*** to make it easier to add data to a table or update the existing data. **(Figure 6)**

To make the information in the table look neat and clear on the printed page, you can create a ***report*** which pulls information from a table. **(Figure 7)**.

To pull selected information from the table, you create a ***query***. **(Figure 8)**

One field in each table must be a ***primary key***. The primary key holds a unique item that identifies each record. Each record might have a unique record number as the primary key, for example.

Tables can be related to other tables so they share a common field.

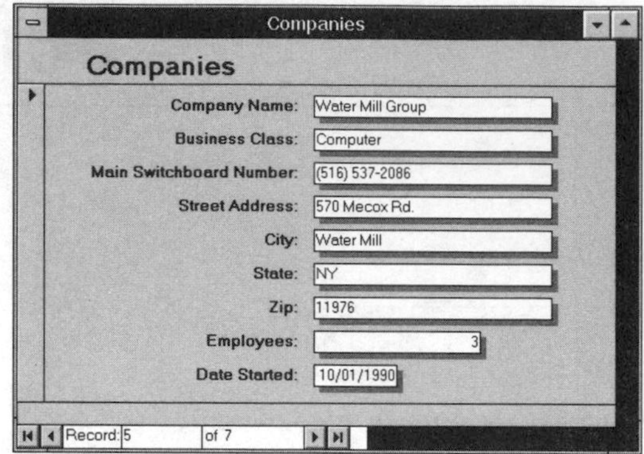

Figure 6. *A form.*

One record. *One field.*

Table: Companies

Company Name	Business Class	Main Switchboard Number	Street Address	City	State	Zip	Employe
CMM, Inc.	Publishing	(312) 555-4254	37 Rock Road	Chicago	IL	60619	
Lola's Care	Service	(516) 555-9384	4 Main St.	Bridgehar	NY	11987	
VPI	Media	(212) 555-4242	397 Park Ave. So.	New York	NY	10016	
Water Mill Group	Computer	(516) 537-2086	570 Mecox Rd.	Water Mill	NY	11976	
Wein Events	Service	(212) 555-4200	140 Charles St.	New York	NY	10014	
B&B	Advertising	(212) 555-4958	590 Third Ave.	New York	NY	10022	1

Record: 1 of 6

Figure 5. *A table.*

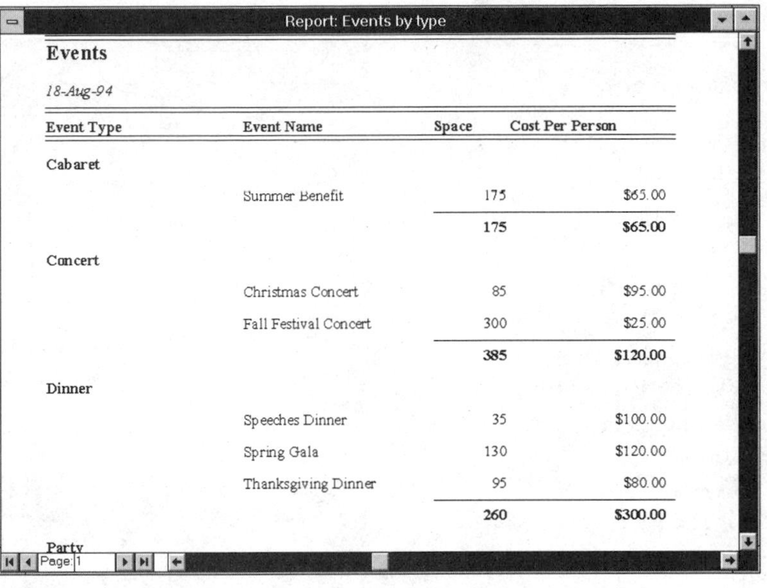

Figure 7. *A report.*

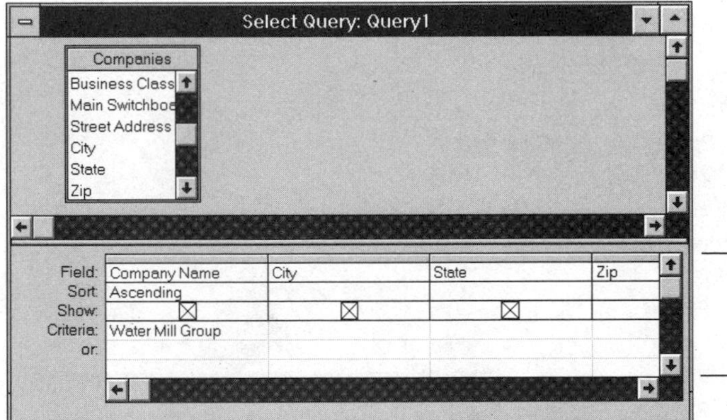

This query finds all entries that have a company name of "Water Mill Group."

Figure 8. *A query.*

Creating a Table with the Table Wizard

The Table Wizard helps you start a new table and set up the fields. It provides dozens of sample fields that you might find in both Business and Personal databases.

1. Click the Table tab in the Database window. **(Figure 9)**
2. In the Database window, click the New button.
3. On the New Table dialog box, click the Table Wizards button. **(Figure 10)**
4. On the Table Wizard dialog box, click Business or Personal to choose a database type. **(Figure 11)**
5. Click a table on the list of Sample Tables.
6. Double-click a field on the list of Sample Fields to add the field to the list of "Fields in my new table."
7. Continue adding other fields from the same sample table or other sample tables you choose on the Table Wizard dialog box until you have all the fields you need.
8. Click Next to move to the next step.
9. On the next Table Wizard dialog box, enter a name for the table. **(Figure 12)**
10. Choose either *Let Microsoft Access set a primary key for* me (to let Access create the primary key field) or *Set the primary key myself* (to make decisions in a separate Table Wizard step about how the primary key should be established.) **(Figure 13)**
11. Click Next to move to the next step.

    If you chose Set the primary key myself: Select a field from the drop down list on the following Table Wizard dialog box. **(Figure 14)** Then choose whether Access should add numbers

Figure 9. *The Table tab of the Database window.*

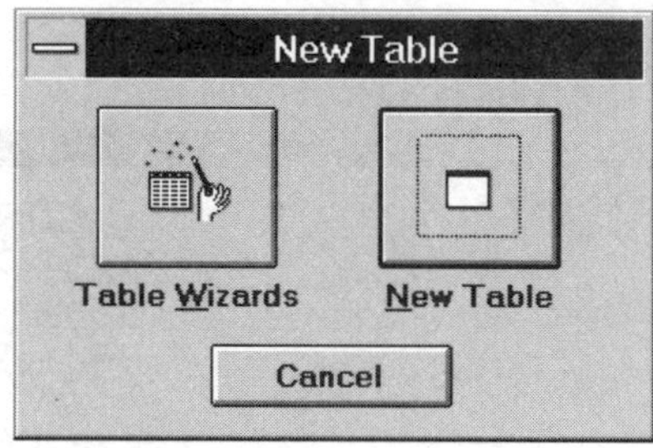

Figure 10. *The New Table dialog box.*

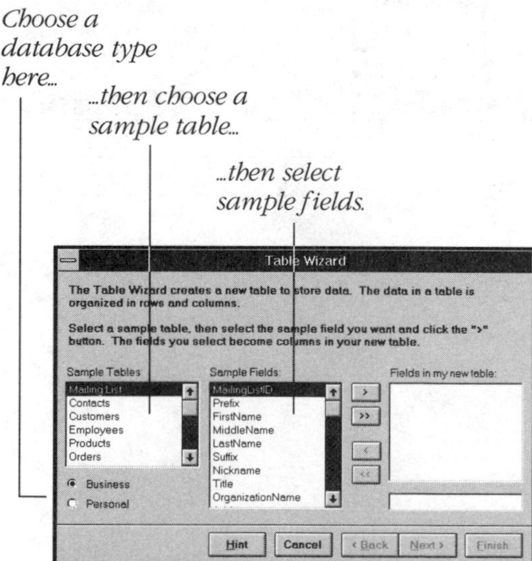

Figure 11. *Table Wizard dialog box.*

Access

Enter a name for the table here.

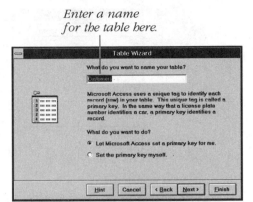

Figure 12. *Table Wizard dialog box.*

automatically or whether you'll enter numbers or text in the primary key field. Click Next.

If you have already created other tables, you can choose how to relate the new table to an existing table:
On the next Table Wizard dialog box, choose one of the existing tables to relate to the next table, then click Change. **(Figure 15)** On the next dialog box, choose one of the three options to define a relationship between the two tables, and then click OK.

12. On the final Table Wizard dialog box, choose an option and then click Finish. **(Figure 16)**

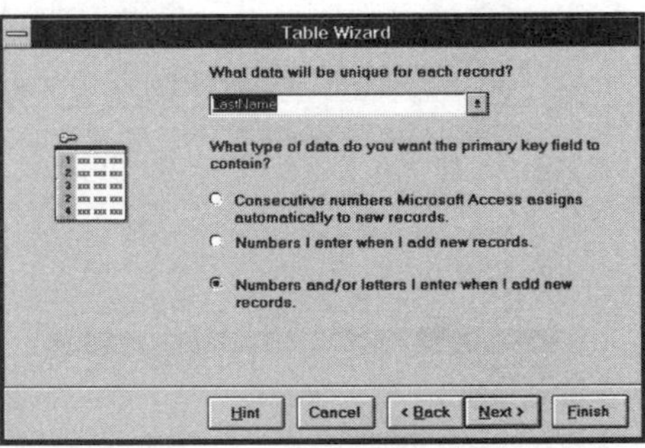

Figure 13. *Table Wizard dialog box.*

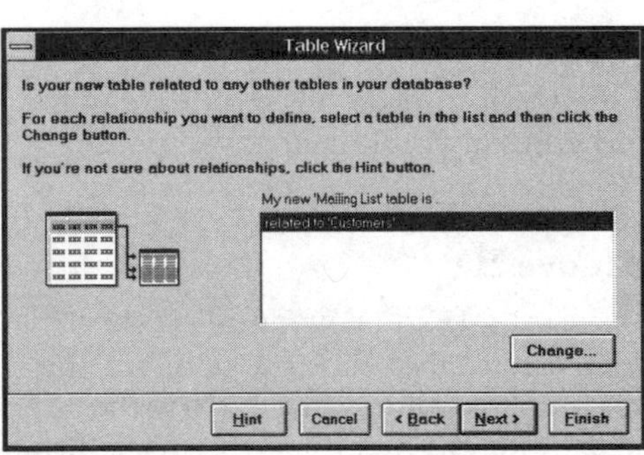

Figure 14. *Optional Table Wizard Step.*

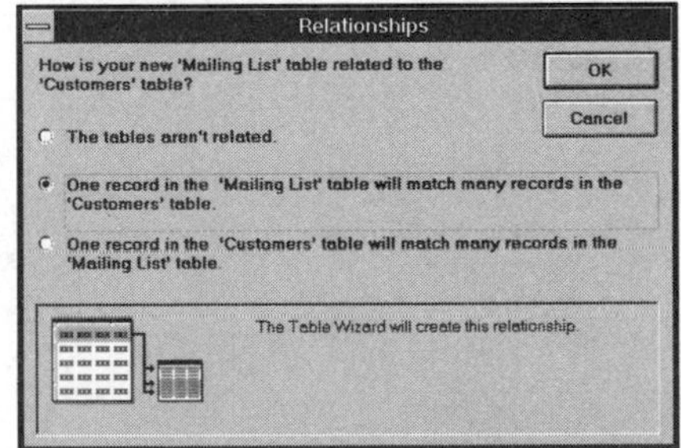

Figure 15. *Relationships dialog box.*

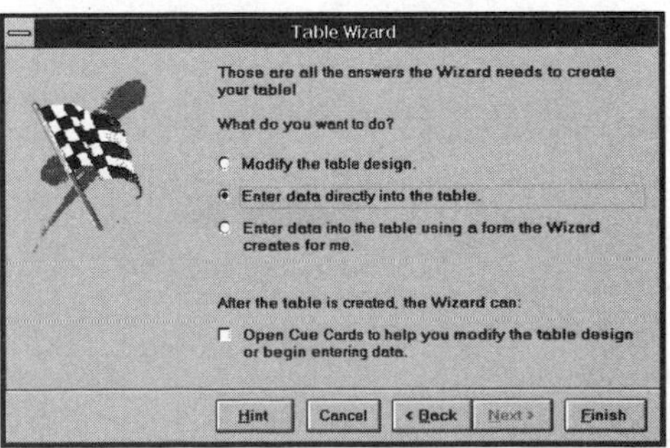

Figure 16. *The Final Table Wizard dialog box.*

Adding a Field

Access

Adding a Field to the Table in Design View

1. On the Table tab of the Database window, choose a table and click Design. **(Figure 17)**
2. In the Table window, click a blank row in the Field Name column. **(Figure 18)**
3. Enter a field name and press Tab to move to the next column. **(Figure 19)**
4. Choose a data type from the drop-down list in the Data Type column and press Tab to move to the next column. **(Figure 20)**
5. Enter a description for the field in the Description column.
6. Click the Save button or choose Save from the File menu to save changes to the table. **(Figure 21)**

✔ Tips

- If a table is already open for data entry and editing, you can click the Design View button in the Table Datasheet toolbar to switch to Design view. **(Figure 21)**
- To insert a field between two other fields on the list, click the name of the field that should be just **below** the new field and then click the Insert Row button. Click a row and then click the Delete Row button to delete a field. **(Figure 21)**

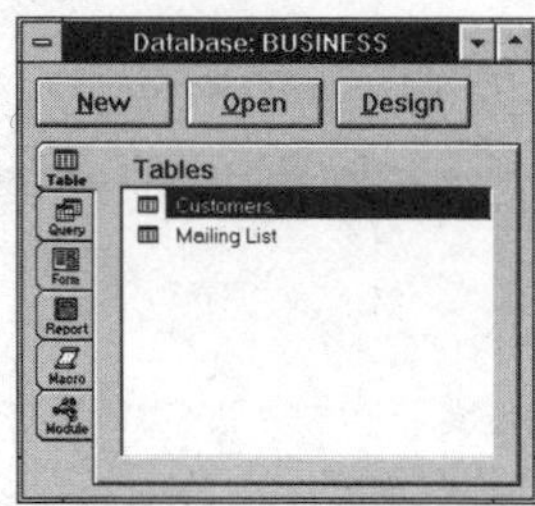

Figure 17. *The Database window.*

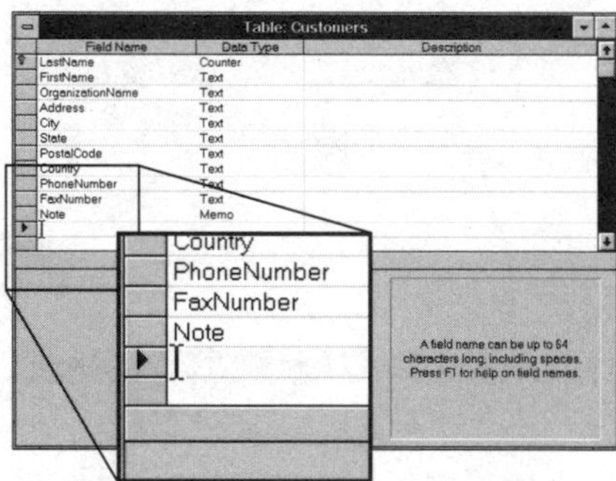

Figure 18. *Click a blank row in the Field Name column.*

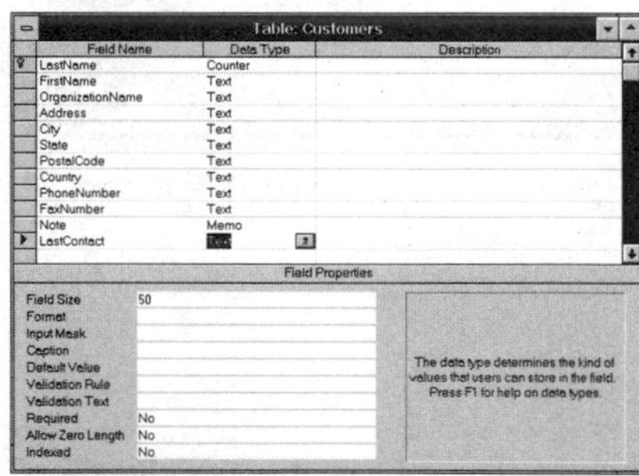

Figure 19. *Enter a field name and press Tab.*

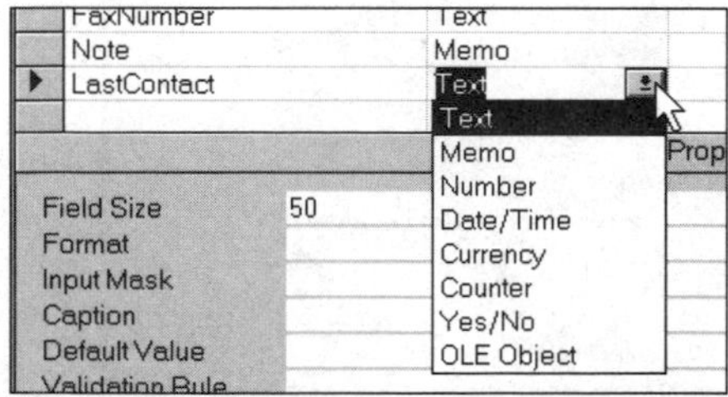

Figure 20. *The drop-down data type list.*

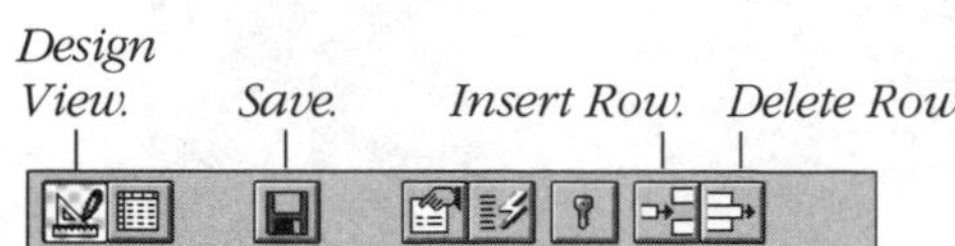

Figure 21. *The Save button.*

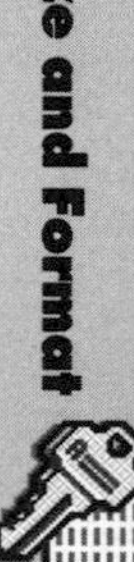

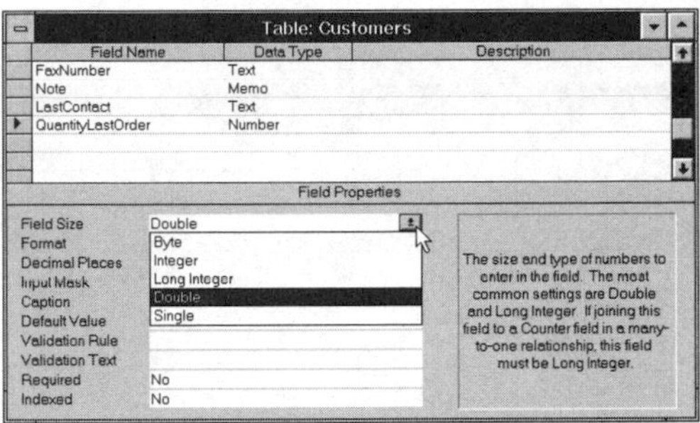

Figure 22. *Drop-down list for a number field.*

Table: Customers

Field Name	Data Type
LastName	Text
FirstName	Text
OrganizationName	Text
Address	Text
City	Text

Field Properties

Field Size	35
Format	@
Input Mask	
Caption	Last Name
Default Value	
Validation Rule	
Validation Text	
Required	No
Allow Zero Length	No
Indexed	Yes (No Duplicates)

Figure 23. *Formatting the LastName field to require an entry.*

Setting the Field Size and Format

1. On the Tables tab of the Database window, choose a table and click Design.
2. On the Table window, click the name of the field to format.
3. Click the Field Size text box and then enter a number if the field is text or choose from the drop-down list of options if the field is a number or other data type. **(Figure 22)** *See Table 31-1 below for the Number Field Size Options.*
4. Click the Format box and then, if the field is a text field, enter one of the symbols shown in Table 31-2. **(Figure 23)**
5. Click the Save button or choose Save from the File menu to save changes to the table.

✔ Tips

- For a text field, you can enter any field size between 0 and 255. The default is 50.
- When setting the field size for a Number field, choose the option that requires the least number of bytes but is still suitable for your data. *See Table 31-1.*

Table 31-1. *Number Field Size Options*

Integer	Accepts numbers from -32,768 to 32,767. Occupies 2 bytes.
Long Integer	Accepts numbers from -2,147,483,648 to 2,147,483,647. Occupies 4 bytes.
Single	Stores numbers with six digits of precision, from -3.402823E38 to 3.402823E38. Occupies 4 bytes.
Double (default)	Stores numbers with 10 digits of precision, from -1.79769313486232E308 to 1.79769313486232E308. 8 bytes.

Table 31-2. *Text Formatting Symbols*

@	A text character is required in the field (either a character or a space).
&	A text character is not required.
<	All characters entered will become lowercase.
>	All characters entered will become uppercase.

Entering a Caption and Default Value for a Field

A caption appears at the top of a field in the table and next to the field on a form. Changing the caption name does not change the field name. You may prefer to use "First Name" as the caption for a field called "fname," for example.

1. On the Table tab of the Database window, choose a table and click Design.
2. On the Table window, click the name of the Field to format.
3. Click the Caption box text and enter the text that will be used to label the field on the form. **(Figure 24)**
4. Click the Default Value text box and then enter the default entry. **(Figure 25)**
5. Click the Save button or choose Save from the File menu to save changes to the table. **(Figure 26)**

✔ Tip

- If you don't set a caption name, the field name is used.

Enter a field caption.

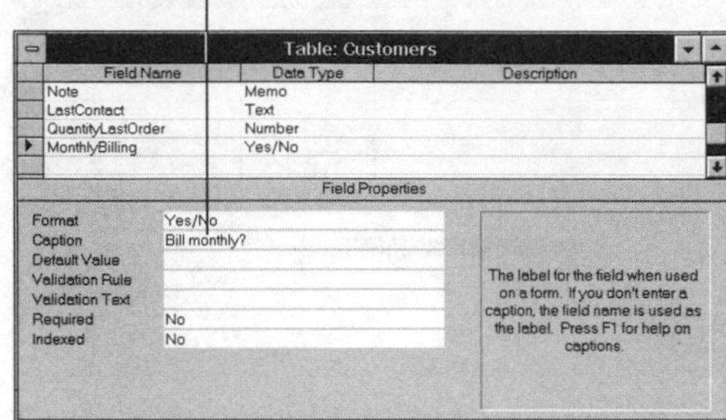

Figure 24. *The Table window.*

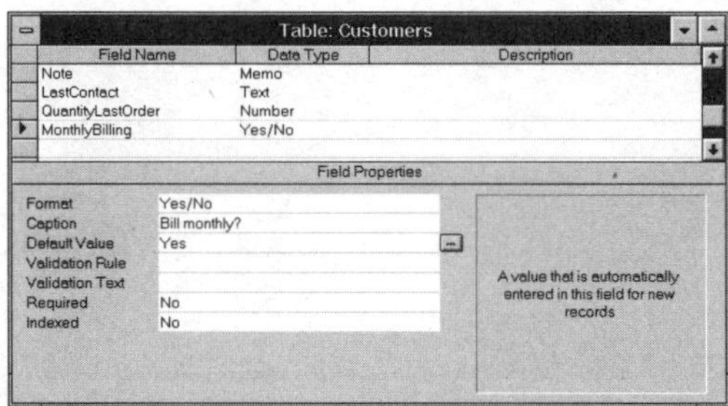

Figure 25. *Entering Yes as the default value for a Yes/No field.*

Save button.

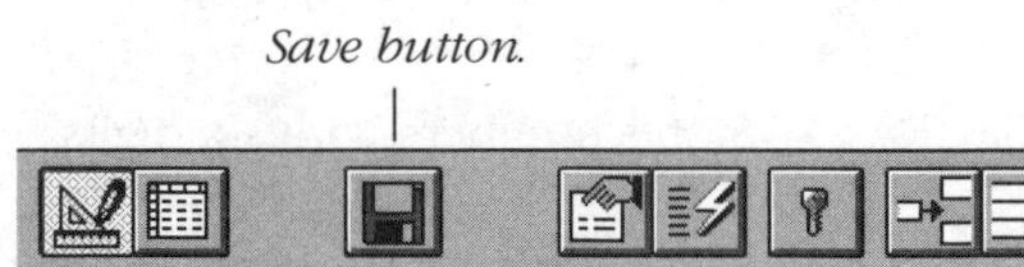

Figure 26. *The Save button.*

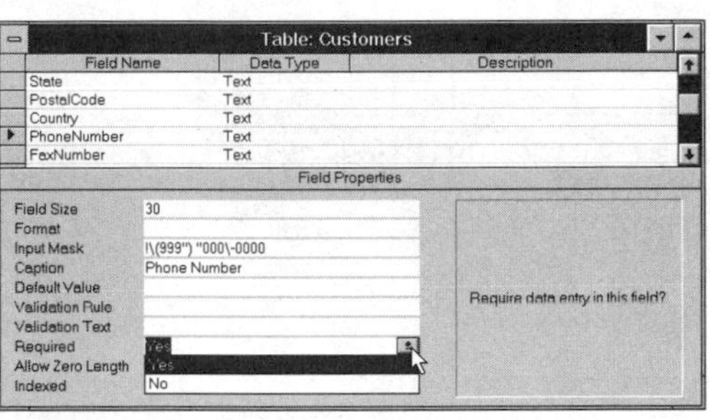

Figure 27. *The options on the Required drop-down list.*

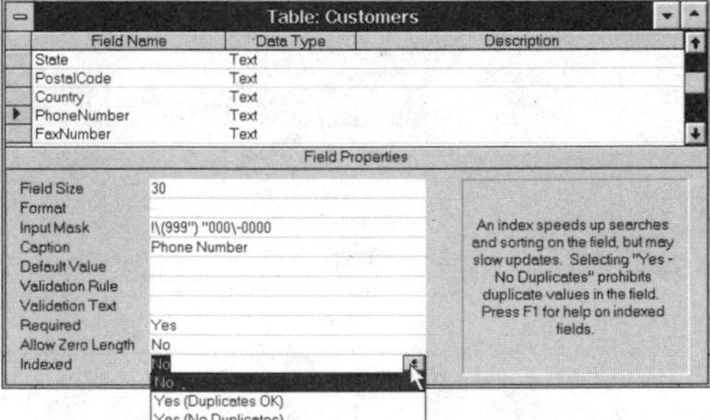

Figure 28. *The options on the Indexed drop-down list.*

Figure 29. *The Indexes button.*

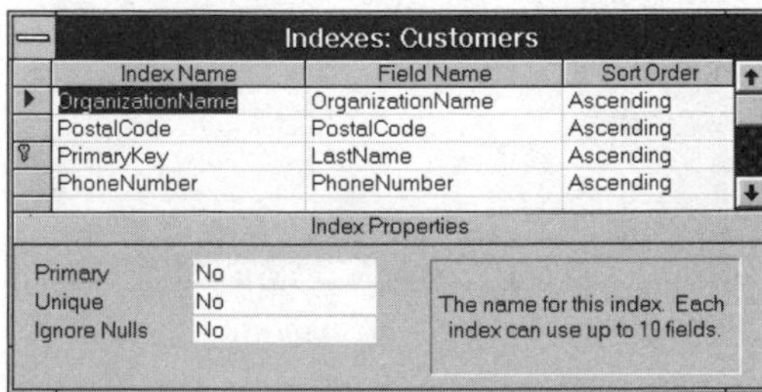

Figure 30. *The Indexes window.*

Requiring/Indexing a Field

A *required* field must have an entry before the record can be saved. An *indexed* field is specially prepared so it can be searched much faster.

1. On the Tables tab of the Database window, select a table and click Design.
   or
   If the table is already open, click the Design View button.
2. On the Table window, click the name of the Field to format.
3. Click the Required text box and choose Yes or No from the drop-down list. **(Figure 27)**
4. Click the Indexed text box and choose an option on the drop-down list. **(Figure 28)** *See Table 31-3 for the Indexed options.*

✔ Tips

- Primary key fields are automatically indexed.
- To view a list of fields that are indexed, click the Indexes button on the Standard toolbar while the table is shown in Design view. **(Figures 29–30)**

Table 31-3. ***Indexed options***

No	This field is not indexed.
Yes (Duplicates OK)	This field is indexed and duplicates are allowed.
Yes (No Duplicates)	This field is indexed and each entry is unique.

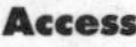

Saving the Table

You must save each table that you create and also save any changes to a table.

1. While the Table window is open, click the Save button on the Table Design toolbar. **(Figure 31)**

   or

   Press Ctrl+S.

   or

   Choose Save from the File menu. **(Figure 32)**

If the table is new, its name is added to the list of tables in the Database window. **(Figure 33)**

Figure 31. *The Save button.*

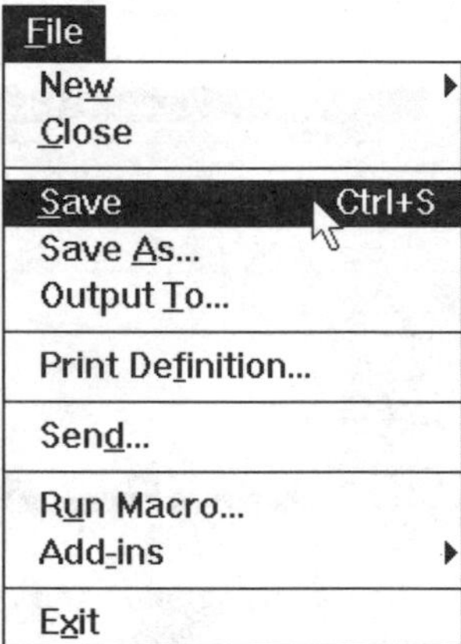

Figure 32. *The File menu.*

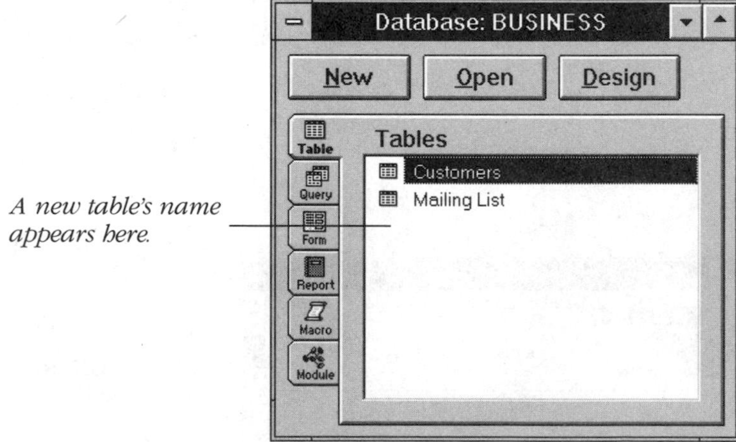

Figure 33. *The Database window.*

Creating a Form 32

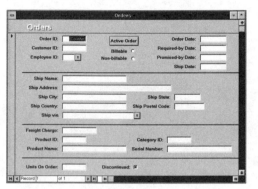

About Forms and Controls

Each object on a form is called a *control*. Controls can be labels, text boxes, blanks, empty fields, checkboxes, buttons, radio buttons, and several other types of graphical objects. **(Figure 1)** The controls on a form display when you are entering or editing a table with the form and they also print when you print the form.

When the Form Wizard creates a form, it places controls on the form automatically. You can modify the controls or add new controls in Design view. **(Figure 2)**

Figure 1. *Controls on a form.*

Access

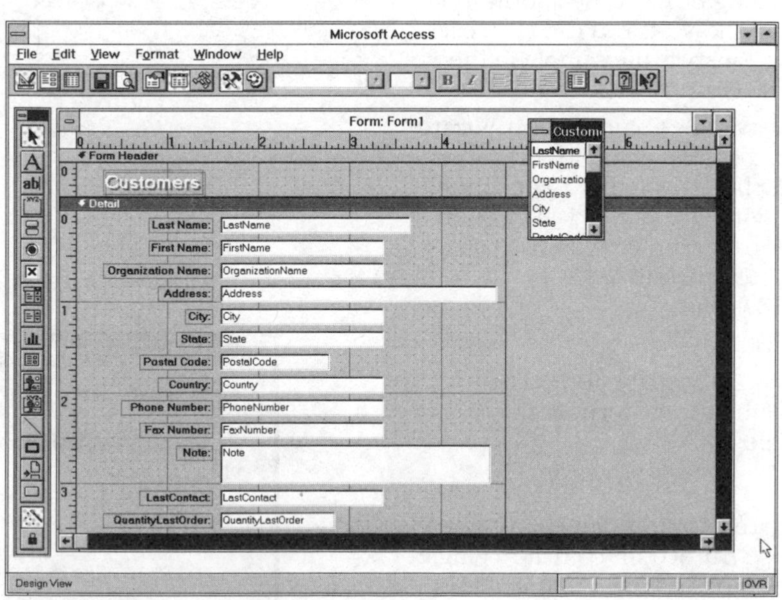

Figure 2. *A form in Design View.*

Creating a Single-Column Form with the Form Wizard

1. Click the Form tab in the Database window. **(Figure 3)**
2. Click the New button in the Database window.

   or

   From the File menu, choose New and then choose Form.
3. On the New Form dialog box, choose a table from the drop-down list of tables. **(Figure 4)**
4. On the New Form dialog box, click the FormWizards button.
5. On the Form Wizards dialog box, double-click Single-Column. **(Figure 5)**
6. On the Single-Column Form Wizard dialog box, double-click each field to include and then click Next. **(Figure 6)**

   or

   Click the >> button to include all the fields in the table and then click Next.
7. On the following Single-Column Form Wizard dialog box, choose a form style and then click Next. You can click each button and inspect the sample in the dialog box. **(Figure 7)**
8. On the last Single-Column Form Wizard dialog box, enter a name for the form and then choose whether to open the form showing the table's data or open the form in Design View so you can modify the form's design. **(Figure 8)**
9. Click Finish.
10. Press Ctrl+S to save the form. Then enter a name for the form in the Form Name dialog box.

✔ Tip

- On the Form Wizards dialog box, you can choose AutoForm to create a Single-Column, Embossed form that includes all the fields in the table.

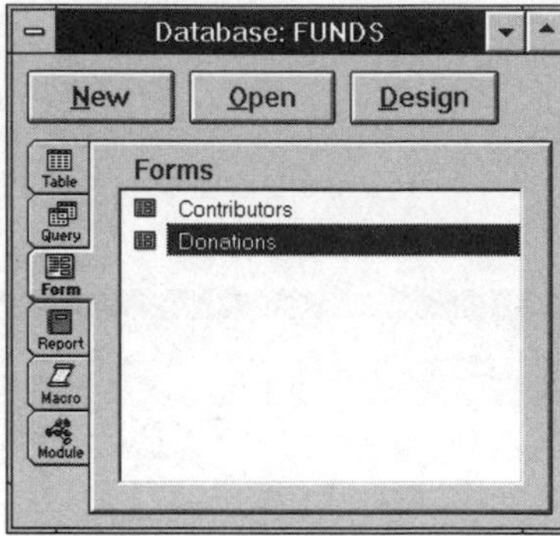

Figure 3. *The Form tab.*

Click here to pull down the list of tables.

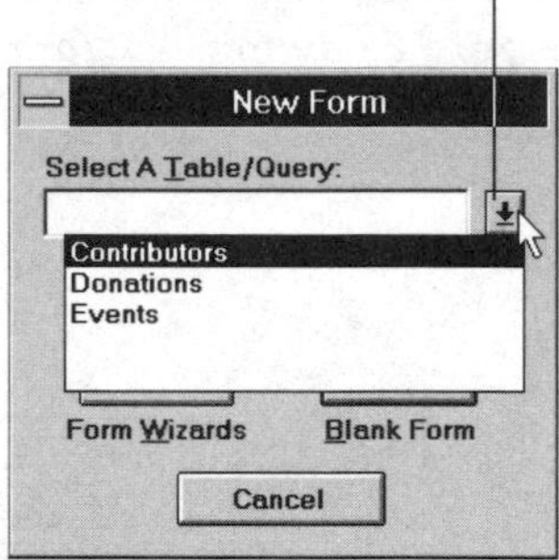

Figure 4. *The drop-down list of tables.*

Double-click here.

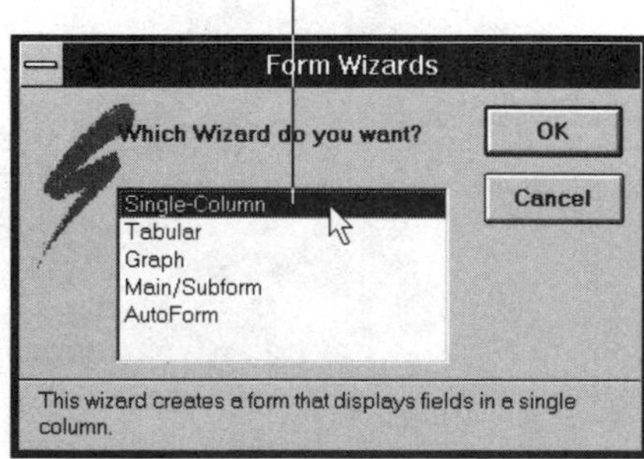

Figure 5. *The Form Wizards dialog box.*

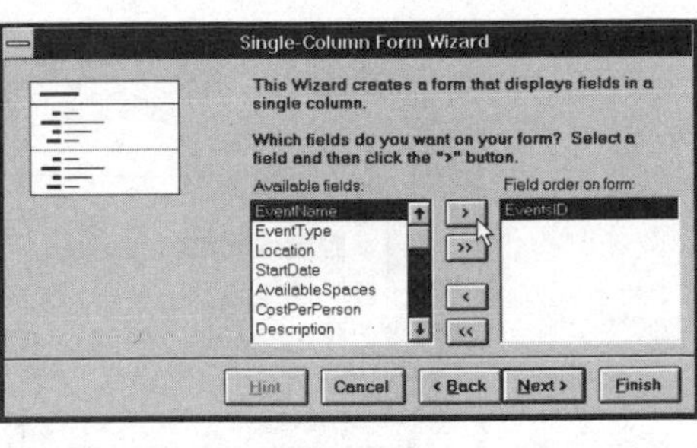

Figure 6. *The Single-Column Form Wizard dialog box.*

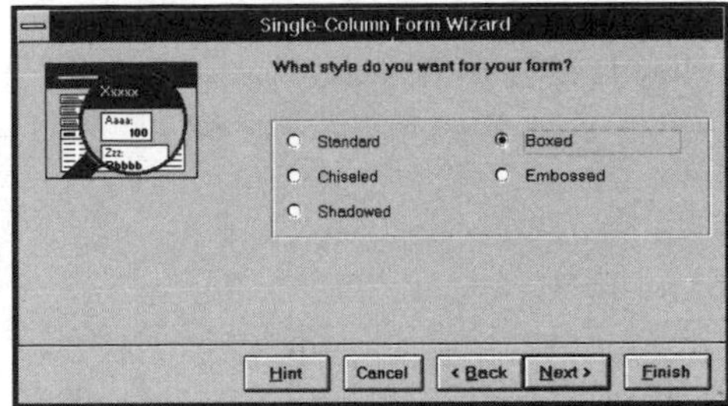

Figure 7. *The second Single-Column Form Wizard dialog box.*

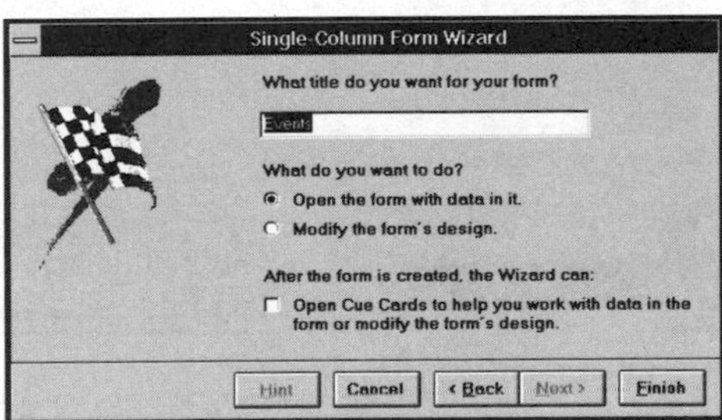

Figure 8. *The last Single-Column Form Wizard dialog box.*

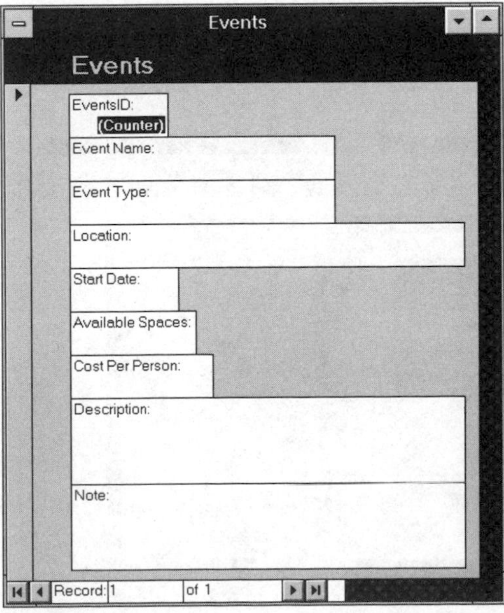

Figure 9. *A typical Single-Column form.*

Opening the Form in Design View

To modify the form that the Form Wizard has created, you must switch to Design view.

1. In the Database window, click the form tab. **(Figure 10)**
2. Select a Form and then click the Design button.

   or, if you are currently using the form to enter or edit data

1. Click the Design View button on the Standard toolbar. **(Figure 11)**

   or

   From the View menu, choose Form Design. **(Figure 12)**

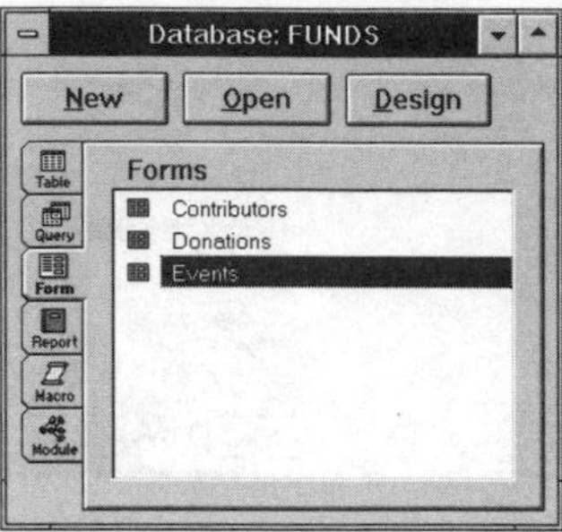

Figure 10. *The Form tab of the Database window.*

Design View button.

Figure 11. *The Design View button.*

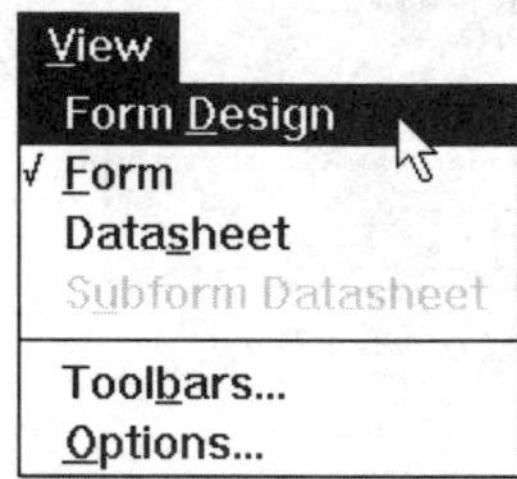

Figure 12. *The View menu.*

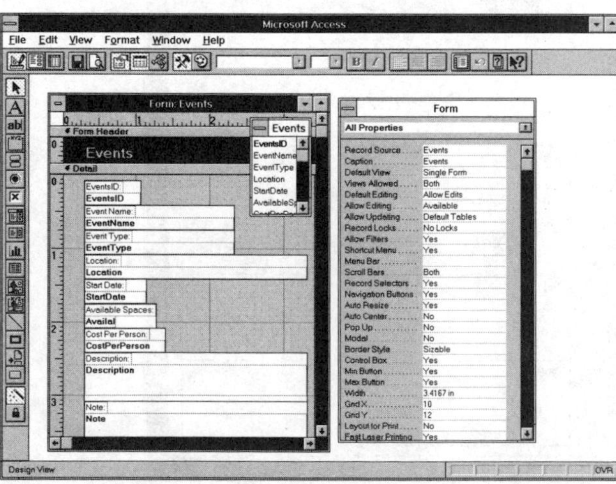

Figure 13. *A form in Design view.*

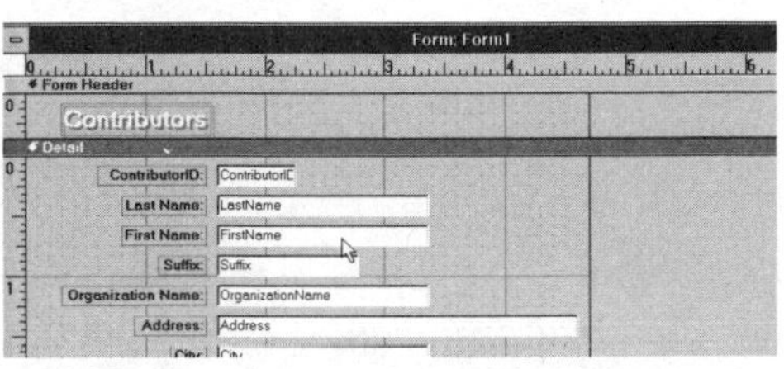

Figure 14. *Position the pointer on the control.*

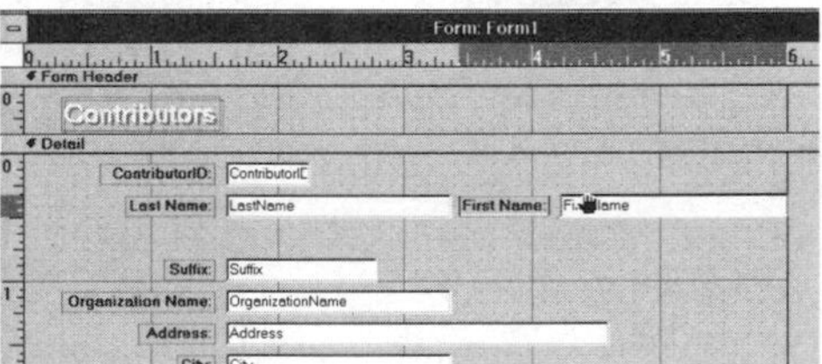

Figure 15. *The control as it is moved to a new position.*

Moving and Sizing Controls

To move a control:

1. Position the mouse pointer anywhere on the control. **(Figure 14)**
2. Hold down the mouse button and drag the control to its new position. **(Figure 15)**
3. Release the mouse button.

To size a control:

1. Drag one of the Size handles around the control to resize the control. **(Figure 16)**

✔ Tips

- Hold down the Shift key as you select several controls or drag a selection box around the controls to select. Then you can move the selected controls simultaneously, as a group.
- The length of a text field remains the same even when you change the size of the text box for the field.

Moving Labels Independently

1. Drag the move handle for a label to move the label independently of the field. **(Figure 16)**

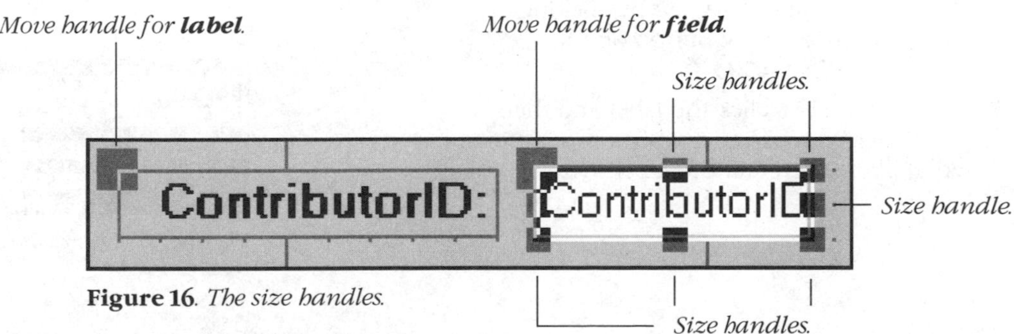

Figure 16. *The size handles.*

Adding and Formatting Labels

Each field on a new form has a label, but you can add additional labels to the form to provide special instructions to the person using the form. For example, you can enter a label for a group of fields that reads "Complete only if non-resident."

1. Make sure the toolbox is visible in Design view. If it is not, click the Toolbox button on the Form Design toolbar. **(Figure 17)**
2. Click the Label button in the toolbox.
3. Click on the form at the location for the new label.
4. Type the label text. **(Figure 18)**

To format the label:

1. Select the label.
2. Use the text formatting controls on the Form Design toolbar. **(Figure 19)**
3. Click the Palette button **(Figure 17)** if you'd like to set a special appearance for the label.
4. Make selections on the Palette dialog box and then close the Palette dialog box. **(Figure 20)**

✔ Tips

- To see the label on the completed form, switch to Datasheet view by clicking the Datasheet View button on the toolbar. **(Figure 21)**
- To edit a label, click the label and then click again to place an insertion point in the label. Then edit the label text.

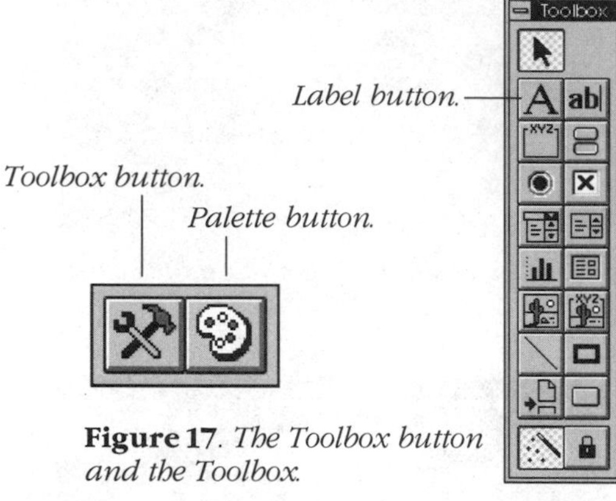

Figure 17. *The Toolbox button and the Toolbox.*

The new label appears where you click.

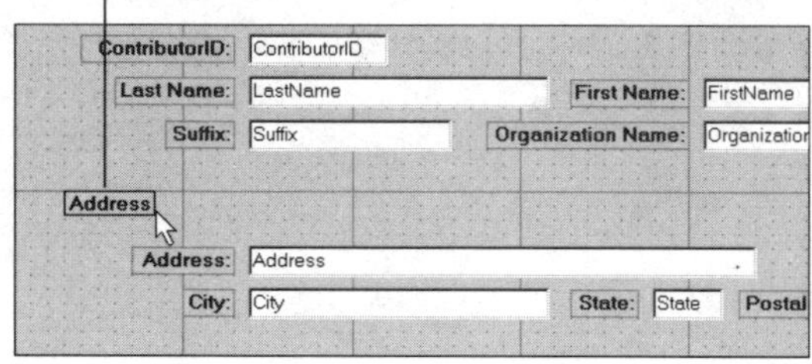

Figure 18. *Click and then type the label text.*

Figure 19. *The text formatting controls.*

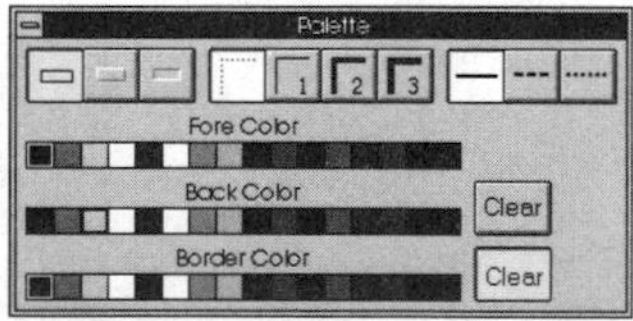

Figure 20. *The Palette dialog box.*

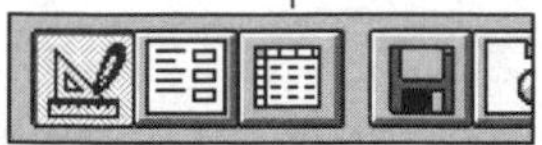

Figure 21. *The Datasheet View button.*

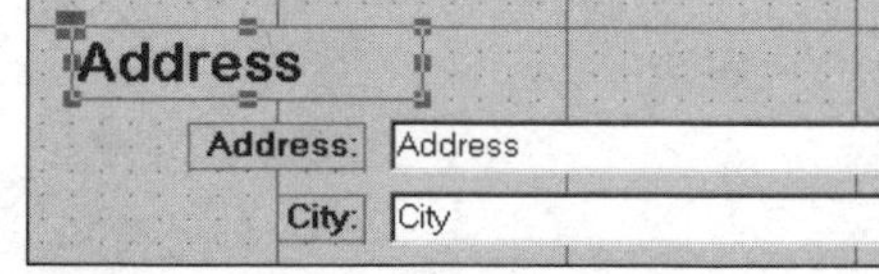

Figure 22. *The formatted label.*

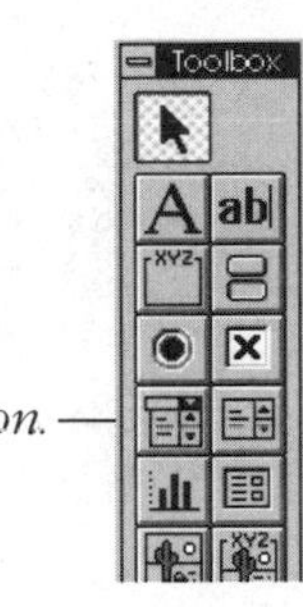

Figure 23. *The Combo Box button.*

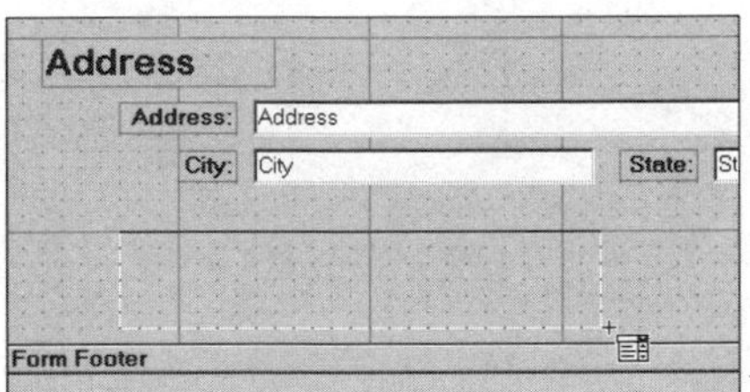

Figure 24. *Drag out a rectangle to place the combo box.*

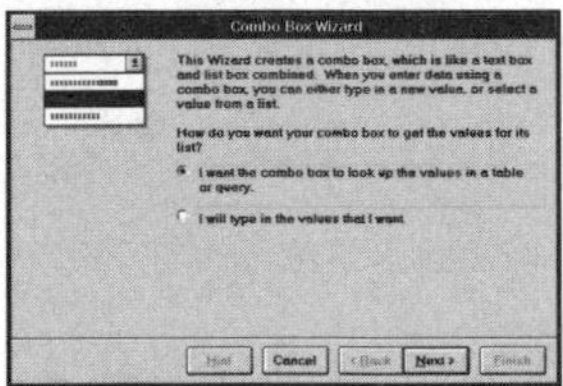

Figure 25. *The Combo Box Wizard.*

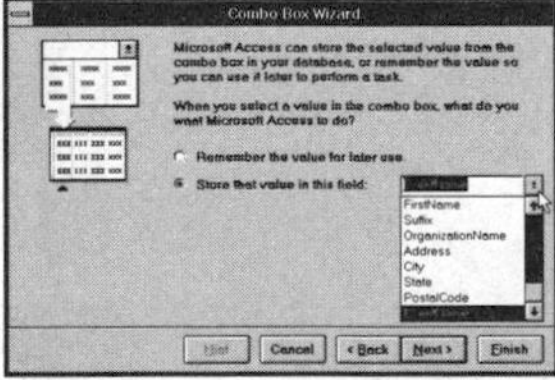

Figure 26. *Choose a field name.*

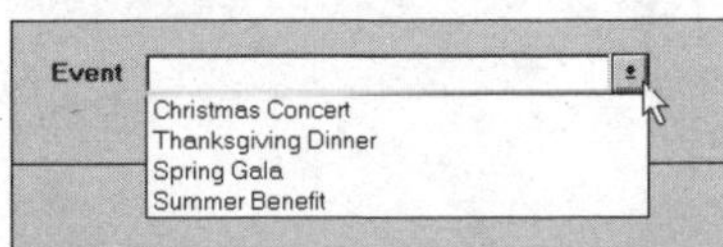

Figure 27. *The completed combo box as it appears on the form.*

Adding a Combo Box

A combo box is an especially useful control for a form. It provides a drop-down list of alternatives or allows the user to type any other entry. The Combo Box Wizard guides you through the steps when you add a combo box.

Combo boxes are only one type of control in the Toolbox. Some other controls also have Wizards that help you create the control.

1. In Design view, click the Combo Box button in the Toolbox. **(Figure 23)**
2. With the crosshair mouse pointer, drag out a rectangle that will contain the combo box. **(Figure 24)**
3. On the first dialog box of the Combo Box Wizard, select "I want the combo box to look up the values in a table or query" and click Next if you'd like the user to select a record from a particular table. The Wizard then takes you through the steps required to select the table. **(Figure 25)**

   or

   Select "I will type the values I want" and click Next to enter a list of alternatives. Then, on the next dialog box, select the number of columns of alternative choices to enter and type the alternatives choices in the columns, pressing Enter after each. Then click Next.
4. On the next dialog box, choose a field name from the drop-down list next to "Store that value in this field:" and click Next. **(Figure 26)**
5. On the last dialog box, supply a label for the combo box and click Finish.

✔ Tip

- If a Combo Box Wizard does not appear when you add a combo box, click the Control Wizards button on the toolbox.

Setting the Form and Control's Properties

The *properties* of a form, a section, or a control are all the settings that govern its appearance and behavior. In the Properties window, you can change every aspect of a form.

1. Click the Properties button on the toolbar. **(Figure 28)**
   or
   Select Properties from the View menu.
2. Click the section, control, or label whose properties you want to inspect. **(Figure 29)**
3. Click the drop-down button next to the Properties text box at the top of the Properties window and then choose a type of properties. **(Figure 30)**
4. Make changes to any of the properties.
5. Close the Properties window.

✔ Tips

- You can also double-click any control to change its properties.
- When you open the Properties window, you may need to drag it to the side to see the fields on the form.
- If a control is "unbound," you must bind it to a field in the table. Enter the name of the field in the Control Source text box in the Properties window.

Figure 28. *The Properties button.*

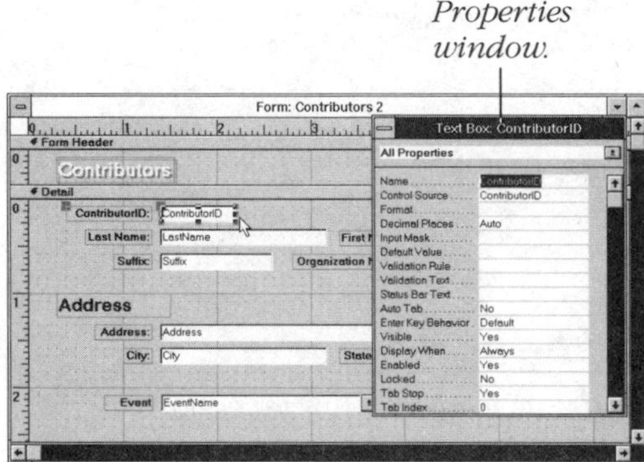

Figure 29. *The Properties window overlays the Form Design window.*

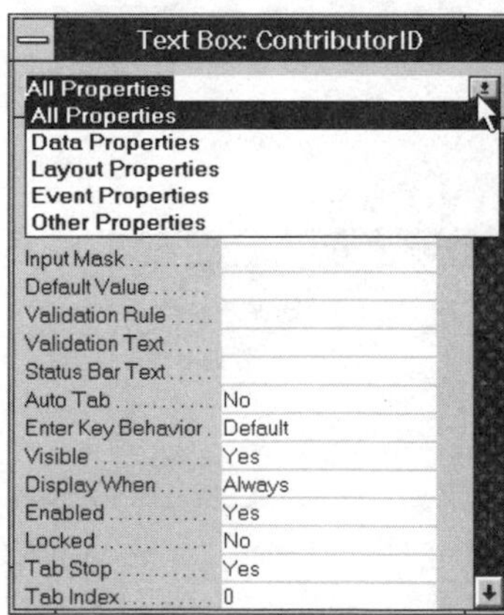

Figure 30. *The Properties drop-down list.*

Entering and Editing Data

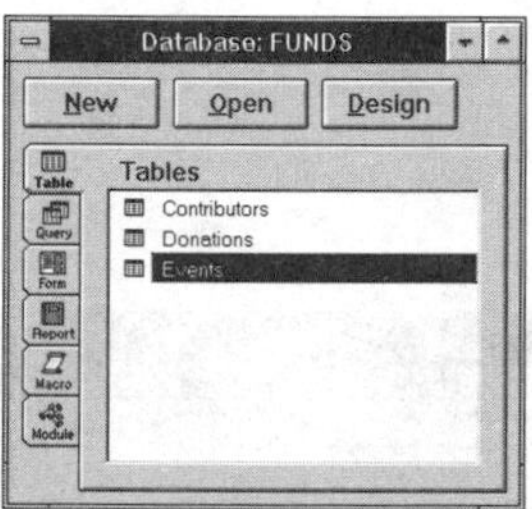

Figure 1. *The Table tab.*

Figure 2. *Press the New button.*

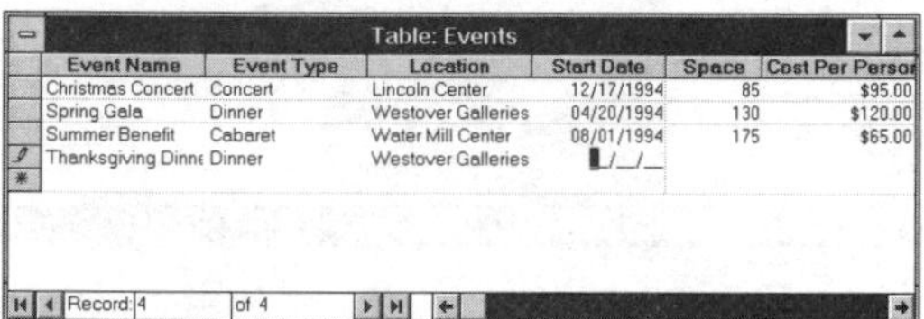

Figure 3. *Enter data and then press Tab.*

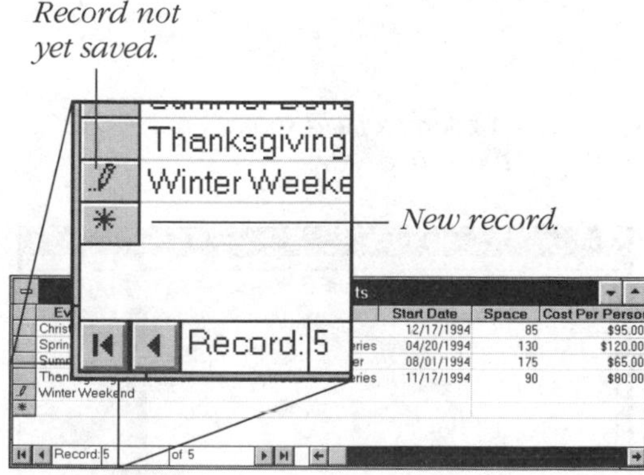

Figure 4. *Press Tab at the end of a record to move to the next, blank record.*

Entering Data into a Table

1. Click the Table tab in the Database window. **(Figure 1)**
2. Double-click a table name.

   or

   Select the table to add to and click Open.
3. Press the New button on the toolbar to add a new record. **(Figure 2)**
4. Enter data into the first field and then press Tab to move to the next field.
5. Continue entering data into fields and pressing Tab to move to the next field. **(Figure 3)**
6. Press Tab after the last field in the record to move to the start of a new record. The record you complete is saved automatically. **(Figure 4)**

✔ Tips

- You do **not** need to do anything special to save each new record. When you move to the next record, the previous record is saved automatically.
- To move to the previous field for corrections, press Shift+Tab.
- Before you begin adding data, a triangle points to the record. While you add data to a record, a pencil symbol appears to the left to indicate that the data is not yet saved. An asterisk appears in the new, blank record created below the record you're adding. **(Figure 4)**

Editing the Data in a Table

1. Click any field in the table to place an insertion point in the field. **(Figure 5)**
   or
   Double-click any word or number in a field to select the word or number. **(Figure 6)**
2. Edit the entry as you would edit text in **Word**.
3. Click a different record to save the changes. **(Figure 7)**

✔ Tips

- To select an entire field, click anywhere in the field and press F2.
- To replace the entry in a field with the entry in the same field of the previous record, click in the field and press Ctrl+'. (Ctrl+apostrophe)
- While you edit a field, the pencil symbol appears to the left of the record to indicate that the changes have not yet been saved.
- To abandon the changes you are making to a field or record, press Esc.
- Click a field with the right mouse button and choose Zoom from the shortcut menu to view the field in its own window. **(Figures 8-9)**

Figure 5. *Click to place an insertion point.*

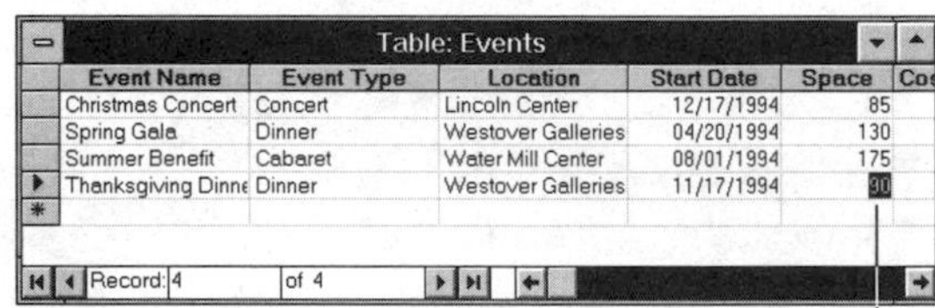

Figure 6. *Double-click a word to select it.*

Figure 7. *Click a different record to save changes to the record you've just finished editing.*

Click a field with the right mouse button.

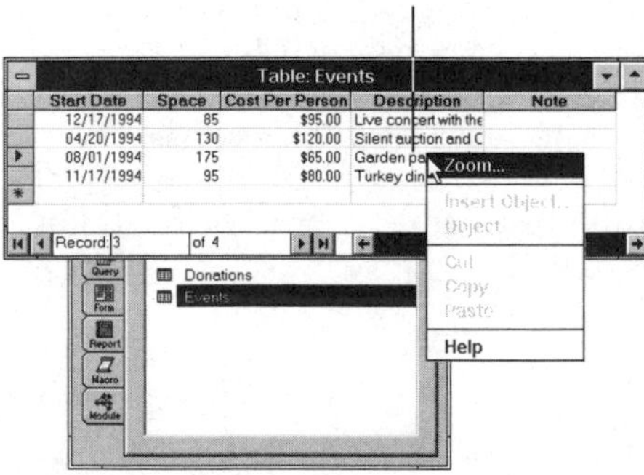

Figure 8. *The Shortcut menu.*

A zoomed field shows the entire entry.

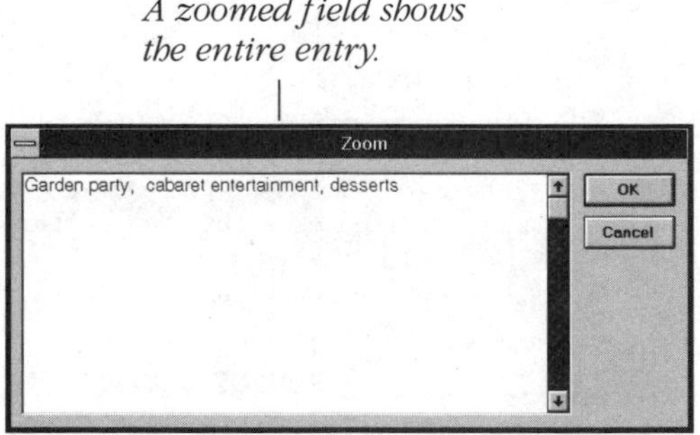

Figure 9. *Zooming into a field.*

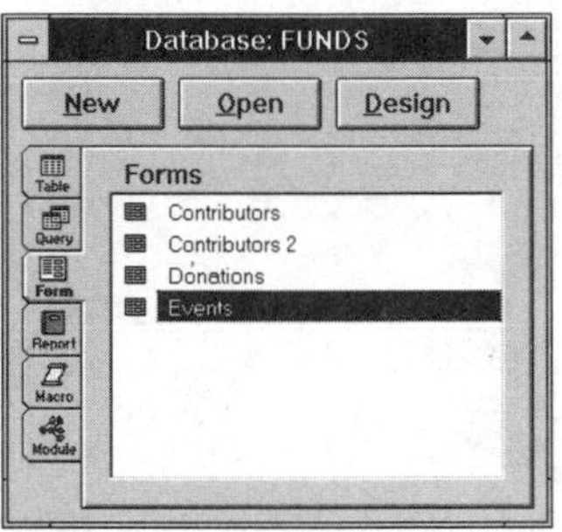

Figure 10. *The Form tab.*

The New button.

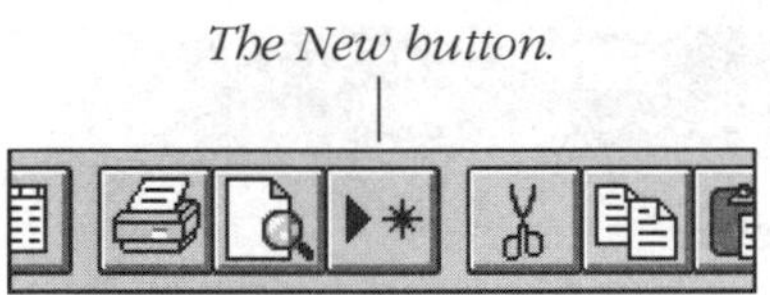

Figure 11. *Click the New button.*

Entering Data in a Form

1. Click the Form Tab in the Database window. **(Figure 10)**
2. Double-click the form name to use.
   or
   Select a form and click Open.
3. Click the New button in the Form View toolbar. **(Figure 11)**
4. Enter data into the first blank field on the form and press Tab. **(Figure 12)**
5. Continue entering data and pressing Tab to move to the next field.
6. Press Tab after the last field to move to the start of a new record. **(Figure 13)**

✔ Tips

- To move to the previous field on a form, press Shift+Tab.
- To jump to a field, click the field.
- You do not need to save each record. The completed record is saved automatically when you move to the next record.

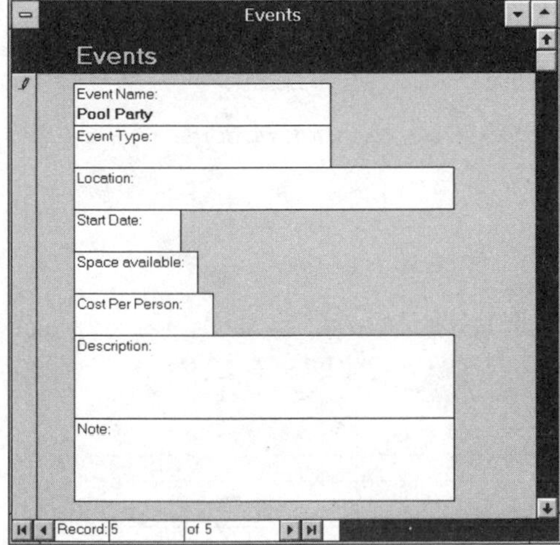

Figure 12. *Enter data into a field and press Tab.*

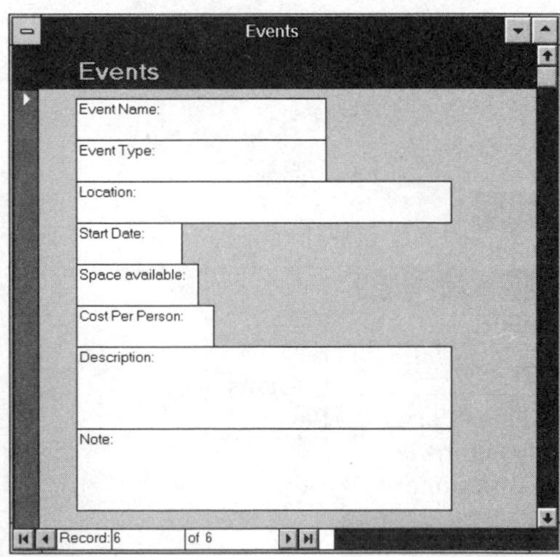

Figure 13. *Press Tab after the last field to move to a new record.*

Viewing Records with a Form

1. Open the form by double-clicking the form name on the Form tab of the Database window. **(Figure 14)**
2. Use the Next or Previous buttons to move forward or backward through the database. **(Figure 15)**

   or

   Press Ctrl+PgDn or Ctrl+PgUp.

   or

   From the Records menu choose Goto, and then choose Next or Previous from the submenu. **(Figure 16)**

✔ Tips

- To jump to the first or last record, press the First or Last buttons, press Ctrl+Up arrow or Ctrl+Down arrow, or choose First or Last from the Goto submenu.
- To jump to a specific record number, select the current record number, type a replacement number, and then press Enter. **(Figure 17)**

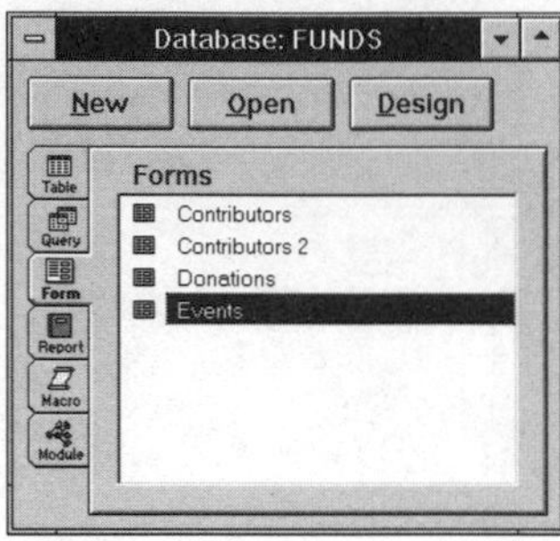

Figure 14. *The Form tab.*

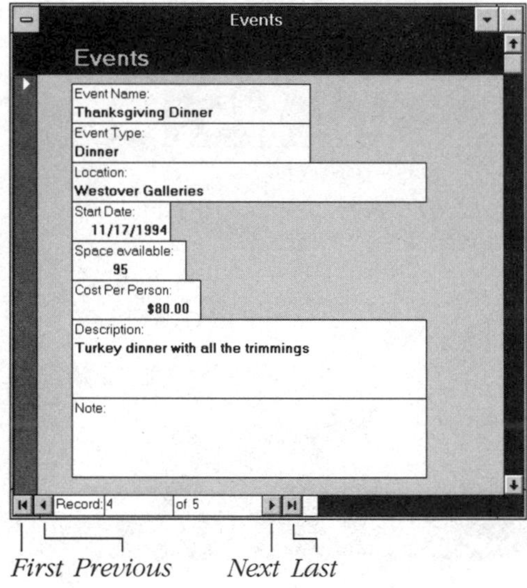

Figure 15. *The navigation buttons.*

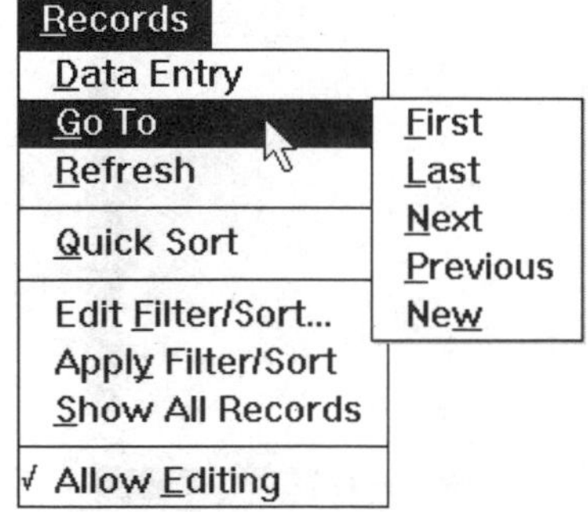

Figure 16. *The Records menu.*

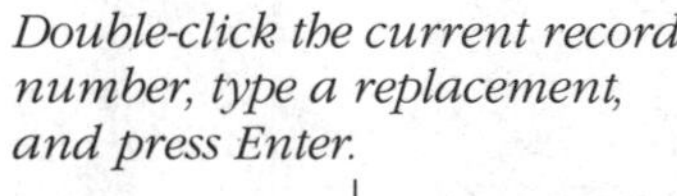

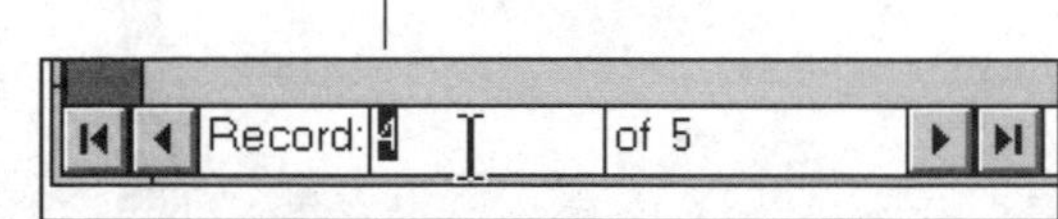

Figure 17. *Jumping to a specific record number.*

Basic Finds, Sorts, and Filters 34

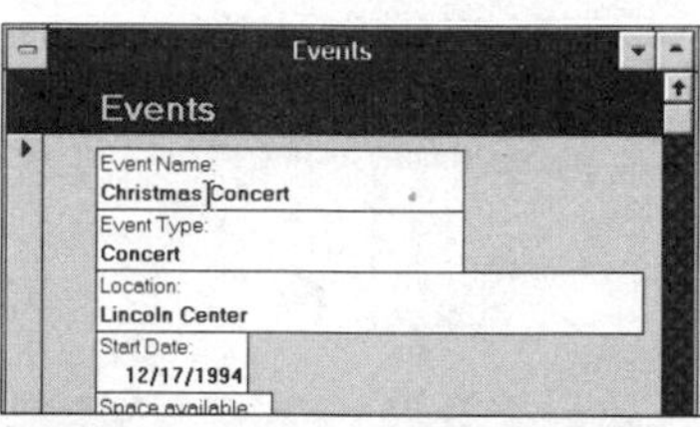

Figure 1. *Click the field that contains the data you want to find, and then click the Find button.*

The Find button.

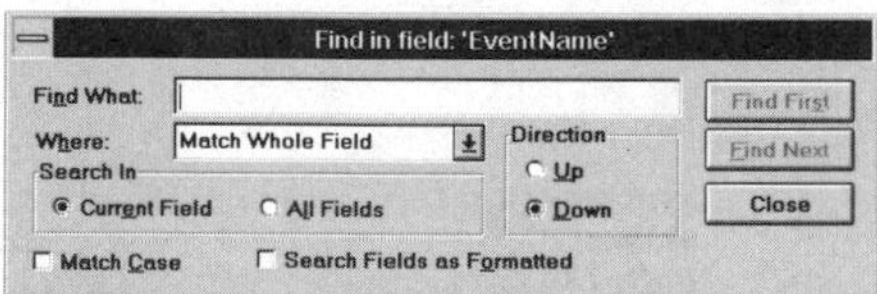

Figure 2. *The Find dialog box.*

Table 34-1. *The Find Dialog Box Options*

Search in Current Field	Restrict the search to the field you clicked in. Fastest.
All Fields	Search in all fields on the form. Takes longer.
Direction	Search **Up** through the table from the current record displayed on the form or search **Down**.
Match Case	Find only records that have the same capitalization as entered in the Find What text box.
Search Fields as Formatted	Search for items as shown in their current Display Format, not as stored in the database.

Finding a Match in the Database

1. Open a form that includes the field that contains the data you want to find.
2. Click in the field. **(Figure 1)**
3. Click the Find button on the toolbar.

   or

   Press F7

   or

   Press Ctrl+F

   or

   From the Edit menu, choose Find.
4. On the Find dialog box, type the entry you want to find into the Find What text box. **(Figure 2)**
5. Click any other options on the Find dialog box that apply. *See Table 34-1.*
6. Click the Find First button to find the first match.
7. Click the Find Next button if the first match was not the item you are looking for.
8. Click Close to close the Find dialog box.

✓ Tips

- When Access reaches the bottom of the table during its search, it asks whether to continue the search from the beginning. If you started halfway down the table, you may want to click Yes to search through the first half of the table.
- Click the Find First button at any time to jump back to the first match found. Then click Find Next to move forward through the matches.

Sorting Records

1. On a form or on the table, click in the field (in any record) upon which you want to sort the data. **(Figure 3)**
2. Click the Sort Ascending or Sort Descending button on the toolbar. **(Figure 4)**

   or

   From the Records menu, choose Quick Sort and then choose Ascending or Descending from the submenu. **(Figure 5)**

✔ **Tip**

- You can create a filter to pull out and then sort a certain subset of the data (all employees who are part time, for example). *See Creating a Filter, page 261.*

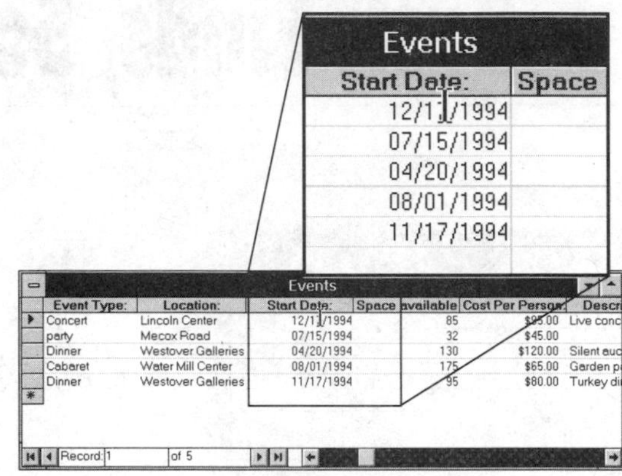

Figure 3. *Click in the Start Date field to sort the data by date.*

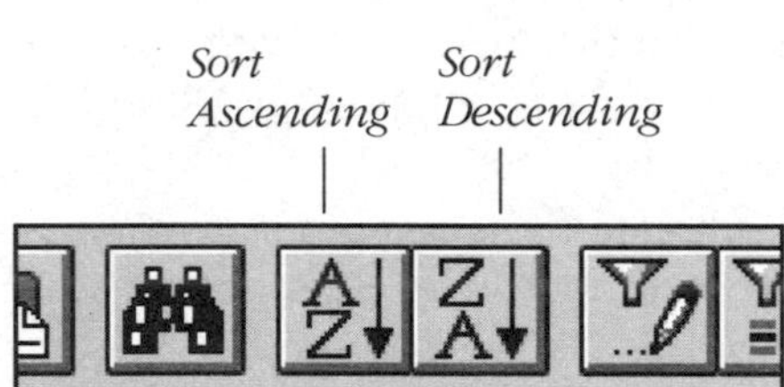

Figure 4. *The Sort buttons.*

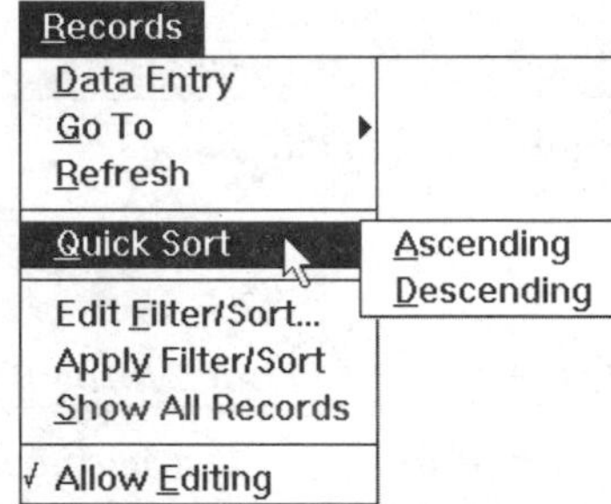

Figure 5. *The Records menu.*

Events

Event Type:	Location:	Start Date:	Space available	Cost Per Person:	Descri
Dinner	Westover Galleries	04/20/1994	130	$120.00	Silent auc
party	Mecox Road	07/15/1994	32	$45.00	
Cabaret	Water Mill Center	08/01/1994	175	$65.00	Garden p
Dinner	Westover Galleries	11/17/1994	95	$80.00	Turkey di
Concert	Lincoln Center	12/17/1994	85	$95.00	Live conc

Record: 2 of 5

Figure 6. *The table sorted by Start Date.*

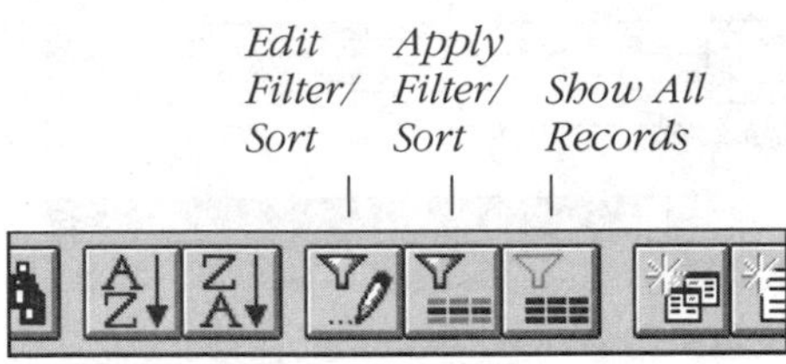

Figure 7. *Filter buttons.*

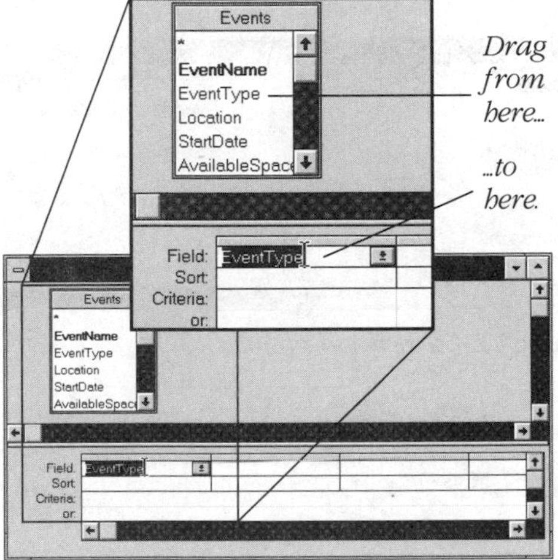

Figure 8. *Drag a field name from the field list.*

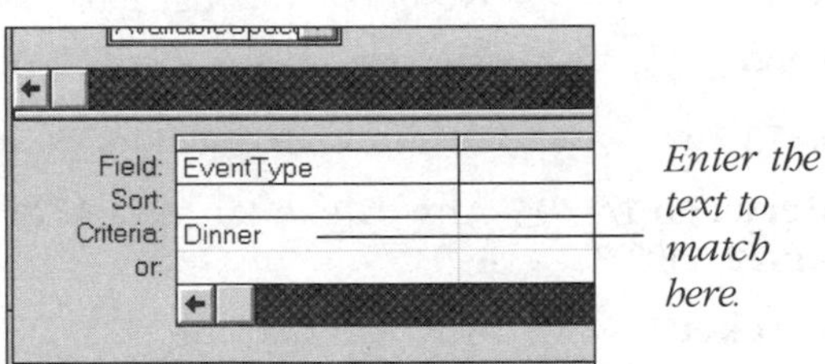

Figure 9. *The Criteria cell.*

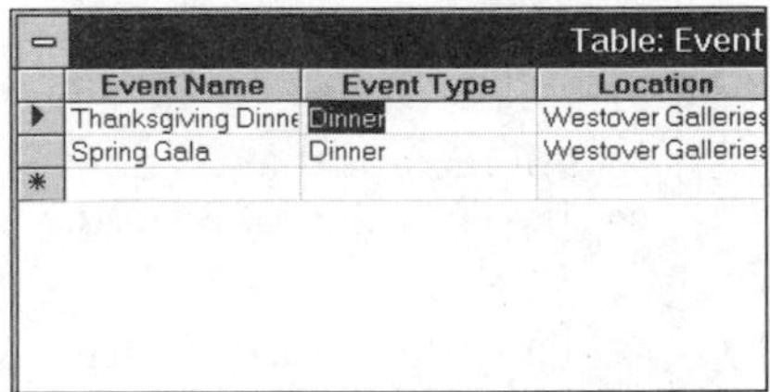

Table: Event

Event Name	Event Type	Location
Thanksgiving Dinne	Dinner	Westover Gallerie
Spring Gala	Dinner	Westover Gallerie

Figure 10. *The filter applied.*

Creating a Filter

A *filter* displays only certain records from a table according to the *criteria* you set. (A filter can display only employees who live in Washington, D.C., for example.)

1. While viewing a form or the table, click the Edit Filter/Sort button on the toolbar. **(Figure 7)**

   or

   From the Records menu, choose Edit Filter/Sort.
2. In the Filter window, drag a field name from the list of fields to the Field cell in the first column below. **(Figure 8)**
3. If you want to sort the data that is found, click in the Sort cell and choose Ascending or Descending from the drop-down list.
4. Into the Criteria cell, type an entry to match. **(Figure 9)**
5. To create a match on a second field, drag a second field name from the field list to the adjoining column in the table below and then repeat Steps 3 and 4 above.
6. Click the Apply Filter/Sort button to close the Filter window and apply the filter.

✔ Tips

- After viewing the filtered data, you can click the Edit Filter/Sort button again, modify or refine the filter, and then click the Apply Filter/Sort button to apply the revised filter to the complete set of data.
- You can save a filter as a query so you can use it again later. *See Saving the Query, page 266.*
- To remove the filter and view all the records in the table, click the Show All Records button in the Standard toolbar. **(Figure 7)**

More Useful Criteria for Filters

If you simply type text or a number into the Criteria cell, Access seeks to match the entry when you apply a filter. You can use an *expression* in a criteria to have Access match a range of values. **(Figures 11-12)** You can also use "or", "not", or "in" as part of a criterion to further refine the acceptable values. Table 34-2 displays samples of criteria you can use.

✔ Tips

- You can type criteria into the Criteria cells of two fields to have the filter match only those records that match both criteria.
- Rather than use "or" in the criteria, you can enter one criteria in the Criteria cell and enter the alternate possibility in the "or" cell.
- After you enter the criteria, Access will add whatever special punctuation it needs. For example, In(TX, FL) becomes In("TX","FL").

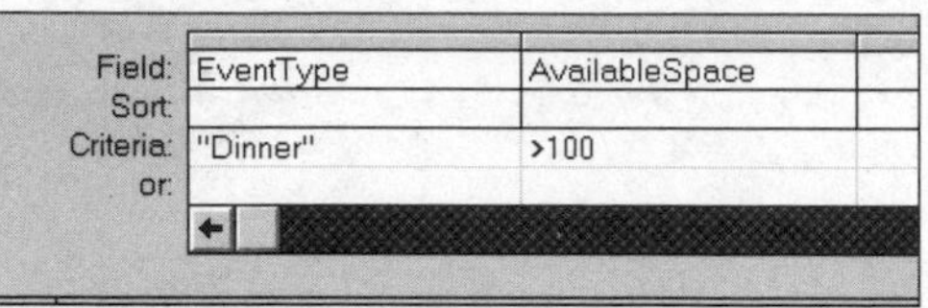

Figure 11. *Sample criteria.*

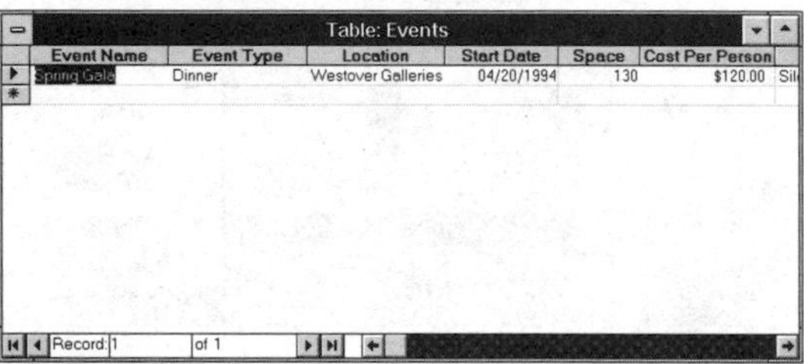

Figure 12. *The criteria applied.*

Table 34-2. *Useful Criteria*

<100	Numbers less that 100.
>200	Numbers greater than 200
<=75	Less than or equal to 75.
Between 1/1/93 and 2/28/93	Any date in Jan. or Feb. of 1993.
market*	Any text that has "market" as its first six letters.
2/*/95	Any date in February, 1995.
France or Spain	Either "France" or "Spain"
Not 20	All records that do not have a value of 20 in the field.
In(TX, FL)	Only those records that have TX or FL in the field.

Using Queries 35

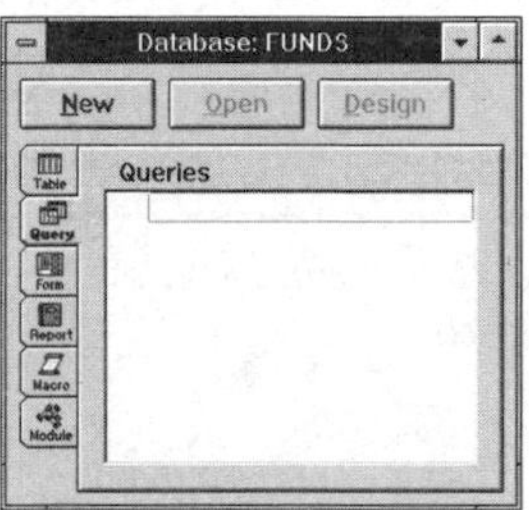

Figure 1. *The Database window.*

Figure 2. *The New Query dialog box.*

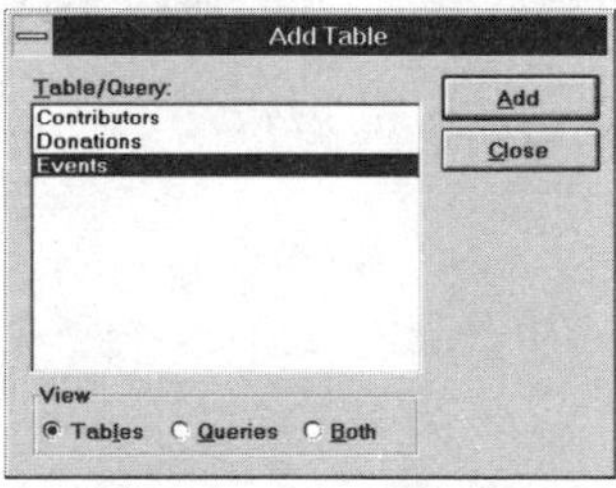

Figure 3. *Click each table to include.*

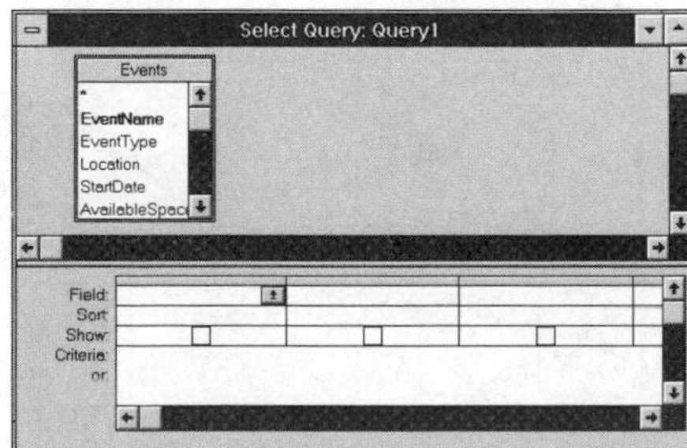

Figure 4. *The tables you have selected appear in the Query window.*

About Queries

When you use a *query*, you are asking the database for specific information that you'd like to view and/or edit. The query is the question.

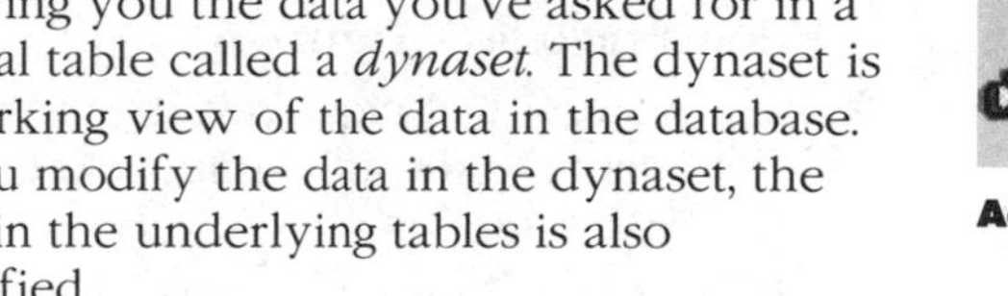

When you run a query, Access responds by showing you the data you've asked for in a special table called a *dynaset*. The dynaset is a working view of the data in the database. If you modify the data in the dynaset, the data in the underlying tables is also modified.

Access provides Query Wizards that help you through more complex queries, but simple queries are easy to create without the help of a Wizard.

Starting a Query

1. In the Database window, click the Query tab. **(Figure 1)**
2. In the Database window, click the New button.
3. On the New Query dialog box, click the New Query button. **(Figure 2)**
4. On the Add Table dialog box, select all the tables that contain information you want included in response to your query. **(Figure 3)**
5. Click Add.
6. Click Close on the Add Table dialog box.

✔ Tip

- Click QueryWizards on the New Query dialog box for help with more complicated queries.

Selecting the Fields

1. On the Select Query dialog box, drag a field name from a field list at the top of the window to a Field cell on the QBE (Query by Example) grid below. **(Figure 5)**
   or
   Click in a Field cell on the QBE grid and then double-click a field name on a field list.
   or
   Click in a Field cell on the QBE grid and choose a field name from the drop-down field list. **(Figure 6)**
2. Use a Step 1 technique to drag the next field name to the adjoining Field cell on the QBE grid.
3. Repeat Step 2 until you have added all the fields that you want in the Dynatable "answer" to the query. **(Figure 7)**

✔ Tips

- In the Select Query window, join lines connect fields in tables that are joined in the database. Fields are joined in tables to form relationships. **(Figure 8)**
- The Show checkboxes in the QBE grid should be checked for all the fields that you want displayed in the dynatable.
- To sort the records in the dynatable, click the Sort cell for the field that you want to sort and then select Ascending or Descending from the drop-down list.

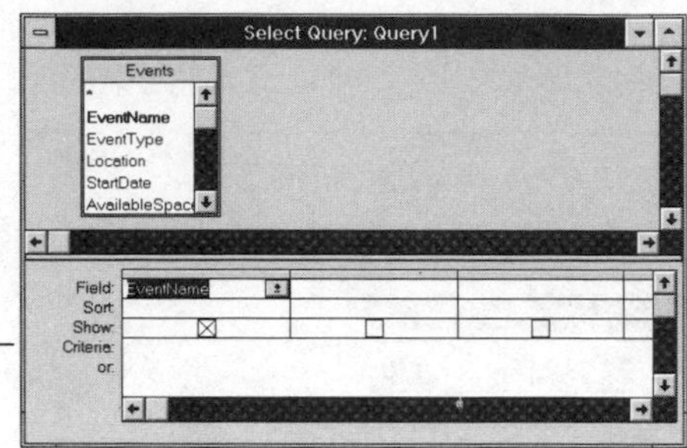

Figure 5. *Drag a field name to a Field cell in the QBE grid.*

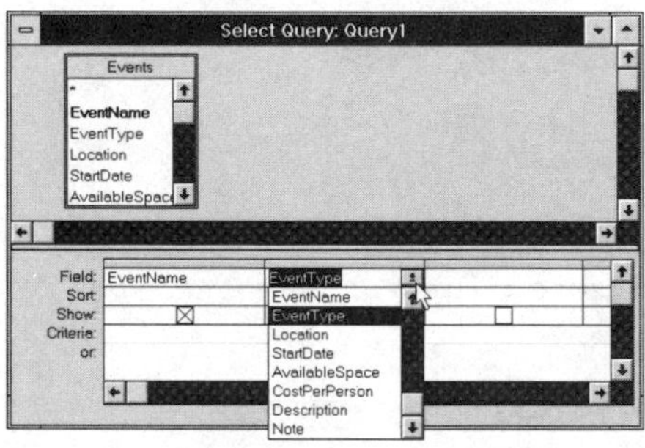

Figure 6. *A drop-down field list.*

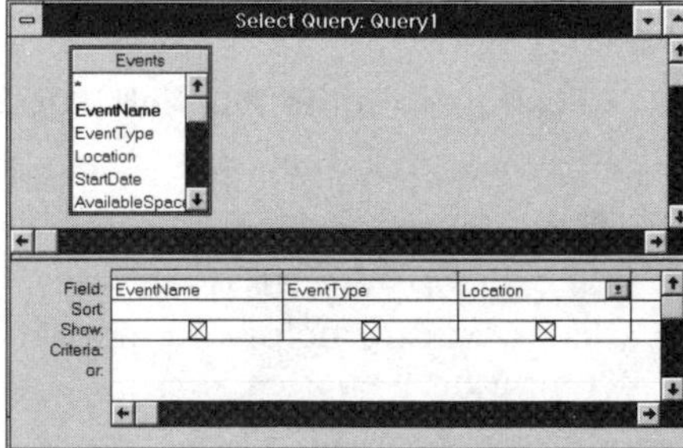

Figure 7. *The completed field cells of a query.*

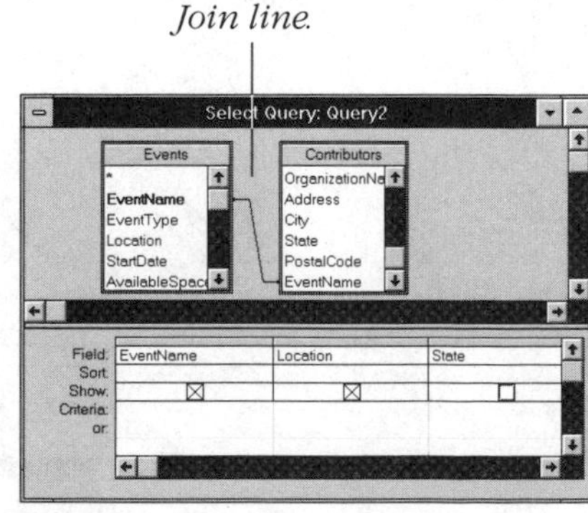

Figure 8. *Join line between the two tables.*

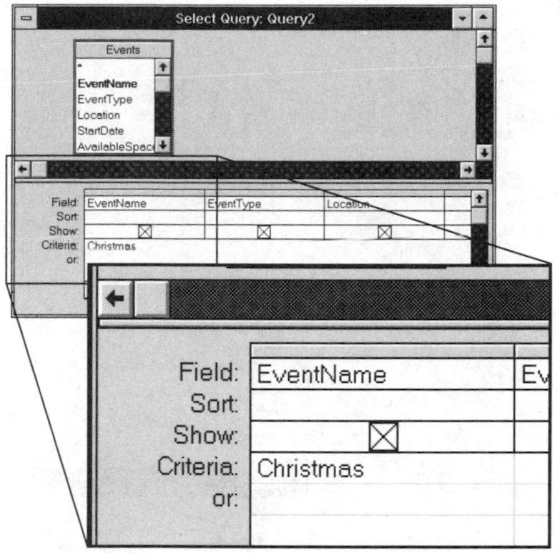

Figure 9. *Enter text or another value to match.*

Entering the Criteria

1. In the Criteria cell for a field in the QBE grid, enter the text or number to match. **(Figure 9)**

   or

   In the Criteria cell, enter an expression to match a range of values. **(Figure 10)**

   or

   Use one of the criteria shown in Table 35-2, page 262.

2. To match two possible values, type the first value in the Criteria cell of the QBE grid and then type the second value in the 'or' cell. **(Figure 11)**

✔ Tip

- When you enter the criteria, you can click the Datasheet view button to see the result of the query. While in Datasheet view, you can then simply click the Design view button to return to the query in progress.

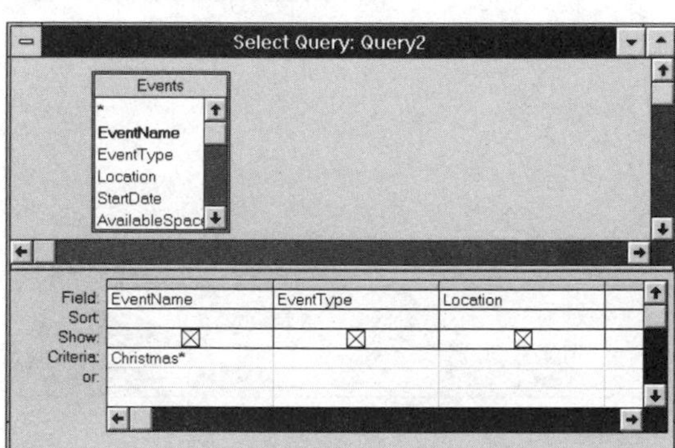

Figure 10. *Enter an expression.*

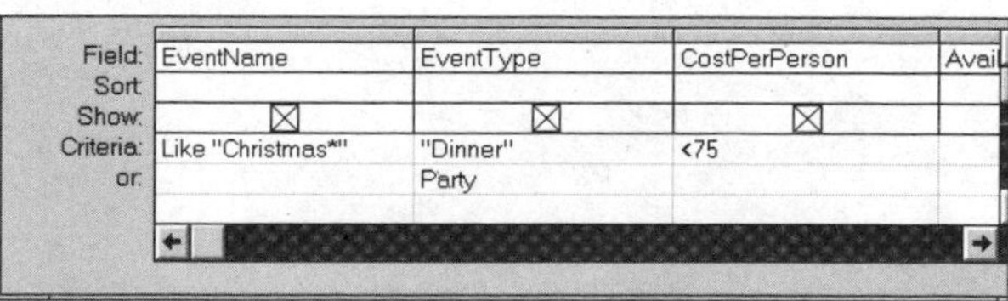

Figure 11. *Use the or cell to create an either/or criterion.*

Saving the Query

1. While the Query window is still open, click the Save button. **(Figure 12)**
   or
   From the File menu, choose Save. **(Figure 13)**
2. In the Save As dialog box, enter a name for the query and click OK. **(Figure 14)**

Figure 12. *The Save button.*

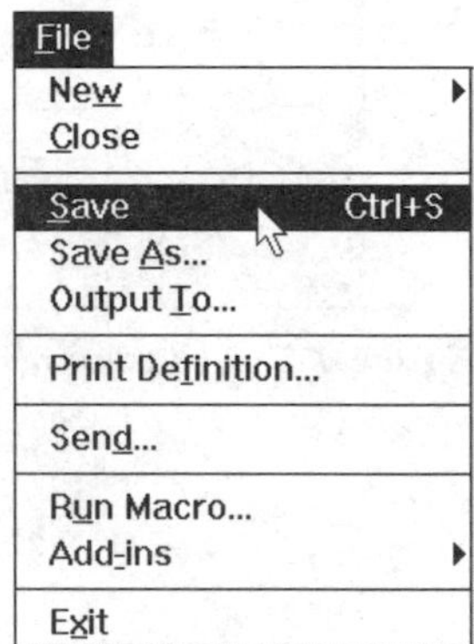

Figure 13. *The File menu.*

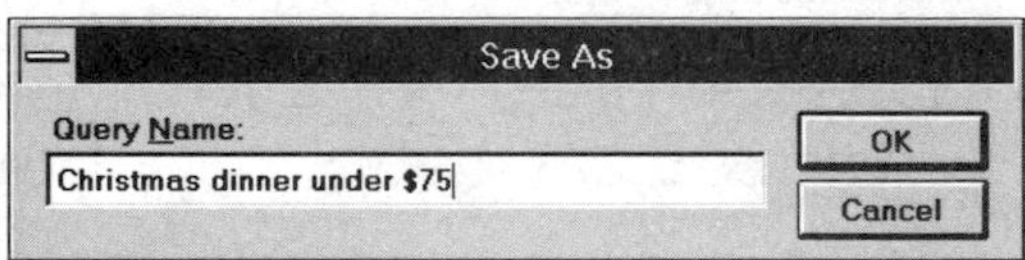

Figure 14. *The Save As dialog box.*

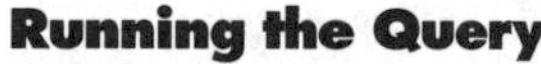

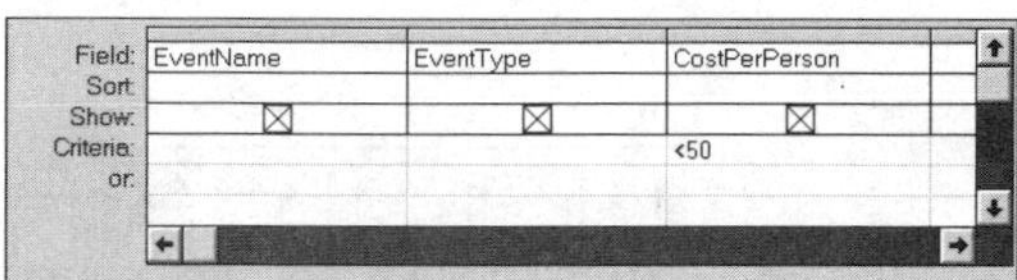

Figure 15. *The query.*

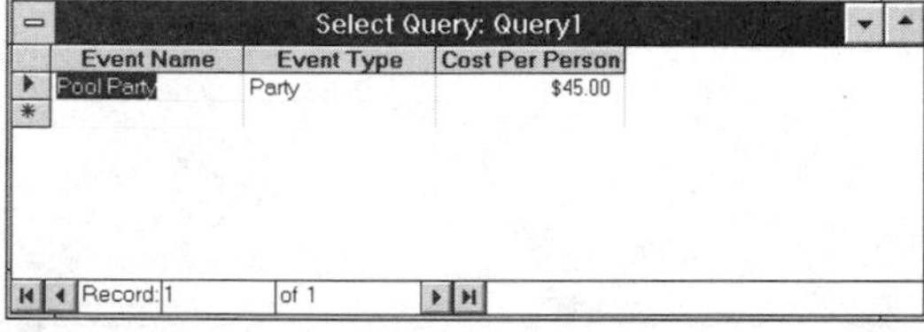

Figure 16. *The dynatable.*

Run button.

Figure 17. *The Run button.*

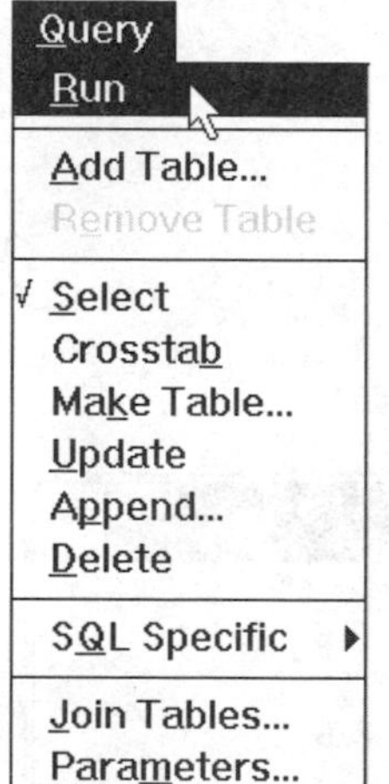

Figure 18. *The Query menu.*

Running the Query

When you run the query, the query opens a dynaset window labeled "Select Query" that displays the result of the query. **(Figures 15-16)** The dynaset shows only the fields included in the query and only the records that match the criteria entered in the query.

1. Click the Run button in the Standard toolbar. **(Figure 17)**

   or

   From the Query menu, choose Run. **(Figure 18)**

Printing the Dynaset

1. While the dynaset is open, click the Print button in the toolbar. **(Figure 19)**

   or

   From the File menu, choose Print.

2. Click OK on the Print dialog box.

Print button.

Figure 19. *The Print button.*

Calculating Totals in a Query

When some of the data in a dynaset is numeric, you might want to see the information tallied up in some way. You can easily sum and average the numbers in a dynaset or determine the minimum and maximum values.

1. While the Query window is open, click the Totals button. **(Figure 20)** A Total row appears in the QBE grid.

   or

   From the View menu, choose Totals.
2. To group the data by the entries in a particular field, choose Group By from the drop-down list in the Total cell for that field. **(Figure 21)**
3. Select an option from the drop-down list in each Total cell of each field in the Query window.
4. Run the Query. **(Figure 22)**

   or

   Click the Datasheet view button.

✔ Tip

- The Total cell of each field must have an entry. If you do not want to total a field, do not include it in the query.

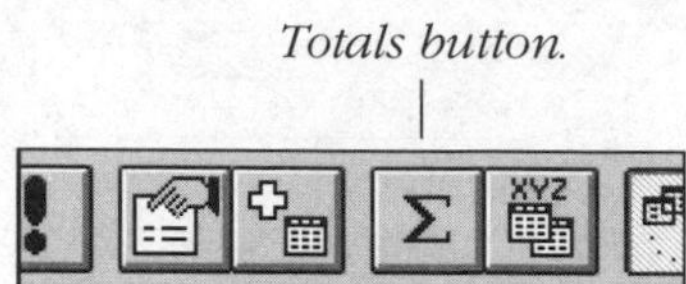

Figure 20. *The Totals button.*

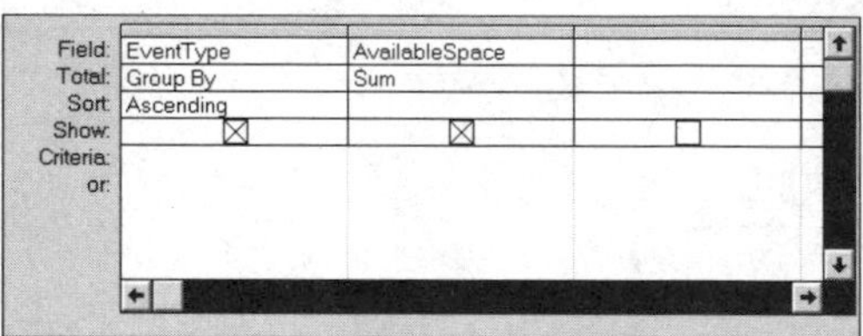

Figure 21. *The Total cells.*

Available Space is summed by type.

Events are grouped by type and sorted in ascending order alphabetically.

Select Query: Query1

Event Type	SumOfAvailableSpace
Cabaret	175
Concert	85
Dinner	225
Party	32

Record: 1 of 4

Figure 22. *The result of the query.*

Creating a Report 36

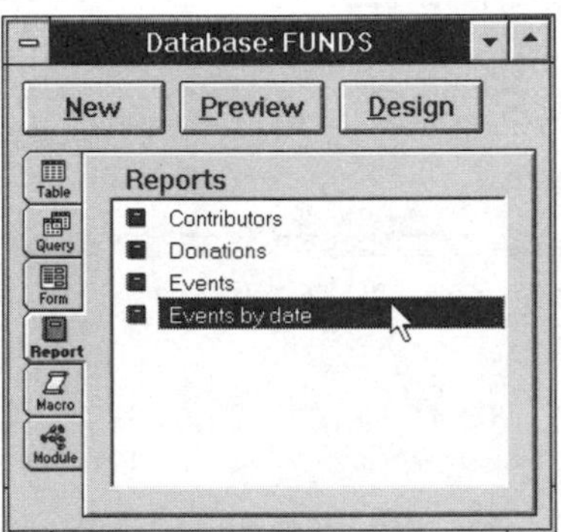

Figure 1. *The Database window.*

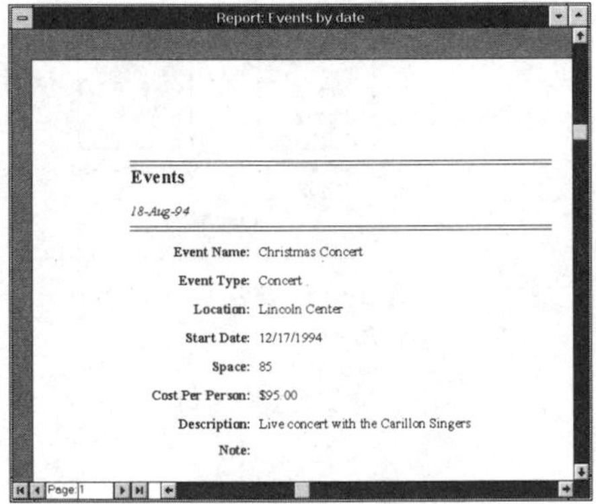

Figure 2. *A report print preview.*

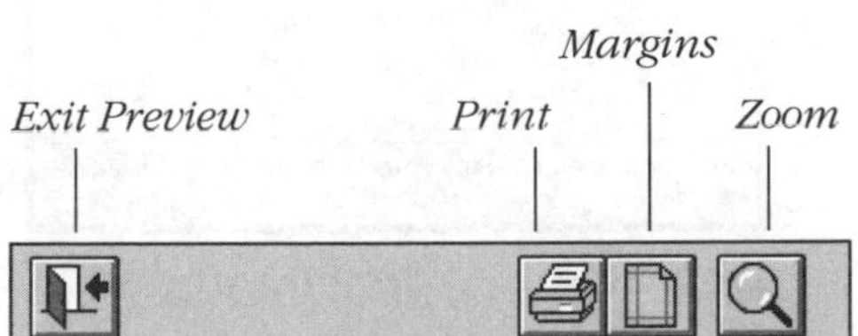

Figure 3. *The Print Preview toolbar.*

Printing an Existing Report

1. Click the Report tab on the Database window. **(Figure 1)**
2. Click a report and then click Preview to view a print preview of the report. **(Figure 2)**

   or, to print the report without previewing it:

   Click the Print button on the Print Preview toolbar. **(Figure 3)**

   or

   From the File menu, choose Print.

Access

✔ Tips

- While previewing a report, click anywhere on the preview to view the full page. Click again on the preview to zoom in.
- Click the Page buttons at the bottom of the window to move from page to page of the preview.
- To close a print preview, click the Exit Preview button on the Print Preview toolbar.

Starting a New Report

1. Click the Report tab on the Database window. **(Figure 4)**
2. On the Database window, click the New button.
3. On the New Report dialog box, select a table or query upon which the report will be based. **(Figure 5)**
4. On the New Report dialog box, click the Report Wizards button.
5. Double-click one of the Wizards on the Report Wizards dialog box. **(Figure 6)**

✓ Tip

- Choose AutoReport to quickly generate a single-column report that includes all the fields in the table.

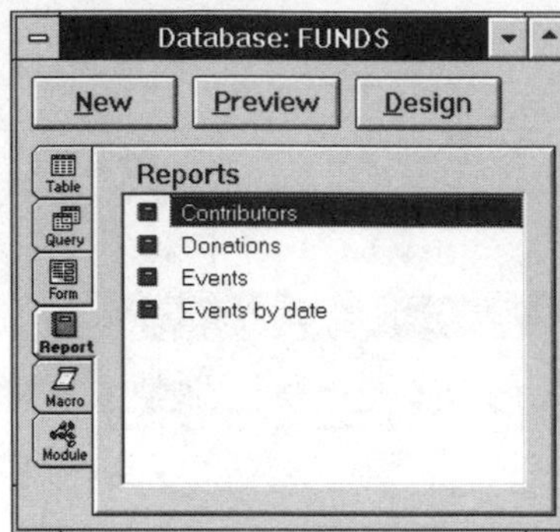

Figure 4. *The Database window.*

Click this pull-down button to select a table.

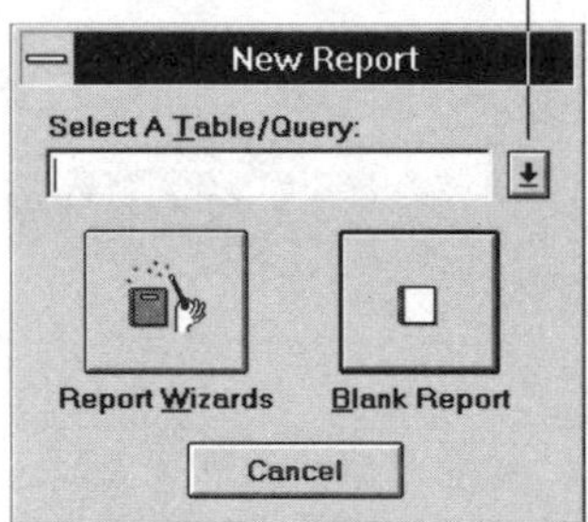

Figure 5. *The New Report dialog box.*

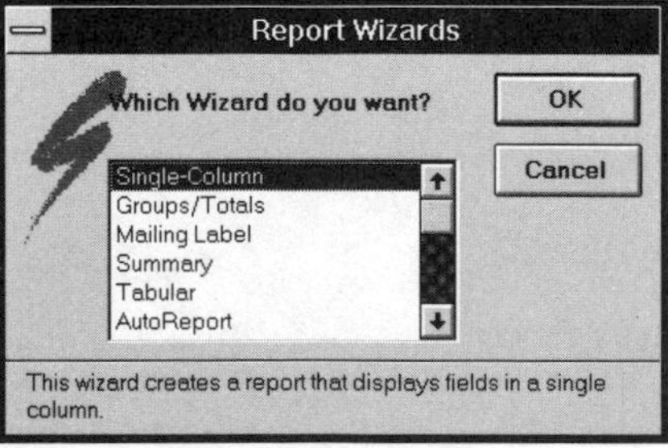

Figure 6. *The Report Wizards dialog box.*

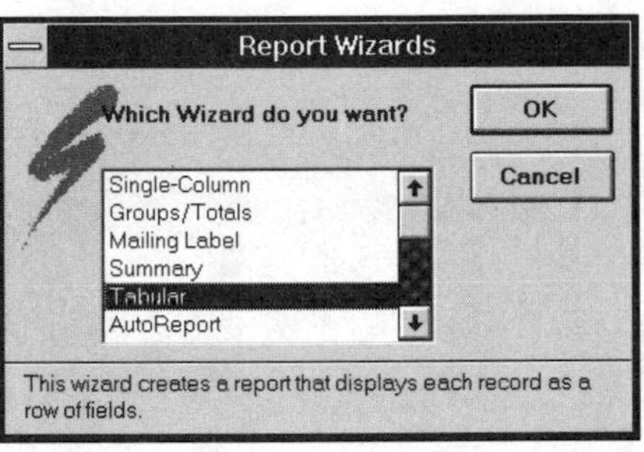

Figure 7. *The Report Wizards dialog box.*

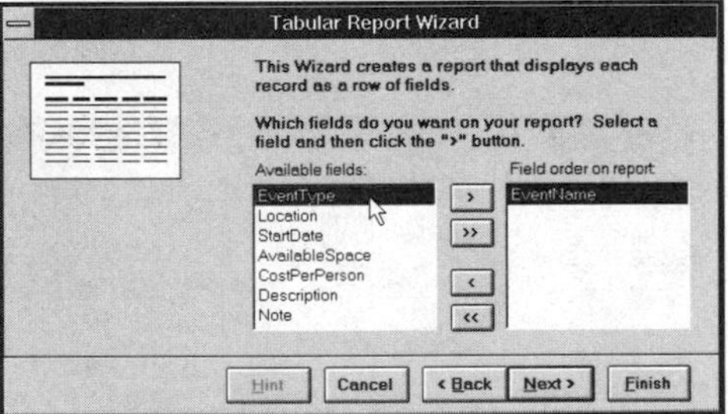

Figure 8. *The Tabular Report Wizards dialog box.*

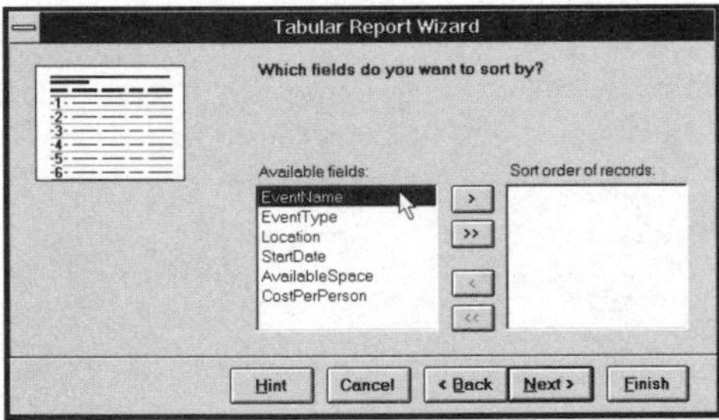

Figure 9. *Tabular Report Wizards dialog box.*

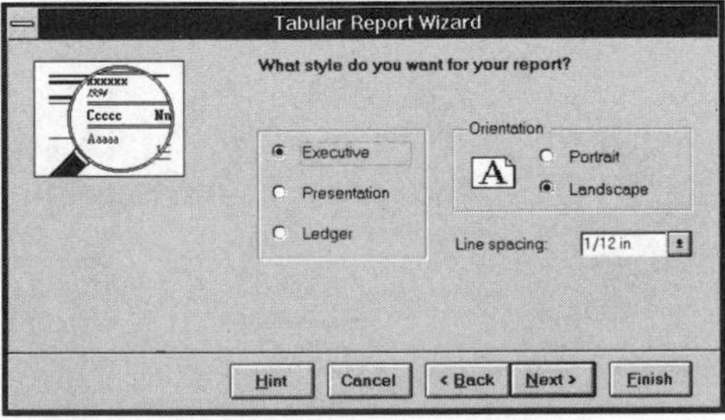

Figure 10. *Tabular Report Wizards dialog box.*

Creating a Tabular Report with the Report Wizard

1. Follow Steps 1-4 on the opposite page.
2. On the Report Wizards dialog box, double-click Tabular. **(Figure 7)**
3. On the Tabular Report Wizards dialog box, double-click each field to include in the report. **(Figure 8)**

   or, to include all the fields in the report: Click the >> button.
4. Click Next.
5. On the next Tabular Report Wizard dialog box, select one or more fields upon which to sort the report and click the > button. Then click Next. **(Figure 9)**
6. On the next Tabular Report Wizard dialog box, select one of the three report styles, select an orientation, and modify the line spacing of the report, if you'd like. Then click Next. **(Figure 10)**
7. On the final Tabular Report Wizard dialog box, enter a report title and then make additional selections according to your preferences. **(Figure 11)**
8. Then click Finish to generate the report.

✔ Tips

- The report appears first in print preview.
- After you generate a report, you must save it by clicking the Save button or choosing Save from the File menu.

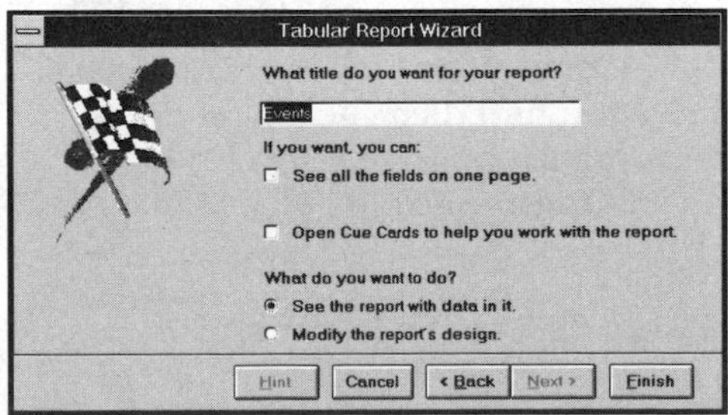

Figure 11. *The Final Tabular Report Wizards dialog box.*

Groups and Totals in a Report

A report can group together similar records (all the employees that have the same department in the "dept" field) and it can total numeric records. **(Figure 19)** The easiest way to create a report with groups and totals is to use the Groups/Totals Wizard.

1. Follow Steps 1-4 in Starting a New Report, earlier in this chapter.
2. On the Report Wizards dialog box, double-click Groups/Totals. **(Figure 12)**
3. On the first Groups/Totals Report Wizard dialog box, double-click the field you plan to group the records by (the department name in the example above). **(Figure 13)** The group fields should be the first field on the report.
4. Double-click each of the other fields in the order you want them on the report and then click Next.
5. On the next Wizard dialog box, double-click the field you plan to group the records by and click Next. **(Figure 14)**
6. On the next Wizard dialog box, choose Normal on the Group drop-down list or choose one of the other options if you are printing a directory. **(Figure 15)**
7. On the next Wizard dialog box, double-click one or more fields upon which to sort the records in the report. Then click Next. **(Figure 16)**
8. On the next Wizard dialog box, choose a report style, orientation, and line spacing. Then click Next. **(Figure 17)**
9. On the final Wizard dialog box, name the report and then choose other appropriate options before clicking Finish. **(Figure 18)**

✔ Tip

- Be sure to save the report after you have previewed it.

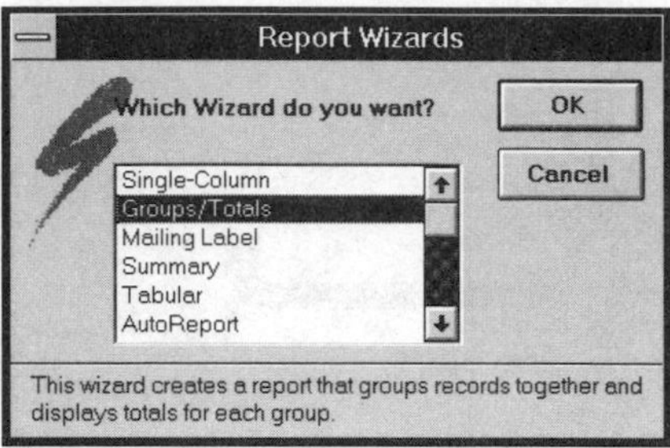

Figure 12. *The Report Wizards dialog box.*

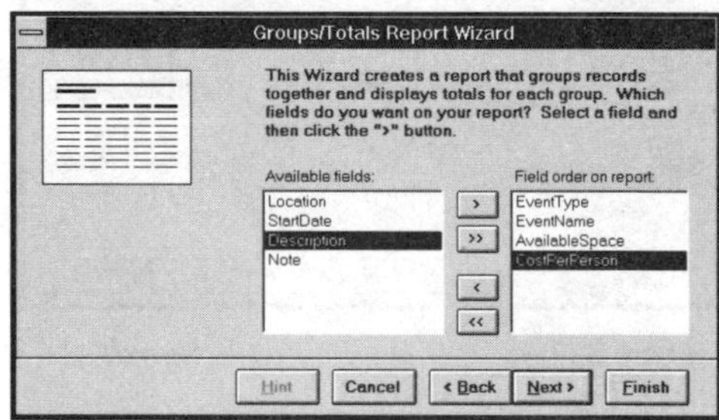

Figure 13. *Make the group field the first field on the report.*

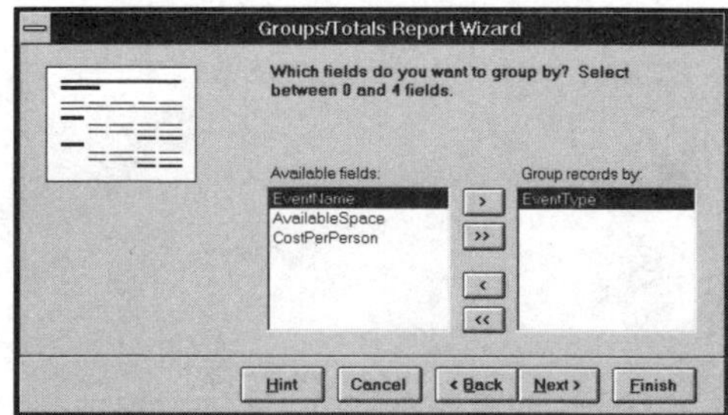

Figure 14. *Double-click the field to use for grouping.*

Access

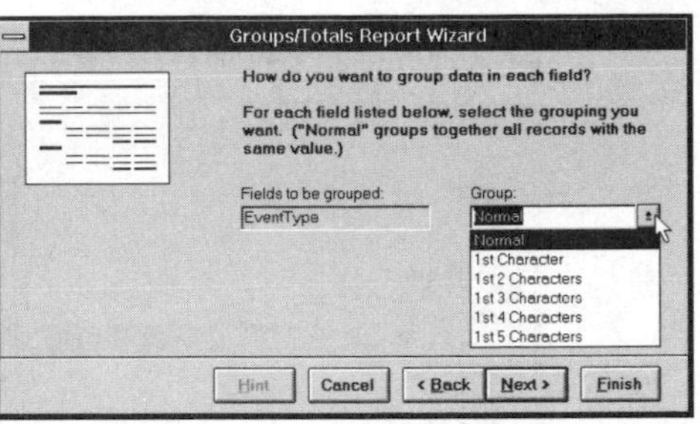

Figure 15. *Select Normal for the group method.*

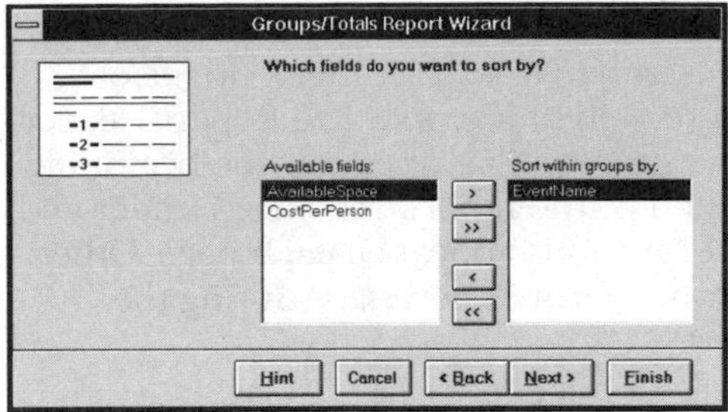

Figure 16. *Select a sort field.*

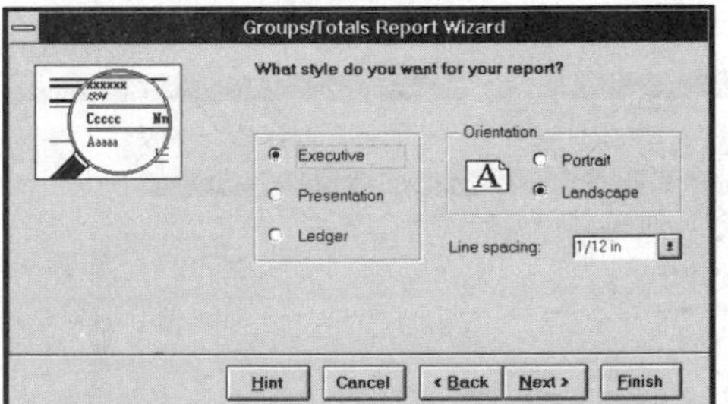

Figure 17. *Choose a report styling here.*

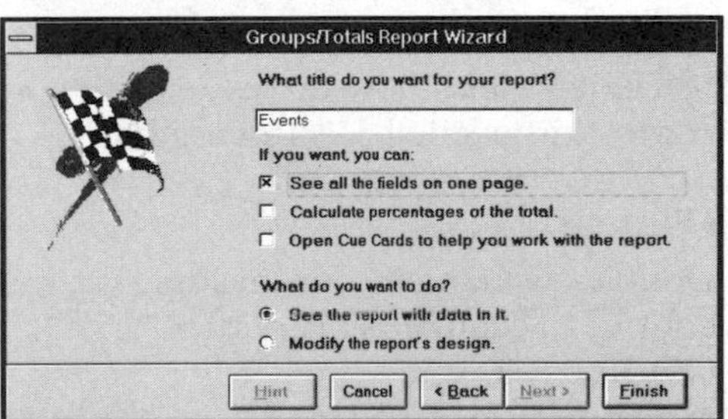

Figure 18. *The final Groups/Totals Report Wizard dialog box.*

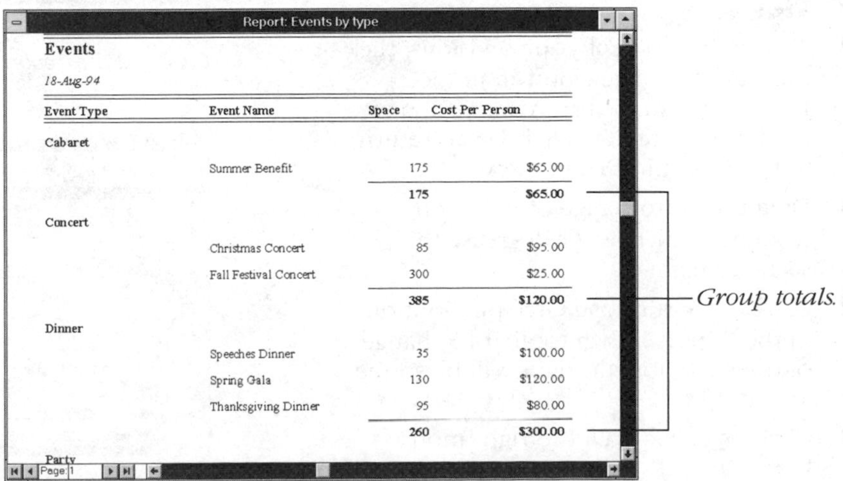

Figure 19. *The grouped report with group totals.*

Revising a Report in Design View

In Design view, you see the contents of each section of a report. The Report Header and Footer sections appear at the beginning and end of the report. The Page Header and Footer sections appear on each page. Other sections repeat as necessary during the report.

Each section contains controls that act just like the controls you use when designing a form.

1. On the Report tab of the Database window, select a report and click Design. **(Figure 20)**
2. In Design view, move or resize the controls as needed. *See Moving and Sizing Controls, page 251.* **(Figure 21)**
3. Double-click any section heading or control to change its properties. **(Figure 22)**
4. To add a field to the report, drag the field from the field list to a report section.
5. Use the tools in the toolbox to add or modify controls, just as you do when designing a form.

✔ Tips

- To see the result of your revisions, click the Sample Preview button in the Report Design toolbar. After you view the sample preview, click Esc to return to the report in Design view.
- Drag the bottom edge of a section heading to increase or decrease the section height.
- Click the Sorting and Grouping button in the Report Design toolbar to change options for how the data will be sorted and grouped.
- Click any field with the right mouse button to see special options on a shortcut menu.

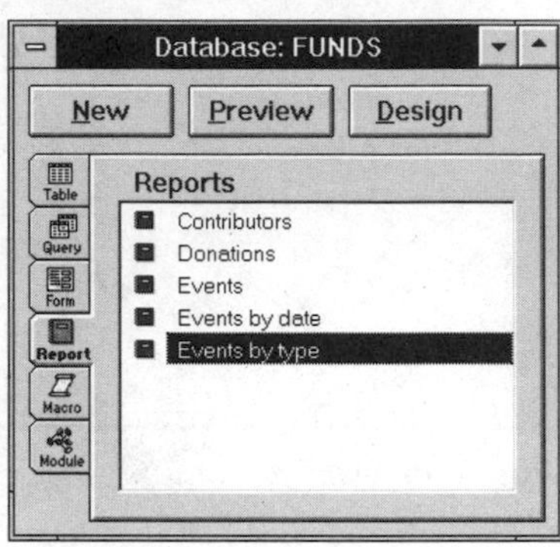

Figure 20. *The Database window.*

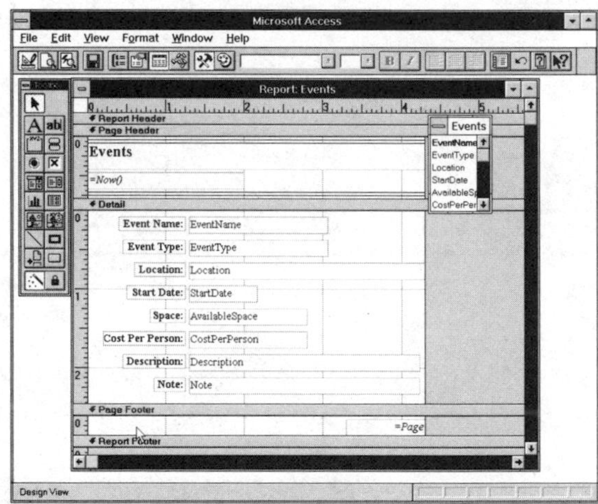

Figure 21. *A report in Design view.*

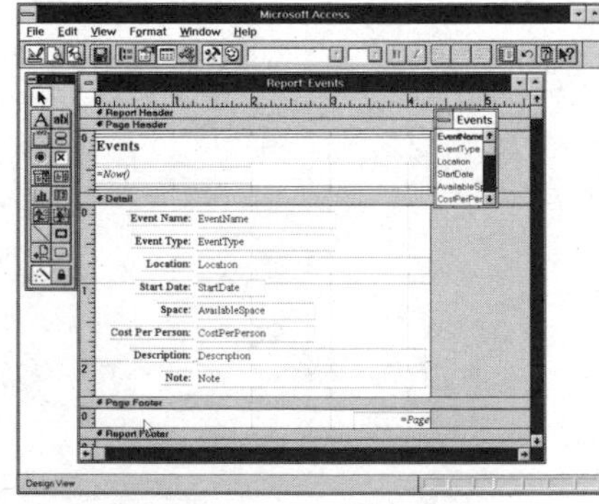

Figure 22. *Double-click a section heading to view its properties.*

Mail 3.2 Communicating

Mail 3.2 Communicating

About Mail

What is Mail?

Microsoft Mail is a communications program that lets everyone on a network send messages back and forth. If you are not connected to a local area network (LAN), you cannot use Mail.

From: LolaW
Date: Wednesday, August 31, 1994 11:20AM
To: SteveS
Subject: Registered: LolaW

Your message
To: LolaW
Subject: Publication Contracts
Date: Wednesday, August 31, 1994 11:09AM
was accessed on
Date: Wednesday, August 31, 1994 11:20AM

Mail lets users compose text messages and attach files created by the Office applications. It also lets users read incoming messages and file messages in folders according to any organization scheme.

Mail includes special capabilities that let you find messages from a particular recipient or messages that contain specific text. It also lets you print messages to maintain a printed record of your electronic correspondence.

The Microsoft Mail system at your organization may have the capability to connect to individuals at other organizations or electronic mail addresses if the proper gateway software is installed. You should check with the individual who administers your system to see whether this capability is available.

The Microsoft Mail Window

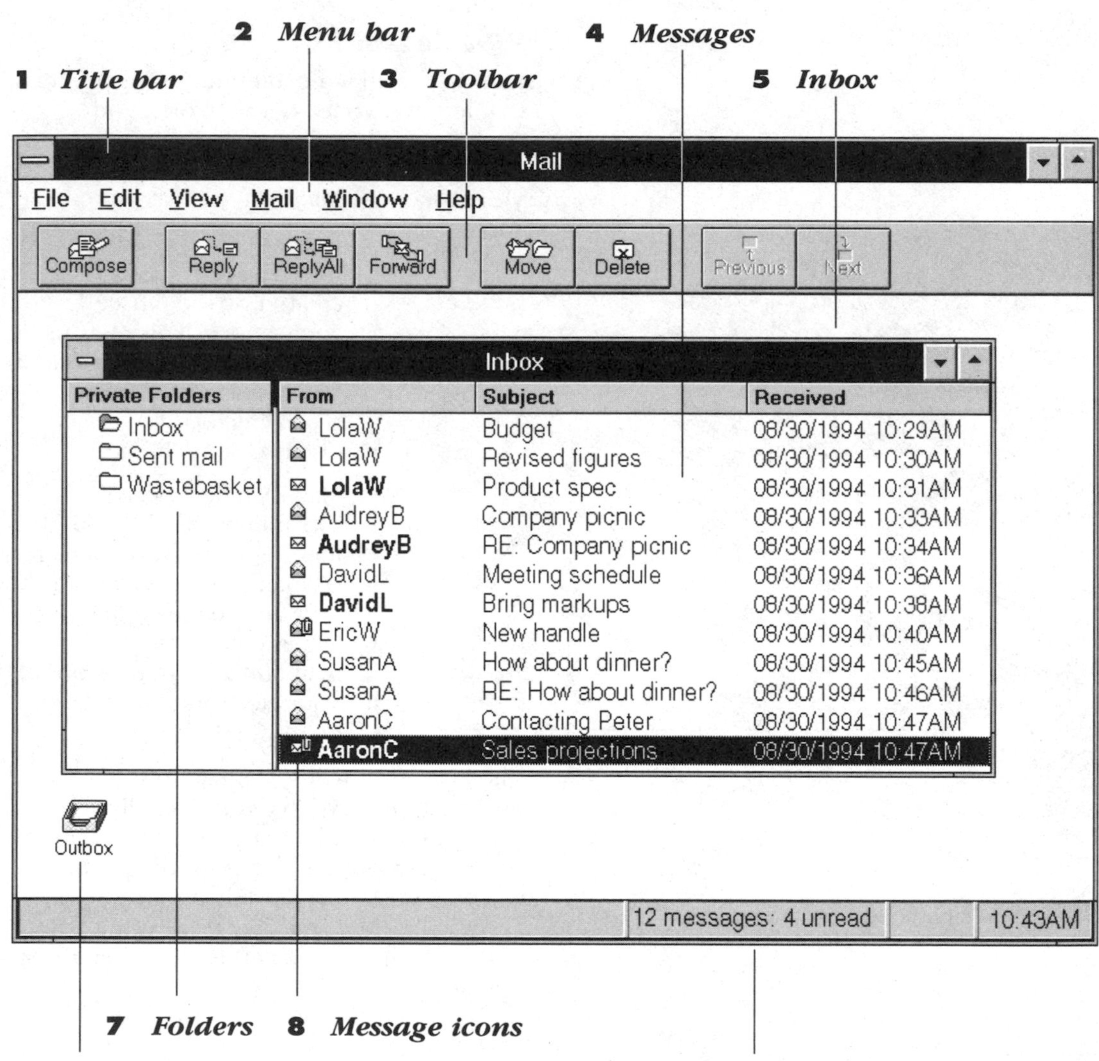

Key to the Microsoft Mail Window

1 *Title bar*

Displays the window name. Drag the title bar to move the window. Double-click the title bar to switch between maximized and restored window.

2 *Menu bar*

Click any name on the menu bar to pull down a menu, or press Alt+the underlined letter of the menu name.

3 *Toolbar*

Toolbar with buttons for message and folder handling.

4 *Messages*

Message headers sorted according to one of the options on the View menu.

5 *Inbox*

Repository of messages that have been sent to you. The Inbox can contain an unlimited number of folders and subfolders for storing messages you've read.

6 *Outbox*

Temporarily stores outgoing messages that the system has been instructed to send, but that have not yet been sent. The Outbox holds outgoing mail when you work offline, perhaps on a portable computer. When you reconnect to the network, the messages are sent from the Outbox.

7 *Folders*

Some folders already exist when you start using Mail. You can add more folders to store messages in any logical arrangement you'd like.

8 *Message icons*

These icons indicate the status of the messages they accompany:

Unread message.

Read message.

Message with an attachment.

Urgent message.

9 *Status bar*

Shows the time and the information about the messages in the open folder.

Starting Microsoft Mail

1. Double-click the Microsoft Mail icon in the Network group of the Program Manager. **(Figure 1)**
2. On the Mail Sign In dialog box, enter your password and click OK or press Enter. **(Figure 2)**

✔ **Tip**

■ You can click the Remember Password checkbox so you don't have to enter your password the next time you start Mail, but this makes your mail accessible to anybody who can use your PC. For security, leave Remember Password unchecked.

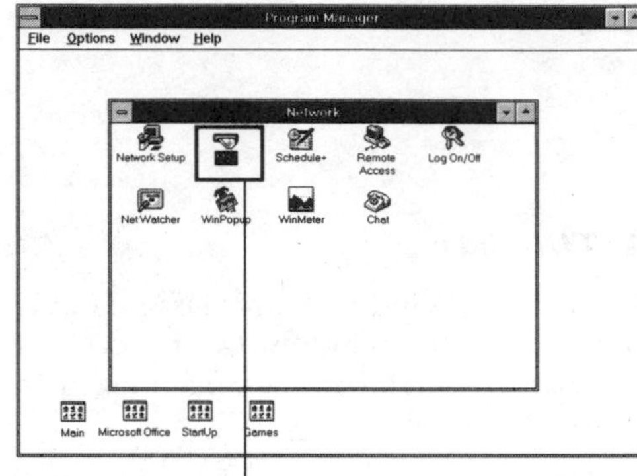

Figure 1. *The Network group.*

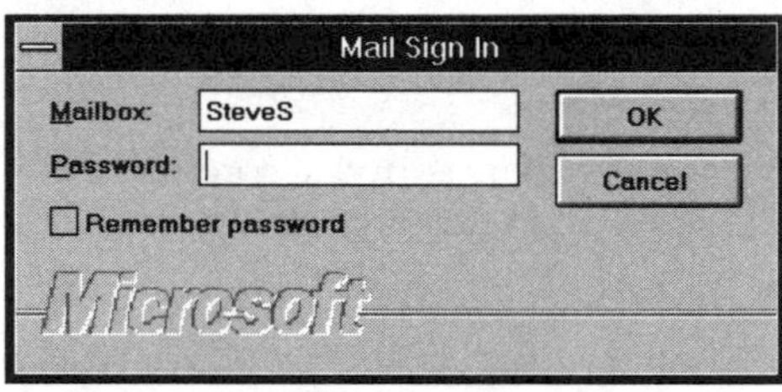

Figure 2. *The Mail Sign In dialog box.*

Quitting Microsoft Mail

1. From the File menu, choose Exit and Sign Out. **(Figure 3)**

   or, to quit mail but remain signed in so other Office applications can send documents using Mail

   From the File menu, choose Exit.

✔ **Tip**

■ If other Office applications are not running, choosing Exit will also sign you out.

Figure 3. *The File menu.*

Reading Messages

Private Folders: Inbox, Sent mail, Wastebasket

From	Subject	Received
LolaW	Budget	08/30/1994 10:29AM
LolaW	Revised figures	08/30/1994 10:30AM
LolaW	Product spec	08/30/1994 10:31AM
AudreyB	Company picnic	08/30/1994 10:33AM
AudreyB	RE: Company picnic	08/30/1994 10:34AM
DavidL	Meeting schedule	08/30/1994 10:36AM
DavidL	Bring markups	08/30/1994 10:38AM
EricW	New handle	08/30/1994 10:40AM
SusanA	How about dinner?	08/30/1994 10:45AM
SusanA	RE: How about dinner?	08/30/1994 10:46AM
AaronC	Contacting Peter	08/30/1994 10:47AM
AaronC	Sales projections	08/30/1994 10:47AM

Figure 1. *The Inbox.*

Private Folders: Inbox, Sent mail, Wastebasket

From	Subject	Received
LolaW	Budget	08/30/1994 10:29AM
LolaW	Revised figures	08/30/1994 10:30AM
LolaW	Product spec	08/30/1994 10:31AM
AudreyB	Company picnic	08/30/1994 10:33AM
AudreyB	RE: Company picnic	08/30/1994 10:34AM
DavidL	Meeting schedule	08/30/1994 10:36AM
DavidL	Bring markups	08/30/1994 10:38AM
EricW	New handle	08/30/1994 10:40AM
SusanA	How about dinner?	08/30/1994 10:45AM
SusanA	RE: How about dinner?	08/30/1994 10:46AM
AaronC	Contacting Peter	08/30/1994 10:47AM
AaronC	Sales projections	08/30/1994 10:47AM
AudreyB	Revised budget attached	08/30/1994 11:00AM

Figure 2. *Double-click a message.*

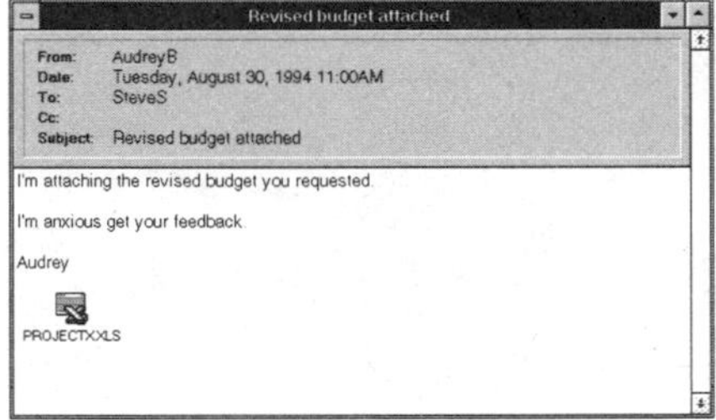

Revised budget attached
From: AudreyB
Date: Tuesday, August 30, 1994 11:00AM
To: SteveS
Cc:
Subject: Revised budget attached
I'm attaching the revised budget you requested.
I'm anxious get your feedback.
Audrey
PROJECTX.XLS

Figure 3. *Reading a message.*

Figure 4. *The View menu.*

Selecting a Message to Read

The Inbox shows a list of messages that have been sent to you. Messages that you have not yet read have a closed envelope icon and the name of the sender is bold. **(Figure 1)**

1. Double-click a message header to open the message. **(Figures 2–3)**

   or

   Use the arrow keys to move the highlight to the message and then press Enter.

2. Press Ctrl+> to read the next message, if you'd like.

   or

   Press Esc to return to the list of messages in the Inbox.

✔ Tips

- You can sort the Inbox by choosing one of the Sort commands on the View menu. **(Figure 4)**
- While reading a message, you can choose Change Font from the View menu to see the message with a monospaced font. Using a monospaced font may be helpful if the message contains text, such as columns, that was arranged with spaces.
- If the message contains an embedded object, double-click the object to open it.

Finding a Message

1. From the File menu, choose Message Finder. **(Figure 5)**
2. On the Message Finder dialog box, enter text to match in one or more text boxes. **(Figure 6)**
3. Press Enter or Click OK. Found messages are displayed in the open space on the Message Finder dialog box. **(Figure 7)**
4. Double-click a message on the list to read the message.

✔ Tips

- By default, the Message Finder checks your Inbox. Click the Where to Look button to specify a different folder or All folders. **(Figure 8)**
- You can minimize rather than close the Message Finder dialog box to keep particular search criteria available for reuse. *See Minimizing Windows, page 12.*

Figure 5. *The File menu.*

Enter text to match in one or more text boxes.

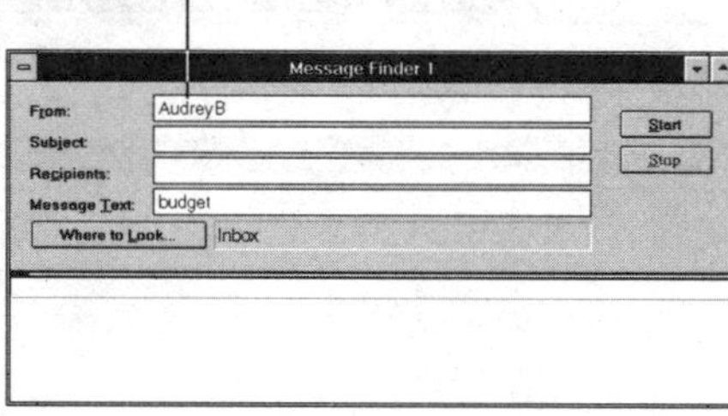

Figure 6. *The Message Finder dialog box.*

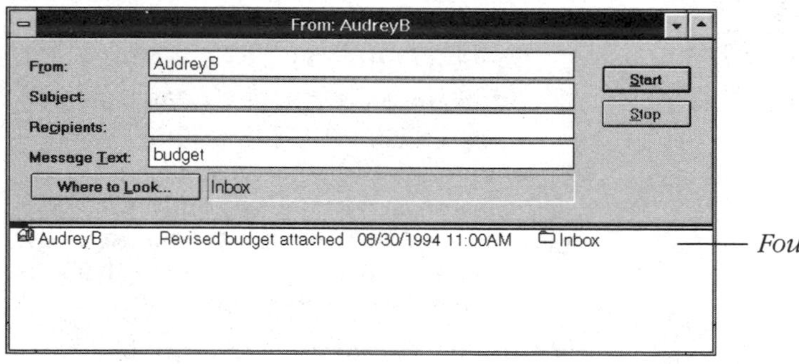

Found message

Figure 7. *Messages found on the Message Finder dialog box.*

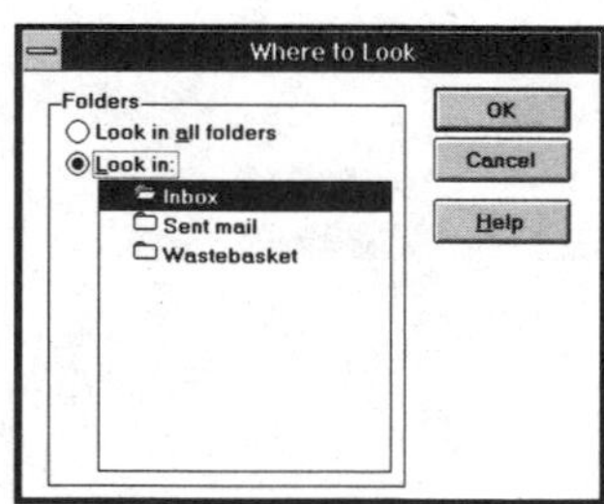

Figure 8. *The Where To Look dialog box.*

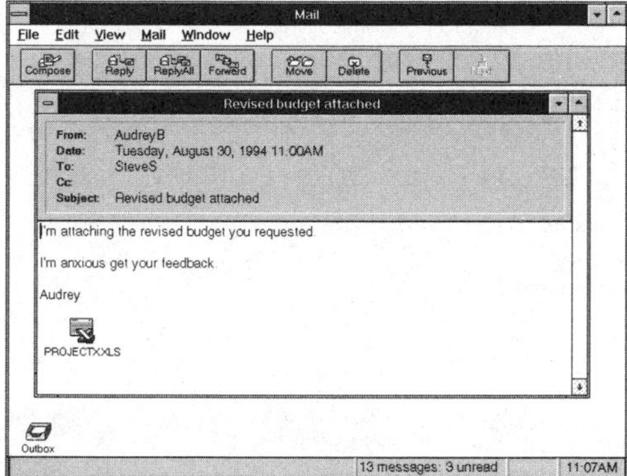

Figure 9. *Open the message.*

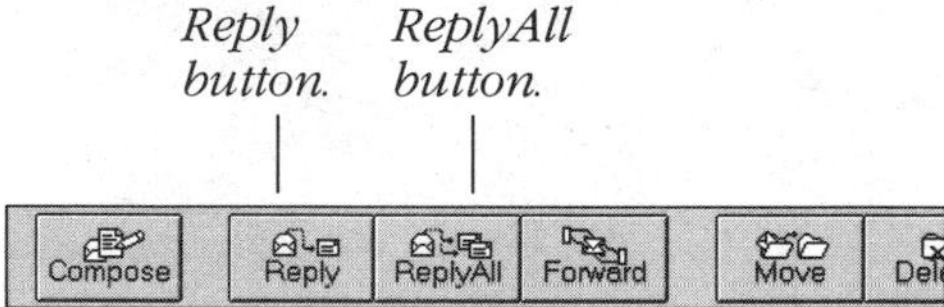

Figure 10. *The Reply buttons.*

Replying to a Message

1. Open the message to which you want to reply. **(Figure 9)**

   or

   Select the message on the Inbox list.
2. Click the Reply button to reply to the sender. **(Figure 10)**

   or

   Click the ReplyAll button to reply to the sender and to all names on the To and Cc lists.
3. Enter the reply text at the current location of the insertion point (above the dashed line). The original message appears below the dashed line. **(Figure 11)**
4. Click Send.

   or

   Click the Attach or Options buttons before clicking Send to customize the message. *See Selecting Message Options, page 289; and Attaching a File to a Message, page 290.*

✔ Tip

- To remove the contents of the original message to which you're replying, delete the original message text before you send the reply.

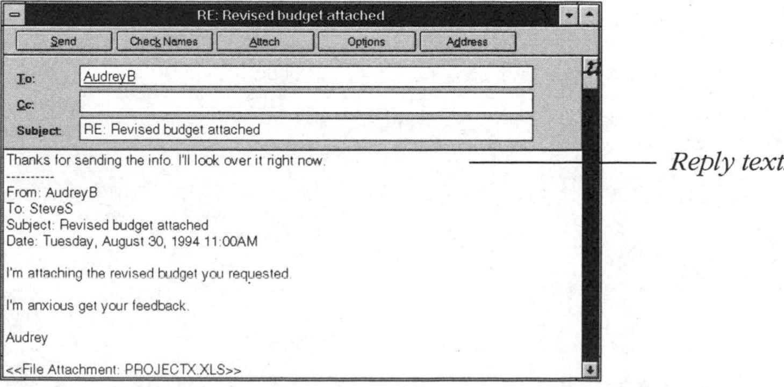

Figure 11. *Enter the reply text above the dashed line.*

Forwarding a Message

1. While reading a message, click the Forward button. **(Figure 12)**

   or

   While viewing the Inbox, drag a message that you want to forward to the Outbox. **(Figure 13)**
2. On the Send Note form that appears, enter an address, optional Cc, and subject after the FW: in the Subject text box. (The FW indicates to the recipient that the message has been forwarded.) **(Figure 14)**
3. Enter any explanatory text to the forwarded message above the dashed lines.
4. Click the Send button.

✔ Tip

■ When you forward a message, you can change the Options or attach files as if you'd created the message. *See Selecting Message Options, page 289; and Attaching a File to a Message, page 290.*

Forward button.

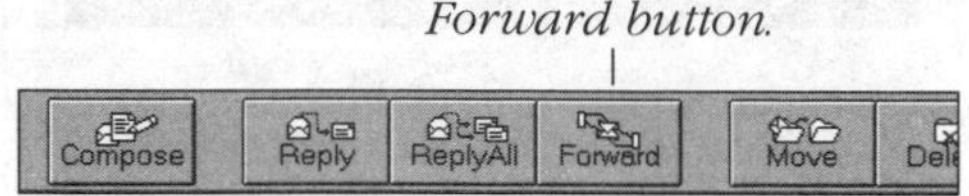

Figure 12. *The Forward button.*

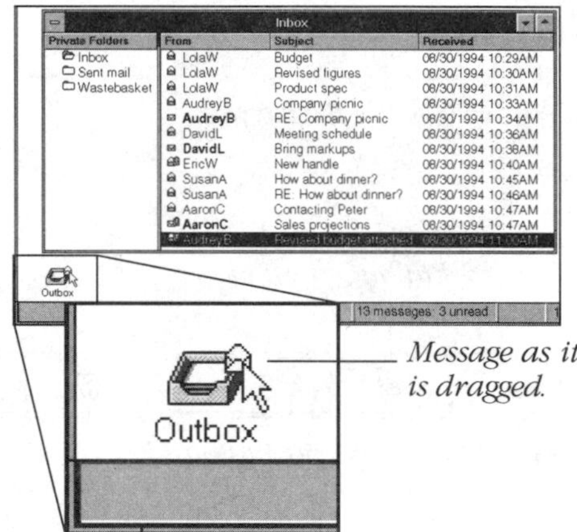

Figure 13. *Drag a message to the Outbox.*

The FW indicates that the message is being forwarded.

FW appears in the subject.

FW: Revised budget attached

Send | Check Names | Attach | Options | Address

To:

Cc:

Subject: FW: Revised budget attached

From: AudreyB
To: SteveS
Subject: Revised budget attached
Date: Tuesday, August 30, 1994 11:00AM

I'm attaching the revised budget you requested.

I'm anxious get your feedback.

Figure 14. *The Send Note form.*

Forwarding a Message

Mail

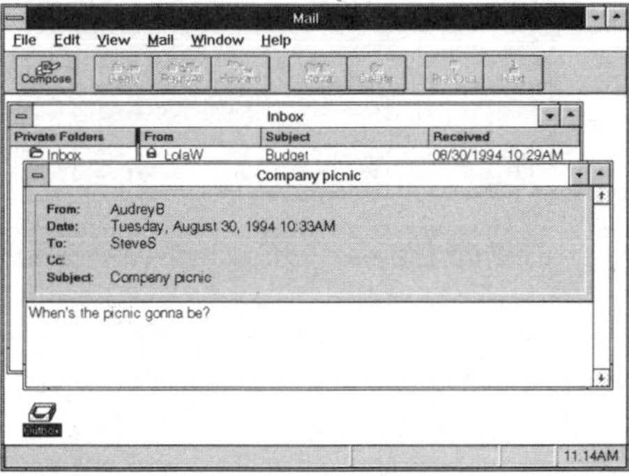

Figure 15. *Open a message.*

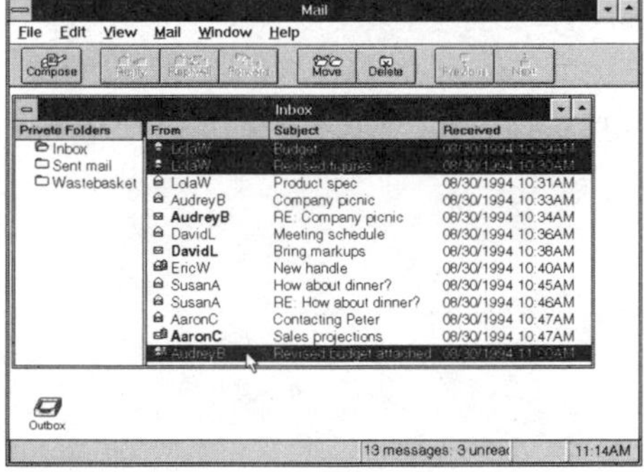

Figure 16. *Selecting multiple messages.*

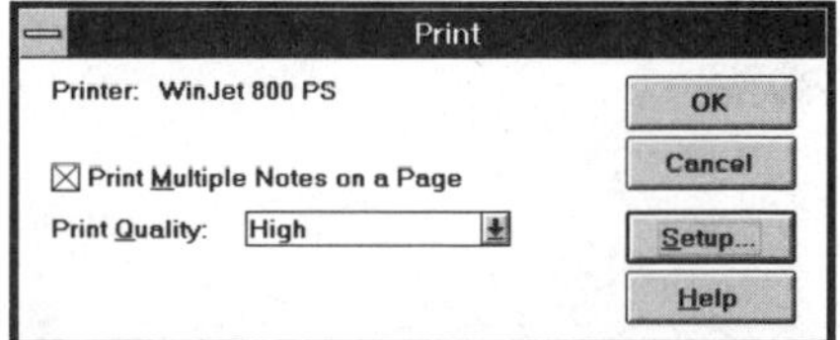

Figure 17. *The Print dialog box.*

Printing a Message

1. Open a message. **(Figure 15)**

or

On the Inbox list of messages, hold down Ctrl and click each message to include in the printout. **(Figure 16)**

2. Press Ctrl+P.

or

From the File menu, choose Print.

3. On the Print dialog box, choose print options and then click OK. **(Figure 17)**

✔ Tips

- Objects that are embedded in the message are printed. Objects that are attached are **not** printed. You must print an attached object from the application used to create it.
- The effect of the Print Quality option depends on your printer.

Deleting a Message

1. Open a message.
or
Select one or more messages on the Inbox list. **(Figure 18)**

2. Click the Delete button. **(Figure 19)**
or
Press Ctrl+D.
or
Press the Delete key on the keyboard.
or
From the File menu, choose Delete.

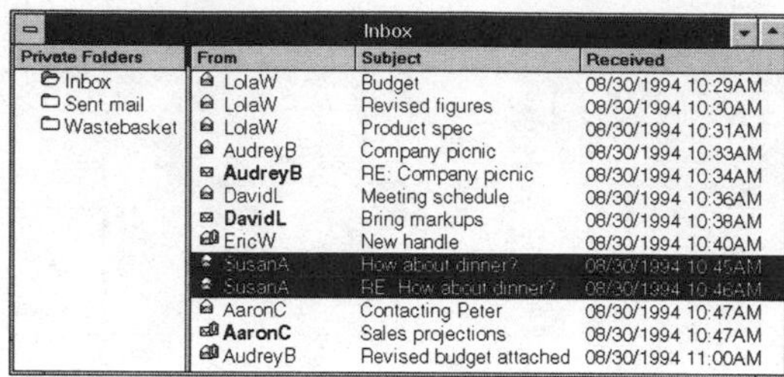

Private Folders	From	Subject	Received
Inbox	LolaW	Budget	08/30/1994 10:29AM
Sent mail	LolaW	Revised figures	08/30/1994 10:30AM
Wastebasket	LolaW	Product spec	08/30/1994 10:31AM
	AudreyB	Company picnic	08/30/1994 10:33AM
	AudreyB	RE: Company picnic	08/30/1994 10:34AM
	DavidL	Meeting schedule	08/30/1994 10:36AM
	DavidL	Bring markups	08/30/1994 10:38AM
	EricW	New handle	08/30/1994 10:40AM
	SusanA	How about dinner?	08/30/1994 10:45AM
	SusanA	RE: How about dinner?	08/30/1994 10:46AM
	AaronC	Contacting Peter	08/30/1994 10:47AM
	AaronC	Sales projections	08/30/1994 10:47AM
	AudreyB	Revised budget attached	08/30/1994 11:00AM

Figure 18. *Select one or more messages on the Inbox list.*

✔ Tips

- Messages that you delete are moved to the Wastebasket folder. To retrieve deleted messages, open the Wastebasket folder and drag the messages back to the Inbox.
- The Wastebasket folder clears when you quit Mail unless you clear the "Empty Deleted Mail folder when exiting" checkbox on the Options dialog box. *See Setting Mail Options, page 298.*

Delete button.

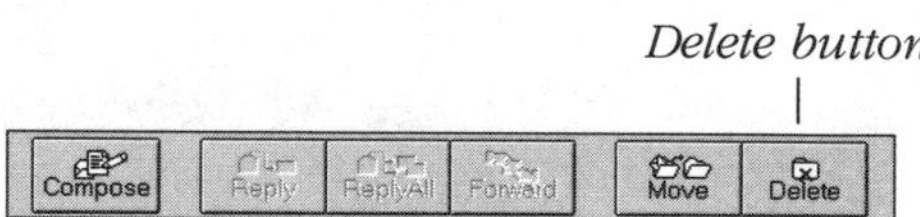

Figure 19. *The Delete button.*

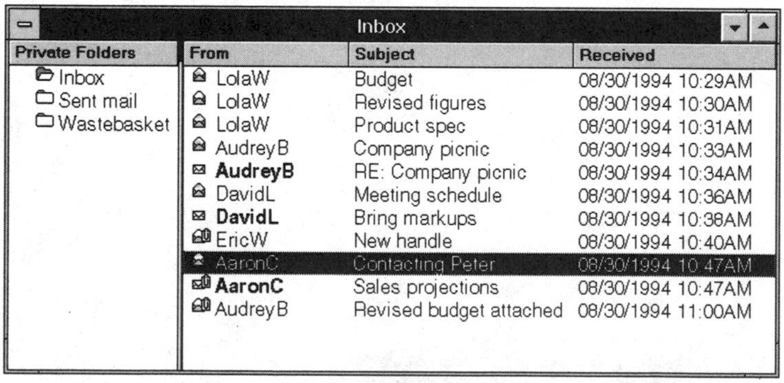

Private Folders	From	Subject	Received
Inbox	LolaW	Budget	08/30/1994 10:29AM
Sent mail	LolaW	Revised figures	08/30/1994 10:30AM
Wastebasket	LolaW	Product spec	08/30/1994 10:31AM
	AudreyB	Company picnic	08/30/1994 10:33AM
	AudreyB	RE: Company picnic	08/30/1994 10:34AM
	DavidL	Meeting schedule	08/30/1994 10:36AM
	DavidL	Bring markups	08/30/1994 10:38AM
	EricW	New handle	08/30/1994 10:40AM
	AaronC	Contacting Peter	08/30/1994 10:47AM
	AaronC	Sales projections	08/30/1994 10:47AM
	AudreyB	Revised budget attached	08/30/1994 11:00AM

Figure 20. *The messages are deleted.*

Sending Messages

Compose button.

Figure 1. *The Compose button.*

Address button.

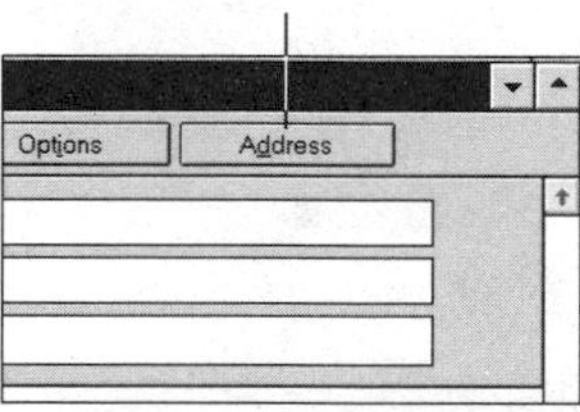

Figure 2. *The Address button.*

Figure 3. *The Address dialog box.*

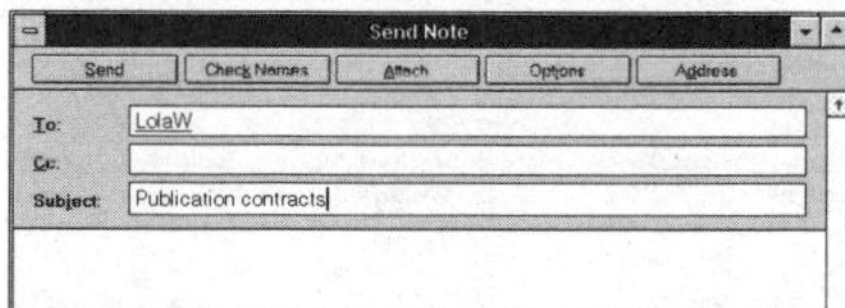

Figure 4. *Enter a subject.*

Starting and Addressing a Message

1. Click the Compose button. **(Figure 1)**
2. On the new Send Note form, click the Address button to select addresses from the Address book. **(Figure 2)**
3. On the Address dialog box, double-click the name of each recipient for the message. **(Figure 3)**

   or

   Drag names from the list at the top to the To or CC boxes below.

   or

   Select names from the list and click the To or Cc buttons.
4. On the Address dialog box, click OK.
5. Enter a message subject in the Subject text box. **(Figure 4)** *Don't skip this step. A subject is helpful when the recipient views his or her Inbox.*

✔ Tips

- In the Address dialog box, type the first few letters of a name to jump to that name on the list. Then press Enter to select the name.
- To view details about a name on the address list, click the name and click the Details button.
- To remove a name from the To or Cc boxes on the Address dialog box, select the name and press the Delete key.
- If you know a recipient's address, you can also type the address into the To text box on the Send Note form without using the Address book.
- The address of an underlined name has been confirmed on the Postoffice List by Mail.

Entering the Text and Sending the Message

1. On the Send Note form, click the message text area.
   or
   After typing the subject, press the Tab key to move the insertion point to the message text area.
2. Type the text of the message. **(Figure 5)**
3. Click the Send button. **(Figure 6)**
   or
   Press Alt+S.

✔ Tips

- Messages you send are transferred to the Outbox temporarily until they are actually sent by the system to the recipient.
- Messages that are successfully sent are transferred to the Sent mail folder where you can review them. **(Figure 7)**

Message text area.

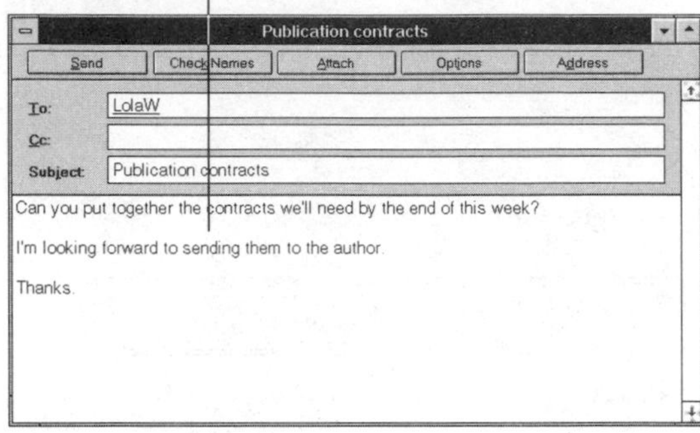

Figure 5. *Type the message text in the message text area.*

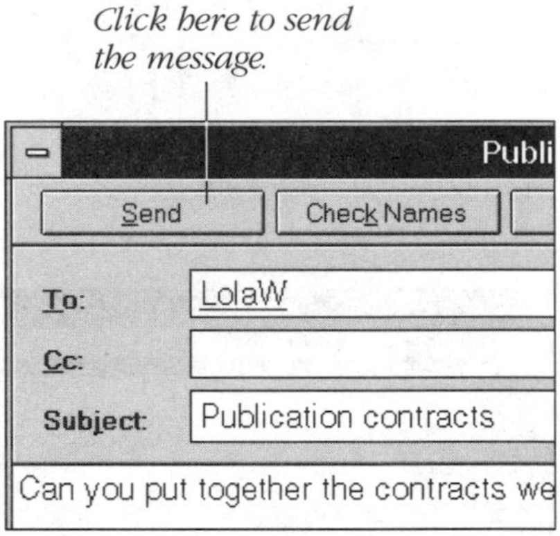

Click here to send the message.

Figure 6. *The Send button.*

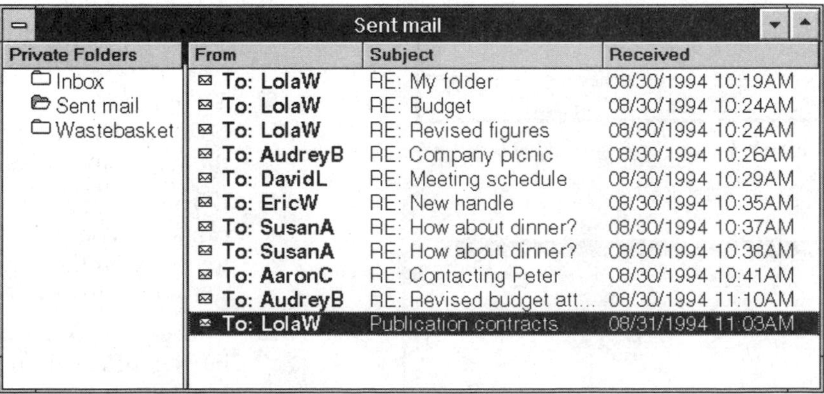

Figure 7. *The Sent mail folder.*

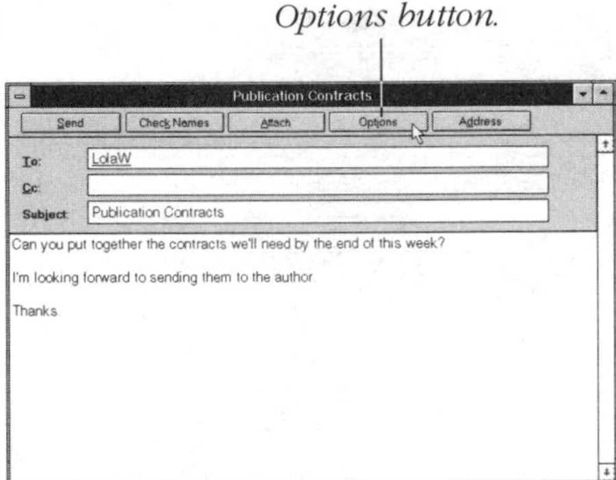

Figure 8. *The Options button.*

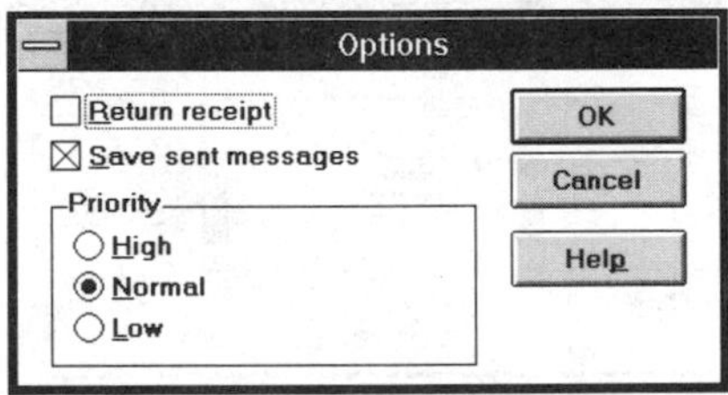

Figure 9. *The Options dialog box.*

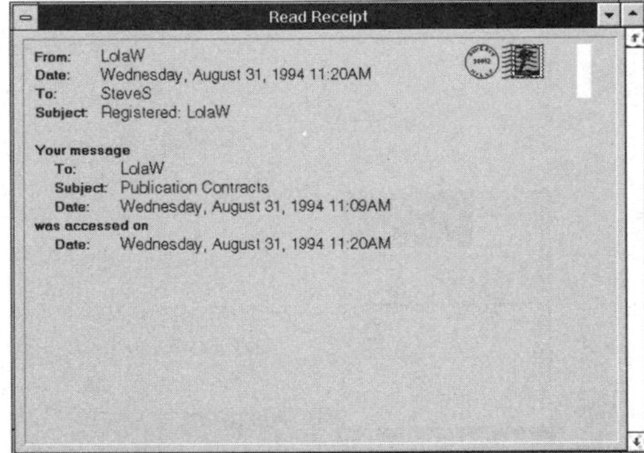

Figure 10. *A return receipt.*

Selecting Message Options

1. While composing a message, click the Options button. **(Figure 8)**
2. On the Options dialog box, click Return Receipt to be notified when the recipient opens the message. **(Figures 9-10)**
3. On the Options dialog box, clear the Save sent messages checkbox if you do not want messages that have been sent to be transferred to the Sent mail folder.
4. On the Options dialog box, choose High, Normal, or Low priority. High priority places an exclamation point next to the message header on the recipient's Inbox. Low priority places a down arrow next to the message header. **(Figure 11)**
5. Click OK.

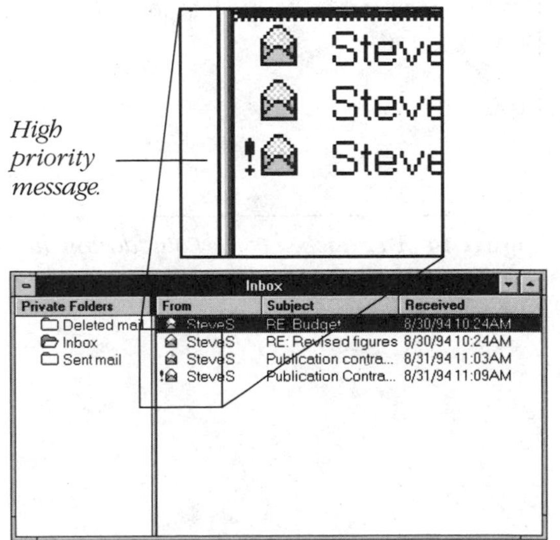

Figure 11. *The recipient's Inbox.*

Mail

Attaching a File to a Message

1. While composing a message, click the Attach button. **(Figure 12)**
2. On the Attach dialog box, select a file and click Attach. **(Figure 13)**
3. To attach another file, repeat Step 2.

✓ Tips

- You can also attach a message by opening the File Manager and dragging a file to the message you are composing.
- You can also drag a file from the File Manager to the Outbox. A Send Note form appears so you can address the outgoing message and add explanatory text.
- A file with an attached message shows a paper clip next to its envelope icon. **(Figure 15)**

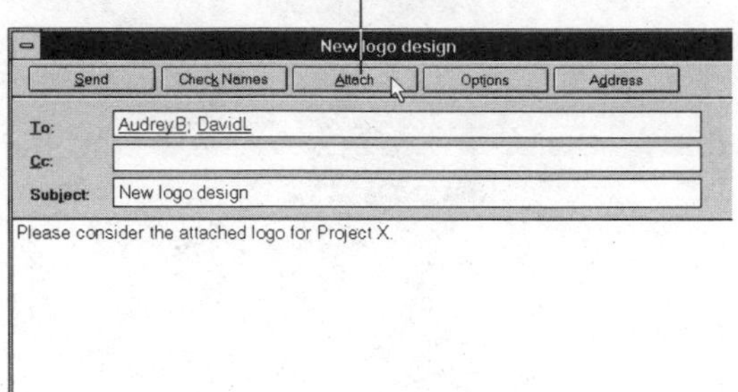

Figure 12. *The Attach button.*

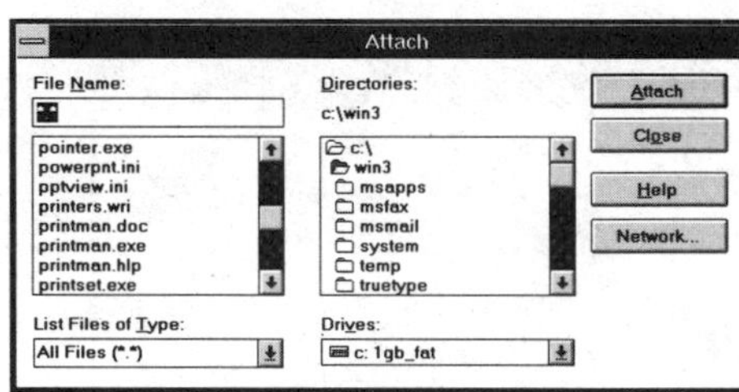

Figure 13. *The Attach dialog box.*

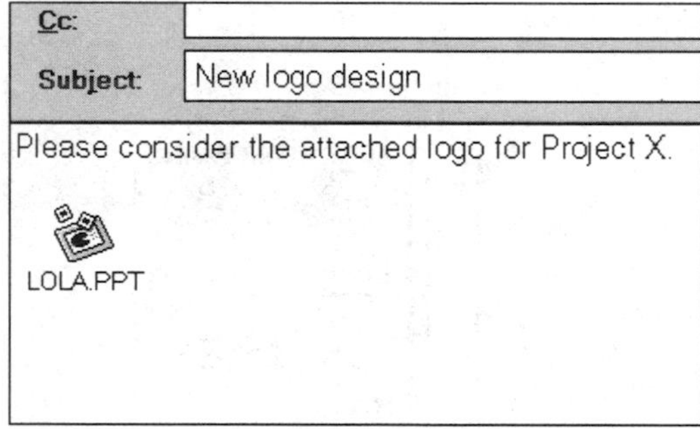

Figure 14. *An attached PowerPoint document.*

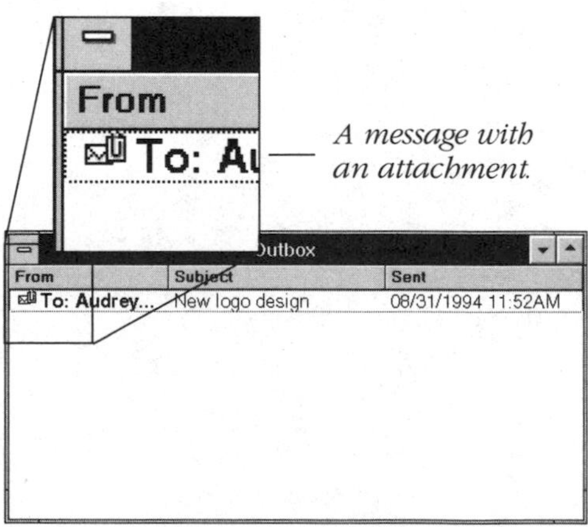

Figure 15. *An outgoing message with an attachment.*

Attaching a File

Mail

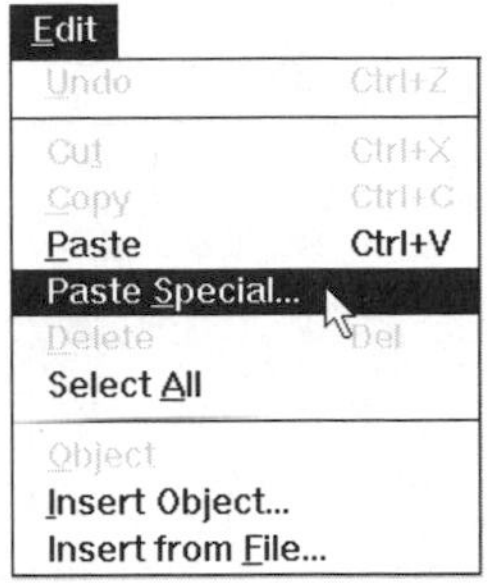

Figure 16. *The Mail Edit menu.*

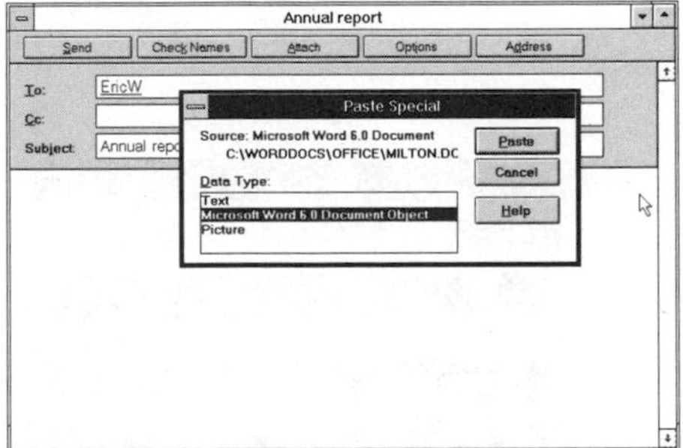

Figure 17. *The Paste Special dialog box.*

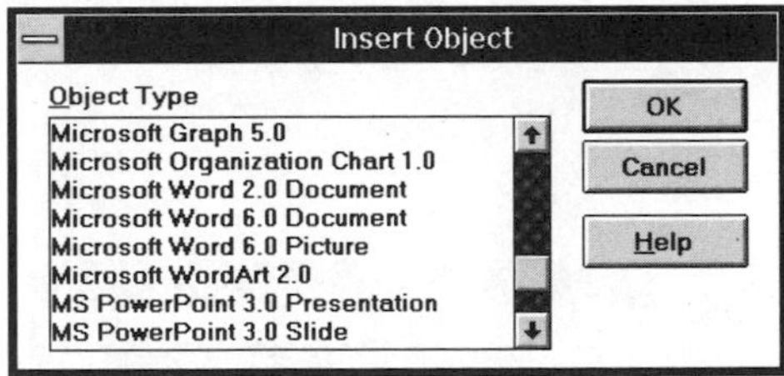

Figure 18. *The Insert Object dialog box.*

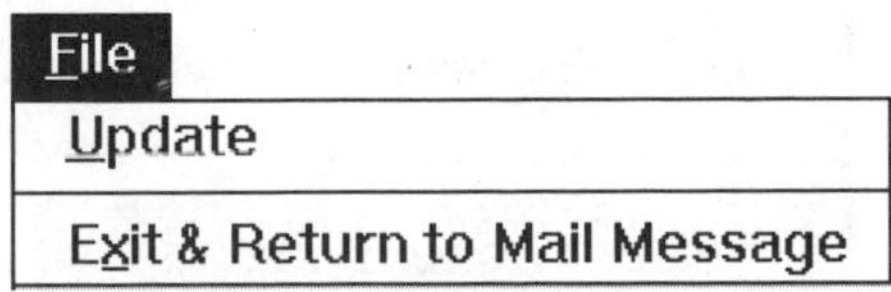

Figure 19. *Another application's File menu.*

Embedding an Object in a Message

1. Create the object in another application, select it, and choose Copy from the application's Edit menu.
2. While composing a message in Mail, choose Paste Special from Mail's Edit menu. **(Figure 16)**
3. On the Paste Special dialog box, double-click the Object data type. **(Figure 17)**

or

1. While composing a new mail message, choose Insert Object from Mail's Edit menu.
2. On the Insert Object dialog box, select an Object type. **(Figure 18)**
3. Create the object in the other application.
4. From the application's File menu, choose Update and then choose Exit and Return. **(Figure 19)**

✔ **Tip**

- You can create a graph to send without using Excel or PowerPoint by selecting Microsoft Graph 5.0 on the Insert Object dialog box.

Mail

Creating a Personal Address Book

1. From the Mail menu, choose Address Book. **(Figure 20)**
2. On the Address Book dialog box, select as many names as you'd like to add to your personal address book. **(Figure 21)**
3. Click the Add Names button **(Figure 21)** or press Ctrl+A.
4. Press Esc.

✔ Tips

- To inspect the Personal Address Book, click the Personal Address Book button on the Address Book dialog box. **(Figure 21)**
- To remove a name from the Personal Address Book, click the name on the Personal Address Book and click Remove. **(Figure 22)**

Using the Personal Address Book

1. While composing a message, click the Address button.
2. On the Address dialog box, click the Personal Address Book button. **(Figure 24)**
3. Use the Personal Address Book as you would the Postoffice Address book.

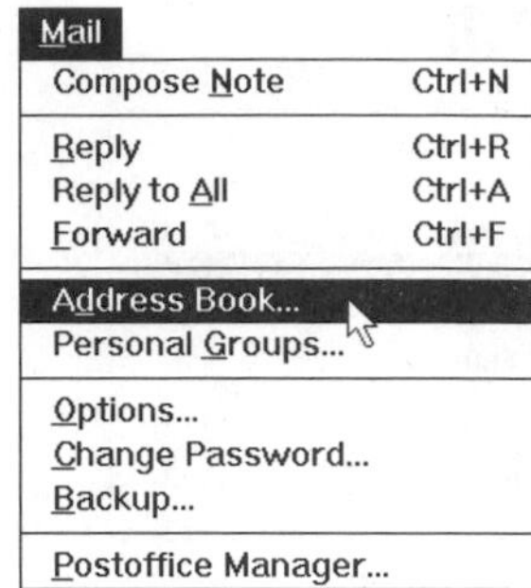

Figure 20. *The Mail menu.*

Select the names to add.

Personal Address Book button.

Add Names button.

Address Book
Directory: Postoffice List
AaronC
AndyE
AudreyB
ClareC
DavidL
EricW
LolaW
SarahR
SteveS
SusanA
Details | Close | Help

Figure 21. *The Address Book dialog box.*

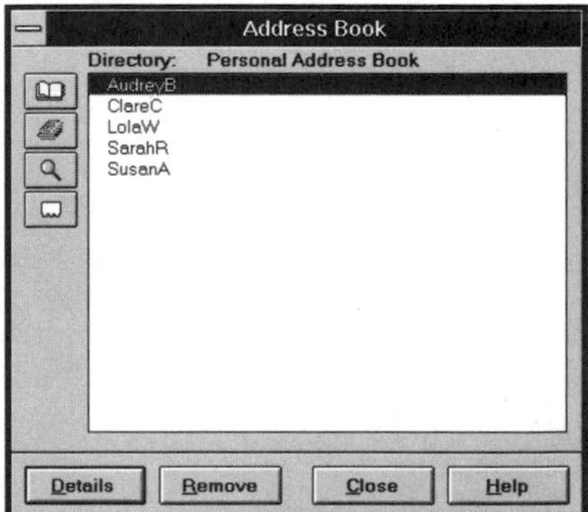

Figure 22. *The Personal Address Book.*

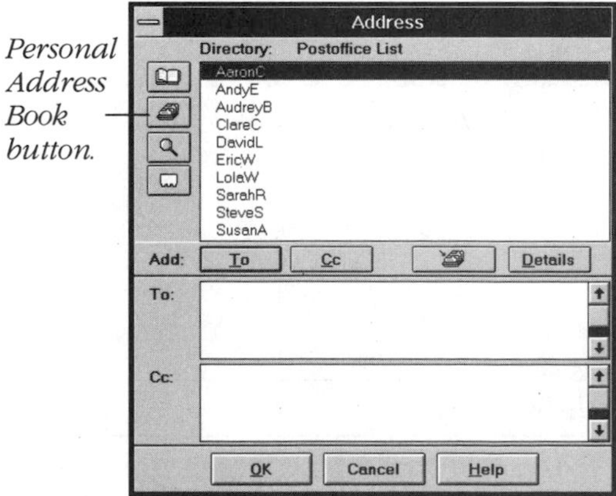

Figure 23. *The Address dialog box.*

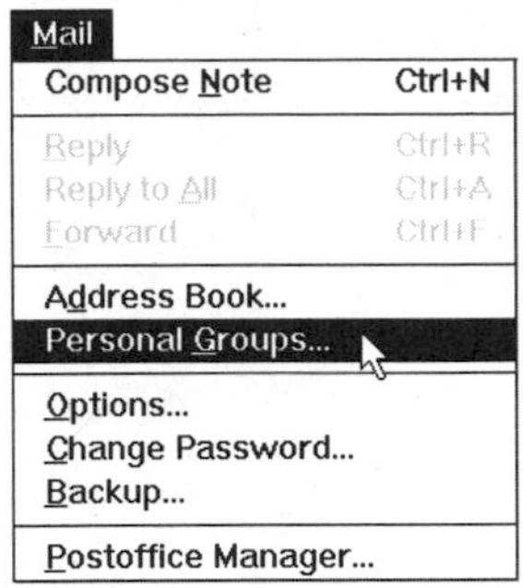

Figure 24. *The Mail menu.*

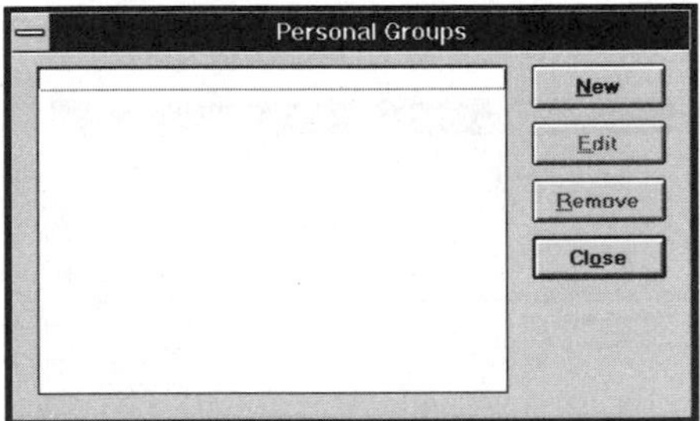

Figure 25. *The Personal Groups dialog box.*

Creating a Personal Group

A personal group is like a distribution list. By entering the personal group name as the recipient of a message, you can automatically send the message to everyone in the group.

1. From the Mail menu, choose Personal Groups. **(Figure 24)**
2. On the Personal Groups dialog box, click New. **(Figure 25)**
3. On the New Group dialog box, enter a name for the group and click Create. **(Figure 26)**
4. On the Personal Groups dialog box, drag names from the Directory list to the Group Members list. **(Figure 27)**
5. Click OK.

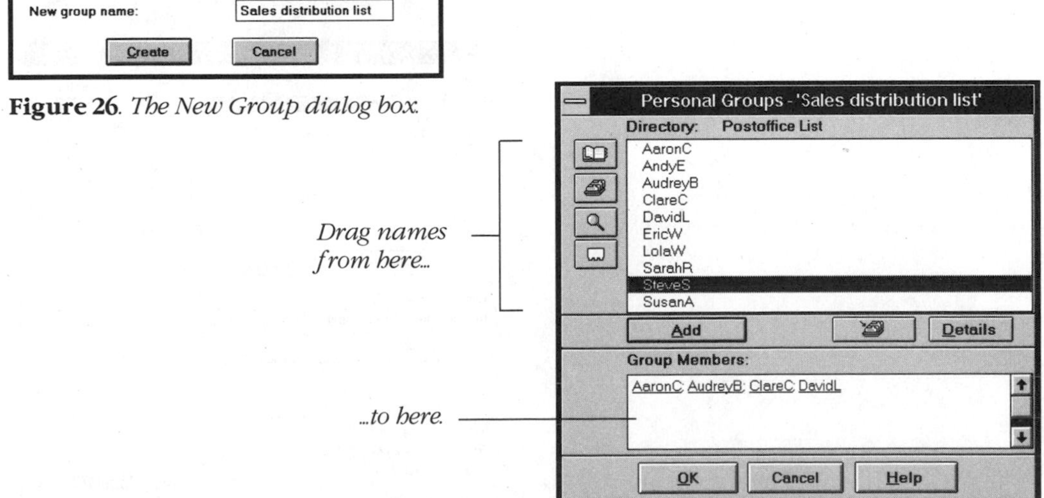

Figure 26. *The New Group dialog box.*

Figure 27. *The Personal groups dialog box.*

Sending a Document from Within an Office Application.

1. From the File menu of the application, select Send. **(Figure 28)**
2. On the Send Note form, enter an address, subject, and any additional text you want in the message body. **(Figure 29)**
3. Click Send to send the document as a Mail message.

✔ Tip

- Choose Add Routing Slip from the application's File menu to automatically send the document to others for their edits or annotations. **(Figure 30)**

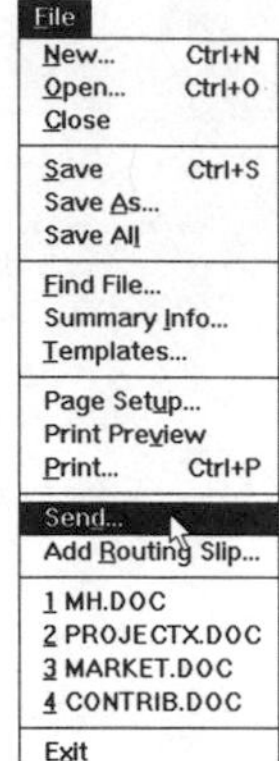

Figure 28. *The File menu of Word.*

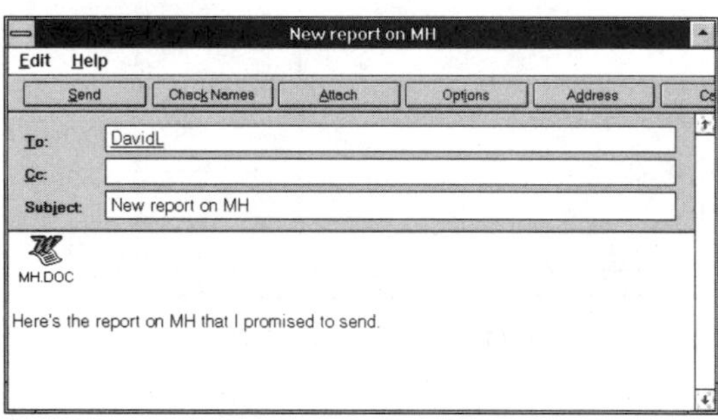

Figure 29. *The Send Note form.*

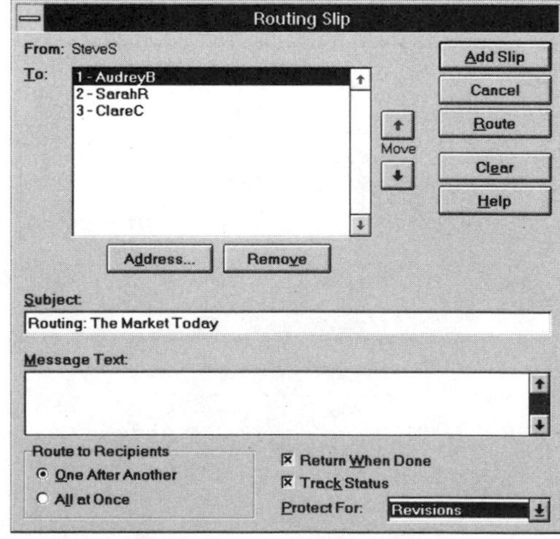

Figure 30. *The Routing Slip dialog box.*

Managing Your Mail

Private Folders	From	Subject	Received
Inbox	LolaW	Budget	08/30/1994 10:29AM
ProjectX	LolaW	Revised figures	08/30/1994 10:30AM
Sent mail	LolaW	Product spec	08/30/1994 10:31AM
Wastebasket	AudreyB	Company picnic	08/30/1994 10:33AM
	AudreyB	RE: Company pi...	08/30/1994 10:34AM
	DavidL	Meeting schedule	08/30/1994 10:36AM
	DavidL	Bring markups	08/30/1994 10:38AM
	EricW	New handle	08/30/1994 10:40AM
	AaronC	Contacting Peter	08/30/1994 10:47AM
	AaronC	Sales projections	08/30/1994 10:47AM
	AudreyB	Revised budget ...	08/30/1994 11:00AM
	LolaW	Registered: LolaW	08/31/1994 11:20AM

Figure 1. *The Inbox.*

Inbox

Private Folders	From	Subje
Inbox	LolaW	Budge
ProjectX	LolaW	Revis
Sent mail	LolaW	Produ
Wastebasket	AudreyB	Comp
	AudreyB	RE: C
	DavidL	Meetir
	DavidL	Bring

Figure 2. *Drag a message to a folder.*

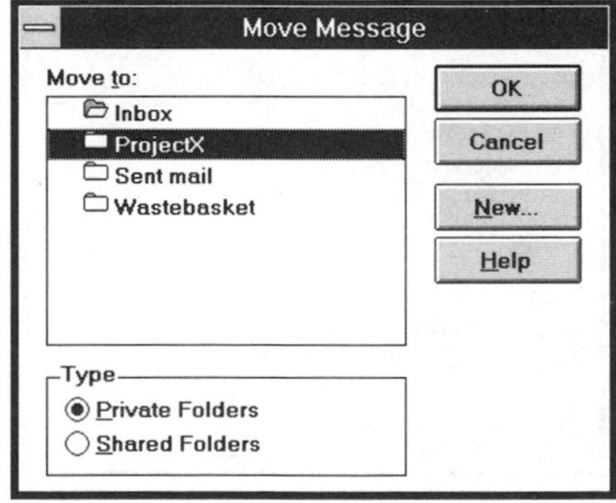

Figure 3. *The Move Message dialog box.*

Filing a Message in a Folder

You can add folders to the list of private folders that you see in the Inbox window and then easily move messages to any folder you create. Folders allow you to organize messages by sender, project, department, or any other plan.

1. On the Inbox, select one or more messages. **(Figure 1)**
2. Drag the selected message or messages to the folder on the list of Private Folders. **(Figure 2)**

   or

   Click the Move button and then select a folder on the Move Message dialog box. **(Figure 3)**

✔ Tips

- The currently open folder shows an open folder icon. **(Figure 4)**
- To view the contents of a folder, double-click the folder name.

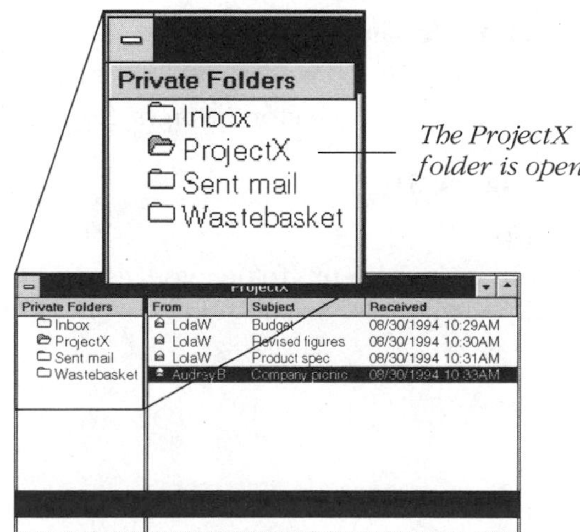

Figure 4. *Folder list.*

Creating Folders

New folders can be Private (only you can view their contents) or Shared (everyone can view their contents).

1. From the File menu, choose New Folder. **(Figure 5)**
2. On the New Folder dialog box, enter a name for the folder and then click either Private or Shared. **(Figure 6)**
3. If you are creating a Shared folder, click Options and then set the options available to other users by clicking the Read, Write, or Delete checkboxes. **(Figure 7)**

✔ Tips

- To add a folder under an existing folder, select the existing folder before choosing New Folder from the File menu. You can also choose to make the new folder a subfolder of an existing folder on the Options dialog box. **(Figure 7)**
- Each folder can have its own Sort order for the messages inside.

Figure 5. *The File menu.*

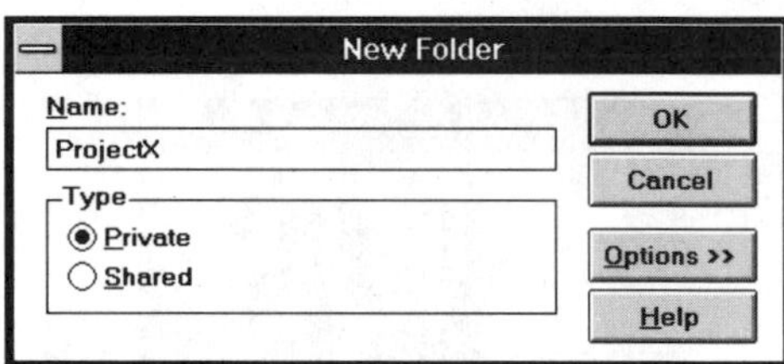

Figure 6. *The New Folder dialog box.*

Figure 7. *The Options dialog box.*

Deleting Folders

1. Click a folder on the Private Folders list.
2. Click the Delete button or press the Delete key on the keyboard. **(Figure 8)**

✔ Tip

- When you delete a folder, you also delete all messages and subfolders it contains.

Figure 8. *The Delete button.*

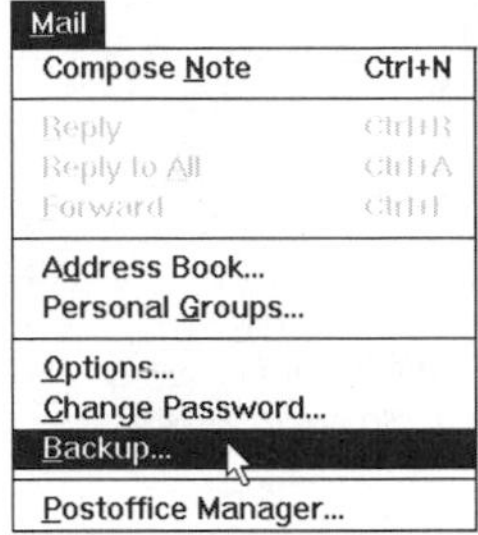

Figure 9. *The Mail menu.*

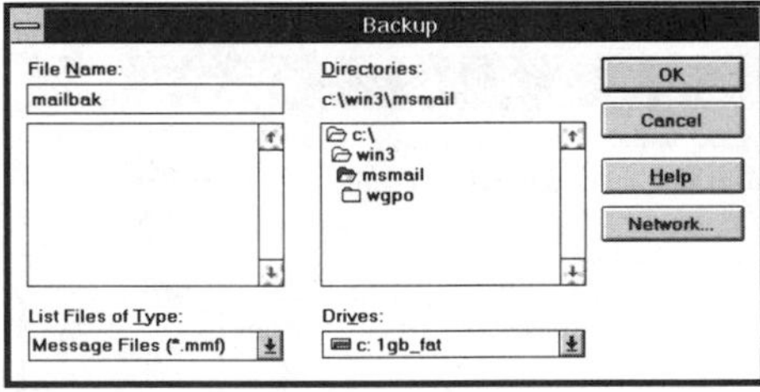

Figure 10. *The Backup dialog box.*

Backing Up Your Messages

Your messages file may be automatically backed up when your system is periodically backed up, but it's still a good idea to back up the message file periodically yourself.

1. From the Mail menu, choose Backup. **(Figure 9)**
2. On the Backup dialog box, enter a new name for the backup file and click OK or press Enter. **(Figure 10)**

Changing Your Password

1. From the Mail menu, choose Change Password.
2. In the Change Password dialog box, enter your existing password into the Old Password text box. **(Figure 11)**
3. Into the New Password text box, enter the new password.
4. Enter the new password again into the Verify New Password text box to confirm it.
5. Click Remember Password if you don't want to have to enter your password each time you start Mail.

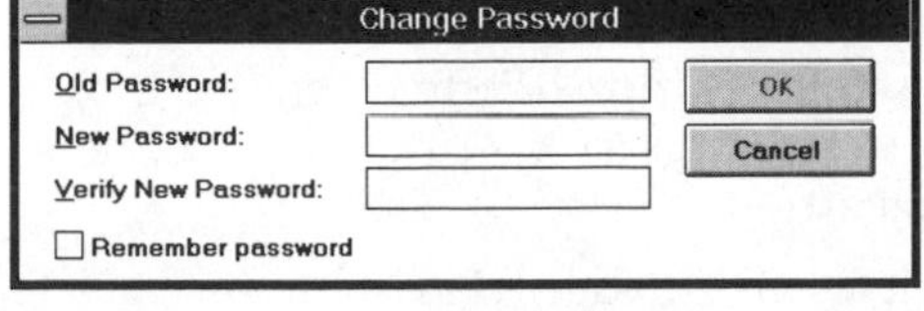

Figure 11. *The Change Password dialog box.*

✔ Tip

- The Remember Password option allows anybody who can use your PC to read and create mail as though they were you. For security, you should leave Remember Password unchecked.

Setting Mail Options

1. From the Mail menu, choose Options. **(Figure 12)**
2. On the Options dialog box, make selections and then click OK or press Enter. **(Figure 13)**

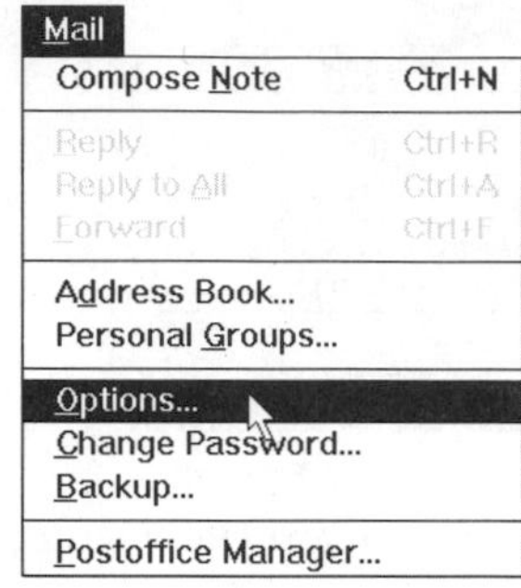

Figure 12. *The Mail menu.*

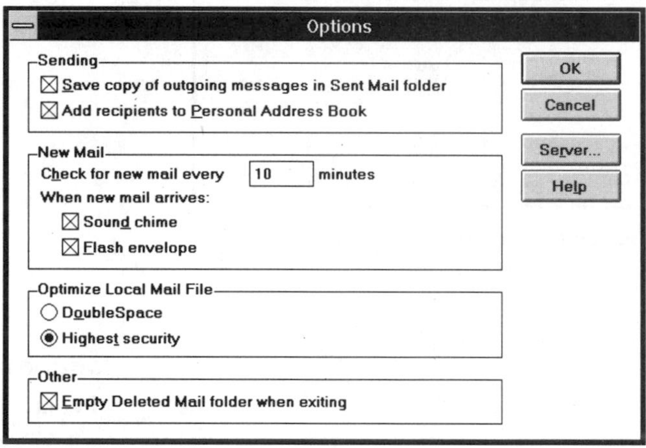

Figure 13. *The Options dialog box.*

Table 40-1. ***Mail Options***

Save copy of outgoing messages in Sent Folder	Sent mail is copied to the Sent mail folder. Otherwise, it is deleted.
Add recipients to Personal Address Book	Automatically adds all recipients of your outgoing messages to your Personal Address Book.
Check for new mail every ☐ minutes	Sets the interval at which Mail will check for incoming messages.
When new mail arrives	**Sound chime** rings a chime when new mail arrives. **Flash Envelope** briefly changes the mouse pointer to an envelope when new mail arrives.
Empty Deleted Mail Folder when exiting	Deletes all messages that are in the Wastebasket whenever you exit Mail.

Combining the Office Applications

Combining the Office Applications

Basic Techniques

Combining Applications

Basic Techniques

About Sharing Information Among the Office Applications

Alone, each Office application is impressive enough, but combined, they form a powerful system that can share information among the applications.

To add specific figures to a memo, you can copy a table of numbers from **Excel** to a **Word** document. To make sure changes to the **Excel** numbers flow through to the **Word** document, you can even create a link between the original numbers in **Excel** and the copy in **Word**. **(Figure 1)**

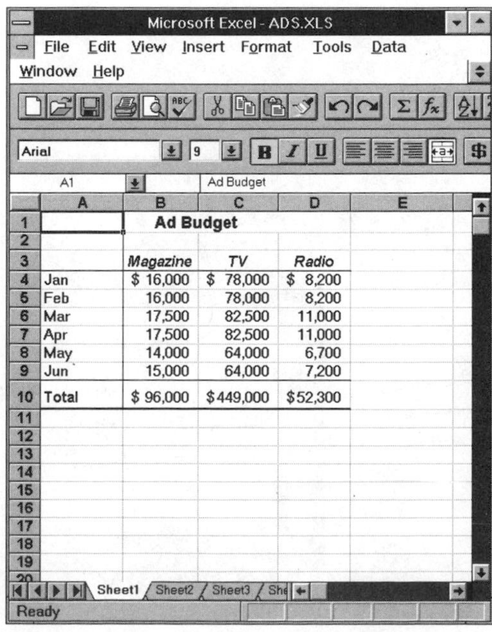

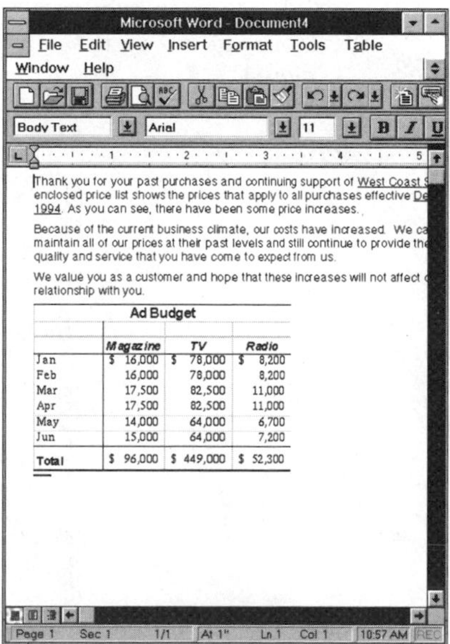

Figure 1. *A table copied from Excel to Word.*

About Dragging and Dropping Among the Applications

The easiest way to move something from one application to another is with *Drag and Drop*. Dragging and dropping *between* applications works just like dragging and dropping *within* an application. You select an item to drag, called an *object*, and then drag between two application windows that are arranged side by side. You can select a range of numbers or a chart in **Excel**, for instance, and drag it to a **Word** memo. **(Figures 2-3)**

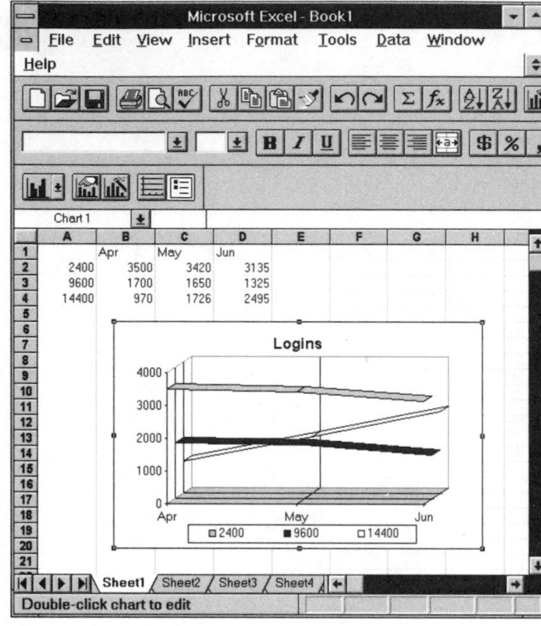

Figure 2. *An Excel chart.*

Table 41-1. *Drag and Droppable Objects*

Word	• Selected text. • A table
Excel	• A cell • Selected range of numbers • A chart • Drawn graphics
PowerPoint	• A slide from Slide Sorter view • Slide show (all slides from Slide Sorter view)
Access	• None

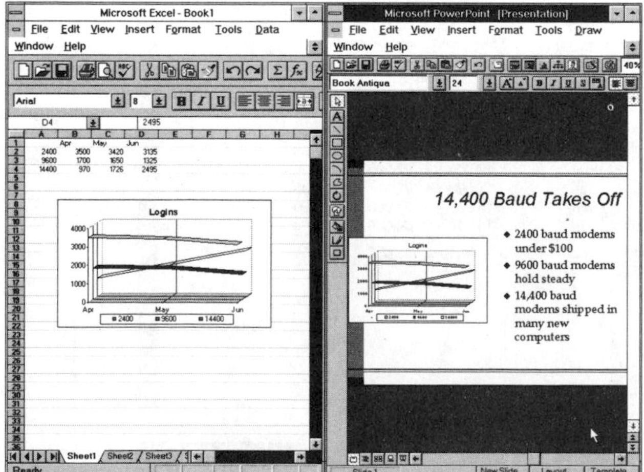

Figure 3. *The Excel chart dragged to a PowerPoint slide.*

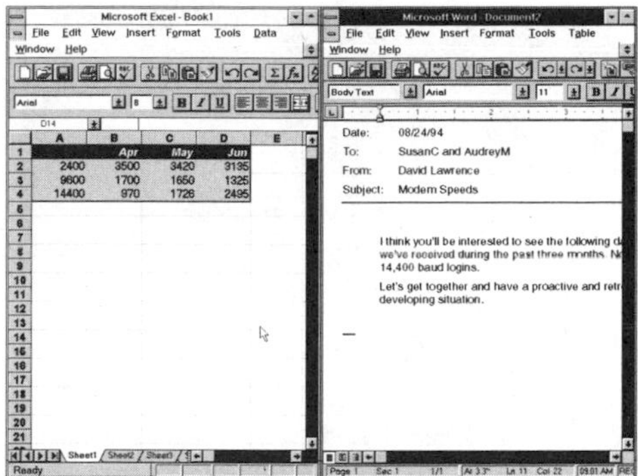

Figure 4. *Excel and Word windows arranged side-by-side.*

Drag and Drop: Moving an Object

1. Arrange the two application windows side by side so you can see both the object and its destination. **(Figure 4)**
2. Select the object. **(Figure 5)**
3. Drag the object to the other window. **(Figure 6)**
4. Release the mouse button to drop the object at its destination. **(Figure 7)**

✔ Tips

- To **copy** rather than **move** an object with Drag and Drop, hold down the Ctrl key as you drag the object. **(Figure 8)**
- When you drag and drop an object, it becomes embedded in the destination application. Any changes to the original are not reflected in the copy unless you establish a link using Copy and Paste Link. *See Linking Objects with Copy and Paste Link, page 307.*

Figure 5. *A selected range in Excel.*

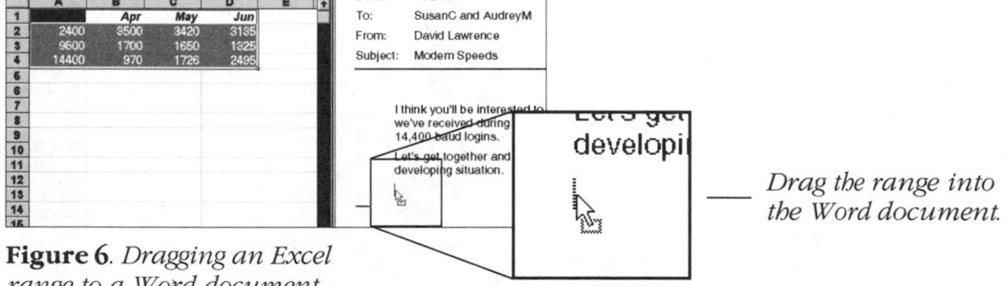

Drag the range into the Word document.

Figure 6. *Dragging an Excel range to a Word document.*

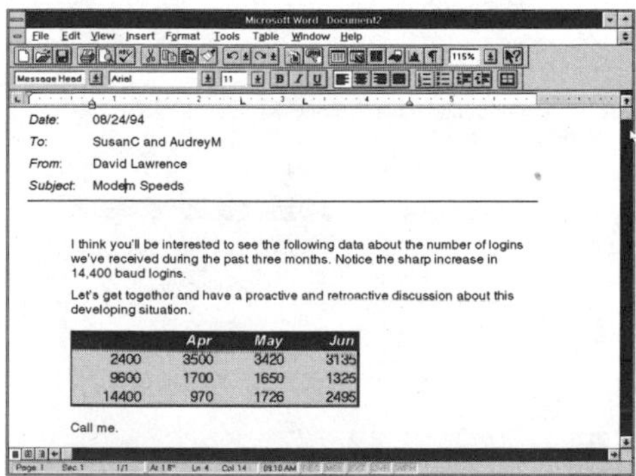

Figure 7. *The range as it appears in Word.*

The plus sign next to the pointer indicates that a copy is in progress rather than a move.

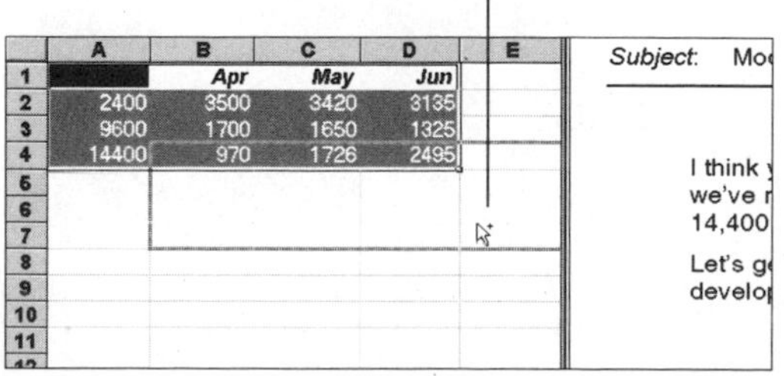

Figure 8. *Copying an object with Drag and Drop.*

Editing an Object After Dragging and Dropping

Even though you've dragged an object to another application, you can still edit the dragged object using the tools of the original application in which it was created. If the original application is a special OLE 2 application, you may even be able to edit the object *in place*.

During in-place editing, the menus, toolbars, and other controls of the originating application temporarily appear in the application window in which you are working.

1. Double-click an object that has been dragged from another application. **(Figures 9-10)**

or

Click the object with the right mouse button and then choose the Edit command on the shortcut menu. **(Figure 11)**

✔ Tip

- If you select an object, you'll see whether you can edit the object in its original application. The status line at the bottom of the application will advise you to double-click if you can edit the object. **(Figure 9)**

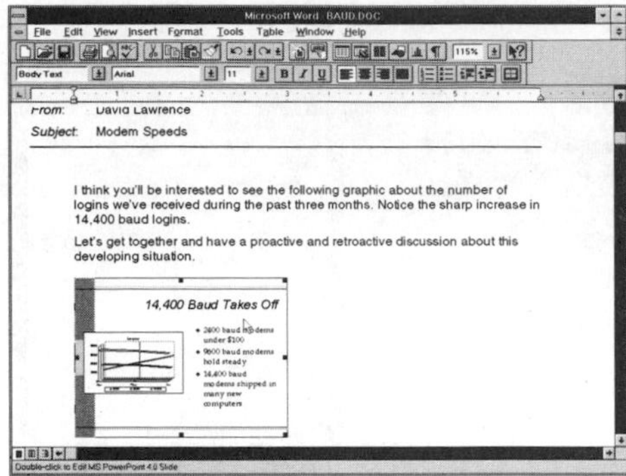

Figure 9. *Double-click a PowerPoint slide in Word to edit the slide in PowerPoint*

The title bar indicates that the slide resides in a Word document.

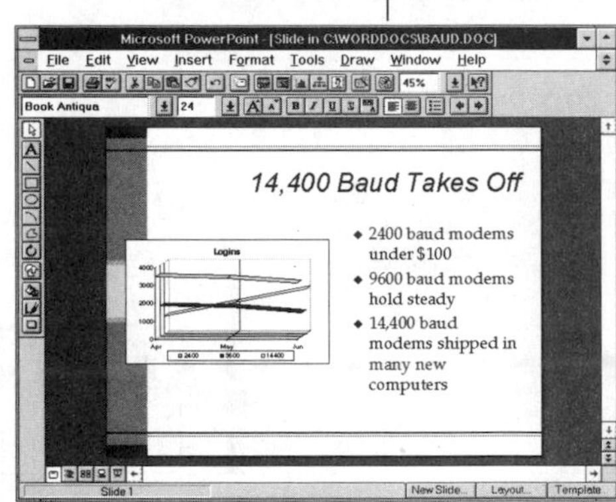

Figure 10. *The slide appears for editing in its originating application.*

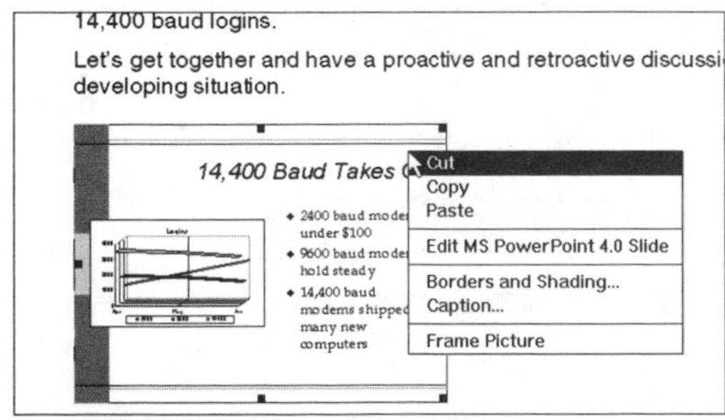

Figure 11. *The shortcut menu for a PowerPoint slide that has been dragged to Word.*

	A	B	C	D
1		Orange	Riverside	
2	2400	65	43	
3	9600	52	45	
4	14400	26	79	
5				
6				
7				

Figure 12. *Selecting an Excel range.*

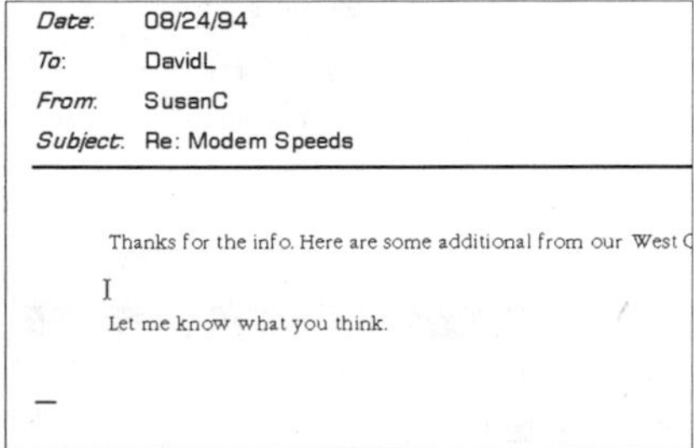

Figure 13. *Click at the destination for the Excel object.*

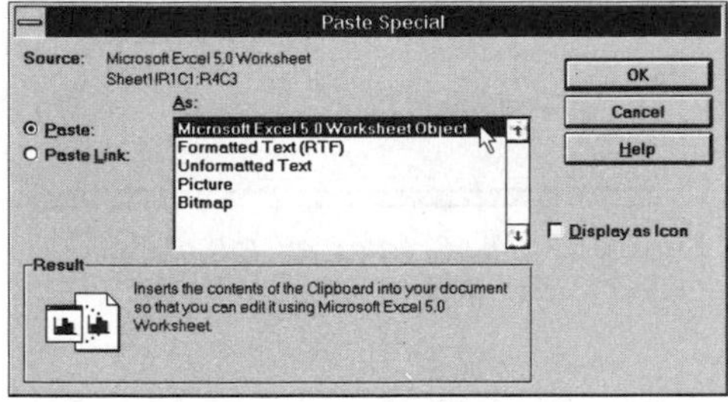

Figure 14. *The Paste Special dialog box.*

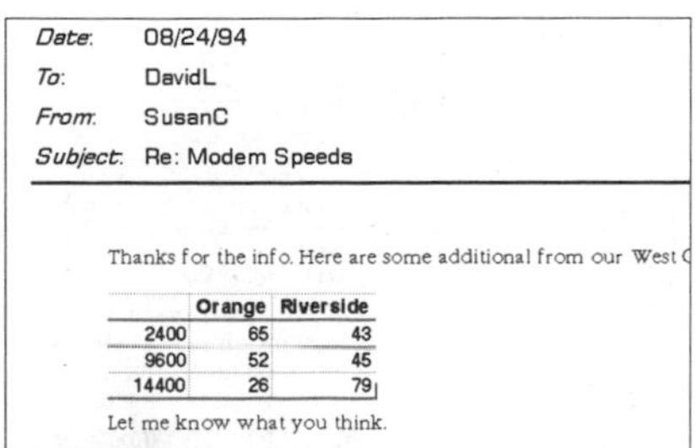

Figure 15. *The Excel range appears in the Word document.*

Embedding an Object with Copy and Paste Special

To transfer an existing object to another application, you can *embed* the object. Embedded objects are not linked to their original application. Instead, all the data for the object is transferred to the destination application. As a result, you can move the destination file to another computer, and the object, which has become an integral part of the destination file, is moved, too. Objects that are dragged and dropped become embedded.

1. Select the object in its originating application. **(Figure 12)**
2. From the Edit menu, choose Copy.
3. Switch to the other application and click at the destination for the object. **(Figure 13)**
4. From the Edit menu of the destination application, choose Paste Special.
5. On the Paste Special dialog box, double-click the item on the list that is referred to as an "object." **(Figure 14)**

✔ Tips

- To edit an embedded object, double-click the object. Either the originating application will open in a separate window or the controls of the originating application will take over the current window. After you edit the object in a separate window, select Update from the File menu, and then Exit and Return from the File menu. If the controls of the originating application take over the current window, click outside the frame that contains the object when you finish.
- Any changes to the original object are not reflected in copies that are embedded in other applications.
- If you move a file with an embedded object to another PC, you must have installed the originating application for the object to edit the object.

Creating an Embedded Object

Rather than embed an existing object, you can create an embedded object in an alternate application on the fly as you work in your main application. This gives you access to the tools of other Office applications at any time as you work.

1. From the Insert menu of your main application, choose Object. **(Figure 16)**
2. On the Create New tab of the Object dialog box, double-click the appropriate object type. **(Figure 17)**
3. In the other application, create the object.
4. From the File menu of the other application, select Update. **(Figure 18)**
5. From the File menu of the other application, select Exit and Return. **(Figure 19)**

✔ Tips

- To edit an embedded object, double-click it.
- If the second application allows in-place editing (the menus and toolbars of the other application appear in the current window) click outside the frame of the new object you are creating rather than follow Steps 4 and 5.

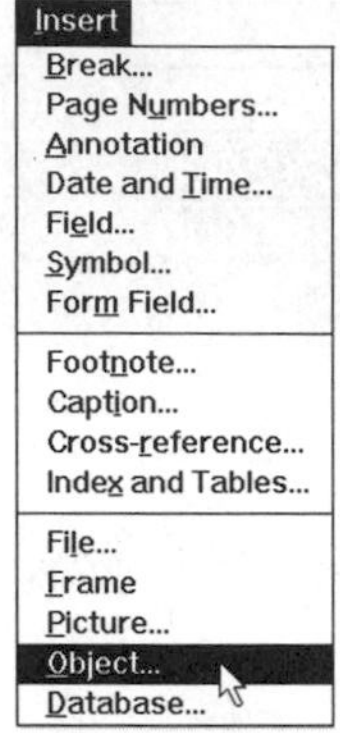

Figure 16. *The Word Insert menu.*

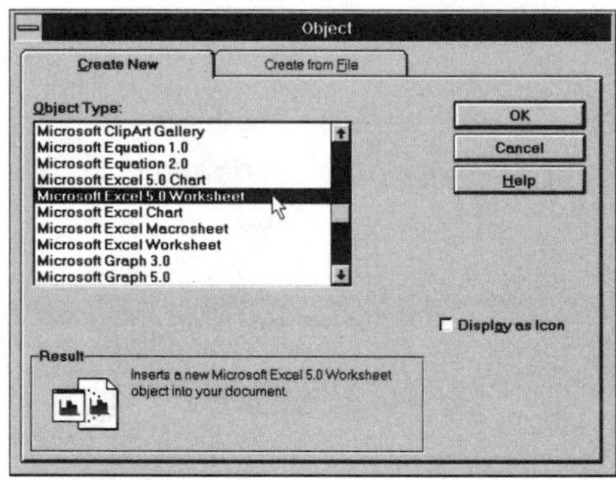

Figure 17. *The Create New tab of the Object dialog box.*

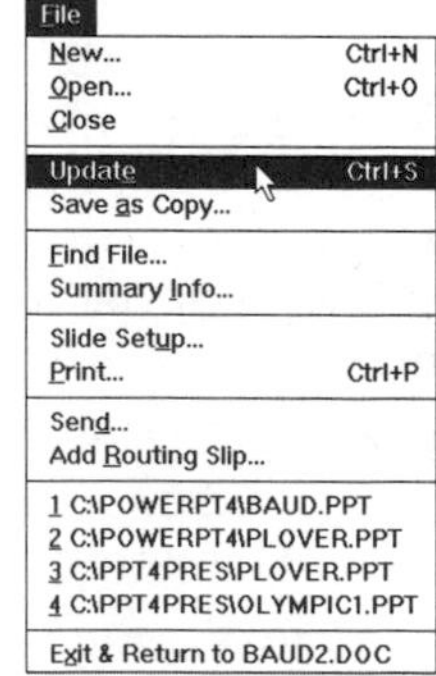

Figure 18. *The File menu.*

Figure 19. *The File menu.*

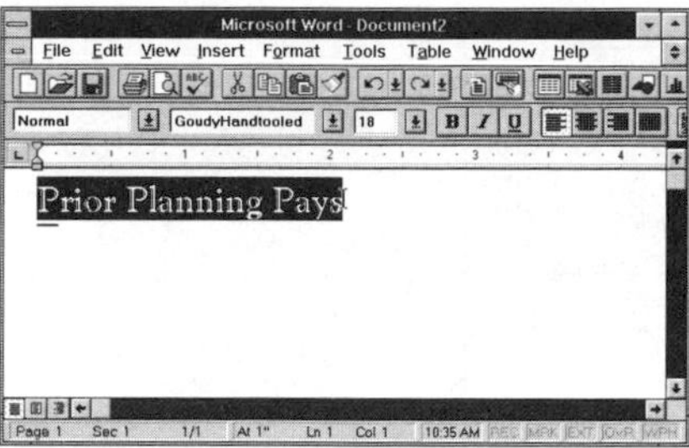

Figure 20. *Select text in Word.*

Linking Objects with Copy and Paste Link

When you *link* rather than embed an object, the object remains in its originating application, but a copy, which is linked to the original, is displayed in the other application. Any changes to the original show up in the linked copy.

By linking an object that needs frequent updating, you can be sure that the changes to the original will flow to all other applications that display a linked copy.

1. Save the file in which you've created the object.
2. Select the object to link. **(Figure 20)**
3. From the Edit menu, choose Copy. **(Figure 21)**
4. Switch to the other application.
5. From the Edit menu of the other application, choose Paste Special. **(Figure 22)**
6. On the Paste Special dialog box, click Paste Link and then double-click the description of the object to link. **(Figures 23-24)**

✔ Tips

- Double-click the pasted copy to edit the original object.
- Each link automatically updates every time you open a document containing links.

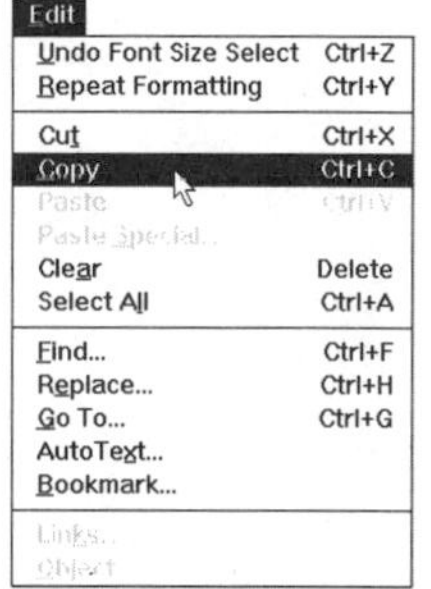

Figure 21. *The Edit menu.*

Figure 22. *The Edit menu.*

Click Paste Link

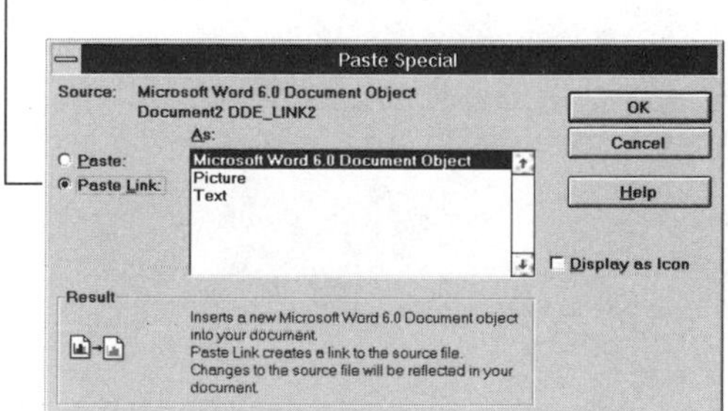

Figure 23. *The Paste Special dialog box.*

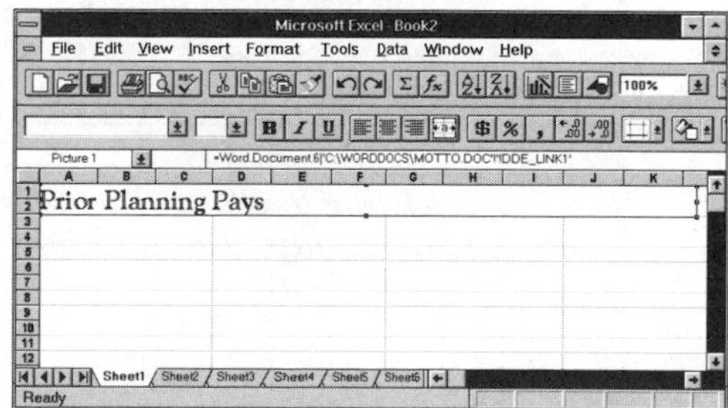

Figure 24. *The linked copy in Excel.*

Updating a Link

Links created with Copy and Paste Link update whenever you reopen the file in which they exist. You can manually update a link at any time, though.

1. From the Edit menu, choose Links. **(Figure 25)**
2. On the Links dialog box, select the link on the list of links. **(Figure 26)**
3. On the Links dialog box, click Update Now.
4. Click OK or Close to put away the Links dialog box.

✓ Tip

- To set the link so that it updates only when you choose Update Now, choose Manual as the Update option on the Links dialog box.

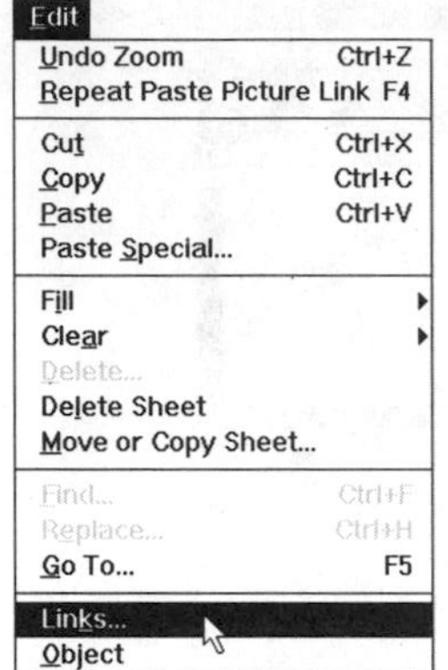

Figure 25. *The Edit menu.*

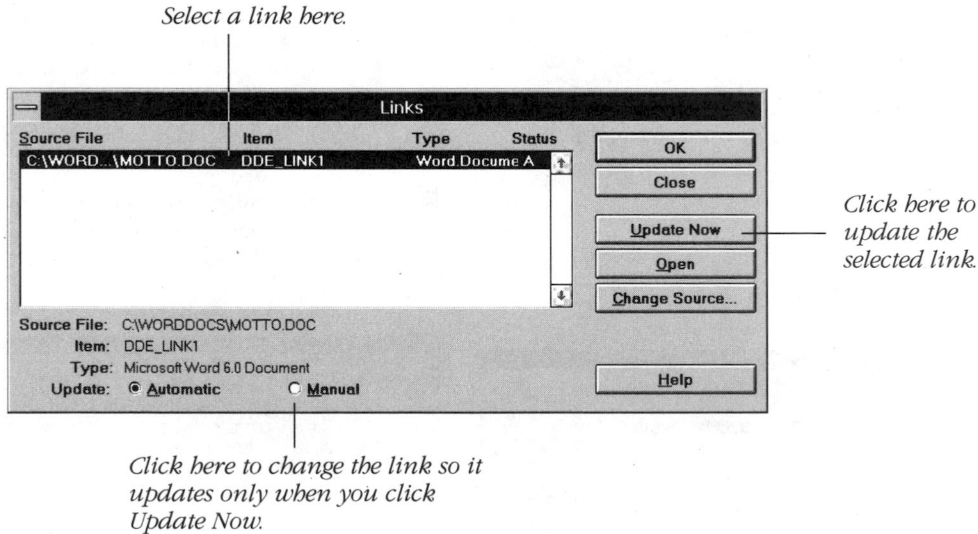

Figure 26. *The Links dialog box.*

Combining Applications

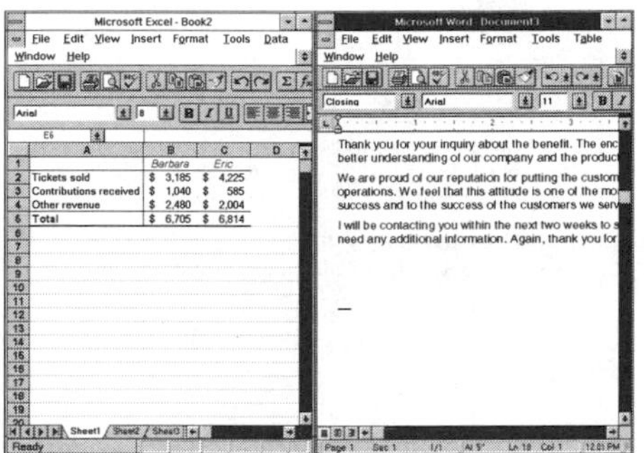

Figure 1. *Word and Excel windows arranged side-by-side.*

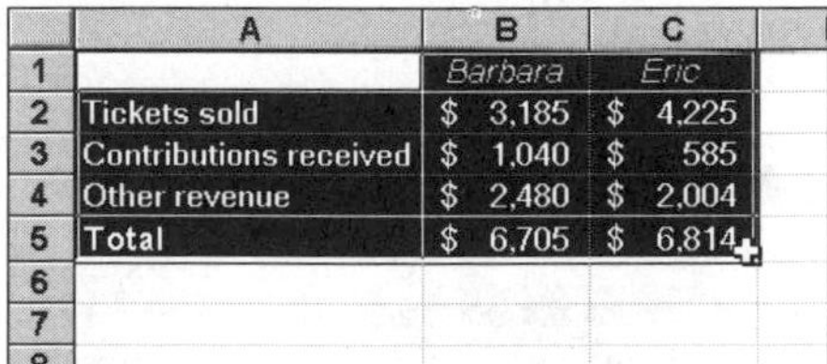

	A	B	C
1		Barbara	Eric
2	Tickets sold	$ 3,185	$ 4,225
3	Contributions received	$ 1,040	$ 585
4	Other revenue	$ 2,480	$ 2,004
5	Total	$ 6,705	$ 6,814
6			
7			
8			

Figure 2. *Select the range to copy.*

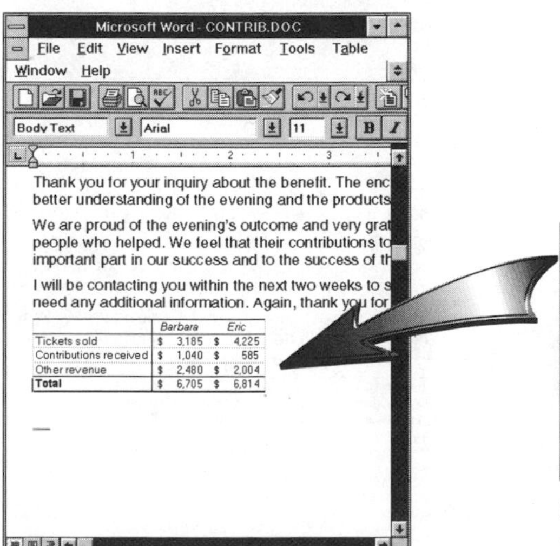

Figure 4. *Release the mouse button to drop the Excel range in the document.*

Excel to Word: Copying Ranges of Numbers

1. Arrange the **Word** and **Excel** windows side by side. **(Figure 1)**
2. Select the range of numbers in **Excel**. **(Figure 2)**
3. Press and hold the Ctrl key.
4. Place the mouse pointer on the border of the range and drag the range to the **Word** window. **(Figure 3)**
5. Release the mouse button when the insertion point is properly positioned in the **Word** document. **(Figure 4)**

✓ Tips

- The **Excel** range becomes embedded in the **Word** document, not linked. Changes to the numbers in **Excel** will not flow through to the **Word** document. *For information about linking numbers, see Excel to Word: Linking Numbers, page 310.*
- To modify the numbers in place using the **Excel** menus and toolbars, double-click the range. Click in the document outside the range to return the **Word** menus and toolbars to the window.

	A	B	C	D
1		Barbara	Eric	
2	Tickets sold	$ 3,185	$ 4,225	
3	Contributions received	$ 1,040	$ 585	
4	Other revenue	$ 2,480	$ 2,004	
5	Total	$ 6,705	$ 6,814	
6				
7				
8				
9				
10				
11				

Figure 3. *Drag the range from the Excel window to the Word window.*

Excel to Word: Linking Numbers

1. Select the range of numbers in **Excel**. **(Figure 5)**
2. From the Edit menu, choose Copy.
3. Switch to **Word**.
4. Position the insertion point at the destination for the copy of the range. **(Figure 6)**
5. From the Edit menu, choose Paste Special.
6. On the Paste Special dialog box, choose Paste Link. **(Figure 7)**
7. On the Paste Special dialog box, double-click Microsoft Excel 5.0 Worksheet Object.

✔ Tips

- Because you pasted a link, any changes to the range in **Excel** will be reflected in the **Word** document. If the **Word** document is not open, the changes will appear the next time you open the document.
- To update the link, choose Links from the Edit menu and then click Update Now on the Links dialog box, or click the range with the right mouse button and choose Update Link from the shortcut menu.
- If you move the document to another PC, you must also move the **Excel** file to the other PC, too.
- To edit the range in **Excel**, double-click the range in **Word.**

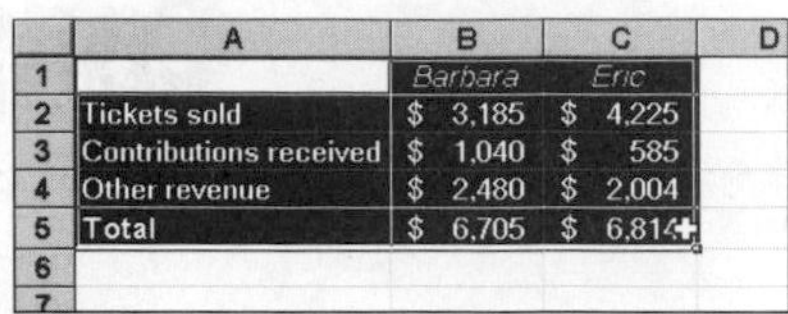

	A	B	C	D
1		Barbara	Eric	
2	Tickets sold	$ 3,185	$ 4,225	
3	Contributions received	$ 1,040	$ 585	
4	Other revenue	$ 2,480	$ 2,004	
5	Total	$ 6,705	$ 6,814	
6				
7				

Figure 5. *Select the range to link.*

Thank you for your inquiry about the benefit. The en
better understanding of the evening and the product

We are proud of the evening's outcome and very gr
people who helped. We feel that their contributions t
important part in our success and to the success of t

I will be contacting you within the next two weeks to
need any additional information. Again, thank you fo

Figure 6. *Click at the destination for the Excel range.*

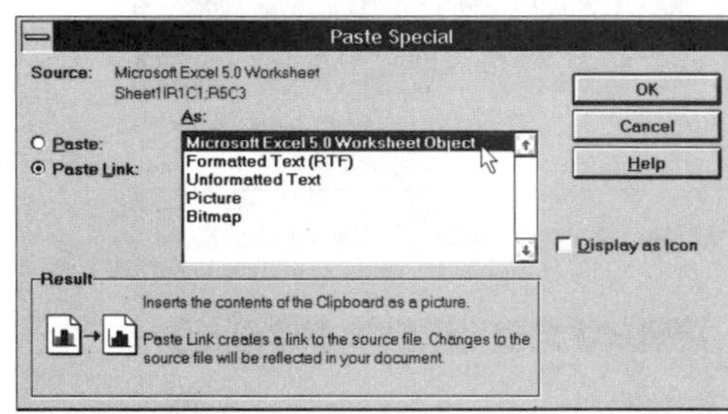

Figure 7. *The Paste Special dialog box.*

Thank you for your inquiry about the benefit. The en
better understanding of the evening and the product

We are proud of the evening's outcome and very gr
people who helped. We feel that their contributions t
important part in our success and to the success of t

I will be contacting you within the next two weeks to
need any additional information. Again, thank you fo

	Barbara	Eric
Tickets sold	$ 3,185	$ 4,225
Contributions received	$ 1,040	$ 585
Other revenue	$ 2,480	$ 2,004
Total	$ 6,705	$ 6,814

Figure 8. *The Excel range copied to a Word document.*

Figure 9. *The PowerPoint Graph slide.*

Click to add title

Presentation - Datasheet

		A	B	C	D	E
		1st Qtr	2nd Qtr	3rd Qtr	4th Qtr	
1	East	20.4	27.4	30	20.4	
2	West	30.6	38.6	34.6	31.6	
3	North	45.9	46.9	45	43.9	
4						

Figure 10. *The datasheet.*

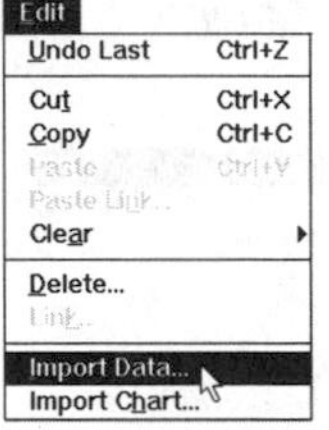

Figure 11. *The Graph Edit menu.*

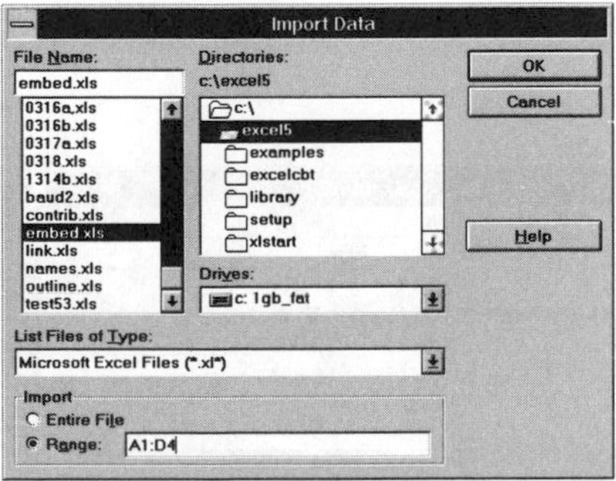

Figure 12. *The Import Data dialog box.*

Excel to PowerPoint: Graphing Numbers

1. In **PowerPoint**, create a slide for a graph. **(Figure 9)**
2. Double-click the "Double click to add graph" placeholder.
3. Click the cell on the datasheet at the upper left corner of the range of cells into which you want to import data from **Excel**. **(Figure 10)**
4. From Graph's Edit menu, choose Import Data. **(Figure 11)**
5. On the Import Data dialog box, select Entire File or Range, depending on whether you want to import all the data in the file or just a range. If you select Range, enter the range address or range name in the Range text box. **(Figure 12)**
6. On the Import Data dialog box, double-click the filename of the worksheet you want. The imported data appears on the worksheet.

✔ Tips

- The data must be on the first worksheet of an **Excel** workbook. Otherwise, you must change the order of the worksheets.
- You can consolidate data from several worksheets in a single **PowerPoint** graph by importing data from different ranges.
- The procedure above imports the data but does not establish a link. *See Excel to PowerPoint: Linking Excel Data to a PowerPoint Graph, page 312.*

Excel to PowerPoint: Linking Excel Data to a PowerPoint Chart

1. In **PowerPoint**, start a Graph slide and double-click the "Double click to add graph" placeholder so the datasheet is open. **(Figure 13)**
2. Switch to **Excel** and then select the range to link. **(Figure 14)**
3. From the **Excel** Edit menu, choose Copy.
4. Switch to **PowerPoint** and click the datasheet cell at the upper left corner of the destination for the data.
5. From Graph's Edit menu, choose Paste Link. **(Figure 15)**
6. On the ChartWizard dialog box, make selections to identify whether the data series are in rows or columns, and whether the first row and column contain labels or data. **(Figure 16)**
7. Click OK.

✔ Tips

- Any changes to the numbers in **Excel** will be reflected in the **PowerPoint** graph.
- To update the link, choose Links from the Edit menu and then click Update Now on the Links dialog box, or click the range with the right mouse button and choose Update Link from the shortcut menu.
- Be sure not to include totals in the data imported. If you **do** include a total row, double-click the row header button for the total row on the datasheet so the row won't be graphed.

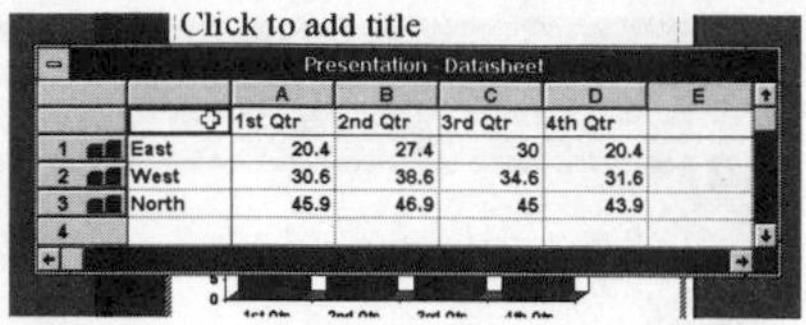

		A	B	C	D	E
		1st Qtr	2nd Qtr	3rd Qtr	4th Qtr	
1	East	20.4	27.4	30	20.4	
2	West	30.6	38.6	34.6	31.6	
3	North	45.9	46.9	45	43.9	
4						

Figure 13. *Open a datasheet for a new graph.*

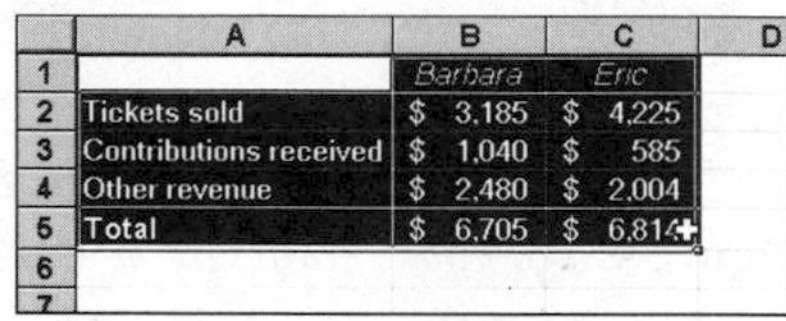

	A	B	C	D
1		Barbara	Eric	
2	Tickets sold	$ 3,185	$ 4,225	
3	Contributions received	$ 1,040	$ 585	
4	Other revenue	$ 2,480	$ 2,004	
5	Total	$ 6,705	$ 6,814	
6				
7				

Figure 14. *Select the range to link.*

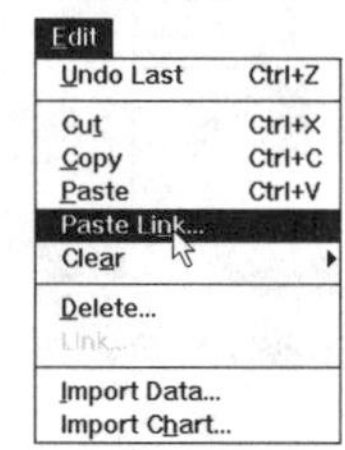

Figure 15. *Graph's Edit menu.*

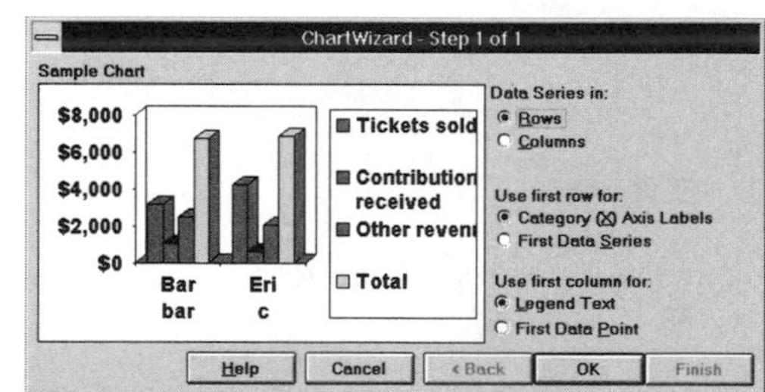

Figure 16. *The ChartWizard dialog box.*

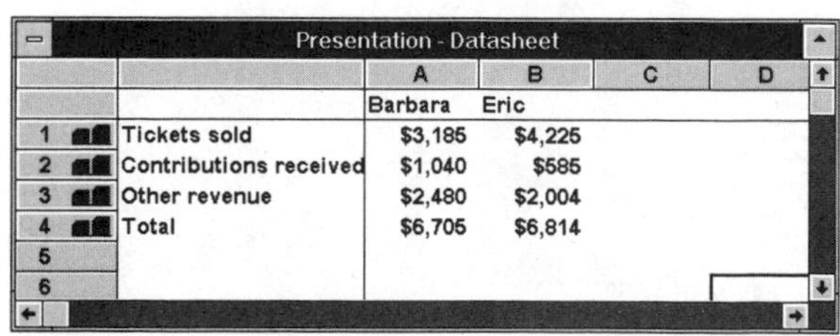

		A	B	C	D
		Barbara	Eric		
1	Tickets sold	$3,185	$4,225		
2	Contributions received	$1,040	$585		
3	Other revenue	$2,480	$2,004		
4	Total	$6,705	$6,814		
5					
6					

Figure 17. *The data appears in the datasheet.*

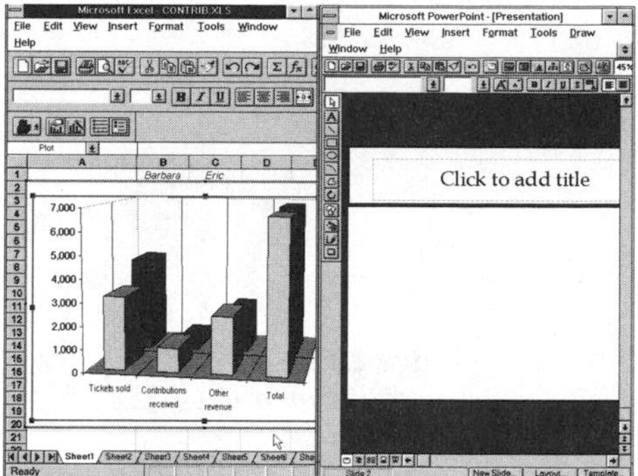

Figure 18. *The Excel and PowerPoint windows arranged.*

Excel to PowerPoint: Excel Chart to a Presentation

1. Arrange the **Excel** and **PowerPoint** windows side by side. **(Figure 18)**
2. Select the chart in **Excel**.
3. Drag the chart to a **PowerPoint** slide. **(Figure 19)**

✔ Tips

- Press the Ctrl key while you drag if you want to **copy** rather than **move** the chart.
- You can also Copy and Paste the chart.
- To edit the chart in **PowerPoint** with **Excel's** menus and toolbars, double-click the chart. **(Figure 20)**

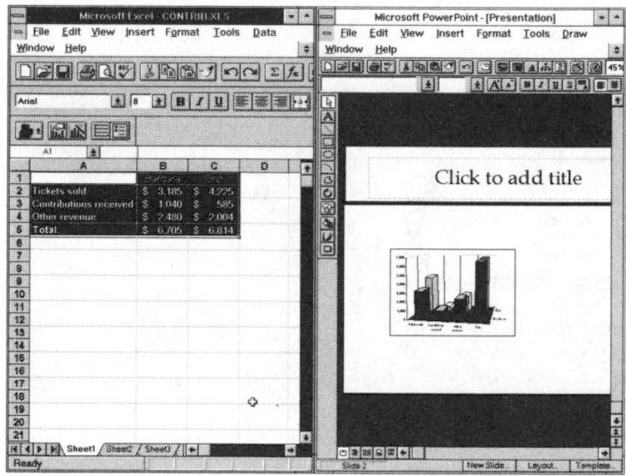

Figure 19. *Drag the chart to a PowerPoint slide.*

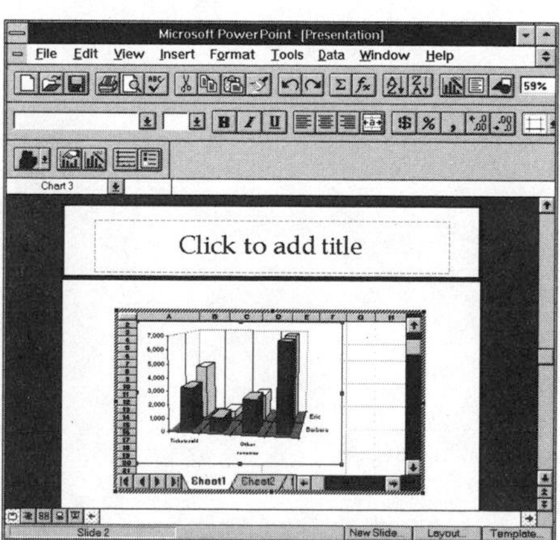

Figure 20. *Editing the chart in PowerPoint with Excel's controls.*

Excel to Access: Excel Database to an Access Table

1. Open the database in **Access**.
2. From the **Access** File menu, choose Import. **(Figure 21)**
3. On the Import dialog box, choose Microsoft Excel 5.0 as the data source. **(Figure 22)**
4. On the Select File dialog box, navigate to and select the **Excel** file from which to import data. **(Figure 23)**
5. On the Import Spreadsheet Options dialog box, choose the table that the data will go to and choose the source spreadsheet name and range. **(Figure 24)**
6. Click OK. The data is imported as specified.

✔ Tips

- If you choose to create a new table, **Access** creates a table named after the spreadsheet you import from.
- If an error occurs during the import, **Access** asks whether to cancel the import process so your existing database remains unharmed.

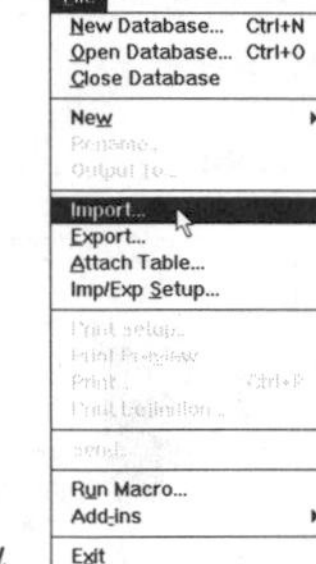

Figure 21. *The Access File menu.*

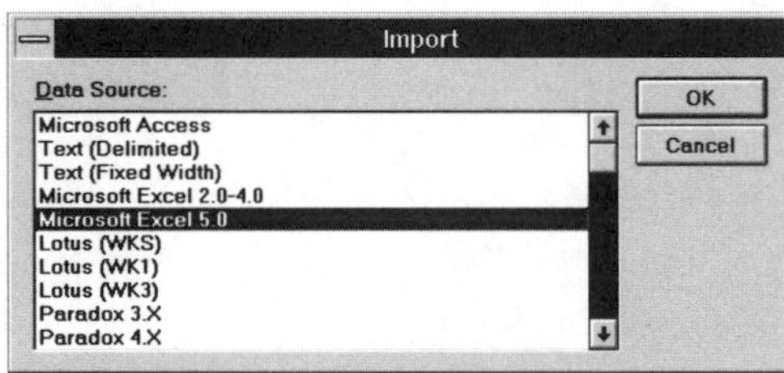

Figure 22. *The Import dialog box.*

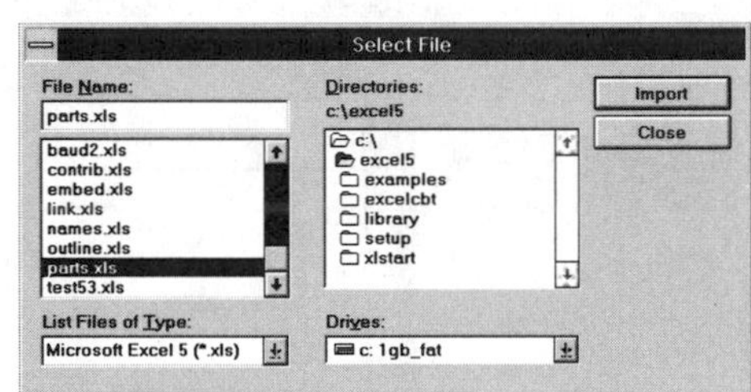

Figure 23. *The Select File dialog box.*

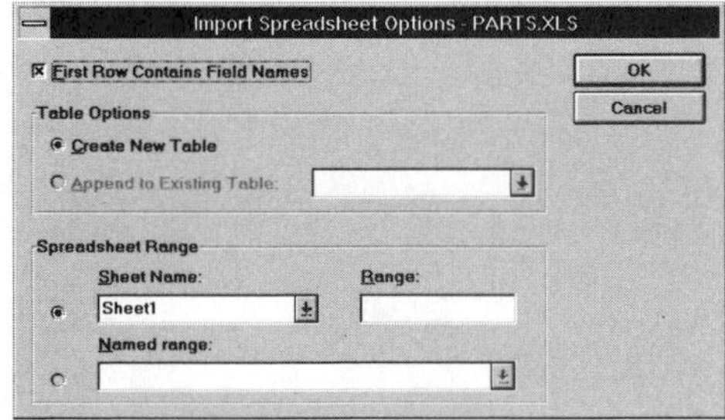

Figure 24. *The Import Spreadsheet Options dialog box.*

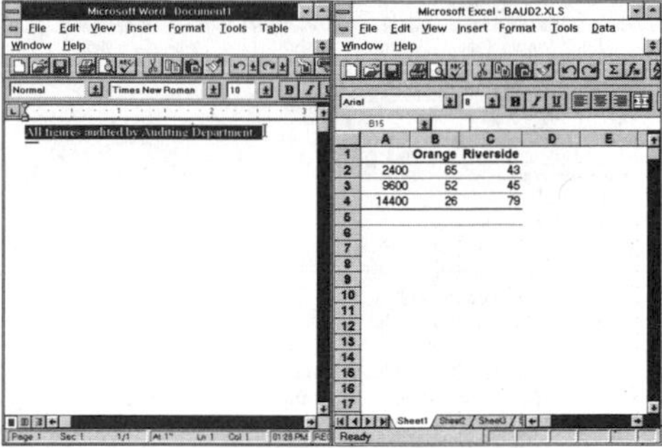

Figure 25. *Select text to copy.*

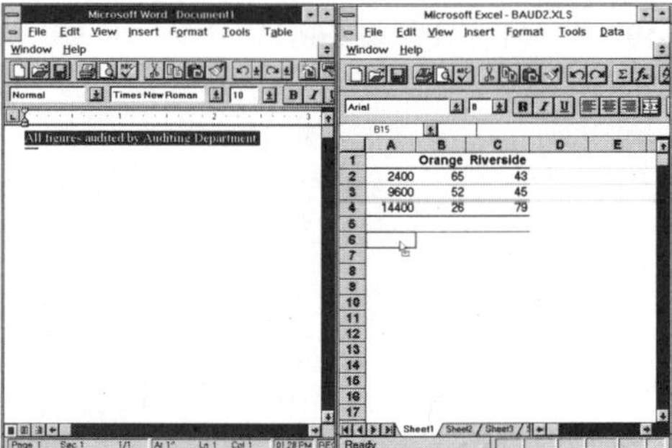

Figure 26. *Drag the text to the Excel or PowerPoint window.*

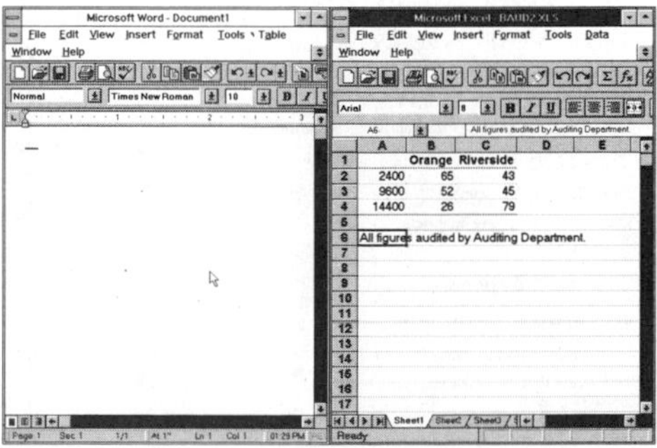

Figure 27. *The text on a PowerPoint slide.*

Word to Excel or PowerPoint: Copying Text

1. Arrange the **Word** window side by side with the **Excel** or **PowerPoint** window.
2. In **Word**, select the text to copy. **(Figure 25)**
3. Place the mouse pointer on the text.
4. Hold down the Ctrl key.
5. Drag the text to a destination cell in **Excel** or to a slide in **PowerPoint**. **(Figure 26)**

✔ **Tips**

- In **PowerPoint**, the text appears as a picture of the text as it was formatted in **Word** so you should format it in **Word** first.
- In **Excel**, the text goes into a cell as though you'd typed it into the cell.
- To edit or format the text after you copy it to **PowerPoint**, double-click the text. Then edit or format the text with **Word's** menus and toolbars. Click outside the text block to return to **PowerPoint's** menus and toolbars.

Word to PowerPoint: Using a Word Outline File

1. Create a presentation outline in **Word** and save it in a file. Each level 1 item will be the title of a new slide. **(Figure 28)**

2. In the Windows File Manager, drag and drop the **Word** outline file to the **PowerPoint** window. **(Figure 29)**

✔ Tips

- Generating the outline in **Word** allows you to use such **Word** tools as the thesaurus.
- You can also use the Present It button to transfer an outline to **PowerPoint**. *See Tip on opposite page.*

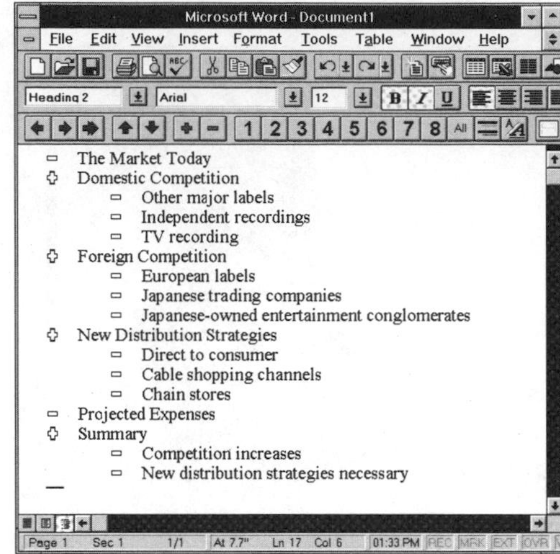

Figure 28. *The presentation outline in Word.*

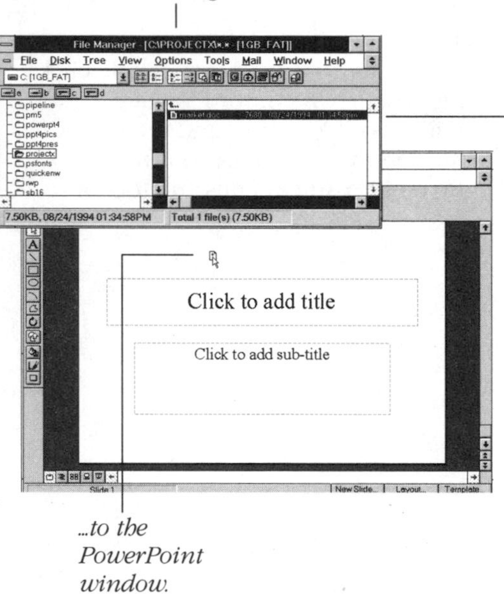

Figure 29. *Drag and drop the outline file to the PowerPoint window.*

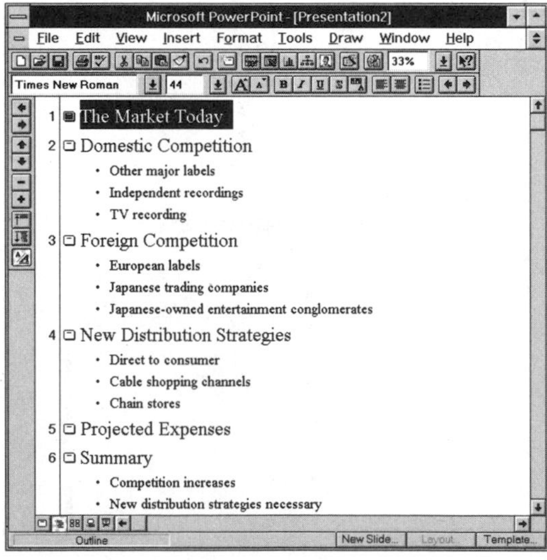

Figure 30. *A new presentation opens in PowerPoint based on the Word outline.*

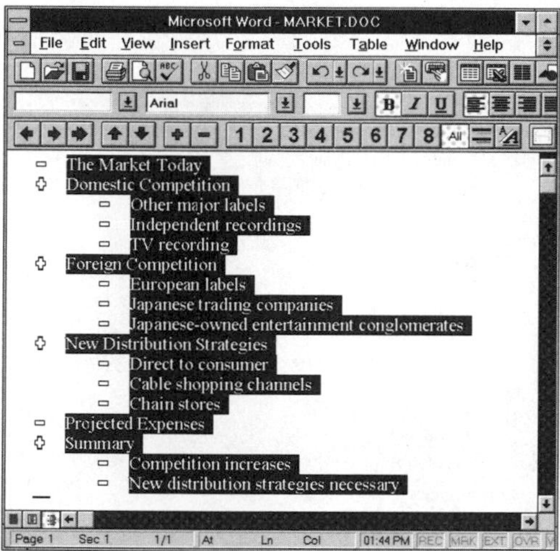

Figure 31. *A selected Word outline.*

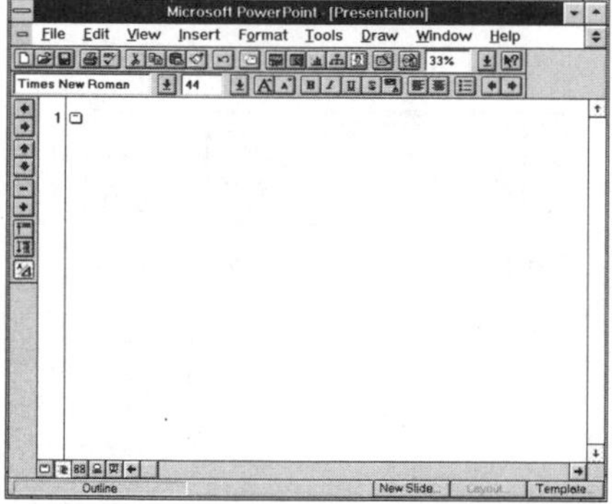

Figure 32. *PowerPoint's Outline view.*

Figure 33. *The Present It Button.*

Word to PowerPoint: Copying a Word Outline to PowerPoint

1. Create and select an outline in a **Word** document. **(Figure 31)**
2. From the Edit menu, choose Copy.
3. Switch to **PowerPoint's** Outline view. **(Figure 32)**
4. Click at the destination for the **Word** outline.
5. From the Edit menu, choose Paste.

✔ Tips

- You can also use **Word's** Present It button **(Figure 33)** to copy an outline to **PowerPoint**, but first you must install the Present It button if it is not already available.

  To install the button, copy the Present It toolbar and Present It macro from the CONVERT.DOT template to the NORMAL.DOT template using the Organizer dialog box, then drag the Present It button from the Present It toolbar to the Standard toolbar.

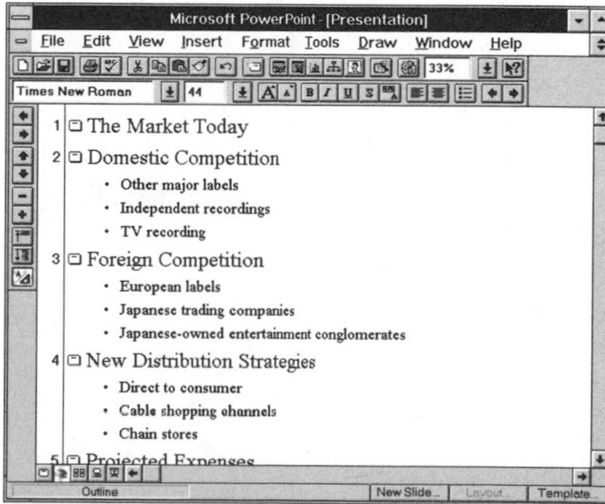

Figure 34. *The outline in PowerPoint.*

PowerPoint to Word: Copying a Presentation Outline to Word

1. Make sure both the **Word** and **PowerPoint** applications are running.
2. Switch to Outline view in **PowerPoint**. **(Figure 35)**
3. Click the Report It button on the Standard toolbar. **(Figure 36)**
4. In **Word**, save the temporary file that is created using a permanent file name. **(Figure 37)**

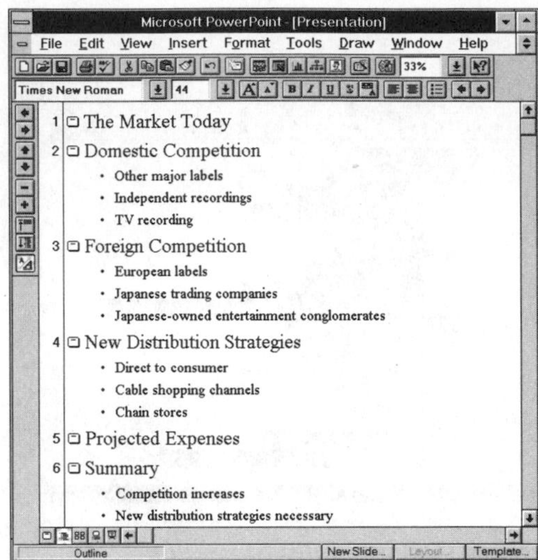

Figure 35. *Outline view.*

Figure 36. *The Report It button.*

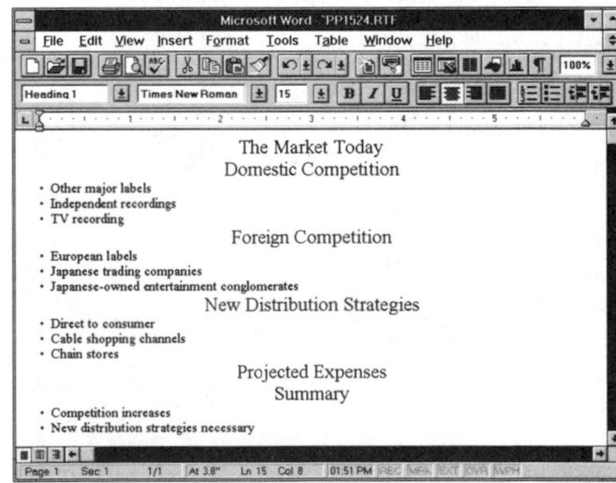

Figure 37. *The outline as it appears in a temporary Word file.*

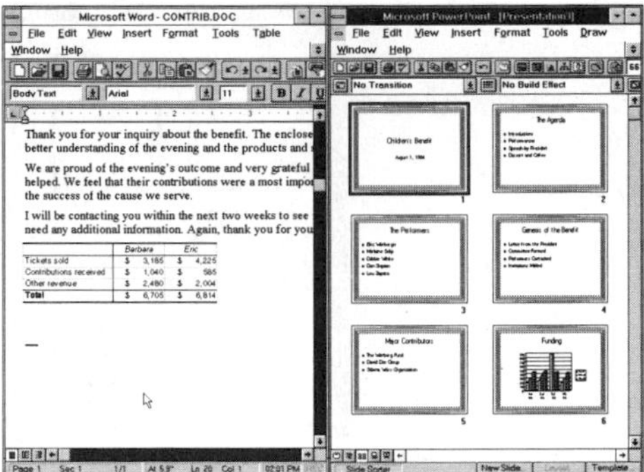

Figure 38. *Slide Sorter view.*

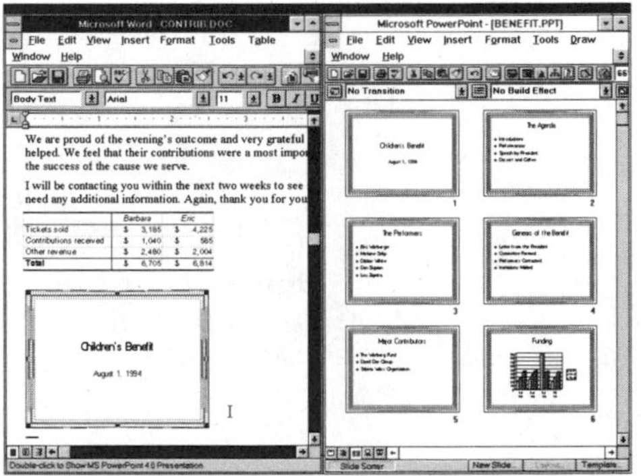

Figure 39. *The first slide of the PowerPoint presentation appears in Word.*

PowerPoint to Word or Excel: Copying a Slide Show to a Word Document

1. Arrange the **PowerPoint** window side by side with the **Word** or **Excel** window.
2. In **PowerPoint**, switch to Slide Sorter view. **(Figure 38)**
3. From the **PowerPoint** Edit menu, choose Select All or press Ctrl+A to select the entire presentation.
4. Press the Ctrl key and drag any slide to the **Word** or **Excel** window. The first slide appears in the other application. **(Figure 39)**
5. Double-click the first slide to run the slide show from **Word** or **Excel**. **PowerPoint** will open to run the show, if necessary.

✔ Tips

- To change the size of the slide in **Word**, select the slide, choose Picture on the Format menu, and then set a scaling percentage. 50% will halve the slide size, for example.
- To change the size of the slide in **Excel**, drag a corner handle of the slide. To maintain the proportions of the slide, make sure the two percentages shown in the status bar in **Excel** are identical.
- To edit the presentation, double-click the first slide or click the slide with the right mouse button and choose Edit MS PowerPoint 4.0 presentation from the shortcut menu.
- Changes made to the presentation after you copy it to **Word** are not reflected in the **Word** slide show unless you link the presentation. *See Linking a Presentation to* Word, *page 320.*

PowerPoint to Word or Excel: Linking a Presentation to Word

1. Create and save the **PowerPoint** presentation in a file. You *must* save the presentation to a file for this procedure to work.
2. Display the presentation in Slide Sorter view. **(Figure 40)**
3. From the Edit menu of **PowerPoint**, choose Select All or press Ctrl+A.
4. From the Edit menu of **PowerPoint**, choose Copy.
4. Switch to **Word** and position the insertion point at the destination for the presentation. **(Figure 41)**
5. From **Word's** Edit menu, choose Paste Special.
6. On the Paste Special dialog box, choose Paste Link and then double-click MS PowerPoint 4.0 Presentation Object as the source. **(Figure 42)**
7. To run the slide show in **Word**, double-click the representative slide that appears. **(Figure 43)**

✔ Tips

- Any changes made to the presentation in **PowerPoint** will be reflected in the **Word** slide show.
- To modify the link, click the slide and then use the Links command on the Edit menu.

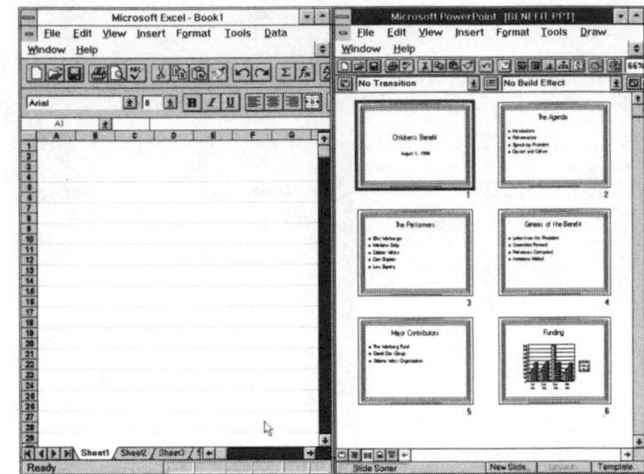

Figure 40. *The presentation in Slide Sorter view*

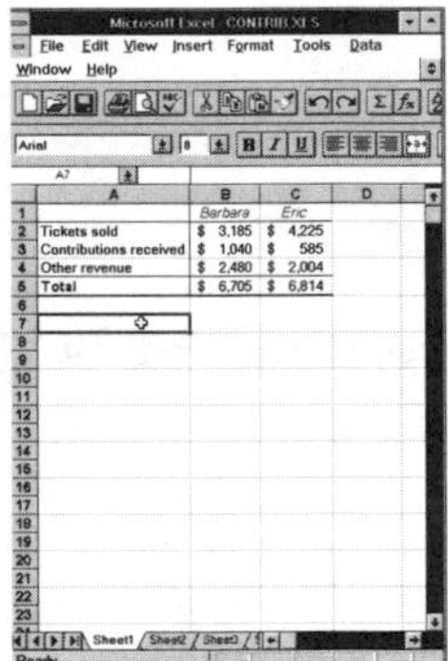

Figure 41. *Click at the destination.*

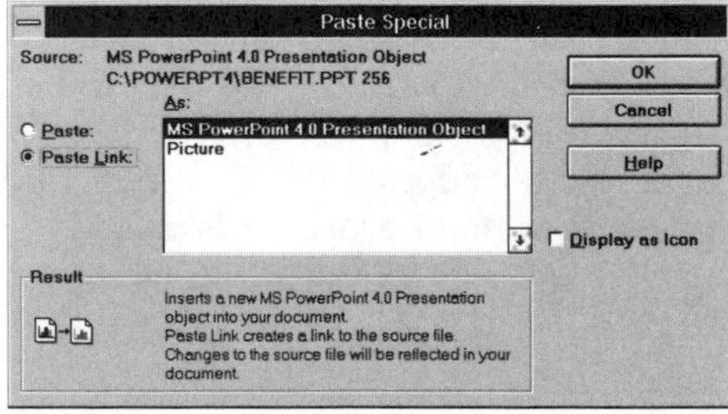

Figure 42. *The Paste Special dialog box.*

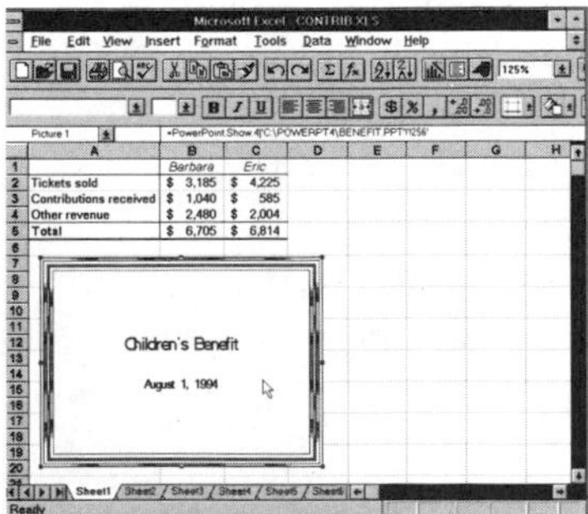

Figure 43. *Double-click the representative slide to start the slide show.*

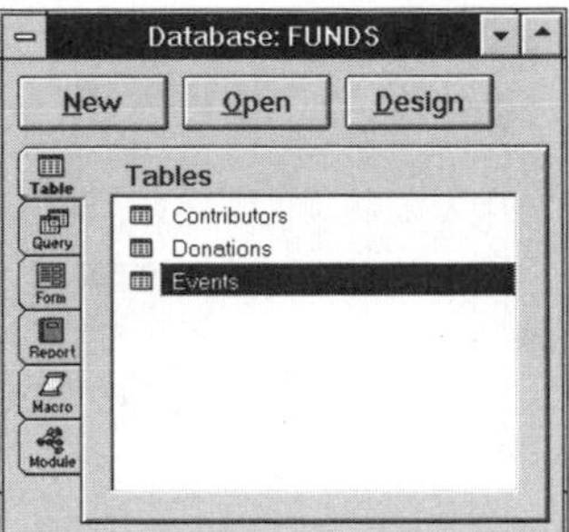

Figure 44. *Select a table in Access.*

Access to Word: Sending Data to a Mail Merge

1. In the Database window of **Access**, select the table that contains the data you want to send to a **Word** mail merge. **(Figure 44)**

   or

   Select a query to pull selected records from an **Access** table. *See Using Queries, pages 263-268.*
2. Click the Mail Merge to Word button on the toolbar. **(Figure 45)**
3. On the Microsoft Word Mail Merge Wizard dialog box, select "Create a new document and then link the data to it." **(Figure 46)**
4. In **Word**, type the text of the merge document, clicking the Insert Merge Field button whenever you want to include information from the **Access** table or query. **(Figure 47)**
5. Check the merge for errors and then print the merge. *See Creating Form Letters with Mail Merge, page 104.*

Mail Merge to Word button.

Figure 45. *The Mail Merge to Word button.*

✓ Tip

- If you've already created a merge document, you can choose "Link your data to an existing Microsoft Word document" on the Microsoft Word Mail Merge Wizard dialog box.

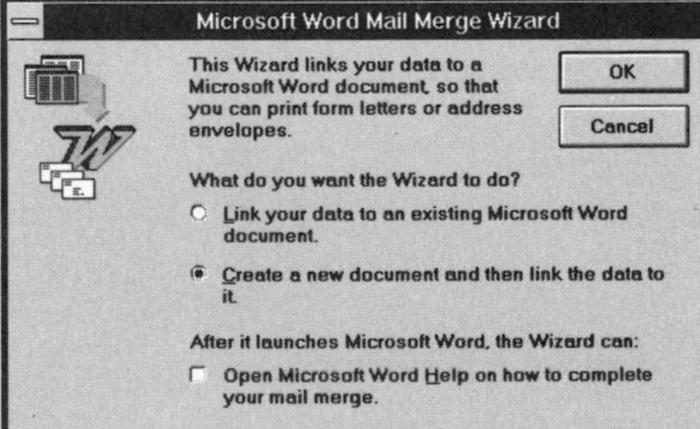

Figure 46. *The Microsoft Word Mail Merge Wizard dialog box.*

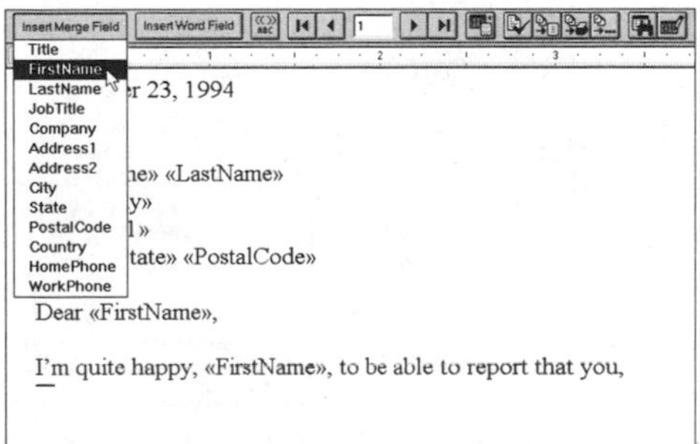

Figure 47. *Choose field names from the Insert Merge Field list as you type the mail merge letter.*

Access to Word: Sending Data to a Mail Merge

Access to Excel: Analyzing Data

1. On the **Access** Database window, select a table, form, or report. **(Figure 48)**
2. Click the Analyze It with MS Excel button on the Database toolbar. **(Figure 49)**

✔ Tip

■ If **Excel** is not already open, **Excel** will be opened and a new worksheet will be created with the same name as the table, form, or report. **(Figure 50)**

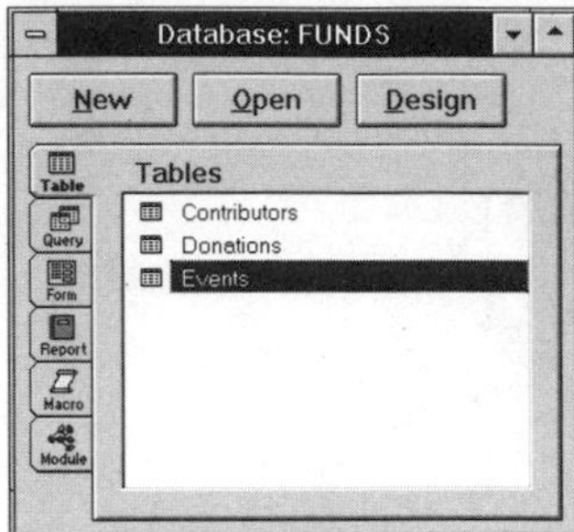

Figure 48. *The Access Database window.*

Analyze It with MS Excel button.

Figure 49. *The Analyze It with MS Excel button.*

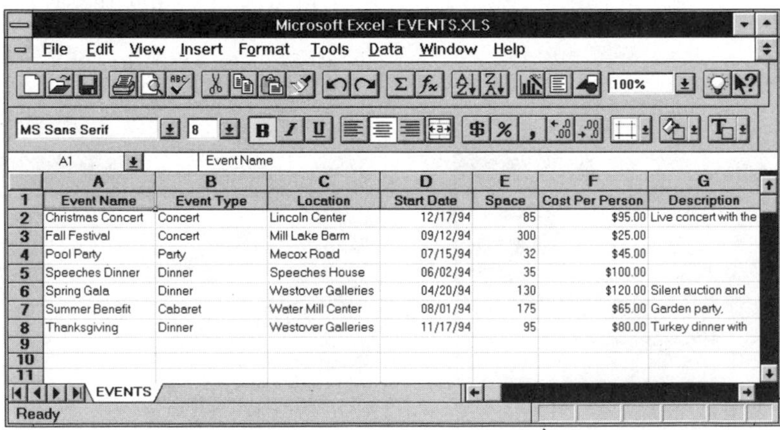

	A	B	C	D	E	F	G
1	Event Name	Event Type	Location	Start Date	Space	Cost Per Person	Description
2	Christmas Concert	Concert	Lincoln Center	12/17/94	85	$95.00	Live concert with the
3	Fall Festival	Concert	Mill Lake Barm	09/12/94	300	$25.00	
4	Pool Party	Party	Mecox Road	07/15/94	32	$45.00	
5	Speeches Dinner	Dinner	Speeches House	06/02/94	35	$100.00	
6	Spring Gala	Dinner	Westover Galleries	04/20/94	130	$120.00	Silent auction and
7	Summer Benefit	Cabaret	Water Mill Center	08/01/94	175	$65.00	Garden party.
8	Thanksgiving	Dinner	Westover Galleries	11/17/94	95	$80.00	Turkey dinner with
9							
10							
11							

Figure 50. *The data from Access appears as an Excel sheet.*

Index

D

E

Index

M

N

Index

Q

R

T

More from Peachpit Press

Microsoft Office For Windows: Visual QuickStart Guide

Steve Sagman

Microsoft Office for Windows combines the top-flight word processor (Word 6), spreadsheet (Excel 5), presentations package (PowerPoint 4), database (Access 2), and e-mail system (Mail)—all the tools for a productive office. What's missing from this integrated suite is a quick and easy way to learn how to use each of the component applications, and then how to put them together. *Microsoft Office for Windows: Visual QuickStart Guide* uses simple step-by-step instructions and more than 1,200 screenshots that show you just how to get up and running—fast. $17.95 *(334 pages)*

The Little PC Book, 2nd Edition: A Gentle Introduction to Personal Computers

Lawrence J. Magid with Kay Yarborough Nelson

Wouldn't you love having a knowledgeable, witty, endlessly patient pal to coach you through buying and using a PC? Well, you do. Popular columnist and broadcaster Larry Magid's expertise is yours in *The Little PC Book,* described by *THE WALL STREET JOURNAL* as "the class of the field." This edition includes the latest on Windows 95, the Internet, CD-ROMs, and more. Includes a handy Windows 95 Cookbook section. $17.95 *(384 pages)*

The Little Windows 95 Book

Kay Yarborough Nelson

Your guide to Windows 95. This easy, informative and entertaining volume spotlights the essentials so you can get to work quickly. Short, fully-illustrated chapters explore the Windows interface in detail, offering numerous tips and tricks. Each chapter includes a handy summary chart of keyboard shortcuts. $12.95 *(144 pages)*

The PC Bible, 2nd Edition

Edited by Eric Knorr

The PC universe is expanding, and the second edition of *The PC Bible* has grown along with it. Twenty industry experts collaborated on this definitive guide to PCs, now updated to include Windows 95 and Internet access. Whether you're a beginning or advanced PC user, you'll benefit from this book's clear, entertaining coverage of fonts, word processing, spreadsheets, graphics, desktop publishing, databases, communications, utilities, multimedia, games, and more. Winner of 1994 Computer Press Award for "Best Introductory How-to" book. $29.95 *(1,032 pages)*

The PC is not a typewriter

Robin Williams

Covers the top twenty things you need to know to make your documents look clean and professional: em dashes, curly quotes, spaces and indents, white space, etc. It's a primer that novices can pick up quickly, and that pros can keep going back to. $9.95 (96 pages)

Real World Scanning and Halftones

David Blatner and Stephen Roth

Here's a book that will save you time and money as you master the digital process, from scanning images to tweaking them, to imagesetting them. You'll learn about optical character recognition software, gamma control, sharpening, moirés, PostScript halftones, Photo CD, and image-manipulating applications like Photoshop and Photostyler. $24.95 *(296 pages)*

The Windows 95 Bible

Fred Davis

Here's absolutely everything you need to know about Windows 95, from installation and interface design to telecommunications and multimedia. This fun-to-read, easy-to-use reference is packed with detailed illustrations, plus insider tips and tricks. Reviewing the previous edition, *THE NEW YORK TIMES* wrote, "Toss out the other Windows books. This one is the best." (Finalist, Computer Press Awards). $29.95 *(1,200 pages, available in May 1996)*

Windows 95 is Driving Me Crazy

Kay Yarborough Nelson

Behind the hoopla and hype surrounding the release of Windows 95 is a lot of dissatisfaction with the performance, compatibility, and interface of Microsoft's new operating system. This is one book that tells you how to make the most of this challenging situation. It's the ultimate problem-solving guide for coping with Windows 95, showing ways to get around the worst problems, better ways of doing certain tasks, what you can and can't do in real-life situations,, and where to get more help. $24.95 *(400 pages)*

Windows 95: Visual QuickStart Guide

Steve Sagman

Windows 95, the long-awaited upgrade of Microsoft's operating system, offers an improved interface, faster performance, and numerous enhancements. This fast-paced, easy-to-read reference guide uses the same approach that's made other books in the Visual QuickStart series so popular: illustrations dominate, with text playing a supporting role. *Windows 95: Visual QuickStart Guide* provides a thorough tour of Windows 95, from introducing the basics, to managing your computer, to communicating online with Windows 95. $14.95 *(192 pages)*

Order Form

USA 800-283-9444 • 510-548-4393 • FAX 510-548-5991
CANADA 800-387-8028 • 416-447-1779 • FAX 800-456-0536 OR 416-443-0948

Qty	Title	Price	Total
	SUBTOTAL		
	ADD APPLICABLE SALES TAX*		
	SHIPPING		
	TOTAL		

Shipping is by UPS ground: $4 for first item, $1 each add'l.

*We are required to pay sales tax in all states with the exceptions of AK, DE, HI, MT, NH, NV, OK, OR, SC and WY. Please include appropriate sales tax if you live in any state not mentioned above.

Customer Information

NAME

COMPANY

STREET ADDRESS

CITY STATE ZIP

PHONE ( ) FAX ( )
[REQUIRED FOR CREDIT CARD ORDERS]

Payment Method

❑ CHECK ENCLOSED ❑ VISA ❑ MASTERCARD ❑ AMEX

CREDIT CARD # EXP. DATE

COMPANY PURCHASE ORDER #

Tell Us What You Think

PLEASE TELL US WHAT YOU THOUGHT OF THIS BOOK: TITLE:

WHAT OTHER BOOKS WOULD YOU LIKE US TO PUBLISH?

PEACHPIT PRESS • 2414 Sixth Street • Berkeley, CA 94710